A Struggle for Power

John Colet

OTHER BOOKS BY THEODORE DRAPER

The Six Weeks' War (1944)
The 84th Infantry Division in the Battle of Germany (1946)
The Roots of American Communism (1957)
American Communism and Soviet Russia (1960)
Castro's Revolution: Myths and Realities (1962)
Castroism, Theory and Practice (1965)
Abuse of Power (1967)
Israel and World Politics (1968)
The Dominican Revolt (1968)
The Rediscovery of Black Nationalism (1970)
Present History (1983)
A Present of Things Past (1990)
A Very Thin Line: The Iran-Contra Affairs (1991)

A Struggle for Power

THE AMERICAN REVOLUTION

THEODORE DRAPER

LITTLE, BROWN AND COMPANY

A *Little, Brown* Book

First published in the United States in 1996
by Times Books, a division of Random House, Inc.
First published in Great Britain in 1996
by Little, Brown and Company

A CIP catalogue record for this book
is available from the British Library.

ISBN: 0 316 87802 2

Typeset by Palimpsest Book Production Limited,
Polmont, Stirlingshire
Printed and bound in Great Britain by
Clays Ltd, St Ives plc.

Little, Brown and Company (UK)
Brettenham House
Lancaster Place
London WC2E 7EN

For Roger

The real cause I consider to be the one which was formally most kept out of sight. The growth of the power of Athens, and the alarm which this inspired in Lacedaemon, made war inevitable.—THUCYDIDES

Scipio Nasica was against the destruction of Carthage because Rome needed a rival to keep sober and alert.—ARNALDO MOMIGLIANO[1]

Pour être bon historien, il ne faudroit être d'aucune religion, d'aucun pais, d'aucune profession, d'aucun parti.[2]

---

[1] Arnaldo Momigliano, *Alien Wisdom* (Cambridge University Press, 1971), p. 26.
[2] Epigraph in Horace Walpole, *Memoirs of the Reign of King George the Second* (London, 1846), vol. 1, p. 237.

CONTENTS

PREFACE

Why another book on the American Revolution? The answer is implicit in the title of this book. Over the many years that books have been written on the Revolution, there have been different interpretations—nationalist, Progressive, social, institutional, constitutional, imperial, ideological. It is obviously possible to learn from all of them, because the Revolution was not a simple, one-sided phenomenon.

Nevertheless, one interpretation may be more central to the nature of the Revolution than others. In my view, the Revolution was basically a struggle for power between Great Britain and its American colonies. Just what this means I prefer the body of this book to make clear. Others have touched on this aspect of the Revolution, but I do not know of any work which has attempted to develop it in much detail.

Since this book is not an academic monograph, I have not used unpublished material. The wealth of published documentation and special studies is so great that it is almost impossible for a single human being to master all of it. I decided that the published material was quite enough for my purposes. The reader will find a great deal of reliance on primary sources in published documentation, for which reason I am most indebted to the various editors who have labored to make them available.

The reader will also find a good deal of citation in the words of the original documents. My aim has been to let many of the actors speak for themselves. In this way, I hope that the reader will gain a more immediate impression of ideas and events than might be possible if I merely summed up what they had to say. I have also kept the original spelling, which is almost always quite clear or at most demands a little effort. I hope that the original spelling will bring the reader closer to the events and their protagonists. It should also be clear that I have not written this book for specialists in particular periods or subjects. My ideal reader is anyone sufficiently interested in the roots of the American Revolution to want to explore an interpretation of why and how it came about.

A Struggle for Power

1

"An accession of Power"

· 1 ·

IN 1759, A "PAMPHLET WAR" of peculiar intensity and significance for the future of the American colonies erupted in England. Before it was over, a large number of pamphlets—then the favorite form of political controversy—were fired off in the effort to influence the British government and public opinion.

Great Britain was then at the turning point of the Seven Years' War, the greatest of the wars in a century of wars. The main enemy was France, long the dominant power in Europe. It was the first true world war, fought in Europe, the West Indies, North America, even India, and wherever the antagonists could get at each other.

The American theater happened to be critical at both the beginning and the end of the war. The American phase came about as a result of a scramble for land in the Ohio valley beyond the Allegheny Mountains. A group of Virginia speculators, organized as the Ohio Company, received a grant of 200,000 acres on condition that it would build a fort to protect prospective settlers. The French in Canada claimed the same territory and were determined to prevent their rivals from settling it. Since the claims of both sides were equally vague and contestable, the decision was bound to go to the one using the most force. Only a spark was needed to start a conflagration.

The spark was struck when the French seized the proposed site of the Ohio Company's fort and constructed one of their own, Fort Duquesne, where Pittsburgh now stands. The lieutenant governor of Virginia, Robert Dinwiddie, who had been clamoring for action against the French presence in the Ohio valley, took the initiative to retake the French fort. The mission was given to Maj. George Washington, then twenty-two years old and an investor with his older brothers in the Ohio Company. Washington's little band set forth in 1754, met a superior French force, fell into its hands as prisoners, and was lucky to get back disarmed but alive.

Washington's mishap—it was little more, since no blood had yet been shed—faced the British government with a difficult decision. Great Britain was unprepared for a land war across the Atlantic, but it was equally reluctant to accept humiliation and let the territory go to the French without a struggle. The war was made unavoidable by secret British instructions in December 1754 to the new commander in chief in the American colonies, Gen. Edward Braddock, to drive the French out of Fort Duquesne. In July 1755, Braddock attempted to capture the fort with about 1,400 British regulars and 450 colonials, the latter under now Lt. Col. George Washington. They met a force of about 900 French and Indians and suffered a disastrous defeat. Braddock himself was killed in a battle in the wilderness, and the French and Indian War, as the American phase of the Seven Years' War came to be known, was set in motion.

It might have remained a war in America or been headed off by some patchy compromise if events in Europe had not moved ominously towards a much larger struggle for power. In 1756, a reshuffle of European alliances took place—France was now allied with Austria and Russia, Britain with Prussia. In August, Frederick the Great of Prussia invaded the kingdom of Saxony, thereby threatening Austria. The new alliance systems came into play. Britain found itself allied with Prussia against a France allied with Austria. The larger Seven Years' War was on.

As a result, the faraway American phase of the war merged with the much larger European phase. Yet in Great Britain itself, a popular impression, frequently encouraged by British ministers, persisted that the war had broken out and had been fought in defense of the American colonies. The great British war leader William Pitt himself said in Parliament that the war had been undertaken "for the long injured, long-neglected, long-forgotten people of America."[1]

The war went badly for the British side for almost three years. When the turn in British fortunes came, it took place in America. In July 1758,

---

[1] Brian Tunstall, *William Pitt, Earl of Chatham* (Hodder and Stoughton, 1938), p. 145; Basil Williams, *The Life of William Pitt, Earl of Chatham* (Longmans, Green, 1913), vol. 1, p. 269.

the French fortress of Louisbourg on Cape Breton Island off the coast of Canada fell to forces under Col. James Wolfe. It was the first British victory of the war. The next year was an annus mirabilis for the British cause. The important French island of Guadeloupe in the West Indies was captured in June 1759, the city of Quebec in September. In 1760, Canada was British.

By this time, both Britain and France were tiring of the war. A decision was still elusive in Europe, but the British victories in America made both sides contemplate a possible peace. It was three years away, but the British "pamphlet war" broke out as a result of the changed circumstances.

• 2 •

The peculiar issue of this bloodless war was "Canada versus Guadeloupe." The necessity to make a choice between them implied that Britain was unable to demand both French colonies as reward for its victories in North America and the West Indies. France, it was recognized, might be ready for peace but not at any price.

But why Guadeloupe? It was the largest and most lucrative of the French "sugar islands." Sugar was an old source of wealth and trade. It had been a costly luxury and medical ingredient until a taste for it in tea and coffee developed in the eighteenth century. Great Britain consumed 10,000 tons in 1700, 150,000 tons in 1800.[2] Britain also had sugar islands in the West Indies, the largest of them Jamaica, but they were less efficient than the French plantations, and all of them produced no more than Guadeloupe alone.[3] Yet the British sugar islands were the source of some of the greatest British fortunes, including that of one of Pitt's main backers, William Beckford, alderman of London and member of Parliament.

In part the argument in these pamphlets was economic. Was the sugar trade of Guadeloupe more desirable than the fur trade of Canada? Was the future increase of population in Canada more promising for the consumption of British manufactures than the limited population of Guadeloupe? Was it more important for British sugar growers to increase their production or to decrease French competition?

But another part of the argument went off in a very different direction.

[2] *The Encyclopaedia Britannica*, 13th ed., vol. 26, p. 44.
[3] One pamphlet gave sugar production in Guadeloupe as at least 100,000 hogsheads annually and estimated the eight British islands—Barbados, Antigua, Montserrat, Nevis, St. Kitt's, Anguilla, Tortola, and Jamaica—at 105,050 hogsheads annually (*Copy of a Letter from a Gentleman in Guadeloupe to his Friend in London*, 1760, in J. Almon, *Anecdotes of the Life of the Right Hon. William Pitt, Earl of Chatham*, 6th ed., 1797, p. 226).

It was significant not only for its immediate bearing on the coming peace but for its revelation of long-suppressed British forebodings about the North American colonies. Fear of the growth of the colonies appeared in so many pamphlets that it was clearly more than a curious aberration on the part of some nervous British officials.

The first pamphlet to raise the issue of Guadeloupe or Canada was entitled *A Letter Addressed to Two Great Men, on the Prospect of Peace; and on the Terms necessary to be insisted upon in the Negociation.*[4] This pamphlet first appeared in December 1759, soon after the fall of Quebec. The "two great men" were William Pitt and the duke of Newcastle, who then shared the main responsibility in the British government. It has been attributed to John Douglas, bishop successively of Carlisle and Salisbury, who supposedly wrote on behalf of Lord Bath, the former William Pulteney, a longtime figure in British politics.[5]

This opening shot clearly favored taking Canada rather than Guadeloupe. It appealed for an early peace—"We have had Bloodshed enough." The French, it said, had always sought "to extend themselves from *Canada,* Southwards, through the Lakes along the Back of our Colonies." The French allegedly aimed to cut off the British colonies from the Indian Nations and open up a route between the St. Lawrence and Mississippi rivers in order to join their colonies of Canada and Louisiana. "The *American* Disputes between the two Nations," the pamphlet asserted, had been "the great Object of the present War." Since the war had begun "principally, with a View to do ourselves Justice in *North America,*" the main aim of the peace treaty should be "the Regulation of Matters on that Continent."

The author knew something about how the American colonies felt about Canada. If Britain did not keep all of it, they "will tell you you have done *Nothing.*" If Canada should be given back, "you lay the Foundation of another War." It was necessary to exclude the French, "*absolutely* and *entirely.*" Britain did not need Guadeloupe, because it had enough sugar islands of its own. On the other hand, the pamphlet cataloged the virtues of the British colonies:

---

[4] A previous pamphlet dated October 17, 1759, of partial relevance to the controversy was entitled *Considerations on the Importance of Canada, and the Bay and River of St. Lawrence.* It was addressed to William Pitt. Its main argument rested on the threat of French naval power, which it contended was based on the fisheries off the coast of Canada; if France were cut off from the fisheries, it "must therefore prove the most fatal Blow they ever felt." The interest of the British-American colonies was only briefly mentioned—"the *British* Empire in the Continent of *America;* which can never be safe, whilst *Canada* is in the Hands of *France*" (pp. 3–4). But this pamphlet was anticipatory; it never touched on the dispute over Guadeloupe.

[5] Clarence Walworth Alvord, *The Mississippi Valley in British Politics* (Arthur H. Clark, 1917; 2d ed., 1960), vol. 1, p. 56 n. 70.

To consider this Affair in its proper Light, it will be necessary to reflect on the infinite Consequence of *North America* to this Country. Our Colonies there contain a Million of Inhabitants, who are mostly supplied with the Manufactures of *Great Britain;* our Trade to them, by employing innumerable Ships, is one great Source of our maritime Strength; by supporting our Sugar Islands with their Provisions, and other Necessaries, they pour in upon us all the Riches of the *West Indies;* we carry their Rice, and Tobacco, and Fish, to all the Markets of *Europe;* they produce Indigo, and Iron; and the whole Navy of *England* may be equipped, with the Products of *English America.* And if, notwithstanding our having lost several Branches of Commerce, we formerly enjoyed in *Europe* and to the *Levant,* we have still more Commerce than ever; a greater Demand for our Manufactures, and a vast Increase of our Shipping; what can this be owing to, but to the Trade to our own *American* Colonies; a Trade which the Successes of this War, will render, every Day, more and more advantageous? If this Matter, then, be considered, in the above Light, by those whom I now address, they will make our *North American* Conquests, the *sine qua non* of the Peace, as being the only Method of guarding our *invaluable* Possessions there, from Usurpations and Encroachments.[6]

Much can be learned from this recital about how the American colonies fitted into the British scheme of things—the protected American market for British manufactures; the dependence of the British navy on American trees for masts; the "triangular trade" between Britain, the North American colonies, and the West Indian colonies. But a forceful reply was not long in coming.

The case against retaining Canada and for obtaining Guadeloupe was first set forth in a pamphlet entitled *Remarks on the Letter Address'd to Two Great Men,* usually attributed to William Burke, a relative of the more famous Edmund. It charged that the earlier pamphlet had been "guided more by old Prejudices than by the true Nature of Things" and would lead Britain to act with "the most wanton Insolence, with the most hateful Oppression."

Instead of concentrating on North America, it argued, "the utmost rational Aim of our Ambition, ought to be, to possess a just Weight, and Consideration in *Europe.*" Canada had never been one of the "Objects for which we began the War." It was not necessary to possess all Canada for

---

[6] I have kept the original spelling and punctuation in this and subsequent citations. The quotations from this pamphlet come from pp. 4, 13, 17, 27, 28, 34.

the British colonies in North America to be safe; a few well-placed forts, and a state of "strength and watchfulness" were enough. If the American colonies believed that nothing had been gained by the war if Canada was not kept, the colonies "must be taught a Lesson of Moderation." If the British colonies, with an advantage of at least ten to one in population and the protection of a great naval power, could not feel secure, "they must blame their own Cowardice or Ignorance, and not the Measures of their Mother Country."

The idea, it went on, of feeling secure "only by having no other Nation near you" had come from the American colonies. It was "the genuine Policy of Savages" and the reason Britain and France had been fighting over "the Sovereignty of Deserts in America, to which neither of us would otherwise have had any right." In fact, the British islands in the West Indies were sure to be more endangered by the French in Guadeloupe than the British colonies in North America by the French in Canada. The British islands supplied only enough for the domestic British market; with Guadeloupe, the British sugar trade could expand to foreign markets; home consumption merely gratified a taste for luxury, whereas foreign markets contributed to greater wealth and power. Guadeloupe produced not only sugar but great quantities of coffee, cotton, and indigo, with sugar alone worth more than all the "fur and peltry" that was all Canada was good for.

Commercially, then, Guadeloupe was said to be far more valuable than Canada. At this point, however, this pamphlet introduced some new and disturbing ideas. One was the commercial competition between the colonies and the mother country:

> To view the Continent of *America* in a Commercial Light, the Produce of all the Northern Colonies is the same as that of *England,* Corn, and Cattle: and therefore, except for a few Naval Stores, there is very little Trade from thence directly to *England.* Their own Commodities bear a very low Price, Goods carried from *Europe* bear a very high Price; and thus they are of Necessity driven to set up Manufactures similar to those of *England,* in which they are favoured by the Plenty and Cheapness of Provisions. In fact, there are Manufactures of many Kinds in these Northern Colonies, that promise in a short Time to supply their Home Consumption. From *New England* they begin even to export some things manufactured, as Hats, for instance.

Worse still, if this trend went on, the northern colonies would gradually have no need of England:

In these Provinces they have Colleges and Academies for the Education of their Youth; and as they increase daily in People and in Industry, the Necessity of a Connection with *England,* with which they have no natural Intercourse by a Reciprocation of Wants, will continually diminish. But as they recede from the Sea, all these Causes will operate more strongly; they will have nothing to expect, they must live wholly on their own Labour, and in process of Time will know little, enquire little, and care little about the Mother Country.

This dire prospect called for some way to forestall it. The obvious means pointed northward:

If, Sir, the People of our Colonies find no Check from *Canada,* they will extend themselves, almost, without bounds into the Inland Parts. They are invited to it by the Pleasantness, the Fertility, and the Plenty of that Country; and they will increase infinitely from all Causes. What the Consequence will be, to have a numerous, hardy, independent People, possessed of a strong Country, communicating little, or not at all with *England,* I leave to your own reflections. I hope we have not gone to these immense expences, without any Idea of securing the Fruits of them to Posterity. If we have, I am sure we have acted with little Frugality or Foresight.

The author almost backed away from discussing this aspect of the question as too delicate or dangerous—but he plunged on anyway:

This is indeed a Point that must be the constant Object of the Minister's Attention, but is not a fit Subject for a Discussion. I will therefore expatiate no farther on this Topic; I shall only observe, that by eagerly grasping at extensive Territory, we may run the risque, and that perhaps in no very distant Period, of losing what we now possess. The possession of *Canada,* far from being necessary to our Safety, may in its Consequence be even dangerous. A Neighbour that keeps us in some Awe, is not always the worst of Neighbours. So that far from sacrificing *Guadaloupe* to *Canada,* perhaps if we might have *Canada* without any Sacrifice at all, we ought not to desire it.[7] And, besides the Points to be considered between us and *France,* there are other Powers who will probably think themselves interested in the Decision of this Affair. There is a Balance of Power in *America* as well as in *Europe,*

---

[7] I have retained the spelling of "Guadaloupe" when it appears in this form in the pamphlets.

which will not be forgotten; and *this is a Point I should have expected would somewhat have engaged your attention.*[8]

The last point was the most telling for the future. A French Canada was a guarantee that the American colonies would be forced to remain British. By keeping Canada, the British would be doomed to give up their American colonies. The British colonies in North America were made up of too "numerous, hardy, independent People, possessed of a strong Country" to remain in subjection to Great Britain much longer. If they were not afraid of the French, as they had always been, they would not need Britain as their protector. With Canada British, the argument went, American independence was not far away.[9]

By this time, however, the idea that the French in Canada held off American independence was already an old one. Peter Kalm, the Swedish botanist, had made the same observation during travels in New York in 1748, even before the outbreak of the Seven Years' War:

> I have been told by *Englishmen,* and not only by such as were born in *America,* but even by such as came from *Europe,* that the *English* colonies in *North America,* in the space of thirty or fifty years, would be able to form a state by themselves, entirely independent on *Old England.* But as the whole country which lies along the sea-shore is unguarded, and on the land side is harrassed by the *French* in times of war, these dangerous neighbours are sufficient to prevent the connection of the colonies with their mother country from being quite broken off. The *English* government has therefore sufficient reason to consider the *French* in *North America* as the best means of keeping the colonies in their due submission.[10]

If Kalm could write this in 1748, Englishmen did not need any particular

---

[8] *Remarks on the Letter Address'd to Two Great Men. In a Letter to the Author of that Piece* (London, 1761), pp. 8–9, 17, 19, 25–28, 32, 36, 49–52.

[9] The British historian W. E. H. Lecky was apparently the first—and for a quarter of a century the only one—to deal briefly with this controversy (*A History of England in the Eighteenth Century,* London, 1882, vol. 3, pp. 268–70). Some of these pamphlets were later discussed by George Louis Beer (*British Colonial Policy, 1754–1765,* Macmillan, 1907, pp. 142–52); William L. Grant, ("Canada versus Guadeloupe, an Episode of the Seven Years' War," *American Historical Review,* July 1912, pp. 735–43); and Alvord (*Mississippi Valley in British Politics,* 1917, vol. 1, pp. 56–63). Alvord listed sixty-five pamphlets dealing with the peace treaty, many of them touching on the Canada-versus-Guadeloupe controversy (vol. 2, pp. 256–64). Their treatment was cursory and devoted primarily to the influence of the pamphlets on the coming peace treaty. I am more interested in what the pamphlets foretold about the coming American independence. In any case, little attention has been paid to the pamphlets for almost seventy-five years.

[10] Peter Kalm, *Travels Into North America,* trans. John Reinhold Foster (London, 1770–71; rev. ed. 1772; reprint, Imprint Society, 1972), p. 138.

originality to pick up the same theme in 1759 and after. But Kalm had merely dropped the idea in the midst of his botanical researches, and it had not been available in an English translation in London until 1770–1772. Nevertheless, the basic thought was so much the same that it must have been in the air in both America and England. Thirty years from 1748 was 1778, three years into the American Revolution.

• 3 •

One American in England was so disturbed by the second pamphlet, the *Remarks,* that he decided to enter the controversy. He was Benjamin Franklin, who had come to London in 1757, only two years before the first pamphlet, and was already well known in scientific circles for his experiments with electricity. Franklin, however, had been sent to London as agent for Pennsylvania and thus had a political role to play. In mid-1760, he produced one of his most famous pamphlets, *The Interest of Great Britain considered. With Regard to her Colonies. And the acquisition of Canada and Guadaloupe,* known as "The Canada Pamphlet."

Franklin was provoked by the argument in the *Remarks* in favor of returning Canada to France in order to check the forces of growth and tendencies towards independence of the British North American colonies. Significantly, his title considered the "Interest of Great Britain," not of the American colonies. His reply, written as if he were an ordinary citizen of the British Isles rather than an American colonist, was intended to reassure the British that the *Remarks'* forebodings about the colonies' unchecked future were without foundation.

Curiously, Franklin had written a previous pamphlet in 1751, but published four years later, with a distinct bearing on the present controversy. It was his *Observations concerning the Increase of Mankind,* which he appended to the new pamphlet as a way of bolstering his argument but which could be read in different ways. It has been described as being "the first statement of the function of the American frontier," as embodying "the first systematic expression of Franklin's expansionism," and as offering "a new economic conception—America as a mercantile empire in itself."[11] It was more than anything else, however, a systematic expression of the rising sense of America's own power.

[11] Carl Van Doren, *Benjamin Franklin* (Viking Press, 1938), p. 217; Gerald Stourzh, *Benjamin Franklin and American Foreign Policy* (University of Chicago Press, 2d ed., 1969), p. 60; Paul W. Conner, *Poor Richard's Politicks* (Oxford University Press, 1965), p. 72.

In one observation, Franklin started with the generally accepted estimate that there were more than "upwards of One Million English Souls in North-America." From this purely demographic premise, he went on excitedly: "This Million doubling, suppose but once in 25 years, will in another century be more than the People of England, and the greatest number of Englishmen will be on this side of the Water. What an accession of Power to the British Empire by Sea as well as Land! What increase of Trade and Navigation! What number of Ships and Seamen!"[12]

In this vein, Franklin wrote as a loyal British subject, which he remained until almost the eve of the Revolution. His "observation" was far from glorifying this accession of power as a strictly American achievement; it was all still dedicated to the greater glory of the British empire. But some British readers could have been less than happy with Franklin's reasoning. By making British superiority depend on American multiplication, he was more or less subtly pushing America into the forefront of the British imperial position.

Other Franklinesque implications were equally double-edged. He calculated just when America would overtake England in population and, by implication, power. Another century, according to this early version of the "American century," would have made the memorable year 1851, which turned out to be just about the time Americans were playing up their "Manifest Destiny." In effect, Franklin was putting forward the idea of an Anglo-American partnership of power. If he was right, however, the balance of power was sure to shift to the American side as it gained in population and power.

Franklin was not one to let go of a good idea. He returned again and again to Great Britain's stake in America and America's contribution to British glory. In 1754, he argued in favor of colonial representation in the British Parliament on the ground that "those, who have most contributed to enlarge Britain's empire and commerce, encrease her strength, her wealth, and the numbers of her people" should be properly rewarded.[13]

On January 3, 1760, just as the Canada versus Guadeloupe controversy was getting started, Franklin wrote a famous letter to his friend Lord Kames, the Scottish philosopher:

No one can more sincerely rejoice than I do, on the Reduction of Canada; and this, is not merely as I am a Colonist, but as I am a Briton. I have long been of opinion, that the Foundations of the

---

[12] *The Papers of Benjamin Franklin*, ed. Leonard W. Labaree (Yale University Press, 1961), vol. 4, p. 233.

[13] Franklin to William Shirley, December 22, 1754, ibid., vol. 5, p. 451.

future Grandeur and Stability of the British empire lie, in America; and tho', like other Foundations, they are low and little seen, they are nevertheless, broad and strong enough to support the greatest political Structure human Wisdom ever yet erected. I am therefore by no means for restoring Canada. If we keep it, all the Country from St. Laurence to the Mississippi, will in another century be fill'd with British People. Britain itself will become vastly more populous, by the immense Increase of its Commerce; the Atlantic Sea will be cover'd with your Trading Ships; and your naval Power, thence continually increasing, will extend your Influence round the whole Globe, and awe the world! If the French remain in Canada, they will continually harass our Colonies by the Indians, impede if not prevent their Growth; your Progress to Greatness will at best be slow, and give room for many Accidents that may for ever prevent it. But I refrain, for I see you begin to think my notions extravagant, and look upon them as the Ravings of a mad Prophet.[14]

Later that same year, when Franklin came to publish his pro-Canada *Observations* in reply to the pro-Guadeloupe *Remarks*, he showed that he did not really think that his notions were so extravagant or the ravings of a mad prophet by essentially repeating them—with a new twist. His problem now was to convince the British that they had nothing to fear from the colonies' territorial expansion or increase of population. He had no intention of recanting his boasts of future colonial development, but he needed to put them in such a way that they would not lead to the idea of American independence.

Franklin knew that what mattered most to the British was their market for manufactured goods. He therefore sought to reassure them that the colonies' territorial expansion was good for British manufactures. If the colonists had more room to spread out, he argued, they were sure to remain largely agricultural. As such, they were destined to be satisfied to be the producers of raw materials and leave manufactures to the British.

Franklin repeated his calculation of 1751 that the American population was doubling every twenty-five years and would in time exceed that of Great Britain. But he hastened to add that such an increase would probably take a century to achieve. Even if the existing colonies stretched only as far as the Mississippi, it would take them centuries to reach a figure of perhaps a hundred million. Meanwhile, the more Americans there were, the more British manufactures they were bound to consume. There was nothing to

[14] Franklin to Lord Kames, January 3, 1760, ibid., vol. 9, pp. 6–7.

worry about, because Great Britain and the American colonies were one people and what was good for a part was equally good for the whole.

As if these assurances were not enough, Franklin played his soothing tune on another string. The colonies, he asserted, were so jealous—in that period meaning suspicious—of each other that they had never been able to unite against the common enemy. If the colonies could not unite to defend themselves against the French and their Indian allies, there was, he said, no reason to fear that "there is any danger of their uniting against their own nation." For them to do so was impossible, not merely improbable, unless they were subject to "the most grievous tyranny and oppression"—a condition then hard to imagine. On this ground, he rejected the supposition that the colonies' "growth may render them *dangerous.*" Meanwhile, according to Franklin, the colonies showed their understanding and public spirit by "the confidence they so justly repose in a wise and good prince [George II], and an honest and able administration."

Franklin's message to the British was that they had nothing to worry about and should prefer Canada to Guadeloupe. There is no reason to believe that he did not honestly believe in what he was saying at this time. He still saw himself as a colonial member of the great British family, as eager as any other member of the family to advance the greater glory of the British empire.

In this pamphlet, Franklin helped to lull the British into the comforting assumption that they were likely to have little or no difficulty with the colonies for a long time to come. To believe him, they had little to fear for as long as a century or more, so long as the colonies had enough land to prefer agriculture to manufactures. By insisting that the colonies could not unite even to defend themselves against the French, he helped to convince the British that the colonies were incapable of uniting in such an unlikely cause as independence from traditional British rule.

While Franklin was in London giving advice to the British, Americans in the colonies soon learned about the Canada versus Guadeloupe controversy. The *South Carolina Gazette* of March 22, 1760, carried a report of the argument for keeping Canada, and an article from *Lloyd's Chronicle* of London in the same vein appeared in the *Boston News-Letter* of May 8, 1760.[15] Thomas Hutchinson, then lieutenant governor of Massachusetts, later recalled that the debate in England was not without effect on the future leaders of the colonial cause:

It was well known in America, that the people of England, as well as

[15] Warren Bertram Johnson, *The Content of American Colonial Newspapers Relative to International Affairs, 1704–1763* (diss., University of Washington, 1962), p. 419.

administration, were divided upon the expediency of retaining Canada rather than the [French West Indian] islands; and it was known that the objection to Canada proceeded from an opinion, that the cession of it by France would cause, in time, a separation of the British colonies from the mother country. This jealousy in England being known, it was of itself sufficient to set enterprising men upon considering how far such a separation was expedient and practicable.[16]

If Hutchinson was right, the British advocates of retaining Canada had put subversive ideas into the heads of the colonies' "enterprising men." If so, it was ironic that British fears helped to bring about just what the British had feared the most.

Another American reaction to the question of Canada's future was recorded by John Adams in his diary on February 1, 1763. He told it as an anecdote about John Erving, Sr., a Boston merchant:

> He has prophesyed so long, and with so much Confidence that Canada would be restored to the French that, because he begins to see his Predictions will not be fullfilled, he is now straining his Invention for Reasons, why we ought not to hold it. He says, the Restoration of that Province can alone prevent our becoming luxurious, effeminate, inattentive to any Danger and so an easy Prey to an Invader. He was so soundly bantered, the other day in the Council Chamber, that he snatched his Hat and Cloak and went off, in a Passion.[17]

Erving apparently had prophesied that Canada would be returned to the French long before 1763. Yet his reasoning was not unlike that of the pro-Guadeloupe pamphleteers. In both cases, the restoration of Canada was seen to have repercussions on the state of the British-American colonies—for Erving, because it would make the colonists "luxurious, effeminate, inattentive to any Danger," for the pamphleteers, because it would encourage the colonies to rebel and seek their independence. One way or the other, the decision whether to take Canada or Guadeloupe could not leave the colonies the same as before.

Adams himself believed that the decision to keep Canada was the dividing line in British policy vis-à-vis the colonies:

Suffice it to say, that immediately upon the conquest of Canada from

---

[16] Thomas Hutchinson, *The History of the Colony and Province of Massachusetts-Bay,* ed. Lawrence Shaw Mayo (Harvard University Press, 1936), vol. 3, p. 73.

[17] *The Diary and Autobiography of John Adams,* ed. L. H. Butterfield (Harvard University Press, 1961), vol. 1, p. 233.

the French in the year 1759, Great Britain seemed to be seized with a jealousy against the Colonies, and then concerted the plan of changing their forms of government, of restraining their trade within narrower bounds, and raising a revenue within them by authority of parliament, for the avowed or pretended purpose of protecting, securing, and defending them.[18]

In some way, whatever it was, the conquest of Canada was vital to the future of the American colonies. The pamphlet war was a portent of things to come at a time when no one could have guessed this from anything that was happening in the colonies.

· 4 ·

Meanwhile, the Canada versus Guadeloupe issue was officially resolved in 1761. Some British statesmen wanted Canada, some Guadeloupe, and at least one influential figure, the duke of Bedford, wanted neither. The "war party," headed by Pitt, wanted to get Canada and almost everything else. Yet the choice was so difficult that Pitt was said to have exclaimed in 1760: "Some are for keeping Canada, some Guadeloupe; who will tell me which I shall be hanged for not keeping?"[19] Others, like the earl of Chesterfield, recommended keeping Canada "as preventives of future war" and because he thought the French were more willing to give up Canada than Guadeloupe.[20] James Douglas, sixteenth earl of Morton, with a particular interest in American affairs, put the security of the British North American colonies first but recognized that giving up Guadeloupe would be "the greatest misfortune that ever attended our Sugar Colonys."[21]

The choice was a difficult one, and uneasiness about keeping Canada was expressed by both Bedford and Morton. Bedford advised Newcastle: "I do not know whether the neighbourhood of the French to our Northern Colonies was not the greatest security of their dependance on the Mother

[18] John Adams to Mr. Calkoen, October 4, 1780, *The Works of John Adams*, ed. Charles Francis Adams (Boston, 1861), vol. 7, p. 266. In his old age, Adams reiterated this point: "It was not until after the annihilation of the French dominion in America that any British ministry had dared to gratify their own wishes, and the desire of the nation, by projecting a formal plan for raising a national revenue from America, by parliamentary taxation" (to H. Niles, February 13, 1818, ibid., vol. 10, p. 284).

[19] Horace Walpole, *Memoirs of the Reign of King George the Third*, ed. G. F. Russell Barker (Lawrence and Bullen, 1894), vol. 1, p. 26.

[20] Lewis Namier, *England in the Age of the American Revolution* (St. Martin's Press, 1930; 2d ed., 1961), p. 276.

[21] Ibid., p. 278.

Country who I fear will be slighted by them when the apprehensions of the French are removed." Morton cited an objection to keeping Canada on the ground "that the awe of the French keeps our Colonys in dependance upon the Mother Country." His answer to this difficulty was to make sure that "the new settlements should be formed into Governments of small extent" and that "the mutual jealousys amongst the several Colonys would always keep them in a state of dependance and it would save a vast expence to Britain in not being obliged to keep up a great number of regular forces which must be maintained if the smallest spot is left with the French upon that Continent."[22]

In the end, the pro-Canada party prevailed. By 1761, the French were resigned to giving up Canada if they could retain Guadeloupe. Other factors delayed the peace treaty for two more years, but these issues were effectively settled. Nevertheless, the "pamphlet war" went on, though it no longer influenced official policy. The persistence of the argument shows that it was not limited to current affairs but had much deeper roots. Our main concern is with the long-term significance, not the immediate political effect.

One pamphlet of 1761 came with a particularly long-winded title: *Reasons for Keeping Guadaloupe at a Peace, preferable to Canada, Explained by Five Letters from a Gentleman in Guadaloupe, to His Friend in London.* In part, it was designed to be an answer to Franklin's pamphlet of the previous year. It expressed the hope that "we shall be wiser than grasp this gilded snake and be bit to death." The "gilded snake" was Franklin's glorification of the rise of American population and strength as a vast boon to British power. This pamphleteer turned Franklin's logic on its head and argued that the Franklinesque view of American progress represented a threat to Great Britain, even its early "ruin."

Franklin's premises were directly challenged:

I say the acquisition of Canada would be destructive, because such a country as North-America, ten times larger in extent than Britain, richer soil in most places, all the different climates you can fancy, all the lakes and rivers for navigation one could wish, plenty of wood for shipping, and as much iron, hemp, and naval forces, as any part of the world; such a country at such a distance, could never remain long subject to Britain; you have taught them the art of war, and put arms in their hands, and they can furnish themselves with every thing in a few years, without the assistance of Britain; they are always grumbling and complaining against Britain, even while they have the French to dread,

[22] Ibid., pp. 276, 278.

what may they not be supposed to do if the French is no longer a check upon them; you must keep a numerous standing army to over-awe them; these troops will soon get wives and possessions, and become Americans; thus from these measures you lay the surest foundation of unpeopling Britain, and strengthening America to revolt; a people who must become more licentious from their liberty, and more factious and turbulent from the distance of the power that rules them; one must be very little conversant in history, and totally unacquainted with the passions and operations of the human mind, who cannot foresee those events as clearly as any thing can be discovered, that lies concealed in the womb of time; it is no gift of prophecy, it is only the natural and unavoidable consequences of such and such measures, and must appear so to every man whose head is not too much affected with popular madness or political enthusiasm.

Therefore, it was alleged that

nothing can secure Britain so much against the revolting of North-America, as the French keeping some footing there, to be a check upon them, if the peace be made with any tolerable attention to our barrier in America, as we may be most certain it will, France must ever after be an enemy too feeble to be dreaded in that corner of the world; but if we were to acquire all Canada, we should soon find North-America itself too powerful, and too populous to be long governed by us at this distance.

There were other considerations. The rate of increase of the American population was particularly threatening, because "the number of people is the great wealth and strength of every country where industry abounds." The American colonies did not need to fear the French in Canada, because they outnumbered them by ten to one. But soon the writer returned to his main theme:

As America increases in people, so she must increase in arts and sciences, in manufactures and trade, while she has the same laws, liberties, and genius we have at home; the more she encreases in these, the less she must want from Britain; the more she rises above a certain pitch, her utility and advantage to Britain must proportionately decline. The period is possibly not at such a distance as some people may imagine, when they may refuse to send you their tobaccoes, but export them to foreign markets themselves; you might send fleets for some time to molest their coasts, but might find yourselves too feeble to send armies that could conquer; the more you waste your strength upon America with any power but France, the more you weaken yourself at home, and become the easier prey to your turbulent and restless European neighbours.

Franklin was challenged on one of his favorite grounds—that the American colonies doubled their number every twenty-five years and, therefore, would need to continue to expand their agriculture westward. On the contrary, the counterargument went, "they must abate of their application in cultivating the ground" and "must naturally put those spare people to learn arts and trades; to make cloaths, shoes, stockings, shirts etc. smiths, carpenters, braziers, and all the trades that flourish in England." It followed that "after this is accomplished, of what utility will they be of [*sic*] to Great Britain?"

This pamphlet went on to praise Guadeloupe and dispraise Canada, but one theme was almost obsessive and came back towards the end:

The sugar islands must always be dependant, but America as she rises to maturity, may endanger our trade and liberty both. It must be absurd to say or think, that when America exceeds us in numbers of people, that she will nevertheless continue dependant; because independancy is grasped at by all mankind since their first creation: how impatient are all the children in England, as they advance in years, to be independant of their natural and fond parents; does not the common conversation of all companies in North-America run upon that subject; when they can ar[r]ive at independancy, they wait for it, and expect it with as much impatience, as a girl of fifteen does for her marriage to break loose from the restraint of a watchful mother. Let no man flatter himself with those empty phantoms, or fancy that he can alter the nature and passions of men, or make them more fond of dependancy in a collective body, than individuals are: it must appear equally absurd to imagine, that North-America as she advances in agriculture, and encreases in numbers of people, will not also encrease in industry, arts, trades, manufactures and sciences; in a country where nature has collected together such profusion of all the materials and conveniences that can invite to such industry, more than any country we know of; and where liberty blossoms and flourishes, with more natural and brilliant lustre, than ever it did in any new established colonies that we read of since the creation of the world: such vain, unnatural, and airy delusions can never have place amongst rational people, who have made the least reflection upon human nature, or observed the uniform experience of past ages.[23]

No sooner did this pamphlet come out than it was answered by another with an even longer title, only part of which read *A Detection of the False Reasons and Facts, Contained in the Five Letters ... By a Member of Parliament.* Virtually everything the former had said about the advantages of Guadeloupe was denied, even that its sugar was commercially more profitable than the Canadian fur trade. To counter the specter of future American commercial rivalry with Great Britain, Franklin's argument was invoked—"that an increase of Territory in *North America* is the best Means to keep our Colonies in a State of *Utility* and *Advantage* to *Great Britain.* For, if their Lands be immense; there can be no Danger of the People's ever becoming so numerous, as to want Employment in that advantageous and useful Way"—agriculture. Most of all, the security of the American colonies was foremost, and it could be assured only by keeping Canada.

Finally, the author dealt with the most dangerous threat of American independence and British decline.

What may be in the Womb of Providence, it is not in the Power of Man to discover ... that there may hereafter rise up a vast Empire of our Brethren in *North America,* are Events that I won't pretend to affirm or deny. But, because this is possible, therefore it must come to pass, is a bad Argument. On the contrary we have all the Reason in the World to believe, That our Brethren in *North America* will *never revolt* from their Mother Country, and that their Increase of Power and Strength is likely to turn out the best Aid to *Britain* against both her foreign and domestic Foes.

The American colonies were governed by "wholesome and equitable Laws," protected from "all Invaders of their Liberty and Property," and admitted to "the Enjoyment of the Rights and Privileges of their Mother Country." Why should there "form the least Idea of a Revolt amongst a People in these happy Circumstances"? Besides, as Franklin had already argued, the colonies were divided too much among themselves ever to unite against such beneficent British rule.

But what if the colonies should be so shortsighted and self-destructive as to revolt and seek independence from Britain? The answer anticipated just what Britain tried to do a decade and a half later:

[23] The citations from this pamphlet come from pp. 6–8, 12, 14, 19, 20, 29, 47, 51, 75–76.

Should the Colonies enter into a Conspiracy against their Sovereign, or presume to act contrary to the true Intent of the Law; or should they pursue Measures to put their Colonies into a State of Offence, to fabricate Weapons of Destruction; to erect Magazines of Naval and Military Stores; to seek for unnatural Alliances; to build Ships of War; or to establish Manufactures and Trade injurious to the Manufactures and Commerce of their Mother Country; *Great Britain* might easily, and ought to interpose with her Power and Authority. The Civil Power faithfully executed, would be sufficient to disarm the Licentious, and all such as were given to Change: And Penal Laws applied to various Circumstances, would effectually restrain the Trade and Manufactures of the Colonies to such a Degree, as to make them subservient, useful and advantageous to their Mother Country.[24]

This pamphleteer was indignant about depending on the French to enable Great Britain to hold on to its American colonies and about unfairly doubting their fidelity: "How badly then does it suit a *British* Pen to seek for Safety to the Power, Dominion, and Commerce of *Great Britain,* in the Arms of her natural Enemy? How scandalous and unjust to stigmatize our Brethren in *North America* with Discontent, Disloyalty, and Rebellion, who have never given the least Reason for such Imputations?"

But the author was willing to admit that Great Britain might be corrupted and so weakened "that there may hereafter rise up a vast Empire of our Brethren in *North America,* with Power to give Laws to all the World." How could the author know this? Because *"North America,* under the *British* Dominion, enjoys every Blessing of a free People." He asked triumphantly: "Can it be possible to form the least Idea of a Revolt amongst a People in these happy Circumstances?" A revolt would deprive the Americans of all their advantages. Great Britain would soon cut off their trade and destroy their navigation—"And without Trade they would make a very wretched Figure in a revolted State." The Americans "ought not to be suspected of approaching towards a Revolution, which would bring manifest Ruin upon themselves."

How easily Great Britain could bring her power and authority to prevent the Americans from doing what was forbidden to them was to be tested fifteen years later. Meanwhile, this pamphleteer consoled himself with

---

[24] *A Detection of the False Reasons and Facts, Contained in the Five Letters, (entitled, Reasons for keeping GUADALOUPE at a Peace, preferable to CANADA; from a Gentleman in Guadaloupe to his Friend in London.) in which The Advantages of both Conquests are fairly and impartially stated and compared* (London, 1761), pp. 45, 49, 50, 51–54.

one more thought. Revolts came from "Idleness, Ignorance, Poverty and Arbitrary Power." But the "richer, the politer, and the more industrious" Americans grew, the more they could be expected to "entertain more exalted Notions of Gratitude and Loyalty to their King and Mother Country." In effect, the danger of an American revolt was bound to come from penury, not from prosperity, from decline, not from a rise. This view was also to be tested shortly.[25]

Thus much of the case for keeping Canada without stirring up American yearnings for independence was based on two calculations that eventually proved to be deceptive. One was that the Americans would have their hands full for so long in the future that it was safe to give them more western land for their increasing population and agriculture. The other was that Great Britain had nothing to fear from the Americans, because they had too many differences among themselves and could never unite in behalf of their own self-government or independence.

Even if these expectations should prove to be delusory, Britain could always use force in the last extremity. In fact, the colonies did in the end enter into what seemed to loyal British subjects to be a "Conspiracy," did pursue measures that put them in a "State of Offence," and did seek an "unnatural Alliance." Within only fifteen years, Britain found it necessary to "interpose with her Power and Authority." To this extent, the pamphleteer was clairvoyant; he merely underestimated how much power and authority it would take to disarm "all such as were given to Change."

· 5 ·

In the critical years before the American Revolution the accession of Canada came up in the colonies. In 1766, an important New York merchant, John Watts, raised it in a peculiar way—that the Americans now regretted that Canada had been taken away from France. He wrote to Gov. Robert Monckton of New York: "The Colonies are extremely incensed at the treatment they have received from the Mother Country & tho' it has not had effects in one sense, it has in another, which I believe will soon be obliterated. They seem to wish Canada again French, it made 'em of some consequence, which in consequence they lost when it was conquer'd, if their reasoning be just."[26]

[25] Ibid., pp. 49–53.
[26] John Watts to Gov. Monckton, May 12, 1766, "The Aspinwall Papers," *Massachusetts Historical Society Collections*, 4th ser., vol. 10 (1887), p. 592.

British opinion began to wonder whether it had not been a mistake to take Canada from the French. In 1768, *The Public Advertiser* published a rumor "that a Negotiation is on the Tapis for restoring Canada to France, in return for one of their Sugar Islands, as the most effectual means of securing the Dependence of America on the Mother Country."[27] In 1773, Josiah Quincy, Jr., of Boston, then in London, dined at "a most superb house," on which occasion a British native expressed the opinion that Great Britain had "committed a most capital political blunder in not ceding Canada to France."[28] In 1774, a writer in *The London Chronicle* contended that a prime cause of the American troubles was that the British had "taken the French off their backs and placed them in a state of security."[29] In his polemical pamphlet *Taxation No Tyranny*, of 1775, Samuel Johnson taunted the Americans: "Let us restore to the French what we have taken from them. We shall see our Colonists at our feet, when they have an enemy so near them."[30]

An irate letter that year in the London *Morning Chronicle* took the same line:

> The American Rebels are constantly boasting of the prodigious services which they rendered *us*, in the course of the last war, when it is notoriously known, that the last war was entered into for their *own* immediate protection; and therefore, whatever efforts they made, were entirely from motives of *private interest*, and not from a generous principle of *attachment* to their Mother Country: while a foreign enemy, indeed, was at their backs, they affected a prodigious deal of loyalty to the present state; but the moment their fears on that head were removed by the cession of all Canada to Great Britain, that moment the dutiful colonies began to change their tone; America was no longer *ours*, but *theirs*.[31]

The next year, another British pamphleteer, replying to the American Declaration of Independence, still raised the old regret that Canada had been taken from the French:

> But, on the other hand, had Canada remained in the hands of the

[27] *The Public Advertiser*, November 7, 1768.
[28] March 8, 1773, *Memoir of the Life of Josiah Quincy Jun.* (Boston, 1825), p. 101.
[29] *The London Chronicle*, September 17, 1774, cited by Fred Junkin Hinkhouse, *The Preliminaries of the American Revolution as Seen in the English Press, 1763–1775* (Columbia University Press, 1926), pp. 104–5.
[30] Samuel Johnson, *Taxation No Tyranny* (London, 1775), p. 84.
[31] *Morning Chronicle*, July 1, 1775, reprinted in *English Historical Documents, 1714–1783*, ed. D. B. Horn and Mary Ransome (Eyre & Spottiswoode, 1957), vol. 10, p. 761.

French, the Colonies would have remained dutiful subjects. Their fears for themselves, in that case, would have supplied the place of their pretended affection for this Nation. They would have spoken more sparingly of their own resources, as they might daily stand in need of our aid. Their former incapacity of defending themselves, would have always recurred to their minds, as long as the objects of their former terror should continue so near their borders.[32]

Thus the American Revolution was haunted by a decision made a decade and a half earlier by the British government. The "pamphlet war" over Canada versus Guadeloupe was only an incident in the making of the British decision, but it has a far larger significance in the development of the Revolution. It reveals a long-standing concern in British circles about the progress made by the American colonies and where it was going to lead. It cast a shadow over the events of the next fifteen years, because it raised the question of what effect the growth of the American colonies would have on the British empire.

· 6 ·

Where did this premonition of Britain's loss of its American colonies, if the French were eliminated in Canada, come from? Why did it arise in 1759–1761? At that time the great controversy over the Stamp Act was still about five years away. The colonists themselves had done nothing and said nothing to trigger such a fear. A colonial agent in London, Benjamin Franklin, did his best to deride the very idea.

In 1759–1761, this strand of British thinking was based on purely objective or nonpolitical factors. It was not a reaction to American grievances and agitation. It had nothing to do with taxes or British soldiers stationed in unwilling colonies. The colonies had not yet given signs that they were aiming at anything resembling independence.

This anticipation of trouble was based solely on power relations, as measured in that century by growth of population and trade. Whether or not these factors motivated the colonies as much as the British thought they must, these premonitions served as the background of future British thinking. Other immediate, practical matters soon divided the colonies and mother country, but they came to be all the more menacing because they

---

[32] [James Macpherson?], *The Rights of Great Britain Asserted Against the Claims of America: Being an Answer to the Declaration of the General Congress* (London, 4th ed., 1776), p. 10.

implied—at least to the British—that something more far-reaching was at stake.

No one can "prove" that the outcome of the Seven Years' War "caused" or "generated" the American Revolution or that the colonies would have continued to fear the French in Canada so much that they would not have dared to make a revolution. All that can be safely said is that influential British opinion was so suspicious of American intentions that the outcome of the Seven Years' War brought out into the open the most extensive forebodings of what to expect from the Americans if they were relieved of the French menace. These suspicions had been long in the making. They intangibly influenced British policy a few years later, when the Americans gave the British more practical and demonstrative causes to worry about the behavior of their American colonies.

2

''Speculative reasoners''

✣

· 1 ·

T HESE PREMONITIONS OF 1759–1761 require an explanation. They did not appear out of nowhere. Yet they did not emerge from any recent evidence that the colonies were aiming at independence. The first British acts which brought on a crisis in British-colonial relations were still three to five years away. Something else must have been behind these alarming forebodings.

By 1759, most of the colonies were over a hundred years old—the oldest, Virginia, about a century and a half. Generations of British ministers had been coping with recalcitrant colonies. Despite the differences among the colonies, some problems had come up again and again in all of them, repeatedly testing the ability of the British imperial system to manage them. Colony after colony, decade after decade, had pushed the colonial system to the limits of forbearance. This experience could not fail to leave a deep institutional imprint on the consciousness of British officialdom.

In order to get behind these premonitions, we need to know what British ruling circles had been told for over a century by their most trusted agents in America. For decades, British administrators had been warning their superiors in London in more or less the same vein. Reports from the colonies had come in month after month, year after year, often in great detail. It would be strange if they did not make a cumulative impression on their readers, especially if they were almost always threatening.

26

· 2 ·

Some aspects of the first or old British imperial system—lack of system might be more nearly correct—help to explain why such premonitions arose, early and late.

The settlement of Jamestown in Virginia in 1607 was England's first colonial experiment. Nothing in its own past experience had prepared England for it. The history of previous empires and colonies was regarded as the only teacher, and its lessons were not reassuring. These were understood to be that colonies were safe and loyal only so long as they were weak and dependent. The farther away they were, the more likely they were to become dangerously rebellious. This ancient wisdom did not bode well for latecoming imperial ventures.

Words can be deceptive here. The American colonies were English in origin but not the work of England as a nation. The first settlements or plantations were financed and established by joint-stock companies primarily interested in profits for their shareholders. The most the government could do was authorize them to conceive, organize, go forth, and take all the risks. The Crown of England gave such authorization in the form of "charters," which were inherited from a much older tradition.[1] Colonization by chartering private companies came naturally to seventeenth-century England. The state lacked the economic resources, administrative apparatus, and sustained will to carry out such enterprises. It was easier, cheaper, and safer to commission companies of "merchant adventurers" to organize and finance the hazardous voyages and precarious settlements, for the same reason that privateers were commissioned to wage naval warfare for a profit.

Colonization was originally an extension of trade and trading companies. Even the Pilgrims of Plymouth were subsidized by London merchants and investors who, as a distinguished American historian put it, "wanted profit, not prayers."[2] Later proprietors, such as William Penn in Pennsylvania, Lord Baltimore in Maryland, and a group of eight in Carolina, took the place of companies, but the practice of colonization by others than the state remained the same.

[1] A *charter* was a document or letter given by the king to a subject or subjects granting certain rights and privileges. It was also called a *patent,* as in the phrase "wee have caused these our Letters to bee made Patent." Thus the terms *charter* and *patent* were used interchangeably.

[2] Charles M. Andrews, *The Colonial Period of American History* (Yale University Press, 1934), vol. 1, p. 344.

A British analysis of the early system stressed its limitations:

Commercial and financial considerations rather than schemes of territorial expansion or missionary enterprise dictated the policy of Elizabeth and the first two monarchs of the House of Stuart. They had no resources available to undertake Imperial development, and they had, therefore, recourse to private enterprise, especially in the form of organized companies, for the individual adventurer had little prospect of success if he relied on his own means, and in fact would have to fall back on the device of seeking to secure the co-operation of others in the exploitation of his patent. The system of concessions meant that the Imperial government had but an indirect authority over the holders of grants; their operations overseas could not directly be controlled by Imperial officers, and recourse must be had to such control as could be exercised on the grantees through their presence from time to time in England.[3]

In later years, right up to the American Revolution, whenever a dispute arose between the colonies and the home government, the former fell back on their charters to obstruct and resist. Charters provided the colonies with a legalistic defense of their "rights." If the ministers of the Crown had been able to foresee that the charters could be used by the colonies as instruments of self-government, they would doubtless have written them differently. This paradox—that the charters lent themselves to colonial self-government—was a critical element from the beginning to almost the end of the colonial period.

Charters were peculiarly double-edged. They acknowledged England's sovereign status at the same time as they left the colonies to their own resources. They became colonial weapons against English rule, because they were so deeply embedded in English constitutional tradition and political structure. They were a prime example of how much the colonial struggle for independence owed to the rule of law derived from the country against which the struggle was waged.

The Crown had long bestowed fiefs or great feudal estates in outlying portions of the kingdom, where the central government could not reach.[4] They were virtually self-governing, because they had to protect and provide for themselves. Out of this custom stemmed the grants to private corporations

---

[3] A. Berriedale Keith, *Constitutional History of the First British Empire* (Oxford University Press, 1930), p. 18.

[4] Louise Phelps Kellogg, "The American Colonial Charter," *Annual Report of the American Historical Association for the Year 1903* (Washington, 1904), vol. 1, p. 192.

or proprietors who were willing to pay the price and take the risks of early colonization.

Merchants had long formed trading companies to engage in foreign commerce. The greatest of these, the East India Company, was chartered in 1600 by Queen Elizabeth to do everything on its own that a national government might do—political, military, judicial, and administrative— and did these things for 250 years. These trading companies provided the prototype for the American colonies as self-subsistent, chartered corporations.

Later, the charter of Massachusetts was temporarily revoked, and the Crown imposed its own direct rule. Eventually, New York, New Jersey, Maryland, Virginia, North and South Carolina, and Georgia went from proprietary status to royal or Crown control. Thus evolved three types of colonial government—charter, proprietary, and Crown.

The basic patterns help to explain why colonists were sent off from England with very few strings attached. The promoters of Virginia and Massachusetts raised their own funds by selling stock with the intention of making a profit, as if they were ordinary business enterprises. Both the Virginia Company and the Massachusetts Bay Company obtained charters from the Crown as self-governing corporations. They were understood to be dedicated to the greater glory of England, but they were left to fend for themselves and were expected to do more for England than England did for them. After all, it did not cost English kings anything to give away land that they did not own and could have done nothing with even if they had owned it.

Another self-determining element came from the kinds of people who left England for the American colonies. Many emigrated because they were deeply discontented, even persecuted, in England. Many others went in search of a better life and the lure of striking it rich quickly. Tobacco held out the promise of huge profits in the Chesapeake region of Maryland and Virginia. The two early "models of English colonization," as they have been called, were far more the creation of Englishmen than of England. The New England model chose America to escape from England, and the Chesapeake model came for individualistic, self-seeking motives. Neither was imbued with the much later colonial mission of national aggrandizement. Whatever the reason, people did not leave England if they wanted the same things that they had had in England.

These influences conspired to make the first colonies self-sufficient and self-regulating. The merchant, craftsman, or yeoman who knew his place and obeyed his superiors in England was not likely to act the same way wrenched from his familiar surroundings. He still considered himself an Englishman and retained a sense of allegiance to his native land. An Englishman transplanted, however, was not the same kind of Englishman.

A propagandistic pamphlet of 1630 in behalf of colonizing Massachusetts illustrates the ambivalent risks of colonization. It instructed prospective settlers that a colony was "a societie of men drawne out of one state or people, and transplanted into another Countrey." Yet, as if this were going too far, it also stated that "a Colonie denying due respect to the State from whose bowels it issued, is as great a monster, as an unnaturall childe." Significantly, the author considered the objection that "such publicke workes cannot be managed but by a publicke purse; Colonies are workes for a State, and not for private persons." He agreed that "Colonies are best undertaken by Princes, assisted with the strength of a whole State." But he countered with Dutch patroons or proprietors in New Amsterdam and England's own Plymouth colony "as examples of what may be done in Colonies by private persons." At that early date, he thought it necessary to deny that Virginia and New England were going to be "a nursery of faction and rebellion," that they would "free themselves from our government," and that "under the colour of planting a Colony they intended to rayse and erect a seminary of faction and separation."[5] If there had been no specter of faction, separation, and rebellion, there would have been no need to deny the possibility.

· 3 ·

England lacked the machinery of government to supervise the colonies closely. In the beginning, it had no special bodies to oversee them. The earliest specifically colonial agency was a commission appointed in 1623 to look into complaints against the proprietary management of Virginia. When the charter of the Virginia Company was annulled the following year, the Crown took direct charge of the colony, which in effect made Virginia the first "Crown colony." It was theoretically administered by the Privy Council, which was in fact too large a body and too preoccupied with other things to pay much attention to a small, faraway appendage.

Another factor in colonial development was the turbulence of the seventeenth century, which was shaken by three political upheavals. In 1644, the outbreak of civil war in the name of a parliamentary Commonwealth by

[5] *The Planters Plea* (London, 1630), reprinted in Peter Force, *Tracts and Other Papers* (Washington, 1836; reprint, Peter Smith, 1963), vol. 2, no. 3, pp. 1, 14, 28, 33–34, 44.

an army under Oliver Cromwell resulted in the overthrow of the monarchy and execution of Charles I in 1649. In 1660, the monarchy was restored under Charles II. In 1688, the Glorious Revolution overthrew James II and brought in William of Orange in an arrangement which resulted in the ultimate supremacy of Parliament. These three events had repercussions in the colonies.

During the Commonwealth phase, Parliament itself took charge of colonial affairs through a Council of State. It was so busy with more pressing matters, though, that the colonies, especially New England, were virtually left to govern themselves. In one respect, however, Parliament made a long-term difference. In 1651, during the Commonwealth period, it passed the first Navigation Act, which restricted all colonial commerce to England; nothing could be brought into or out of the colonies except in English ships. Significantly, however, the Navigation Act stipulated that the colonies were subject to "such laws, orders, and regulations as are or shall be made by the Parliament of England."

With the royalist Restoration in 1660, English policy shifted in favor of Crown colonies. For the most part, decisions were again made by the Privy Council through a standing committee for trade and plantations. Various experiments in the form of subordinate councils for the colonies were tried but never lasted for long. Only starting in 1675 did a Committee for Trade and Foreign Plantations manage to survive for almost twenty years. In any case, the Restoration kings attempted to change little in troublesome New England and set up new colonies in New York, New Jersey, and North and South Carolina to reward favorites. Administration was so lax that the last letter to the Committee for Trade and Foreign Plantations had been received five years before. As late as 1700, William Blathwayt, who as a longtime bureaucrat at the Committee for Trade and Foreign Plantations knew more than anyone else about what had gone on, explained: "Ye Security of our Colonies & rend[e]ring them more usefull to England etc. are common places that have entertain'd us these many years but the means which are very plain have always been opposed or not prosecuted."[6]

In 1696, after the Glorious Revolution, the colonial setup was again reorganized. Parliament passed the legislation which authorized the reorganization; the Privy Council continued to make basic decisions, when it was so inclined. A secretary of state for the Southern Department was responsible for all colonial business. The real work was handled by a new Board of Trade and Plantations, soon shortened to Board of

[6] J. M. Sosin, *English America and the Restoration Monarchy of Charles II* (University of Nebraska Press, 1980), p. 172.

Trade. This board, which lasted until the American Revolution, conducted correspondence with governors, approved or disapproved legislation passed by assemblies, and in general supervised the colonies. In the last resort, however, Parliament could still decide, though it rarely wished to get entangled in colonial affairs.

It was a slow, cumbersome, rickety process. The main concern of the board was not how to administer the colonies efficiently or soundly; it was how to make them commercially profitable to the mother country. The board's staff was small—three to five members generally made decisions. Nevertheless, a number of colonial experts had already begun to make their influence felt, and they carried on irrespective of the regime. The board's most famous member for a short time was the philosopher John Locke, who drew up the constitution of the Carolinas. One member, Martin Bladen, served for almost thirty years. The Board of Trade, however, was not the only bureaucratic agency interested in the colonies. The Treasury, Admiralty, customs, and law officers also had colonial interests and responsibilities. Action could be held up by any one of them.

Even the term *colonies* may cause misunderstanding. These were not colonies in the sense of alien peoples conquered and oppressed by a foreign power. They were not alien; they had not been conquered; and their later grievances were hardly of the kind that they themselves would have described as oppression until the last decade of their colonial status. The term *plantation* was equally applied to the colonies, and, as used by Thomas Hobbes in 1651, it referred to "numbers of men sent out from the Common-wealth, under a Conductor, or Governour, to inhabit a Forraign Country, either formerly voyd of Inhabitants, or made voyd then, by Warre."[7] This seventeenth-century sense is much closer to the origins of the American colonies than to the implication of conquest and exploitation which much later came to be attached to the term *colonies*. We may continue to use it, because it is customary, though at some risk of doing injustice to its particular nature.

The early colonial system was a thoroughly ramshackle affair. The charter and proprietary colonies sprang up without any imperial officials residing in them. Far into the eighteenth century, England had no substantial armed force in the colonies to impose its will. Communication between them and London took weeks and sometimes months. Leading figures in the Privy Council and its committees or councils had no special competence with respect to the colonies, and the membership changed rapidly. Instructions

[7] Thomas Hobbes, *Leviathan, or The Matter, Forme & Power of a Common-Wealth Ecclesiasticall and Civill* (London, 1651), pt. 2, chap. 24.

went out from London, but enforcing them—or even knowing what had happened to them—was another matter. In desperation, agents were sometimes dispatched from England to find out what was going on, only to send back reports about how harshly they were treated. This First British Empire was far from being as impressive as the name may suggest.

• 4 •

And always, there were the charters. They were the umbilical cords which attached the colonies to the mother country. They represented a cultural and political bond without which the colonies would have felt naked and alone. In theory, bands of colonists could have made their way across the ocean and set up on their own. In practice, it was unthinkable to go without the legitimization of the home government. In a sense, the colonies did set up on their own, because their survival was still dependent on themselves. But in a century of cutthroat rivalry among imperial powers, it was indispensable to belong to a greater realm from which future settlers had to come and to which they might return. The tension between separating and belonging was built into the colonial experience.

The first charters betray this tension. The Virginia charter of 1606 made no distinction between the rights of Englishmen at home and those in the colony. It granted the colonists "all Liberties, Franchises, and Immunities" that were "to all Intents and Purposes, as if they had been abiding and born, within this our Realm of *England.*"[8] The second charter, of 1609, however, implied that the colonists were not going to be ruled as if they were in England. It gave the colonizing company "full and absolute Power and Authority to correct, punish, pardon, govern, and rule" all the subjects in its jurisdiction.[9] This transfer of authority to the promoters and investors interposed a power between the English state and the people of the colonies which had unforeseen consequences.

The first charter of Massachusetts Bay, as it was originally called, of 1629, reproduced this tension in a different form. Like other charters, it assured the inhabitants that they were to "have and enjoy all liberties and Immunities of free and naturall Subjects" to all intents and purposes "as yf they and everie of them were borne within the Realme of England." Unlike in Virginia, however, the governor was to be chosen by a general court or

---

[8] Ben Perley Poore, *The Federal and State Constitutions, Colonial Charters, and other Organic Laws of the United States* (Washington, 2d ed., 1878), pt. 2, pp. 1891–92.
[9] Ibid., p. 1901.

convocation of freemen, so that the colony was virtually self-governing from the start. Paradoxically, Massachusetts was given a far greater measure of "liberties and Immunities" than Englishmen enjoyed within the realm.[10]

Most critically, the charters told the fledgling colonies what kinds of governments to set up. In this way, they determined the later relationship between the mother country and the colonies. Here, again, an almost unbearable tension was created. The mother country could only imagine bringing offspring into the world in its own image, but the charter writers could not—or did not—foresee how, in different conditions, their own words might transform that image. In effect, the political ties that originally bound the colonies to the mother country also helped them to shake themselves free.

This metamorphosis came about as a result of the very governmental framework imposed on or chosen by the colonies. If the colonies had actually followed the English model, each would have had the equivalent of a king, a House of Lords, and a House of Commons. Since none of these institutions could exist in the colonies, it was necessary to make do with substitutes or surrogates. The nearest thing in the colonies to the king was a governor, to the House of Lords, a council, and to the House of Commons, an assembly. In general, all colonies had a governor, council, and assembly, though the details varied from colony to colony.

In this scheme of things, the governor was a direct representative of the Crown—but only if he was appointed. In Connecticut and Rhode Island he was not; he was directly representative of the inhabitants. Colonial councils were appointed or elected, but they usually did little more than advise the governor. Assemblies were more like the House of Commons but were limited to acting within each colony, not for the colonies as a whole.

The English system of government had little reality in the colonies. Governors were appointed, removable and responsible to a higher authority in England, as kings were not. Lords were hereditary, but council members were appointed or elected for a single term. Kings could not veto acts of Parliament, but governors could veto acts of assemblies, even if doing so did them little good. In reality, governors were never mistaken for kings, councillors for lords, or members of the assemblies for members of the House of Commons.

The way the colonial charters had come about gave the Crown an advantage over Parliament. The seventeenth-century charters had been granted by kings, not by Parliament, and without any mention of Parliament. As a

_____

[10] Ibid., pt. 1, p. 940.

result, they seemingly tied the colonies to the Crown rather than to Parliament. Governors continued to be appointed by and to represent the Crown, as if nothing had changed in England with the advent of parliamentary supremacy in 1688–89. William and Mary owed their joint crown to an act of Parliament, as did all subsequent British monarchs. But Parliament did not appoint colonial governors; that function remained with the Crown.

Richard Hussey, a king's counsel and member of Parliament, thought it necessary to deny that James I had had the authority to issue any charters to the new colonies. It was a "fatal mistake," he said, for the king to have given the colonies powers in the charters "which the King alone could not give." Thus "an obscurity arose about the colonies and about the administration of them."[11] This "obscurity" was an essential element in the later dispute between Parliament and the colonies. But Hussey spoke in Parliament in 1766, after the upheaval brought on by the Stamp Act, and almost a century and a half too late to do much good.

If, after the Glorious Revolution, Parliament had wished to take to itself the same power abroad that it jealously guarded at home, the colonies would have known more clearly where they stood in the British constitutional scheme. Parliament could always inject itself into colonial affairs, but only if it deliberately chose to do so, which was not often. When it came to colonial matters, Parliament was usually too busy, too divided, or too uninterested to assert itself. Until the 1760s, colonial affairs were generally treated by the secretaries of specific departments of the government; instructions were sent to the governors in the name of the king, not of Parliament. This long neglect made Parliament's sudden incursion into colonial affairs in 1763–1765 all the more startling and unwelcome.

Thus the royal "prerogative" or discretionary power did not die with the Glorious Revolution; it was hedged about but preserved—most of all in the colonies. They held on tenaciously to the privileges granted to them by the royal charters, as if the later history of England had passed them by. The further paradox was that they upheld the royal prerogative as far as it was necessary to protect their charters but were Whiggish parliamentary sympathizers in struggling against the royally appointed governors.

For these reasons, tampering with colonial charters threatened the entire system of chartering, on which much of property rights and local autonomy in England itself was based. The colonies could always hold the English authorities at arm's length—or much farther away—by appealing to their

[11] Richard Hussey, February 3, 1766, *Proceedings and Debates of the British Parliaments Respecting North America, 1754–1783*, ed. R. C. Simmons and P. D. G. Thomas (Kraus International, 1983), vol. 2, p. 141.

charters as if they were so sacred that no king or Parliament could touch them. In 1683, the Massachusetts charter was exalted as "our heavenly Charter; w[hi]ch Jesus Christ hath purchased for us."[12] In 1728, a secular publication gave Providence the credit: "Our charter is the great hedge which Providence has planted around our natural rights, to guard us from an invasion."[13] As late as 1740, Gov. Joseph Talcott of Connecticut solemnly declared that "our Charter, next to the Loyalty we bear to our Sovraigne, and our lives, is the Dearest thing to us on earth."[14] The colonies were so attached to their charters because they obtained privileges from the charters that enabled them to resist British control.

· 5 ·

The three main kinds of colonies—chartered, proprietary, and royal—were different in some ways, but what really mattered in the end was the one way in which they were the same. The charters of all the colonies provided for some sort of elected assembly. And what mattered most of all was that the assemblies were given one power that was total and unconditional: the power over money. Money bills could only originate in the assemblies; without their initiative and approval, nothing could be raised, nothing spent. The Crown and its governors could propose; only the assemblies could dispose. No matter what the title or pomp of office might suggest, the power over money gave the assemblies the ultimate power of decision.

In this respect, the colonial assemblies followed the precedent and tradition of the English Parliament. In their tenacious control of everything and anything having to do with the disposal of their money, the colonies behaved like true Englishmen in England. They fought for their power of the purse as fiercely and as successfully as their English parliamentary forebears had fought for it against the English kings. When James Otis began to contest the right of the British Parliament to tax the colonists, he went all the way back to the Magna Carta and the Glorious Revolution for his precedents.[15]

[12] (Mr. Mathers?) to (Mr. Gouge?) at Amsterdam, October 3, 1683, in *Edward Randolph*, ed. Robert Noxon Toppon (Prince Society, 1899), vol. 3, p. 315.

[13] *New England Weekly Journal*, March 18, 1728, cited by Lawrence H. Leder, *Liberty and Authority* (Quadrangle Books, 1968), p. 109.

[14] *Talcott Papers: Correspondence and Documents during Joseph Talcott's Governorship of the Colony of Connecticut, 1724–1741* (Collections of the Connecticut Historical Society, 1896), vol. 4, pp. 286–87.

[15] James Otis, *The Rights of the British Colonies Asserted and Proved* (1765), reprinted in Bernard Bailyn, ed., *Pamphlets of the American Revolution, 1750–1776* (Harvard University Press, 1965), pp. 430–33.

He could do so because the colonies had been set up with assemblies that imitated the House of Commons in the one respect that could prove to be the undoing of the entire system.

In 1679, during the reign of Charles II, the most influential and most orthodox colonial official, William Blathwayt, saw where control of the money-power was going to lead. He warned that colonial assemblies "have left his Majesty but a small share of the Sovereignty and may as well question that which remains" by declaring that "the revenue ought to arise from them and that the disposall of it and the power of receiving the accounts is belonging to them."[16] Blathwayt was rewarded the following year by appointment as the surveyor and auditor general of revenues in the royal colonies. But he was never able to get control of colonial revenues.[17] The main interest in his warning of 1679 is how early the money problem was recognized and how little or nothing could be done about it even during the Restoration.

In effect, the locus of money-power implied that the assemblies had the final authority in the colonies, as Parliament had in England. The charters implicitly surrendered to the colonies the very power that made the difference between form and substance. The tension between the two was not resolved without a struggle that went on for decades, beginning long before the premonitions of 1759–1761.

· 6 ·

The early English colonial system had only itself to blame. It arose in an age of placemen, appointed to political office to give them easy pickings at public expense. The colonies were ideal for this purpose because they were required to support hungry freeloaders at no cost to the royal Exchequer. The flaw in the system was the colonies' reluctance to coöperate.

Governors spent much of their time complaining to their superiors in London about how little power they had and how much they suffered at the hands of incorrigible assemblies. The root cause of their distress was their dependence on assemblies for their salaries, because it was English policy to spend as little as possible on, and to make as much as possible out of, the colonies. For well over a century, the British ruled the colonies on the cheap, expected them to be self-supporting, and got the most out of them

[16] Cited by Stephen S. Webb, "William Blathwayt, Imperial Fixer: From Popish Plot to Glorious Revolution," *William and Mary Quarterly*, January 1968, p. 7.

[17] Gertrude Ann Jacobsen, *William Blathwayt* (Yale University Press, 1932), pp. 162–85.

for the least. Colonies were self-supporting by taxing themselves for their own administrative costs. Without success, governor after governor cried for relief from monetary dependence on their assemblies.

Some governors abused their sinecures mercilessly or had been appointed on dubious grounds. Gov. Benjamin Fletcher of New York made a fortune selling favors. Govs. Robert Hunter of New York and Alexander Spotswood of Virginia were rewarded for being old soldiers who had fought with Marlborough at Blenheim. Gov. Samuel Shute of Massachusetts was another deserving colonel. Lord Cornbury was described by an early English historian as "illiterate, frivolous, and poor."[18] Governors were appointed for the royal or Crown colonies who never set foot in them; these officials held more lucrative appointments elsewhere, had lieutenant governors serve in their stead, and divided the spoils, such as they were, with their substitutes. Gov. James Glen of South Carolina was appointed in 1738 and did not arrive until 1743, because he was simultaneously inspector of seigniories in Scotland and preferred to stay there for the first five years of his term.[19]

In the mid-eighteenth century, Cadwallader Colden of New York, who knew as much about the colonies as anyone, thought that opposition to governors came naturally to the colonists and that anyone who opposed almost any governor could become a popular favorite:

> The *English* seemed to have little Regard to the Qualification of the Person they sent, but to gratify a Relation or a Friend, by giving him an Opportunity to make a Fortune; and as he knew that he was recommended with this View, his Counsels were chiefly employed for this Purpose.
>
> By this Means an *English Governor* generally wants the Esteem of the People; while they think that a Governor has not the Good of the People in View, but his own, so they on all Occasions are jealous of him; so that even a good Governor, with more Difficulty, pursues generous Purposes and publick Benefits, because the People suspect them to be mere Pretences to cover a private Design. It is for this Reason, that any Man, opposing a Governor, is sure to meet with the Favour of the People, almost in every case.[20]

Assemblies reacted defensively to the endemic corruption and waste. As

[18] George Chalmers, *An Introduction to the History of the Revolt of the American Colonies* (1782; reprint, Boston, 1845), vol. 1, p. 356.

[19] Edward McCrady, *The History of South Carolina under the Royal Government, 1719–1776* (Macmillan, 1899), p. 250.

[20] Cadwallader Colden, *The History of the Five Indian Nations of Canada* (1st ed., 1747; 2d ed., London, 1750), pp. 120–21.

one lieutenant governor put it, "The general disposit[i]on of the people as well without doors as within" to give salaries to governors for no more than from year to year derived from the hope "thereby to restrain a governor from running into excesses."[21] Controlling salaries could lead to challenging the Crown. Governor Spotswood once explained that members of his assembly objected to Queen Anne's control of salaries on the ground that "by the same rule she appoints £1200 she may appoint £12,000."[22] Saving money was one of the main campaign promises of candidates for assemblies. Governor Hunter recognized that men were elected "by the popular argument of having saved the Country's money, some have got the Election secured to themselves, who have always been, and ever will be refractory in what relates to the expence of Government."[23]

Unfortunately for governors and other appointed officials, they had to live. Someone had to pay for them. Assemblies were expected to do the paying and invariably balked. The colonists did not like to part with money and vastly enjoyed making governors grovel for it. Instead of fixed salaries, the assemblies liked to dribble out "gifts" or "presents." These handouts had the advantage of signifying that the assemblies were paying governors for good behavior and only as much as they were considered worth—to the colonists. Only in the four southern colonies, Virginia, Maryland, and North and South Carolina, were definite sums set aside to pay governors. Payments elsewhere were sometimes voted for no more than six months if the governors were particularly obnoxious or uncooperative. By keeping governors on a short financial leash, assemblies made sure that they understood where the real power was located. A governor was hardly a dictator; he was forced to act like a politician, getting along by currying favor and expending limited sources of bribery.

Thus the colonists had the upper hand economically, though governors theoretically had the upper hand politically. So long as governors depended on the assemblies for their livelihood, the colonists were in effect the governors' paymasters. Ostensible political supremacy could never hold out against actual economic supremacy. This imbalance put the governors at the colonists' mercy, so long as the home government refused to support its colonial officials in the style to which they thought themselves entitled. This economic advantage of the colonists had nothing to do with the relative economic strengths of the colonies and the mother country; so long as governors

---

[21] Lt. Gov. George Clarke of New York to the Council of Trade and Plantations, February 18, 1738, *Colonial Papers, America and West Indies* (London, 1969), vol. 44, p. 33.

[22] Ibid., 1710–June 1711, p. 259.

[23] Ibid.

had to come to the colonists for their financial support, the political position of governors lacked an economic underpinning, and the economic position of the colonists more than made up for their assumed political inferiority.

In essence, England found itself with an empire before it could afford to have one or had foreseen what it would entail. A major reason was that the financial structure of government in Great Britain was so rickety. The British Treasury never had enough money to pay for the mother country's current expenses and salaries. The old, wasteful, and hopelessly inefficient system of farming out the collection of taxes to professional revenue gatherers, who were often more interested in what they could get out of it than in what they turned over to the government, was still employed. Lotteries were a main source of income. Official salaries were both inadequate and long delayed. Treasury officials did not know where or when they were going to get their own salaries. Officeholders paid themselves by resorting to the sale of offices, wholesale extortion, plural jobholding, and other sharp or desperate practices. Colonial officials were among the least of the home government's financial worries. When the officials complained, they were advised to squeeze more money out of the penny-pinching colonials.

In 1698, William Blathwayt received a report from John Usher, a former lieutenant governor of New Hampshire, about Lord Bellomont, who had replaced Fletcher as governor of New York:

> Am Sorry to Se[e] and hear of Soe much Slightt and contemptt he metes with; that as poore as I am would nott for the province undergoe the Same. The truth is any person true to the Kings interestt, and for putting comands from the King in Execution, shall mete with enemys enough, in which the Earl [Bellomont] is noe small Sharor. I finde this place to be Some whatt a kind [akin] to province New Hampshire, unless they can have all matters goe according to theire oun will, though never Soe much ag[ains]tt the Kings prerogative and interestt; and for kepeing there [their] purses tyed up, though in the issue tend to theire own damage. I thoughtt [for] a person of the Earls quality with thatt justice, honor, and integrity, they would [have] redily manifested greatt Loyalty; butt Loyalty is founded on Selfe interestt, which judge a Sandy foundation. . . .
>
> In these parts of the world, a person nede noe more trouble then to be invested with the Kings Comistion [Commission] and Comands and be faithfull therein.[24]

Thus was set up a system that was more than and different from a mere division of power. It can best be described as one of dual power. A division of power might have left ultimate power with the English Crown or its colonial representatives. The ultimate power, however, was the assemblies' power over the purse. Yet it came into conflict with the political institutions and patterns of behavior of the age, which had long dictated deference to the English Crown and formal obeisance to its conventions. A reality struggled to break out of this shell many decades before it finally succeeded.

In its political form, the American Revolution was brought about by British actions which attempted to reduce the power of assemblies and eventually led them to bid for all power. As Jack P. Greene has put it, "Their quest for power became the most important single feature of colonial political and constitutional development, eventually comprising a significant element in the Revolutionary movement that produced the dismemberment of the first British Empire."[25]

· 7 ·

The first premonitions of an American "quest for power" came almost as soon as settlers arrived in New England. A number of seventeenth-century thinkers gave ample warning that the American colonies were bound to rebel against English rule. They posed for the first time the crucial question: Under what conditions would the American colonies seek to break away from their mother country and strike out on their own? Their answers hinted that the early British imperial system was fundamentally self-destructive.

The distinction of having been the first of the gloomy prophets may well go to Sir Ferdinando Gorges, the archenemy of the Massachusetts colony and first proprietor of Maine. Gorges was vexed because the Plymouth colony, the first to arrive aboard the *Mayflower* in 1620, had been settled in defiance of a grant which had recently been given to him and associates of the entire territory stretching from present-day Philadelphia to Newfoundland. He was especially upset because the Plymouth separatists and later the Puritan dissenters defied the authority of the English established church. By the 1630s, an influx into Massachusetts of several thousand religious dissenters enabled the Puritan leadership

[25] Jack P. Greene, *The Quest for Power* (University of North Carolina Press, 1963), p. 1. Greene's study deals only with the lower houses of the legislature in the southern colonies— Virginia, North Carolina, South Carolina, and Georgia—in the period between the Glorious Revolution of 1688–89 and the American War for Independence. His "quest for power" is not the same as that dealt with in this book.

to drive out the agents and settlers whom Gorges had managed to send over.

Gorges had much to complain about by the time he wrote "A Briefe Narration" of his efforts to promote colonization in America. As a result of the emigration to Massachusetts, Gorges recalled, James I had ordered none to go without a license and—here we come to the heart of the matter—

> take the Oaths of Supremacy and Allegiance, so that what I long before prophesied, when I would hardly get any for money to reside there, was now brought to passe in a high Measure, the reason of that restraint was grounded upon the severall complaints, that came out of those parts, of the diverse sects and schimes [*sic*] that were amongst them, all contemning the publique Government of the Ecclesiasticall State; And it was doubted, that they would in short time, wholly shake off the Royall Iurisdiction of the Soveraigne Magistrate.[26]

Just when Gorges made—or claimed to have made—this statement is unclear. It must have been sometime after the substantial migration to Massachusetts in the 1630s. In any case, he published his memoir in 1658, and even if his prophecy was retroactive it was still one of the earliest. The religious implications of the New Englanders' nonconformism were not lost on Gorges or on other officials during the die-hard reign of Charles I and the anti-Puritan persecution of Archbishop Laud.

A rival claim for an even earlier warning may be made for one of Laud's informers in New England, George Burdett. He was a popular preacher who moved from Salem to Dover, New Hampshire, and to York, Maine, before returning to England. Burdett must have been a marked man, because one of his reports to England in 1639 was supposedly "found" in his study by his alleged persecutors. This report contained these incriminating lines: "That he delayed going to England, that he might fully inform himself of the state of the place as to allegiance, for it was not new discipline which was aimed at, but sovereignty; and that it was accounted perjury and treason, in the general court, to speak of appeals to the King."

In this early period, the alleged threat of American "sovereignty" came from small, weak settlements determined to govern themselves for religious reasons, which, in the context of the time, could not be dissociated from political self-rule. Thus there was an old and deep religious substratum in

---

[26] Sir Ferdinand Gorges, "A Briefe Narration of the Originall Under takings of the Advancement of Plantations into the Parts of America" (London, 1658), reprinted in *Sir Ferdinando Gorges and the Province of Maine,* ed. James Phinney Baxter (Prince Society, 1890), vol. 2, p. 60.

all the subsequent strivings, especially in New England, towards a larger measure of autonomy and finally independence.

Another early sense of trouble ahead on more political grounds appeared in a pamphlet by Maj. John Child, published in 1647. Four years earlier, a loose confederation, called the United Colonies of New England, had been formed for self-defense and mutual assistance. This independent action of the existing four New England colonies was apparently one of the things that had aroused Child's suspicions. He was concerned that New England was setting a bad example to parts of Great Britain itself, especially Ireland, Wales, and Cornwall. He pointed to New England as evidence that there could be "a plot against the laws and liberties of English subjects." Referring to statements made by Edward Winslow, the agent in England of Plymouth and Massachusetts Bay, Child warned darkly:

> And, by the way, mark, reader, his [Winslow's] great boasting, *that they are growing into a nation;* high conceits of a nation breed high thoughts of themselves, which make them usually term themselves *a state;* call the people there their subjects; *unite four governments together, without any authority from the king and Parliament;* and then *term themselves the United Colonies;* are publicly prayed for by that title, not giving forth their warrants in his majesty's name, no, not in the time of the most peaceable government.

These reasons excited Child to raise the alarm that New England's effrontery might be infectious: "For, being begun at this plantation, by the same rule others might seek it should extend to all other plantations; and then, why not to Ireland? And why shall not example, custom, and fair pretences bring it into Wales and Cornwall; and so over England?"[27]

According to Child, the New Englanders' original sin was that boasting of growth had brought on "high thoughts of themselves," and such thoughts had led to nothing less than speaking of themselves as *"a state."* His agitation was premature. The New England Confederation was formally abolished without difficulty in 1684. Yet he had hit on something that continued to bother some Englishmen more and more. If the colonies were *"growing into a nation,"* for whatever reason, they had already become to such distant English observers as Child a potential rival and threat.

[27] Chalmers, *Introduction to the History of the Revolt,* vol. 1, p. 88.

· 8 ·

Far more distinguished thinkers also considered the relationship between a mother country and its colonial children. The idea of a mother and child connection was early introduced by Thomas Hobbes in his *Leviathan* of 1651. One type of colony came about, according to Hobbes, "when a Colony is set[t]led, they are either a Common-wealth of themselves, (as hath been done by many Common-wealths of antient time)." In this case, the original commonwealth was a "Metropolis" or "Mother" to the colony and required "no more of them, then Fathers require of the Children, whom they emancipate, and make free from their domestique government, which is Honour, and Friendship."

But the second type, Hobbes went on, "remain united to their Metropolis, as were the Colonies of the people of *Rome;* and then they are no Common-wealths themselves, but Provinces, and parts of the Common-wealth that sent them." Hobbes merely defined the two types and did not enter into their contemporary relevance to the existing English colonies.[28] Nevertheless, his view assumed that there was more than one type of colony and implied that the American colonies were not necessarily of the second kind.

Five years later, the subject was taken up in more detail by James Harrington in *The Common-wealth of Oceana,* a thinly disguised scheme for reforming the English constitution. Later, Harrington was one of the American colonists' intellectual heroes and major influences. To James Otis, over a century later, he was "the great, the *incomparable* Harrington."[29] For John Adams, Harrington's judgments were "often eternal and unanswerable by any man."[30] One passage, cherished by the Founders, in which Harrington had briefly referred to the West Indies, as America was commonly called as late as the end of the seventeenth century,[31] provided the advanced thought of the eighteenth century with a key text: "For the colonies in the *Indies,* they are as yet babes that cannot live without suckling the breasts of their mother-Cities, but such as, I mistake, if when they come of age they do not wean themselves:

[28] Hobbes, *Leviathan,* p. 131.
[29] Otis, *Rights of the British Colonies,* p. 423.
[30] John Adams, *A Defence of the Constitutions of Government of the United States of America* (1776), in *The Works of John Adams,* ed. Charles Francis Adams (Boston, 1861), vol. 4, p. 410.
[31] Charles M. Andrews, ibid., p. 302.

which causeth me to wonder at Princes that delight to be exhausted in that way."[32]

Harrington's words have been taken to mean that England would cease to be able to hold on to her far-flung colonies as soon as they had come of age and could take care of themselves.[33] A large part of his chapter on the rights and limitations of governors was reprinted in the *Massachusetts Spy* of February 13, 1772. On the eve of the Revolution in 1775, John Adams gave this interpretation to the sentence just cited: "This was written 120 years ago; the colonies are now nearer manhood than ever Harrington foresaw they would arrive, in such a period of time."[34] In the year of the final American victory, the Reverend Ezra Stiles, then president of Yale College, explained that the new American principles of government and religion had "realized the capital ideas of Harrington's *Oceana*."[35] Historians have agreed on Harrington's foresight. One English historian read this passage as having foreshadowed "the final separation of George III's reign."[36] Another viewed Harrington's rather matter-of-fact words as "his sympathetic prophecy of American independence."[37] An American historian praised Harrington for having shown "keen insight" and wrote that "his conclusion was sound."[38] But Harrington had written too early for his words to relate to the actual issues of the 1760s and 1770s in the colonies; he was only useful to stress that when the colonies had come of age they would have a right to their own place in the sun.

Harrington's insight was reflected in a remarkable discussion about the problem of New England that took place at a meeting of the Council for Plantations in London on May 26, 1671. We know the exact place, time, and subject, because one of the commissioners sworn in that day was John Evelyn, the famous diarist. The commissioners, who included the leading figures of the regime, insisted on getting more information about the people of New England because, as Evelyn recorded, they appeared to be "very independent as to their reguard [sic] to old England, or his Majestie, rich and strong as now they were." The commissioners debated in what manner

[32] *James Harrington's Oceana,* ed. S. B. Liljegren (Carl Winter, 1924), p. 20.

[33] Charles Blitzer, *An Immortal Commonwealth* (Yale University Press, 1960), pp. 128–35.

[34] John Adams in *Novanglus, and Massachusettensis; or Political Essays, etc.* (Boston, 1819), p. 82.

[35] Ezra Stiles, "The United States Elevated to Glory and Honor," cited by Nathan O. Hatch, *The Sacred Cause of Liberty* (Yale University Press, 1977), p. 134.

[36] Basil Williams, *The Whig Supremacy, 1714–1760* (Oxford University Press, 1939; reprint, 1952), p. 298.

[37] H. F. Russell Smith, *Harrington and His Oceana* (Cambridge University Press, 1914), p. 153.

[38] George Louis Beer, *British Colonial Policy, 1754–1765* (Macmillan, 1907), p. 166.

to write for information because "the Condition of that Colonie was such, as they were able to contest with all our Plantations about them, & feare there was, of their altogether breaking away from all dependance on this nation." Some members wanted to send "a menacing Letter" to New England, but others, "who better understood the touchy & peevish humor of that Colonie, were utterly against." At another meeting, on June 6, it was decided to send "onely a conciliating paper at first" in order not to make a bad situation worse or until they had more information, since, in Evelyn's words, "we understood that they were a people al most [sic] upon the very brink of renouncing any dependance of the Crowne." On August 3, the decision was made to send a commission to New England to find out "whether they were of such power as to be able to resist his Majestie & declare for themselves as Independent of the Crowne, as we were told, & which of late years made them refractorie."[39]

For colonies to become "rich and strong" was, then, the most alarming of danger signals. However exaggerated this notion of New England's riches and strength may have been at the time, it points to what, in this hardheaded English view, was most likely to bring about colonial separatism. If the circumstances were right, it was believed, the wish was bound to follow.

At the very end of the seventeenth century, this line of reasoning was again put forward by Charles Davenant, an outstanding economic theorist and government official. In a work published in 1698, he summed up the various strands of informed opinion that had emerged in England. The main objection to the colonies, according to Davenant, was "that they drein this Kingdom of People, the most important Strength of any Nation." Nevertheless, Davenant was not an extreme pessimist. The colonies could be "of no Damage to the State" unless—and this was the great question of the next century—"they acquire abroad, such Riches, Power and Dominion, as may render them in process of Time, formidable to their Mother Country."

Davenant felt that they had not yet arrived at this formidable state; they were still a "Spring of Wealth" to England. If they were no longer such a boon, he wrote, "it must be through our own fault, and Misgovernment, if they become independent of *England*." Therefore, Davenant warned, "we may let 'em grow (more especially *New-England*) in Naval Strength, and Power, which if suffer'd we cannot expect to hold 'em long in our Subjection." He strongly opposed permitting New England to build warships, as others had proposed, because "some such Courses may indeed drive 'em, or put it

39 *The Diary of John Evelyn*, ed. E. S. de Beer (Oxford University Press, 1959), pp. 554–57.

into their Heads, to erect themselves into Independent Common-Wealths."
The way to make sure that the American colonies would not turn against
England and become detrimental to its interests was to "keep a strict Eye
upon their conduct, and chiefly watch their Growth in shipping of Strength,
or in Number of Inhabitants."

Then came a passage which most lucidly reflected the current state of
advanced opinion: "Colonies are a Strength to their mother Kingdom, while
they are under good Discipline, while they are strictly made to observe
the Fundamental Laws of their Original Country, and while they are kept
dependent on it. But otherwise, they are worse Members lopp'd from the
Body Politick, being indeed like offensive Arms, wrested from a Nation, to
be turn'd against it, as occasion shall serve."

In the end, however, Davenant refused to despair. He denied that the
colonies could of themselves become dangerous to England. According to
him, only "Arbitrary Power as shall make them desperate, can bring 'em to
rebel."[40]

In another work the following year, Davenant was even more optimistic.
He professed to doubt that "the Greatness these Colonies can arrive at,
in a Natural Course, and in the progress of Time, can be dangerous to
England."[41] In Davenant's work, one can clearly discern the tension that
had taken hold in England between fearing the colonies and appreciat-
ing them.

One of the most optimistic of the British prophets was Daniel Defoe, the
journalist and novelist. He wrote and published *A Review of the State of the
British Nation,* an early journal, single-handedly. He turned the pessimistic
view of colonial progress on its head and argued that just the opposite was
true: "To make them great, rich, populous and powerful, is the only, or at
least most effectual Way to make their Independency for ever impossible,
and to put them out of all Fear of such a State; nay, tho' it were allow'd
to be the Desire, or Inclination, or Design, *call it which you please,* of the
People there, which was never yet proved, no nor reasonably suggested."
Defoe knew that "our famous Politicians" differed with him: "Make them,
say these Gentlemen, great and rich, and strong, give them People and
Money, and they'll bid you Defiance, and set up for themselves." He
admitted that *"potentially,* they can, yet Politically they cannot; in their
Senc[s]es they cannot, without putting a full Stop to their Prosperity,

---

[40] Charles Davenant, *Discourses on the Publick Revenues and on the Trade of England,* pt.
2, discourse 3, "On the Plantation Trade" (London, 1698), pp. 195–207.

[41] Charles Davenant, *An Essay upon the Probable Methods of making a People Gainers in
the Ballance of Trade* (London, 1699), p. 207.

and immediately letting their own Hands to their own Destruction." For example, he believed that New England and New York owed their growth to their market in England and that it was only necessary to "double-lock the Door against their Prosperity, and consequently have them secure against an Independency." But he wrote this in 1707, and time would tell how long the colonies would be satisfied to have no more than an English market for their goods.[42]

Defoe and other prophets were "speculative reasoners," as David Hume called them in his mid-eighteenth-century *History of England*. Hume understood them to foresee that the colonies, "after draining the mother country of inhabitants," were bound to achieve independence.[43] What is most striking about this speculative reasoning is that it most frequently rested on a calculus of power rather than of rights, grievances, or ideologies. When the colonies came of age and made themselves rich and strong, they were bound to become dangerous and rebellious. The urge for independence was directly related to the measure of power, as its components were then understood. A century before the American Revolution, some of the most acute and influential political minds in England were already convinced that the worst could happen, had to happen, or was already happening.

The practical vulnerability of the empire and the ideas which suffused it combined to make politically minded Englishmen extraordinarily sensitive to forebodings of rising colonial power and its implications for colonial dependence on the mother country. As we shall see, for almost the entire life of the colonies, there was plenty of reason to be apprehensive of their final destination, even when the colonies could not acknowledge it to themselves. If power, not ideology, was driving the colonies on to their appointed breakaway, self-awareness was not needed until the very last stage of the process.

---

[42] [Daniel Defoe], *A Review of the State of the British Nation*, December 23 and 27, 1707, pp. 539–40, 547–48.
[43] David Hume, *The History of England* (orig. ed., 1759; reprint, Oxford, 1836), vol. 2, p. 164.

3

"He is the Patriot"

· 1 ·

Bʀɪᴛɪsʜ ɢᴏᴠᴇʀɴᴏʀs ᴄᴏᴍᴘʟᴀɪɴᴇᴅ ɪɴᴛᴇʀᴍɪɴᴀʙʟʏ about the defiant behavior of the American colonists, and particularly the assemblies. They complained that they were dealing with an incipient or even fully matured spirit of independence long before the colonists were willing to admit it to themselves. These signs and portents filled the reports which went back to London.

To show how deeply rooted they were, we may examine the records of typical governors from four major colonies—Virginia, Massachusetts, New York, and Pennsylvania. The four have been chosen for their relative importance, geographical distribution, and different types of government— Virginia a southern "Crown colony," Massachusetts a northern "charter colony," New York another Crown colony, and Pennsylvania a middle "proprietary colony." One governor has been chosen from each of these colonies to give some idea of what had been put into the heads of British authorities in the decades leading up to the 1760s. There is little need for more, because almost all the other governors sent similar reports. We will consider the colonies in order of their settlement.

In Virginia, governors did not govern. George Hamilton, earl of Orkney, was appointed governor of Virginia in 1704. He was an old soldier who had fought with Marlborough at Blenheim, and this appointment was his reward. But it was not his only reward, and he preferred to pay personal attention to other duties that were more lucrative. He remained the nominal governor for thirty-three years without once setting foot in the colony. His sinecure was not unique; it was built into the system of rewarding favorites by enabling them to live in the style they were thought to deserve.

But Virginia had to have a representative of the Crown, for which reason stand-ins were appointed as lieutenant governors. Orkney had no fewer than four successive lieutenant governors, each of whom gave him half of their stipend. The first one, Edward Nott, served only one year, 1705–6, without making much of an impression. His successor was Col. Alexander Spotswood, a Scot, whose correspondence with his superiors in London makes the most illuminating reading about what was going back to England early in the eighteenth century.

At thirty-four, Spotswood was another soldier who had served with Marlborough at Blenheim, had been wounded, and had earned as his reward an appointment in Virginia, though he had to share it with Orkney. Spotswood has been singled out as one of the better governors.[1] He was not, therefore, among those who can be lightly dismissed as hopelessly corrupt or totally unfitted for the job.

Spotswood's political education began early. After only six months in the colony, he told the Board of Trade in London that his main problem was

> the inclinations of the Country being rendered more misterious by a new and unaccountable humour obtained in several Countys of excluding the Gentlemen from being Burgesses, and choosing only persons of mean figure and character: by what I have yet heard, the business of taking up Land is the Chief Grievance they have recommended to their Burgesses to get redressed. . . . it being the temper of the people here never to favour any Undertaking unless they can see a particular advantage arising to themselves.[2]

After a year in the colony, Spotswood discovered how hard it was to get the House of Burgesses, as the local assembly was called, to part with money, even for defense. In July 1711, he wanted to build a fort at Point Comfort and met with inevitable resistance, which he explained as follows: "I knew very well it would be in vain to expect the least Assurance from the Assembly, unless they were first assured that they should not be charged

---

[1] Evarts Boutell Greene, *The Provincial Governor in the English Colonies of North America* (Harvard University Press, 1898; reprint, Peter Smith, 1966), p. 49. Louis B. Wright refers to him as "that able administrator" (*The First Gentlemen of Virginia*, Huntington Library, 1940, p. 300).

[2] *The Official Letters of Alexander Spotswood, Lieutenant Governor of the Colony of Virginia, 1710–1722* (Virginia Historical Society, 1882), vol. 1, pp. 19, 41.

with the maintenance of a Garrison, which is an annual expence they will never be prevailed with to lay on the Country, however necessary it may be for its Security."[3]

By the end of 1711, he had learned so much about the colonists that he felt qualified to tell London what the trouble was. He explained that it was due to

> that unhappy humour of the Country in choosing their Representatives, persons of mean understandings. . . . Such people being rarely possessed with a publick Spirit, and generally bringing along with them the same penurious temper in their publick Transactions that governs them in their private capacitys. It is no wonder if this irreconciles them to all measures wherein Expence of money is required, and puts them upon unjustifiable means to save their own pockets, tho' at the Risque of their Country's safety.[4]

It was not only a matter of personal economy; it was also the best way to get elected to the assembly. Spotswood pointed out that "the late Burgesses hope to recommend themselves to the populace upon a received opinion among them, that he is the best Patriot that most violently opposes all Overtures for raising money, let the occasion be what it will."[5]

Just how the assembly encroached bit by bit on the prerogatives of the governor was explained by Spotswood in 1713. Governors had been accustomed to handing out grants of land, one of their most effective means of gaining and rewarding supporters. But grants of land in Virginia were handled by the General Court, made up of the council and assembly, in which the governor did not have a veto, and the courts were even ordering governors to grant patents or legal documents, so that the governor could not

> dispense the favours of the Crown, according to the merits and qualifications of the person. This Custome being suffer'd so long to prevail, is now pleaded as the Right of the people, And all restrictions of that method look'd upon as so many infringements of their Liberty, and her Maj[es]ty's fav'r seems to them a new term, w'th which they are not acquainted, or at least they forget ye meaning of.[6]

[3] Spotswood to the Council of Trade, July 25, 1711, ibid., p. 88.
[4] Spotswood to the Council of Trade, December 28, 1711, ibid., p. 132.
[5] Spotswood to the Council of Trade, February 8, 1711, ibid., p. 140.
[6] Spotswood to the Lords Commissioners of Trade, February 11, 1713, ibid., vol. 2, p. 14. The reference to "her Majesty" is to Queen Anne.

Of all these cries of alarm, the most anguished came at the end of 1713, in reference to a proposed reform in tobacco cultivation and prevention of frauds in tobacco payments. Here again, Spotswood tried to explain what elections to the assembly were like and what made a successful candidate:

> There are a set of People whom all the meaner sort of Planters cry up for honest, for Lovers and Patriots of their Country, and for Friends to ye Poor, and this general Character often sets them up for candidates in the Election Field, (where the Votes and humours of the lowest Mob do at present decide who shall be the Representatives in Assembly). . . . But a few Years' Observation had made me perceive y't [that] the Vulgar in these parts reckon him only the Honest Man who inclines to favour their Interest. He is ye lover of this Country who in all Controversies justifies the Virginian, and [in] all Dealings is ready to help him to overreach the Forreigner: He is the Patriot who will not yield to whatever the Governm't proposes, and can remain deaf to all Argum'ts that are used for ye raising of Money, and lastly, him they call the poor man's Friend who always carrys Stilliards [scales] to weigh to the needy Planter's advantage, and who never judges his Tobacco to be Trash. Of this set of People there was such a number in ye lower House that it was w'th some Address and great struggle ye Bill was got to pass there, for tho' their Understandings be not above the level of their Electors, and that they could not advance one solid Argument against it, yet they readily discover'd y't this Bill was to cut y'm [them] out of their Popular interest and profitable way of living, and thereupon they oppos'd it most violently with their Nays.7

By 1715–16, after about six years in Virginia, Spotswood saw a more sinister motive for the opposition. He began to complain that the assembly's bills were guilty of "encroachment upon the prerogative of the Crown."8 He was especially wrathful against "men who look upon every benefit that accrues to their Soveraign as so much taken from themselves; who envy his Majestie the profits of his own proper Estates and Revenues, and are offended if at their request His Maj[es]tie doth not apply them to such uses as they think most proper."9

Spotswood spotted more such disrespect in 1718. The burgesses were

---

7 Spotswood to the Lords Commissioners of Trade, December 29, 1713, ibid., p. 50.
8 Spotswood to the Lords of Trade, October 24, 1715, ibid., p. 134.
9 Spotswood to the Lords Commissioners of Trade, May 23, 1716, ibid., p. 153.

called into session to deal with regulation of the Indian trade and defense of the frontiers. The lieutenant governor's requests were voted down by "the Party who have always their Eyes very quick to watch all Advantages for lessening the power of the Crown."[10] Another issue concerned whether officials should take oaths as Virginians and not as "Counsellors for the King." Spotswood did not always get the expected answer:

This, My Lords, is no imagined Equivocation that I suppose they might use, but it is a real Distinction w[hi]ch I have heard actually contended for in Council, and upon a Question put at the Board, I have had from one of these Gent[leme]n in two Different Opinions at the same time, telling me plainly y't one he gave me as Acting for the people of Virg[ini]a, and the other as Councellor for the King.[11]

Spotswood came to believe that there was nothing superficial about this "real Distinction" between acting for Virginia and acting for the king. It was, he added,

a distinction that has taken root in too many of the present Members of the Council, and, in truth, this is the very ground Work of Our Discord, for which I perceive the Creolian[12] is uppermost in all their Judgments. I cannot but take them for unfaithfull Counsellors, and while they prove me to be Staunch for his Maj'ty's Rights, they w[i]ll think me a Gov[erno]r not for their purpose, and for that Reason Strive to blast my Credit, as they have been endeavouring of late years by Anonymous Papers and other indirect means.[13]

A governor's lot was not a happy one:

Whatever undutiful behaviour they use towards their Soveraign, or inhumanity to their fellow Subjects, no Governor must reprove them on pain of having his Speeches and Messages voted Scandalous, and his modest Expostulations represented to his Soveraign as a Crime. And lastly, none of this Party must be removed from any Office he enjoys, let his Conduct be never so irregular, but a numerous Chain of Relations shall combine, and ye most notorious Offenders Courted and Encouraged to bespatter the Character and Traduce the Administration of that Governor who has the boldness to attack

[10] Spotswood to the Board of Trade, June 24, 1718, ibid., p. 279.
[11] Spotswood to the Board of Trade, August 14, 1718, ibid., p. 291.
[12] This term then meant a person born in the colony of European descent.
[13] Ibid., p. 291.

any one of this formidable Party, that the disturbing the quiet of his Government and blasting his Reputation is the certain Consequence of his falling under their displeasure, and if, by spreading the most false Reports, they can so far poison the minds of the People as to obtain a number of men of like principles to be chosen Burg[omaster]'s, The publick Interest of the Country, as well as the Service of the Crown, shall be thwarted and opposed, Unjust Laws projected, under pretence of publick Liberty.[14]

This anti-Spotswood, anti-Crown party or faction, as Spotswood referred to them, was not made up of the discontented and unwashed poor. His main enemies and critics were among the richest and most eminent planters in the colony. Foremost among them was William Byrd II, owner of 43,000 acres of land and about 220 slaves, and author of the famous diary.[15] Another was Philip Ludwell, so highly placed that Spotswood stayed at his house on first arriving in Virginia. Ludwell served in a high office until Spotswood succeeded in removing him. By 1718, after eight years in Virginia, Spotswood wrote in desperation to the earl of Orkney:

> Wherefore I take ye Power, Interest and Reputation of the King's Governor in this Dominion to be now reduced to a desperate Gasp, & if the present Efforts of the Country cannot add new Vigour to the same, then the Haughtiness of a Carter, the Hypocrisy of a Blair, the Inveteracy of a Ludwell, ye Brutishness of a Smith, the Malice of a Byrd, the Conceitedness of a Grymes, and the Scurrility of a Corbin, with about a score of base disloyalists & ungrateful Creolians for their adherents must for the future Rule this Province.[16]

These names were among the best-known and most influential in the colony. They invariably controlled the assembly and often even the council. They had the inestimable advantage of using the financial monopoly of the assembly for their own ends. A governor who did not have independent sources of money to get things done had to come pleading or begging to get things done for him in the assembly. The struggle in Virginia was waged between two centers of power, one an extension of the Crown with its local beneficiaries and hangers-on, the other a native elite with its own network of relatives and dependents. These contending political forces were already so

---

[14] Ibid., p. 314.

[15] *The Correspondence of the Three William Byrds of Westover Virginia, 1684–177*, ed. Marion Tinling (University Press of Virginia, 1977), vol. 1, p. 313.

[16] Spotswood to Orkney, December 22, 1718, cited by Leonidas Dodson, *Alexander Spotswood* (University of Pennsylvania Press, 1932), p. 257.

fully formed that Spotswood referred to them as parties—the "Governor's and the Country's Partys."[17]

At this early date, Spotswood was faced with a constitutional issue that worked in favor of his enemies. If the threefold colonial system of governor, council, and assembly was similar to the British system of king, Lords, and Commons, and if Parliament had established its supremacy as a result of the Glorious Revolution, then the assemblies were also entitled to supremacy in the colonies. Spotswood's attempt to get over this dangerous analogy was one of the first of its kind:

> What is urged from the Parliamentary practice in England cannot well be deployed here, the Immemorial possession of the one bearing no proportion to ye Modern Practice of these new Colonys, where the Concessions of the Soveraign, either by his Letters Patent, the Laws of the Mother Kingdome, or those w[hi]ch the people are allowed to make for themselves, seem to be the Basis of all the Privileges they can Claim.[18]

In effect, this argument was an expression of the constitutional dilemma of British rule in America. On the one hand, the colonies owed their very existence and form of government to charters issued to them by the British "Soveraign" and "Mother Kingdome." On the other hand, the same charters gave the colonies privileges, especially in the powers allotted to assemblies, that worked against British sovereignty overseas and the mother-and-child relationship as the child grew up. The threefold arrangement in the colonies had been inspired by and superficially resembled that in England without the same historical and social underpinnings. Once a struggle for power between the two elites developed in the colonies, the analogy with the British system served to undermine rather than to uphold the British model.

In the end, Spotswood had to go. The opposition wore him down until his superiors in London decided that he had exhausted his usefulness. In 1722, Spotswood was removed. As early as 1718, he had begun to detect that there was more to the opposition than particular grievances; the object was "lessening the power of the Crown." The governor's authority had been reduced to a "desperate Gasp," and the colonial opposition "must for the future Rule this Province." Yet at this time, the issues were mainly land and

---

[17] Spotswood to Mr. Secretary Craggs [secretary of state], May 20, 1720, *Official Letters of Alexander Spotswood*, vol. 2, p. 341. Spotswood also used the term "Popular Party" (Spotswood to the Board of Trade, September 27, 1718, p. 300).

[18] Spotswood to the Board of Trade, August 14, 1718, ibid., p. 289.

taxes—or whatever had to do with the power over money. No ideological factors had entered into these controversies. The colonies still expected decisions to be made in London, where William Byrd had been sent as agent of the burgesses and had stayed for over three years protecting his political allies and undermining Spotswood. Long before the colonists were ready or willing to acknowledge it, Spotswood suspected where all this was going to lead.

• 2 •

In Massachusetts, governors had always faced more opposition than in Virginia. After the Glorious Revolution, which was not so glorious in America, Massachusetts sent three emissaries—Increase Mather, followed by Elisha Cooke and Thomas Oakes—to London to negotiate the terms of a new charter. The three originally agreed on what they wanted—a return to the political status quo ante, in which the assembly was dominant. Mather, the leading negotiator, had been told in 1688, before the accession of William III, that only Parliament could authorize the return of the old charter, and for various reasons he wasted a year trying unsuccessfully to get such a bill passed. After William came in, Mather turned his attention to the new king, who had obtained a ruling from the lord chief justice to the effect that he could decide what was best for the colony. New to the country and the job, William cautiously consulted and acted with the consent of the Privy Council and Lords of Trade. Mather had to feel his way as the new order was gradually worked out.

That order proved to be a mixed blessing. It did not represent a full-fledged transfer of power from the Crown to Parliament but settled for a shifting and often indeterminate balance between them, especially if Parliament chose to be passive or was too divided to assert itself. The Crown still retained a major share of control in the colonies, where conditions changed much less drastically than the colonies had hoped.

William rudely disappointed Mather. The blow came in April 1691, when the king was told that he could constitutionally decide the form of government for the colonies. He decided that he wanted to continue to appoint governors and give them the power to veto legislation by the popular assembly. The secretary of state, Lord Nottingham, advised the king to resist Mather's demands on the ground that they would amount to a "copartnership in the government." This rebuff hinted at what had been in the ministerial minds—that the real issue was the colony's bid to return to virtual independence, a status which the new regime was as determined as its predecessor to reject.

Nevertheless, Mather's persistence partially paid off. The new charter confirmed the appointment of a governor, lieutenant governor, and secretary of the colony by the king. But he consented to appoint as the first governor Mather's nominee, Sir William Phips, a native of Maine, then part of Massachusetts. The chief compromise came in the makeup of the "General Court," composed of the governor, a council of twenty-eight members, and a house of representatives or assembly consisting of two representatives elected by the freeholders of each town or inhabited place. In other colonies, the councils were generally appointed by the king at the recommendation of the governor; they were chosen from among the well-to-do and more prominent local figures. In Massachusetts, however, the council was going to be chosen by the General Court as a whole, in which the assembly predominated, though the councillors were to be subject to the approval of the governor.

Whatever the formalities, the most telling influence was likely to flow, as usual, from wherever the money-power was. Here the General Court in which the assembly predominated had the last word. The assembly controlled the salaries of governors and judges. Since the council, after the first one, was also elected, there was much less difference between it and the assembly than in the other colonies, where it was appointed. A governor could easily be isolated, with his sole recourse a veto, which he was apt to use only at the cost of future estrangement, endangering the annual allocation of his salary.

With a heavy heart, Mather debated with himself whether to accept the new charter. He finally concluded that it was the best that could be obtained in the circumstances. In his account of the negotiations, Mather persuaded himself that the new General Court was going to have "as much Power in New-England as the King and Parliament have in England." He particularly stressed the power of the General Court to impose taxes and the expectation of "Protection and Assistance from England, as the Matter shall require, more than formerly." He listed all the things the governor could not do without the consent of the council—appoint sheriffs, pack juries, choose judges who acted against consciences, make laws or levy taxes, interfere with anyone's religion. He described the new setup as based on two negatives—"the King's Governour has a Negative Voice in all Acts of Government," and "the People have a Negative on him."

The other two agents, Cooke and Oakes, were never reconciled to the charter of 1691. Cooke was particularly intransigent. One of the wealthiest men in Boston, he steadfastly refused to change his mind and was debarred from sitting in the council by Governor Phips after having been elected to it in 1693. Cooke and his adherents regarded Mather's acceptance of the new charter as little short of treason. The feud between the incipient parties dominated Massachusetts politics for years to come. At this early date, the leading figures divided into two camps—those who rejected any British control in principle, and those who reluctantly accepted it as the lesser evil.

The result was a halfway house. It gave something to everyone, and everything to no one. The British had their royal governor, with a veto over colonial legislation. The colonists had their council and assembly, the former partially dependent on the governor's assent, the latter not dependent on him at all. Both were increasingly responsive to the popular will and had a financial stranglehold upon any headstrong governor. The charter of 1691 was a compact of dual power, and it became increasingly unstable as Massachusetts grew in population, wealth, and self-confidence.

A typical governor in the first half of the eighteenth century was Samuel Shute, another British colonel. In 1721, he explained how the House of Representatives bullied governors. When the assembly decided to do nothing about his allowance until he had signed all the bills it wanted, he wrote to the Board of Trade: "I can't help complaining here how unavoidable a necessity a Governour of this province is sometimes under, either of agre[e]ing to what may not be for H.M. [His Majesty's] interest, or of incurring the displeasure of the House to the risk of his support."[19] That same year, the Board of Trade reported to the king about Massachusetts:

> Thus, altho' the Government of this Province be nominally in the Crown, & the Governor appointed by your Majesty, yet the unequal Balance of their constitution having lodged too great a power in the Assembly, this province is, & is always likely to continue in great disorder. They do not pay a due regard to your Majesty's Instructions; they do not make a suitable provision for the maintenance of their Governor, & on all occasions they affect too great an independence on their Mother Kingdom.[20]

In 1722, London was told that the House of Representatives had usurped

[19] *Colonial Papers, America and West Indies,* March 1720–December 1721, 1933, p. 372.

[20] "State of the British Plantations in America, in 1721," Representation of the Lords Commissioners for Trade and Plantations to the King, September 8, 1721, *Documents Relative to the Colonial History of the State of New-York,* ed. E. B. O'Callaghan (Albany, 1856), vol. 5, p. 597. [Hereafter cited as *New York Documents.*]

both the legislative and much of the executive powers in the colony. Not only were its members allotting a salary to the governor and lieutenant governor at only six-month intervals but they were "likewise appoint[ing] the salary of ye Treasurer every year, whereby they have in effect ye sole authority over that important office, which they often use to intimidate the Treasurer from obeying the proper orders for issuing money. By all which means the House of Representatives are in a manner the whole Legislative, and in a good measure the executive power of the Province."[21]

Shute's complaints piled up. He assured the board, "as I have often done, that the people here pay little attention or no defference to any opinion or orders that I receive from the Ministry at Home."[22] Confirmation came from the British agent Thomas Moore, who was sent by the secretary of state for the Southern Department, Lord Carteret, "to discover all things new and strange in H.M. Plantations." Moore decided to start with New England, where he was bound to be most shocked by what he heard. In 1723, he wrote to Carteret in a style mimicking what the Americans were saying:

> We are all politicians yet have no will to forbear speaking of treason, of which I have heard more in one day, than in all my life before, such as H.M. [His Majesty] has no business in this country, he is our nominal King, but has not one foot of ground among us, neither he or his deputys or Governours have anything to do here, the Country is ours not his. ... Yet still H.M. shall be heartily prayed for by us, as our titular King, but we ourselves must have the uncontroulable power, to act despotically as we please, and to mend the matter delude H.M. with sham addresses, pretending loyalty, false accounts of affaires by our Agents, blindfolding the Com[m]issioners of Trade, with chimeras instead of realities, telling every thing but the truth, so that the true state of this country has never yet been known to H.M. or his Ministers, but all huddled upon secrecy and juggle. No wonder then the disease is become desperate, since the sickness was never knowen, seeing their phrenzie running so high as to deny H.M.'s right here, what wonder then his Governour is called blockhead, and has dead dogs and cats throwen into his coach.[23]

The scholarly British editor of the documents containing this report was so struck by it that he made this telling comment: "The state of opinion, in fact, so far as Massachusetts was concerned, was not far different now

---

[21] *Colonial Papers,* 1722–23, 1934, p. 325.
[22] Ibid., pp. 157–58.
[23] Ibid., p. 257.

[1723] from that which prevailed in the American Revolution. What was different was the presence at the earlier period of the danger from the French and Indians, the political and financial position of Great Britain, and the actions of the British Government as influenced by it."[24]

By 1726, the board could no longer pretend that Shute would get money from the assembly. "But as it is doubtful whether the people of New England will pay a ready obedience to H.M. orders," it proposed that Shute should be paid out of the "royal bounty" to enable him to discharge the expenses of a voyage. "But if the people of New England shall not comply with H.M. directions herein," its members still insisted, "we know no other method so effectual to reduce them to compliance, as to lay a state of that Province before the Parliament."[25] Reference to Parliament, as if the people of New England were more likely to obey it than the king, was a sure sign that the board had reached its wit's end and did not know any longer what to recommend.

Another year passed, and in 1727, the new king, George II, ordered the Massachusetts council and assembly to establish a fixed salary for "Our Governor."[26] His order was ignored, just as Queen Anne's edict twenty-four years earlier had been. By 1732, the board informed the House of Commons that the trouble had come about because "the power [in Massachusetts] seems to be divided between the King and the People; but in which the People have much the greater share."[27]

It is clear that the reports which went back to London from Massachusetts for well over a century fed into the stream of British resentments and frustrations with respect to the colonies. Later Americans were accustomed to think that only the colonists had trials and tribulations. This one-sidedness would have come as a surprise to British ministers and officials.

· 3 ·

In New York, Robert Hunter, commissioned in 1709, was one of the better and more unusual governors. An acquaintance of the eminent British writers Joseph Addison and Dean Swift, he was a person of some literary pretensions. Despite a recognition of his superior abilities, he was not saved from complaining bitterly to London about his lot.

[24] Ibid., p. viii.
[25] Ibid., 1726–27, 1936, pp. 126–27.
[26] Ibid., p. 244.
[27] Ibid., 1732, 1952, p. 53.

After relating how the assembly had done all sorts of things of which he disapproved, Hunter hit on what was really at stake: "Now, my Lords, unless it could be supposed that Her Majesty [Queen Anne] could rest satisfyed to have her Governour and Council here made Cyphers, Her Authority in their persons trampled under foot, and matters of Government for the future managed by the caprice of an Assembly, I firmly hope for and promise myself a speedy and effectual Remedy."[28] By this time—1710—London was being told that governors had become "Cyphers," and one of the best of them could only hope that there might be a "Remedy."

A forlorn Hunter reported the following year that nothing had changed and a remedy was as far away as ever:

> Now, My Lords, what course to take in such a juncture I know not, the Officers of the Government are starving, the Forts on the Frontiers in ruine, the French and French Indians threatening us every day, noe publick money nor credit for Five pounds on the publick account, and all the necessary expence of the Government supply'd by my proper credit, particularly ffire and candle and repeaires for all ye garrisons, and noe hopes that I can think of for any remedy here, ffor as to the calling of a New Assembly, I shall either have all the same members, or such others who will returne with greater ffury. The Resolutions of putting themselves on the same foote with the Charter Governments being too general to be allayed by any measures that can be taken on this side, I would faine hope that the next Pacquet will bring us some Releif in Her Majesty's Resolutions with relations to this Government, ffor without that you must expect to hear of nothing but confusion.[29]

Hunter filled pages with these lamentations—his inability to get little more than half of his allotted salary from the assembly, the hopelessness of getting anything from the assembly for the ordinary expenses of the government or defense against enemies. As he tired of asking for a miracle cure from London, Hunter began to express his own premonitions of disaster:

> I have wearyed my Lord Dartmouth [secretary of state] and ye Lords of Trade with ye grievances of this government; my sufferings are of small consequence, but I'll venture once more to affirme that

---

[28] Governor Hunter to the Lords of Trade, November 28, 1710, *New York Documents,* vol. 5, p. 185.

[29] Governor Hunter to the Lords of Trade, May 7, 1711, ibid., p. 209.

without a speedy & effectuall remedy her Maj[es]ty can make noe state of any government in this place, and in a little time ye disease may prove too strong for ye cure.

Thereupon Hunter, who was better educated than most governors, ominously recalled the warning of James Harrington in the previous century:

A greater assertor of liberty, one at least that understood it better than any of them, has said; That as Nationall or independant Empire is to be exercised by them that have ye propper ballance of dominion in the nation; soe Provinciall or dependant Empire is not to be exercised by them that have ye ballance of dominion in the Province; because that would bring ye government from Provinciall and dependant, to Nationall and independant. Which is a reflexion that deserves some consideration for ye sake of another from ye same person, to witt: That the Colonies were infants sucking their mother's breasts, but such as, if he was not mistaken, would weane themselves when they came of age.[30]

In effect, Hunter came to believe that the "propper ballance of dominion" had been so upset in the colony in favor of the assembly that a change from dependent to independent and from provincial or colonial to national had come about. His own experience, he implied, bore out Harrington's speculations.

If anything more were needed to convince Hunter that time was growing short, it was an irreconcilable controversy between the governor and council on one side and assembly on the other over the control of the money-power. No issue was more far-reaching and fundamental.

The occasion for the dispute was the passage by the assembly of some money bills which the council tried to amend. When the assembly refused to budge on its monopoly of deciding on what to spend money and how much to spend, Hunter reacted with something akin to horror:

But now the mask is thrown off; they [assembly] . . . have but one short step to make towards what I am unwilling to name. The Connecticut scheme is what they have in their heads, and if I be not mistaken they are f[l]attered by some at home with the hopes of obliging the Crown to that concession by their undutifull practices. The various & dissonant modells in the Charter and Proprietary Governments is [sic]

[30] Governor Hunter to Secretary St. John, September 11, 1711, ibid., p. 256.

apparently the spring which move thes[e] perplexities in most of the Provinces. Let them be never soe well, each conceives an opinion that their neighbours are better whilst upon another foot of government.

In the infancy of the Colonies the Crown was lavish of priviledges, as necessary for their nurseing; but a full grown boy makes commonly but indifferent use of that indulgence requisite towards a child. If it is expected that ye Colonies, now they are grown up, should be a help and of some use to their parent country, there is an evident necessity of an uniformity in their governments. Upon that alone, amongst other things, an uniformity in worship intirely depends; a thing more to be wish't than hoped for as they now stand. For altho' I cannot accuse our missionaries of want of either zeale or industry, their progress is but inconsiderable and their proselytes few. How indeed can it be otherwise when both the legislative and executive powers are lodg'd in such hands as are likelier to pull it up by the roots than plant it; and ye people they are to work upon are generally obstinate, the whimsicall & factious who flock hither for elbow room to exert their talents.[31]

Hunter here reflected the conviction of officials in London that the colonies could not be made obedient and deferential unless all of them were converted into royal colonies on the model of New York. It was not that the system in New York was working well but rather that colonies such as Massachusetts and Connecticut would no longer make New Yorkers feel that the others were better off and want to emulate them. Yet this aim of achieving uniformity, which went back to the royalist Restoration, was always frustrated, because there were conflicting interests in Parliament, and the charter colonies pulled all the political strings at their disposal in London to sidetrack it. Despite its acknowledged superiority, Parliament was still loath to interfere in the administration of the colonies, which were considered to be the Crown's sphere of influence and which had obtained their charters from the Crown.

After Hunter's private outburst to London, the struggle over the money-power came out publicly and appeared in the assembly's journal. The council, favorable to the governor, argued that it had a right to amend the bills, because it was part of the legislature with the same status as that of the assembly, both of them having received their mandates "by the mere Grace of the Crown." In effect, the council presented a double challenge to the assembly. Were the two houses of equivalent status, even in the sphere

[31] Governor Hunter to Secretary St. John, January 1, 1711, ibid., pp. 296–97.

of money bills? And, even more telling, were both no more than puppets of the Crown, without a life of their own?

When the assembly continued to insist that its money bills could not be amended, the council protested that it "knew of no Power the Crown has given to the Assembly to take the Right from the Council by any Resolves of theirs." This brought from the assembly a reply that went to the heart of the matter and anticipated the great debate on colonial rights half a century later. The language is stiff and antiquated, but the meaning is sufficiently clear to warrant exact quotation:

> 'Tis true the Share the Council have (if any) in the Legislation, does not flow from any Title they have, from the Nature of that Board, which is only to advise, or from their being another distinct State or Rank of People, in the Constitution from which they are not, being all Commons, but only from the meer Pleasure of the Prince, signified in the Commission.
>
> On the contrary, the inherent Right of the Assembly have to dispose of the Money, of the Freemen of this Colony, does not proceed from any Commission, Letters Patent, or other Grant from the Crown, but from the free Choice and Election of the People; who ought not to be divested of their Property (nor justly can) without their Consent.
>
> If the Lords Commissioners for Trade and Plantations, did conceive no Reason, why the Council should not have the Right to amend Money Bills, is far from concluding there are none; the Assembly understand them very well, and are sufficiently convinced of the Necessity they are in, not to admit of any Incroachment so much to their Prejudice.[32]

The essence of this reply is contained in the words "the free Choice and Election of the People; who ought not to be divested of their Property (nor justly can) without their Consent" and cannot "admit of any Incroachment so much to their Prejudice." The assertion of an "inherent Right" cut the assembly at least partially free from dependence on the Crown for its raison d'etre. The opposition to depriving anyone of property without the free "Consent" of an elected body was a further step in the direction of self-determination. Taxes were considered to be a form of depriving someone of property. The "Consent" of the governed by their free choice and election was tantamount to a declaration of popular rule. It had been the custom of governors to complain about the encroachment of the assemblies on the prerogatives of the Crown; now the tables were

[32] *Journal of the General-Assembly of New York*, November 17, 1711, vol. 1, p. 307.

turned, and an assembly was refusing to admit any "Incroachment" on its rights and privileges.

A week later, the assembly came through with another ringing declaration: "The Obstructions made by the Council, in the passing of Money Bills here, will wholly debilitate this Colony, in this, as well as all other sole disposing whereof, ought justly to reside in the Owners, or their Representatives, and is a Right which the Assembly never can recede from, without betraying the Trust reposed in them, by their Electors."[33]

After this, an impasse prevailed. Six months later, Hunter told the assembly that he had been in the colony for two years and had not received a farthing for the support of the government. The assembly's pretensions were "groundless and will not be allowed here." He had been assured by the Board of Trade that the council could amend money bills. Yet there was little he could do about it. He ended pathetically that, if he did not prevail, "I must rest satisfied with the Comfort of having done my Duty, in Admonishing you, and the Testimony of a good Conscience, for what have I neglected within the Compass of my Power, by Night or Day, for your Service? And whose Ox or whose Ass have I taken?"[34]

A modus vivendi was reached months later. Hunter announced that the "contending Parties have agreed, as to the Necessity of settling such a Revenue, and to differ only about the Measures and Means."[35] After all this, the Board of Trade informed the secretary of state, Lord Dartmouth, that the New York Assembly had given a "very ill example to her Majesty's other Governments in America, who have most of them already shewn too much inclination to assume pretended rights tending to an independency of the Crown of Great Britain."[36]

After five years of futile struggle with the assembly, Hunter begged to be taken out of his misery:

> Now my Lords in this wretched posture are our affairs on this side and the ill humour as grown much upon forebearance, the letters wrote to me and ordered to be communicated to them by the former Lords Commissioners of Trade, taxing their conduct with undutifulness[,] disloyalty and disrespect, being intirely disregarded, and even in their house called by the mannerly name of bullying letters, even these who would be distinguish'd by the name of friends

[33] Ibid., November 23, 1711, p. 308.
[34] Ibid., May 1, 1712, pp. 309–10.
[35] Ibid., September 17, 1712, p. 321.
[36] Lords of Trade to the Earl of Dartmouth, April 1, 1713, *New York Documents*, vol. 5, p. 359.

to the Government, never think of settling any support otherwise than from year to year & that in the pitiful manner it has been lately done[.] If for some hidden causes that I cannot guess at this Govern[men]t is to be continued on this wretched foot, it will be great charity in your Lordships to acquaint me with it speedily, that I may make it my most humble application to His Majesty [George I] to put me into some station how mean soever whereby I may be enabled to do him effectual service, and get bread for a numerous family who's life with my own I have devoted to that use.[37]

A recent biographer says that Hunter possessed "the firmness of character, clear judgement, intelligence, and ruthlessness that would make him a top flight officer."[38] None of these qualifications helped him. Where money was concerned, a good governor could be treated as roughly as a bad one. The issue was not so much whether a governor was good or bad as whether he challenged the claims of assemblies to decide on all matters that they considered to be in their domain.

At about this time, official British opinion was reflected in the view of George Chalmers that the New York government "was really changed; from being monarchical, it had already become democratical."[39]

· 4 ·

As a proprietary colony, Pennsylvania was distinct from a charter colony such as Massachusetts or a Crown colony such as New York. Yet, in essentials, it was not so different. William Penn's own experiences show that owning a colony was not the same as governing it.

With the exception of Georgia, Pennsylvania was the last colony to be founded. Like the others, it had as its birth certificate a charter. In 1681, Charles II granted one to William Penn as the sole proprietor of a vast tract of 45,000 square miles, west of New Jersey, south of New York, and north of Maryland, the last, under Lord Baltimore, the only other proprietary colony. Converted to Quakerism, a persecuted sect, at the age of twenty-three, Penn conceived of making his land a home for them.

---

[37] Governor Hunter to the Lords of Trade, May 21, 1715, ibid., p. 404. To his friend Dean Swift, Hunter wrote that "I have spent three years of Life in such torment and vexation, that nothing in Life can ever make amends for it" (cited by Lawrence H. Leder, *Robert Livingston, 1654–1728, and the Politics of Colonial New York,* University of North Carolina Press, 1961, p. 229).

[38] Mary Lou Lustig, *Robert Hunter, 1666–1734* (Syracuse University Press, 1983), p. 11.

[39] George Chalmers, *An Introduction to the History of the Revolt of the American Colonies* (1782; reprint, Boston, 1845), vol. 2, p. 255.

Even as a proprietor, Penn was bound by the terms of his charter as the other colonies were bound by theirs. One of its terms hinted that he, too, might have trouble with a popular legislature. It gave him "free, full, and absolute power" to make laws but on condition that they were made with "the advice, assent, and approbation of the Freemen of the said Countrey, or the greater parte of them, or of their Delegates or Deputies." How he could have absolute power if he had to have the consent of the freemen was not explained.

Before going forward with his plans for settlement, Penn undertook to give his future colony a form of constitution, which he called a "Frame of Government." His first ideas of how to govern the colony were so nebulous that he tried to avoid making any concrete commitment on the ground that good men were more important than good laws. But this advice was not good enough for the good men who came to Pennsylvania. In the end, after three more versions of the Frame, he settled for a government made up of a governor, a council, and an assembly, as in the other colonies. In 1701, however, discontent in the rapidly growing colony brought forth another constitutional document, or "Charter of Privileges." It shifted all legislative power to the assembly, which gained the right to prepare and pass bills into law and to "have all other Powers and Privileges of an Assembly, according to the Rights of the free-born Subjects of *England, and as is usual in any of the King's Plantations in America.*"[40] Pennsylvania thus obtained a unicameral legislature, the only one in the colonies. The council remained, but only as an advisory body to the governor.

Penn's long-distance governance of Pennsylvania was a textbook case of maladministration. He spent only two periods in the colony, each less than two years. When he was not there, he worked through deputy or lieutenant governors, whom he chose haphazardly. If good intentions were enough, William Penn might well be considered the most farsighted and benevolent of American founders. Yet he brought on himself so much "Care and Vexation," as he once put it,[41] in his "Holy Experiment" that one might imagine there were two William Penns—the ideal and the real.

Penn's management of money was as faulty as his judgment of men. To finance his scheme, he sold shares to about 600 investors. In what amounted to an advertising campaign, he persuaded about 4,000 people to emigrate to Pennsylvania. Since they bought plots of land from him, he was in effect

---

[40] Ben Perley Poore, ed., *The Federal and State Constitutions, Colonial Charters, and other Organic Laws of the United States* (Washington, 2d ed., 1878), pt. 2, pp. 1509–40.
[41] Penn to the Board of Trade, April 28, 1700, *The Papers of William Penn* (University of Pennsylvania Press, 1987), vol. 3, p. 595. [Hereafter cited as *Penn Papers.*]

a real estate speculator and absentee landowner. As a salesman, he was phenomenally successful and managed to sell almost three-quarters of a million acres. But he was so careless about money that he drove himself hopelessly into debt.[42] In 1692, the colony was taken away from him and a Crown-appointed governor put in charge; the colony was restored to him two years later. In desperation, he tried, without success, to sell the colony to the Crown. By 1704, he bewailed his "free Colony for all Mankind" as "a perfect ruine to me & my family."[43] In another outburst of self-pity, he lamented, "I have Spent all my days, mon[e]y, and pains, & Interest to a mean purpose."[44] In 1708, at the age of sixty-three, after a quarter of a century of "great pains & incredible expences,"[45] he spent nine months in a debtors' prison. He was constantly forced to defend himself in London against charges of illegal practices and to protect his interest in Pennsylvania from being taken over by the Crown.[46]

Nicholas More, one of Penn's favorites, was his choice as Speaker of the Assembly and chief justice. By 1684, More had made himself so unpopular that he was impeached as "a public enemy in the Province and territories, and a violator of the privileges of the freemen in Assembly met." He was saved from arrest and trial by ill health and an early death.[47] An early deputy governor, Capt. John Blackwell, was another disaster. Penn soon received complaints that Blackwell's "governing is harsh[,] unkind & arbitrary."[48] Blackwell met with such resistance that by 1689 he implored Penn, "I now only wayt for the hower [hour] of my deliverance; for I see tis impossible to serve you in this place."[49] His deliverance came when Penn removed him from office, though Penn thought "I had a treasure in him."[50]

Penn's further choices were almost uniformly unfortunate. Another lieutenant governor was his cousin William Markham, who pleased no one and was ordered dismissed by the Board of Trade.[51] A successor, John Evans, was picked up in company with William Penn, Jr., by a constable in "a disreputable resort," and young Penn was charged with assault while

[42] Richard S. Dunn, "Penny Wise and Pound Foolish: Penn as a Businessman," *The World of William Penn* (University of Pennsylvania Press, 1986), p. 37.

[43] Penn to Roger Mompesson, February 17, 1705, *Penn Papers*, vol. 4, p. 335; Penn to Robert Harley, February 9, 1703–4, p. 258.

[44] Penn to James Logan, July 5, 1704, ibid., p. 282.

[45] Penn to Friends in Pennsylvania, June 4, 1710, ibid., p. 676.

[46] For example, "To the Board of Trade," August 26, 1701, ibid., pp. 76–79.

[47] Joseph J. Kelley, Jr., *Pennsylvania: The Colonial Years, 1681–1776* (Doubleday, 1980), p. 55; William Robert Shepherd, *History of Proprietary Government in Pennsylvania* (Columbia University, 1898), p. 256.

[48] *Penn Papers*, vol. 3, p. 248.

[49] Kelley, *Pennsylvania*, p. 64.

[50] William Penn to Hugh Roberts, December 10, 1689, *Penn Papers*, vol. 3, p. 266.

[51] From the Board of Trade, September 12, 1699, ibid., pp. 576–77.

resisting arrest.[52] Yet Penn's political adversities were no handicap to the growth of the colony. By 1700, Philadelphia had surpassed New York in population and was drawing abreast of Boston as the largest city in North America. Immigrants from Germany and elsewhere poured in and gradually made the Quakers a minority in their own homeland.

Pennsylvania politics took on a turbulence and complexity similar to those in other colonies and completely escaped from Penn's control. Quaker factions fell out among themselves, and rival interests challenged the old order. As Philadelphia increased in size and importance, Quaker manners and customs so failed to predominate that by 1697 one of Penn's most faithful informants reported to him that "things goe wrong heare; wickedness growes & Vice so much Raignes in the grocest [grossest] manner to the sorrow and Reproach of gods people & Is a stumbling blocke in the way of many."[53]

David Lloyd was another of Penn's miscalculations. Lloyd, born in Wales in 1656, worked for Penn in England in the litigation which had threatened his proprietorship towards the end of James II's reign. That Lloyd was not a Quaker did not inhibit Penn from using him. In 1686, at the age of thirty, Lloyd accompanied Penn on his second visit to Pennsylvania and stayed there. Penn appointed him attorney general; his entire career seemed bound up with Penn. Yet Lloyd soon showed his independence by resisting the authority of Penn's new deputy governor, Blackwell, who retaliated by dismissing him.

Lloyd soon accumulated land of his own, was elected to a seat in the assembly, and began to build up a political following. By 1689, according to his biographer, he had "placed himself squarely in opposition to the proprietary prerogative on nearly every issue."[54] He became a Quaker and was thus able to take the lead within the still dominant political establishment. Lloyd's recalcitrance attracted the attention of Edward Randolph, now surveyor general in the American colonies, a fearsome royal watchdog. Randolph duly reported to the Board of Trade that "David Lloyd the present Atturny Generall in Pennsilvania has Declared that he served for the Province only and thereupon refused to put Severall forfeited Bonds in suit."[55] Serving the province only was tantamount, to Randolph, to lèse-majesté. Pennsylvania's laws brought from Randolph an accusation

---

[52] Shepherd, *History of Proprietary Government,* p. 299; David Lokken, *David Lloyd: Colonial Lawmaker* (University of Washington Press, 1959), charitably says it was apparently a "drinking house" (p. 151).

[53] Robert Turner to William Penn, December 9, 1698, *Penn Papers,* vol. 3, p. 533.

[54] Lokken, *David Lloyd,* p. 33.

[55] *Edward Randolph,* ed. Robert Noxon Toppon (Prince Society, 1898), vol. 2, p. 219.

that always lingered in the background of these controversies. In a letter to the Board of Trade, he charged that the colonists "shew themselves independent from the Crown, not acknowledging his present Majeste King William ye Third to be their Soveraign Lord & King."[56] Another indefatigable enemy, Robert Quary, head of the court of vice admiralty, wrote to the Board that the Pennsylvanians were a "perverse, obstinate and turbulent people who will submit to no laws but their own, and have a notion that no Acts of Parliament are of force among them except such as particularly mention them."[57] A few years later, Quary was still at it and again informed the Board that members of the assembly were "resolv'd to have all the Governm[en]t and powers into their own hands, they insist to have the sole regulation of all Courts, and the nomination of all officers to sett [sit] when, and as often and as long as they please on their own adjournments, they have fill'd a volume with votes and resolves, and what they call their rights and priviledges, so that they have banish'd all [royal] Prerogative and Governm[en]t but what is lodged in the Assembly."[58]

In 1704, Lloyd openly declared war on his former benefactor. Together with a group of like-minded Quakers in the assembly, he sent to England a scathing indictment of Penn, in the form of a traditional "Remonstrance." It accused Penn of unfulfilled promises, mismanagement, violation of his own charter, and various other malpractices, but appealed to him not to make a deal with the British government at their expense—"Do not Surrender the Government whatever Terms thou may, by so Doing, make for thy Self and Family, Which we Shall Deem no less than a betraying us."[59]

For the better part of almost four decades, Lloyd dominated Pennsylvania politics. When Penn died in 1718, Lloyd was chief justice of the Pennsylvania Supreme Court. By the time Lloyd died in 1731, at the age of seventy-five, Pennsylvania had changed so much that many of the old ways and controversies were receding into a vanishing past. By 1738, only a third of the 85,000 inhabitants were Quakers, though they still controlled most of the wealth and seats in the assembly.[60]

Lloyd belonged to the first generation of colonial politicians in Pennsylvania. Though he insisted to the end on the legislative priority of the Pennsylvania Assembly, he could never bring himself to question the overall authority

[56] Randolph to the Board of Trade, April 26, 1698, ibid., vol. 5, p. 173.

[57] Quary to the Board of Trade, September 6, 1698, Colonial Papers, cited by Lokken, David Lloyd, p. 82.

[58] Quary to the Board of Trade, June 28, 1707, Colonial Papers, vol. 18, 1706–June 1708, p. 490.

[59] Penn Papers, vol. 4, pp. 295–303.

[60] Kelley, Pennsylvania, pp. 204–5.

of the king and Parliament. It was within the existing imperial system that he—and others like him in all the colonies—sought to enlarge the self-rule of the assembly, in which endeavor he was largely successful.

Lloyd's achievement is all the more noteworthy in that it came in the first quarter of the eighteenth century, long before we have been accustomed to think of such aggressive and sustained political challenges to unrestrained British rule. All the governors in our four colonies—as in most of the others most of the time—were beset by the same pressures from colonial elites and their political domination of the assemblies. British officials already saw them as heading towards a goal of independence or at least some form of colonial autonomy. If the political direction in London had been different, a showdown might have come much earlier than it did.

4

''Fashionable reading''

❧

• 1 •

THE FIRST HALF OF THE eighteenth century produced more "speculative reasoners." Whatever their political sympathies, they reasoned in much the same way as their predecessors about future colonial independence.

John Trenchard and Thomas Gordon have been called the most important "publicists and intellectual middlemen" to have "shaped the mind of the American Revolutionary generation."[1] They first published their views in a weekly, *The Independent Whig*, after which they produced the more famous *Cato's Letters*, a series of political essays in *The London Journal* between 1720 and 1723. They belonged to the tradition of the "old Whigs," who upheld the supposedly earlier, purer Whiggish ideals of anticlericalism and antiautocracy. Trenchard and Gordon are best known for their indefatigable campaign against the corruption and backsliding of the reigning Whig party under Sir Robert Walpole, the dominant figure in British politics between 1721 and 1742. Their ruthless criticism of contemporary British politics and society and their passionate appeal for more liberty and equality fed into that stream of colonial thought which was most restless and aspiring. *Cato's Letters* were reprinted in whole or in part in colonial periodicals throughout the next half century; edition after edition in book form, at least six by 1755, came across the Atlantic.

One of the letters, entitled "Of Plantations and Colonies," appeared in

[1] Bernard Bailyn, *The Ideological Origins of the American Revolution* (Harvard University Press, 1967), p. 35.

The London Journal of December 8, 1722. It seemed to deny that the American colonies were ready to break away, but it discussed at length under what conditions they might want to do so. Like James Harrington, Cato used the metaphor of "weaning." The colonists could not have missed the message in the following passage:

> I would not suggest so distant a Thought, as that any of our Colonies, when they grow stronger, should ever attempt to wean themselves from us; however, I think too much Care cannot be taken to prevent it, and to preserve their Dependencies upon their Mother-Country. It is not to be hoped, in the corrupt State of human Nature, that any Nation will be subject to another any longer than it finds its own Account in it, and cannot help itself. Every Man's first Thought will be for himself and his own Interest, and he will not be long to seek for Arguments to justify his being so when he knows how to attain what he proposes. Men will think it hard to work, toil, and run Hazards, for the Advantage of others, any longer than they find their own Interest in it, and especially for those who use them ill: All Nature points out that Course: No Creatures suck the Teats of their Dams longer than they can draw Milk from thence, or can provide themselves with better Food: Nor will any Country continue their Subjection to another, only because their Great-Grandmothers were acquainted.

Trenchard and Gordon also told the British what to do if they wished to hold on to the American colonies. They reasoned that there were only two ways to prevent the colonies from throwing off their dependence—by keeping it out of their power to do so or by keeping it out of their will or desire. The first way could only be accomplished by the use of force, the second "by using them well." But, they believed, force could not work, because it would destroy the colonies themselves and make them useless. Only "liberty and encouragement" were apt to be successful. Unless violence was used against them, however, the northern American colonies were sure to increase in "People, Wealth, and Power."

Cato addressed the colonies as if they were already another nation. No two nations, the authors warned, could remain friends for long without mutual interests, which alone could bind them together. They then returned to the conditions which might lead the colonies to break away:

> The Interest of Colonies is often to gain Independency; and is always so when they no longer want Protection, and when they can employ themselves more advantageously, than in supplying Materials

of Traffick to others: And the Interest of the Mother-Country is always to keep them dependent, and so employed; and it requires all their Address to do it; and it is certainly more easily and effectually done by gentle and insensible Methods, than by Power alone.[2]

This analysis of the relationship between the American colonies and their mother country was uncannily prophetic. It hit on just those aspects of the connection which were going to put them further and further apart— the colonies' growing self-interest in independence, the declining need for protection, and the futility of force.

Cato's views were familiar to Americans before the Revolution. In 1753, the conservative Reverend Samuel Johnson of Connecticut complained to the archbishop of Canterbury that "among other pernicious books the *Independent Whigg* grows much in vogue."[3] In 1765, during the Stamp Act crisis, the Reverend Jonathan Mayhew, the influential pastor of the West Congregational Church in Boston, recalled a passage in *Cato's Letters* that now seemed to him almost a prophecy. The passage was the one previously cited, beginning with the words "It is not to be hoped" and ending with "only because their Great-Grandmothers were acquainted." Mayhew also wrote to the rich English colonial sympathizer Thomas Hollis, recommending this extract for publication in London newspapers. It duly appeared in the *Saint James Chronicle* of London and the *Evening-Post* of Boston.[4] In one of the most famous colonial pamphlets of the Stamp Act period by John Dickinson, a passage from *Cato's Letters* was cited at length.[5] According to John Adams, *Cato's Letters* and all the writings of Trenchard and Gordon "became fashionable reading" in 1770.[6]

The problem with attributing too much importance to such influences from the seventeenth century and the first quarter of the eighteenth century is that for decades they became virtually dormant. The colonial leaders took what they needed from the past, but only when they needed it. *Cato's Letters* had appeared long before the colonies had any of the grievances that immediately preceded the Revolution, and it is a mistake to read back influences that were grasped at almost on the eve of the Revolution.

[2] [John Trenchard and Thomas Gordon], *Cato's Letters* (London, 6th ed., corrected, 1755), vol. 4, p. 9.

[3] *Documents relative to the Colonial History of the State of New-York*, ed. E. B. O'Callaghan (Albany, 1856), vol. 6, p. 777. [Hereafter cited as *New York Documents*.]

[4] Charles W. Akers, *Called unto Liberty* (Harvard University Press, 1964), pp. 202, 208.

[5] John Dickinson, *The Late Regulations respecting the British Colonies* (Philadelphia, 1765), reprinted in Bernard Bailyn, ed., *Pamphlets of the American Revolution, 1750–1776* (Harvard University Press, 1965), p. 689.

[6] John Adams to Dr. J. Morse, January 5, 1816, in *The Works of John Adams*, ed. Charles Francis Adams (Boston, 1861), vol. 10, p. 202.

At the time they first appeared in London, the more immediate influence of *Cato's Letters* was that they directed British attention to the prospect and prerequisites of colonial independence. Their British readers could have been alerted to the conditions that might endanger British rule in the colonies, such as "when they no longer want Protection" or would do better by controlling their own trade. Trenchard and Gordon did not advocate colonial independence; they rather coolly advised that it was in Britain's own interest to keep the colonies in a state of contented dependency, which was more easily and effectively achieved "by gentle and insensible Methods, than by Power alone." These were, in fact, Walpole's methods, and Cato's strictures were far more relevant to British policy almost a half century later.

Not long after the appearance of *Cato's Letters*, British readers were assured that there was little to fear from the American colonies. This advice again came from Daniel Defoe. In 1728, he maintained that forebodings of colonial independence were "preposterous," because the colonies were so dependent on Great Britain. Colonial prosperity did not alarm him, because it meant increased trade and "in particular an Encrease of the Consumption of our Manufactures."[7]

The same argument was put forward soon afterwards by a more serious authority, Joshua Gee, a leading economic writer and adviser to the British government. He speculated about what would happen if New England "should ever attempt to be independent of this Kingdom." He thought it most likely that New England would lose so much trade that it would be driven "to the utmost Difficulties to subsist," or that Britain would subdue the colony by placing a standing army in it. He agreed, however, that *"New-England* has shown an uncommon stif[f]ness, very different from that Regard they ought to have for their Mother-Country, or a true Sense of the protection and great Tenderness which has been extended to them." Yet he admitted that the relationship was not one-sided. Britain's shipbuilding industry depended on the timber from New England, without which, he wrote, "we should soon sink in our Navigation." Nevertheless Gee argued against the "Objection made by some Gentlemen, which is, that if we encourage the *Plantations,* they will grow rich and set up for themselves, and cast off the *English* Government." He saw little ground for "such Doubts and Jealousies."[8]

---

[7] [Daniel Defoe], *A Plan of the English Commerce, Being a Compleat Prospect of the Trade of this Nation, as well as the Home Trade as the Foreign* (London, 1728), pp. 361–63.

[8] Joshua Gee, *The Trade and Navigation of Great-Britain Considered, etc.* (London, 3d ed., 1731), pp. 71–75.

A much weightier thinker, Francis Hutcheson, a Scottish professor of moral philosophy and teacher of Adam Smith, seemed in part to address himself to the future of the American colonies. He taught from 1730 to 1746 at Glasgow University, where his lectures were made into a book. It appeared in print in a short version in Latin in 1742 and in English in 1747. His fuller *System of Moral Philosophy* came out in 1755, nine years after his death. Both shorter and longer versions were used as texts in the colonies, where one of his subjects must have been of particular interest. It was, as Caroline Robbins put it, "a theory about the right of resistance to the policies of the mother country."[9]

Hutcheson's theory made the right of resistance dependent on how the mother country treated the colonies. In the main passage which deals with this subject, he taught that colonies oppressed by a mother country did not have to tolerate it, but he also seemed to go somewhat further—that it was wrong for a mother country to hold on to colonies once they were fully grown and "sufficient by themselves." The entire passage was a remarkable anticipation of future events:

> If the plan of the mother-country is changed by force, or degenerates by degrees from a safe, mild, and gentle limited power, to a severe and absolute one; or if under the same plan of polity, oppressive laws are made with respect to the colonies or provinces; and any colony is so increased in numbers and strength that they are sufficient by themselves for all the good ends of a political union; they are not bound to continue in their subjection, when it is grown so much more burdensome than was expected. Their consent to be subject to a safe and gentle plan of power or laws, imports no subjection to the dangerous and oppressive ones. Not to mention that all the principles of humanity require that where the retaining any right or claim is of far less importance to the happiness or safety of one body than it is dangerous and oppressive to another, the former should quit the claim, or agree to all such restrictions and limitations of it as are necessary for the liberty and happiness of the other, provided the other makes compensation of any damage thus occasioned. Large numbers of men cannot be bound to sacrifice their own and their posterity's liberty and happiness, to the ambitious views of their mother-country,

[9] Caroline Robbins, " 'When It Is That Colonies May Turn Independent': An Analysis of the Environment and Politics of Francis Hutcheson," *William and Mary Quarterly*, April 1954, p. 215. Another treatment of Hutcheson appeared in her later book, *The Eighteenth-Century Commonwealthman* (Harvard University Press, 1959), pp. 185–96, but her article deals more directly with Hutcheson's views on the relationship between colonies and mother countries.

while it can enjoy all rational happiness, without subjection to it; and they can only be obliged to compensate the expences of making the settlement and defending it while it needed such defence, and to continue, as good allies, ready to supply as friends any loss of strength their old country sustained by their quitting their subjection to it. There is something so unnatural in supposing a large society, sufficient for all the good purposes of an independent political union, remaining subject to the direction and government of a distant body of men who know not sufficiently the circumstances and exigencies of this society; or in supposing this society to be governed solely for the benefit of a distant country; that it is not easy to imagine there can be any foundation for it in justice or equity. The insisting on old claims and tacit conventions, to extend civil power over distant nations, and form grand unwieldy empires, without regard to the obvious maxims of humanity, has been one great source of human misery.[10]

It would be easy to imagine that Hutcheson was thinking, when he wrote these words, of the American problem in the late 1760s or 1770s. But he was writing in the 1730s or 1740s, when no American was giving him cause to have such thoughts. Part of a chapter from his book was published in the *Massachusetts Spy*—in 1772. As with Trenchard and Gordon, the embattled Americans looked backward to Hutcheson for what they needed to go forward.

· 2 ·

Such premonitions were not limited to the British Isles. France also had its speculative reasoners.

The first remarkable forewarning was found and brought to light by the American historian Francis Parkman, in a *"mémoire"* of 1710–11 found in the French naval archives. It noted that "there is an antipathy between the English of Europe and those of America, who will not endure troops from England even to guard their forts." If the French in Canada should fall, it continued, "Old England will not imagine that these various provinces will then unite, shake off the yoke of the English monarchy, and erect themselves into a democracy."[11]

[10] Francis Hutcheson, *A System of Moral Philosophy* (London, 1755; facsimile reprint, Hildesheim, 1969), vol. 2, bk. 3, pp. 308–9.
[11] Francis Parkman, *A Half-Century of Conflict* (1892; reprint, Little, Brown, 1910), vol. 1, pp. 154–55.

In 1720, a pamphlet published in London attempted to frighten the British about an alleged French plan to plant settlements on the Mississippi River. These settlements, it was said, "whether we have War or Peace with the *French*, will not only prove hurtful, but destructive at last, to our Plantations in *America*, and consequently weaken in a very sensible manner the Strength and Power of *England*, by drying up the Streams that convey thither the greatest Part of their Wealth, and lopping off the most valuable Branches of the *British* Trade and Navigation." If the French were permitted to go ahead with their settlements, it went on, "they will find it a Matter of no great Difficulty, with the Assistance of the *Indians*, to invade from thence and *Canada, all the* English *Plantations at once*, and drive the Inhabitants into the Sea, unless they come to be enabled by some extraordinary Means, which is a thing rather to be *wish'd for* than *depended on*, to provide infinitely better, than they can at present for their Safety and Preservation."[12]

In the next decade, the marquis d'Argenson, Louis XV's secretary of state for foreign affairs, left a notable collection of *Pensées*, which reflected on his life and times. After almost three decades of enmity, Great Britain and France had temporarily called off their feud in 1717 in the form of a triple alliance with Holland. But the tie with France had begun to loosen by the early 1730s and gave d'Argenson reason to think about the condition of the British colonies in America. In 1733, one of his *Pensées* looked forward to Britain's future loss:

> Another great event is being prepared on this globe. The English have vast, rich, orderly domains in North America; they have a new England, a parliament, governors, soldiers, an abundance of white inhabitants, riches, laws, and—what is worse—a naval force.
>
> I say that one fine morning you will see these dominions separate themselves from England, rise and *set up an independent republic*, as Holland did with respect to Spain. These English colonists already refuse to obey; they have their own will. The white people who have come there to live have done so to remain permanently. They do without almost everything that comes from Europe. One day, when they are driven to the extreme, their limit overreached, will they not be able to say: Why should we be dominated by

[12] *Some Considerations on the Consequences Of the French Settling Colonies on the Mississippi . . .* (London, 1720; reprint, Historical and Philosophical Society of Ohio, 1928), pp. 26, 28.

England from Europe? Let us be our own masters and work only for ourselves.

D'Argenson also contemplated the future greatness of America a hundred years before another Frenchman, Alexis de Tocqueville:

> What is going to happen? Is anyone thinking about this? That country, fully familiar with our skills, always in communication with us as a result of the perfection of their ships, will in a short time make themselves masters of all America, especially of its gold mines. What a difference it will really make to have a government that works for itself and does so locally instead of having a government of appointees!
>
> But patience—America will in several centuries make great progress in growth of population and refinement.
>
> Such has been the future of colonies in all times. First they give recognition and respect to their creators, of whom they were extracted, as Eve was from Adam's rib; then they seek to separate themselves. They cost much, and I ask, what profit do they bring?

Just how the separation was going to take place was already clear to d'Argenson:

> They must continually invent experiences of tyranny as the reason for their submission, and blame it for holding back their commerce and their sustenance, thereby costing them untold amounts of money. Yet they disobey, revolt and end by making themselves into independent republics.
>
> We will create in America new sovereignties which will soon become rich and populated, acting by themselves without waiting for orders from Europe; while today they suffer the unhappy condition of Roman slaves who obtain nothing for themselves and only for their masters.
>
> England will be the first to take this route, by necessity, and without which their reasoning will not help them. Stupid policies— don't you think?

D'Argenson also foresaw where British permissiveness and inaction were bound to lead: "I know that the English govern their colonies with moderation, but the English have no less to fear, since it is a moderation of necessity. The colonies are well aware of this. Subject peoples do not tolerate a mild regime for long; contempt begins where gratitude ends.

Moreover, self-interest alone is enough when it is a matter of exchanging the good for the better."[13]

D'Argenson was not the only French reasoner to see so far ahead. Another in the next decade was the "celebrated" and "great" Montesquieu, as he was called by his American admirers. Montesquieu's admiration of the British political system carried over to the British colonies, which he thought had been granted the same type of government. In agreement with Walpole, he advised a commercial nation, situated far from its colonies, to increase "its commerce rather than its domination." As if addressing Great Britain and its American colonies, he went on: "Moreover, as one loves to establish what one has at home, it will give to the people of its colonies the form of its own government: and as this government brings with it prosperity, we will see great peoples arise in the very forests to which they were sent to inhabit."[14]

Still another was the precocious French economist and statesman Turgot, then only twenty-three years old. In 1750, Turgot delivered a discourse at the Sorbonne titled "On the Successive Progress of the Human Spirit." In it, he observed: "Colonies are like fruits which hold to the tree only until their maturity; when they can take care of themselves they have done what has been done since Carthage—*what America will do one day.*"[15]

Montesquieu foresaw that a great people was destined to arise in the distant British colonies. Turgot took the next step and forecast that they were sure to break away.

· 3 ·

D'Argenson's views did not persuade the French government to give up its North American colonies. Count de Maurepas, the secretary of state in charge of naval affairs, had very different ideas about the French colonies.

---

[13] *Mémoires et journal du Marquis d'Argenson* (Paris, 1858), vol. 5, pp. 386–89. This authoritative edition prints these "thoughts" from an article written in 1733 under the heading "Colonies." In his *Prophetic Voices concerning America* (Boston, 1874), Charles Sumner, the first collector of such prophecies, apparently used an earlier edition and attributed these lines to *Pensées sur la Réformation de l'Etat*, written between 1733 and 1745 (pp. 37–38). Sumner's translation is also somewhat different, but the sense is usually the same.

[14] *Oeuvres Complètes de Montesquieu*, ed. André Masson (Editions Nagel, 1950), vol. 1, p. 438 (bk. 19, chap. 27).

[15] *Oeuvres de M. Turgot* (Paris, 1808), vol. 2, p. 66. The editor appended this note to these words: "It was in 1750 that M. Turgot, only twenty-three years old, and sent to a seminary for the study of theology, foretold, foresaw the revolution which established the United States and which separated them from the Europe[an] power apparently most capable of holding its colonies under its domination."

As much as d'Argenson was anticolonial, Maurepas was procolonial. D'Argenson was in charge of foreign affairs for less than three years, ending in 1747. Maurepas held office from 1723 to 1749, when he was dismissed and exiled from Paris for having perpetrated a witticism at the expense of madame de Pompadour, and it took him another quarter of a century to make a political comeback. Meanwhile, he was responsible for turning French policy in the direction of the colonies across the Atlantic.

Maurepas's basic thinking was typical of the time. "Commerce creates riches," he held, "and consequently the power of states." From wealth and power he went on to the role of the navy and colonies. Naval forces were absolutely necessary for the support of commercial shipping, from which it followed that "maritime states which have the greatest naval forces can take possession not only of the greatest share of commerce but of colonies." At a time when few French officials recognized the importance of colonies in this imperial scheme, Maurepas was their chief proponent.[16] He is even said to have had a scheme whereby the French colonists in North America would befriend the British colonies as if they were natural allies and thus "one day help them to break the yoke of England"—a remarkable anticipation of the Franco-American alliance during the American Revolution.[17]

Even before the British, then, the French were moving towards making the North American colonies the chief battleground in the European struggle for power. Colonies which had long been neglected as distant outposts were now made to decide the fate of their mother countries. The reversal of roles was implicit in a statement made in 1748 by Edmond-Jean-François Barbier, a disciple of Maurepas, that the loss of France's colonies in North America would bring about the absolute ruin of French commerce.[18]

But by far the most extraordinary premonition of what was at stake in the French and British colonies was expressed by another Frenchman two years later. He was Marquis Roland-Michel Barrin de la Galissonière, a naval officer who was able to put his ideas into practice.

Galissonière fortuitously served as deputy governor of New France, as Canada was called, from September 1747 to September 1749. Marquis de La Jonquière, the regularly appointed governor, had been wounded in a naval engagement on his way to take over the post and captured by the British. Galissonière, who had often visited the colony previously during

[16] Maurice Filion, *La Pensée et l'action de Maurepas vis-à-vis du Canada, 1723–1749* (Editions Leméac, 1972), pp. 43, 47, 105, 139.
[17] Roland Lamontagne, *Aperçu structural du Canada au XVIIIe siecle* (Editions Leméac, 1964), p. 27.
[18] Filion, *La Pensée et l'action*, p. 106.

his voyages, was pressed into service as a substitute. The Swedish botanist Peter Kalm described Galissonière as "a nobleman of uncommon qualities," short and somewhat humpbacked, with a surprising knowledge of scientific matters, especially natural history.[19]

In his two years in Canada, Galissonière formed the conviction that the British were planning to drive the French out of North America. He believed that the only way to prevent this expulsion was to erect a line of forts between Canada and the French colony of Louisiana to the south. To make up for the British-American advantage in population, Galissonière envisaged a barrier of military posts, trading stations, and forts in the Illinois and Ohio country, then the no-man's-land between Canada and Louisiana. In effect, he aimed to enclose the British-American colonies between the Atlantic and the Allegheny Mountains to prevent them from outflanking the French colonies from the south and north.[20]

When Jonquière was released, Galissonière returned to France and in 1750 submitted his *Mémoire sur les colonies de la France dans l'Amérique septentrionale,* perhaps the single most remarkable document of its time. Its logic led inexorably to the first battle of the Seven Years' War.

Galissonière admitted that Canada, relatively poor and sparsely populated, had been and was likely to remain a burden to France—a reason why Maurepas had met with such opposition from d'Argenson and others. Yet, Galissonière argued, it "is of the greatest importance and absolutely necessary not to neglect any means or spare any expense to assure the preservation of Canada, since it is only in this way that we can succeed in saving America from the ambitions of the British, and since the progress of their empire in this part of the world is what is most capable of giving them superiority in Europe."

After a lengthy examination of Canada's regions and resources, Galissonière came back to his main point:

> Finally, we must spare nothing to strengthen our colonies, since we can and must think of them as the barrier of America against the encroachments of the English, for only they can make up for the lack of naval forces, and what they will cost will save considerably more

[19] Peter Kalm, *Travels Into North America,* trans. John Reinhold Foster (London, 1770–71, rev. ed. 1772; reprint, Imprint Society, 1972), pp. 406, 475. Galissonière has also been described as "short and stooped slightly," but otherwise "good-looking" (Martti Kerkkonen, *Peter Kalm's American Journey,* Helsinki, 1959, p. 106).

[20] Roland Lamontagne, *La Galissonière et la Canada* (Presses de l'Universitaires de France, 1962); Lionel Groulx, *Roland-Michel de la Galissonière, 1693–1758* (University of Toronto Press, 1970). Lamontagne gives his full name as Roland-Michel Barrin de la Galissonière.

expense spent otherwise with much less certain results, especially if we permit ourselves to be reduced to the necessity of getting help from France to support them in time of war. And since they cannot be left to depend on their own resources alone, without giving them up in some way to the English, whose superiority in America and the wealth that they draw from there to the exclusion of other nations, would very surely give them the superiority in Europe.[21]

As usual with prophets of alarm, Galissonière's worst fears—that the British-American colonies would soon take possession of all other colonies in North America and even in the West Indies—were premature. Like others, he took off from the increasing power of the British colonies in order to make his point about where it was all going to lead. Unlike others, however, he was mainly interested not in the prospect of American independence but in what the ascendancy of the British colonies would mean for Europe.

The French in Canada, he urged, were the means to prevent the British from gaining the upper hand in Europe by deriving such great benefit from their American colonies. The French, he thought, had a military advantage to offset the odds against them; they had more and better alliances with the Indian tribes and could lead them to fight against the British-Americans, because more French colonists were able to live like Indians. He recognized that France could not hope to equal the British in naval power on the high seas, which left a French attack on the British possessions as the only recourse.

The distinctive feature of Galissonière's reasoning was the link between power in the colonies and power in Europe. If the British were drawing so much commercial and naval benefit from their American colonies, they were using it to get the better of their European rivals, among which France had the most to lose. Instead of defeating British aims on the continent, which had been shown to be an expensive and futile course for all concerned, an indirect assault on British interests could be launched against the American colonies with allegedly deadly effect. At the same time, Galissonière raised the specter of an inevitable British-American assault on French Canada, thus giving his military policy a defensive as well as an offensive justification.

One way or the other, the British-American colonies were thrust by this

---

[21] The French original appears in Lamontagne, *La Galissonière et la Canada.* There is a somewhat different translation in *New York Documents,* vol. 10, esp. pp. 223–24 and 232, and in Groulx, *Roland-Michel de la Galissonière,* p. 61.

reasoning into the center of European politics. Willy-nilly they became more important to others as they rose in their own self-esteem. That such speculations were taken seriously in France suggests that they were in the air and did not depend on anyone's individual insight.

· 4 ·

Back in England, at about the same time that Galissonière was telling the French how important the North American colonies were, a British official in North Carolina was impressed by much the same thought. He was James Abercromby, who left two book-length treatises on colonial affairs: the first written about 1752, the second about 1774. They were never published in his lifetime and, in fact, did not appear in print until 1986. Nevertheless, they were studied by some American historians and given the highest praise. Charles M. Andrews regarded the first work so favorably that he said it "will give the reader, better than any printed pamphlet of which I know, an insight into the working of the British system, with all its defects and deficiencies."[22] The editors of the recently printed edition agree that "the two treatises together constitute the fullest, most systematic, and most original contemporary analysis of the British imperial system as it existed on the eve of the American Revolution."[23]

Abercromby's career was almost unique for a British official. No British minister had ever visited the American colonies, and no member of the Board of Trade, despite its manifold business with them. Abercromby was a Scot appointed in 1730 at the age of twenty-three as attorney general and advocate general of the court of vice admiralty in South Carolina. He held those posts—and others, including two terms in the assembly—for the next fourteen years. From 1748, he served as colonial agent in London for North Carolina and Virginia, the latter post until the outbreak of hostilities in 1775. From 1761 to 1768, he sat in Parliament and voted against the repeal of the Stamp Act.

In his first work, which concerns us now, he immediately concurred with one of Galissonière's main ideas. In his crabbed, convoluted prose,

---

[22] Charles M. Andrews, *The Colonial Period of American History* (Yale University Press, 1934), vol. 4, p. 409 n. 1.

[23] *Magna Charta for America:* James Abercromby's "An Examination of the Acts of Parliament Relative to the Trade and the Government of our American Colonies" (1752) and *"De Jure et Gubernatione Coloniarum,* or An Inquiry into the Nature, and the Rights of Colonies, Ancient, and Modern" (1774), ed. Jack P. Greene, Charles F. Mullett, and Edward C. Papenfuse, Jr. (American Philosophical Society, 1986).

he saw the American colonies in European terms and emphasized their importance for influencing the European balance of power:

> How therefore, to make Natural, and Political Ties, between the Mother Country and these Colonies, insomuch, as it regards, the Interior Interest of this Kingdom, but likewise, from the Share, that well Adapted rules of Policy, For the Government, and Trade, of these our Colonies, must have, in Maintaining, the Independency, of the Sovereignty of this Nation, amidst Contests in Europe, for universal Dominion; for, wherever, and whenever, such Contests happen it will be found, That the Auxiliary power of American Colonies, (as the Source of Maritime power) in some Shape or other, will Contribute, to the Support, or overthrow, of European Nations. . . . It is now, from Experience Evident, that a very great Accessory power, may be Derived from thence, to the Principal States, And [that] no European Nation [can be] so Blind, but to See with envy, the particular benefit, Arising to this Nation, from these our American Colonies.

Abercromby was a rather orthodox mercantilist. It was not going to be easy, he saw, to get that "particular benefit" and make the colonies "Subservient to the Interest of the Principal State," because some of them "from their first Establishment, Stand, upon a kind of Independency." He set himself the task of proposing changes in the governing of the colonies to realize the "benefit" and hold back the "Independency." He made a lengthy series of proposals to restrict the colonies and especially to get British officials to carry out British laws and instructions or be removed and fined. Above all, he wanted Parliament to pay more attention to the colonies:

> It is surprizing, that Considering the Connection, and Intercourse that these Kingdoms have with their Plantations, Considering how powerfull in Strength and Wealth the American Plantations are become, and daily becomeing more and more so, and Considering, how much this Kingdom is Interested in Maintaining a Natural as Well as Political Tye between the Mother Country and the Colonies, for, of all Alliances, that, with the Plantations, is the Most Natural, most prudent, and most beneficial to the Strength and to the Wealth of this Kingdom; from these Considerations therefore, it becomes amazing, that the Parliament of Great Britain have not hitherto attended to the Interior Government of these Colonies, by taking under their Consideration, the different Powers Exercised by the

Several Colonies, in making of Laws, and how far such Powers at this time of the Day are, or are not, now Consistent with the Policy and Interest of the Mother Country; or admitting of no Inconsistency in such Powers, how far the Same are duly Exercised.

In one text of this work, Abercromby summed up what was bound to happen if Parliament did not act: "That the Plantations are either to be Governed by the Arbitrary Rule of the Sovereign or are to becom[e] Independent of this Kingdom, for *Imperium in Imperio* cannot long Subsist."[24] He was a forerunner of those British ministers and officials who looked to Parliament to play a larger and more controlling role to put the colonies in their place as a subordinate element in the British system.

Not long afterwards, the colonial problem was taken up by Dean Josiah Tucker of Bristol and later of Gloucester in England, one of the most remarkable figures of the age, with unconventional views on religion, economics, and politics. Tucker's thoughts on what to do about the colonies changed over the years. He initially put his mind to the problem of a colonial breakaway in 1749 with the aim of trying to prevent it. To do so, he believed, the best way was to encourage trade with the "plantations," still a common term for the colonies. Either Britain could promote trade with them and support their growth or they would be forced to go to other markets and— sacrilege from the mercantilist point of view—permit "other Nations to *come* and *trade* with them." Tucker was afraid that the colonies would make their own manufactures instead of getting them from Britain. His recipe for an exchange of commodities was to make them serve a "MUTUAL BENEFIT.—A mutual Benefit is a MUTUAL DEPENDENCE." Then he came to the main point:

> And this Principle alone will contribute more to the preserving of the Dependency of our Colonies upon their Mother Country, than any other Refinement or Invention. For, if we are afraid, that one Day or other they will revolt, and set up for themselves, as some seem to apprehend; Let us not *drive* them to a Necessity to *feel* themselves *independent* of us; As they *will* do, the Moment they perceive, that they can be supplied with all Things from *within* themselves, and not *need* our Assistance. If we would keep them still dependent upon their Mother Country, and in some Respects *subservient* to

[24] Ibid., pp. 45, 148–49, 169 n. 159. The editors' introduction contains a far more easily understood summary of Abercromby's work (pp. 12–23).

her *Views* and *Welfare;*—Let us make it their INTEREST always so to be.[25]

Here Tucker stressed self-interest as the key to colonial dependence. As soon as the colonies perceived that they could supply themselves with all the things that they had been accustomed to get from Britain, they would necessarily turn to thoughts of independence. British policy had to aim at keeping the colonies dependent, but it had to be a mutual dependence— an enlightened view in the mid-eighteenth century. Tucker later changed his mind and decided that it was best for Great Britain to get rid of the colonies altogether.

Tucker's earlier view followed a line of thought that went back at least a century in English speculative reasoning about the colonies. It has been relatively neglected in recent historical work on the background of American revolutionary thought.

For there were two parallel British traditions. One went back to the republican thought of Milton, Sydney, Locke, and others in the seventeenth century and to the Commonwealthmen or "Real Whigs" in the first half of the eighteenth century. This intellectual trend has been minutely studied, because it provided the Founding Fathers with an armory of rights, concepts, and rhetoric with which to justify the struggle for independence. The colonial leaders ransacked the storehouse of ancient and modern history and literature for precedents, heroes, and inspiration. Recent scholars have been impressed less by the break with the past that the American Revolution represented than by the transmission of an ideological inheritance and its application to the American colonies.[26]

But there was another British tradition. It was mainly concerned with the power rather than the right of a colony to seek independence. This line of thought went back to Maj. John Child's alarm in 1647 about the earliest colonies "growing into a nation"; to James Harrington's reference in 1656 to the colonies' inclination to wean themselves when they "come of age"; to Charles Davenant's warning in 1698 that "Riches, Power and Dominion" made colonies formidable; to Cato's prophecy in 1722 that the colonists would "not be long to seek for Arguments to justify" their desire for

[25] Josiah Tucker, *A Brief Essay on the Advantages and Disadvantages Which Respectively Attend France and Great Britain with Regard to Trade* (London, 1749; 3d ed., 1753), pp. 93–96.

[26] Some of the best-known works of this kind are Clinton Rossiter, *Seedtime of the Republic* (Harcourt, Brace, 1953); Robbins, *Eighteenth-Century Commonwealthman;* Richard M. Gummere, *The American Colonial Mind and the Classical Tradition* (Harvard University Press, 1963); H. Trevor Colbourn, *The Lamp of Experience* (University of North Carolina Press, 1965); Bailyn, *Ideological Origins of the American Revolution;* J. G. A. Pocock, *The Machiavellian Moment* (Princeton University Press, 1975), pt. 3.

independence and that colonies often saw that independence was in their self-interest as soon as they felt that they no longer needed protection; and to Josiah Tucker's forecast in 1749 that the colonies would feel themselves to be independent as soon as they did not need protection.

This realistic, hardheaded tradition had more to say to British rulers than to potential American rebels. It warned successive British governments that they had better keep the colonies in a state of dependence if they wanted to hold on to them. Such a policy did not occur to British minds only after the colonists had made their first overt moves to throw off the British connection; it had long antedated colonial disaffection and disobedience. The danger of permitting the colonies to "come of age" or obtain "Riches, Power and Dominion" had hung over British colonial policy almost from the beginning. It was largely ignored during the Walpolian years to mid-century, but its very neglect had permitted the colonies to "come of age" and, in fact, to increase their "Riches, Power and Dominion."

5

"What subordination? What Obedience?"

IF INFLUENTIAL BRITISH THINKERS were so alert to what was going on in the colonies and how it was bound to end, why did British governments do no more to prevent it from happening? Why did they not force the issue while they were best able to do so? Why did they wait so long?

The answers go back to the very nature of the early British imperial system. British policy required that the colonies should support themselves, all the while contributing to Great Britain's benefit. Yet, by supporting themselves, the colonies lessened their dependence on Great Britain, and by contributing to British commercial profit, they increasingly made Great Britain dependent on themselves. The results reversed the first axiom of imperial rule—that colonies should always be dependent on the mother country.

This system could prevail only so long as it rested on colonial goodwill or colonial submission to superior force. Neither was sufficient in the long run. The colonists were perfectly willing to pay lip service to the Crown and, if necessary, say all the right things, but not if doing so cost them anything they were unwilling to pay. Until trained, regular troops were sent over to fight in the Seven Years' War in 1756, the British military establishment in the colonies was made up of four understaffed companies stationed in New

York. The colonies were expected to defend themselves. They even took the initiative and supplied all the troops in the successful assault on the French fortress of Louisbourg in 1745. For well over a century, it was British policy to rule the colonies on the cheap, to get the most out of them for the least.

The colonies went their own way for so long, despite the forebodings of subordinate officials, largely because their superiors in the Privy Council and Parliament, where decisions were made, had other, weightier things to preoccupy them. The latent struggle for power in the colonies was influenced by more pressing struggles for power on the continent.

During the first half of the eighteenth century, just when the colonies were gathering strength and reaching political maturity, the colonial problem was far less urgent than the struggles against France and Spain. While Great Britain was embroiled in Europe, it was in no mood or condition to deal forcefully across the Atlantic with its own people, as it still thought of them. Once Great Britain went over to an anti-French policy under William III, its money and its energies were fully engaged in one war after another. The first war with France—known as King William's War in its American phase—went on from 1689 until 1697. Then came the War of the Spanish Succession—called Queen Anne's War in America—from 1701 to 1713. The oddly named War of Jenkins' Ear against Spain dragged on from 1739 to 1748. Meanwhile, the War of the Austrian Succession—King George's War in America—occurred between 1740 and 1748. All these wars were inconclusive; one merely prepared the way for the next. While they went on, the British external outlook was more continental than colonial.

Only the successful conclusion of the Seven Years' War—or the French and Indian War, as it was called in America—of 1756–1763 enabled Great Britain to gain a breathing spell from these wars. Not until then was Britain free to turn its full attention to the festering colonial problem in America.

Internally, British rulers also had other things to think about. For about three decades after the Glorious Revolution, British administrations suffered from extreme instability and rapid turnover of high offices. A Jacobite uprising in 1715 to restore a descendant of James II to the throne contributed to the sense that it was more important to concentrate on affairs at home than on symptoms of future colonial disaffection.

All the greater, therefore, were the relief and satisfaction that greeted the stable rule finally established by Sir Robert Walpole from 1721 to 1742 and continued by his successors, the brothers Henry Pelham and the duke of Newcastle, until 1756. This remarkably long, seemingly cohesive period of thirty-five years—partially extended for another six years until Newcastle was forced out of his last office in 1762, after forty-five years of continuous service—was the colonial calm before the storm. It may be thought of as the middle period of colonial development—between the first century of infancy and growing pains, through a near half century of lusty adolescence, to a final decade of prerevolutionary coming of age. The best chance the British had to rein in the colonies came in this period.

For much of this period, Great Britain was at peace in Europe and at peace with itself. It was a time of intense self-absorption and self-aggrandizement. The favorite Walpolian motto, *quieta non movere,* which had the same implication as "don't rock the boat" or "let well enough alone," summed up the ideals of the age—to put stability and security first, to prefer the profits of commerce and industry to the spoils of war, to make no changes that threatened to offend anyone or jeopardize anything. Walpole's style of government, based on patronage and preferment, taught British ministers for decades to come how to manage the system.

Parliament's role was ambivalent. It was reluctant to increase the powers of the Crown in the colonies in ways that might shift the balance at home. The favorite colonial reform of royal officials—to establish a uniform pattern of colonies directly accountable to the Crown without the interposition of old colonial charters—could never get through Parliament. Yet ministers and officials acknowledged Parliament's ultimate jurisdiction in colonial affairs by threatening to take their complaints to Parliament. They rarely carried out their threats, however, and when they did they were not welcome, because Parliament was not anxious to take responsibility for colonial policy.

Governors, though totally responsible to the Crown, knew that they were caught between two fires. When Governor Belcher of Massachusetts complained grievously about his lack of funds, he confided to a colonial agent in London that "I must walk very circumspectly lest the King's ministers shou'd imagine I am not zealous enough for the honour of the Crown, and lest the House of Commons shou'd think I bear too hard upon the priviledges of the people. I'll endeavour to steer as nicely as I can between both."[1] In 1744, the Board of Trade tried to get Parliament out of the way by presenting a bill to give royal instructions to the colonies all the force of acts of Parliament. It was rejected on its first reading.[2] Benjamin Franklin later recalled that the bill had been "thrown out by the Commons, for which

---

[1] Belcher to Richard Partridge, November 1, 1731, "The Belcher Papers," *Massachusetts Historical Society Collections,* ser. 6, vol. 6, p. 38.
[2] James A. Henretta, *"Salutary Neglect"* (Princeton University Press, 1972), p. 325.

we adored them as our friends and friends of liberty, till by their conduct towards us in 1765 it seem'd that they had refused that point of sovereignty to the king only that they might reserve it for themselves."[3] Franklin thus recognized that Parliament had played a different role vis-à-vis the colonies in the first half of the eighteenth century than in the third quarter. In its earlier role, Parliament had been reluctant either to increase or to diminish the power of the Crown. Walpole's strategy was to do as little as possible to disturb the Crown, Parliament, and the colonies.

British politics reacted upon the colonies long before the colonies reacted upon British politics. Whatever was wrong or troublesome in the colonies was long not permitted to disturb the good life in Great Britain. The profits of merchants counted far more than the complaints of administrators. The Board of Trade advised less and less; the chief figures in the government cared less and less for its advice. The board virtually ceased to figure as an active factor in British colonial policy between 1724 and 1748.[4] It had long been the one body that had consistently pushed for a hard line against colonial pretensions; when it was reduced to inconsequence and ineffectiveness, no one else was interested enough to take up the slack. The unconcern was not inadvertent; it was governmental policy under Walpole and Newcastle. They did not force issues raised by the colonies, because they did not have the inclination or will to do so, not because they did not have sufficient provocation or challenge.

Edmund Burke later dubbed this policy "salutary neglect." Walpole could safely pursue such a policy because the colonies were not yet ready to take advantage of it. Even then, however, they had made enough progress and had shown enough willingness to stand their ground to persuade Walpole that he could face them down only by stirring up the kind of turbulence he was determined to avoid.

· 2 ·

From the perspective of the entire eighteenth century, Sir Robert Walpole and the duke of Newcastle had aided and abetted the American Revolution without, of course, intending to do so.

---

[3] John Bigelow, *The Life of Benjamin Franklin* (J. B. Lippincott, 1875), vol. 1, pp. 367–68. In a letter to James Bowdoin, January 13, 1772, Franklin said that the bill had been thrown out because it had been opposed by colonial agents (ibid., p. 367).

[4] Basil Williams, *The Whig Supremacy, 1714–1760* (Oxford University Press, 1939), p. 294. Charles M. Andrews preferred the dates 1730 to 1748 (*The Cambridge History of the British Empire,* Cambridge University Press, 1929, vol. 1, p. 413).

Walpole was the longest-lasting chief minister in British history—*prime minister* was then used as a term of reproach, suggesting someone who wished to usurp too much power. He combined the posts of first lord of the Treasury and chancellor of the Exchequer for twenty-one years, which enabled him to control the entire administration. Walpole's era established the House of Commons as the dominant factor in what had formerly been seen as a balanced, threefold governance of king, Lords, and Commons. The chief ministers had previously come from the House of Lords; Walpole was the first to emerge from the House of Commons and stay there for all the years of his ministry. His downfall had started with the protests against the Excise Bill of 1733—a British phenomenon which showed that the colonists were not the only ones with an aversion to paying taxes.

Walpole mainly devoted himself to domestic administration. His man in charge of colonial affairs was Thomas Pelham, the duke of Newcastle. He was both the most precocious product and the most shameless practitioner of patronage politics, the consuming political game of the age. Walpole made Newcastle secretary of state for the Southern Department in 1724, when he was not yet thirty-one years of age. Without any previous experience in foreign affairs, Newcastle was put in charge of relations with southern Europe and the colonies, the joint responsibilities of his department. He was rich, titled, and intelligent enough to play most successfully according to the existing rules of the game, not sensitive enough to know or care where they would lead. His political longevity was legendary, even exceeding Walpole's. He remained in the same post for the next twenty-four years, a record never equaled. After Walpole's fall in 1742, the duke's younger brother, Henry Pelham, succeeded as head of the government and Newcastle moved from the Southern to the Northern Department, responsible for relations with northern Europe, then considered to be higher in status. When Henry Pelham died prematurely in 1754, Newcastle succeeded him and held the chief post intermittently until 1762. His unprecedented career extending over forty-nine years—from lord chamberlain in 1717 at the age of twenty-four to lord privy seal in 1766 at the age of seventy-three—made him the most durable British politician of that or any other century.

A revealing example of how the British colonial system pretended to work and how it really worked occurred in 1729, after Newcastle had been on the job for five years. He had been importuned for so long by Governor Burnet of Massachusetts about the latter's uncertain and inadequate salary that something apparently had to be done about it. On June 16 of that year, Newcastle sent Burnet an official message that put the gravest interpretation upon the Massachusetts disobedience. He had made up his mind, he wrote, that

> there is too much reason to think, that the main drift of the Assembly, in refusing to comply with what has been so frequently and so strongly recommended to them, is to throw off their dependance on the Crown; which proceeding can in no wise be justified by their Charter, and never will be allowed by His Majesty. This obstinance of theirs has produced the final determination of laying the whole matter before the Parliament.[5]

This was for the record. Privately, Newcastle drafted another letter to Burnet the same day with a rather different message. He advised the Massachusetts governor that "it were to be wished the bringing things to that extremity [Parliament] might be avoided." He authorized Burnet to accept the salary that had been offered to him, providing it should cover his entire tenure in office. He also directed Burnet to make the comedown look as if it were his own idea and did not come from the British government.[6] The salary was never allotted for Burnet's entire tenure, and Newcastle never went to Parliament to bring the matter to a head.

The implications of this empty threat to lay the whole matter before Parliament were not lost on another governor, Spotswood of Virginia. Col. William Byrd of Westover discussed the Burnet affair with Spotswood sometime later. Spotswood told Byrd that "if the Assembly in New England would stand Bluff, he did not see how they cou'd be forct to raise Money against their will, for if they shou'd direct it to be done by Act of Parliament, which they have threaten'd to do, (though it be against the Right of Englishmen to be taxt, but by their Representatives), yet they wou'd find it no easy matter to put such an Act in Execution."[7]

Putting such an act in execution could have been done only by resorting to force. Such a desperate measure had already been proposed by Thomas Burnet, brother of Governor Burnet. He had suggested that "an independent Company be sent thither under him as Captain to take possession of the Fort, which will be the only means to bring these people to have respect for the Government."[8] Nothing of the sort happened—for the next forty years.

---

[5] *Colonial Papers, America and West Indies* (London, 1969), 1728–29, 1937, p. 413.
[6] Ibid., pp. 413–14.
[7] *The Writings of Colonel William Byrd of Westover in Virginia* (New York, 1901), pp. 365–66.
[8] Cited by Henretta, *"Salutary Neglect,"* pp. 71–72.

· 3 ·

The double face of the Walpole-Newcastle colonial policy was strikingly shown by some of the stickiest parliamentary legislation of the period— the Molasses Act of 1733. The bill was introduced as a result of complaints from the British islands in the West Indies, whose economy was based on the production of sugar, against the competition of the French sugar islands— St. Dominique, Guadeloupe, and Martinique. The British West Indies— Antigua, Barbados, Jamaica, Montserrat, and St. Christopher—were such an immense source of wealth that they were considered at the time to be more important to the empire than the North American colonies.

Molasses, a by-product of the islands' sugar mills, was turned into rum in New England. There were so many distilleries in Rhode Island, Massachusetts, and Connecticut that they were known as the Rum Coast. Rum, to a degree hard to believe in a later and much different world, was essential to the New England economy. It was one of the main means of profitable exchange for furs from the Indians and slaves and ivory from Africa, as well as in intercolonial trade. Some of the greatest early New England fortunes were based on the rum trade, most of which was carried on illegally. Boston alone was said to have about fifty distilling houses. Nothing could set off a panic in New England more surely than tampering with this trade.

The trouble arose because the British islands could not supply all the molasses needed by the North American distilleries or supply them as cheaply as the French islands. The French West Indian molasses manufacture and the New England rum production were as if made for each other. The French islands could not send their molasses to France, because the French preferred wine and brandy to rum. Moreover, France could not supply its sugar islands with the provisions they needed. What France did not want and could not pay for, New England wanted and could pay for, with enthusiasm. By Walpole's time, an immensely important trade had developed between the French islands and the New England colonies. The French islands provided most of the molasses which the New Englanders made into rum. In exchange, New England sent flour, meat, fish, horses, lumber, and other commodities to the French islands. With the profits made in the rum trade, New England was able to pay for most of its imports from Great Britain, which it could not otherwise afford to do owing to its unfavorable balance of trade with its mother country.

Everyone benefited—except the British sugar islands. Their lobby in London, made up mainly of absentee owners of plantations in the upper altitudes of British society and politics, commanded far more influence than anything the plain Americans could muster. The result was the Molasses Act, which was designed to cut off the French-American trade by putting a 100 percent duty upon non-British sugar.

The West Indian planters had got what they wanted by crying in the right places that they faced ruin. The Americans also cried ruin in as many places as they could reach. The agent of Massachusetts and Connecticut in London foretold funereally that the act was bound to ruin "many thousand families there."9 Richard Partridge, the New York agent in London, brought up the argument of nonrepresentation in Parliament to denounce the act as "divesting them of their rights and privileges as ye King's natural born subjects and English men in levying subsidies upon them against their consent when they are annexd to no county in Great Britain, have no Representatives in Parliam[en]t, nor any part of ye Legislature of this Kingdom."10

Walpole was ostensibly faced with a choice between ruining either one group of British colonies or another. He was equal to the challenge. By passing the act, he legally appeased the British West Indian planters. By doing little or nothing to enforce it, he appeased the New England rum merchants. Smuggling was not a particularly American vice. Professor J. H. Plumb remarks in his biography of Walpole: "It is difficult for us to comprehend the immensity of eighteenth-century smuggling. Walpole had first-hand knowledge. Not much of the linen used at Houghton [Walpole's country house] during his early life had passed through the customs. Even when Secretary at War he had been engaged in smuggling his wines up the Thames."11

Smuggling had long been part of the British way of doing business whenever excise duties made desirable commodities, such as brandy and tobacco, too expensive. As much as 192,515 gallons of brandy and 1,061,268 pounds of tobacco were seized by the customs between 1723 and 1733, all of which was estimated to be only one-tenth of the total amount smuggled into the country in those years.12 Smuggling was another American habit, much complained of by the English, which showed that the Americans were, as they claimed to be, good and true Englishmen.

---

9 *The Colonial Merchant,* ed. Stuart Bruchey (Harcourt, Brace and World, 1966), p. 70.
10 *Colonial Papers,* 1733, publ. 1932, p. 66.
11 J. H. Plumb, *Sir Robert Walpole: The King's Minister* (Cresset Press, 1960), p. 237.
12 Derek Jarrett, *Britain, 1688–1815* (St. Martin's Press, 1965), p. 192.

Walpole suffered his first humiliating defeat by being forced to withdraw an excise bill in 1733. The uproar which this bill aroused in Great Britain was strikingly like that which the Stamp Act set off in the colonies three decades later. The bill was furiously attacked as the end of British liberty and enslavement by customs officers. Almost in the same words as a later colonial slogan, British crowds chanted, "Liberty, Property, and No Excise." Walpole himself barely escaped without personal injury. As he was walking towards his carriage during the excise debate in Parliament, he was grabbed by his cloak and saved from serious violence only by the intervention of his son, Edward, and a friend, Gen. Charles Churchill.

Walpole's explanation of why he surrendered to the opposition on the excise issue casts some light on his refusal to drive the colonists into the same sort of resistance. He declared that "in the present inflamed temper of the people, the act could not be carried into execution without armed force; that there would be an end of the liberty of England, if supplies were to be raised by the sword."[13]

Later in the same decade, Walpole again showed what a healthy respect he had for troublemaking Americans. After he had been forced to withdraw his bill for excise taxes in Great Britain, Walpole was urged to make up for the loss by imposing direct taxes on the colonies. Again the resemblance to the Stamp Act crisis is marked. In 1739, Sir William Keith and others had argued for the need to employ a small number of regular British troops in the colonies against the French threat. They recommended a duty on stamps to pay for the force and gave assurance that the Americans would "chearfully comply" so long as the money was spent for protective service and for no other purpose.[14] Walpole is supposed to have given this reply to the proposal: "I have old England set against me, and do you think I will have new England likewise?"[15]

He also is said to have given this fuller explanation for his refusal:

> I will leave that for some of my successors, who have more courage than I have, and are less a friend of commerce than I am. It has been a maxim with me during my administration, to encourage the trade

[13] William Coxe, *Memoirs of the Life and Administration of Sir Robert Walpole* (London, new ed., 1800), vol. 1, p. 236 (attack on Walpole); 239–40 (Walpole's explanation).

[14] "Some Remarks on the most rational and effectual Means that can be used in the present Conjuncture for the Future Security and Preservation of the Trade of Great Britain, by protecting and advancing her Settlements on the Northern Continent of AMERICA," in *Two Papers on the Subject of Taxing the British Colonies in America* (J. Almon, 1767), pp. 8–10. The other paper was called "Proposal for establishing by Act of Parliament the Duties upon Stampt [*sic*] Paper and Parchment in all the British Colonies."

[15] John Morley, *Walpole* (Macmillan, 1889), p. 168.

of the American colonies to the utmost latitude (nay, it has been necessary to pass over some irregularities in their trade with Europe); for, by encouraging them to an extensive growing foreign commerce, if they gain £500,000, I am convinced that, in two years afterwards, full £250,000 of their gains will be in his majesty's exchequer, by the labour and produce of this kingdom; as immense quantities of every kind of our manufactures go thither, and as they increase in their foreign American trade, more of our produce will be wanted. This is taxing them more agreeably both to their own constitution and to ours.[16]

Here we have the fundamental issue of British colonial policy, later identified with Edmund Burke and others but originally stated with cold precision by Walpole. The vital choice was between trade and taxes. So long as trade with the colonies was rising and making Great Britain richer and richer, Walpole was willing to give up other benefits from them. He was even willing to overlook infractions of the navigation and trade acts so long as colonial earnings ultimately accrued to ever greater British profits. Much of what came out openly in the 1760s and 1770s lies buried in the evasions of the 1730s.

The chief lesson of the molasses-rum imbroglio was that the American colonists could evade and violate British laws with virtual impunity. If the British government did not find some way to mollify them, they were just as likely as their British compeers to take direct or indirect action to defend their interests. Parliamentary supremacy meant less in America than it had come to mean in Great Britain; Parliament to the Americans was but another component of British power over the colonies, to be obeyed or defied depending on what colonial interests were.

In the thirty years after the Molasses Act, the annual remittance from customs duties in the colonies to Great Britain amounted to less than £2,000; the cost of collection was £7,000.[17] As one of the leading British officials later pointed out, smuggling was a highly political act: "That Connection [of the colonies with Great Britain] is actually broken already, whenever the Acts of Navigation are disregarded; and for so much of their Trade as is thereby diverted from its proper Channel, they are no longer *British* colonies, but Colonies of the Countries they trade to."[18]

[16] This is the version given by William Gordon, *The History of the Rise, Progress, and Establishment of the Independence of the United States of America* (New York, 1789), vol. 1, pp. 92–93. Gordon's work was the first published history of the American Revolution.

[17] [Thomas Whately], *The Regulations Lately made concerning the Colonies, and the Taxes Imposed upon Them, considered* (London, 1765), p. 57.

[18] Ibid., p. 92.

Consistency, however, was not an outstanding British characteristic. If Walpole's attitude towards trade, the acts of navigation, smuggling, and customs in the colonies had prevailed throughout the British administration, a good deal of mutual hostility could have been avoided. But British customs officials were stationed in American ports to enforce the acts of navigation, to punish smuggling, and to collect customs duties. When these officials were thwarted and discredited, Americans were not likely to be impressed by British decrees—or the power to enforce them.

· 4 ·

To be a customs official in the colonies, especially in New England, was not a peaceful occupation. One case in Boston in 1724 was fully reported to the lords commissioners of the Treasury in London.

The brigantine *William and Mary* was caught clandestinely bringing in goods from Spain. Its master, W. Whipple, was charged with the crime. Informants were almost always necessary to get convictions. Two witnesses, who gave evidence against him, "were so grossly affronted by some merchants and others in a riotous manner" that the comptroller of customs, William Lambert, was obliged to apply to the court for their protection. At the public trial the two witnesses

> again appeared and on their examination they were scuriously [scur-rilously] treated by many that appeared in the Court and as soon as the Judge had left the Court some merchants and masters of ships with a great number of other persons in a violent and mobbish manner assaulted the said evidences [witnesses] kicked and pushed them downstairs and beat one of them so unmercifully dragging him thro' the streets that it is not yet known what may be the consequence and if the Sheriff had not come to his assistance and taken him into his house it is generally beleived [sic] he would have been murdered, and they even threatened to use the Judge of the Court and the Officers of the Customs in the same manner in case sentence was given against them all which appears more fully by several affidavits sent home to Governor Shute remaining in his hands.[19]

Another case was reported from North Carolina the following year. Christopher Gale, the collector of customs in the port of Beaufort, claimed

[19] *Colonial Papers,* 1724–25, vol. 29, pp. 82–83.

that he had been insulted by Deputy Governor George Burrington in public court. Gale's house was even broken into "with intent to murder him, so that he was obliged to leave the Government and his office." Gale, who had previously served as chief justice in Roanoke, tried to account for his tribulation: "He knows no reason for such behaviour, unless it be for his supporting the Naval Officer and Collector of Customs in the port of Roanoake [sic] and advising them when applied to as Chief Justice, for the interest of H.M. Revenue and support of trade, when they were the one of them imprison'd and the other publickly threaten'd and insulted for only doing the duty of their office."[20]

If Walpole had decided to enforce the Molasses Act in the colonies, London would no doubt have been deluged with such reports. Judges, sheriffs, and naval officers were already confronted with small-scale warfare to protect smugglers and intimidate informants. Walpole avoided making a bad situation worse by putting expediency above principle—or even making expediency into a principle of government. It was when his successors sought to make the enforcement of a parliamentary act a matter of principle that Edmund Burke looked back longingly to Walpolian expediency, which he misnamed neglect. It was rather because Walpole was quite aware of what had been happening in the colonies and what they could not be made to do willingly that he took the easy way out.

One element—the prospect of colonial independence—in any conflict between British and American interests was rarely missing. It was typically brought out by Col. Martin Bladen, a longtime member of the Board of Trade. Bladen had conceived of the strategy of inflicting a prohibitive duty on imports from the French West Indies instead of simply disallowing them. When he was confronted with the argument that the proposed bill would result in the ruin of the North American colonies, he replied "that the duties proposed would not prove an absolute prohibition, but he owned that he meant them as something that should come very near it, for in the way the northern colonies are, they raise the French islands at the expense of ours, and raise themselves also to[o] high, even to an independency."[21] Bladen saw, as previous speculative reasoners had seen, that the British colonies would not "raise themselves . . . [too] high"—a close relative of Maj. John Child's "growing into a nation" and James Harrington's "come of age"— without ultimately aiming "even to an independency."

Bladen had also tried to convince Newcastle of the merit of establishing

[20] Ibid., p. 317.
[21] Leo Francis Stock, ed., *Proceedings and Debates of the British Parliaments respecting North America* (Carnegie Institution of Washington, 1937), vol. 4, p. 182.

a new settlement in Nova Scotia. It would, he argued, "drain great Numbers of Inhabitants from New England, where they are daily aiming at an independency & very much Interfere with the Trade of their Mother Kingdom."[22] Independency and trade were somehow intermingled in these efforts to crack down on the exasperating New Englanders.

Bladen's recipe for putting the colonies in their place called for the appointment of a captain general and general governor over all of them to tidy up the administrative structure—goal from the Stuart period. Since colonies were supposed to be subordinate to the mother country, according to official British thinking of the time, Bladen was appalled by the shocking reality. Writing in 1739, he burst out:

> What subordination? What regard to the Trade and Interest of Great Britain? What Obedience to her Laws? could be expected from American Principalitys, and Independent Common Wealths, established at so vast a Distance from their Mother Country? For such in Effect are the Proprietary and Charter Provinces—Distinct Governments—Various in their Forms—Seperate [*sic*] in their Legislatures—Absolute within their respective Dominions—hardly accountable for their Laws or Actions to the Crown—And impatient of Subjection to that Power, from which they draw their Origin, and to whom alone they must be indebted, for their Preservation, in time of danger.[23]

Walpole and Newcastle were unmoved by these outcries of British colonial officials. They were politicians, and, as politicians do, they lived for the day, the month, or the year, and preferred to leave a showdown with American insubordination to their successors, so long as Americans were sufficiently mollified by a policy of appeasement. One wonders what might have resulted if the showdown had come earlier and Walpole had been less complaisant. As it happened, the opening of the prerevolutionary crisis in 1761 went directly back to the Molasses Act of 1733.

[22] Cited by Henretta, *"Salutary Neglect,"* p. 96.
[23] "Martin Bladen's Blueprint for a Colonial Union," ed. Jack P. Greene, *William and Mary Quarterly*, October 1960, p. 524.

6

''This Million doubling''

❦

· 1 ·

EVERY AGE HAS ITS OWN sense of what the foundation of power is.
By the eighteenth century, reigning political thought held that the most
important basis of power and wealth was population.

The principle was already well established by the time it was codified
by the high authority of Charles Davenant in 1699. He held that
people were "the first Matter of Power and Wealth."[1] Three decades later, the popularizer Daniel Defoe simply stated that numbers
are "the Wealth and Strength of the Nation."[2] Even an unorthodox
thinker, Josiah Tucker, asserted in the middle of the century that
"Numbers of People are the Strength, as Industry is the Riches of
a Country."[3] In his classic work three-quarters of the way through
the century, Adam Smith still believed that "the most decisive mark
of the prosperity of any country is the increase in the numbers of
its inhabitants."[4] John Adams went somewhat further a few years

[1] Charles Davenant, An Essay upon the Probable Methods of making a People Gainers in
the Ballance of Trade (London, 1699), p. 24.

[2] [Daniel Defoe], A Plan of the English Commerce, Being a Compleat Prospect of the Trade
of this Nation, as well as the Home Trade as the Foreign (London, 1728), p. 18.

[3] Josiah Tucker, The Elements of Commerce and Theory of Taxes (London, 1755), in Josiah
Tucker: A Selection from His Economic and Political Writings, ed. Robert Livingston Schuyler
(Columbia University Press, 1931), p. 64.

[4] Adam Smith, An Inquiry into the Nature and Causes of the Wealth of Nations, ed. Edwin
Cannan (Modern Lib. ed., 1937), p. 70.

later by making population "the surest indication of national happiness."[5]

If population brought power, wealth, prosperity, and happiness, the Americans were sure to possess all these at a rate never before known. The growth of the population of the American colonies was an unheard-of phenomenon.

The most impressive thing about the population of the American colonies was not merely the leap in numbers; it was even more the rate of growth. The population of England and Wales has been estimated at 6.5 million in 1750 and 7.5 million in 1770—an increase of less than 15 percent.[6] Between 1720 and 1750, the population of Great Britain actually declined and did not rise until after 1780.[7] The population of the thirteen colonies is believed to have been 1,260,000 in 1750 and 2,312,000 in 1770—an increase of almost 100 percent.[8] In effect, the American population doubled about every twenty-five years; the English hardly doubled in a century.

The American demographic explosion did not go unnoticed in Great Britain. It provoked repeated outbursts of alarm, one reason for which was the fear that the colonies were draining the mother country of its people. Opinions differed, but debate shows from early in the century that the growth of the American population was closely watched and apprehensively examined. This inordinate sensitivity to the movement of people provided the background for Jeremiah Dummer's warning to the colonists in the first quarter of the century that their increasing numbers and wealth were being interpreted as symptoms of their coming revolt.

Dummer was the London agent of Massachusetts and Connecticut from 1710 to 1721. In 1712–13, he was so worried about efforts to get Parliament to nullify the New England charters and unite them into a single Crown colony that he wrote the first draft of a pamphlet against any such plan. With some additions, it was published in 1721 as *A Defence of the New-England Charters,* which John Adams later called "both for style and matter one of our most classical American productions."[9] In it, Dummer said that "one

---

[5] John Adams, "A Defence of the Constitutions of Government of the United States of America," in *The Works of John Adams,* ed. Charles Francis Adams (Boston, 1861), p. 554.

[6] James A. Williamson, *A Short History of British Expansion* (Macmillan, 1958), vol. 2, p. 10. Another estimate is 6.140 million in 1751 and 7.052 million in 1771, or slightly less than that of Williamson (Phyllis Deane and W. A. Cole, *British Economic Growth, 1688–1959,* Cambridge University Press, 1962, p. 6).

[7] Charles M. Andrews, "The American Revolution: An Interpretation," *American Historical Review,* January 1926, p. 222.

[8] Evarts B. Greene and Virginia D. Harrington, *American Population Before the Federal Census of 1790* (Columbia University Press, 1932), pp. 5–6.

[9] John Adams to William Tudor, August 11, 1818, *Works of John Adams,* vol. 10, p. 343.

meets with from people of all conditions and qualities" a disconcerting view: " 'Tis said, *that their increasing numbers and wealth, jointed to their great distance from Great Britain, will give them an opportunity, in the course of some years, to throw off their dependance on the nation, and declare themselves a free state, if not curbed in time, by being made entirely subject to the crown.*"

Dummer professed to see "neither reason nor colour" to this charge and replied that the colonies were then in such bad shape economically that "there is far more danger of their sinking, without some extraordinary support from the crown, than of their ever revolting from it." In any case, he added, they were so different from one another that "they never can be supposed to unite in so dangerous an enterprise." Even if "they would be hardy enough to put it in execution," he continued, "it would be good policy to keep them disunited."[10]

But American numbers and wealth could lend themselves to a different interpretation. By midcentury, they were made into an argument for expelling the French from Canada, gaining British superiority in Europe, and establishing Great Britain as the dominant world power. This grandiose prospect is usually attributed to Benjamin Franklin, but it was first put forward by Governor Shirley of Massachusetts, a friend of Franklin's.

In 1745, Shirley sent a message to the duke of Newcastle appealing for the conquest of all Canada. He argued that

> from the Healthfulness of the Climates on this Continent and the Surprizing Growth of it's [sic] Inhabitants within the last Century it may be expected that in one or two more centuries there will be such an addition from hence to the Subjects of the Crown of Great Britain, as may make 'em vye [sic] for numbers with the subjects of France, and lay a foundation for a superiority of British Power upon the Continent of Europe at the same time that it secures that which the Royal Navy of Great Britain has already at sea.[11]

The idea must have been in the air. In any case, Franklin took it up six years later and made it into a fully developed theory of imperial expansion. In his *Observations concerning the Increase of Mankind,* as we have seen, he turned Dummer's old foreboding on its head and gave Great Britain reason for rejoicing at the growing American population instead of being frightened by it.

---

[10] From the reprint in London in 1765, pp. 72–73 (italics in original).
[11] *Correspondence of William Shirley,* ed. Charles Henry Lincoln (Macmillan, 1912), vol. 1, pp. 284–85.

After Franklin, others took up the threat or promise of American population growth. In 1755, the year that Franklin published his *Observations*, a leading British popular magazine made its readers aware of the colonies' standing in population and urban development, as it was later called. It reported that Massachusetts was "in many parts as populous as *England*." America already contained more people than the Kingdoms of Naples and Sicily, Sardinia, Portugal, Spain, Denmark, Sweden, Prussia, and Holland. Boston was "as large and as well built" as any city in England, except London.[12]

In fact, Philadelphia and New York had surpassed Boston in population. Philadelphia, the largest American city by the 1750s, was comparable in size to Bristol, Manchester, and Norwich.[13] The five most important American urban centers—Philadelphia, New York, Boston, Charleston, and Newport—increased in population between 1743 and 1760 by 33 percent, or about 8 percent more than the general population. The growth of these cities was markedly greater than that of their British contemporaries. The average colonial townsman was better off, enjoyed better educational facilities, and could get ahead far more quickly than British city dwellers.[14] Yet it should not be forgotten that only 7 to 8 percent of the colonial population on the eve of independence lived in towns, defined as urban places with 2,500 or more inhabitants.[15]

One English writer calculated that, if the American population doubled every twenty-five years, it would reach 32 million by 1865. "Little doubt can be entertained," he warned, "that this vast country will in time become the greatest and most prosperous empire that perhaps the world has ever seen." In 1766, another writer estimated the number of American colonists at 3 million on the way to doubling, whereupon he asked: "And how are we to rule them?" A newspaper told its readers that the white inhabitants in the American colonies would come to 21.5 million in another century, which led it to pose this question: "Is not this an alarming Circumstance?"[16]

The circumstances were not alarming to everyone. One who was not alarmed, for reasons that showed that Franklin was not alone in his thinking, was John Mitchell, the author of a well-informed work on the condition of

[12] *The Gentleman's Magazine, and Historical Chronicle,* January 1755, pp. 15–18.

[13] Ralph Davis, *The Rise of the Atlantic Economies* (Cornell University Press, 1973), p. 276.

[14] Carl Bridenbaugh, *Cities in Revolt: Urban Life in America, 1743–1776* (Alfred A. Knopf, 1955), pp. 4–5, 210–11.

[15] John J. McCusker and Russell R. Menard, *The Economy of British America* (University of North Carolina Press, 1985), p. 250.

[16] Cited by Fred Junkin Hinkhouse, *The Preliminaries of the American Revolution as Seen in the English Press, 1763–1775* (Columbia University Press, 1926), pp. 42–43, 106.

the American colonies and their relationship with Great Britain published in 1767. Mitchell was an eminent botanist and mapmaker as well as an acute political observer. An Englishman, he knew the colonies well, having lived in Virginia for many years.

In Mitchell's opinion, it would have been alarming, from the point of view of British self-interest, if the population of the colonies were not increasing so fast. He estimated the British population at the time to be between 5.5 and 6.0 million. This was too few, he thought, to manage all of Britain's far-flung affairs at home and abroad. Only the North American colonies could supply "this deficiency and want of people." The main problem for him was how the colonists, doubling their number every twenty or thirty years, could "subsist by a dependence on *Great Britain*." If they remained dependent on Britain, the colonies would make her rich and unbeatable— "the great increase of the colonies would be a constant addition to the power and wealth of this nation," bringing about "a *balance of power* more in favour of *Great Britain*, than that which has cost such immense sums to preserve at home," as well as "the only equivalent it has, or can expect, for that great superiority, in numbers, which our enemies have over us in *Europe*." His chief concern was that British economic policy was forcing the colonies to become independent, "whether they will or not." Mitchell was worried that British policy failed to recognize the colonies' importance and that it held back from encouraging them to go on spreading out and increasing in numbers.[17]

Early schemes of colonial union usually referred to the growth of population as a reason for going ahead with such a plan. One, by William Smith, Jr., of New York in 1765–1767, proposed that the conflict brought on by the stamp tax crisis be resolved by forming an American parliament based on representatives or deputies chosen by the various colonial assemblies. The Crown was to retain its former veto on colonial legislation, and Parliament its legislative supremacy in all cases relating to "Life, Liberty and Property," with the exception of taxation. Smith gave as his first reason in favor of the scheme that "the Colonies are universally agitated, by Suspicion, Fear and Disgust; and doubling by their own Growth in less than thirty years, will in *Fifty*, equall the Inhabitants of Great Britain and Ireland. Unforeseen Events in Europe, may accelerate this momentous Increase."[18] A decade later, in his proposal for a union between Great Britain and the American

---

[17] [John Mitchell], *The Present State of Great Britain and North America* (London, 1767), pp. vii–x.
[18] William Smith, Jr., "Thoughts upon the Dispute between Great Britain and her Colonies" (1765–1767), *William and Mary Quarterly*, January 1965, p. 116.

colonies to avert the imminent Revolution, Joseph Galloway gave as one reason for the plan America's "increasing numbers, and consequently her growing strength and power."[19]

Population thus gave Americans their first demonstrable sense of present and growing power. Long before the Revolution, Americans were told and told themselves how numerous they were, how much more numerous they were going to be, and how numbers added up to wealth and power. Even a population of little over 1 million was considered eminently respectable by mid-eighteenth-century standards, and the 2 million reached by 1770 was regarded as a formidable leap. The decade of the 1780s still holds the record for the most rapid rise in the percentage of increase of population in all of American history.[20] It was this rate of increase that impressed contemporaries the most. If population was the foundation of wealth and power, America could be expected to double its wealth and power every twenty-five years or so. To the eighteenth-century mind, this single circumstance was staggering in its implications.

· 2 ·

Population gave birth to the earliest American futurology. Political implications were drawn from it before, during, and after the American Revolution.

In 1770, the Town of Boston produced a fiery pamphlet protesting the "Boston Massacre," during which five colonists were killed. Most of the pamphlet was given over to the events that took place on March 5 of that year. The authors, however, felt it necessary to make a more political statement in a few pages of "Observations," appended to the narrative and intended to clear up "the present and future state of *Great-Britain* and her colonies."

In this pamphlet, the current state of Britain was glowingly described. With the considerable help of the colonies, Great Britain had risen "to her present opulence and greatness, which so much distinguish her among the powers of *Europe.*" But much more of both opulence and greatness was possible if only Great Britain realized that "the means of this greatness are held out to her by the colonies" and treated them with the kindness

---

[19] [Joseph Galloway], *A Candid Examination of the Mutual Claims of Great-Britain and the Colonies* (New York, 1775), p. 43.
[20] J. R. Pole, *Foundations of American Independence, 1763–1815* (Bobbs-Merrill, 1972), p. 218.

and justice necessary "to avail herself of those means." Americans were increasing rapidly and "will be in a short time a prodigious addition to his majesty's subjects." By its productive abilities, "what a fund of wealth and power will America be to her!" If the connection with the colonies were maintained, "she would then be a mighty empire: the greatest, consisting of people of one language, that ever existed." Franklin had not wasted his time trying to teach the British more or less the same thing two decades earlier.

But the most notable contribution of this pamphlet was a statistical demonstration of what the British had to gain from the increase of colonial population owing to its effect on British exports to the colonies. Some colonial statistician had gone to the trouble of drawing up a table showing the prospective relationship of exports and population from 1766 to 1866:

In 1766: £1,737,065 for 2 million colonists
    1786:   3,474,130 " 4   "   "
    1806:   6,948,260 " 8   "   "
    1826: 13,896,520 " 16   "   "
    1846: 27,793,040 " 32   "   "
    1866: 55,586,080 " 64   "   "

In conclusion, the authors commended these observations to the attention of Parliament, which was advised to consider "whether any revenue whatever, even the greatest that America could possibly produce, either without or with her good will, would compensate the loss of such wealth and power."[21] Thus population entered into the deal which the colonists hoped to make with the British at that time—to leave their revenues alone in exchange for the "wealth and power" the colonies could contribute to the mother country through their growing population and trade.

As the Revolution approached, colonial leaders increasingly exploited the political implications of population growth. In 1772, Samuel Adams argued that it was absurd to expect Americans to have their property disposed of by a House of Commons 3,000 miles away when "the inhabitants of this country in all probability in a few years will be more numerous than those of Great Britain and Ireland together."[22] Just how many years it would take to outnumber the British was figured out in 1775 by Edward Wigglesworth, a politically minded professor of divinity at Harvard University. In a pioneer

[21] A Short Narrative of the horrid Massacre in Boston ... with some Observations on the State of Things prior to that Catastrophe (Boston, 1770), p. 46 n. Reprinted in Frederic Kidder, History of the Boston Massacre (Albany, 1870), esp. pp. 120–21.
[22] The Writings of Samuel Adams, ed. Harry Alonzo Cushing (G. P. Putnam's Sons, 1906), vol. 2, p. 359.

study of American population, he took off from the familiar assumption that "the British Americans have *doubled* their number, in every period of twenty-five years from their first plantation." To this premise he immediately added: "A rapidity of population not to be parallaled [*sic*] in the annals of Europe! It has never been equalled since the patriarchal ages." Whereas Franklin had expected Americans to outnumber Englishmen by 1851, Wigglesworth improved on that date by calculating that the numerical advantage would go to the Americans by 1825. If the "unhappy contest" between the two sides were settled amicably, as he still hoped it would be, "such an union of interest and affection would succeed, as would render them the envy of *Europe* and the glory of the WORLD."[23]

In the same year, the Reverend Ebenezer Baldwin used the same reasoning for higher purposes. He delivered a sermon in which population was pressed into service of the idea that the colonists were likely to be "the Foundation of a great and mighty Empire," which would become "the principal seat of that glorious Kingdom, which Christ shall erect upon the Earth in the latter Days." In a lengthy footnote, Baldwin inevitably took as his starting point the doubling of population every twenty-five years and then explained that "that meant a nation of 40 million in 1876. Allowing for growth "but half so fast' in the next century, the empire in 1976 would boast 92 million." Therefore, "at about this time," Baldwin triumphantly concluded, "the American Empire will probably be in its Glory."[24]

Another demonstration of the divine function of population growth came from the Reverend Ezra Stiles in 1783. He delivered an election sermon in Connecticut in which he foresaw that "before the millenium, the English settlements in America, may become more numerous millions, than that greatest dominion on earth the chinese empire." If this should prove to be the case, he exulted, "how applicable would be the text, when the Lord shall make his American Israel, *high above all nations which he hath made.*"[25]

A single example a few years later shows how "rapid multiplication" continued to inspire American visions of future greatness. Writing to James Aaron Burr in 1801, Thomas Jefferson made population the key to his creed of territorial expansionism. "However our present interests may restrain us within our own limits," he confided, "it is impossible not to look forward to distant times, when our rapid multiplication will expand itself beyond

---

[23] Edward Wigglesworth, *Calculations on American Population* (Boston, 1775), pp. 5, 7, 24.

[24] Ebenezer Baldwin, "The Duty of Rejoicing under Calamities and Afflictions" (New York, 1776), pp. 38–40 n, cited by James West Davidson, *The Logic of Millennial Thought* (Yale University Press, 1977), p. 249.

[25] Ezra Stiles, *The United States elevated to Glory and Honor* (New Haven, 1783), p. 36 (italics in original).

those limits, & cover the whole northern, if not the southern continent, with a people speaking the same language, governed in similar forms & by similar laws."[26] Two years later, the opportunity came for Jefferson to expand existing limits with the purchase of the Louisiana Territory, even though he was dubious about its constitutionality.

In the eighteenth century and after, the growth of American population was so unprecedented that it was considered to be virtually inexplicable. The Reverend John Witherspoon of Princeton thought it so great that "no political calculations have yet been able to understand or lay down rules for [it]."[27] In England, William Pulteney, a friend of David Hume and Adam Smith, noted that the Americans "have gone on encreasing in wealth and population, in a manner never before experienced in the world."[28] Dr. Richard Price, the English advocate of the American cause, described the increase as "never before known." He foretold: "The probability is that they will go on to increase; and form a mighty Empire, consisting of a variety of states, all equal or superior to ourselves in all the arts and accomplishments which give dignity and happiness to human life."[29] And Thomas Malthus, the founder of modern population study, acknowledged that the rapidity of increase of population in America was "probably without parallel in history."[30]

The lesson of all this is that, from early in its history, the future of America was made to influence its present. This sense of immanent greatness was one of the factors which enabled the colonies to defy the greatest empire in the world just when it seemed to have reached the zenith of its power after the Seven Years' War. At the foundation of this temerity was a simple, startling statistic—that the Americans doubled their population about every twenty-five years. Endless variations were played on this theme, all pointing upwards and onwards.

· 3 ·

Population did not perform its miracles by itself. Population begat wealth;

[26] *The Works of Thomas Jefferson,* ed. Paul Leicester Ford (G. P. Putnam's Sons, 1905), vol. 9, p. 317.

[27] *The Miscellaneous Works of the Rev. John Witherspoon* (Philadelphia, 1803), p. 291.

[28] William Pulteney, *Thoughts on the Present State of Affairs with America and the Means of Conciliation* (London, 4th ed., 1778), p. 12.

[29] Richard Price, *Observations on the Nature of Civil Liberty, the Principles of Government, and the Justice and Policy of the War with America* (London, 5th ed., 1776), p. 42.

[30] T. R. Malthus, *An Essay on the Principle of Population* (1798; reprint, Royal Economic Society, 1926), p. 105.

wealth was the offspring of trade; population, wealth, and trade laid the foundations of power. Such was the conventional wisdom during the American colonies' coming of age.

The economic spirit of the age had been most pithily expressed by Sir Josiah Child at the end of the seventeenth century: "Foreign trade produces riches, riches power, power preserves trade and religion."[31] It was again most authoritatively set forth in the early eighteenth century by William Wood, the high priest of British mercantilism. His creed contained these rules: "Our *Foreign Trade* is now become the Strength and Riches of the Kingdom. . . . Without being Rich and Populous, a Nation can never be great and Powerful . . . all Nations have been Powerful in proportions to their application to *Commerce*. . . . 'Tis *that* which gives Life and Strength to any Nation . . . our *Trade* and *Navigation* are greatly *encreased* by *our Colonies and Plantations* . . . they are a *Spring* of *Wealth* to this *Nation*."[32]

Commerce and power were linked all through the eighteenth century. Sir William Keith made the association in 1738: "Trade may justly be considered to be the Arteries and Sinews of the Body Politic, by which its easy Motion is continued and preserved: That it is likewise the Fountain of Riches, and consequently of Strength and Power."[33] Another version of 1747 reads: "All states and Kingdoms have flourished, and made a Figure in proportion to the Extent of their Commerce."[34] Thomas Whately, the most influential British official in colonial policy in his time, published a work on British trade and finances in 1766, with this as his opening sentence: "That the wealth and power of Great-Britain depend upon its trade, is a proposition, which it would be equally absurd in these times to dispute or to prove."[35] In the same year, Edmund Burke asserted that "liberty and commerce" were "the true basis of its [Britain's] power."[36]

The American colonies conformed almost classically to this economic model. Nine out of ten Americans worked on the land, but agriculture was a source of profit only if it went beyond a subsistence level and produced enough for export. A subsistence economy would have been static, and the American colonies were anything but that. New England,

[31] Cited by Jacob Viner, *Studies in the Theory of International Trade* (George Allen & Unwin, 1955), p. 112.

[32] William Wood, *A Survey of Trade* (London, 1718; 2d ed., 1722), pp. 4, 10, 62, 135.

[33] William Keith, *History of the British Plantations in America* (London, 1738), p. 6.

[34] R. Campbell, *The London Tradesman,* cited in *English Historical Documents, 1714–1783,* ed. D. B. Horn and Mary Ransome (Eyre & Spottiswoode, 1957), vol. 10, p. 495.

[35] [Thomas Whately], *Considerations on the Trade and Finances of this Kingdom . . .* (London, 1766); reprinted in *A Collection of scarce and interesting tracts* (London, 1787), vol. 2, p. 69.

[36] Edmund Burke, "A Short Account of a Late Short Administration," *The Works and Correspondence of the Right Honourable Edmund Burke* (London, 1852), vol. 3, p. 2.

for reasons of soil and climate, was predominantly commercial or engaged in industries, such as shipbuilding, that were closely linked with commerce. The middle Atlantic colonies had mixed economies that also depended on trade, internal and external, for growth. The southern colonies raised huge surpluses of staples, especially tobacco, for export.

The increase of population again tells much of the story. A demographic growth of 500 percent between 1700 and 1760 was made possible only by the attendant economic growth that attracted thousands of immigrants and encouraged an extraordinary natural increase. The ability of the colonial economy to absorb so many people was implicit evidence that growth of the economy and of population went together with a continuity and rapidity that had never been equaled.

The first half of the American eighteenth century was particularly dynamic. Between 1720 and 1750, population more than doubled— from 466,185 to 1,170,760. Exports nearly doubled—from £468,188 to £814,768. Imports more than quadrupled—from £319,702 to £1,313,083. The twenty-year period from 1750 to 1770 was somewhat less striking but still marked a substantial advance. Population almost doubled—from 1,170,760 to 2,148,076. Exports increased from £814,768 to £1,015,535. Imports went from £1,313,083 to £1,925,571. These figures are rough and need to be taken as only approximate or suggestive.[37]

The most remarkable economic growth came in the second quarter of the eighteenth century—precisely the Walpolian period. By 1729, the Board of Trade received this kind of admonition:

> The more powerful our Plantations grow, the more it behoves [sic] us to have a watchfull Eye upon their Conduct, more especially such of them, as have few or no Staple Commodities of their own to Exchange with us, and whose product is generally the same as that of Great Britain, which lays them under strong temptations of interfering with us in our Manufactures, Commerce, Shipping and Navigation, as is very much the case of all the Colonys to the Northward of Virginia, but more particularly of the Massachusetts Bay.[38]

A century which made fetishes of population and commerce as the greatest engines of power and progress could only marvel. The American

[37] *Historical Statistics of the United States: Colonial Times to 1970* (U.S. Department of Commerce, Bureau of the Census, Bicentennial Ed., 1975), pt. 2, pp. 1168, 1176. For a criticism, see McCusker and Menard, *Economy of British America*, p. 214.

[38] "Some Considerations upon the Present State of the Massachusetts Bay, 1729," cited in M. H. Smith, *The Writs of Assistance Case* (University of California Press, 1978), p. 152.

colonies were still inferior to such European powers as Great Britain and France in absolute terms, but the colonies were superior to them in rates of growth in both population and economic development, which held the greatest promise or threat for the future. Two American economic historians summed up the prerevolutionary period: "For European Americans in British North America and the British West Indies, the years just before the American Revolution were a 'golden age'; they were better off not only than their predecessors or than most of their contemporaries elsewhere in the world but also than their descendants were to be again for some time to come."[39]

· 4 ·

The British took note of the growing power of the colonies. Their view was largely dictated by the mercantilist doctrine that dominated British policy.

Mercantilism was peculiarly candid about its bias in favor of the mother country. Colonies were worth having only to the extent that they benefited the imperial power. The principle was stated without inhibition by Sir Charles Hedges, secretary of the Board of Trade, in a message to Governor Cornbury of New York in 1706: "The Plantations are to be valued as they are more or less valuable to England."[40] Colonies were expected to furnish raw materials for British manufactures, which were in turn to enjoy a monopoly of the colonial market. The success of the system depended theoretically upon the colonies' importing more than they exported, thus assuring the mother country of a favorable balance of trade. In the best of all mercantilist worlds, competition between the mother country and the colonies was nonexistent.

This system had been put in place by the Navigation Acts of the seventeenth century. The principle of the division of labor—manufacturing for Great Britain, raw materials for the colonies—was not altogether one-sided. The production of tobacco was banned in Great Britain to give the southern colonies a monopoly of that precious commodity. If all the American colonies had been like the southern ones producing staples for the British market, the system would have worked according to plan. The bone that stuck in the mercantilist throat was the northern colonies. They

[39] McCusker and Menard, *The Economy of British America*, p. 51.
[40] *Colonial Papers, America and West Indies* (London, 1969), 1706–June 1708, vol. 18, p. 3.

lived by trading, shipbuilding, and other mercantilist ventures—the mirror image of Great Britain itself. They broke through the mercantilist barrier by trading with the French sugar islands and wherever they could send their merchant shipping. Great Britain had long tolerated this practice, despite the mercantilist rule that all colonial trade was supposed to go through British ports and from there be transshipped. The British were forced to give the northern colonies more leeway, because the northern colonies could not have paid for their British imports if they had not made profits from their trade with Europe and elsewhere.

British mercantilism was not strictly enforced, but to the extent that it was enforced it rubbed the northern colonists the wrong way, and it prepared them for insubordination to the extent that they successfully evaded it.

The one untouchable part of the British system was the manufacturing monopoly. So important was the American market to the British woolen industry that legislation to prevent the colonists from making their own woolen goods went back to 1699. Hats were added to the prohibition in 1732 and iron production in 1750. The pressure to curb the colonists came from British manufacturing lobbies, which were prominently represented in Parliament and which made colonial nonrepresentation even more onerous.

Nevertheless, at a very early date, worries arose in Great Britain about whether the colonies were more dependent on Britain than Britain on the colonies. The question came up as early as 1689, when most of the American colonies were less than fifty years old and their inhabitants numbered no more than about 100,000. It was raised by Dr. Benjamin Worsley, then the leading British authority on the colonies. As secretary of the Council of Trade set up in 1651 by the first of the Navigation Acts and later secretary of the new Council for Trade and Plantations formed in 1672, Worsley was the Crown's leading adviser on colonial affairs for a quarter of a century.[41]

In 1668, he composed a "Proposition" on the colonies for the earl of Shaftesbury, shortly afterwards appointed head of the council. In it Worsley introduced the idea that the "plantations" in America no longer depended on England but rather England on them. He supported this view by observing that Britain was already incapable of carrying on without the colonies' trade. The European market, he noted, had been contracting; the colonies had to fill the gap. He preferred the colonial to the European trade because, he thought, the former "swell[s] not just one part of the nation but would distribute itself far more equally for the benefit of the many than had

[41] Charles M. Andrews, *Colonial Period of American History* (Yale University Press, 1938), vol. 4, p. 58.

the earlier exchange with Europe." Optimistically, he advocated measures to help the colonies increase their population and improve their conditions, because "the Empire of England likewise that is hereby rendered the most August[,] formidable and Considerable abroad."[42]

A similar appreciation of the colonies came later in the century. In 1689, a British official advised the earl of Nottingham, a privy councillor, that the West Indies and the North American colonies contained "about 3, or 400,000 subjects that furnish a full third part of the whole Trade and Navigation of England. Here is a great Nursery of Our Sea Men, and the Kings Customs depend mightily thereon."[43]

Perhaps the most authoritative seventeenth-century view was stated by Charles Davenant in 1698. He observed that "colonies are a strength to their mother kingdom, while they are under good discipline, while they are strictly made to observe the fundamental laws of their original country, and while they are kept dependent on it." Otherwise, they were worse than useless, "being indeed like offensive arms wrested from a nation, to be turned against it as occasion shall serve." Colonies, then, could be potentially hostile and dangerous as well as friendly and advantageous. Meanwhile, Davenant was optimistic about the American colonies. He did not think that "the greatness these colonies may arrive at in a natural course, and in the progress of time, can be dangerous to England." In general, he surmised, "our colonies while they have English blood in their veins, and have relations in England, and while they can get by trading with us, the stronger and greater they grow, the more this crown and kingdom will get by them; and nothing but such an arbitrary power as shall make them desperate, can bring them to rebel."

The main thing to fear, he believed, was the development of manufactures in New England. Though he discounted the danger, he warned that an effort by New England "to set up manufactures, and to clothe, as well as feed their neighbours, their nearness and low price would give them such advantages over this nation, as might prove of pernicious consequence." This and other causes for alarm could only be avoided by keeping the colonies dependent upon "their mother countrey, and not to suffer those laws, upon any account, to be loosened, whereby they are tied to it, for otherwise they will become more profitable to our neighbours than to us."[44]

[42] David S. Lovejoy, *The Glorious Revolution in America* (Harper & Row, 1972), pp. 4–5.
[43] *The Glorious Revolution in America*, ed. Michael G. Hall, Lawrence H. Leder, and Michael T. Kammen (University of North Carolina Press, 1964), p. 67.
[44] Charles Davenant, *Discourses on the Public Revenue, and on the Trade of England* (London, 1698), reprinted in *The Political and Commercial Works of Charles D'Avenant*, ed. Sir Charles Whitworth (London, 1771), vol. 2, pp. 10–11, 22, 24–25.

Well into the next century, outstanding British thinkers continued to worry about the same questions. In 1718, William Wood took the position that "colonies and Plantations are both Strength and Riches to their MOTHER COUNTRY while *they* are strictly made to observe the Laws of it." He acknowledged the fear of manufactures in the northern colonies, but it seemed "very remote" to him.[45] In 1731, Joshua Gee also reflected the fear of the colonies in British political and commercial circles by seeking to allay it. He admitted that there were fears "in the Minds of some People" that the colonies would set up their own manufactures if they were encouraged to go on raising hemp, flax, silk, and other commodities. His solution was to give the colonies bounties for raw materials so that there would be no advantage for them to go in for manufactures. He was less worried than others, because he did not think that New England could get along alone, and anyway, a standing army could be placed in the colony to make sure of its obedience. Still, Gee recognized that British trade depended on building ships, for which the supply of timber from New England was so indispensable that without it, he wrote, "we would soon sink in our Navigation."[46]

Another attack on the subject was made in a pamphlet that came out in London in 1755. It was written by Ellis Huske, an Englishman who had come to New England in his mid-thirties, published a newspaper for a time, served as postmaster in Boston, then spent two decades in New Hampshire. He was in a sense half-English, half-American, and his purpose at the time was to convince the British public to seize the opportunity to get rid of the French in Canada.

Huske was most eloquent about "the vast Importance of the Northern Colonies." The British West Indies depended on them for their "very Being," the British navy and merchant marine needed the colonies for their masts and seamen. All this was preparatory to his most telling blow:

> But what will your *Landholders, Manufacturers, Artificers, Merchants,* &c. say of the Importance of your Colonies, and the necessity of going to War to regain and preserve them entire, if it cannot be done by other Means, when they reflect that if they are lost, they will lose one Third of their Property and Business in general; for it is certain, that full one Third of our whole Export of the Produce and

[45] Wood, *Survey of Trade,* pp. 148, 154.
[46] Joshua Gee, *The Trade and Navigation of Great-Britain Considered, etc.* (London, 3d ed., 1731), pp. 71–73, 75, 104.

Manufactures of this Country is to our Colonies, and in proportion as this diminishes or increases, their Estates and Business must increase or diminish.

Huske concluded by giving the colonies credit for having "enabled us to make the figure we do at present, and have done for upwards of a Century past, in the Commercial World, from whence we have derived Wealth, Power and glory, and the greatest Blessings given Man to know."[47]

This was just what Americans wanted the British to think if the latter were to be induced to fight an all-out war against the French in North America. But the British did not need to get this sort of inspiration from an Englishman living in America. British readers could find a similar rationalization for their dependence on the colonies even in their own popular journals. One such exhortation appeared in *The Monthly Review* in 1756:

> Our Plantations were always of great Consequence, but they are now of the *utmost* Consequence to the Nation; for at least one half of our Commerce depends upon them, as the whole of our Strength and Happiness depends upon our Commerce. Our Wealth produces Liberty, and our Wealth was produced by Trade; whatever affects the latter will lessen the former: And whenever we lose our Trade, we must gradually feel the effects of Poverty and arbitrary Power.[48]

Or if confirmation was wanted from a more authoritative source, it could be obtained from one of the weightiest economic authorities, Malachy Postlethwayt, in a book published in 1757. He first made sure to put his stamp on the oldest of British principles: "Colonies ought never to forget what they owe to their mother country, in return for the prosperity and riches they enjoy. Their gratitude in that respect, and the duty they owe, indispensably oblige them to be immediately dependent on their original parent, and make their interest subservient thereunto." But many pages later, he alluded to the American colonies in such a way that some readers may have wondered who was subservient to whom: "Thus Great Britain deprived of its subjects, dominions, and trade in and to America, our merchants will be ruined, our customs and public funds sink, our manufactures want a vent, our lands fall in value, and, instead of

---

[47] Ellis Huske, *The Present State of North-America* (London, 1755), pp. 56–58.
[48] *The Monthly Review or, Literary Journal* (London), vol. 14, 1756, p. 37.

decreasing our public debts will be encreased, without the least prospect of payment."

Postlethwayt also made a clear connection between the balance of trade and the balance of power. "It is plain," he asserted, "that of several nations, that whose general balance [of trade] is always most in its favour, must become the most powerful." This principle led him to pronounce that it was necessary "to throw the balance of trade so effectually into the hands of Great Britain, as to put the constant balance of power in Europe into her hands."[49] According to this equation, anything that threatened Great Britain's trade threatened its power in Europe. With so much British trade dependent on the American colonies, it followed that the latter were capable of determining not only the British balance of trade but the British balance of power in Europe.

From Worsley in 1668 to Postlethwayt in 1757, almost a century, the British view of the colonies was peculiarly paradoxical. On the one hand, the *idée fixe* of British policy was the need to keep the colonies in a state of dependence. On the other hand, the dependence of the colonies was made all the more necessary by the equally deep-rooted idea that Great Britain was getting to be fatally dependent on them. The tension between these two convictions increased unbearably as the eighteenth century advanced.

Some aspects of colonial dependence on Great Britain had little or nothing to do with legal or administrative constraints. Colonial trade was protected by the British navy on the high seas. In the circumstances of that day, the value of such protection was incalculable, though the colonists took it for granted so long as they felt they were entitled to all the rights and privileges of Englishmen. If the British navy was dependent on New England masts, those masts served the interests of new as well as old England. British brokers and bankers charged handsomely for their services, especially for the transshipment of colonial wares from British ports to Europe and elsewhere. But they also provided real services, such as credit, commercial intelligence, and staff work, not easily replaceable. How hard they were to replace came out after the Revolution, when the British readily reestablished their former credit and commercial ties with the new American states.

Whatever the American grievances in the first six decades of the century, the two sides were held together by a real community of interests. The dependency was not one-way; if it had been, the American Revolution might have come earlier.

[49] Malachy Postlethwayt, *Britain's Commercial Interest Explained and Improved* (London, 1757), vol. 1, pp. 153, 480; vol. 2, pp. 386, 551.

· 5 ·

Statistics of population growth and its collateral effects were not the only signs that the American colonies were growing up. Something else was noted—how well Americans lived. The better Americans lived, the more apt they were to stir up suspicions that they were doing too well to remain a dependency for long. Prosperity was a symptom of growing power, and growing power was never far from the specter of independence.

The connection among prosperity, power, and self-determination worried Jeremiah Dummer as early as 1720. In a letter home, he expressed "great satisfaction" with what he had been reading in the journals of the assembly—"frequent accounts of your laying out new townships, settling ministers and schools, enlarging your new townships, regulating trade and manufactures, and doing many other things which show the growing state of the province, and the good order of the government." But all was not well, he wrote, because "that which gives me pleasure, gives others pain." The others were in England, where he had to defend the interests of the colony. His explanation of what gave pain to those others is one of the most revealing documents of the period, a good half century before the American Revolution:

> People here are very apt to read these things with jealous eyes; and when they find in the same journals, that all business is transacted in the Council and Assembly, and conferences managed between the two houses with the same decency and solemnity as in the parliament of Great Britain, they fancy us to be a little kind of sovereign state, and conclude for certain that we shall be so in time to come, and that the crown will not be able to reduce us at so great a distance from the throne.

Dummer was so troubled that he questioned whether it was wise to print the journals and worried how to keep the good news from the wrong eyes in England. He explained:

> Now, though these fancies are the most absurd and unreasonable in the world, yet when men have once taken them into their heads, it's hard to get them out again. I have therefore ever found, since I have had the honour of serving the province, that our greatest prudence is to lie quiet and as unobserved as we can; and that the less show

we make to the world, the safer we are from the stroke of publick as well as private envy.[50]

The colonies could hardly keep themselves from being observed or make less show in the world, however dangerous it might be. By mid-century, foreign observers were coming in increasing numbers to see the new phenomenon for themselves. Of the three most famous European visitors between 1748 and 1760, one was Swedish, one German, and one British.

The first was Peter Kalm, a Swedish botanist and agriculturalist, who traveled in Pennsylvania, New Jersey, New York, and Quebec for two years, 1748–1750. He left vivid impressions of some American cities, Philadelphia in particular. To his eyes, it had risen to "grandeur and perfection," and "its fine appearance, good regulations, agreeable situation, natural advantages, trade, riches and power, are by no means inferior to those of any, even the most ancient towns of *Europe.*" Pennsylvania itself, he reported, "now vies with several Kingdoms in *Europe* in number of inhabitants." As for the English colonies in North America in general, they "have increased so much in number of inhabitants and in their richness, that they almost vie with Old England."[51]

The next was Gottlieb Mittelberger, a German immigrant who lived in Pennsylvania from 1750 to 1754. "In this province," he later wrote, "even in the humblest or poorest houses, no meals are served without a meat course; and no one eats bread without butter or cheese, even though the bread is as good as ours." The people were "amply fed." All trades and professions "bring in good money." No beggers were visible. "It is no wonder, therefore, that this beautiful country, already extensively settled and inhabited by wealthy people, has excited the envy of France." Mittelberger recorded two sayings which he said were current in Pennsylvania. One went: "Pennsylvania is a heaven for farmers, paradise for artisans, and hell for officials and preachers." The other was "It is a paradise for women, a purgatory for men, and a hell for horses."[52]

American towns especially impressed British visitors. One of the most impressionable was Lord Adam Gordon, a Scottish army officer and member of Parliament, who began a tour of the American mainland in 1764 and went as far north as Quebec the following year. Some of his observations follow:

---

[50] *Massachusetts Historical Society Collections*, 3d ser., vol. 1, 1825, reprint 1846, p. 145.

[51] Peter Kalm, *Travels Into North America*, trans. John Reinhold Forster (London, 1770–71, rev. ed., 1772; reprint, Imprint Society, 1972), pp. 38, 137.

[52] Gottlieb Mittelberger, *Journey to Pennsylvania*, trans. and ed. Oscar Handlin and John Clive (Harvard University Press, 1960), pp. 48–49, 51, 77, 93.

Charleston: The streets are straight, broad, and airy, the churches are handsome, the other places of worship are commodious, and many of the houses belonging to individuals are large and handsome, having all the conveniences one sees at home.

South Carolina: Upon the whole, this is undoubtedly one of the most opulent and most increasing colonies in America, and bids fair to exceed all the others if it advances to the like proportion as it has done for forty years past.

Williamsburg: Much resembles a good country town in England.

Philadelphia: The noble city of Philadelphia . . . is perhaps one of the wonders of the world, if you consider its size, the number of inhabitants, the regularity of its streets, their great breadth and length, their cutting one another all at right angles, their spacious public and private buildings, quays and docks, the magnificence and diversity of places of worship (for here all religions who profess the name of Christ are tolerated equally), the plenty of provisions brought to market, and the industry of all its inhabitants. One will not hesitate to call it the first town in America, but one that bids fair to rival almost any in Europe.

Boston: This is more like an English old town than any in America.[53]

Travelers' tales may be discounted. These, however, were the kinds of reports that made Europeans believe that the American colonies were doing exceptionally well and catching up with the European world. In particular, the cities of America, young as they were, seemed to have grown magically to rival Europe's.

A popular British publication, *The Gentleman's Magazine,* gave its readers the following assessment of American cities and colonies in 1755:

New Hampshire and Maine: Well known for its fishery . . . most famous for the excellent masts and yards that it furnishes to the royal navy of *England* which you could not get in such abundance, not on such conditions, in any country of the world; for they do not take a guinea from you: But for all their fish, masts, &c. you pay them in goods.

Massachusetts or New England: There are in it many hundreds of fine houses, and *Boston* is as large and much better built than *Bristol,* or indeed than any other city in *England, London* excepted.

[53] *Narratives of Colonial America, 1704–1765,* ed. Howard H. Peckham (R. R. Donnelley & Sons, 1971), pp. 245, 246, 249, 259, 290.

Rhode Island: Newport is the capital, and has an excellent harbour; the town is much bigger than our city of *Worcester,* and contains three times the number of inhabitants.

Connecticut: A colony that few people in *England* have heard of, and yet no part of *England* has so many fine market towns, in many of which are from 3 to 500 houses . . . the consumption of our manufactories in this country is very great, and the product of all the provisions, horses, and lumber that they export to other countries, comes to *London* for goods.

New York City: Contains about 5000 houses, all of Brick and stone; which in shape excell the same number in any part of *London,* and their town house is little inferior to *Guild-Hall.* Their streets are better paved than those of *London* . . . in this city are six large markets, and none in *Europe* are supplyed with provisions so good, so plentiful, and so cheap.

New Jersey: Within these 25 years past, it is become very prosperous, and very populous.

Philadelphia: It contains 5000 houses, and for its bigness, is as fine a city as any on the globe. . . . The houses are well built, their town house elegant, and their market-place equal to any in *Europe.*

Virginia: The people live in great plenty, but are not quite so numerous as in some other colonies, because they employ Negroes in the raising of their tobacco.

North Carolina: It is a very fruitful country.

South Carolina: Charles-Town is the capital of this province, and is about as big as the city of Gloucester. . . . All this country has every necessary, and most of the conveniences of life.[54]

More serious readers could get very much the same sort of information in almost the same words from a seemingly more authoritative source, such as William Burke's *An Account of the European Settlements in America,* published in 1757 and once attributed to the more famous Edmund, to whom William was related. The book conscientiously summed up what was known or thought about the colonies at the time. Among its observations were these:

New England: In no part of the world are the ordinary sort so independent, or possess so many of the conveniences of life. . . . The most populous and flourishing parts of the mother country hardly make a better appearance.

54 *The Gentleman's Magazine* (London), January 1755, pp. 15–17.

Pennsylvania: The people free and flourishing.

Philadelphia: A splendid and wealthy city.

Charleston: The planters and merchants are rich and well bred; the people are showy and expensive in their dress and way of living; so that everything conspires to make this by much the liveliest and politest place, as it is one of the richest too, in all America.[55]

No English reader of these published accounts could have doubted that the American colonies were unusually prosperous and getting more so all the time, even if some of the information was imaginative. No one could have thought of the colonists as poor and downtrodden as a result of British unfairness or exploitation. If there was an ulterior motive in these descriptions, it was to show how much Great Britain had to gain from the colonies and how much reason they had to be thankful for British protection and generosity.

"It must have been clear to an impartial observer of 1760," concluded Carl Bridenbaugh, "if he was familiar with the European scene, that the five colonial communities [Philadelphia, New York, Boston, Charleston, and Newport] matched English and Continental provincial cities and, in more ways than one, bettered their models."[56]

· 6 ·

Ordinary life in the colonies also compared favorably with that in Europe at the time.

In general, the rich were not as rich as wealthy Europeans, but the poor were much less destitute and desperate. The scarcity and high cost of labor, particularly of skilled labor, enabled colonial laborers to command real wages estimated at 30 to 100 percent higher than those of contemporary English workmen.[57] Indentured servants were often treated callously, but they could get some land when they had worked off their indentures and set up on their own. Benjamin Franklin's maternal grandmother had been an indentured servant who had married her employer. Colonial society was clearly stratified, but there was far less of the disdain for hard labor that was common in wealthy, aristocratic British circles. The news went forth

---

[55] [William Burke], *An Account of the European Settlements in America* (London, 1757; reprint, Boston, 1835, attributed to Edmund Burke), pp. 259, 275, 307.

[56] Bridenbaugh, *Cities in Revolt*, p. 210.

[57] Richard B. Morris, *Government and Labor in Early America* (Columbia University Press, 1946; reprint, Northeastern University Press, 1981), p. 45.

to Europe, as an Irish immigrant urged friends at home in 1725, to come over, "it being the best Country for Working folk and tradesmen of any in the world." Unlike the British, colonial workmen took an active part in local politics, so much so that British officials complained that at town meetings, "the lowest Mechanicks discuss upon the most important points of government, with the utmost freedom." The votes of such "Mechanicks" often decided elections to the assemblies and helped to make them allergic to paying governors' salaries.[58]

The economic odds still seem to have favored the ordinary colonists in the second half of the eighteenth century. In 1762, Nathaniel Ware, the comptroller of customs in Boston, informed the British Treasury that "the very lowest orders" in the colonies "are really better fed, clothed, and every way accommodated than the most industrious and discreet of our journeymen artificers in London."[59] Americans in England had similar impressions. Joseph Trumbull of Connecticut, visiting England in 1764, wrote back from Liverpool: "We in New England know nothing of Poverty & want, we have no idea of the thing, how much better do our poor people live than 7/8 of the people of this much Famed Island."[60] Benjamin Franklin toured Ireland and Scotland in 1772 and was struck by the social and economic gulf between the rich and poor, as a result of which he was led to reflect: "I thought often of the Happiness of New England, where every Man is a Freeholder, has a Vote in publick Affairs, lives in a tidy warm House, has plenty of good Food and Fewel [fuel], with whole Cloaths from Head to Foot, the Manufacture perhaps of his own Family."[61]

New England always benefited from a comparison with the old. *American Husbandry,* a work published on the eve of the Revolution, expressed the current view:

> Respecting the lower classes of New England there is scarcely any part in the world in which they are better off. The price of labour is very high, and they have with this advantage another no less valuable, of being able to take up a tract of land whenever they are able to settle it. . . . This great ease of gaining a farm, renders the lower class of people very industrious; which, with the high price of labour, banishes

[58] Ibid., pp. 44–53; Chilton Williamson, *American Suffrage from Property to Democracy, 1760–1860* (Princeton University Press, 1960), p. 39.

[59] Cited by John L. Bullion, *A Great and Necessary Measure* (University of Missouri Press, 1982), p. 67.

[60] Williamson, *American Suffrage,* p. 39.

[61] Franklin to Joshua Babcock, January 13, 1772, *The Papers of Benjamin Franklin,* ed. Leonard W. Labaree (Yale University Press, 1961), vol. 19, p. 7.

everything that has the least appearance of begging, or that wandering
destitute state of poverty, which we see so common in England.

The same work distinguished between the more or less affluent farmers
in both countries. British substantial farmers were "incomparably richer,"
but the poorer type were much better off in New England, where "the little
freeholders and farmers live in the midst of plenty of all the necessaries of
life; they do not acquire wealth, but they have comforts and abundance."[62]
This was, at any rate, what Americans told themselves, and it helped
to make them feel superior to the mother country. It also contributed
significantly to the makeup of the colonial assemblies and the conspicuous
role of relatively modest farmers and tradesmen in deciding who was to
be elected to them.

Whatever idealization there may have been in these testimonials, recent
scholarship has arrived at results remarkably consistent with eighteenth-
century impressions. The impressions themselves should not be dismissed;
they made up the climate of opinion within which policy, which could not
wait for quantitative historians two centuries later, was made.

One study by Alice Hanson Jones has found that colonial per capita
income and wealth got off to a strong and very early start. They had
apparently reached "very high levels" within twenty-five or thirty years
of settlement, with growth in per capita real wealth rising fairly steadily,
if slowly, thereafter. The continued migration to the colonies, mainly for
economic improvement, and the rapid rate of natural population increase,
facilitated by an ample food supply, indicate that the average income there
could not have been "greatly lower" than in England. By 1774, on the eve
of the Revolution, the colonies might have come "very nearly on a par in per
capita income with England, but somewhere lower in wealth."[63] Elsewhere,
she says that the American standard of living in 1774 was "probably the
highest achieved for the great bulk of the population in any country up to
that time."[64]

Another study found that the colonies had become "economically
self-sufficient" by the beginning of the eighteenth century. In this view,
"the levels of income per free colonist on the eve of the American
Revolution was certainly extraordinarily high." Probate records and wealth

[62] *American Husbandry* (1776), pp. 52–53.

[63] Alice Hanson Jones, *Wealth of a Nation to Be* (Columbia University Press, 1980),
pp. 67–68, 72.

[64] Alice Hanson Jones, "Wealth Estimates for the American Middle Colonies, 1774," *Economic
Development and Cultural Change*, vol. 17, no. 4, pt. 2 (1970), p. 130. McCusker and Menard
seem to agree with this estimate (*Economy of British America*, p. 268).

estimates "tentatively show that the average free colonist fared better than his or her typical British counterpart by the end of the colonial period and probably even as early as the latter part of the seventeenth century." More than two-thirds of the world population in the third quarter of the twentieth century lived in countries with average incomes below that of the average American two hundred years earlier.[65]

Still another study has told the same story even more optimistically. It points out that British economic regulations, despite some inconveniences, "affected no more than 5 to 8 per cent of gross colonial output," when they were not ignored, as was often the case. The other 95 or 92 percent could hardly have done better under prevailing conditions. "Given the existing technology and the availability of natural resources," it appears that "this commercial-agricultural society was probably functioning at near maximum efficiency. Indeed, by the mid-eighteenth century, if not earlier, the typical inhabitant of the mainland colonies was almost certainly enjoying the highest standard of living in the contemporary world."[66]

Wealth was far more evenly distributed in colonial America than in Great Britain or on the continent. Though there were rich and poor in the colonies, according to another study, "probably in few societies in history have the means of subsistence been so widely distributed among the mass of the people as in colonial America."[67] If so, a feeling of surging power in the colonies was likely to be shared more widely than elsewhere, because more people participated in and benefited from it.

At the top of the colonial social structure was a group whose wealth compared favorably with all but the richest British counterparts. By the 1760s, it has been estimated, "the largest proprietors—and no one else in all of English America—were receiving colonial revenues comparable to the incomes of the greatest English noblemen and larger than those of the richest London merchants."[68] In land, livestock, producer and consumer

[65] Gary M. Walton and James F. Shepherd, *The Economic Rise of Early America* (Cambridge University Press, 1979), pp. 142–43.

[66] Edwin J. Perkins, *The Economy of Colonial America* (Columbia University Press, 1980), pp. 12–13.

[67] Stuart Bruchey, *The Roots of American Economic Growth, 1607–1861* (Harper & Row, 1965), p. 59.

[68] John M. Murrin and Rowland Berthoff, "Feudalism, Communalism, and the Yeoman Freeholder: The American Revolution Considered as a Social Accident," in *Essays on the American Revolution,* ed. Stephen G. Kurtz and James H. Hutson (University of North Carolina Press, 1973), p. 267.

goods, the three main regions—northern, middle, and southern—were almost on the same level.[69]

More recent American historians have stressed the uneven and unequal social structure of the American colonies. There were marked differences between a relatively small, rich class at the top, a much larger group in the middle, and a substantial majority at the bottom.[70] By the end of the colonial period, the top 5 percent of inventoried estates in Boston contained 46 percent of the probated wealth, with 55 percent in Philadelphia. A class of genuinely poor people, between 10 and 20 percent of the population, appeared in Boston in the 1740s and in New York and Philadelphia by the 1760s.[71] But our main interest here is in how American society was regarded abroad, especially in Great Britain. What impressed foreign travelers was "the comfortable circumstances of even the humble, the virtual absence of an impoverished class, and the opportunity of the poor man to rise."[72] To a European eye and mind, the Americans as a whole had risen on the social scale to such an extent that they represented a new force in the economic and political world.

· 7 ·

Most alarming of all was the increasing Americanization of British trade. Two things happened in the eighteenth century that made colonial trade a crucial factor in British economic development. One was the growth of American-British trade; the other was the decline of European-British trade. Together these trends pushed the American colonies into the forefront of British economic and political concerns.

Despite some ups and downs, the trade with the colonies climbed higher and higher decade after decade. British exports to the colonies rose from

[69] Alice Hanson Jones, table 9.3. For more discussion of differences and similarities, see James A. Henretta, "Wealth and Social Structure," in his *Colonial British America*, pp. 272–75.

[70] Jackson Turner Main, *The Social Structure of Revolutionary America* (Princeton University Press, 1965); Gary B. Nash, *Race, Class, and Politics* (University of Illinois Press, 1986).

[71] Henretta, "Wealth and Social Structure," p. 278. Gary B. Nash, "Urban Wealth and Poverty in Pre-Revolutionary America," *Journal of Interdisciplinary History* 6 (1976). Bruce C. Daniels, "Long Range Trends of Wealth Distribution in Eighteenth Century New England," *Explorations in Economic History* 11:2 (Winter, 1973–74): 123–25.

John Adams already knew that there was an aristocracy in colonial America, as for example in Connecticut: "The state of Connecticut has always been governed by an aristocracy, more decisively than the empire of Great Britain is. Half a dozen, or, at most, a dozen families, have controlled that country when a colony, as well as since it has been a state" (*Works of John Adams*, vol. 6, p. 530).

[72] Main, *Social Structure of Revolutionary America*, pp. 221–22.

£267,205 for the decade 1700–1710 to £471,342 for 1720–1730. Then they jumped to £812,647 during 1740–1750, and to £1,763,409 for 1760–1770. Imports from the colonies for the same periods increased from £265,783 to £518,830 to £708,943 to £1,044,591.[73]

At the beginning of the eighteenth century, as Edmund Burke pointed out, the colonial trade had amounted to one-twelfth of total British trade; by 1775, it was better than one-third.[74] The great British cities, especially London and Bristol, flourished primarily because their trade had expanded. Around half of all British exports of copperware, ironware, glassware, earthenware, silk goods, printed cotton and linen goods, and flannels went to colonial consumers. Between two-thirds and three-quarters of all exported British cordage, iron nails, beaver hats, linen, and Spanish woolen goods went to the colonies. British sugar refiners sent one-third of their overseas trade to the colonies.[75] As the colonial period came to a close, the North American trade constituted by far the largest and fastest-growing segment of Britain's foreign commerce, and foreign commerce was the principal dynamic element in the entire British economy.

Meanwhile, the heavily protected European market was increasingly closed to British commerce. The European share in British trade dropped from 78.9 percent in about 1700 to 48.8 percent in about 1773 and continued to decline for the rest of the century, to only about 21 percent of exports and 29 percent of imports in 1797–98.[76] As the European markets contracted, the American and West Indian markets took up the slack. British manufacturers and merchants were not sorry to shift from the European to the American markets, because the latter were largely protected from competition—at least to the extent that the Americans were willing to go along with or could not get around the protectionist system.

In 1769, an influential article published in both Virginia and Maryland, signed by "Atticus" and sometimes attributed to George Mason, showed how the colonists tried to take advantage of this presumed dependence:

> It is acknowledged that upon the whole, the Wealth, the Trade, the Shipping, and the maritime Power of *Great-Britain*, have increased beyond the Idea of former Times.

[73] John Lord Sheffield, *Observations on the Commerce of the American States* (London, 6th ed., 1784), App. 9, p. 24.

[74] March 22, 1775, *Proceedings and Debates of the British Parliaments Respecting North America, 1754–1783*, ed. R. C. Simmons and P. D. G. Thomas (Kraus International, 1983), vol. 5, p. 603.

[75] McCusker and Menard, *Economy of British America*, p. 286.

[76] Walton and Shepherd, *Economic Rise of Early America*, p. 75; Deane and Cole, *British Economic Growth*, p. 34.

This she owes to her *American* colonies. They have made her ample Amends for the decay of all her other Commerce: Here is her Grand-Market for all her various Manufactures, and hence is she principally supplied with gross Materials.

This is the only Trade in which she cannot be rivalled, and which nothing but her own Tyranny and Folly can ever deprive her of.[77]

Who, then, had economic power over whom? In theory, Great Britain controlled the terms of American trade and with it the American economy, even if the control had loopholes. In practice, the greater the scale of the American trade, the more dependent on it the British became. If the colonists had to buy from the British, the British had to sell to them. The more the colonies bought, the more they counted as trading partners. The more lopsided the British economy became in relation to the colonies, the greater the cost to Great Britain if ever the colonies decided to change the rules of the game. "America," a pro-British apologist declared, "is a *Hen* that lays her *Golden Eggs* for Britain."[78]

The early American historian David Ramsay wrote of the change in the colonial attitude after the repeal of the Stamp Act in 1766:

Elevated with the advantage they had gained, from that day forward, instead of feeling themselves dependent on Great-Britain, they conceived that, in respect to commerce, she was dependent on them. It inspired them with such high ideas of importance of their trade, that they considered the Mother Country to be brought under greater obligations to them, for purchasing their manufactures, than they were to her for protection and the administration of civil government. The freemen of North America, impressed with the exalting sentiments of patriotism and of liberty, conceived it to be within their power, by future combinations, at any time to convulse, if not bankrupt the nation, from which they sprung.[79]

This relationship extended to the unfavorable colonial balance of trade, which forced the colonists to go deeply in debt to the merchants of

[77] *Virginia Gazette* and *Maryland Gazette*, May 11, 1769, reprinted in *The Papers of George Mason*, ed. Robert A. Rutland (University of North Carolina Press, 1970), vol. 1, pp. 106–7. The editor thinks that the ideas in this article were borrowed from Mason but that the identity of the author has not been fully established.

[78] Egerton Leigh, *Considerations on certain Political Transactions of the Province of South Carolina* (London, 1774), p. 75, reprinted in *The Nature of Colony Constitutions*, ed. Jack P. Greene (University of South Carolina Press, 1970), p. 118.

[79] David Ramsay, *The History of the American Revolution* (Philadelphia, 1789), vol. 1, pp. 74–75.

the mother country. In the quarter of a century before the Revolution, the colonies as a whole bought more than they sold and thus traded themselves into a state of massive indebtedness. British merchants and financial houses were pleased to extend huge credits at high rates of interest. At least four-fifths of American imports were said always to have been bought on credit.[80] The colonial debt in 1775 was estimated to equal the importation for about a full year.[81] All the elements of the mercantilist system conspired to lure British manufacturers, merchants, and bankers to favor the American market at the expense of British trade with the rest of the world—to their ultimate undoing.

Nevertheless, the colonies, especially in the north, had to trade with countries outside the British orbit in order to be able to pay their debts to British creditors. In the period 1768–1772, for which comprehensive trade figures are available, 55 percent of all North American colonial exports went to Great Britain, leaving 45 percent for the rest of the world, mainly the West Indies and southern Europe.[82] The British had to tolerate this non-British colonial trade in order to make viable much of the colonial trade with Great Britain.

The more the British Americanized their commerce, the more they— and the Americans—felt that the British could not do without the Americans. The more the balance of trade favored Great Britain, the more the Americans went into debt. The more they went into debt, the more they were able to threaten to bring down the mercantilist house of cards by refusing to trade or pay their debts.[83] The more the colonists threatened to break off commercial relations, the closer they came to breaking off political as well as economic ties with the mother country. The more valuable the colonies were to Great Britain, the more they valued themselves. "The progress of the early British American economy over the colonial period had been sufficient to make

---

[80] Sheffield, *Observations*, p. 200.

[81] Samuel Chase, "Notes of Debates in the Continental Congress," in *The Diary and Autobiography of John Adams*, ed. L. H. Butterfield (Harvard University Press, 1961), vol. 2, p. 217.

[82] James F. Shepherd, "British America and the Atlantic Economy," in *The Economy of Early America*, ed. Ronald Hoffman, John J. McCusker, Russell R. Menard, and Peter J. Albert (University Press of Virginia, 1988), p. 9.

[83] This has been the traditional view. More recently, American economic historians have partially challenged it. "The colonists paid for their purchases overseas," James F. Shepherd has stated. "Though there was a high degree of *interdependency* among the participants in this eighteenth-century Atlantic economy that stemmed from the relatively high levels of overseas trade, the colonists were not in a position of *dependency*." But he quickly added that "an approximately balanced current account means only that colonial indebtedness abroad was not increasing. A large amount of indebtedness existed, and on balance this ran from American debtors to British creditors" (*Economy of Early America*, p. 17).

independence thinkable by the 1770s," say John J. McCusker and Russell R. Menard.[84]

What eventually brought down the mercantilist system in the colonies was its inherent contradictions. In the most favorable interpretation of mercantilist doctrine, it benefited both sides by enabling British trade to operate in a protected market and by permitting the colonies to find a secure market for their raw materials. A crucial flaw was that all the colonies were not producers of raw materials. The northern colonies were just as commerce oriented as Great Britain. Another flaw followed from the state of colonial development. Mercantilism was a dependency theory, and the less dependent the colonies became on Great Britain, or the more dependent Great Britain became on them, the more the theory was undermined.

All these alarming circumstances were held in abeyance, however, so long as there was a still more alarming circumstance. Until the British and Americans could settle their accounts with the French, they were in no position to settle their accounts with each other.

[84] McCusker and Menard, *Economy of British America*, p. 326.

7

"A Sort of Independency"

Bᵧ THE MIDDLE OF THE eighteenth century, two struggles for power were going on simultaneously. One dragged on locally and inconclusively between British officials and American colonists. The other was waged all over the world between the two great rivals of the century, Great Britain and France.

Whatever the ostensible reasons, chiefly the succession to various European thrones, the prize of the Franco-British struggle was the balance of power in Europe. In three wars between them, from 1689 to 1697, from 1702 to 1713, and from 1740 to 1748, the American colonies had been far from the main action. They had taken part in the wars without changing the essential character of the larger contest. Nevertheless, the colonies had gradually emerged as a factor to be reckoned with.

In the first war, Massachusetts troops under Sir William Phips had captured the French stronghold of Port Royal in Nova Scotia in 1690, but it had been recaptured by the French the following year. Another expedition from the colonies had retaken the same objective in 1710, but it was again given up in the peace treaty. The next colonial victory, however, was far more impressive and more indicative of the future.

In the 1740–1748 war, known as the War of the Austrian Succession in Europe and as King George's War in America, the British side won exactly one battle—and it was won by the American colonists. The scene of the first great colonial military triumph was the walled fortress of Louisbourg on Cape Breton Island, which was a major French trading as well as military base, guarding the entrance to Canada. The initiative for the attack came from Massachusetts, not from London, and its leader was William Pepperrell, the commander of the Maine militia, not a British general. The main promoter of the expedition was Gov. William Shirley, an ambitious, enthusiastic, imperial-minded lawyer. Pepperrell and over 3,000 volunteers, most of them from Massachusetts, supported by a British fleet under Commodore Peter Warren, succeeded in forcing the surrender of the fortress in June 1745.[1]

On the news of the victory, Shirley wrote to Pepperrell that his army had brought "glory to the New England arms which must make a shining part of the English history to the latest posterity."[2] It was the first time that colonial forces could make such a boast. The news was received with less joy in London. British arms had done so poorly on the continent that, as a British historian put it, "this solitary conquest seemed a source of embarrassment rather than congratulation" to the duke of Newcastle and other British officials.[3] The chief minister, Henry Pelham, regretted the capture of Louisbourg "as a stumbling-block to all negotiation" for peace instead of welcoming it as a boost to British morale.[4] It was no embarrassment to ordinary people in Great Britain, who, it is said, made Louisbourg "the darling object of the whole nation . . . ten times more so than ever Gibraltar was."[5] The Pelham ministry tried to relieve some of the embarrassment, much to Shirley's displeasure, by giving most credit for the victory to Warren, who was made an admiral. When Shirley heard that Warren intended to take command on land at Louisbourg, he threatened that the discontents of the colonists were so great that "they will soon burst out, I am afraid, into an unquenchable flame" if Warren carried out his plan.[6]

More light was shed on British motives the following year, when Shirley, still seeking more conquest, submitted a plan for the invasion and conquest of all Canada, in which colonial troops were to make the main effort. The

[1] The story is told in detail by Douglas Edward Leach, *Arms for Empire* (Macmillan, 1973), pp. 186–87, 224–41.
[2] *Correspondence of William Shirley*, ed. Charles Henry Lincoln (Macmillan, 1912), vol. 1, p. 234.
[3] Basil Williams, *The Life of William Pitt, Earl of Chatham* (Longmans, Green, 1913), vol. 1, pp. 135–36.
[4] W. Coxe, *Memoirs of the Administration of the Right Honourable Henry Pelham* (London, 1829), vol. 1, p. 284.
[5] Richard Lodge, ed., *The Private Correspondence of Chesterfield and Newcastle, 1744–1746* (London, 1930), p. 75, cited by John A. Schutz, *William Shirley* (University of North Carolina Press, 1961), p. 105.
[6] *Correspondence of William Shirley*, vol. 1, pp. 236–37.

duke of Bedford, then head of the Admiralty, is said to have objected "on account of the independence it might create in those provinces, when they shall see within themselves so great an army, possessed of so great a country by right of conquest."[7] Bedford, it seems, favored an expedition to conquer Quebec in 1746 but apparently not on Shirley's terms.[8]

In the end, the colonists were sorely disappointed. With the peace treaty of Aix-la-Chapelle in 1748, the British returned Louisbourg and Cape Breton Island to the French in return for French concessions in Europe. The treaty was clearly no more than a truce, as both sides prepared for another war. The return of Louisbourg came as a shock to New England, where it was regarded as a betrayal. It signified that Great Britain was still oriented towards Europe and regarded the colonies as no more than a bargaining point, despite the efforts that colonial spokesmen had made to convince the British politicians and public that the colonies held out the promise of a greater British empire.

Something of the American attitude was conveyed in a letter by a Pennsylvania merchant to a business acquaintance in London:

> I wish your ministry could be brought to judge rightly of the value and consequence North America is to Great Britain and the danger of the French gaining some settlements in some part of what is now possessed by the English. If they should once get masters in America, England could never hold the balance again according to my present apprehensions. Less than half a century may enable North America, if no uncommon accident happens, to become very formidable—I mean that English part of it—as they are capable to furnish within themselves everything necessary for naval armaments of the growth and manufacture of those countries, gunpowder excepted and for this nothing but saltpetre is wanting. And as the people increase greatly their number, in time to come will furnish great quantities of all things necessary without being obliged to call on Europe for them.[9]

This colonial rationale for taking precedence in Great Britain's own interest anticipated Franklin's *Observations* by three years. It implied

[7] This statement was attributed to the duke of Bedford by George Chalmers, *An Introduction to the History of the Revolt of the American Colonies* (1782; reprint, Boston, 1845), vol. 2, p. 242. It was frequently cited by nineteenth-century American historians (see Arthur Buffinton, "The Canada Expedition of 1746," *American Historical Review*, April 1940, p. 555).

[8] Basil Williams, *The Whig Supremacy, 1714–1760* (Clarendon Press, 1939; reprint, 1952), p. 247.

[9] Cited by Anne Bezanson, R. S. Gray, and M. Hussey, *Prices in Colonial Pennsylvania* (Philadelphia, 1935), pp. 275–76, and by Leach, *Arms for Empire*, pp. 251–52.

that the British should depend on America rather than on Europe, that the balance of power in Europe required the mastery of North America, and that the growth of American population was the key to all of these benefactions. The Pelham ministry, with Newcastle in charge of foreign affairs, wanted peace more than anything else and was not disposed towards letting colonial ambitions stand in the way.

Yet the inconclusive war and unsatisfactory peace helped to bring about a turning point in Britain's strategic outlook. A new generation of British politicians began to question the traditional policy based on expensive and unreliable continental allies. The Americans were only too glad to offer themselves as an alternative.

· 2 ·

Walpole's "old system" had made the balance of power in Europe the chief consideration. This concentration on the continent had been influenced by the fact that the British kings were also electors of Hanover, where both George I and George II had been born and to which they felt a more intimate attachment than to the adopted land of their kingships. George I was not even able to speak English, and George II spoke it with a marked German accent. The Hanoverian connection had required that England's colonial interests be made secondary and if necessary sacrificed to the needs of the European balance of power, as the return of Louisbourg to France in 1748 demonstrated. Continental and colonial policies were thus intertwined; as the old system or "continental strategy" played up the former, it underplayed the latter.

Yet the British responsibility for Hanover was enormously expensive. It hinged on continental alliances paid for with huge annual subsidies, especially to the Prussia of Frederick the Great. Walpole had all he could do to prevent Great Britain from being dragged into continental intrigues, and even he had not been able to prevent a war with Spain in 1739, one of the main reasons for his undoing three years later. Apart from its expense, the continental strategy had a basic flaw—it was based on Great Britain's weakest military branch, the army, instead of on its strongest, the navy.

By the middle of the century, a group of rising British politicians began to challenge the traditional policy as wasteful and futile. Walpole's successor at the head of the government, Henry Pelham, had been forced to patch together a "broad bottom ministry" to buy off the different personal and political groups and interests that had arisen under Walpole. The bottom was broad enough to hold old-timers, such as the duke of Newcastle, his brother, and William Pitt, the antithesis of all that Walpole and Newcastle had stood for. But Pelham died prematurely in 1756; his weak and divided administration permitted a new generation of British leaders to come forward and prepare to dominate the next decade of British politics.

The younger generation had first made a name for itself during Walpole's time in fierce opposition to both his domestic and foreign policies. In this phase of their formative period, they had already hinted at the direction in foreign affairs they wished to take.

William Pitt, the rising star, born in 1708, had entered the House of Commons in 1736 at the age of twenty-eight. He had made himself the scourge of the Hanoverian connection, favoring what he called an "insular" rather than a "continental" policy. He had savagely protested that "this great, this powerful, this formidable kingdom is considered only as a province to a despicable electorate," meaning Hanover.[10] He had later made known that his opposition to Walpole was also motivated by the latter's failure to maintain British interests in America.[11] Pitt's first cabinet post of paymaster general of the armed forces, which he assumed in 1746, did not put him directly in touch with colonial affairs. Another graduate of the anti-Walpole school of British politics, John Russell, fourth duke of Bedford, close to Pitt at the time, had more to do with the colonies.

In 1744, at the age of thirty-four, Bedford was awarded the office of first lord of the Admiralty in the Pelham ministry. Two years later, he succeeded Newcastle as secretary of state for the Southern Department in direct charge of the colonies, while Newcastle shifted over to the Northern Department. The so-called War of the Austrian Succession was then in its sixth year, with two more to go. The colonial capture of Louisbourg in 1745 had apparently disturbed Bedford so much that he did not think it was a good idea to encourage colonial forces to take more of Canada.

Bedford was responsible for bringing in two other new men of much greater consequence for future colonial policy. When he was still at the Admiralty, he was instrumental in the appointment of George Grenville, one year his junior, as a lord of the Admiralty. Grenville had entered Parliament in 1741 at the age of twenty-nine as one of Pitt's small entourage; his association with Bedford enabled him to start on a governmental career which, two decades later, put him at the center of the colonial crisis.

Bedford was also instrumental in the promotion of an even younger man, George Montagu, second earl of Halifax; he added Dunk to his name when

[10] Williams, *Life of William Pitt*, vol. 1, p. 106.
[11] O. A. Sherrard, *Lord Chatham: Pitt and the Seven Years' War* (Bodley Head, 1955), p. 93.

he married the daughter of Sir Thomas Dunk, who made the addition of his name to that of Halifax a condition of the marriage. In 1748, Halifax was appointed president of the Board of Trade, in direct charge of business with the colonies, though it took him a few more years to get full control. Only thirty-two at the time of his appointment, Halifax quickly moved to lift the board out of its long doldrums. His predecessor, Lord Monson, had held the post for two decades, all through Walpole's period, and was notorious for his do-nothing policy; he did not even bother to answer his mail.[12] In 1749, Halifax brought into his board the even younger Charles Townshend, who had been presented with a seat in Parliament two years earlier at the age of twenty-two.

Halifax was the first of the new men to put his personal stamp on colonial affairs, and much that happened in the next quarter of a century was set going by him. He was hardworking, tough-minded, and power hungry. Horace Walpole, who rarely had a good word for anyone, took him to be "fond of power and business . . . jealous of his own and country's honour" and gave him credit for having "as much as he could counteracted the supineness of the [Pelham] Administration."[13] When Halifax was being considered as head of the Southern Department as well as the Board of Trade, Newcastle warned against the move: "He is so conceited of His parts that He would not be there one Month, without thinking He knew as much, or more of the Business than any one Man."[14] George Bancroft later made him out to be one of the monsters of British officialdom—"without sagacity, yet unwilling to defer to any one . . . a presumptuous novice."[15] In fact, Halifax was all the more dangerous to the colonists because he was a quick learner and a hard-driving executive.

Thus four of the leading characters in the unfolding colonial crisis— Pitt, Grenville, Halifax, and Townshend—were brought together in the

[12] According to Horace Walpole, "It would not be credited what reams of paper, representations, memorials, petitions, from that quarter of the world [America] lay mouldering and unopened in his office" (*Memoirs of the Reign of King George the Second*, ed. Lord Holland, London, 2d ed., rev., 1847, vol. 1, p. 396).

[13] Ibid., p. 397. Walpole was much more censorious of Halifax in his *Memoirs of the Reign of King George the Third*, ed. G. F. Russell Barker (Lawrence and Bullen, 1894), vol. 1, p. 216.

Halifax has not been well served by published scholarship. Two works on him are unpublished doctoral dissertations: Robert Alan Blackey, *The Political Career of George Montague Dunk, 2nd Earl of Halifax, 1748–1771: A Study of an Eighteenth Century English Minister* (New York University, 1968), and Steven Gregory Greiert, *The Earl of Halifax and British Colonial Policy: 1748–1756* (Duke University, 1976).

[14] Newcastle to Pelham, September 2, 1750, cited by James A. Henretta, *"Salutary Neglect"* (Princeton University Press, 1972), p. 305.

[15] George Bancroft, *History of the United States* (1852 ed.), vol. 4, p. 37.

ministry of the unlikely Henry Pelham thanks to the traditional policy of buying off potential oppositionists. Later they went their own ways as the temptations of office and changing political conditions came between them. At this time, however, they were recognized as a distinctive political group or tendency, with Pitt their acknowledged leader and mentor. That he should have led them in the beginning was all the more ironic in light of the fierce disagreement which Pitt had with the other three on colonial policy two decades later.

When Halifax took on the job as head of the Board of Trade, the third war with France had just come to an inconclusive end. It provided a breathing space permitting both sides to reassess their positions in the Americas and prepare for the next round of hostilities. In these circumstances, Halifax's first task was to inform himself of what had been going on in the colonies and to figure out what the British could do about it.

He soon learned, if he did not know already, that Great Britain did not have much real power in running the colonies. Complaints of British inadequacy had been coming in from governors for years, without anyone's taking much notice of them. Profits from the colonies, not power over the colonies, had preoccupied Halifax's predecessors. On taking office, Halifax could have found this lament from Gov. Lewis Morris of New Jersey in 1745: "The too great and unwarrantable encroachments of Assemblies in more than one of the northern plantations, seems to make it necessary that a stop some way or other should be put to them, & they reduced to such propper & legall bounds as is consistent with his majestie's prerogatives and their dependance; to prevent a growing evill which, if time gives more strength to, may be difficult to cure."[16] Or he could have read this message from Gov. George Clinton of New York in 1746: "By these Means all the Officers of the Government are become dependent on the Assembly, & the King's prerogative of judging the merit of his Servants & of appointing such persons as he may think most proper is wrested out of the hands of his Governour of this Province, and the King himself (as far as in their power) deprived of it."[17]

Just as he was assuming his post in 1748 came this anguished cry of pain from Gov. James Glen of South Carolina:

> By a long loose administration it [dependence on the Crown] seems
> to be quite forgotten, and the whole frame of Government unhinged,
> the political balance in which consists the strength and beauty of

[16] *The Papers of Lewis Morris*, Collections of the New Jersey Historical Society (New York, 1852), vol. 4, pp. 225–26.

[17] *Documents relative to the Colonial History of the State of New-York*, ed. E. B. O'Callaghan (Albany, 1856), vol. 6, p. 461.

the British Constitution, being here entirely overturned, and all the Weights that should trim and poise it being by different Laws throwen into the Scale of the People. . . . Almost all the Places of either profit or trust are disposed of by the General Assembly. . . . A Governor has no power either to reprove them or remove them.[18]

A huge file of these denunciations and entreaties had accumulated by the time Halifax came to inform himself about the business of the board. If we may trust Newcastle's warning about his conceit, Halifax soon thought he knew, and was actually in a position to know, more about what was going on in the American colonies than anyone else in the British government. Unlike the others, however, what he came to know he also came to act on.

The result was a document produced by the Board of Trade shortly afterwards entitled "Some Considerations relating to the present Condition of the plantations; with Proposals for a better Regulation of them." Most of these "Considerations" had been floating around for years in bureaucratic circles, without much effect on official policy.

One "Consideration" explained why the colonies had become a potential danger to Great Britain and why something had to be done about it: "The British Empire in America is of that large Extent, already settled so many Leagues backward from the Coast; daily encreasing and emproving, by the Numbers yearly born there, and by the new Settlers from Europe, that it is become the utmost Consequence to regulate them, that they may be usefull to, and not rival in Power and Trade their Mother Country." From increasing extent and growing numbers, the end was already in sight: "For unless some Care be taken, the People born there, are apt to imbibe Notions of Indepen[denc]y of their Mother Kingdom."

Privileges had been given to encourage the early settlements without

> any Imagination, that from thence, such Settlements would have established a Sort of Independency of their Mother Kingdom, as some of them, are inclinable to do, and as the others too probably may, by Reason of their great Encrease of Inhabitants, and their being thereby enabled to furnish themselves by their own Labour and Industry, with great part of the Manufactures, that are now sent from hence.

But nothing could be done with the colonies as then constituted. It was necessary to "revise" their constitutions "before any Law can be expected

[18] Glen to Board of Trade, October 10, 1748, in *Great Britain and the American Colonies, 1606–1763*, ed. Jack P. Greene (University of South Carolina Press, 1970), pp. 261–67.

to be of Service there: And any Law without a coercive Power to inforce the same, will be of little Consequence in any Colony, unless that Colony be made to acknowledge a Dependence on the Mother Kingdom."

Whereas the colonies regarded their charters to be sacrosanct, this document argued that they were revocable

> for it can never be supposed, that any Powers or Priviledges, granted only to encourage Settlements in America, by the Crown, were ever intended to discharge any Part of it's [sic] People, from their Allegiance and Dependence, and yet retain a Right of being protected by the Crown. Nor can it be imagined, that this happy regulated Monarchy, should ever intend to establish such little independent Commonwealths; in some of which the Governors, who are chosen annually by the People, give no Security for the due Observance of the Laws of Trade and Navigation, or even take the Oaths of Allegiance, that we know of; From which it is but easy to judge, what Effect, any other Laws here, without a coercive Power, would have among them.

Practical proposals followed. Times had changed. It was no longer possible to deal easily with the business from the colonies. Now they required "the constant Application and Attendance of Persons versed in the History of them." It was recommended, therefore, that the Board of Trade should become "the sole Office of Correspondence with the Plantations, and wherein all Matters relating thereto, were to be discussed for his Majesty's Information." Governors should be given sufficient "security" so that they would not be dependent on assemblies for their salaries or perquisites, "but by His Majesty's Appointment."[19]

This document summed up all that previous officials had warned against and what future officials were to be guided by. It perceived the colonies to be "little independent Commonwealths." It recognized that the Mother Kingdom did not have the "coercive Power" to make them do anything they did not want to do. It pinpointed the weakest link in the British chain of colonial authority—the dependence of the governors on the assemblies for their salaries and perquisites. It sought to tighten the British administration at home by making the Board of Trade the only intermediary between the home government and the colonies—a jurisdiction which the board did not achieve until 1752. An exception was then made for unusually important

[19] Ibid., pp. 267–71, for the complete text.

cases requiring the immediate attention of the secretary of state for the Southern Department, who still retained the policy-making role. Halifax did not rest until he had succeeded five years later in getting greater recognition of his position by being authorized to attend meetings of the cabinet when American affairs were discussed.

Parliament, which had also neglected the colonies, was brought into play. In 1750, it was prevailed on to pass an Iron Act, which prohibited the colonies from manufacturing finished iron products. In 1751, Parliament also passed a Currency Act, prohibiting the colonies from issuing paper money. In 1753, Halifax tried to set a precedent in New York by ordering the newly appointed governor, Sir Danvers Osborne, to get "a permanent revenue settled by law upon a solid foundation for defraying the necessary charges of government."[20] This instruction did as much good as had all previous orders of this type.

· 3 ·

The slide to another war with France began during Halifax's tenure at the Board of Trade. The initiative came from both sides, as if each were bent on giving the other cause for fear and retaliation.

On the French side, Galissonière was as good as his word. The immediate casus belli was a struggle for control of the land beyond the Alleghenies. Until well into the 1740s, it had been left to the fur traders, who went in and out of the forest trails without political entanglement. The French had far more at stake than the British in the region, because the fur trade was virtually the economic raison d'être of Canada, whereas the British colonies had developed a far more advanced and varied economy. Short of manpower, the French had adopted a policy of befriending the Indian tribes; their traders, missionaries, and officials had learned to live peacefully with the Indians. The British-American traders were notorious for their crude mistreatment and fraudulent practices, reports of which were particularly disturbing in London. The early French Governor Frontenac had established a post on the shore of Lake Ontario, now Kingston, before the end of the seventeenth century, and French penetration had long preceded the British-American push west.

Competition for the Indian trade was the chief source of French-British rivalry in the first half of the eighteenth century. Both sides had established

[20] *Royal Instructions to British Colonial Governors, 1670–1776*, ed. Leonard Woods Labaree (Appleton-Century-Crofts, 1935; reprint, Octagon Books, 1967), vol. 1, pp. 190–93.

a few posts, mainly in the northwest of the territory along the Ohio River, without gaining any decisive advantage.

By the time Galissonière came along towards the end of the 1740s, the stakes had risen. The main prize was no longer beaver skins; it was occupation of and sovereignty over territory. Galissonière's arrival in Canada came soon after the first serious efforts by British-American interests to settle the land beyond the Alleghenies. Virginia made the initial move in 1745 with a concession of 100,000 acres to entrepreneurs. A group of prominent Virginians, backed by British financiers, formed the Ohio Company in 1747, the year of Galissonière's arrival, and petitioned the Crown for 200,000 acres of land in the upper Ohio region. The company promised to settle 200 families in the first seven years and also to erect a fort and maintain a permanent garrison.

The larger purpose of the grants was set forth in a petition of 1748 from the London merchant who was most instrumental in organizing the company—to "greatly promote the consumption of our own British manufactures, enlarge our commerce, increase our shipping and navigation, and extend your majesty's empire in America."[21] The Board of Trade approved the grant the following year on the ground that such a settlement west of the mountains was desirable to increase the security of the colonies, encourage trade with the Indians, and deter the French from occupying the same territory.[22] The claims of both countries to the land were equally flimsy and far-fetched, but in that century such niceties were no obstacles to an imperial rivalry.

The American initiative was mainly pushed by Gov. Robert Dinwiddie of Virginia, a protégé of Halifax. Dinwiddie, born near Glasgow, had made his career in the Americas from 1722 to 1758, starting with sixteen years on the island of Burmuda and ending with seven years as lieutenant governor of Virginia. He was a zealous, obedient servant of the Crown, an interested shareholder in the Ohio Company, and an imperial expansionist of the stripe of Governor Shirley of Massachusetts. Virginia's second charter had given her all the territory "from Sea to Sea"—though hardly anyone in 1609 knew where the western "Sea" was or how to get there wherever it was. Yet the language of the grant by James I was taken to give Virginia a particular claim to the territory which the French under Galissonière's program were now threatening and in which the Ohio Company had been handed its thousands of acres without knowing where they were.

[21] Louis Knott Koontz, *Robert Dinwiddie* (Arthur H. Clark, 1941), p. 166.

[22] Clarence Walworth Alvord, *The Mississippi Valley in British Politics* (Arthur H. Clark, 1917, 2d ed., 1960), vol. 1, pp. 87–88; Koontz, *Robert Dinwiddie*, pp. 157–58.

The Ohio Company was made up of "the cream of Virginia aristocracy," including three Washingtons, one of them the seventeen-year-old George, who was sent out in 1749 to survey the land.[23] Land speculation was a favorite means of get-rich-quick colonial fortune hunting, and the Ohio venture was no exception. It differed from most land-grab schemes only in having the full backing of the British government, which was mainly interested in providing a buffer against the French.

The plan of the Ohio Company to establish a post in the Ohio valley threatened to cut the French line of communications between Canada and Louisiana and to get in the way of the lucrative French fur trade throughout the west. The British-American initiative drove Galissonière to take preventive counteraction. In 1749, before his departure, he sent an expedition under Capt. Céleron de Bienville to explore the Ohio territory and place leaden plates with inscriptions proclaiming French possession along the route of the mission. The detachment seized and imprisoned British-American traders encountered on the way; some of them were sent to France. The French showed by this and later actions that they were grimly determined to gain exclusive possession of the vast trans-Allegheny area, oust the British-Americans from it, and thus contain the latter between the ocean and the mountains. By mid-century, each side was provoking the other, one move leading to another.

Galissonière's action soon brought British cries of alarm. "The Governor of Canada is making Incroachments in the most unwarrantable manner," wrote Col. Edward Cornwallis, governor of Nova Scotia, to Col. Robert Napier, adjutant general and chief military aide of the duke of Cumberland, captain general of the British army, in 1749. "On pretence of hindering us to make Settlements before the limits are settled he has sent Detachments to three different Places near the Entrance of the Peninsula, so as to pour in the Savages upon us & succour them as he pleases."[24]

Meanwhile, Halifax and Dinwiddie worked together to drive the French out of the virgin land. In 1752, Halifax showed that he was willing to take the most aggressive action by advocating the demolition of the main French fort at Crown Point on Lake Champlain. Thereupon Dinwiddie sent him alarming news of French incursions south of Lake Erie and proposed erecting British forts on the Ohio River to hold back the French. Halifax proceeded to warn the earl of Holdernesse, the secretary of state for the

---

[23] Kenneth P. Bailey, *The Ohio Company of Virginia and the Westward Movement, 1748–1792* (Arthur H. Clark, 1939), p. 35.

[24] *Military Affairs in North America, 1748–1765*, ed. Stanley Pargellis (D. Appleton-Century, 1936), p. 8.

Southern Department, that unless measures to stop the French were immediately taken, the British colonists were not going to be able to put up any settlements in the area. In June 1753, Dinwiddie sent an even more frightening message to Halifax—that the French were about to invade the Ohio valley. Halifax seized this opportunity to carry out his intention of "stampeding the other ministers into adopting an aggressive policy toward the French," as his most recent biographer has put it.[25]

Halifax took the line that the French not only were determined to take over the unsettled land from the Alleghenies to the Mississippi but also were threatening to conquer the existing British colonies along the Atlantic. He announced that the French had already invaded Virginia and had driven British subjects from "their Settlements in a great panick"—none of which had actually happened; no such settlements had even existed.[26] The result was just what Halifax and Dinwiddie wanted to achieve. On August 23, 1753, war was virtually ensured by an order of the British cabinet to all colonial governors to tell the French to get out and, if they refused, to "repell force by force" and "to drive them out by force of arms."

Despite their agitation against the French, the British colonies were unprepared for war. They guarded their individual autonomy so jealously that they prevented themselves from acting together. Further, they were far behind the French in gaining the support of the Indians, an important factor in wilderness fighting.

Halifax now conceived an unprecedented plan to unite the British colonies against the French. To get them to act together, he proposed appointing a British commander in chief over them. To win the sympathy of the Indians, he asked the governors of the six most endangered colonies to meet with six of the Indian "nations" or tribes belonging to the Iroquoian confederation, known as the Six Nations. For this purpose, he proposed a congress of colonial commissioners to meet at Albany, New York.

While Halifax was making converts to his plan on the British side, Dinwiddie was faced with a more serious French challenge. Galissonière's policy of driving the British out of the area and building forts gained official approval in Paris shortly after his return there. In April 1754, a French force estimated at a thousand was sent out to thwart the building of the first British fort, which the Ohio Company had promised to set up and which a small garrison was constructing. The French captured the partly built fort and garrison without trouble and quickly made it

[25] Greiert, *Earl of Halifax*, p. 294.
[26] Ibid., p. 295.

into a formidable stronghold—where Pittsburgh now stands. In May 1754, Dinwiddie in revenge sent out a party, under the command of Lt. Col. George Washington, which attacked a French force and killed its commanding officer.

By this time events were taking over in America. Halifax had set in motion an extraordinary gathering to win over the Indians and establish a unified command against the French. Before the meeting could take place, however, the first blood was spilled in an unofficial war that had not been authorized in London or Paris. From faraway Europe, the stakes in the western American wilderness could only have appeared to be minimal. To make it the occasion for the decisive struggle for power of the eighteenth century, it was necessary to engage in the kind of reasoning that Galissonière had shared with Halifax—that command of the Ohio and Illinois territory was sure to decide the fate of the old French and British colonies, that the old colonies were bound to decide the fate of Great Britain and France, and that the balance of power in Europe hinged on control of land to which only the Indians had any reasonably convincing claims.

· 4 ·

The Albany Conference of June 1754 was one of the landmarks of the colonial period. Later it was regarded as the last chance to avoid an open break between Great Britain and its American colonies. This view was subsequently encouraged by Benjamin Franklin, the most creative American mind at the conference. Looking back, in the year before his death, he reflected that the plan which he had espoused or something like it might have delayed the separation of the colonies for perhaps another century.[27]

The conference itself was unprecedented. Never before had such a distinguished group of colonial delegates assembled for a task of such magnitude. The twenty-three delegates came from seven colonies, though only the two from Rhode Island had been elected by a legislature. The invitation had been sent out by Lt. Gov. James De Lancey of New York on instructions from the Board of Trade. Only the Massachusetts delegates were instructed to discuss "articles of Union and Confederation"; the rest were limited to the matter of relations with the Indians. The delegates included Thomas Hutchinson, then a member of the Massachusetts Council; Chief Justice

[27] *The Papers of Benjamin Franklin*, ed. Leonard W. Labaree (Yale University Press, 1961), vol. 5, p. 417. [Hereafter cited as *Franklin Papers.*] The documents of the Albany Conference have been published widely; for convenience, I have used the texts in this source.

Stephen Hopkins of Rhode Island; Richard Wibird, Speaker of the Assembly and later governor of New Hampshire; Dep. Gov. William Pitkin of Connecticut; Atty. Gen. William Smith of New York; Benjamin Franklin and Speaker of the Assembly Isaac Norris of Pennsylvania; President of the Council Benjamin Tasker, Jr., of Maryland; and some others equally notable in their colonies. Even without authorization from all the colonial legislatures and without delegates from all the colonies, the makeup of the conference was as representative and influential as its sponsors could have hoped for.

That this conference did not delay the break with Great Britain for another century or even a full quarter of a century is evidence of a cleavage that could not be bridged by the best of intentions or the most able of men. The conference, in fact, showed why the British and Americans were so far apart and, in that sense, brought the ultimate separation that much closer. It was at best a missed opportunity, more important for why it was missed than for what made it an opportunity.

It was not what Halifax had called for. He had envisaged setting up a string of British forts, designating a commander in chief of the colonial forces, and appointing a single commissary or commissioner to take general charge of Indian affairs. The conference had no authority to take such steps. The delegates represented with one exception only themselves, not the legislatures of their colonies. Whatever they might have decided would still have had to go back to the various assemblies to be ratified and then to the British government to be approved. It was a mark of the times that the British government had found it necessary to put its proposals before a group of Americans and no longer felt that it alone could decide what was best for both Great Britain and the colonists. In effect, the British now proposed and the Americans disposed.

Instead of doing what Halifax had asked for, the conference soon went out of control. He had envisaged a number of concrete, limited objectives, in no way to change the fundamental relations of the colonies to each other or to the mother country. The main theme of the conference, however, turned out to be something far more ambitious and radical—nothing less than a "Plan of Union."

It was the brainchild of Franklin. Three years earlier, he had come to more or less the same view as Halifax about the Indian problem and its resolution. He had come to believe that "securing the Friendship of the Indians is of the greatest Consequence to these Colonies" and that it was necessary for this purpose "to unite the several Governments." He preferred "a voluntary Union entered into by the Colonies themselves" instead of "one impos'd by Parliament" and optimistically thought that the former "would be perhaps not much more difficult to procure" than the latter.[28] By the time he conceived of the plan presented at Albany, he knew better.

The Albany plan provided for a "General Government," with a president general appointed by the Crown and a Grand Council made up of members chosen by the colonial assemblies. It gave the president general a veto over the actions of the Grand Council, thus perpetuating a form of dual power. But the individual colonies were to be deprived of the authority to deal with the Indians separately, as they had been accustomed to do. Indian treaties, trade, and purchases of land were to be reserved to the president general and Grand Council. The Union was also to be responsible for new settlements and forts in the Ohio valley and Great Lakes. For these purposes, the president general was empowered "to make Laws And lay and Levy such General Duties, Imports, or Taxes" as were deemed necessary.[29] Franklin explained that the laws made by the president general and Grand Council were to be limited to paying for settlements, soldiers, and the Indian trade. Nothing in the new body was intended to "interfere with the constitution and government of the colonies; who are to be left to their own laws, and to pay, levy, and apply their own taxes as before."[30]

In short, the plan was severely limited in its "Union," though it was called a "Plan of Union." But what attracted most attention was not its limitations but its superimposition of a new type of government, however limited in scope, on the existing colonial regimes. The Albany group realized that the colonies could never be induced to accept a "general government" over themselves which assumed powers that had previously belonged to the individual colonies or the Crown. To get around the expected resistance by the colonial assemblies to any such broader scheme, the Albany Plan turned to the British Parliament for its enactment. The very first sentence in the document made "humble application" for an "Act of the Parliament of Great Britain" that "one General Government may be formed in America." As Franklin later wrote to a friend in London, "Every Body cries, a Union is absolutely necessary; but when they come to the Manner and Form of the Union, their weak Noddles are presently distracted. So if ever there be an Union, it must be form'd at home by the Ministry and Parliament."[31] By looking to Parliament for the decision, the Albany Conference recognized what was later contested—that Parliament

---

[28] Ibid., vol. 4, pp. 117–18.
[29] Ibid., vol. 5, p. 390.
[30] Ibid., p. 413.
[31] Ibid., p. 454.

had the right and power to legislate for the colonies and, indeed, was the only source capable of uniting the colonies even in their own defense.

The plan also suggested that control of taxation by the individual assemblies was not sacrosanct. It called for a double system of taxation— one as formerly by each assembly for its own colony, the other by order of the president general and Grand Council for the general defense. It was a top-heavy arrangement, designed ostensibly to leave all the old elements in place while shifting some powers to the new and more inclusive body.

Dual power still pervaded the Albany Plan. The reason for it was the acute realization of the group that it had no chance if it appeared to undermine the power of either the Crown or the colonies. A preliminary sketch which served as a basis of the discussion betrayed the awareness of this double jeopardy yet admitted that both the Crown and the colonies would have to surrender some part of their past power to the new entity: "In Such a scheme the Just Prerogative of the Crown must be preserved or it will not be Approved and Confirmed in England. The Just Liberties of the People must be Secured or the Several Colonies will Disapprove of it and Oppose it. Yet some Prerogative may be abated to Extend Dominion and Increase Subjects and Some Liberty to Obtain Safety."[32]

The concessions to the Crown were considerable. It was given the appointment and support of the president general. His agreement was necessary for all acts of the Grand Council. New laws were required to be, as always, "not repugnant but as near as may be agreeable to the Laws of England." Such laws had to be transmitted to and approved by the king-in-council, to remain in force if not disapproved of within three years after presentation.

The concessions to the colonial assemblies were also significant. The new "government" could raise and pay soldiers, build forts, and equip vessels, but it could not impress men in any colony without the consent of its legislature. The financial accounts were to be reported annually to the assemblies. Each colony could also maintain its own military and civil establishments in their existing state.

These stipulations show that the Albany reformers were acutely sensitive to the necessity for preserving some semblance of a balance of power among the new general government, the British government, and the traditional colonial governments. Franklin tried to put the best possible

---

[32] Ibid., p. 361.

face on the proposed arrangement by pretending that nothing had really changed:

> The power proposed to be given by the plan to the grand council is only a concentration of the powers of the several assemblies in certain points for the general welfare; as the power of the President General is of the powers of the several governors in the same points.
>
> And as the choice therefore of the grand council by the representatives of the people, neither gives the people any new powers, nor diminishes the power of the crown, it was thought and hoped the crown would not disapprove of it.[33]

These pious thoughts and hopes proved to be futile. To concentrate powers in a new level of government, especially in the realm of defense at a time of imminent war with France, was not likely to escape notice. To shift power away from the assemblies and governors, even if by consent of the Crown and assemblies, could not fail to be a shift of power. It was on this shift more than on anything else that the plan stood or fell.

The similarities and differences between the Halifax and Franklin conceptions were striking. Both were immediately motivated by the French threat and the Indian problem. Both saw that some form of united colonial action was necessary to meet these pressing needs. Both provided for a chief military executive, a commissioner for Indian affairs, and western forts. Then they went their separate ways. Halifax sought to impose such unity primarily by putting a British commander in chief and a commissioner of Indian affairs over the colonies' separate arrangements. He was not giving up any imperial power; a centralized control of the armed forces and outlying fortifications, dictated by a rejuvenated British administration, was bound to increase imperial power over the colonies.

Franklin and others at Albany wanted to create a new level of centralized control, formally shared by Great Britain and the colonies but far more likely to interpose another and more formidable barrier between Great Britain and the colonies. The president general might well have been a distinguished colonial, such as Franklin himself, if he and the Grand Council were to work in harmony and not to reproduce the stultifying wrangles between the royal governors and colonial assemblies. More than anything else, however, a Grand Council made up wholly of colonial representatives would not be easily accepted in London. In the past, the British government had been able to deal with the colonies individually

---

[33] Ibid., pp. 404–5.

and, on occasion, to play one off against another. The Grand Council would have confronted the British government with something entirely new—a forum in which all the colonies could work together in a community of interests.

In the end, only Halifax's original proposals were carried out without benefit of the Albany meeting. Maj. Gen. Edward Braddock was soon appointed commander in chief of the forces in America, and Col. William Johnson was put in charge of relations with the Six Nations. Franklin later reasoned that his plan would have enabled the colonies to unite in their own defense, and thus no army from Great Britain would have been necessary to fight in the American phase of the coming Seven Years' War. In that case, there would have been no occasion for keeping a British army in America after the war or for raising revenue in America to support it. Not without some sadness, he contemplated the likelihood that the "terrible Expence of Blood and Treasure" might have been avoided and "the different Parts of the Empire might still have remained in Peace and Union."[34]

If the Albany Plan of Union did represent such a last chance, it sheds a new light on the breaking point between Great Britain and the American colonies. The die, then, was cast a decade before the Stamp Act or any of the subsequent grievances that exacerbated but did not generate the basic contentions. It was cast because neither side could bring itself to accept a shift in the balance of power between them, even though it might have made the relationship more flexible and effective against the common enemy. The purpose of the Albany Plan was not to sever the ties between Great Britain and the colonies; in Franklin's mind, the plan was a last-ditch effort to readjust the relationship in order to cope with new conditions and an impending crisis. Franklin, then and for two more decades, was not anxious to sever those ties. He was trying to improve them, and his failure showed that the British-American struggle for power could not be averted by an administrative reshuffling.

· 5 ·

That a distinguished group of colonial leaders should have agreed in 1754 that something was drastically wrong with the way the colonies were organized and, even more remarkably, on what to do about it was

---

[34] Ibid., p. 417.

significant enough.[35] Still more significant was the total and hopeless failure of the attempt.

On the colonial side, it failed ignominiously. Not a single assembly voted in its favor. Even in Pennsylvania, the reaction was so hostile that the plan was taken up in the legislature when Franklin was absent, which he thought "not very fair, and reprobated it without paying any attention to it at all, to my no small mortification."[36] The plan was virtually ignored in Virginia, Maryland, and South Carolina. In Rhode Island it was permitted to languish in the General Assembly for about half a year, then no action was taken on it.[37] It was rejected by the New Jersey Assembly. It did no better in Connecticut. In Massachusetts, the plan was considered at length, but the outcome was the same—disapproval. It did better in New York, where "broad approval" was given but no positive action taken.[38]

As soon as the assemblies had a chance to think about the Albany Plan, they did not like it at all, despite its distinguished sponsors, many of whom also cooled off when they came home. Governor Shirley of Massachusetts explained that the assemblies "don't like the plan concerted by the Commissioners at Albany w[hi]ch all of 'em conceive to infringe upon their Colony-liberties & privileges."[39] He pointed to Rhode Island as a bad example. Despite its inhabitants' increase in numbers and wealth

> the reins of their government prove now so loose that a spirit of mobbism prevails in every part of it; they pay no regard to the Kings instruction, and very little or none to Acts of Parliament, particularly to Acts of Trade, in which they seem to look upon themselves as freebooters, as their government was not originally calculated for preserving their dependency upon Great Britain, they have little or no appearance of it among them now, and their example hath by degrees infected His Majesty's neighbouring governments with irregularities which they might not otherwise have gone into.[40]

Such a colony, Shirley maintained, had no reason to give up any part of its

[35] Franklin described the plan as "pretty unanimous" and said later that "it was unanimously agreed to" (ibid., pp. 394, 417).

[36] *Benjamin Franklin's Autobiographical Writings,* ed. Carl Van Doren (Viking Press, 1945), p. 732.

[37] Stephen Hopkins, *A True Representation of the Plan formed at Albany, in 1754,* for uniting all the British Northern Colonies, with introduction and notes by Sidney S. Rider (Providence, 1880), p. 44.

[38] There is a colony-by-colony report on actions taken in Lawrence Henry Gipson, *The British Empire Before the American Revolution* (Alfred A. Knopf, 1942), vol. 5, pp. 141–55.

[39] Cited by Gipson, ibid., pp. 165–66.

[40] *Correspondence of William Shirley,* vol. 2, p. 115.

charter in favor of "establishing a General Government and *Imperium* over all Colonies to be comprized in the Union." Others were less independent but no less jealous of their old charter rights or what they conceived those rights to be. One attack on the plan in Rhode Island charged that the Albany Plan "would revoke all His Majesty's Government Commissions in North-America, and destroy every Charter, by erecting a Power above Law, over the several Legislatures."[41] The New Jersey Assembly contended that the plan would "strike at the very vitals of the constitution of that province."[42] In Massachusetts the main reason given was that "in its operation, it would be subversive of the most valuable rights & Liberties of the several Colonies included in it; as a new Civil Government is thereby proposed to be establish'd over them with great & extraordinary power to be exercis'd in time of Peace, as well as war ... inconsistent with the fundamental rights of these Colonies, and would be destructive of our happy Constitution."[43] Connecticut, which had one of the freest charters, even opposed the plan on the ground that it "might in time be of dangerous consequence to his Majesty's interest," as if its assembly were worried about British power in the colonies.[44]

In short, the colonies would have nothing to do with the Albany Plan of Union, because they believed that it lessened the power to rule themselves, which they thought their charters gave them.

The British did not like the plan for much the same reason—the preservation of their power. When Newcastle asked George Onslow, the Speaker of the House of Commons and the one who knew the temper of the House best, for his opinion of the plan, Onslow told him that such a bill would meet with hard going in Parliament, because of the "ill Consequence to be apprehended from uniting too closely the Northern Colonies with Each Other; An Independency upon this Country being to be apprehended from Such an Union."[45] When Newcastle turned to Charles Townshend, who had recently transferred from the Board of Trade to the Admiralty, he received more bad news. Townshend told him that the assemblies would never agree on a joint plan, because it was "impossible to imagine that so many different representatives of so many different provinces, divided in

[41] Philoletes, "A Short Reply to Mr. Stephen Hopkin's [Hopkins's] Vindication," *Rhode Island Historical Tracts* (Providence, 1880), p. 51.

[42] *New Jersey Archives*, vol. 16, p. 492, cited by Gipson, *British Empire Before the American Revolution*, vol. 5, p. 146.

[43] Josiah Willard, secretary of the colony, to William Bollan, its agent in London, December 31, 1754, cited in *Commonwealth History of Massachusetts*, vol. 2, p. 461.

[44] Cited by Gipson, *British Empire Before the American Revolution*, vol. 5, pp. 148–49.

[45] Greiert, *Earl of Halifax*, p. 334.

interest and alienated by jealousy and inveterate prejudice, should ever be able to resolve upon a plan of mutual security and reciprocal expense." At best, according to Townshend, Parliament would have to impose such a plan on the colonies. But even if it did so, he foresaw from the colonies the same old trouble that had thwarted the British in everything else they had tried to do:

> I am certain the Assemblies of the provinces will never pass the act of supply requisite to support the scheme of union in such a manner as his Majesty may confirm it. It is well known to those who have attended to the affairs of America that the provinces have for many years been engaged in a settled design of drawing to themselves the ancient and established prerogatives wisely preserved in the Crown as the only means of supporting and continuing the superintendency of the mother country, and their manner of doing this has been by their annual bills of supply, in which they have appointed all the officers of the Crown by name to be employed in the Exchequer, substituted warrants for drawing out public money in the place of the Governor's, and in one word dispossessed the Crown of almost every degree of executive power ever lodged in it; it is as certain that whenever the bill of supply to follow this scheme of a general concert is passed, the same provinces will insert into it the same scheme of encroachments, and then the Crown will be reduced either to purchase this security to the colonies by sacrificing our only security for their dependence upon us, or to have a partial supply in consequence of a general fund to be settled, or to drop the whole design of a union upon this plan.[46]

Townshend, having been at the Board of Trade for almost six years, knew as much about the colonies—or had read as many complaints from governors—as anyone in the British government. His reaction to the Albany Plan was revelatory of what such British ministers had in mind when they thought of the colonies. Instead of the plan, Townshend proposed that Parliament should force the colonies to provide a permanent revenue for their own and British security by taxing colonial imports and exports.[47] He never thought through his parliamentary bill, and it was one more British intention that had to wait for over a decade to take on any reality.

Some colonial officials also knew what was irking the British. The Massachusetts agent in London, William Bollan, sent word that members

[46] Lewis Namier and John Brooke, *Charles Townshend* (St. Martin's Press, 1964), p. 40.
[47] Ibid., pp. 38–39.

of Parliament had in mind "a Design of gaining power over the Colonies," apparently by presenting their own plan to unite the colonial forces.[48] Governor Shirley, who had been wavering, advised the secretary of state in charge of the colonies that "the prerogative is so much relaxed in the Albany Plan, that it doth not appear well calculated to strengthen the dependency of the Colonies upon the Crown; which seems a very important article in the consideration of this affair."[49] Franklin later blamed both sides. "The Crown disapprov'd it," he explained, "as having plac'd too much Weight on the democratic Part of the Constitution; and every Assembly as having allow'd too much to Prerogative."[50]

The fiasco of the Albany Plan was another symptom of a persistent struggle for power. The plan was not rejected on its merits. Both sides agreed that the colonies needed a greater degree of unity to survive the threat of the French and Indians. But neither side would tolerate a plan that impinged on its power. When it was considered at all, the only thought given to it was how it bore on the powers, prerogatives, and privileges of the existing governmental structure. Once it was seen by all that the balance of power had to change if the plan was implemented, it never had a chance.

· 6 ·

Yet the mortal threat of France to the American colonies had long been a staple of colonial opinion. The danger had been flaunted as early as 1720 by a pamphleteer whose purpose was to make his readers take fright at the French possession of Louisiana. Any new French settlements threatened to ruin British trade in America, and, in the words of the pamphleteer, "all our Colonies, unless much better regulated and secured than they are at present, may one time or other, *be entirely taken from us.*" If war broke out, the French would "find it a Matter of no great Difficulty, with the Assistance of the *Indians,* to invade from thence [Louisiana] and *Canada, all the* English *Plantations at once,* and drive the Inhabitants into the Sea." He appealed for "some extraordinary Means" to provide for the safety and preservation of the British colonies, but he was not optimistic about getting them. One trouble was that "his Majesty's Dominion on this Continent is canton'd into so many petty independent States or Common

[48] *Massachusetts Archives,* December 4, 1754, vol. 6, p. 169, cited by Gipson, *British Empire Before the American Revolution,* vol. 5, p. 151.

[49] *Correspondence of William Shirley,* vol. 2, p. 117.

[50] *Franklin Papers,* vol. 5, p. 417.

Wealths, whereof there is scarce one that can expect Relief or Assistance from another, in the most imminent Danger. . . . I think it naturally follows, that some time or other, the *Mississippi* will drown our Settlements on the Main of *America.*"[51]

In 1732, James Logan, formerly William Penn's right-hand man and colonial secretary of Pennsylvania, warned the British government that "the American Plantations are of such Importance to Britain, that the Loss of them to any other Power, especially to France might be its own ruin."[52]

The same point was made in connection with a colonial demand that had little to do with the larger issue. In 1738, the General Assembly of New York wanted to substitute elections every three years for those every seven years. A memorandum sent to London argued that the more frequent elections would benefit the welfare and prosperity of the colony, thus strengthening it against France, which was said to be "Extrem[e]ly Jealous of its Interests, and ever watchfull to seize on every Advantage for the Extension of their settlements upon the Lands undoubtedly belonging to the British Crown." Then came a most ominous warning: "That a fatal blow will be given to this British Interest both in Europe and America, if this Country should ever fall into the hands of the ffrench."[53]

In 1744, Governor Shirley of Massachusetts, forever trying to get the British to attack the French in Canada, urged the duke of Newcastle to support a combined colonial land army and British naval force to invade Cape Breton Island. Shirley held out all sorts of inducements—it would "give his Majesty's subjects the whole Furr trade," make them "Masters of an entire Territory of about eighteen hundred miles extent" from Georgia to Newfoundland, bring about "the Growth of their Numbers, to which it would be difficult to set Limits." The value of this territory, he assured Newcastle, would represent an increase of "Natural Wealth and power" so great that it "may be reckon'd a more valuable Territory to Great Britain than what any Kingdom or State in Europe has belonging to it." Otherwise, he warned darkly, the French would become so strong that they might

---

[51] *Some Considerations on the Consequences Of the French Settling Colonies on the Mississippi* . . . (London, 1720; reprint, Historical and Philosophical Society of Ohio, 1928), pp. 16, 28, 41. This pamphlet was assigned by Justin Winsor to Dr. James Smith of South Carolina, but it was attributed by Bradley W. Bond, Jr., in the introduction, to someone from New England, and written early in the summer of 1718. On the other hand, the author's praise of Virginia is so enthusiastic that he may very well have been a Virginian.

[52] James Logan, "A Quaker Imperialist's View of the British Colonies in America: 1732," ed. Joseph C. Johnson, *Pennsylvania Magazine of History and Biography*, April 1936, p. 130.

[53] E. B. O'Callaghan, ed., *The Documentary History of the State of New-York* (Albany, 1851), vol. 4, p. 245.

possibly in time "think of disputing the Mastery" of the entire northern continent.[54]

After the French had surrendered Louisbourg, Shirley advised the Board of Trade that the North American continent "may be justly looked upon in its Increase to be an inexhaustible Source of Wealth and Power to Great Britain." He also gave a number of reasons, one of which was particularly revealing, why the British should put a garrison in the town and a squadron of warships in the port of Louisbourg:

> It would by it's [sic] vicinity to the Brittish colonies and being the Key of them, at least of the most principal of 'em, give the Crown of Great Brittain a most absolute hold and Command of 'em, if ever there should a time come when they should grow Restive and dispos'd to shake off their Dependency upon their Mother Country; the possibility of which I must freely own seems to me from the Observations I have been able to make upon the spot, at the Distance of some Centuries farther off than I have heard it does to some Gentlemen at Home.[55]

It was then 1745, thirty years before the first shot fired at Lexington, yet Shirley, a native son, thought it well to reassure his superiors in London that they did not have to worry, at least immediately, about the colonies shaking off their dependency, even though others were less optimistic about the time it would take. But it was best to make sure by putting a garrison and stationing a squadron of warships at Louisbourg. After Louisbourg was returned to the French in the peace treaty of 1748, Shirley used Galissonière's subsequent efforts to build up a French system of forts to urge a similar policy on the part of the British, again for the purpose of "securing the Benefit of the Trade of the Colonies to their Mother Country, and creating a Dependency of 'em upon her."[56]

In 1750, Gov. Roger Wolcott of Connecticut continued to remind the Board of Trade that the French were inveterate enemies. At the end of that year, he wrote that "the French at Canada are threatning to Drive us and all the English on the Continent into the Sea and are advancing in their Settlements nearer and nearer towards us," though none had been made within Connecticut.[57] The next war with the French was being prepared.

And in London, Halifax at the Board of Trade made himself the

[54] *Correspondence of William Shirley*, vol. 1, pp. 163–64.
[55] Ibid., p. 244.
[56] Ibid., pp. 478–80.
[57] Wolcott to Board of Trade, December 31, 1750, *The Wolcott Papers, Collections of the Connecticut Historical Society* (Hartford, 1916), vol. 16, p. 25.

mouthpiece of related ideas, but from a distinctively British point of view. He delivered a speech in Parliament in 1755, on the eve of the formal declaration of war, which summed up the new imperial outlook of the younger generation of British ministers, not yet in the first rank.

Halifax's main theme was that the American colonies were more important than Britain's European allies. He expressed scorn for "running about Europe in search of allies who can be of no service to us." Instead, Great Britain should make greater efforts to win over many of the American Indians who weighed down "upon the back of our colonies of Virginia, Maryland, Pennsylvania and New York." Better to make alliances with the Indians, who now preferred to join forces with the French, than to purchase allies in Europe "at the expence of large annual subsidies." The choice before England, he maintained, was between purchasing continental allies to defend Hanover and concentrating on defending the American colonies against the French. For, he exclaimed, it was not in Britain's power to purchase continental allies

> without neglecting entirely the prosecution of the war by sea and in America, and should our trade and plantations be exposed to the ravages of the French, a national bankruptcy would probably in a very few years ensue, which would render us unable to continue the war in Europe for the defence of Hanover, or to prosecute the war by sea and in America, or even to defend ourselves here at home.[58]

According to this line of reasoning, the loss of the American colonies was sure to bring about Great Britain's bankruptcy and even incapacity to defend its own territory. Halifax's thinking was not original; it was just what colonists had been trying for years to make the British believe: that it was necessary once and for all to get rid of the French threat in North America, not only in the colonists' own interest but in that of Great Britain itself. To make the leap from the colonies to the mother country, colonial spokesmen had raised the specter of what would happen to Great Britain if France succeeded in taking over the British colonies. By the 1750s, this type of propaganda from the colonies was becoming ever more strident and urgent.

At about the time Halifax made his parliamentary speech, a pamphlet was published in Boston that more than any other expression of the period insisted on the crucial importance of the American colonies to Great Britain. It was written in the mid-1750s by William Clarke, who dedicated it to

[58] *Parliamentary History,* vol. 15 (1755), col. 637.

Governor Shirley. The work first evoked the memory of Louisbourg as the event that allegedly gave "Peace to *Europe.*" It then paid its respects to the increase of colonial population—that Massachusetts doubled its numbers every twenty years, and that the colonies as a whole could expect to reach 3 million in thirty years. The author next turned his attention to the vital importance of the British colonies and what their loss would mean for Great Britain. His purpose was clearly to persuade Great Britain to declare all-out war against France:

> The Prince, who holds Possession of the *English* colonies in *North-America,* will be in a Condition to keep the Sovereignty of the Atlantic Ocean, thro' which the homeward bound Trade from the East and West-Indies generally passes. . . .
>
> [If Great Britain lost the American colonies, French naval power] would increase to such a Degree of Superiority over that of *Great-Britain,* as must entirely destroy her Commerce, reduce her from her present State of Independency to be at last nothing more than a Province of *France.*
>
> That these Colonies are of such Consequence to the Trade, Wealth and Naval Power of *Great-Britain,* and will in future Times make so much larger Additions to it, that whilst she keeps them entire, she will be able to maintain not only her Independency, but her Superiority as a Maritime Power. And on the other Hand, should she once lose them, and the *French* gain them, *Great-Britain* herself must necessarily be reduced to an absolute Subjection to the *French Crown,* to be nothing more than a *Province of France.* [59]

Greater inducement for Great Britain to eliminate France from North America could hardly be imagined. As if the balance of power in Europe were not enough, the ante had now been upped to include the very existence of Great Britain as an independent state. Clarke was clearly a member of Shirley's circle and reflected the obsessive eagerness of those around the Massachusetts governor to drive the French out of Canada. Almost any argument was good enough to convince the British that they had as much or more at stake as the colonies in the blood feud with the French. Yet Clarke's approach was not all that uncommon. It was not very different from that of Halifax's message to Parliament that same year—that French "ravages" of the British colonies would make Great Britain unable "to defend ourselves here at home."

[59] [William Clarke], *Observations on the late and present Conduct of the French* . . . (Boston, 1755), pp. 4, 37, 43–45, 47.

A better-known American propagandist, William Livingston, took a similar line the following year. Livingston was a great admirer of Shirley and later served as the state of New Jersey's first governor.[60] In another work designed to whip up sentiment against the French, after fighting had already begun, Livingston boasted that the American colonies "may be made an inexhaustible magazine of wealth" and that without them "Great Britain must not only lose her former lustre, but, dreadful even in thought! cease to be any longer an independent power." If Britain lost her American possessions to France, it would be "An Event my lord, of the most tremendous consequence to us—to you—to the Protestant religion—to the peace of Europe—yes—to the peace and happiness of all Mankind."[61]

These appeals against the French threat were merely among the most extreme of the colonial alarms. In one form or another, they had been coming with increasing shrillness from the colonies. In 1750, the Massachusetts Assembly had petitioned George II for military aid as "subjects of the Crown of Great Britain, and the Dread which proceeds even from the most distant prospect of being ever subjected to the Yoke, and Tyranny of the French."[62] As war approached, the appeals began to take on a more self-pitying tone and to plead that the colonies could not defend themselves. The most anguished cries came from Massachusetts. A message from the Massachusetts Assembly to Governor Shirley in January 1754 accused the French of taking such measures "as threaten great danger, and perhaps in time, even the intire [*sic*] destruction of this province (without the interposition of his majesty) notwithstanding any provision we can make to prevent it."[63] By the end of the year, the Massachusetts Council and Assembly begged Shirley to use his good offices to convince the king that "we apprehend it *impossible, in the present distressed circumstances of the province, to maintain a force necessary for the defence of so extensive a frontier; and therefore we must humbly rely upon his majesty's paternal*

[60] "Of all our plantation governors . . . Mr. Shirley is the most distinguished for his singular abilities. . . . He is a gentleman of great political sagacity, deep penetration, and indefatigable industry" (*Massachusetts Historical Society Collections*, 1st ser., vol. 7, pp. 69–70). In his later literary efforts, Livingston was called "Washington's right-hand propagandist" (Philip Davidson, *Propaganda and the American Revolution, 1763–1783*, University of North Carolina Press, 1941, p. 379).

[61] William Livingston, *A Review of the Military Operations in North America* (London, 1758), pp. 6, 98.

[62] Public Record Office, A. 40, Nova Scotia, 1751, vol. 63, p. 189, cited by Lawrence Henry Gipson, *The British Empire Before the American Revolution* (Alfred A. Knopf, 1958), vol. 6, p. 7.

[63] See the group of colonial appeals in [William Knox], *The Controversy between Great Britain and her Colonies Reviewed* (London, 1769), pp. 114–15.

goodness . . . for assistance."[64] These sentiments were also exchanged in private correspondence. In the summer of 1755, Thomas Hancock, uncle of John Hancock and founder of the family fortune, wrote a letter to his agent in London, Christopher Kilby, with the familiar refrain: "For God's sake then let us Root the French blood out of America. . . . it will be the Salvation of England for in 40 years this very America will absolutely take all the Manufactory of England, a Noble Return for their assistance[,] a Good Interest 40 per Cent for their Outsett at Least," and "whoever keeps America will in the End (whether French or English) have the Kingdom of England."[65]

In 1755, a lengthy study called *State of the British and French Colonies in North America* appeared in London to fire up the British against the French and to reassure the British that they had nothing to fear from the Americans. The author accused former British governments of having encouraged the disunity of the colonies in order to maintain their dependence and prevent them from seeking independence. But, like Franklin at this time, he professed to see no danger of a colonial breakaway:

> Indeed this disunion among the provinces has been kept up in good measure by a pernicious maxim, which in some former reigns prevailed in their mother country, like that which seems to prevail there still, of ruling by parties, or division. The bad effects of which may be seen in the present distressed and distempered state of the colonies, by which the maxim *divide et impera*, which appears to have operated more for the interest of the *French* than of *Great Britain:* former governments might likewise have had another pretence for keeping up the disunion among the colonies, namely, the danger, in an united state, of their throwing off dependence and setting up for themselves. But this can never reasonably be supposed to happen, were they ever so rich, as well as strongly united, unless they were driven to that extremity, by usage which would make *Britons* themselves impatient of subjection. However, to suppose any such danger at present, or for many ages to come, is ridiculous; since they can never do any thing while they want a fleet, and *Britain* has one to restrain them. So long as this shall be the case, if ever they should revolt, it would never be with design to set up for themselves: they would be under a necessity to seek the protection of some other power.

[64] Ibid., p. 127 (italics in original).
[65] W. T. Baxter, *The House of Hancock* (Harvard University Press, 1945), p. 132.

In any case, the specter of "their throwing off dependence and setting up for themselves" was always there and had to be exorcised. Meanwhile, the great danger came from the French. If they succeeded in taking over the trans-Allegheny country, "they would in time be masters of all the *British* colonies." Only two choices remained—to drive out the French or to *"out-fort,* as well as *out-settle* them." At this stage before the war, the latter policy was the least the British could adopt.[66]

Another work that same year by the geographer Lewis Evans appeared in Philadelphia and warned the British that the Americans might prefer independence if they were not treated right. Evans advised the British to fight French expansionism, not that of the Americans, in the area beyond the Alleghenies:

> Supposing the Colonies were grown rich and powerful, what Induce-
> ment have they to throw off their Independency? . . . But while they
> are treated as members of one Body, and allowed their natural
> Rights, it would be the Height of Madness for them to propose
> an Independency, were they ever so strong ... and for that reason
> it becomes those who would regard the future Interest of Britain and
> its Colonies to suppress the Growth of the French Power and not the
> English, in America.[67]

Repeatedly, anti-French agitation was combined with reassurances against American independence, as if to blunt the fear that getting rid of the French in Canada was an invitation to the Americans to strike out on their own. As for the Americans, they were caught in a peculiar dilemma. They could not resist boasting of how great and wealthy they were or were about to become, at the same time pleading how weak and vulnerable they were in the face of the French in Canada. British-Americans of the type of Benjamin Franklin solved the problem by fervently believing that all American gains were sure to accrue to the greater influence and grandeur of the British empire, but the need for reassurances of American loyalty showed that there was considerable doubt in Great Britain about holding down a growing America without the aid of the French threat.

---

[66] The complete title is *State of the British and French Colonies in North America With Respect to Number of People, Forces, Forts, Indians, Trade and other Advantages* (A. Millar, 1755). The work is allegedly made up of "Two Letters to a Friend," the first and longest dated December 10, 1754, the second March 14, 1755.

[67] Lewis Evans, *An Analysis of a General Map of the Middle British Colonies in America* (Philadelphia, 1755), p. 32.

8

''Combustible material''

As WAR WITH FRANCE approached, a new British military strategy clashed with the old. Unlike the old, which was based on the army and European alliances, the new stressed the navy and the American colonies. The dispute was generally known as the "continental strategy" versus the "maritime strategy."

The struggle between them came out openly in Parliament in November 1754. The debate was set off by a government request for military supplies against French "encroachments." As Col. Henry Conway put it, "every one knows, that the pretensions set up by the French, and the encroachments they have made upon us in America, are such as we cannot tamely submit to." The question was what to do about it. Another speaker, Thomas Potter, held that the French advantage in Europe in population and army was so great that Great Britain could protect itself only by means of the old strategy of continental alliances. Yet he criticized the government for having been too restrained "when it is so well known that the French have actually attacked us, and have murdered a great number of our people, as well as robbed many others, in America." He contended that "we ought to have declared war against them, the moment we heard of their attacking us in America."

Henry Legge wanted to seek redress first by negotiation and to form a new anti-French confederacy in Europe only after peaceful efforts had failed. He defended the government against having "any design to sacrifice any of our rights in America, to the obtaining of a dishonourable and precarious peace" but cautioned that it was dangerous to "insinuate our being resolved to assert our rights in America to their utmost extent" on the ground that doing so would alarm some European courts unconcerned with the strictly British-French dispute.

Most revealing was the action advocated by William Beckford, one of William Pitt's main backers, a wealthy alderman of the City of London and representative of leading financial and commercial interests. Beckford strenuously rejected the idea that "it is impossible for us to contend with France, without the assistance of a powerful alliance upon the continent of Europe." He even blamed past alliances for the growth of France's foreign commerce and foreign plantations. "If the French persist in refusing to us justice," he asserted, "let us attack them upon our own element the ocean; If we attack them any where by land, let it be in America, where we are sure of the utmost assistance our colonies can give, without subsidy or reward."

Sir Robert Walpole's brother, Horatio, went back to the need for continental allies, while paying tribute to the pressing importance of the colonies—"for it is to them we owe our wealth and our naval strength." The earl of Egmont, an old opponent of Sir Robert Walpole's policies, came out for standing "single and alone in a naval war with France," though he was willing to accept allies if, he said, they "apply to us for assistance, instead of our applying to them" and "without putting us to such an expence as must interrupt or interfere with the prosecution of the war by sea or in America." Finally, the government's spokesman, Atty. Gen. William Murray, later more famous as the earl of Mansfield, defended the continental system of European alliances on the ground that the loss of neither trade nor colonies would frighten France so much as "a party of German hussars approaching near the purlieus of Versailles," as had happened in the time of Marlborough, a half century earlier.[1]

Such was the division of political opinion in Great Britain on the eve of the Seven Years' War. The new maritime-American strategy was clearly gaining ground, but the old line continued its hold on government policy. Yet even those who wanted to fight as before on the continent did not deny the primacy of colonial interests; the argument was mainly over means, not ends. The French "encroachments" in the American wilderness could not be accepted by any important British politician.

The odds still favored the traditionalists. Funds for subsidies were voted

[1] *Parliamentary History,* vol. 15 (1754), cols. 338–39 (Conway), 342–46 (Potter), 347, 350 (Legge), 354, 358 (Beckford), 364–65 (Walpole), 368, 370 (Egmont), 372 (Murray).

and alliances held in reserve. Yet British official opinion was disturbed by the new strategy. Even Newcastle, who had difficulty making up his mind, wrote: "Sea war, no continent, no subsidy, is almost the universal language." He was willing to go no further than the defense of Hanover, which could not be given up without alienating George II.[2] The new generation of British politicians wanted to go much further. The duke of Bedford was opposed even to defending Hanover. "The only war we can carry on is a sea war, and an American one," he believed, "though we have done hitherto like pirates, rather than a great nation."[3] William Pitt wrote that he favored "our insular plan, by declaring that we mean to enable his Majesty to defend the dominions of England, and not to lay the foundations for continental operations."[4]

Further evidence of support for the new strategy was the appearance of a new political weekly, *Monitor,* first issued in August 1755. It argued for the inevitability and desirability of another war with France on condition that "it should be energetically fought by naval means alone for Britain's true interests in America." The paper was put out by another Beckford, Richard, and largely represented financial and mercantile interests in the City.[5]

A publication in Philadelphia provided an extended exposition of the favorite colonial strategy. It held that the colonies were an object of the highest importance to Great Britain and, therefore, that it was more important for Great Britain to carry on the war with France in America than in any other part of the world, since all the money spent in such an effort would circulate in the colonies and eventually return to the mother country. As a result of the British advantage of open ports, easy navigation, and the greatest store of provisions, a war in America was supportable for a much longer time and with less expense by the British than by the French.[6]

Thus the Americans were well aware of the debate in England on the old and new strategies and their allotted role in them. From having been at the periphery of the world struggle for power, they were suddenly promoted to occupying a central role in determining the next winner and loser.

[2] Carl William Eldon, *England's Subsidy Policy Towards the Continent During the Seven Years' War* (diss., University of Pennsylvania, 1938), p. 17.

[3] *The Grenville Papers,* ed. William James Smith (London, 1852), vol. 1, p. 146.

[4] Pitt to Grenville, December 1755, ibid., p. 152.

[5] Marie Peters, *Pitt and Popularity* (Oxford University Press, 1980), pp. 43, 146–47.

[6] *American Magazine,* November 1757, reprinted in *Boston News-Letter,* September 15, 1758.

As the *Monitor*'s espousal of the maritime strategy shows, the essential reason for the shift in the British outlook was economic. The ever-increasing commercial importance of the colonies made them worth more to the British than anything that could be gained on the continent. The main British motivation was summed up by the earl of Holdernesse: "We must be merchants while we are soldiers, that our trade depend upon the proper exertion of our maritime strength; that trade and maritime force depend upon each other, and that the riches which are the true resources of this country depend upon its commerce."[7] Pitt's colonial policy has been described as based on the fundamental principle that France was "chiefly if not solely to be dreaded as a maritime and commercial power."[8]

Thus anguished calls from the colonies to be protected from France came together with a new credo in both Great Britain and France making their North American colonies critical to their economic and imperial welfare. Each side easily convinced itself that the other intended to strike at it in the new world.

• 2 •

The American aspect of the Seven Years' War was reinforced by the way it began.

The irrepressible conflict broke out in such a way that the British could tell themselves they were fighting in behalf of the American colonies. When the Ohio Company, on the British-American side, received its 200,000 acres on condition that a fort be built to protect prospective settlers, the French were determined to prevent the deal from being consummated.

Then followed the events which brought on the war—Maj. George Washington's failed attempt to take possession of the French fort, the British decision to appoint Gen. Edward Braddock as commander in chief for the colonies as a whole, Braddock's disastrous defeat in the second effort to drive out the French.

At first the reason given in London was that the colonies had brought the embarrassment on themselves by their failure to contribute to their own defense. Lord Hardwicke, the lord chancellor, protested to Newcastle, "Tis monstrous that People will not help themselves." Newcastle in turn explained to Lord Granville, the influential president of the Privy Council:

[7] Julian S. Corbett, *England in the Seven Years' War* (Longmans, Green, 1918), vol. 1, p. 189.
[8] Kate Hotblack, *Chatham's Colonial Policy* (George Routledge & Green, 1918), p. 49.

" 'Tho We may have Ten Times the Number of People in our Colonies, They don't seem to be able to defend Themselves, even with the Assistance of Our Money." Yet Newcastle shared the general opinion that, whatever the shortcomings of the Americans, they could not be permitted to suffer the humiliation unrevenged and let the territory go to the French without a struggle. He wrote to Hardwicke: "Every body is full of North America, and our Defeat there. . . . Something must be resolv'd and *that Something* must be (if possible) Effectual."[9]

The European phase of the larger war was officially declared in June 1756, after new alliances had been formed between Great Britain and Prussia on the one hand and between France and Austria on the other. Later that year, William Pitt entered the government as secretary of state for the Southern Department, in charge of the American colonies, with the duke of Newcastle as head of the Treasury. These two, formerly far apart, now worked together with tolerable harmony to wage the war. The European alliances into which Great Britain entered were clearly inconsistent with the previous antialliance and antisubsidy policy of Pitt and his supporters; they opened Pitt up to the charge that he had betrayed his previous policies by accepting the alliances and the subsidies made necessary by them, and by sending British troops to the continent.[10] Though he was only the southern secretary, Pitt was long given credit for having guided the military side of the war, and his enormous reputation has rested on its outcome.

Thus the Seven Years' War started as if it were a struggle to protect the interests of American land speculators. Their interests were inflated as if their fate could threaten the loss of the American colonies as a whole. The fate of the colonies was stretched as if it were capable of deciding the balance of power in Europe and, in the last extremity, the future of Great Britain as an independent nation. Or it could be said that the rivalry between Great Britain and France to decide the balance of power in Europe was what made a local quarrel over a primitive little fort in Indian country, far from any settled habitation, the opening shot in the first world war in modern times.

In Great Britain itself, a popular impression, frequently encouraged by British ministers, persisted that the war had broken out and had been fought in defense of the American colonies. Pitt himself is said to have declared in Parliament that the war "has been undertaken not to defend Hanover, but

---

[9] James A. Henretta, *"Salutary Neglect"* (Princeton University Press, 1972), p. 338.
[10] This aspect of Pitt's career is discussed at some length by Jeremy Black, *William Pitt* (Cambridge University Press, 1992), chap. 3.

for the long-injured, long-neglected, long-forgotten people of America."[11] That someone of Pitt's stature should make the colonies and not Europe the main reason for the greatest war of the century was something new in British and world politics.

· 3 ·

The war did not go according to plan. At first nothing seemed to go right for the British and their allies. Europe was the scene of one setback after another; even Hanover was occupied by the French. The news was no better from America; the earl of Loudoun, the British commander, paid the price by being recalled at the end of 1757.

At about this time, however, the tide of battle in Europe began to change in favor of Prussia's Frederick the Great, the main British ally. Pitt's determination to take the offensive in North America also paid off; the fortress of Louisbourg was captured for the second time in July 1758 by a force under Col. James Wolfe, the first British victory of the war. The next year was an annus mirabilis for the British cause. The French-Canadian capital of Quebec fell in September 1759 to forces, mainly British regulars, in the legendary battle in which both commanders, Wolfe and Montcalm, died under fire. In the West Indies, the French sugar island of Guadeloupe surrendered to a British naval assault. In Africa, Gorée fell to British forces; in India, Madras was successfully defended and Surat was captured. Another British ally, Prince Ferdinand of the German principality of Brunswick, defeated the French in a major battle at Minden. Montreal was taken in 1760. By that year, the war in Canada was effectively over.

By this time, all the contestants were ready to look for a way out of the war. A decision was still elusive in Europe; only in North America had it been possible to strike a knockout blow. Abortive peace negotiations between the French and British took place early in 1760. Within the British cabinet, some of the most influential ministers, including Newcastle and Hardwicke, fearing that the war was bankrupting the country, favored ending it on moderate terms. Against them Pitt held out for a war to the finish against French naval power and against any further French threat to British interests. The issue came to a head with Pitt's insistence in 1761

[11] This is the version in Brian Tunstall, *William Pitt, Earl of Chatham* (Hodder and Stoughton, 1938), p. 145. Basil Williams has a slightly different version: "Why was this present war undertaken if not for the long-injured, long-neglected, long-forgotten people of America?" (*The Life of William Pitt, Earl of Chatham,* Longmans, Green, 1913, vol. 1, p. 269).

on declaring war against Spain after it had entered into a Bourbon family compact with France. Pitt was overruled and resigned; his departure brought to an end the British will to prosecute the war to the bitter end. The peace treaty of Paris in 1763 officially ended a war that had been running down since his departure.

Pitt's war policy put the American colonies into contemporary world politics on a level they had not achieved before. His initial impulse had been to make the colonies the foremost factor in the struggle with France. He apparently abandoned this strategy during the first two years of the war, when he had conducted it in the traditional continental way and without any progress in the colonies to show for it. But once the American phase of the war came into its own in 1768, he was able to regain his old ground and come out ahead, even if he failed to taste the full fruits of victory.

Pitt later interpreted the European and American fronts of the war as if they had been two sides of the same coin. It has been claimed for him that he sought to weaken France in Europe in order to defeat France in America.[12] Two of Pitt's most famous statements seem to express this view of what he had achieved—that "America has been conquered in Germany" and that the campaign in America was "where England and Europe are to be fought for."[13] Both made America the crucial point of the entire war, at least from the British point of view as Pitt saw it—a stunning reversal of all previous British strategy.

A late-eighteenth-century American historian saw the change in a way that shows the point had not been lost on the American revolutionary generation:

> The rivalship of these two countries [France and Great Britain] was placed on a critical poise, which both apprehended would be finally cast by the preponderance of the certain though remote power, which must in the destiny of things, arise from America. Who should possess this country? was then one of the most important questions that could be made: And, although it might be too latent to be interesting to the body of either nation in Europe, yet it was open to the view of the real politicians of both, and from local causes, made a more general impression on the people of the American Colonies.[14]

[12] This is the main argument in the work of Sir Julian S. Corbett, *England in the Seven Years' War*, e.g., vol. 1, p. 291.

[13] Horace Walpole, *Memoirs of the Reign of King George the Third*, ed. G. F. Russell Barker (Lawrence and Bullen, 1984), vol. 1, p. 76; Williams, *Life of William Pitt*, vol. 1, p. 334.

[14] George Richards Minot, *Continuation of the History of the Province of Massachusetts Bay, From the Year 1748* (Manning & Loring, 1798), pp. 175–76.

Though Pitt was more America-minded than most British ministers, the course of the war could not leave any of them unaffected. The colonies were thrust into the foreground of British political consciousness, with grave consequences in the next decade. Walpole's generation could still afford to neglect the colonies, however benignly. Pitt's generation and even more the next one could not regard the colonies with such indifference. Events in the colonies had made the difference between victory and defeat, and even, as some thought, survival and submission.

Pitt spent recklessly to win the war, with the result that he left to his successors the problem of paying for it. Without the huge cost of the war, the main postwar colonial grievances could not have arisen in just the way that they did. If the war had been less expensive, Great Britain would not have piled up an enormous debt. If Great Britain had not piled up such a debt, it would have been less likely to tax the American colonies. If the colonies had not been taxed, they would have had less incentive to defy and ultimately to rebel against British policy and jurisdiction. The American Revolution could have happened without the Seven Years' War, but not in the same way and at the same time.

· 4 ·

The colonial behavior in the war also helped to prepare the way for future events.

The conduct of this war was unlike any other the colonies had ever engaged in. For one thing, a British commander in chief took charge of the entire force in all the colonies. Such an office had never before existed; each colony had been accustomed to raise its own militia, commanded by its own local officers—if and when it was raised at all, and then always for limited periods and specific purposes, determined in advance by the colonial assemblies. To the colonists, royal governors were bad enough, but they were at least restricted to individual colonies. The war demanded a much greater central control from London. As never before, the highest British authorities, from the king down, were preoccupied with the affairs of the colonies.

The British military system was unsuited to colonial conditions. British soldiers were sent across the ocean to fight in the American backwoods, to which their training was ill-adapted. The British army was still organized by the contract system—regiments were raised by higher officers, generally of distinguished lineage, who did the recruiting in return for a money bounty for each recruit. Commissions were sold. Promotions were purchased. Mercenaries were hired. Released debtors, pardoned criminals, and impressed paupers and vagrants filled the lower ranks. The system was both extremely expensive and absurdly inefficient.

Thousands of British officers and soldiers were given a unique opportunity to see for themselves what the American cities and countryside, homes and workshops, were like. If the British needed any more convincing about the alleged affluence and progress of the colonies, many of them had only to keep their eyes open. Among the most impressed were British officers, who were wined and dined by the wealthier colonial hostesses.

A colonial pamphleteer later regretfully explained why some British officers and visitors wondered why they had to support such rich colonies:

> During the war, we had great intercourse with England—officers of the army were continually passing and repassing, many of them sons of the best families. Gentlemen on their travels extended their routs [*sic*] to America; and even Peers of the realm landed on our shores. Flushed with the joy of victory, and pleased with the men by whom we conquered, we lavished the fruits of industry in social banquets. We displayed a parade of *wealth* beyond the bounds of moderation and prudence; and suffered our guests to depart with *high ideas of our riches*—these were communicated to their friends at home, and the tale went around.[15]

In one of his postwar pamphlets, John Dickinson alluded to the war period:

> We are informed, that an opinion has been industriously propagated in *Great-Britain,* that the colonies are wallowing in wealth and luxury, while she is labouring under an enormous load of debt. Never was there a greater mistake. This opinion has arisen from slight observations made in our cities during the late war, when large sums of money were spent here in support of fleets and armies. Our productions were then in great demand, and trade flourished. Having a number of strangers among us, the people naturally not ungenerous or inhospitable, indulged themselves in many uncommon expenses. But the cause of this gaiety has ceased, and all the effect remaining is, that we are to be treated as rich people, when we are really poor.[16]

[15] A Citizen of Philadelphia [Richard Wells], *A Few Political Reflections Submitted to the Consideration of the British Colonies* (Philadelphia, 1774), p. 32 (italics in original).

[16] *The Late Regulations respecting the British Colonies on the Continent of America considered* (Philadelphia, 1765), in *The Writings of John Dickinson,* ed. Paul Leicester Ford (Historical Society of Pennsylvania, 1895), vol. 1, pp. 232–33.

The first historian of the American Revolution, William Gordon, later identified those Dickinson called the "strangers among us" for whom the colonists had run up such "uncommon expenses":

> The disposition to tax the *Americans*, unless they would tax themselves equal to the wishes of the ministry, was undoubtedly strengthened by the reports of their gaiety and luxury, which reached the mother country; it was also said, that the planters lived like princes, while the inhabitants of *Britain* laboured hard for a tolerable subsistence. The officers lately returned, represented them as rich, wealthy, and even overgrown in fortune.[17]

Judging from what Lord Loudoun, the first British commander in chief, told William Pitt about New Jersey during the war, the southern planters were not the only ones who made such an impression. Loudoun described the people of New Jersey as "almost whol[l]y employed in [Agri]Culture, where each Man lives in great affluence on his own Lands, and saves considerably more every Year, by which they are all Rich."[18] Whether or not the colonists were as affluent as British officers thought they were, the impression was undoubtedly widespread and became a factor in the formation of future British policy. Those who had been vaguely conscious of the progress of the colonies were now apt, at first sight, to exaggerate it. Even when they compared the colonies with conditions at home, the former came off very well.

The war was an economic bonanza for the colonies. The British themselves helped to make the war years a time of unparalleled colonial prosperity. Specie, which had always been in short supply in the colonies, became plentiful as unprecedented amounts of hard money came in to support the land and naval forces. Colonial privateers had never had such abundant and profitable pickings. Colonial merchants notoriously charged far more for providing food and supplies to the armed forces than had been customary in the local trade. Benjamin Franklin estimated that Great Britain had spent £2 or £3 million sterling per year—a massive sum—in the colonies on its fleet and army.[19]

Great Britain also reimbursed the colonies for the cost of colonial recruits.

[17] William Gordon, *The History of the Rise, Progress, and Establishment of the Independence of the United States of America* (London, 1788; New York, 1789), vol. 1, pp. 122–23.
[18] Loudoun to Pitt, April 25, 1757, in *Correspondence of William Pitt when Secretary of State with Colonial Governors*, ed. Gertrude Selwyn Kimball (Macmillan, 1906), vol. 1, p. 42. [Hereafter cited as *Pitt Correspondence with Colonial Governors.*
[19] *The Papers of Benjamin Franklin*, ed. Leonard W. Labaree (Yale University Press, 1961), vol. 9, p. 76.

This influx of money more than made up for the economic dislocation caused by the war.

· 5 ·

Dual power was nothing new in the colonies. But now it became far more manifest and flagrant as a result of the exigencies of the war. It forced itself on the attention of British commanders in chief and their superiors in London with an urgency that the problems of the governors never had. The peacetime pleas of the governors could be ignored, or governors could be recalled if they did not get along with assemblies. A war fought in the colonies was another matter. The same power that had thwarted governors could thwart British commanders, with far more serious consequences.

The full force of the wartime problem hit Loudoun. At every turn he had to come to the colonies for help or cooperation—recruits, funds, quarters, and all the needs of a partly foreign, partly local army. When Loudoun arrived in 1756, he did not fully realize what he was going to be up against. He assumed that it would be enough for a commander in chief to give orders or even to make no more than suggestions. To his astonishment and chagrin, he learned that he had to negotiate with the assemblies as if they were sovereign powers. If they wished to do what he wanted them to do, his plans might go more or less smoothly; if they disagreed with him or merely wished to assert their power of obstruction, he was virtually helpless.

A few months after arriving in the colonies, Loudoun reported what he had found to the duke of Cumberland, the king's son and head of the army: "The truth is governors here are ciphers; their predecessors sold the whole of the king's prerogative, to get their salaries; and till you find a fund, independent of the province, to pay the governors, and new model the government, you can do nothing with the provinces."[20] After a period of frustration and indecision, Loudoun decided to give way and accept a procedure which he personally detested. The war was no time to fight with the colonies as well as with the French.

For the colonies, it was a time to assert themselves more than ever before, because more was wanted from them. They were determined to fight off increased British control, even for the most exclusively military purposes. In each colony, assemblies voted whether to give Loudoun local troops and

---

[20] Loudoun to duke of Cumberland, November 11, 1756, cited by Robert Zemsky, *Merchants, Farmers, and River Gods* (Gambit, 1971), p. 99.

money. Some dictated how the troops could be used and the money spent. Loudoun found that he could only plead and cajole; he could not order or requisition. British commanders and royal governors reported piteously throughout the war on their frustrations and failures in the face of resistance and defiance by assemblies.

In Maryland, for example, the assembly voted a small sum that happened to be in the treasury for recruits on condition that they were to be used how and where the assembly itself directed. Loudoun was precluded from having even indirect control over them inside or outside the colony. Later the assembly agreed to furnish 200 men on condition that they remained in Maryland, then reconsidered and withdrew the offer.[21]

Loudoun reported to Pitt that Gov. Horatio Sharpe of Maryland and the assembly were conducting their own battle over "the Provincial Troops raised by them, the Command of which Troops, the Assembly insist on wresting out of His hands as Governor, and indeed out of the King's hands, and would take into their own hand the Sole Command and destination of them." In the same message, Loudoun complained that "the Universal plan in this Country is, to throw all Expences off themselves and lay it on the Mother Country."[22] When Governor Sharpe asked the assembly to pay the garrison at Fort Cumberland with provincial funds, the assembly refused and, Loudoun reported, "not only insisted on our Troops being withdrawn from Fort Cumberland, but likewise" that none of them "should be subject to any account whatever to the Commands of the Earl of Loudoun or any other of His Majesty's generals." The Maryland dispute was resolved when Loudoun capitulated and gave assurances that he would "make good the Expences" of keeping the garrison at Fort Cumberland, which would otherwise have fallen to the enemy. Brig. Gen. John Forbes subsequently informed Pitt that "I can have but very little dependence of Maryland doing any Good for the Service."[23]

The same sort of losing battle with the local assembly was fought in Pennsylvania. Loudoun's successor, Maj. Gen. Jeffrey Amherst, told Pitt that he had done his best to persuade the Speaker of the Assembly and some of its principal members to pass a "supply bill," but that they were determined to refuse. He was forced to violate his instructions in order to get any bill passed, otherwise "not a Man could be raised and the remains of the 1400 Men supposed to be kept up would be disbanded in a weeks

[21] Eugene Irving McCormac, *Colonial Opposition to Imperial Authority During the French and Indian War* (University of California Press, 1914), pp. 69–71.

[22] *Correspondence of William Pitt with Colonial Governors*, vol. 1, pp. 185–87.

[23] Ibid., p. 236.

time."[24] Gen. John Stanwix later had to make a deal with the Pennsylvania assembly by agreeing that the assembly "have tack'd on to This Bill, some favourite Clauses of their Own."[25]

In Virginia, only vagrants or those with no means of support or employment could be enlisted for duty outside the colony. Forbes so lost his patience with recruits from both Pennsylvania and Virginia that he wrote to Pitt:

> I vainly at the beginning flattered myself that some very good Service might be drawn from Virginia, & Pennsylvania Forces, but am sorry to find that a few of their principal Officers excepted, all the rest are an extream bad Collection of broken Innkeepers, Horse Jockeys, & Indian Traders, and that the Men under them, are a direct copy of their Officers, nor can it well be otherwise, as they are gathering from the scum of the worst of people, in every Country, who have wrought themselves up, into a panick at the very name of Indians who at the same time are more infamous Cowards, than any other race of mankind.[26]

The case of Massachusetts was particularly significant, because it concerned the authority of the British Parliament to determine the conditions for fighting the war. Loudoun had to apply to Gov. Thomas Pownall to obtain quarters for one of his battalions. Pownall directed the recruiting officers to apply to the local magistrates. The magistrates refused to provide quarters for a reason crucial to the whole subsequent history of the colonial challenge to British rule. They replied that "the Act of Parliament on this Point, did not extend to America, and that there was no Law of this province impowring [sic] them to Billet Soldiers, told the Officers that they could not be justified in doing it, by Law, and refused to do it." Loudoun insisted. Pownall backed Loudoun with a strong message to the Massachusetts legislature. Under pressure, the two houses passed a bill permitting quartering of the troops. But the last word was said by the legislature, not by Parliament, Pownall, or Loudoun.[27]

If the outcome had been all that mattered, Loudoun should have been satisfied. He was not. In principle, it had been a Pyrrhic victory for him. Loudoun had taken the position that "the Act of Parliament in the Article of Quarters doth extend to North America." In that case, he did not need the act of the Massachusetts legislature to get quarters for his troops. The

[24] Ibid., vol. 2, p. 88.
[25] Ibid., pp. 130–31.
[26] Ibid., vol. 1, p. 342.
[27] Ibid., pp. 128–29.

incident—and there were many more of the same kind—confirmed the colonial contention that the writ of the British Parliament did not extend to the colonies and that an act of Parliament could be enforced only if the colonial legislature independently enacted it or something similar. The issue was not whether the troops should be quartered; it was agreed that they had to be quartered somewhere. The dispute was simply and solely over the decision-making power. Where was it—in London or in Boston? If the latter in the case of quartering troops in wartime, what else was excluded from the writ of Parliament? Was a parliamentary act valid only if and when it was countersigned by a colonial assembly?

These questions were implicit in the stand taken by the Massachusetts legislature that an act of Parliament on the quartering of troops did not apply to the colonies. Loudoun reluctantly accepted the practical way out of the impasse through the mediation of Governor Pownall, who had put enough pressure on the Massachusetts legislature to get it to accede independently. Most of the differences between the commanders in chief and the colonial authorities were settled similarly. Nevertheless, the crucial issue of power or decision making was raised during the Seven Years' War in a way that could not be evaded forever. The overhanging question after the war was bound to be whether a showdown could be postponed for very much longer.

The reports to London show that British commanders and governors realized full well what was at stake. Gov. James Hamilton of Pennsylvania informed Pitt that he had been obliged "to do violence to my own Judgment, and to make a Sacrifice both of the property, and just powers of Government of the Proprietary's of this Province to the Assembly, who would take no steps towards forwarding the Service recommended, but at the price of obtaining the most unjust advantages over their Proprietaries, with whom they are contending."[28] Gov. Pownall wrote: "Such is the defective State of the Governments that there cannot on the Continent be produced an instance of the Governors being able to carry his Majesty's Instructions into Execution where the People have disputed them."[29] Gov. Benning Wentworth of New Hampshire complained: "At present I have his Majesties Commission and Instruction for my Government, and direction, but from the incroachments Made by the Assembly, both are in a manner Rendered useless."[30] By September 1756, Loudoun concluded that the war would have to be fought and won from England—"the King must trust in this country

[28] Ibid., vol. 2, p. 276.

[29] Cited by Jack P. Greene, "The Seven Years' War and the American Revolution: The Causal Relationship Reconsidered," in *The British Atlantic Empire Before the American Revolution,* ed. Peter Marshall and Glyn Williams (Frank Case, 1980), p. 87.

[30] Ibid.

to himself, and those he sends . . . for this Country will not run when he calls."[31]

An economic war of nerves was also waged between the British authorities and the colonial trading interests. War or no war, New England traders were determined to continue the interchange with the French sugar islands in the West Indies. For the New Englanders, that trade was still an economic necessity. From the British standpoint, it was trading with the enemy. Colonial vessels delivered foodstuffs to the French islands, including supplies for French warships. The profit on the trade was apparently even greater than in peacetime.

As the war dragged on, this trade came to impress the British war leaders as little short of treason. In 1757, Loudoun denounced the "lawless set of smugglers, who continually supply the Enemy with What Provisions they want, and bring back their goods in Barter for them."[32] Two years later, a British vice admiral condemned the "vile Illicit Trade" as "infamous and barefaced."[33] Pitt himself could stand it no longer. In 1760, the last effective year of the American war, he complained bitterly against an "illegal and most pernicious Trade," carried on by Americans with the French enemy, "supplying with Provisions, and other Necessaries, whereby they are, principally, if not alone, enabled to sustain, and protract, this long and expensive War." He ordered "the most speedy and effectual Stop to such flagitious Practices, so utterly subversive of all Law, and so repugnant to the Honor, and well-being of this Kingdom."[34]

By the end of 1757, Loudoun had lost the confidence of Pitt, who was displeased by Loudoun's backers in London, some of his decisions in the field, and his difficulties with the colonial authorities. Pitt wanted to raise large bodies of provincial troops to wage the war, which required giving way to the colonies. He introduced a system of paying for provincial troops, which the assemblies then voted for. The cost of the war was immensely increased, but the enrollment of colonial troops went forward. Nevertheless, in 1758 the British Army in North America consisted of some 20,000 regulars, "nearly independent of provincial aid in provisioning, transport, and scouting." Provincials fought in 1759 and 1760, but for the most part they acted as a workforce, mainly repairing and building forts and roads.[35]

[31] Loudoun to Sir Charles Hardy, September 16, 1756, cited by Stanley McCrory Pargellis, *Lord Loudoun in North America* (Yale University Press, 1933), p. 186.

[32] Lawrence Henry Gipson, *The British Empire Before the American Revolution* (Alfred A. Knopf, 1953), vol. 8, p. 82.

[33] Ibid., p. 81.

[34] *Correspondence of William Pitt with Colonial Governors*, vol. 2, pp. 320–21.

[35] Pargellis, *Lord Loudoun in North America*, pp. 354–55.

The contribution of the colonies to the war effort varied. Massachusetts, Connecticut, and Virginia did the most. Some other colonies, such as South and North Carolina and Pennsylvania, did little more than defend their own borders. British regulars did more for New York and New Jersey than the colonies did for themselves. One review of the colonial contribution concluded that "the record of Connecticut is perhaps the most highly creditable, while that of Maryland is without question the least so."[36] On the whole, the northern colonies did the most, the southern colonies the least. All of them put together contributed far less than the British regular forces, who were responsible for most of the offensive warfare against the French in Canada.

Historians have recognized that the controversies during the Seven Years' War prefigured those after the war. One study pointed out: "The grounds upon which the colonists claimed exemption from British taxation and restrictions in the later period were by no means new; they had been asserted again and again in substantially the same terms during the war with France. The conditions in the two periods were similar and they called forth similar ideas, protests, and demands on the part of the Americans."[37] Loudoun's biographer gives this explanation for his behavior:

He failed to realize that each of these popularly-chosen groups was in its own way as immovable, as potent, as parliament, and was already hide-bound by a set of precedents of its own making which yielded to no authority. They were all dedicated to the continuance of a struggle in which they had already registered far more gains than losses, the advancement of their powers at the expense of the Crown. When Loudoun loomed on their horizons, they were by tradition and temperament forced to regard him, the Crown's supreme military representative, as much of a foe to their constitutional advancement as any governor had ever been, and they employed the same tactics which had won them success before.[38]

To some extent, the colonies had been fighting a two-front war. They had contributed to the common cause in unequal measure, depending on how close each one was to the enemy. Whatever they did, they were determined to do it on their own terms. When their interests conflicted with what the British wanted, they held out tenaciously, by passive resistance as well as by

[36] Lawrence Henry Gipson, *The British Empire Before the American Revolution* (Alfred A. Knopf, 1949), vol. 7, p. 328.
[37] McCormac, *Colonial Opposition to Imperial Authority*, p. 2.
[38] Pargellis, *Lord Loudoun in North America*, p. 170.

outright opposition. The French were external enemies—but not so much that it was impermissible to trade with them. The British were made to feel as if they were internal enemies whenever they wanted something the colonies were unwilling to give. Above all, the colonies were unwilling to give up any of their rights and privileges, even if their recalcitrance meant impeding the war effort and driving the British commanders to distraction.

The British experience in the colonies during the war strongly influenced British policy after the war. It seems to have taught the British lessons that proved costly to themselves in the postwar period. One was that the colonies could not be depended on to defend themselves, even in the greatest danger to their own safety and well-being. Another was that every colony was interested only in its own self-interest and could not be persuaded to unite with the others, whatever the extremity. Only a British initiative, it was believed, could make the colonies act together.

British commanders were little impressed with the fighting quality of the colonial recruits. One of the most disparaging was Gen. James Wolfe, the hero of Louisbourg and Quebec, whose opinion of his colonial troops was scathing. "The Americans," he said, "are in general the dirtiest, most contemptible cowardly dogs that you can conceive. There is no depending on them in action. They fall down dead in their own dirt and desert by battalions, officers and all. Such rascals as those are rather an encumbrance than any real strength to any army."[39] Yet Wolfe also thought that "this will, some time hence, be a vast empire, the seat of power and learning."[40] Evidently two such ideas could exist in the same British head in the late 1750s. Colonial soldiers paid back the British by regarding them as hidebound and smug, better on parade than in primitive colonial conditions.

On both sides, these lessons were not without foundation. But they were gained in a war in which Britons and Americans were willy-nilly fighting together, with the former in command and paying most of the bills. The British were in for quite a few surprises when they tried to apply what they thought they had learned before and during the war to the struggles that arose between them and the colonies afterwards.

· 6 ·

We have come full circle from where we began. We started with the "pamphlet war" of 1759–1761, which raised the question whether it was

[39] Lawrence Shaw Mayo, *Jeffrey Amherst* (Longmans, Green, 1916), p. 108.
[40] Beckles Willson, *The Life and Letters of James Wolfe* (Heinemann, 1909), p. 395.

in the British interest to end the Seven Years' War by requiring France to give up the sugar island of Guadeloupe or the fur-bearing expanse of Canada. Great Britain had come out of the fighting with both, but the dominant ministers in the cabinet decided that they could not demand both from a France that was weakened and tired but not by any means knocked out. The issue was complicated by the presumed effect that a choice between Guadeloupe and Canada would have on the British colonies in North America.

Out of this debate arose a related historical question: To what extent was the outcome of the Seven Years' War responsible for the American Revolution? A brief review of some opinions from the time of the war itself to the middle of the twentieth century shows what a long tradition there is of binding the two events together.

During the Seven Years' War, the marquis de la Capellis, a high French official, continued the French tradition of predicting that the British would not be able to keep their North American colonies if the French were driven out of Canada. In 1758, he declared that a British conquest of Canada "would be one more cause acting to hasten her ruin by favouring the defection of her colonies in North America." He thought that the colonies "will soon be richer than Old England and will undoubtedly shake off the yoke of the mother country."[41]

This line of thought was similar to the view of a London newspaper on the eve of the Revolution that

> while a foreign enemy, indeed, was at their backs, they affected a prodigious deal of loyalty to the present state; but the moment their fears on that head were removed by the cession of all Canada to Great Britain, that moment the dutiful colonies began to change their tone; America was no longer *ours,* but *theirs;* the champions for *Constitutional Rights* would no longer obey the voice of the *Constitution;* from petitions which we could not grant, they proceeded to acts of outrage which we could not overlook.[42]

A British pamphleteer the following year put the case in much the same way:

> Had Canada remained in the hands of the French, the Colonies

[41] Cited by Guy Fregault, *Canada: The War of the Conquest,* trans. Margaret M. Cameron (Oxford University Press, 1969), pp. 231–32.

[42] From a letter signed "Poor Old England" in *Morning Chronicle,* July 1, 1775, in *English Historical Documents, 1714–1783,* ed. D. B. Horn and Mary Ransome (Eyre & Spottiswoode, 1957), vol. 10, p. 761.

would have remained dutiful subjects. Their fears for themselves, in that case, would have supplied the place of their pretended affection for this Nation. They would have spoken more sparingly of their own resources, as they might daily stand in need of our aid. Their former incapacity of defending themselves would have always recurred to their minds, as long as the objects of their former terror should continue so near their borders. But their habitual fears from France were, it seems, removed only to give room to their ingratitude to Great Britain.[43]

Francis Parkman later made the same point in the strongest terms:

More than one clear eye saw, at the middle of the last century, that the subjection of Canada would lead to a revolt of the British colonies. So long as an active and enterprising enemy threatened their borders, they could not break with the mother-country, because they needed her help. . . . If, by diplomacy or war, she [France] had preserved but half, or less than the half, of her American possessions, then a barrier would have been set to the spread of the English-speaking races; there would have been no Revolutionary War; and for a long time, no independence.[44]

In the mid-twentieth century, a distinguished American historian, Lawrence Henry Gipson, arrived at a similar point of view:

In fact, it would seem that the very magnitude of the victory won by the British in the course of this war . . . laid the sure foundation for future American independence. . . . Now, at last freed from the age-long menace of foreign foes along their borders, these men [of British America]. . . . were stirred with the vision of a great future on the North American continent and of a high mission that must not be denied them.[45]

Another eminent American historian, Arthur Schlesinger, asked how it came about that the colonies, relatively isolated from one another, were able to unite against the British policies of 1764–65. He answered that the basic factor was "the ousting of France from North America by the Peace of 1763. By eliminating England's ancient enemy as

43 [James Macpherson?], *The Rights of Great Britain Asserted Against the Claims of America: Being an Answer to the Declaration of the General Congress* (London, 4th ed., 1776), pp. 15–16.

44 Francis Parkman, *Montcalm and Wolfe* (orig. ed., 1884), from the Introduction.

45 Lawrence Henry Gipson, *British Empire Before the American Revolution* (Alfred A. Knopf, 1946), vol. 6, p. 18.

an ever-present danger it not only weakened the colonists' sense of military dependence on the homeland but also their sense of political dependence."[46]

And on the British side, a notable historian also of this century, Sir Lewis Namier, believed that "with the removal of the French, the road to independence, and even to a French alliance against Great Britain, was opened for the Colonies."[47]

These views from so many sources of the connection between the Seven Years' War and the American Revolution cannot be lightly dismissed. They are based on an assessment of long-term factors that antedated the immediate differences which arose between Great Britain and the American colonies in the mid-1760s. These factors recalled the basis of the "pamphlet war" of 1759–1761, which dealt with the increased population, expanded trade, and augmented self-confidence of the colonies. They went back to Maj. John Child's thought in the mid-seventeenth century that New England's boasts of growth would lead to "high thoughts of themselves" and bring them ultimately to see themselves as "a state," and to James Harrington's idea at about the same time that colonies would come of age and wean themselves. In this view, the French threat in Canada had held the Americans back from asserting themselves because they needed British protection. With the French gone, the Americans were sure to find reasons to throw off the British mantle and declare their independence.

Yet the future was not so simple. If the elimination of the French threat was all that was needed to break down the dependence of the colonies on Great Britain, the Revolution should have come soon after the war. Instead, it waited for fifteen years of tense and tumultuous crises. There was no simple transition from the Seven Years' War to the American Revolution. The early American historian David Ramsay thought that "the rapid increase of their numbers, and extension of their commerce" needed only a "spark" to set the "combustible material" on fire. Grievances had not been lacking for a long time, but grievances by themselves do not determine how seriously they will be regarded or whether they will be pushed as far as a conflict. Whatever the particular inequities, compensating advantages and inhibiting factors also prevailed. What changed markedly through the

[46] Arthur M. Schlesinger, *Prelude to Independence* (Alfred A. Knopf, 1958), p. 55.
[47] Lewis Namier, *England in the Age of the American Revolution* (St. Martin's Press, 1930; 2d ed., 1961), pp. 281–82.

Seven Years' War was the power relations between Great Britain and the colonies. The French threat had given the British a preponderance of power over the Americans without the British having done anything to earn it. The Revolution had to wait for a further change in this relationship of power, when special grievances could seem to be unacceptable to the colonial political consciousness.

What may be said with confidence is that the outcome of the Seven Years' War was a necessary but not a sufficient condition for the American Revolution. Other things had to happen after the war for a "spark" to set the "combustible material" on fire.

9

''The *winners*
and the *losers*''

· 1 ·

IF THE END OF THE Seven Years' War opened the road to the Revolution, the road still had to be traveled. Fifteen years intervened between the effective end of the war in North America in 1760 and the violent outbreak of the Revolution in 1775. As it happened, the opening of the revolutionary era was long believed to have come in 1760 or 1761. It was supposedly located in the writs of assistance case, as described by John Adams, who first made it the beginning of "the resistance to the British system for subjugating the colonies." He dated the start of resistance as 1760, though he was inconsistent and also put it in 1761.[1] The earliest histories of the American Revolution by contemporaries mentioned it in different ways.[2]

---

[1] "The resistance to the British system for subjugating the colonies, began in 1760" (Adams to William Wirt, January 5, 1818, in *The Works of John Adams,* ed. Charles Francis Adams, Boston, 1861, vol. 10, p. 272). "The commencement of their disputes with Great Britain, in 1761" (Adams to the abbé de Mably, 1782, vol. 5, p. 492). Adams sometimes used both dates, as in his letter to H. Niles, February 13, 1818, vol. 10, p. 282.

[2] The first history by William Gordon says: "From this period may be dated, the fixed, uniform, and growing opposition, which was made to the ministerial plans of encroaching upon the original rights and long established customs of the colony" (*The History of the Rise, Progress, and Establishment of the Independence of the United States of America,* vol. 1, p. 113). M. H. Smith, *The Writs of Assistance Case* (University of California Press, 1978), thinks that Gordon was probably influenced by Adams (p. 236). Ramsay's history does not mention it at all and starts with 1764. Mercy Warren's history of 1805 also ignores it and starts with 1765.

Adams's version was enshrined in the mid-nineteenth century in George Bancroft's history, in which the case was described as the first dim outline of America's "vision of her own independence."[3]

In essence, the case was fairly simple. A writ of assistance was a legal directive enabling a customs officer to get assistance in making an arrest. Smuggling and other illegal practices were old English customs, which the writs were intended to combat. A parliamentary act had introduced such writs in England in 1662, and another parliamentary act had applied them to America in 1696. Customs officials particularly needed help to conduct searches for illicit goods hidden in homes or other private buildings, traditionally regarded as privileged sanctuaries.

Such writs had not been used by customs officials in the colonies for over half a century, because it had been customary for the officials to conduct searches on their own authority. In 1756, however, they were required to get authorization from the Superior Court in Massachusetts. Only seven such writs had been issued between 1756 and 1760. In the latter year, however, a group of over sixty leading merchants and shippers brought an action challenging the writs of assistance for the first time. All or most of the plaintiffs were known to deal in smuggled goods in a colony where smuggling was a way of business, if not of life.

Smuggling was big business. British Treasury officials estimated the annual value of European manufactures smuggled into North America at nearly £500,000.[4] What was most irksome to the American merchant-smugglers was that they had for years been happily carrying on a smuggling trade with Europe, the Caribbean, and wherever their ships could reach, without risk until the unexpected crackdown represented by the toughened writs of assistance. An outstanding smuggler, William Cooper, later one of the most active merchants in important patriot committees, complained to a correspondent in 1768: "You know what has been called an illicit trade has been wink'd at by all former Administrations, it being eventually more profitable to Britain than the Colonies. . . . We feel for our Mother Country as well as for our selves, but charity begins at home."[5]

In 1760, however, William Pitt had ordered governors to enforce the laws against "this dangerous and ignominious Trade" and bring "such

---

[3] George Bancroft, *History of the United States*, (Little, Brown, 1852), vol. 4, pp. 415–19. Bancroft, however, had some qualms and put in a long footnote that admitted Adams "in his extreme old age" had conflated recollections from 1761 to 1766 (pp. 416–17). Bancroft was preceded by William Tudor in his *Life of James Otis* (Boston, 1823), which closely followed Adams's letters to Tudor.

[4] John W. Tyler, *Smugglers and Patriots* (Northeastern University Press, 1986), p. 13.

[5] Ibid., p. 17.

heinous Offenders to the most exemplary and condign Punishment."[6] As Gov. Stephen Hopkins of Rhode Island, who was just such a merchant, explained to Pitt, the colonies engaged in illicit trade because they produced too much flour, beef, and other products to be consumed by themselves, and, anyway, their profits enabled them to buy more British manufactures.[7] Little guilt was attached to smuggling in the colonies, because they thought it was a method of survival and because it indirectly benefited the British as well as themselves.

Thus the case contained the basic elements of later causes célèbres. The law had been on the books for a long time and had applied equally to Great Britain and America. What made it obnoxious was that it was now going to be enforced. In addition, the newly appointed chief justice of the Massachusetts Superior Court, in charge of the writs, was Thomas Hutchinson, who was also lieutenant governor and probate judge. He was already considered by other aspiring personalities and families to have too much personal and family power. One rival family, the Otises, believed that Col. James Otis, Sr., had been cheated out of the appointment as chief justice.

The plaintiffs were represented by two of the most eminent lawyers in the colony, Oxenbridge Thacher and James Otis, Jr., the latter a son of the colonel. The issue was apparently technical. Thacher, the senior advocate, argued that the Superior Court did not have jurisdiction, because it was not a court of exchequer. Otis took a different line of attack. He did not question the validity of writs of assistance as such; he questioned the existing writ on the ground that it was general, not specific. The distinction came about because customs officials were accustomed to ask for the authority to make use of writs at their discretion for the duration of a monarch's reign. Since George III had ascended the throne in 1760, it had been necessary for the collector of customs in Salem and Marblehead to ask for a renewal of the general writ. When the case was brought before the Superior Court in February 1761, Otis's argument basically rested on a mistaken assumption—that general writs in America conflicted with British practice. He was thus led to plead his case in large part as if he were defending the true fundamentals of British law rather than mounting an American campaign against them. When it turned out that he had been misled about the British denial of general writs, his case fell apart, and the ultimate verdict at a second hearing in November 1761 went against him

[6] *Correspondence of William Pitt with Colonial Governors,* ed. Gertrude Selwyn Kimball (Macmillan, 1906), vol. 2, pp. 320–21.

[7] Ibid., p. 377.

and Thacher. Once the case was settled, commercial life went on as usual in Massachusetts, and no more protests against the writs were registered.

Yet, owing to John Adams, the case was long considered the spark that set off the prerevolutionary process. Twenty-five years old, Adams was then a law student and attended the trial as part of his apprenticeship. He hurriedly jotted down some notes as the lawyers argued both sides of the issue. These notes were skimpy, garbled, and at times unintelligible, as such notes tend to be. Some weeks later, Adams composed a longer version of his original notes, a so-called abstract, in which he clearly jumbled fact and literary embellishment.[8] Decades later, in his old age, he told the story again and again, adding more and more frills and flourishes, now obviously incapable of separating fact from fiction.

Besides Adams's version of the proceedings, there is another by Chief Justice Hutchinson. He gave the case a strictly legal interpretation, based on the argument over general versus special writs of assistance. Nothing in Hutchinson's brief summary would lend itself to an incipiently revolutionary challenge to British rule by Otis.[9] The entire burden of evidence for it rests on Adams's original notes and later "Abstract."

The only semblance of such a challenge in the original notes rested on a single sentence, which, taken out of context, could be made to anticipate the colonial rejection of parliamentary authority. It read: "As to Acts of Parliament, an Act against the Constitution is void: an Act against natural Equity is void: and if an Act of Parliament should be made, in the very Words of this Petition, it would be void."

But these assertions did not challenge British legal doctrine, which had never held that acts of Parliament could violate the "Constitution" or "natural Equity," whatever they might mean in this context. When Adams came to write the "Abstract," however, he gave Otis much stronger language. He now had Otis calling these writs "instruments of slavery on the one hand, and villainy on the other," "the worst instrument of arbitrary power, the most destructive of English liberty, and the fundamental principles of the constitution, that ever was found in an English law-book." Otis supposedly said that he was arguing "in favour

---

[8] Adams's "Abstract" presents a difficult—if not impossible—problem of how much can be accepted as Otis's original speech and how much Adams's later embellishment. Since there is no other record like Adams's, the point remains moot. In his magisterial work, M. H. Smith comments that the abstract filled out the "skeletal fragments" in the original notes to "almost unrecognizable transfiguration" (*Writs of Assistance Case*, p. 246).

[9] Thomas Hutchinson, *The History of the Colony and Province of Massachusetts-Bay*, ed. Lawrence Shaw Mayo (Harvard University Press, 1936), vol. 3, pp. 67–68. [Hereafter cited as *Hutchinson's History*.]

of British liberty." The parliamentary passage in the notes was repeated in shortened form: "No Acts of Parliament can establish such a writ: Though it should be made in the very words of the petition it would be void."

Except for the overheated rhetoric, there is still nothing in this expanded version that remotely resembles a challenge to British sovereignty or an incipient call for American independence. If there had been, it would presumably have attracted a great deal of attention at the time. But the trial went totally unreported in the Boston press, and only the final verdict in November 1761 was noted, without any fanfare. It even passed almost completely unrecorded in the records of the Superior Court.[10] If the case was as pivotal and had such a thunderous effect on him as Adams later claimed, it could be expected to appear in the diary which he kept at the time. In the diary, however, he made only one reference to it in all of 1761, and it hardly bears out his later enthusiasm.[11] Adams himself later told Mercy Warren, the sister of James Otis and author of an early revolutionary history, that the case would have been forgotten if he had not made notes.[12] Yet in later years Adams also claimed that the case "made a deep impression upon the public, which never wore out"; "American independence was then and there born"; "in the month of February, 1761, James Otis electrified the town of Boston, the province of Massachusetts, and the whole continent, more than Patrick Henry did in the whole course of his life"; and "Mr. Otis's oration against *writs of assistance* breathed into this nation the breath of life."[13] The more Adams wrote about it in his old age, the more rhapsodic he became.

It has been shown that Adams was wrong in so many details that he cannot be trusted in this case.[14] Seventeen sixty was merely the year that the writ of assistance was applied for; 1761 was the year of the trial at which Otis allegedly made his portentous speech; Adams confused both events years later. He also erred in making it seem that the writs of assistance case had

[10] Smith, *Writs of Assistance Case*, pp. 171, 231, 248.

[11] The diary for April 1761 notes that Col. Josiah Quincy "saw an Abstract of the Argument for and against Writts of Assistants—and crys did you take this from those Gentlemen as they delivered it? You can do any Thing! You can do as you please! Gridley did not use that Language. He never was Master of such a style! It is not in him—&c" (*The Diary and Autobiography of John Adams*, ed. L. H. Butterfield, Harvard University Press, 1961, p. 210). Whatever this is taken to mean, it can hardly be made into a glorification of Otis's handling of the case.

[12] Correspondence between John Adams and Mercy Warren, *Massachusetts Historical Society Collections*, 5th ser., vol. 4, p. 355. Adams was displeased because the case had been left out of Warren's *History of the Rise, Progress and Termination of the American Revolution* (Boston, 1805). This was the third history of the American Revolution, after Gordon and Ramsay.

[13] Adams to Mr. Calkoen, October 4, 1780 (*Works of John Adams*, vol. 7, p. 266); Adams to William Tudor, March 29, 1817, vol. 10, p. 247; Adams to William Wirt, January 5, 1818, vol. 10, p. 272; Adams to H. Niles, January 14, 1818, vol. 10, p. 276.

[14] By M. H. Smith in his *Writs of Assistance Case*.

come up because orders had been sent from England telling customhouse officers to apply for them; writs had been used previously, though not in great numbers, and no such orders had been sent. The writs had little or nothing to do with the later issue of taxation; they were simply a means of enforcing the existing laws against smuggling.

Yet the case cannot be totally ignored, if only because of the fame which it enjoyed for so long. If nothing else, it is an example of revolutionary mythology and a warning against taking every word of the Founders as holy writ. For all his great abilities and immense contribution, Adams was a man of enthusiasms and eccentricities. He was bent on giving James Otis the honor of having initiated the revolutionary process, though Otis did not need this inflated reputation and soon earned his distinction fairly, without Adams's help. In fact, Francis Bernard, who came to Massachusetts as governor in 1760, thought the colony at that time was unusually loyal. "This people," he informed the Board of Trade, "are better disposed to observe their contract with the Crown than any other on the continent that I know."[15] He had been governor of New Jersey and had some basis of comparison.

Still, the case represented a minor effort on the part of Massachusetts's merchants, accustomed to the profits of smuggling, to challenge a restraint on their trade. Customs officials by themselves were virtually helpless searching for smuggled goods; they were far more dangerous if they could get assistance. In this sense, the merchants were trying to protect themselves against an official threat to their way of doing business.

One of Adams's reconstructions of the case shows how he rewrote the past to fit in with the future of colonial resistance:

Suffice it to say, that immediately upon the conquest of Canada from the French in the year 1759, Great Britain seemed to be seized with a jealousy against the Colonies, and then concerted the plan of changing their forms of government, of restraining their trade within narrower bounds, and raising a revenue within them by authority of parliament, for the avowed or pretended purpose of protecting, securing, and defending them. Accordingly, in the year 1760, orders were sent from the board of trade in England to the custom-house officers in America, to apply to the supreme courts of justice for writs of assistance to enable them to carry into a more rigorous execution certain acts of parliament called the acts of trade (among which the famous act of navigation was one, the fruit of the ancient English

[15] John Gorham Palfrey, *History of New England* (Little, Brown, 1905), vol. 5, p. 225.

jealousy of Holland) by breaking open houses, ships, or cellars, chests, stores, and magazines, to search for uncustomed goods.[16]

This explanation significantly ties the new British "jealousy against the Colonies" to the British conquest of Canada. That "jealousy" antedated 1759—the capture of Quebec—but took a different turn by 1760, as the Guadeloupe versus Canada pamphlets show. There were, however, no such orders from the Board of Trade, and, in fact, there had been recourse to writs of assistance as early as 1755.[17]

Yet James Otis was a great innovator. John Adams merely gave him too much credit for the wrong achievement. Otis may or may not have been responsible for the first protorevolutionary ideas in 1761, but he was certainly the one who gave them their earliest expression in 1762.

· 2 ·

James Otis was both the first and the strangest of the great prerevolutionary spokesmen. He was a descendant of one of the first settlers, with four generations of Otises behind him. His father, known as Col. James Otis, was primarily engaged in commerce and practiced law on the side. As Speaker of the House of Representatives, he was someone to be reckoned with politically. He had apparently set his heart on getting an appointment to the Superior Court as a further sign of rising political and social status. When an allegedly promised appointment to a vacancy did not come through in 1760, he was said to have turned against the "court party" of the governor, Francis Bernard, and to have conceived a deep enmity for the successful candidate, Thomas Hutchinson. Gossip linked the father's grievances with the son's zeal in taking on antiestablishment causes.

Whatever the reason, the political disaffection of James Otis, Jr., came about suddenly. He had received the best American education of the time at Harvard College. By temperament and inclination, he seems to have been a scholarly type, but, like so many of his background, he had turned to the law to support himself. In 1760, the same year as the political storm over his father's failed appointment to the Superior Court and the preliminary legal action against the writs of assistance, he brought out a book, *The Rudiments of Latin Prosody*, for use in Latin schools. A similar work on Greek prosody

---

[16] Adams to Mr. Calkoen, October 4, 1780, *Works of John Adams,* vol. 7, p. 267.
[17] Joseph R. Frese, "James Otis and Writs of Assistance," *New England Quarterly,* December 1957, p. 496.

was never published. As late as 1760, he also served as advocate general in the Massachusetts court system, a post which required him to argue cases on behalf of the provincial government. He resigned this office when he decided to take on the merchants' case against the writs of assistance. Thus his career seems to have changed course abruptly sometime at the end of 1760 or the beginning of 1761. Whatever the reason, the case for the first time plunged him into partisan politics. Whether or not it created the kind of sensation ascribed to it by John Adams, it probably helped to get Otis elected to the House of Representatives in May 1762.

Otis's social and political position indicates that this early resistance was no incipient rebellion by the lowly and oppressed. He represented a colonial elite that was already high in the political and social scale and wished to go higher. Except for the unfulfilled ambition of his father, which the son allegedly swore to avenge, no other reason for his headlong political about-face of 1760–61 has ever been offered or appears from the circumstances of his previous life. As a lawyer, he could have been expected to defend the commercial interests which were chafing at what they took to be unwarranted British interference in the way they had been accustomed to do business. The younger Otis, however, was no mere legal mouthpiece. He was capable of giving his advocacy an ideological cast that set him apart in the controversies in which he was engaged.

Other ambitious colonial politicians had long made careers representing the popular cause in assemblies against royal governors and their appointees. If Otis had done no more than this in his first year in the House of Representatives, he would not have done anything particularly new or notable. It was how he went about making himself heard that made him stand out.

His chance came about as a result of another squabble, seemingly so petty that it hardly appears to have been worth the trouble. This incident does not present the problem of authentic source material that has bedeviled the writs of assistance case, because Otis had his side of the dispute published in a pamphlet in his own name that same year.

Sometime at the end of the summer of 1761, a different kind of minor crisis arose in the fishing towns of Salem and Marblehead. Governor Bernard reported that a majority of the leading merchants and fishermen in the towns had raised an alarm about the presence off the coast of a French privateer, allegedly endangering their fishing vessels. They demanded immediate protection, with the result that the governor and the provincial council agreed to send a sloop, *Massachusetts,* to cruise in the endangered waters for a maximum of one month. The sloop was outfitted, twenty-four men added to its crew, and a bounty offered to encourage enlistment for the duty. The total expense of the operation was said to have amounted in one version to no more than £300 or £400, or in another version, by Otis's biographer, to only about £72.[18]

After Otis had entered the House of Representatives the following May, the incident was raked up to embarrass the governor. In September, a committee of the assembly, already dominated by Otis, challenged the action of the governor and council in language never before employed in such a "remonstrance," as it was traditionally called. Since it was written by Otis, he took it upon himself to defend its unusual violence of expression.

The objection was not to what the governor and council had done but to how they had done it. The facts were not in dispute. Otis conceded that the governor and council "doubtless meant well as to the protection of the fishery."[19] The entire issue turned on whether they should have voted any expenditures for the sloop and its crew without prior authorization by the House of Representatives. Otis's resolution denounced any expenditure for the sloop and its crew without the assembly's prior authorization, even in an emergency, as of such enormity that "it would be of little consequence to the people whether they were subject to George or Lewis [Louis], the King of Great Britain or the French King, if both were arbitrary, as both would be if both could levy Taxes without Parliament." This coupling of the two kings, when their countries were still officially at war, was too much for Governor Bernard, who refused to accept the message until the offending words were expunged.

Otis, however, was not to be put off so easily. In his pamphlet, he spent several pages defending this alleged disrespect and making sport of the entire hubbub over it. He finally agreed to recognize that "the King of Great-Britain is the best as well as the most glorious Monarch upon the Globe, and his subjects the happiest in the universe," while "the French King is a despotic arbitrary prince, and consequently his subjects are very miserable," without, however, appearing to be contrite or apologetic.

The point of the quarrel was hardly new. Assemblies had been jealous of their sole control of public money for as long as there had been colonies. What was new was Otis's way of defending the assemblies'

---

[18] The details appear in the pamphlet by James Otis, *A Vindication of the Conduct of the House of Representatives of the Massachusetts-Bay* (Boston, 1762). A reprint was edited by Charles F. Mullett, "Some Political Writings of James Otis," *University of Missouri Studies,* July 1, 1929, pp. 13–44. A slightly different version of the events appears in *Hutchinson's History,* vol. 3, pp. 70–71, where the figures are given as £300 to £400; Otis's biographer, William Tudor, has Otis say that the figure was about £72 (*Life of James Otis,* p. 117).

[19] Mullett, "Some Political Writings of James Otis," p. 32.

asserted monopoly of financial power. He chose to make a stand on a case that stretched that power to its most extreme limits. The expenditure on behalf of the merchants and fishermen of Salem and Marblehead had been made at their demand, in an emergency, and for a relatively small sum of money. Thus Otis was forced to base his case on principle pure and simple. The practice in this affair might be inconsequential, but the principle could be made to seem all-important and incapable of compromise.

Perhaps Otis's most daring move was to introduce the term *taxes* into the controversy. Any expenditure, however small and well-meaning, he argued, "is in effect taking from the house their most darling priviledge, the right of originating all Taxes." He then made a breathtaking leap to the next charge, that "it is in short annihilating one branch of the legislature. And when once the Representatives of a people give up this Priviledge, the Government will very soon become arbitrary."

It was at this point that he injected the startling passage equating the British and French kings "if both could levy Taxes without Parliament." Here was another audacious implication—that the colonial assembly was akin to the British Parliament in its capacity to levy taxes. In a later passage, Otis made this parallel explicit: "A house of representatives here at least, bears an equal proportion to a Governor with that of a house of Commons to the King." In fact, he went on, the former was even more privileged, because a governor was merely a fellow subject, "tho' a superior, who is undoubtedly intitled to decency and respect; but I hardly think to quite so much Reverence as his master." He again came back to the parallel by calling the assembly "the great council of this province, as the British Parliament is of the Kingdom."

Extreme cases may make bad law, but they can make good politics. Otis succeeded in creating an extreme case by pushing to the furthest limits the possible violation of principle of assembly control of monetary matters. "If the Governor and Council can fit out one man of war, inlist men, grant a bounty and make establishments," he asked, "why not for a navy, if to them it shall seem necessary, and they can make themselves the sole judges of this necessity?" It was "a grievous event, a terrible misfortune, and a dreadful example to inferiors" for the governor and council to misapply money, whatever the circumstances. "All things are possible," Otis claimed, and another governor and council might take money out of the treasury and "divide and pocket it among themselves." Above all, any such appropriation represented "a tax upon every inhabitant," and if the assembly's right to originate taxes was taken away from it, its power "may be said to be annihilated" and "arbitrary" government was on its way.

Otis's denunciation changed nothing; it was only a "remonstrance" or protest. Nevertheless, it anticipated grievances and arguments that were soon to have the most serious practical consequences. The dread word *taxes* was introduced into the long-standing political tug-of-war between governors and assemblies. *Taxes* usually referred to special assessments or levies based on property stipulations or particular purchases. Otis stretched the term to refer to any appropriation from an existing treasury.

Gov. Bernard did not deny that "the business of originating the Taxes most certainly belongs to the Representatives of the People," by which he meant local, colonial-imposed taxes. But he contended that the governor and council were empowered to issue "Money out of the Treasury." As a result, he pleaded: "When this Distinction is considered; how can this Act, whether right or wrong, be applied to the Right of originating Taxes, annihilating one Branch of the Legislature and making the Government arbitrary?" The distinction was never cleared up, because Otis was interested in staking out a political position rather than in getting anything undone that had been done. Still, he had somehow contrived to link the assembly's control over money with the explosive issue of taxation.

Otis was thus able to raise a cry over the first half of the later revolutionary protest against "taxation without representation." The issue of representation did not arise in 1762, because an act of Parliament was not at issue and the colonists were fully represented in the assembly. Sixty-one years later, however, Otis's biographer, William Tudor, made good the lack by giving Otis credit for having laid down the maxim that "taxation without representation was tyranny."[20] It became another legend embedded in the American tradition. With somewhat greater reason, however, Tudor asserted that "this trifling expenditure may be considered as one of the preparatory causes of the Revolution."[21] He also saw that it taught the public "to look at principles, and to resist every insidious precedent inflexibly." Otis's resistance in 1762 was purely rhetorical, but he had succeeded in making a mountain of principle and precedent out of a molehill of administration and expenditure.

Otis first showed how to turn a difference over a relatively minor practical issue into an irreconcilable dispute over a major principle. He managed to aggravate the alleged official misconduct by imagining what it could lead to in the most extreme, hypothetical circumstances. In such a dispute, the final verdict could come only through a struggle for power, as Otis

---

[20] Tudor, *Life of James Otis*, p. 118.
[21] Ibid.

himself seemed to suggest. In a brief preface to his pamphlet, he made these prophetic observations:

> The world has been and will be pretty equally divided, between these two great parties, vulgarly called the *winners,* and the *losers;* or to speak more precisely between those who are discontented that they have no Power, and those who never think they can have enough.
>
> Now, it is absolutely impossible to please both sides, either by temporizing, trimming or retreating; the two former justly incur the censure of a wicked heart, the latter that of cowardice, and fairly and manfully fighting the battle out, is in the opinion of many worse than either.[22]

Thus Otis as early as 1762 had posed the decisive question of the prerevolutionary period: Was it going to be possible to appease those in the colonies who were discontented for lack of enough power and those in Great Britain who thought that they already had given up too much power to the colonies? Could a struggle for power be settled by "temporizing, trimming or retreating" or would it be necessary to fight "the battle out" to a finish? No one in the colonies at this time, when almost everyone was euphoric about the imminent peace ratifying a British-American victory in the Seven Years' War, saw so clearly and daringly ahead. Otis's insight can only be appreciated in retrospect, for it was no more than a flash of intellectual lightning in its own day. Adams was right about Otis's unique and unprecedented contribution to the American Revolution, but he was wrong about the time and the occasion.[23]

Above all, Otis's pamphlet shows that an initial spark came from the American side before any substantial move was made by the British government to hold down or tax the Americans. It was a spark that did not set off a flame until British actions made these premature words come alive.

· 3 ·

These British actions were not long delayed. David Ramsay, it will be

---

[22] Otis in Mullett, "Some Political Writings of James Otis," p. 14 (italics in original).

[23] It is significant that Otis's pamphlet of 1762 has been reprinted only in the 1929 compilation edited by Charles F. Mullett, now rare except in the largest libraries. It is not included in the valuable *Pamphlets of the American Revolution, 1750–1776,* Bernard Bailyn, ed. (Harvard University Press, 1965), in which Otis's first pamphlet dates from 1764.

recalled, thought that there were three main factors in the prerevolutionary process—"combustible materials" as well as a spark and a flame.

These materials were contributed by the British in 1763–64. They had little to do with Otis and the writs of assistance case, which were local phenomena with minimal repercussion in London. British policy went ahead after the official end of the Seven Years' War in 1763 by virtue of the rethinking of British-American relations, as exemplified by the Canada versus Guadeloupe dispute, not in response to Otis or his once celebrated case.

One aspect of the change in British policy was the emergence of Parliament as the chief and sometimes the only arbiter of American policy. Previously the American lobbies and agents had done their business mainly with the Board of Trade, which was a relatively small organization with members who were known to the Americans. Between 1715 and 1764, American interests had rarely petitioned the king or Parliament directly. From 1764 on, American suitors found that colonial decision making had shifted to Parliament, which was far more impervious to American persuasion than the Board of Trade had been.[24] In effect, Parliament had awakened to the importance of colonial issues and had decided to use its long dormant power over the colonies. The Americans were not prepared to influence Parliament and watched helplessly as it passed one bill after another of the greatest moment to American interests. In the end, all the Americans could do was to deny that Parliament had any power over them.

British colonial policy admittedly took a sharp turn in 1763–64. It was marked by four measures that for good reason increasingly disturbed the American colonists. They were the Proclamation of October 1763, the so-called Sugar Act of April 1764, the establishment of vice admiralty courts at the same time, and the Currency Act of September 1764. In addition, the Stamp Act was also announced in 1764, to take effect the following year. Each of these acts struck at important colonial interests; cumulatively, they represented a radically new colonial policy to be carried out by radically new means.

It is not hard to see why the colonists felt that they were set up as losers in every one of these innovations and why they came to see that they had to resist by every possible means. But to understand why an irreconcilable conflict was set in motion in these years it is equally necessary to see why British ministers felt that such measures

[24] Alison Gilbert Olson, *Making the Empire Work* (Harvard University Press, 1992), pp. 158–59.

were right and necessary. These acts were not put over surreptitiously by conniving ministers; they went through the British Parliament almost without objection from any quarter. Only later, after colonial protests began to come in, was it realized that something had gone wrong, and even then there was British unanimity about Parliament's authority to take these actions. In the argument that followed, each side stressed what was most advantageous to it and for the most part talked past the other side. Each British measure had a rationale which anyone in the same position might have approved and anyone on the receiving end might have resisted.

For the end of the Seven Years' War had produced an unmistakably new situation in North America and had confronted the British administration with obviously new problems requiring some sort of new policy. There was the physical assimilation of a vast new territory from Canada to Louisiana and from the Appalachians to the Mississippi, larger than all the old coast-bound colonies combined. The new land beyond the Appalachian Mountains was British to do with as the British government pleased—this much was admitted in 1764.[25] It was as if Great Britain had been given a second chance in America to set up new colonies without any of the encumbrances of the old, without those exasperating charters from a previous century and those colonial politicians who knew how to take advantage of every loophole and opportunity. Such a windfall had never been considered seriously before and urgently demanded a great new intellectual effort on the part of the administration headed by George Grenville, itself in office only since April 1763.

Grenville and his cabinet were not given much time to make up their minds. The greatest Indian uprising of the century, led by Pontiac, chief of the Ottawas, broke out in May 1763, though the news was not received in London until July. It was largely brought about, a twentieth-century historian has written, because of the colonists' practice of "buying vast tracts of land for insignificant sums, of forcing removal of the Indians, of replacing intractable chiefs with compliant ones, of failing to keep their

[25] Gov. Thomas Fitch of Connecticut maintained that the old colonies should not be made to bear any of the cost of "the new and large acquisitions" because "they do indeed properly belong to the crown, and will finally be disposed of and settled for the benefit of the crown and the nation in general, and not for the advantage of the colonies in particular" (*Reasons Why the British Colonies in America Should Not Be Charged with Internal Taxes*, 1764, reprinted in Bailyn, *Pamphlets of the American Revolution*, p. 404). Oxenbridge Thacher pointed out: "The colonies are no particular gainers by these acquisitions. None of the conquered territory is annexed to them. All are acquisitions accruing to the crown" (*The Sentiments of a British American*, 1764, in ibid., p. 492).

treaties."[26] The removal of French power had deprived the Indians of their allies against American colonial encroachments. The British cabinet was faced with a blazing crisis in precisely the territory taken over from the French. Pontiac's Indians were still assisted and encouraged by French settlers remaining in the area. At the same time, American colonists on the western frontier of Pennsylvania, Maryland, and Virginia were exposed to more Indian raids. Reports of Indian massacres alarmed all the colonies. The British cabinet was belatedly informed of the fall of one British post after another as it considered what to do about the trans-Appalachian territory in the late summer of 1763. The uprising did not die down until September 1763 and continued to simmer until 1766.

For the British, a new Indian policy was inextricably interwoven with the need for a new policy for the territory. Moreover, it called for a new policy for an old problem. British leaders had long believed that the colonies had made themselves vulnerable to the French by mistreating the Indians. As previously noted, one of the foremost members of Grenville's cabinet, Lord Halifax, had been responsible as long before as 1754 for calling together the Albany Conference for the main purpose of winning over the Indians and establishing a unified command against the French. In 1755, he had asserted in Parliament that it was more important to make alliances with the Indians than to buy the support of European allies.[27] A decade later, the Indian problem was more intractable than ever and the defense of the former French territory still in question.

The British answer was the Proclamation of 1763. It attempted to resolve the Indian problem by separating the Indians from the white population in the colonies. Its most important provision made it illegal for the British-American colonists to buy land or settle west of the Allegheny Mountains, where few white settlers were as yet to be found. The entire region between the Alleghenies and the Mississippi was reserved for the Indian tribes, except for white traders who were to be licensed to sell goods to the Indians and buy the highly prized furs from them. British officers were empowered to enforce this virtual partition of the British domain south of Canada and north of Louisiana. The proclamation did not close the door on all future expansion of the old colonies across the Alleghenies if such was the eventual need, but even then it carefully restricted eventual transfers of property to lands purchased from formal Indian councils by a representative of the Crown, not by individual land speculators.

[26] Howard H. Peckham, *Pontiac and the Indian Uprising* (Princeton University Press, 1947), p. vii.
[27] *Parliamentary History,* vol. 15 (1755), col. 637.

But it was not that easy and clear in practice. Land speculation was just as much in the business blood of the colonists as smuggling. The activities of the Ohio Company had helped to bring on the Seven Years' War, and with the peace in 1763 its promoters could hardly wait to put their long-postponed plans into execution. Col. George Washington headed a movement of Virginia veterans who had been promised compensation in the western lands in return for their military duty. Washington and other notables from Virginia and Maryland formed a new Mississippi Company to obtain 2.5 million acres of land east of the great river. A western "land craze" gripped the wealthy and influential in many of the middle Atlantic colonies.[28]

Now all this was threatened, permanently or temporarily. The hardest hit were the fur traders and land speculators. The traders were supposed to be so closely regulated that they were forbidden to show their wares to the Indians except at appointed posts in the presence of an official commissary, whose responsibility it was to set fair prices for both the goods sold and the peltry bought. Control of the small traders who rushed into the Indian territory after 1763 proved to be expensive and impractical; the old colonies with their own ambitions across the Alleghenies refused to cooperate. Lax enforcement of the proclamation did the Indians little good and merely infuriated the trading interests, large and small, that had made skins and furs one of the main sources of enrichment in the colonies.

The land speculators never reconciled themselves to the proclamation. As they correctly surmised, it was more a temporary expedient to get over a crisis in Indian relations than a consistent policy that successive British governments could sustain. Four years after the proclamation had gone into effect, George Washington reflected the typical attitude of those who wished "to secure a good deal of Land," even where it was then officially prohibited. He wrote to a surveyor who had fought under him during the recent war that he wanted him

> to secure some of the most valuable Lands in the King's part which I think may be accomplished after a while notwithstanding the Proclamation that restrains it at present and prohibits the Settling of them at all for I can never look upon that Proclamation in any other light (but this I say between ourselves) than as a temporary expedient to quiet the Minds of the Indians and must fall of course

[28] Clarence Walworth Alvord, *The Mississippi Valley in British Politics* (Arthur H. Clark, 1917; 2d ed., 1960), vol. 1, pp. 94–95.

in a few years especially when those Indians are consenting to our Occupying the Lands.

This commission was not without its risk; it clearly entailed violating the proclamation's main intent. Therefore, Washington went on to caution his agent in an unusually long and revealing sentence:

I wou[l]d recommend it to you to keep this whole matter a profound Secret, or trust it only with those in whom you can confide and who can assist you in bringing it to bear by their discoveries of Land and this advice proceeds from several good Reasons and in the first place because I might be censurd for the opinion I have given in respect to the King's Proclamation and then if the Scheme I am now proposing to you was known it might give alarm to others and by putting them upon a Plan of the same nature (before we cou[l]d lay a proper foundation for success ourselves) set the different Interests a clashing and probably in the end overturn the whole all of which may be avoided by a Silent management and the [operation] snugly carried on by you under the pretence of hunting other Game which you may I presume effectually do at the same time you are in pursuit of Land which when fully discovered advise me of it and if there appears but a bear [*sic*] possibility of succeeding any time hence I will have the Lands immediately Surveyed to keep others off and leave the rest to time and my own Assiduity to Accomplish.[29]

It is unlikely that Washington and other Virginia gentlemen felt any particular guilt in making such efforts to evade or outwit a British edict, however well-intentioned, that went against their accustomed practices and immediate interests. The proclamation does not seem to have caused much of a stir in the colonial press.[30] It was easily ignored, because it was largely unenforced and unenforceable. Nevertheless, it was the first step taken by the British government after the official end of the Seven Years' War to change the rules of doing business in the newly conquered territories. New treaties with Indians in 1768 made the proclamation a dead letter. The bill of particulars in the Declaration of Independence against the king of Great Britain did not specifically mention the Proclamation of 1763 but alluded in general to "raising the conditions of new Appropriation of Lands." The proclamation was one of the first of the "combustible

[29] Washington to William Crawford, September 21, 1767, *The Writings of George Washington*, ed. John C. Fitzpatrick (Government Printing Office, 1931), vol. 2, pp. 468–71.
[30] Richard L. Merritt, *Symbols of American Community, 1735–1775* (Yale University Press, 1966), p. 169.

materials" that led to far more explosive protests, resistance, and, finally, violence.

After a few years, it became clear to Gen. Thomas Gage that the measures taken to enforce the proclamation had failed of their purpose. He reported that the new British forts in the region could not take care of the trade with the Indians, because the American traders ignored them and made their own deals with the Indians outside the forts. He opposed the idea of building up the settlements to form "respectable Provinces" for a reason that went to the heart of growing British anxieties. The new American West between the Allegheny Mountains and the Mississippi River, he advised London, could not be developed economically to the advantage of Great Britain. Instead, the people in the region would be forced in a few years "to provide Manufactures of some kind for themselves." Then came Gage's revealing inference: "And when all Connection, upheld by Commerce, with the Mother-Country shall cease, it may be suspected that an Independency on her Government will Soon follow."[31]

This line of reasoning was typically British. It combined manufactures with independence, even in the far-fetched case of the new western territory. It put the prospect of future independence in the forefront of British policy for a region that did not yet have a sizable settlement. It condemned the proclamation to futility and failure.

· 4 ·

One thing led to another. From the start, the proclamation clearly needed implementation. Conquered Frenchmen and warlike Indians did not disappear with the peace treaty. If the trans-Appalachian territory and Canada were British in fact, separate from the older American colonies, it was up to the British to make sure that hostile forces were restrained and hungry interlopers kept out. The fighting force that had put down Pontiac's rebellion and had suffered most of the casualties had been largely made up of British regulars, not colonial volunteers. Most of the colonies had always resisted permitting their manpower to be used outside their individual borders. Garrison duty was foreign to the colonial temperament and had never been successfully imposed on colonial recruits during the late war, even within the old colonies. Only British regulars could be sent to the posts beyond the mountains.

[31] Gage to Lord Hillsborough, November 10, 1770, *The Correspondence of General Thomas Gage with the Secretaries of State, 1763–1775* (Yale University Press, 1931), vol. 1, p. 275.

Such considerations led the Grenville ministry to put in place the next link in the chain. It was an increase in the British Army in North America on a permanent basis from 3,755 men to 10,000—7,500 in North America and 2,500 in the West Indies. Most of this force was stationed in the West beyond the Alleghenies, but it did not bode well that so many British troops were for the first time readily available in the event of trouble. Such a potential military threat had never faced the old colonies before. One of the reasons that they had been able to defy British governors so easily was that the latter had virtually no force behind them and had never even asked for any, for no previous British government would have sent troops except to put down a foreign foe. The only military force the British had had in the colonies before 1763 was made up of the four independent companies in New York, with only four lieutenants and 400 privates, which were considered "the most contemptible of all" British units anywhere.[32]

It took some time for the old colonies to realize the full implications of the Proclamation of 1763. A protest in Massachusetts in 1764 against the financial effect of the new policy accepted the proclamation itself as evidence of the "wisdom and real concern for the good" of the colonists.[33] Soon, however, the new British force strung out in North America gave the colonists reason to raise the old English cry of alarm against a "standing army" and its inevitable use as an instrument of oppression.

From the perspective of London, the North American army had been enlarged for perfectly sound reasons. Indeed, British officials thought that they had acted in the interest of the old colonies. Yet there was always a double edge. One leading official explained that "the security of the old colonies and the advantages obtained by the peace depend upon preserving these in safety and subjection."[34] Safety may have come first, but subjection was not far behind.

Somewhat later, the proposed injection of 7,500 British troops into the West led to one of the more disagreeable disputes with the colonies. In order to get to the Alleghenies, it was necessary to pass through populated areas between the coast and the mountains. Since these marches took days, the troops had to be put up en route. The British did not have quarters in the settled areas and searched for ways to solve the problem.

By this time, in early 1765, the answer was not easy. General Gage,

[32] Stanley McCrory Pargellis, "The Four Independent Companies of New York," in *Essays in Colonial History* (Yale University Press, 1931), pp. 96–123.

[33] *Considerations Upon The Act of Parliament* (Boston, 1764), reprinted in Bailyn, *Pamphlets of the American Revolution,* p. 361.

[34] [Thomas Whately], *Considerations on the Trade and Finances of this Kingdom,* . . . (London, 1766), reprinted in *A Collection of scarce and interesting tracts* (London, 1787), vol. 2, p. 99.

the British commander in chief, reported to Welbore Ellis, the secretary at war, that "the Difficultys in carrying on the Service in North America increase very fast." Colonists protested that the Mutiny Act, which covered this and other military matters in Great Britain, did not apply to America, because the colonies were not specifically mentioned. The problems of the military were getting to be so grievous that "it will soon become difficult in the present Situation, to keep Soldiers in the Service, or possible to quarter or March them." Gage reported: "Soldiers are seduced from the King's Service, Deserters protected and secreted, Arms Cloaths &ca purchased, Quarters and Carriages refused without incurring any Penalty."

Gage proposed that Parliament should amend the Mutiny Act to make it apply to North America, and to billet troops in private houses if they could not otherwise be sheltered.[35] When such a bill was brought into the House of Commons, however, it met with strong opposition. After much dissension, the measure was amended to put up troops in empty houses, barns, and similar places but not in private houses. One of the pro-American merchants in London, David Barclay, brought up a consideration that was already in British minds: "As this law will increase the power of the Commander-in-chief in America, it may not be improper to remark, what every body seems to agree in, that if America ever throws off its dependence on this country, it will most probably be attempted by some aspiring genius amongst the military."[36] Whatever the subject, American independence was not far away. In any case, a similar problem came up in the Quartering Act almost a decade later.

The proclamation and the new British Army in North America brought on an even more serious and intractable problem. Soldiers cost money, and more soldiers cost more money. The smaller force had cost between £80,000 to £90,000 a year; the larger force drove the expense above £275,000 a year. Military supplies increased in cost by about £60,000 a year, mainly for the American account. The total came to what was then the staggering sum of about £320,000 yearly.[37]

A British administration facing a crushing load of debt from past wars was scarcely in a position to meet this added expense without squeezing additional money out of somewhere. British taxes had already risen to what was considered their maximum feasible peak, far greater than anything the colonists had to pay; the British landed interest, which most members of

[35] Gage to Ellis, January 22, 1765, *Gage Correspondence*, vol. 2, pp. 262–66.

[36] *The Grenville Papers*, ed. William James Smith (London, 1852), vol. 3, p. 12 n. 2.

[37] Whately, *Considerations*, p. 99. The figure of £320,000 was estimated by George Louis Beer, *British Colonial Policy, 1754–1765* (Macmillan, 1907), p. 267 n. 1.

Parliament represented, was especially hard hit, and any attempt to make it pay more was viewed as politically insurmountable. By tradition, British policy had always looked to the colonies to support themselves, even to pay for those British-appointed officials, such as governors, representing the Crown rather than the colonies. If the additional money had to come from somewhere, it was clearly going to come from the colonies. Since the British ministry professed to believe that the new army in America was there to protect the old as well as the new territory, it seemed only fair to the British mind to ask the colonies to pay the bill.

· 5 ·

From mid-1763 on, the British ministry began to look around for sources of additional revenue from the colonies. As usual in the initial phases of these proceedings, the British did not intend to disturb the colonists any more than was absolutely necessary. The approach, as the earl of Egremont, then secretary of state for the Southern Department, in charge of the colonies, told the Board of Trade, was to be whatever was "least Burthensome & most palatable to the Colonies."[38] It took a year for Parliament to act on what must have seemed at the time like a brilliant idea.

For three decades, the "Molasses Act" of Walpole's neglectful day had rested undisturbed in the legislative record. It had provided for a duty of sixpence on a gallon of imported molasses, a rate so high that the rum manufacturers of New England could not afford to pay it and the British government could not bring itself to enforce it. From 1733 to 1763, the act had brought in only £21,652, or no more than £700 a year.[39] It had cost more to administer the act than it was worth. Parliament was told in 1762 that the revenues had amounted to between £1,000 and £2,000 a year, and the cost of collection to the customs between £7,000 and £8,000 a year.[40] This dead letter of a law suddenly came to life as ministers sought to get more money out of the colonies. The brilliant idea was that, if the British Exchequer could get very little out of sixpence a gallon of molasses, perhaps it could get more by lowering the rate to what the rum manufacturers might be willing to pay.

The problem was how low to reduce the duty to make it profitable on all sides. The British Treasury first thought of fourpence a gallon; George

[38] Beer, *British Colonial Policy,* p. 275.
[39] Thomas C. Barrow, *Trade and Empire* (Harvard University Press, 1967), p. 177.
[40] George Grenville to Horace Walpole, September 8, 1763, *Grenville Papers,* vol. 2, p. 114.

Grenville, chancellor of the Exchequer, seemed to lean towards two; the colonial agents in London urged one.[41] In the end, the Sugar Act of April 4, 1764, settled on three. It was only one of twelve duties imposed at the same time, but the act took its name from that imposed on "molasses and syrups." To sweeten this pecuniary pill, the drafters added a provision they thought would make the whole thing more appealing or at least less obnoxious to the colonists. Instead of going into the general British budget, as with other taxes and duties, all the money brought in by the Sugar Act was specifically reserved "for defending, protecting, and securing" the British colonies in America. It was thus intended to help pay for the newly enlarged British Army in North America and for nothing else.

One word, however, crept into the act that had not been used in the original Molasses Act or any other legislation of this kind. The guilty word was *revenue*. The preamble said that "it is just and necessary, that a revenue be raised in your Majesty's said dominions in America" to defend, protect, and secure them. Duties had previously been imposed in the name of regulating the trade of the empire, a purpose which the colonists had always recognized. *Revenue* implied that something different was now being attempted, more like a direct tax to pay for British expenses, not in behalf of the traditional trade and navigation laws.

As if this were not enough, the Sugar Act promised to be only the beginning of such measures. If the expected revenue from the Sugar Act had been large enough, the Grenville ministry might have stopped there or would not have had a plausible reason to go further in the same direction. The act itself hit at a relatively small number of influential colonists in New England—those with interests in the rum trade. The chances are that agitation against the Sugar Act, especially in New England, would still have shattered the postwar calm, but it might have played itself out, as other grievances had done. Unfortunately, the revenue from the Sugar Act was expected to fall far short of what Great Britain needed to support the army in North America. All the measures of 1764 brought in no more than £45,000, about one-seventh of the army's cost.

Grenville was thus driven to insert into the Sugar Act itself a clause that "it may be proper to charge certain stamp duties in the said colonies and plantations." The future Stamp Act was in this way linked with the Sugar Act a year before the former was actually enacted. The colonial reaction to the first, therefore, had to take the second into account. Some British opinion later held that it had been a mistake to give the colonists a year

---

[41] Jasper Mauduit to Speaker of the House of Representatives of Massachusetts, December 30, 1763, *MHS Collections*, 1st ser., vol. 6 (1799), p. 193.

to prepare for the Stamp Act, and that Grenville's program might have stood a better chance of succeeding if he had struck more quickly.[42]

The colonial agents in London were caught in the middle during the negotiations to set the duty on molasses. They had tried to get a lower duty, but they did not oppose the principle that the colonies should "bear the charge" of their "own government and defence."[43] The agents did not get an official reaction from the colonies in time to change their own attitude or warn off the British ministers with whom they were dealing. The Massachusetts agent, Jasper Mauduit, advised the Massachusetts leadership that the British government was determined that "a practicable duty should be paid, and the payment of it enforced" and that "to attempt to controvert either of these, would be to no manner of purpose." Just as the act was being passed in Parliament, he was told to insist on no duty at all, and after it was passed, he was ordered to work for its repeal.[44]

Other well-known Americans did not take such a hard line. One of those who viewed these measures with more or less public equanimity was Benjamin Franklin. In a pamphlet published in April 1764, Franklin scoffed at the "Bug bear" of a standing army. "It is very possible," he granted, "that the Crown may think it necessary to keep Troops in America henceforward, to maintain its Conquests, and defend the Colonies; and that the Parliament may establish some Revenue arising out of the American Trade, to be apply'd towards supporting those Troops. It is possible, too, that we may, after a few Years Experience, be generally very well satisfy'd with that Measure, from the steady Protection it will afford us against Foreign Enemies, and the Security of internal Peace among ourselves without the Expence or Trouble of a Militia."[45]

At the end of that month, however, Franklin privately wrote to a British correspondent in a different vein. He now took the line that the colonists could do little about the trade, duties, troops, and fortifications that Parliament was deciding for America. Then he pressed the practical argument that any cut in the colonial trade with the West Indies was bound to hit back at British exports to the mainland colonies, which would then no longer be able to afford them. Instead of denouncing

[42] *An Impartial History of the War in America between Great Britain and Her Colonies from Its Commencement to the end of the Year 1779* (London, 1780), pp. 50–51.

[43] Letter of Jasper Mauduit, February 11, 1764, *MHS Collections*, 1st ser., vol. 6 (1799), p. 195.

[44] Thomas Cushing to Mauduit, April 9 and June 22, 1764, *Jasper Mauduit*, Charles Grenfill Washburn Collection (*MHS*, 1918), pp. 158–60.

[45] *The Papers of Benjamin Franklin,* ed. Leonard W. Labaree (Yale University Press, 1961), vol. 11, p. 169.

the injustice of the British actions, he appealed to British self-interest on the ground that "what you get from us in Taxes you must lose in Trade." He chided the British for wanting too much for themselves: "Nature has put Bounds on your Abilities, tho' none to your Desires. Britain would, if she could, manufacture and trade for all the World; England for all Britain;—London for all England; and every Londoner for all London. So selfish is the human Mind!"[46] The ambiguity in Franklin's attitude in 1764 is evidence of how far the revolutionary process still had to go to win over influential, moderate colonial opinion. Not for the last time, Franklin seemed to be facing two ways—publicly unconcerned about the new army and its effect on colonial revenues, privately concerned enough to play on British self-interest against British actions, without arguing the rights and wrongs of the case.[47]

Just then, the British were equally convinced that only colonial selfish-ness could explain resistance to these "least Burthensome & most palatable" measures. It was widely believed in Great Britain that the mother country had fought a long war, had gone deeply into debt, and was now obliged to provide protection for the ungrateful colonial children who refused to pay even part of the costs. The typical attitude of British officialdom was later expressed by William Knox: "The duty of six pence a gallon upon foreign molasses, which had been paid thirty years before Mr. Grenville was first commissioner of the treasury, was no grievance, *because it had never been collected;* but when that gentleman reduced the duty to three pence, all liberty was at an end—for he took measures for the Colonies to pay the three pence."[48]

· 6 ·

The measures taken to make the colonies pay the threepence were the last link in the chain of British innovations—the "combustible material"— in 1764.

[46] Franklin to Peter Collinson, April 30, 1764, ibid., pp. 181–83.

[47] In his well-known biography of Franklin (Viking Press, 1938), Carl Van Doren said, on the basis of this letter to Collinson, that "Franklin saw injustice and danger at once" (p. 321). But Van Doren ignored Franklin's virtual acceptance of the British actions in the pamphlet earlier that month and tendentiously distorted the letter to Collinson to make Franklin more "revolutionary" in this period than he actually was. Franklin did not complain about British "injustice." If the reader had been told about the passage in Franklin's pamphlet that same month, he might have wondered what Franklin was supposed to have seen "at once."

[48] [William Knox], *The Controversy between Great Britain and her Colonies Reviewed* (London, 1769), p. 44.

The chief step was a provision put into the Sugar Act in April of that year to deal with violations of the whole trading system. The trade and navigation acts had long been enforced in both England and America by vice admiralty courts, so called because they were headed by naval officers or those appointed to act in their stead. For the better part of a century, North America had had eleven such courts. Colonial governors were nominally given the title of vice admiral, and they in turn chose judges to do the work. The jobs were mainly honorific; most judges carried on other activities to support themselves. Their jurisdiction covered everything from seamen's wages to the forfeiture of ships and cargoes in violation of the trade and navigation acts.

Until the end of the seventeenth century, trade and revenue cases had been tried in the colonies in common-law courts. Since customs officials and other Crown officers could rarely get convictions in these courts, equal jurisdiction had been granted in 1696 to the vice admiralty courts. As a result, customs officials could choose whichever type of court they thought best suited their purposes. One difference particularly separated the two types of courts in the colonial mind—trials in the common-law courts were decided by juries, those in the vice admiralty courts by a single judge. Nevertheless, the procedure in the vice admiralty courts was so much less complicated and more expeditious that most merchants and seamen had long preferred them to the common-law courts. Vice admiralty judges, however, were no more likely than customs officials to reject the blandishments of colonial smugglers and other pressures. In effect, the trade and navigation acts were little more than a dead letter in both types of courts, which was the main reason there had been so few protests against the vice admiralty courts, despite their lack of jury trials.

The first sustained attempt to undermine the authority of the vice admiralty courts did not come in Boston until 1761, as a result of a legal counterattack by a group of merchants threatened with penalties for illegal trade. That the courts were unwilling or unable to enforce the commercial restrictions, either because local juries would not convict or because local judges were politically vulnerable, had been an open secret for decades.

In 1763, with the official end of the Seven Years' War, a British crackdown started. Parliament passed a statute empowering naval officers to seize vessels in the illegal trade on the high seas instead of permitting the vessels to get into the countless inlets and bays along the Atlantic coast from which they could surreptitiously unload their cargoes. Governors were warned to cooperate in carrying out this military measure against "this iniquitous Practice" or risk the king's extreme displeasure.[49] A naval patrol of forty-four vessels was put in place to haul off suspected smugglers.

In 1764, another and even more objectionable method of dealing with the problem was made part of the Sugar Act. The main obstacle to strict enforcement had always been the necessity for the vice admiralty courts to limit their jurisdiction to individual colonies, where local pressures and intrigues were most intense. The new act contained a provision which set up a superior vice admiralty court with jurisdiction over violations of the trade laws in all of North America. Owing to the location of the North American fleet at Halifax, Nova Scotia, the new court was located there. Other vice admiralty courts had always been presided over by local, colonial judges; a British judge was brought over to inaugurate the new court, away from colonial politics and collusions. Now seized vessels and cargoes were to be sent all the way to Halifax and the trials held there.

In the end, the Halifax court had little to do, because government officials in the colonies were reluctant to transfer their cases so far away. In 1765, a change was made, giving the Halifax court appellate jurisdiction, without adding to its business. When the Stamp Act was put through that year, all the colonial courts, including the one at Halifax, were empowered to try any case of violation, thus extending the vice admiralty court's jurisdiction to the collection of revenue as well as the enforcement of the trade and navigation acts. The uproar over the Stamp Act brought the vice admiralty courts into even greater disrepute and made their judges still more vulnerable to colonial discontent.[50]

The fate of the vice admiralty courts tells as much as anything else why the British stirred up so much trouble in 1764 and what came of it. From the British point of view, the new court of general jurisdiction was a plausible expedient to get around the colonial influence in the local courts, both vice admiralty and common law. The superior court need not have been located in far-off Halifax; it seems to have been put there merely to please the admiral commanding the North American fleet, for whom the location was most convenient. Plans were later made but were never carried out to set up the same type of court at Boston, Philadelphia, and Charleston.

The main effect of the vice admiralty courts in general and the Halifax court in particular was to give the American colonists an additional reason

[49] Earl of Egremont to the Governor of New York, July 9, 1763, *Colden Papers, Collections of the New-York Historical Society for the Year 1922*, publ. 1923, vol. 6, p. 223.

[50] Carl Ubbelohde, *The Vice-Admiralty Courts and the American Revolution* (University of North Carolina Press, 1960), pp. 3–80.

to protest against the whole new colonial system that the British were trying to work out in 1763–64. The vice admiralty courts were objectionable because they did not conduct jury trials, and the Halifax court was doubly objectionable because it was so far away. It profited little for the British to point out that vice admiralty courts without juries had operated in the colonies without protest for many decades before 1764, and that the move to Halifax would have been unnecessary if the old courts had been capable of enforcing statutes that had never been questioned so long as they were unenforced.[51]

The ultimate irony is that even the Halifax court proved a futile makeshift that harmed the British far more than the Americans. Like the old system of collecting molasses duties, it cost more than it took in.

· 7 ·

The British barrage of legislation for the colonies in 1764 was unprecedented. It is necessary to go back to the bad old days of the Restoration in the previous century, when efforts had been made to beat the New England colonies into submission, to find a similarly sustained British offensive. Only the proclamation had come in 1763, and then towards the end of the year. The other measures were concentrated in 1764; if any one year was the starting point of the prerevolutionary era, this one has the best claim to the title.

To the British, each of the measures made good sense. No one decision stood by itself; each created the necessity for the next. All seemed to follow reasonably and inexorably from the legacy of the Seven Years' War. The greatest military triumph of the century had in no more than a few months given rise to the greatest British crisis of the century. If there had been no war and no victory, there would have been no newly acquired western territory and no problem of what to do with it. If there had been no vast new territory, there would have been no Proclamation of 1763. If there had been no Proclamation of 1763, there would have been no need for an army on the spot to enforce it. If there had been no increase in the British

[51] Stamp taxes had existed in England since 1694. Violations since 1711 had been brought before two or more justices of the peace only, without a trial by jury. But English cases were brought before a court in one's own neighborhood or county, not an admiralty judge far away. Colonial justices of the peace were, however, far more amenable to popular influence. The differences between the two systems are well treated in David S. Lovejoy, "Rights Imply Equality: The Case Against Admiralty Jurisdiction in America, 1764–1776," *William and Mary Quarterly,* October 1959, pp. 459–84.

Army in North America, there would have been no incentive to make the colonies pay for at least part of its cost. If the cost had not been so high, the additional revenue from the Sugar Act would not have been needed. If the revenue from the Sugar Act had been enough, there would have been no need to get additional revenue from the Stamp Act. Throughout this period, the huge debt built up during the war haunted British ministers and made them almost desperate for means to cut it down or at least not add to it.

These decisions were not made haphazardly, though the proclamation was somewhat hurried by the flare-up of Pontiac's rebellion. About a year of sustained ministerial and bureaucratic planning and consultation had gone into the final determination. No one British minister was responsible, though George Grenville as head of the government came to get most of the blame. Each measure was deliberately submitted to Parliament and approved by it without opposition.

Israel Mauduit, the brother of the Massachusetts agent in London, had warned that "Parliament will most certainly concur" with Grenville to make America "bear the charge of its own government and defence."[52] Two days after the Sugar Act was passed, he tried to rid his employers of any illusions about the parliamentary reaction: "The present sense of Parliament is such, that I should only flatter and deceive the General Court, if I led them to imagine, that any one Man of Consequence there would stand up in his place, and avow an opinion that America ought not to bear at least the greater part of the expense of its own Government; or that Acts of Parliament (tho' not Orders of Council) were not obligatory upon all his Majesty's Subjects in all parts of his Dominion."[53]

Grenville was not the only one obsessed by the need to cut the British debt, and the Americans were not the only ones to suffer from it. Grenville's immediate predecessor as chancellor of the Exchequer, Sir Francis Dashwood, had already brought in a budget calling for an excise tax on cider of four shillings per hogshead, despite the fact that Walpole had been forced to drop a similar measure thirty years earlier and had never recovered from the defeat. Cider in the West Country counties of England was just as much a political powder keg as molasses in New England. Grenville had inherited the cider tax and had decided to push it through Parliament, despite the fierce opposition of William Pitt. The analogy with the Sugar Act was even closer, because the cider tax was enforceable without trial by local juries. Grenville admitted that it was

[52] *MHS Collections*, 1st ser., vol. 6, pp. 194–95.
[53] Ibid., p. 363.

"odious" but "unavoidable."[54] The opposition called the measure "a new and frightful plan of taxation" and argued that it would set a precedent permitting any minister to "levy any sum of money that he pleases." The country, it cried, was on the high road to "tyranny and oppression."[55] The uproar over the cider and similar taxes continued in Great Britain until Grenville gave up his office; the Cider Act was repealed in 1766. Grenville himself thought of the American and British taxes in the same way. The Americans did not like their new tax, but "the [British] western country desires an exemption from cider, the northern from a duty on beer." The true way "to relieve all," he told Parliament, "is to make all contribute their proper share."[56]

A proclivity for smuggling and a prejudice against taxes were not peculiar to the colonists. They were doing what came naturally to the British of their time, and they were not marked out as special victims. There was, however, one important difference—the cider counties had representatives in Parliament, the molasses-into-rum colonies did not. The parliamentary record is full of denunciations of the cider tax; there were no molasses representatives from the colonies to provide the same. Yet so few British residents were actually represented in Parliament that this difference could hardly have impressed them as much as it did the colonists. In British politics, it was difficult to see why the colonists should not pay a tax on molasses if the British were required to pay a tax on cider.

With equally good reason, from their point of view, the Americans did not like the new British actions. The Proclamation of 1763, if enforced, condemned the old colonies to subsist within the relatively narrow confines between the Atlantic and the Alleghenies. Land speculation of the Ohio Company type, long encouraged, was now held back or indefinitely postponed. The irrepressible fur traders were going to be tied up in bureaucratic knots. Merchants saw suspected vessels hauled all the way to Halifax and trials held there. The new standing army was supposed to protect the Indians from the colonists and vice versa, but few colonists wanted the Indians protected against them. The army, even if spread out in the western territory and outlying posts, gave the British, for the first time, a force stronger than mere words to deal with potential colonial defiance. All the more galling was a tax levied on the colonists to pay for

[54] *The History, Debates and Proceedings of the Houses of Parliament of Great Britain from the year 1743 to the year 1774*, March 7, 1764 (London, 1792), vol. 6, p. 132.

[55] Ibid., p. 195.

[56] *Proceedings and Debates of the British Parliaments Respecting North America, 1754–1783*, ed. R. C. Simmons and P. D. G. Thomas (Kraus International, 1983), February 6, 1765, vol. 2, p. 10.

these soldiers. A duty of threepence a gallon on molasses was worse than one of sixpence, because a smaller duty that had to be paid was worse than a larger duty that was almost never paid.

Who was right? The question cannot be answered without asking another question: Right for whom? Each side had good enough reasons to persuade itself that it was right. In each case, right coincided with self-interest; the clash of rights was also a clash of interests. Seen this way, the incipient Revolution could be decided only by the capitulation of one side or the other, by some sort of compromise between them, or by a final conflict that would separate them forever. It took ten years to resolve which one of these choices it was going to be. During this time, the British almost capitulated on at least two occasions; people of goodwill on both sides could not make up their minds how far to go and continued to hope for a settlement satisfactory to all; and a general sense of an impending break did not set in for a decade. Why there was no way to avoid an armed struggle is the most demanding question of the American Revolution.

10

"Our British Privileges"

❧

· 1 ·

THE IMMEDIATE EFFECT OF THE end of the Seven Years' War was favorable to the imperial cause in the colonies. It inspired pride in the common victory and satisfaction that the colonies had been liberated from a century-old fear of the French. No intimation of the coming struggle spoiled the celebrations of 1763.

Only two years later, the struggle was so far advanced that it erupted into colonial violence. There had never before been a movement and an ideology in the colonies such as emerged in this period. Once they took shape, they could not be held back or shunted aside. Whatever portents or preliminaries there had been in previous years, this was unlike anything that had ever happened in the colonies.

Such a phenomenon was driven by a new and irresistible force. An irreconcilable element had entered into the old connection, one that could lead only to the total victory of one side or the other. Such an element was not present in the colonial opposition to the Proclamation of 1763, the new vice admiralty court in Halifax, or even the Sugar Act and its duty on molasses, much as they were detested.

Before the Stamp Act, governors and other British officials had warned that sooner or later the American colonists were going to break away. But these suspicions and intimations were long buried in musty archives, and we know about them only because a small army of scholars winkled them out many years later. The American colonists were not bothered by them at the time, because they did not know about them.

The Stamp Act was different. It released into the public arena the fatal virus that infected both sides and made it impossible for them to coexist within the same body politic. It produced a cause the colonies thought worth fighting for. It took another ten years for the full implication of opposition to the act and its successors to work itself out, because both sides were reluctant to face the ultimate outcome. They struggled vainly to find some way out, only to find themselves more firmly imprisoned in it.

The ultimate question is: What was there about this tax that brought on the beginning of the end of an association that was a century and a half old? To understand why it happened, it is necessary to appreciate the peculiar significance taxation had in the political culture the British and British-Americans had in common.

· 2 ·

Much as the Americans disliked all taxes, and especially the stamp tax, it was not the tax itself that brought them to the breaking point. Whatever the cost of it to some colonists, mainly merchants, lawyers, and printers, it was not so crushing that it could have brought about a revolutionary cleavage. British historians are still trying to show that, as taxes go, the British government had done its best to remove the sting from this one.[1] None of this worked, because something else in the act transcended practical considerations, something more important than whether the tax was large or small in its totality.

The clue to the puzzle of this singularly swift transition was the peculiar nature of taxation in eighteenth-century British thought. Both sides shared the Whiggish doctrine that came out of the Glorious Revolution of 1688–89,

---

[1] "Great care had been taken to make the Stamp Act acceptable to the colonies. The total tax envisaged was small. The wide range of duties, which averaged only about 70 per cent of their equivalent in Britain, had been devised to provide an equitable distribution of the burden. All money raised by both this tax and the 1764 molasses duty would be handed over to army paymasters in the colonies. There was never any foundation to the contemporary and historical myth that Britain would drain money from America. The two revenue measures would cover only one-third of the annual army cost in the colonies, now being estimated at £350,000, and Britain would have to cover the balance. The Stamp Act, moreover, was to be administered by leading resident colonists, not by officials sent out from Britain. This decision was implemented as soon as the legislation had passed. The key post was that of Stamp Distributor, one for each colony. It would provide income, power, and prestige, and was bestowed as patronage: for colonial resistance was not anticipated in London at the time, even by men, such as Benjamin Franklin, recently arrived from America" (Peter D. G. Thomas, "The Grenville Program, 1763–1765," in *The Blackwell Encyclopedia of the American Revolution*, ed. Jack P. Greene and J. R. Pole (Blackwell, 1991), pp. 110–11.

the defining British event for the next century. What set them apart was that they took their ideological positions from different aspects of the common heritage. After almost a century, it was broad and loose enough to contain its own conflicts and contradictions, in Great Britain itself and between the British and Americans.

The reason the Stamp Act could pit American Whigs against British Whigs is that taxation meant far more than a way to gain revenue. Taxes were something apart, because they impinged crucially on property and sovereignty. The colonial ideologists knew their Locke, the fountainhead of Whiggism, and played endless variations on his themes. The colonists would have had to read and remember only a single paragraph in John Locke's *Second Treatise of Government* to know what to think about taxes, property, consent, and representation:

> 'Tis true, Governments cannot be supported without great Charge, and 'tis fit every one who enjoys his share of the Protection, should pay out of his Estate his proportion for the maintenance of it. But still it must be with his own Consent, i.e. the consent of the Majority, giving it either by themselves, or their Representatives chosen by them. For if any one shall claim a *Power to lay* and levy *Taxes* on the People, he thereby invades the *Fundamental Law of Property,* and subverts the end of Government. For what property have I in that which another may by right take, when he pleases to himself?

But Locke also taught that "there can be but *one Supream Power,* which is *the Legislative,* to which all the rest are and must be subordinate."[2] In the British system, the "legislative" was represented by Parliament, which, according to Locke, took precedence over the "Executive Power." There was much more to Locke than these basic ideas, but they are enough to suggest that both sides of the revolutionary struggle could look back to Lockean thought for support of their fundamental positions—one to the doctrine of consent and representation, the other to the supremacy and sovereignty of Parliament.[3]

The colonial ideologists had no need for great originality to base their arguments on consent and representation. They found them ready-made

---

[2] *Two Treatises of Government,* 2d Treatise, chap. 13, no. 149.

[3] The latter principle was reiterated with emphasis by William Blackstone in the first volume of his *Commentaries on the Laws of England,* which came out in 1765, the same year as the Stamp Act: "There is and must be in every state a supreme irresistible absolute and uncontrolled authority in which the *jura summa imperii* or rights of sovereignty reside, and this supreme power is by the constitution of Great Britain vested in the King Lords and Commons."

in the accepted political system of their future enemies.[4] In fact, Benjamin Franklin had clearly stated the colonial case against parliamentary taxation of the colonies as far back as 1754, ten years before Grenville served notice that such a tax was coming. In a letter to Governor Shirley of Massachusetts, Franklin had defended his plan of union at the Albany Conference, which had provided for a Grand Council in which the colonies would be represented and which would have the power of taxation. He had written: "That it is suppos'd an undoubted Right of Englishmen not to be taxed but by their own Consent given thro' their Representatives. That the Colonies have no Representatives in Parliament." Therefore, the colonies had the right to tax themselves without the interference of Parliament.[5] Franklin had not pushed this idea once his plan of union had been rejected, but that he had had such a plan shows how deeply rooted colonial resistance to the parliamentary stamp tax was.

If anything had been gained in the Glorious Revolution, it was the fundamental principle of parliamentary supremacy. But the balance of powers between the Crown and Parliament was more complex and questionable in the colonies. Kings still insisted that they had special prerogatives in the colonies, but they could not do whatever they pleased, because they had to take into consideration what Parliament was ready and willing to let them do or not do. In effect, the balance shifted, depending on how much interest Parliament was prepared to take in colonial affairs. When Parliament passed the Stamp Act, it raised the question of whether parliamentary supremacy crossed the ocean and included the colonies. Until the Stamp Act, it was generally thought to have done so. Parliament had passed legislation restricting colonial trade and manufactures whenever it was pleased to do so. But it had never acted in the field of colonial taxation, and to this extent the invocation of parliamentary supremacy in the colonies was new.

In the American case, parliamentary supremacy was challenged by the doctrine of colonial consent. If the colonists had to give their consent to parliamentary taxation, Parliament was not completely sovereign over them. If Parliament was sovereign, the colonists did not have to consent to its legislation. The same problem did not arise in Great Britain because

[4] Whether the Founding Fathers were "Lockean liberals" has become a matter of dispute. I am here concerned solely with the derivation of the doctrine of consent on the one hand and of parliamentary supremacy on the other, both of which clearly went back to Locke. In the first case, James Otis in *The Rights of the British Colonies Asserted and proved* (1764) and *A Vindication of the British Colonies* (1765) cited Locke repeatedly as the supreme authority.

[5] Franklin to Shirley, December 4, 1754, *The Papers of Benjamin Franklin*, ed. Leonard W. Labaree (Yale University Press, 1961), vol. 5, pp. 444–45.

it was assumed that the British people were represented in Parliament, though only about one in ten was permitted to vote; the rest were said to consent through an esoteric process of "virtual representation." But the British people did not have assemblies through which they could make their political will known. That the Americans raised the problem of consent signifies that they challenged Parliament's power over them in at least one vital respect. If the Americans were right in this one case, they were tearing a hole in the structure of British sovereignty over them.

The American radicals later called themselves Whigs and their opponents Tories. But much of the intellectual argument was between American Whigs and British Whigs, each side using a different aspect of Whiggish doctrine. Just as American Whigs took their stand on the principle of consent, British Whigs such as George Grenville took their stand on the principle of British sovereignty. Because it was closely linked with sovereignty, Grenville was unwilling to give up the power of taxation under any circumstances. He informed William Knox, who had worked for him and was willing to compromise:

> But I own I cannot think that we ought for any consideration of Revenue from thence, even if it could amount to a million a year instead of 200,000£., as you propose, to give up and sell for ever the right of sovereignty and taxation in the Parliament of Great Britain over its colonies. . . . If Great Britain, under any conditions gives up her right of taxation she gives up her right of sovereignty, which is inseparable from it, in all ages and in all countries.

Grenville was such a staunch parliamentarian that, with reference to how the colonies might have their contributions apportioned, he declared: "God forbid that we should ever give that power to the King without Parliament."[6] For such British Whigs, the supremacy of Parliament over the Crown and colonies mattered most; it signified the continued dependence of the colonies on Great Britain. For American Whigs, consent to taxation was uppermost; it stripped Parliament of the right to tax them or to do anything else that went along with the power of taxation. Until almost the very end of the prerevolutionary struggle, the Americans fought the British ideologically with Britain's own ideological weapons—or at least those that served their purpose. It was not for nothing that ideological lawyers, who were most likely to know how to manipulate the British system, played such a prominent part before the Revolution.

[6] Grenville to Knox, June 27, 1768, July 15, 1768, *The Manuscripts of Captain H. V. Knox,* Historical Manuscripts Commission (Dublin, 1909), vol. 6, pp. 96, 97.

In the end, the argument over taxation was an argument over power. The struggle to deprive Parliament of its power over taxation struck at the heart of British power in the colonies and spilled over everything else. The Americans began by fighting on this narrow front only. The Revolution occurred because it could not end there. In a sense, the end was in the beginning, which is why the stakes in the struggle against the Stamp Act were so high.

The struggle between Great Britain and its American colonies developed in the form of action-reaction cycles. First one side made a move, then the other side made a countermove. Basically, however, the pattern of moves remained the same. The first cycle of 1763–1766 was determining and much of what happened later was repetition.

The opening action was British. In March 1764, Grenville served notice in connection with the Sugar Act that a stamp tax was coming, though he did not put it through until the following February. He delayed because he wanted more time to prepare the ground, but the delay gave colonial legislators time to decide what to do about it, and it did not take them long to figure out how to react.

The first response came from Massachusetts. In May of that year, a committee of the town of Boston struck back. Its reaction to Grenville's measures came in the form of instructions to newly elected members of the Assembly on how to deal with the recent British measures, especially the forthcoming stamp tax. These instructions were drafted by Samuel Adams but most likely reflected the views of a closely knit group of local notables who shared a common background. Adams's instructions were soon published in the Boston press and from there spread to other colonies. Curiously, Adams himself knew how hard it was to collect taxes from the colonists; he was then a collector of taxes for the town of Boston and had so much trouble that he had inserted a notice in a Boston newspaper threatening "steps of the law being taken, *without distinction* of persons" if delinquents did not pay up.[7] He was obviously not opposed to all taxes, only to British-imposed taxes, and against them he waged a much loftier campaign.

The Adamses belonged to an old Boston family, going back to the early seventeenth century. Sam's father was a man of "ample fortune" who operated a brewery and actively engaged in local politics, finally succeeding in getting himself elected to the Massachusetts assembly. Sam attended Harvard and studied law but never finished. He inherited the

[7] William V. Wells, *The Life and Public Services of Samuel Adams* (Little, Brown, 1865), vol. 1, pp. 37, 45–49.

brewery and one-third of his father's property but had no aptitude for business and lost most of it. He was so impecunious that he was forced to accept handouts from friends and neighbors. Until he was over forty, Sam Adams was a failure in everything but politics, but in this he proved to be an outstanding success.

Much of the colonial side of the great revolutionary debate in the next decade was contained in a few lines of Adams's instructions:

> For if our Trade may be taxed why not our Lands? Why not the Produce of our Lands & every thing we possess or make use of? This we apprehend annihilates our Charter Right to govern & tax ourselves—It strikes at our Brittish Privileges, which as we have never forfeited them, we hold in common with our Fellow Subjects who are Natives of Britain: If Taxes are laid upon us in any shape without our having a legal Representation where they are laid, are we not reduced from the Character of free Subjects to the miserable State of tributary Slaves?[8]

The arguments were all there—the magnification of any tax into total dispossession of all property; the recourse to the charter as the guarantee of self-government as well as self-taxation; the appeal of British subjects against the British government; the connection between parliamentary taxation and representation in Parliament; the ultimate definition of the struggle against taxation as one between freedom and slavery. Put this way, the struggle was bound to go on and to be different from any other in the past. The stress on representation made it seem that the colony wanted to be represented.

In June, the Massachusetts assembly took the initiative to form an incipient all-colonies movement. It called on all the other colonies to protest both against the sugar duty and prospective stamp tax. Again the emphasis was on representation. The Massachusetts call asserted that

> those Measures have a Tendency to deprive the Colonists of some of their most essential Rights as British Subjects and as Men, particularly the Right of assessing their own Taxes, and being free from any Impositions but such as they consent to by themselves or Representatives.[9]

Soon colonies were vying with each other to reject the approaching stamp

---

[8] *The Writings of Samuel Adams*, vol. 1, p. 5.
[9] Committee of Massachusetts House of Representatives to Connecticut, June 25, 1764, *Collections of the Connecticut Historical Society*, vol. 18, pp. 284–85.

tax. A special session of the Rhode Island assembly appointed a committee of correspondence to confer with the other colonies on measures to obtain a repeal of the Sugar Act and to prevent passage of the Stamp Act. Its agent in London was instructed "to do every thing in his power, either alone or by joining with the agents of the other governments, to effect these purposes." By October 1764, a growing sense that each colony could accomplish little by acting alone was reflected in a message from the Rhode Island assembly to the Secretary of the Connecticut assembly: "If all the Colonies were disposed to enter with Spirit into the Defence of their Liberties; if some Method could be hit upon for collecting the Sentiments of each Colony, and for uniting and forming the Substance of them into one common Defence of the whole, and this sent to England, and the several Agents directed to join together in pushing and pursuing it there in the properest and most effectual Manner, it might be the most probable Method to produce the End aimed at."[10]

An expanded anthology of colonial complaints came from the General Assembly of New York in October 1764. It denounced "certain Designs, lately formed, if possible, to induce the Parliament of *Great-Britain,* to impose Taxes upon the Subjects *here,* by Laws to be passed *there*" as calculated to "reduce the Colonies to absolute Ruin." The "Exemption from the Burthen of ungranted, involuntary Taxes, must be the grand Principle of every free State.—Without such a Right vested in themselves, exclusive of all others, there can be no Liberty, no Happiness, no Security; it is inseparable from the very idea of Property, who can call that his own, which may be taken away at the Pleasure of another?" The British Parliament, it held, was not the supreme legislature of the entire empire; Parliament was merely the head of "one Part of a Dominion" taxing another part.

This petition exemplifies the twofold nature of the attack on parliamentary taxes. As a practical matter, they were "ruinous"; as a matter of principle, they were inadmissible. The practical part might have been negotiable; the principle struck at the root of the imperial connection. If the denial of this "grand Principle" robbed the colonies of all liberty, happiness, security, and even the "idea of Property," and if the empire was made up of autonomous parts, the implications were fundamental and shattering to the existing relationship between Great Britain and its American colonies.

But it was typical of this early period that other statements in the same document went in a different direction. It also protested that there was no "Desire of Independency upon the supreme Power of the Parliament." The

[10] Rhode Island General Assembly's Committee to George Wyllys, October 8, 1764, ibid., pp. 290–92.

very thought of such a desire was rejected with the "utmost Abhorrence," because the colonies still needed "protection." It was agreed that Parliament had the authority "to model the trade of the whole Empire," even with "a necessary Regard to the particular Trade of *Great-Britain.*" A deal was offered—Parliament could remain in command of colonial trade "but leave it to the legislative Power of the Colony, to impose all other Burthens upon it's own People." In effect, the deal amounted to continued British control of trade in exchange for leaving everything else, particularly taxes, to the colonies.

One long sentence embodies the political rhetoric of the period, combining protestation, lamentation, and threat:

> The General Assembly of this Colony have no desire to derogate from the Power of the Parliament of *Great-Britain;* but they cannot avoid deprecating the Loss of such Rights as they have hitherto enjoyed, Rights established in the first Dawn of our Constitution, founded upon the most substantial Reasons, confirmed by invariable Usage, conducive to the best Ends; never abused to bad Purposes, and with the loss of which Liberty, Property, and all the Benefits of Life, tumble into Insecurity and Ruin: Rights, the Deprivation of which, will dispirit the People, abate their Industry, discourage Trade, introduce Discord, Poverty and Slavery; or, by depopulating the Colonies, turn a vast, fertile, prosperous Region, into a dreary Wilderness; impoverish *Great-Britain,* and shake the Power and Independency of the most opulent and flourishing Empire in the World.[11]

Here the choice was stark for both the colonies and Great Britain itself—on one side, all that was good and beneficial; on the other side, all that was bad and ruinous. This appeal contains a contradiction that the colonial polemicists were never able to clear up. They did not wish to "derogate" or detract anything from the power of Parliament but insisted that Parliament could not touch established colonial "Rights," which effectively derogated from that power. It may also have escaped the New York authors that it might not please British readers to be told that British "Power and Independency" depended on how the colonies were treated.

Other petitions to the king, Lords, and Commons came from still a third province, Virginia. They went somewhat beyond the Adams-Otis approach but not so far as the New Yorkers'. The king was asked to protect the right of the colonists to be governed by their own laws "respecting their internal

[11] New York Petition to the House of Commons, October 18, 1764, in *Prologue to Revolution,* ed. Edmund S. Morgan (University of North Carolina Press, 1959), pp. 8–14.

polity and Taxation as are derived from their own Consent." The Lords were told that freedom could not exist where taxes were laid without consent and without representation. The Commons were informed that the American subjects were not constitutionally represented in Parliament but also that in practice they could not be represented. There was in addition an implied threat that "anticonstitutional Power" on the part of Great Britain "may be dangerous in its Example to the interiour Parts of the *British* Empire, and will certainly be detrimental to its Commerce."[12]

Two reactions from New Jersey in 1764 were revealing. One came in a letter from Daniel Coxe to Joseph Reed, the Philadelphia lawyer who later corresponded with the earl of Dartmouth and ended in the revolutionary camp. Coxe, also a lawyer in Trenton, went the opposite way. He was a member of a notable family which, like many, were divided in their loyalties, showing how persons of the same background chose different paths. Daniel, with large interests in land and from 1771 to the Revolution a provincial councillor, remained a staunch Tory and was forced to flee to England. The most famous member of the family, Tench Coxe, was another Tory, but with a difference. A young businessman, he sided openly with the British after British troops marched into Philadelphia in 1776, went over to the revolutionary side as soon as the British evacuated the town in 1778, and lived long enough to become assistant secretary of the Treasury in the administration of John Adams and to become the most influential political economist in the early republic.

When Daniel Coxe wrote to Joseph Reed on April 12, 1764, the time had not yet come to take sides. He reacted angrily to the British demands as if he were an ordinary, normal member of the American elite: "What in the name of Sense has possess'd the English Nation or rather its parliament. . . . My God! What Madness this is." He complained bitterly against the British policy of draining the colonies of gold and silver, of favoring the British West Indian colonies at the expense of the North American mainland, of preventing the old colonies from expanding westward. But then he wondered whether there was a fundamental explanation for the British animosity—"they seem somehow to be afraid We may grow too Strong for Infancy, & apprehend our Indepen[den]cy, or perhaps more truly they seem to understand little of Us, our Interest, or their own, respecting Us, and what will become of Us I cannot tell if such be their present temper."[13] In 1764, a future Tory could still entertain such sentiments. Yet Coxe had

[12] Ibid., pp. 14–17.
[13] Coxe to Reed, April 12, 1764, *New Jersey in the American Revolution, 1763–1783*, ed. Larry R. Gerlach (New Jersey Historical Commission, 1975), pp. 5–6.

expressed thoughts that had come out openly in the British pamphlets of 1759–61—"too Strong for Infancy" and fear of "Independency."

More officially, a committee of correspondence of the New Jersey legislature instructed the colony's agent in London, Joseph Sherwood, to make known that "we look upon all Taxes laid upon us without our Consent as a fundamental infringement of the Rights and priveleges Secured to us as English Subjects and by Charter." He was told to cooperate with other agents "to Show the Colonies are unanimously of One Mind."[14]

By 1764, then, at least six colonies, among them the most populous and important—Massachusetts, New York, Virginia, New Jersey, Rhode Island, and Connecticut—had taken their stands against the new British policy, especially on the key issue of taxes.[15] They varied in their emphases but agreed substantially on the main points. Taxes required consent; consent required representation in Parliament; if the requirements were not met, ruination and slavery were sure to follow. In Virginia, representation was already written off as impracticable. If the colonies suffered, they would drag Great Britain down with them. New York and Virginia insisted that their exemption from parliamentary taxation was a matter of "right," not merely of expediency, though they also argued the case for expediency.

Hard questions remained. How could "supreme Power" belong to Parliament if it did not have the power to tax the colonies? Why, in principle, was it right for Parliament to have power over trade but not taxes? How could Americans consider themselves to be as British as their British compatriots if the latter could be taxed by Parliament but the former could not? What kind of polity would emerge in the colonies if they took charge of everything but their trade? How long was trade likely to remain a British prerogative if everything else was taken away from British authority? What would such a division of power, even if it were feasible, do to the existing fabric of the British political and imperial system?

The answers to such questions were still some time off. Advanced colonial thinkers and activists had started something they were not immediately prepared to finish. For the time being, they were content to live with contradictions and ambiguities. Yet it is remarkable how many

[14] Ibid., pp. 7–8.

[15] The petitions from Connecticut and Rhode Island were similar to the pamphlets by Governor Fitch of Connecticut and Governor Hopkins of Rhode Island. Pennsylvania also sent instructions to its agent, Richard Jackson, for "the Right of assessing their own Taxes, and of being free from any Impositions but those that are made by their own Representatives." But it held out a plan under consideration "to grant the necessary Aids to the Crown, and to contribute to their general Defence" (*Letters and Papers of Benjamin Franklin and Richard Jackson, 1753–1785*, ed. Carl Van Doren, American Philosophical Society, 1947, pp. 183–86).

basic questions had been broached in but a few months after the Grenville ministry had made its first move. Equally remarkable is the unanimity of colonies that before had not often been able to agree or act together.

· 3 ·

That America had grown up sufficiently to take on Great Britain was now shown in another way. Until the crisis brought on by the stamp tax, Americans had not been notable for political expression. They had not yet taken to the political pamphleteering that had long flourished in Great Britain. Above all, no American had been bold enough to argue affairs of state with the British government.

The first significant American political pamphlet by James Otis, published in 1762 in connection with the writs of assistance case, had been directed against Governor Bernard of Massachusetts, not Parliament. But it had stated a principle that could later be applied to a parliamentary tax. Otis had held that "the power of taxing is peculiar to the general assembly" and that "all taxation ought to originate in the House." He cited Locke at length as his supreme authority, including a dictum on taxes.[16] Otis did not apply his reasoning to an act of Parliament; that was still to come, but the germ of the idea was present in this pamphlet.[17]

The annus mirabilis of American political pamphleteering came in 1764. Four extraordinary pamphlets appeared that year, one in New Haven, two in Boston, and one in Rhode Island. They were extraordinary because they revealed a mastery of political theorizing and controversy never before exhibited in the colonies, and because they presented a united front despite the distances and differences that separated their authors.

The New Haven pamphlet was the work of a group of Connecticut legislators headed by Gov. Thomas Fitch. The governor took the lead because in Connecticut he was popularly elected and represented the people rather than the Crown. This presentation of the colonial case shows that it had been reduced to a few basic formulas. Laws, especially

[16] Locke's dictum that legislatures "must not raise taxes on the property of the people, without the consent of the people, given by themselves or deputies.

[17] James Otis, A Vindication of the Conduct of the House of Representatives of the Massachusetts-Bay (Boston, 1762), pp. 23 (Locke) and 39 (power of assembly). Otis's biographer, William Tudor, claimed that Otis in this pamphlet had shown "that taxation and representation are inseparable," which read into this pamphlet the later stamp tax controversy (The Life of James Otis, Boston, 1823, p. 122). Tudor had received in 1818 a letter from John Adams making an even more expansive claim for this pamphlet (The Works of John Adams, ed. Charles Francis Adams, Boston, 1861, vol. 10, pp. 310–11).

taxes, required consent; consent required representation; but the colonies were too far away to be represented in Parliament; therefore, "legislative authority," including taxes, must be vested in the colonial legislatures, where alone the colonists were represented.

But this pamphlet represents an early stage of the colonial argument and also shows how far it still had to go. One line of thought was peculiarly double-edged. It maintained that, without the authority to impose taxes or duties, "the general rights of legislation would be of no avail" to the colonial legislatures. By the same reasoning, however, Parliament would be deprived of its "general rights of legislation" over the colonies. Whichever was right, one or the other was sure to suffer a loss of power.

Another double-edged argument was based on an extreme case. It took this form:

> If these internal taxations take place, and the principles upon which they must be founded are adopted and carried into execution, the colonies will have no more than a shadow of legislation left, nor the King's subjects in them any more than the shadow of true English liberty; for the same principles which will justify such a tax of a penny will warrant a tax of a pound, an hundred, or a thousand pounds, and so on without limitation; and if they will warrant a tax on one article, they will support one on as many particulars as shall be thought necessary to raise any sum proposed.[18]

In effect, the question Where would it end? forced both sides to look at the stamp tax as if it were decisive for all legislation. The British were bound to ask themselves the same question. If Parliament could not tax stamps without consent, it could not tax anything without consent; if so, it was left with "no more than a shadow of legislation." The stamp tax might be large or small, necessary or not, but when it was made into a matter of principle, it became a monster for both sides.

But the Connecticut authors were not ready to go to the bitter end. For one thing, they made a distinction between "internal" taxes, such as the one on stamps, and "external" taxes, such as commercial duties. By distinguishing between the two, they left open a large area for parliamentary control, despite the contrary implications of their broader anti–stamp tax argument. They went so far as to acknowledge that "the Parliament of Great Britain is most certainly vested with the supreme authority of the

[18] [Thomas Fitch et al.], *Reasons Why the British Colonies, in America, Should Not Be Charged with Internal Taxes* (New Haven, 1764), reprinted in Bernard Bailyn, ed., *Pamphlets of the American Revolution* (Harvard University Press, 1965), p. 393.

nation, and its jurisdiction and power most capacious and transcendent." They protested that "the colonies will be far, very far from urging or even attempting anything in derogation of the power or authority of that august Assembly, or pretending to prescribe bounds or limits to the exercise of their dominion." They explicitly conceded that

> nothing in the foregoing observations, be sure, is intended by way of objection but that the crown by its prerogative or the Parliament by its supreme and general jurisdiction may justly order and do some things which may affect the property of the American subjects in a way which, in some sense, may be said to be independent upon or without the will or consent of the people, as by regulations of trade and commerce and the like, and by general orders relative to and restrictions of their conduct for the good of the whole.[19]

In practice, if not in theory, the British were offered a deal. If they gave up the power to tax, the colonies were willing to permit them to keep the power to regulate trade and commerce. This trade-off depended on the distinction between "internal" and "external" taxes, which continued to muddle the issue for some time. It was a dubious distinction, as this passage recognized by admitting that it "in some sense" violated the principle of popular consent. The colonies were not yet ready for a total break and were looking for a way out of the impasse created by their rebellion against taxes.

The Connecticut authors also agreed that the new trans-Allegheny lands belonged to the Crown, not the colonies, and that, therefore, the latter should not bear any expense for them.[20] It was another concession that the colonies would live to regret.

· 4 ·

James Otis was the author of the most famous of the Boston pamphlets in 1764.[21] It shows that the colonists had not yet thought through their objections to the stamp tax. More than others, it locates Otis politically in the past as well as in the future.

Otis was a true believer in consent and representation. He was as good

[19] Ibid., p. 394.
[20] Ibid., p. 404.
[21] James Otis, The Rights of the British Colonies Asserted and proved (Boston, 1764), reprinted in Bailyn, Pamphlets of the American Revolution, pp. 419–82.

a Lockean as anyone else—*"The supreme power cannot take from any man any part of his property, without his consent in person or by representation"* and *"Taxes are not to be laid on the people but by their consent in person or by deputation."* Taxation was his main bogey, and he made lack of consent to it equivalent to "an entire disfranchisement of every civil right." On the other hand, he was willing to accept parliamentary dictation in matters of trade and commerce. He wanted the colonial assemblies to be recognized as provincially "subordinate," with no taint of independent status, and held that the colonies were "subordinate dominions."[22] He led the colonists in their early disaffection but in his own individualistic way.

Otis was at his most idiosyncratic in his attitude to the British Parliament. He saw where the dispute between Parliament and the colonies might lead and sought to head off a parting of the ways by prematurely raising the most troublesome questions of all: What if Parliament refused to accede to the colonial demands? Where was the greater loyalty—to the supremacy of Parliament or the claims of the colonial legislatures? Otis boldly—or perhaps rashly—answered this question in advance. There was no escape from obedience to Parliament, even if it was wrong in this instance. He attributed to the king and Parliament "the most pure and perfect intentions of justice, goodness, and truth that human nature is capable of" and insisted that "a most perfect and ready obedience is to be yielded to it while it remains in force." He made this absolute declaration of submission to the higher authority:

> The power of Parliament is uncontrollable but by themselves, and we must obey. They only can repeal their own acts. There would be an end of all government if one or a number of subjects or subordinate provinces should take upon them so far to judge of the justice of an act of Parliament as to refuse obedience to it. If there was nothing else to restrain such a step, prudence ought to do it, for forceably resisting Parliament and the King's laws is high treason. Therefore let Parliament lay what burdens they please on us, we must, it is our duty to submit and patiently bear them till they will be pleased to relieve us.[23]

To Otis it was necessary to find the "middle road" between "subordination, absolute slavery, and subjection on the one side, and liberty, independence, and licentiousness on the other."[24] If such a middle road

---

[22] Ibid., pp. 446–47, 461, 456–57, 470.
[23] Ibid., p. 448.
[24] Ibid., p. 452.

had existed, the Revolution might have been avoided, but it took ten years to find out whether it existed or not.

The second Boston pamphlet of 1764, by Oxenbridge Thacher, published soon after Otis's, was less likely to get its author into trouble, though the two were largely in agreement. Thacher, too, gave the British credit for good intentions. He could see that "no design is formed to enslave them, and that the justice of the British Parliament will finally do right to every part of their dominions." He also thought that the colonies had no more than a "subordinate legislature subject to the control of the mother state." But he objected to double taxation—by the colonies' own legislatures and now by the British Parliament. With the Connecticut group, he agreed that the newly conquered territory beyond the Alleghenies was British rather than colonial.

Thacher, however, contributed a somewhat different line of reasoning. He criticized the new taxes on the ground that they were bound to harm Great Britain as well as the colonies. He reminded the British that "everybody knows that the greatest part of the trade of Great Britain is with her colonies." If the colonies could no longer afford to carry on this trade, they would be forced to make their own manufactured goods instead of importing them from Great Britain—or be reduced to the skins of beasts as the Indians were "and sink into like barbarism." Did Parliament, he asked, want to kill the "hen that every day laid her a *golden egg?*"

Thacher's was at this early stage the authentic voice of the British-American. As he put it, "He is not ashamed to avow a love to the country that gave him birth; yet he hath ever exulted in the name of Briton."[25] He died the next year, before he could witness the transition from British-American to plain American.

The last pamphlet, published towards the end of 1764, was the work of Stephen Hopkins, the governor of Rhode Island, the other colony that elected its own chief executive.[26]

It, too, started from the Lockean premise—"British subjects are to be governed only agreeable to laws to which themselves have some way consented, and are not to be compelled to part with their property but

[25] [Oxenbridge Thacher], *The Sentiments of a British American* (Boston, 1764); reprinted in Bailyn, *Pamphlets of the American Revolution,* pp. 490–92, 496–97.

[26] [Stephen Hopkins], *The Rights of Colonies Examined* (Providence, 1764). Though the title page says 1765, it was authorized to be published by the General Assembly in November 1764 and first published in the *Providence Gazette* on December 22, 1764 (William E. Foster, *Stephen Hopkins: A Rhode Island Statesman* [Rhode Island Historical Tracts, Providence, 1884], pt. 2, p. 51. Bailyn puts it in 1765, though he says that it was "published with the endorsement of the Rhode Island Assembly in December [1764]" (*Pamphlets of the American Revolution,* p. 500).

as it is called for by authority of such laws." But it was much harsher in its application of the principle than the others; anything less amounted to "the miserable condition of slaves." The Crown, it contended, had always treated the colonies as "dependent, though free," without explaining how they could go together, but now "the scene seems to be unhappily changing."

To change it back again, Hopkins offered the same kind of deal as the Connecticut pamphlet but differently expressed. It was based on the distinction between "matters of a general nature," such as commerce and credit, and the particular matter of taxation. For this reason, he proposed a division of labor between Parliament and the colonial legislatures, the former to take charge of the concerns common to the entire British empire and the latter "to take care of its interests and provide for its peace and internal government." Hopkins chose to "pass by" the question of colonial representation in Parliament and merely asked that the colonies be given notice of every new measure that affected their rights, liberties, or interests.

A striking aspect of Hopkins's work is the different way in which he discussed the molasses tax and the stamp tax. He objected to the first on practical grounds and argued that Rhode Island was peculiarly dependent on foreign molasses and its own distilleries. When it came to the stamp tax, however, he adopted a different tone. He could hardly control his rhetoric: "For it must be confessed by all men that they who are taxed at pleasure by others cannot possibly have any property, can have nothing to be called their own. They who have no property can have no freedom, but are indeed reduced to the most abject slavery."

He scoffed at the idea that "the people in Britain have a sovereign authority over their fellow subjects in America." The British empire was an "imperial state, which consists of many separate governments each of which hath peculiar privileges," so that "all laws and all taxations which bind the whole must be made by the whole," not by the British people alone. The House of Commons had acted by virtue of "mere superiority and power." The colonies, he protested, had always raised the money requested by the Crown; this was the only constitutional way. One of the most striking allusions went back to the conquest of Canada in the Seven Years' War: "Hard will be the fate, yea cruel the destiny, of these unhappy colonies if the reward they are to receive for all this is the loss of their freedom; better for them Canada still remained French, yea far more eligible that it ever should remain so than that the price of its reduction should be their slavery."[27]

After these pamphlets, hard questions remained. Was there a really essential difference between internal and external taxes? Should the colonies accept continued British control of their commerce in return for getting the British to give up the power of internal taxation? What did a surrender of the power to tax do to the fundamental relationship between Great Britain and its colonies? Were they subservient dependencies of a British imperium; were they separated but equal parts of one whole; or did they have "separate governments," each with its own constitutional separation of powers?

The larger questions had never before been thrust into the public arena. The new taxes could not be handled the way the old molasses tax had been finessed, by a tacit agreement to keep them on the books but not to enforce them. By the 1760s, the British government was determined not to continue on the slippery slope of abdication. Above all, the colonial ideologists were determined to resist the new taxes in principle and found the way to do so by raiding Britain's own armory of received political wisdom. An irresistible force was moving towards an immovable object.

· 5 ·

Meanwhile, British governing circles faced the same problems.

A comforting British assumption had always been that the thirteen colonies were too widely separated and too divided by self-interest and cross-purposes to be capable of challenging British rule effectively. The fiasco of the Albany Conference in 1754 had seemingly confirmed this settled conviction. The colonies had gone their separate ways even during the Seven Years' War, despite what they had claimed was the deadly threat from France.

In the past, the British had not deliberately adopted a policy of "divide and rule," because it had not been necessary to do so. The way the colonies had originally been settled and developed was enough to favor a more passive version of "divide and rule"—to the extent that the colonies were ruled at all. If the British had not been so confident—with some reason—that the colonies would not and could not get together on almost anything, they might have acted differently.

In 1764, the first step towards a colonial united front against the already

[27] Bailyn, *Pamphlets of the American Revolution*, pp. 507–8, 512, 516, 520.

enacted Sugar Act and the projected Stamp Act was the proposal for joint action by the Massachusetts representatives. Gov. Francis Bernard of Massachusetts was quick to sense trouble. He lost no time alerting the Board of Trade that there was more to the proposal than met the eye:

> Altho' This may seem at first sight only an Occasional measure for a particular purpose, yet I have reason to believe that the purposes it is to serve are deeper than they now appear. I apprehend that it is intended to take this opportunity ... to lay a foundation for connecting the demagogues of the several Governments in America to join together in opposition to all orders from Great Britain which don't square with their notions of the rights of the people. Perhaps I may be too suspicious; a little time will show whether I am or not.[28]

In London, a remark had already been dropped that also hinted of the crisis to come. On March 7, 1764, when Grenville for the first time mentioned in Parliament that he intended to introduce a bill to tax the Americans, he set off an exchange of which we have only a tantalizingly brief record. A parliamentary diary kept by James Harris, an associate of Grenville, contains this entry: "[Grenville] Gave us some general idea of his plan, particularly as to the taxing America. Beckford rambled—hoped regard would be had to the American legislatures etc. Charles Townshend answered strongly for Government—that our plan of expenses being so great, America ought to share."[29]

William Beckford was a follower of William Pitt; Charles Townshend was president of the Board of Trade. Beckford's allusion to the American legislatures was peculiarly intuitive of just where the neuralgic political point was going to be. American legislatures had always had a monopoly of taxation in the colonies; in what way the British government could have a "regard" for the colonies' taxing power if Parliament broke their monopoly was precisely the problem that Grenville had not yet begun to face. Townshend's reply reflects an official British desire to sidestep Beckford's stab in the dark and to decide the matter on purely practical grounds.

Grenville himself was still uncertain just how to get the money that he wanted from the colonies. He told American agents who visited him soon

---

[28] Bernard to Board of Trade, June 29, 1764, Bernard Papers, vol. 3, p. 157, cited in Edmund S. Morgan and Helen M. Morgan, *The Stamp Act Crisis* (University of North Carolina Press, 1953), p. 103.

[29] Cited by Lewis Namier and John Brooke, *Charles Townshend* (St. Martin's Press, 1964), pp. 114–15.

after his first announcement that he was not "sett upon this tax, if the Americans dislike it and preferr any other method of raising the money themselves." He asked the agents to write to the colonies, "and if they choose any other mode I shall be satisfied, provided the money be but raised."[30] This version of Grenville's approach, by one of the Americans present, suggests that the British minister was more interested in getting money to pay for the British forces in America than in how he got it. The only other "mode," however, was requisitioning, which let each colony decide for itself how it was going to raise its quota. This method had never worked in the colonies, even during the recent war against the French. Grenville, therefore, has been suspected of duplicity.[31] It is just as likely that he had not yet worked out a definite plan and was toying with different methods without having fully thought through the consequences of any of them.

The idea that the colonies should somehow get together to make a contribution in order to forestall parliamentary legislation was not altogether outlandish. When Benjamin Franklin considered the matter in June 1764, he thought it not unlikely that the colonies would agree on a "general Tax, as a Stamp Act, or an excise on Rum, &c. or both," instead of quotas for each colony.[32] Governor Bernard told the Massachusetts agent, Richard Jackson, in August 1764 to "interpose on the behalf of the province that they may at least have the liberty of enacting internal taxation themselves: which I have no doubt, but that they will readily do, when it shall be positively required of them."[33] When four American agents, including Franklin, who had recently arrived in London, met with Grenville on February 2, 1765, they made just such a proposal—that "the several Colonies might be permitted to lay the Tax themselves."[34] The choice seemed to be between a tax on stamps by Parliament or some equivalent action by the colonial assemblies to prevent Parliament from setting a precedent.

Grenville and his closest associates always claimed to have chosen the tax on stamps because it was the least onerous measure they could think of. There is no reason to doubt the original intention. Grenville told the

[30] "Israel Mauduit's Account of a Conference between Mr. Grenville and the Several Colony Agents," in *The Jenkinson Papers, 1760–1766*, ed. Ninetta S. Jucker (Macmillan, 1949), p. 306. Israel Mauduit was the brother of Jasper Mauduit, the agent for Massachusetts, and had attended the conference for him. Other versions confirm this account.

[31] Morgans, *Stamp Act Crisis*, pp. 60, 66.

[32] Franklin to Jackson, June 25, 1764, *Letters and Papers of Franklin and Jackson*, p. 168.

[33] Bernard to Jackson, August 18, 1764, cited in *Prologue to Revolution*, p. 29.

[34] Jared Ingersoll to Thomas Fitch, February 11, 1765, *Prologue to Revolution*, p. 33.

agents, according to one of them, that he wanted to raise money in America "by means the most easy and least objectionable to the Colonies" and to give them an opportunity to state their objections.[35] Thomas Whately, the official who actually drafted the Stamp Act for Grenville, said that the delay had been motivated "out of Tenderness to the Colonies." The tax on stamps had been chosen as "the easiest, the most equal and the most certain."[36]

Grenville also tried to win over the colonists by appointing an American in each colony to act as stamp collector. One of those who were willing to meet him more than halfway was Benjamin Franklin, the agent for Pennsylvania. His response shows that even someone who opposed the stamp tax saw it as merely a special case without larger implications for the American-British relationship. Franklin obtained the appointment of John Hughes, to whom he wrote that, while he still wanted to get the tax repealed, "in the meantime, a firm Loyalty to the Crown and faithful Adherence to the Government of this Nation, which it is the Safety as well as Honour of the Colonies to be connected with, will always be the wisest Course for you and I to take, whatever may be the Madness of the Populace or their blind Leaders, who can only bring themselves and Country into Trouble, and draw on greater Burthens by Acts of rebellious Tendency."[37] Franklin's reaction to the stamp tax suggests that Grenville had reason to be surprised at the upheaval it produced.

Yet the solicitude on the ministry's part indicated that it realized there was something different and exceptional about a tax on stamps and that it had to be handled with unusual delicacy. Whatever Grenville and his close associates may have thought they were doing to make the tax more palatable to the colonists, it was soon enough apparent that the problem was what they wanted to do, not how they were going about doing it.

By the end of 1764, Grenville had reason to know what the real trouble was and where it was coming from. The import of the colonial pamphlets and petitions did not escape the British authorities. The two that seem to have disturbed them most came from Massachusetts and New York.

On December 11, 1764, the Board of Trade reported to the king that the resolutions and proceedings of both assemblies "treated the acts and resolutions of the legislature of Great-Britain with the most indecent disrespect." The Privy Council advised the king to direct that copies

---

[35] Charles Garth to Committee of Correspondence of South Carolina Assembly, June 5, 1764, *English Historical Review*, vol. 54, 1939, pp. 646–48.

[36] [Thomas Whately], *The Regulations Lately made concerning the Colonies, and the Taxes Imposed upon Them, considered* (London, 1765), p. 101.

[37] Franklin to Hughes, August 9, 1765, *Franklin Papers*, vol. 12, pp. 234–35.

of these acts and resolutions be presented to Parliament. They were, however, not considered when their contents became known, because "they denied the power of Great-Britain" and "were found to contain expressions questioning the jurisdiction of parliament."[38]

If there was a year of decision, it was 1764. The way had been prepared the year before with the official end of the Seven Years' War and the promulgation of the first measures which the colonies considered hostile to their interests. But it was in 1764 that the colonies began to find their ideology of resistance and to rally their forces. It was also in 1764 that the British began to realize that they were up against something more serious than the usual colonial discontents. Both sides had no way of knowing how deep was their estrangement.

· 6 ·

Nevertheless, the pamphlets of 1764 were only a beginning of the Americans' efforts to rationalize their resistance to the British offensive.

Until now, the pamphleteers were all of one mind, however differently they may have stated their views. Early in 1765, however, the first pamphlet to express an opposing view appeared. It was the work of Martin Howard, Jr., of Rhode Island, who took aim at the previous year's publications of Stephen Hopkins and James Otis. Howard, like the others, was a lawyer who briefly emerged from obscurity and might have quickly returned to it if he had not provoked Otis into writing another pamphlet to answer him.

Howard's polemic is notable as an unqualified defense of the British cause by an American. He accused Otis of having perpetrated a "disguised" expression of the "dangerous and indiscreet position" that the colonies "have rights independent of, and not controllable by the authority of Parliament." Hopkins was charged with an even graver offense—having claimed that "the House of Commons have not any sort of power over the Americans." Howard presented a number of arguments in rebuttal that were endlessly repeated in the years to come. It was "the essence of government that there should be a supreme head"—in this case Parliament. It represented "every British subject, wheresoever he be." If the jurisdiction of Parliament was "transcendent and entire," it could levy taxes as well as regulate trade. Howard was also one of the first

[38] *The Conduct of the Late Administration Examined, Relative to the American Stamp-Act* (London, 1767), pp. 15–16, note a; [William Knox], *The Claim of the Colonies To An Exemption from Internal Taxes Imposed By Authority of Parliament, Examined* (London, 1765), p. 35.

to make an important distinction between the jurisdiction of Parliament and the exercise of that jurisdiction. The first was untouchable; only the second was amenable to expediency or utility. The first was off-limits to the colonies, but they could "remonstrate, petition, write pamphlets and newspapers without numbers" within the bounds of the second. Howard was no great controversialist, but he saw some things clearly, especially the significance of this distinction between principle and practice.[39]

The main interest in Otis's reply is how he tried to deal with this distinction. He indignantly said that neither he nor Hopkins had ever contemplated "an independent, uncontrollable provincial legislative" or had denied that "the Parliament of Great Britain hath a just, clear, equitable, and constitutional right, power, and authority to bind the colonies by all acts wherein they are named," including taxes of all kinds. Otis went on, however, to make the same distinction that Howard had made—that it did not by any means follow that " 'tis always expedient and in all circumstances equitable for the supreme and sovereign legislative" to tax the colonies, especially if they were not represented in Parliament. Otis repeatedly affirmed parliamentary supremacy over the colonies, or else "the colonies would be independent, which none but rebels, fools, or madmen will contend for." Yet he insisted that the right of taxing the colonies was not the same as "the mode of exercising it." The latter could be inequitable and unreasonable, which is what Otis consistently maintained. As for colonial representation in Parliament, he still believed in it but now admitted that the present American generation would get very little out of it, because they were still too few to make a difference in Parliament. But he held out the prospect of future growth of population in the colonies in a way that might have seemed ominous to British readers:

> Is it to be believed that when a continent of 3000 miles in length shall have more inhabitants than there are at this day in Great Britain, France, and Ireland, perhaps in all Europe, they will be quite content with the bare name of British subjects, and to the end of time supinely acquiesce in laws made, as it may happen, against their interest by an assembly 3000 miles beyond sea, and where, should they agree in the sentiments with the Halifax gentleman [Howard], it may be thought that an admission of an American member would "sully and defile the purity of the whole body"? One hundred years will give this continent more inhabitants than there are in the three kingdoms.

[39] Martin Howard, Jr., *A Letter from a Gentleman at Halifax* (Newport, 1765), reprinted in Bailyn, *Pamphlets of the American Revolution*, pp. 532–44.

This was written by one who more than any other American opponent of the stamp tax was willing to concede to Parliament maximum power over the colonies, at least in principle. Howard soon struck back with a pamphlet charging that Otis had changed his mind and now embraced his own view of absolute parliamentary authority. Then Otis came back once again and succeeded in confusing even his well-wishers by agreeing that the colonies were already represented in Parliament—"virtually, constitutionally, in law and in equity." Nevertheless, during the same year, he put out another pamphlet in which he seemed to retreat to his previous position that actual representation was better than virtual representation and that every man of sound mind should be able to vote for his parliamentary representative.[40]

Otis's political fate shows where the colonial struggle for a nascent revolutionary political line was heading. He was the first great victim of the fast-moving colonial radicalism in 1765. In 1764, he could still safely assert that it was necessary to obey Parliament, even if that body was wrong on a particular issue. In 1765, he could no longer get away with essentially the same position. He had changed less than had the colonial opinion around him. As one study of his political career put it, the patriot had become a recreant.[41] Even John Adams thought his old hero had been "corrupted and bought off." He recalled in his old age: "The rage against him [Otis] in the town of Boston seemed to be without bounds. He was called a reprobate, an apostate, and a traitor, in every street in Boston."[42] Otis was accused of making a shady deal with the radicals' bugbear, Lieutenant Governor Hutchinson. The first historian of the American Revolution, William Gordon, was so embarrassed when he came to write about Otis's statements on Parliament's supreme power that he claimed they had been "extorted" from him because he feared "being called to an account for the part he had acted" previously, thereby depriving Otis of both integrity and courage.[43]

Otis's unforgivable sin was that he saw at this early stage, and before anyone else was ready to avow it, that refusal to affirm parliamentary

---

[40] James Otis, *Brief Remarks on the Defence of the Halifax Libel on the British-American-Colonies* (Boston, 1765), and *Considerations On Behalf of the Colonists in a Letter to a Noble Lord* (Boston, 1765), both reprinted in *University of Missouri Studies*, October 1, 1929, pp. 109–25; Martin Howard, Jr., *A Defence of the Letter from a Gentleman at Halifax* (Newport, 1765).

[41] Ellen E. Brennan, "James Otis: Recreant and Patriot," *New England Quarterly*, December 1939, pp. 691–725.

[42] *Works of John Adams*, vol. 10, pp. 295–97.

[43] William Gordon, *The History of the Rise, Progress, and Establishment of the Independence of the United States of America* (New York, 1789), vol. 1, p. 119.

supremacy over the colonies was bound to lead them towards independence and make rebels of them. He had led them against the Sugar and Stamp acts but, from the radical revolutionary point of view now evolving, not for the right reasons or in the right way. By 1765, he was already an embarrassment. The revolutionary process needed a different spokesman, one more suited to the new stage of political awareness reached by the colonial movement.

· 7 ·

Otis's successor as chief spokesman was Daniel Dulany, who came out with still another pamphlet later in 1765. He was a Maryland lawyer and politician from a wealthy, influential family. His main contribution was a reasoned attempt to reconcile the subordination of the colonies to Great Britain with their freedom from taxation by the British government. He tried to have it both ways by taking as his point of departure the premise that "there may very well exist a *dependence* and *inferiority* without absolute *vassalage* and *slavery*," or, as he also put it, "I acknowledge dependence on Great Britain, but I can perceive a degree of it without slavery, and I disown all other." The British regulation of colonial trade, he argued, was permissible and even necessary for due subordination; the tax on stamps went too far and, inferentially, suggested vassalage and slavery.

Dulany also labored to show that "virtual representation" was not applicable to the colonies, which could give their consent to taxes only through their own assemblies. The attractiveness of his argument was that it made an effort to give the British what was "necessary or proper for preserving or securing the dependence of the colonies" and to give the colonies what was presumably not necessary or proper "for that very important purpose."

It was an adroit performance. Dulany gave all the stock arguments against the stamp tax—charters, consent, representation, unfairness—without making them seem to challenge the traditional British-American connection. His pamphlet offered as an alternative the method of requisition, whereby the colonies would tax themselves in their own ways. He protested that the question was one "of *propriety,* not of power," and immediately followed with the revealing remark that "though some may be inclined to think it is to little purpose to discuss the one when the other is irresistible, yet are they different considerations." He also played it safe, so far as any practical action was concerned, by claiming that he could show the invalidity of a parliamentary law while at the same time recommending a "submission" to it. Instead of coming out forthrightly in Otis's fashion to call for ultimate obedience, Dulany coyly cautioned that "I shall say nothing of the use I intend by the discussion." In effect, he put the colonial case in its most moderate and conciliatory form, giving to both sides what he thought was in their best interests to avoid a break between them.[44]

Dulany's skillful political footwork paid off in England, where two editions of his pamphlet soon came out. William Pitt cited it favorably in the House of Commons. Other sympathetic British politicians praised it. More editions came out in New York and Boston.[45] It was a great success for a while—but only for a while.

· 8 ·

Finally, another contribution to the American cause came forth at the end of 1765. It was the work of John Dickinson, an unlikely agent of revolution. He was born into a rich, landholding family in Maryland, spent three years studying law at the Middle Temple in London, and came home to practice in Philadelphia. His father's death in 1760 made him one of the largest landowners in Pennsylvania; he was elected to the Pennsylvania Assembly in 1762. In local politics, he was opposed to the group around Benjamin Franklin that wanted to make Pennsylvania into a Crown colony in order to get rid of the proprietorship.

Dickinson's approach differed from that of Otis and Dulany. Theirs was largely political and jurisdictional; his brief was almost entirely economic, weighed down with flourishes of erudition from works by Postlethwayt and Tucker, and *Cato's Letters*. He succeeded, however, in giving his economic analysis of the consequences of the stamp tax an inflammatory tone by making it seem to be catastrophic or apocalyptic. In the same month his pamphlet appeared, he published a broadside against the tax in this vein: "ROUSE yourselves therefore, my dear Countrymen. Think, oh! think of the endless Miseries you *must* entail upon yourselves, and your Country, by touching the pestilential Cargoes that have been sent to you. Destruction lurks within them.—To receive them is Death—is worse than Death—it is SLAVERY!"[46]

---

[44] Daniel Dulany, *Considerations on the Propriety of Imposing Taxes in the British Colonies* (Annapolis, 1765), reprinted in Bailyn, *Pamphlets of the American Revolution*, pp. 610–58.

[45] Aubrey C. Land, *The Dulanys of Maryland* (Johns Hopkins Press, 1955), pp. 266–67.

[46] Sandra Sarkela Hynes, *The Political Rhetoric of John Dickinson, 1764–1776* (diss., University of Massachusetts, 1982), p. 98.

His pamphlet was somewhat more subdued. The Stamp Act, he maintained, was going to draw off "as it were, the last drops of their blood." The tax was going to be easy on the wealthy and "fall on the necessitous and industrious, who most of all require relief and encouragement." The colonies were being "treated as a rich people when we are really poor." British manufacturers and merchants would suffer along with the colonists, who would spend less the more they were taxed. Towards the end, Dickinson exclaimed:

> What man who wishes the welfare of America can view without pity, without passion, her restricted and almost stagnated trade, with its numerous train of evils—taxes torn from her without her consent— her legislative Assemblies, the principal pillars of her liberty, crushed into insignificance—a formidable force established in the midst of peace, to bleed her into obedience—the sacred right of trial by jury violated by the erection of arbitrary and unconstitutional jurisdictions—and general poverty, discontent, and despondence stretching themselves over his unoffending country?

Dickinson let drop other revealing remarks. He reminded the British that "it may justly be said that the FOUNDATIONS OF THE POWER AND GLORY OF GREAT BRITAIN ARE LAID IN AMERICA." He denied British allegations that the colonists were "designing and endeavouring to render themselves independent," but he did so in such a way that the threat of independence could still be held out if the British persisted in their oppressive and arbitrary measures. This manner of denying that Americans wanted to be independent was much used in this period: "Evils are frequently precipitated by imprudent attempts to prevent them. In short, we never can be made an independent people except it be by Great Britain herself; and the only way for her to do it is to make us frugal, ingenious, united, and discontented"—topped off by a quotation along the same lines from *Cato's Letters.*

Another observation by Dickinson turned on a common British view of the outcome of the Seven Years' War. The usual British contention was that the colonies would never have dared to become so obstreperous if the French still threatened them from Canada. Dickinson informed the British that the colonists were firmly persuaded that "they never would have been treated as they are if Canada still continued in the hands of the French." Yet, in the end, Dickinson—like so many others at the time—backed away from the awful precipice and assured his British readers that the colonists' resentment "is but the resentment of dutiful children who have received unmerited blows from a beloved parent."[47]

The ideological pamphlets of 1765 were not matched in quantity or quality until 1774, the eve of the Revolution. Dickinson produced another outstanding pamphlet in 1768, but he was exceptional. The great controversialists of 1764–65 were, with few exceptions, unable to keep up with the onrushing revolutionary tide. Otis was left behind in 1765. Fitch, after eleven years as governor of Connecticut, was defeated in 1766 and died a loyalist. Thacher died in 1765 and never had another chance to prove how revolutionary he really was. Dulany dropped out of active opposition to British rule and went through the Revolutionary War a neutral. Dickinson was never forgiven for refusing to sign the Declaration of Independence. Only Governor Hopkins of Rhode Island did not falter throughout the revolutionary struggle.

These men raised questions of principle and power, which they could not resolve but which once let loose lived a life of their own. They raised them in a rhetorical manner that made them seem to be matters of life or death, freedom or slavery. A stamp tax could be compromised if it was regarded as nothing more than a tax, but freedom or slavery could not. The men of 1764–65 started something they could not finish, but the end was implicit in their beginning. Otis may have believed that acts of Parliament had to be obeyed even if they were wrong; others could be persuaded by him that such acts were wrong and therefore should not be obeyed. If parliamentary taxes required colonial consent, and consent required colonial representation in Parliament, some might begin by advocating representation, but others might soon reject representation on the ground that it was impracticable and inequitable.

For the British, the Stamp Act was not likely to bring in so much money that it was worth stirring up an irreconcilable conflict. Thomas Whately of the British Treasury estimated that the sale of stamps would bring in no more than one-third of what was needed to pay for the new forces. He expected the military establishment in the colonies to cost at least £300,000 annually and the American taxes to bring in at most £100,000 annually. Britain would still have to send £200,000 to the colonies to make up the difference.[48] Yet once the decision was made to impose the stamp tax, the British were stuck with it,

[47] John Dickinson, *The Late Regulations respecting the British Colonies* (Philadelphia, 1765), reprinted in Bailyn, *Pamphlets of the American Revolution*, pp. 669–91.

[48] Whately to John Temple, June 12, 1765, *Massachusetts Historical Society Collections*, 6th ser., vol. 9, 1897, p. 59.

until they were persuaded to back away by the intensity of American resistance.

The political agenda was set in 1764–65, a decade before it was fully worked out in theory and practice. Its leading spokesmen were too extreme for the old order and not extreme enough for the new. Its most representative figure was the tragic James Otis, who never recovered his ideological influence and died in the very year of the final triumph of the American Revolution, after having suffered periods of insanity resulting from a blow received in a quarrel with a British official. He has been punished even by historians and editors of collected works; there has been no published biography of him since 1823 and no collected edition of his works, though many lesser figures have received both.[49]

In 1765, too, the issue of the power of Parliament over the colonies made its appearance. Otis had tried to avoid it in 1764 by agreeing in advance that Parliament had such power, though it had been used badly in this specific case. In May 1765, Gov. Bernard pressed this view to its ultimate conclusion. He advised the Massachusetts legislature to give "a respectable submission to the decrees of Parliament" because "in an empire, extended and diversified as that of Great Britain, there must be a supreme legislature, to which all other powers must be subordinate."[50] In the next ten years, this principle was repeated ad nauseam by British officials and propagandists; it was the rock on which the entire pro-British case rested. By September 1765, Bernard thought it necessary to warn that "the right of the Parliament of Great Britain to make laws for the American colonies, however it has been controverted in America, remains indisputable at Westminster."[51]

Colonial agents in London tried to warn the colonies against challenging the power of Parliament. One such caution came from Richard Jackson, the agent for Connecticut:

> I know that such [arguments] as tended to overturn ye Power of ye Parliament would have none [i.e., no weight], & indeed prove abundantly too much; in every State there must be a supream

---

[49] As early as 1805, Mercy Warren, sister of James Otis, complained in her history that Otis was "a character neglected by some, and misrepresented by other historians." *History of the Rise, Progress and Termination of the American Revolution* (Boston, 1805), vol. 1, p. 89 n. There is an unpublished dissertation, *James Otis of Massachusetts—the First Forty Years, 1725–1765*, by Hugh F. Bell, Cornell University, 1970.

[50] May 30, 1765, *Speeches of the Governors of Massachusetts from 1765 to 1775; and the Answers of the House of Representatives to the Same* (Boston, 1818; reprint Da Capo Press, 1971), pp. 34–35.

[51] September 25, 1765, ibid., p. 40.

Legislature, which must necessarily have Power over every part of ye State that is intitled to the Protection of the Government. . . .

I say Arguments ag[ains]t the Power of Parliament prove too much because they prove that not a single Act of Parliament binds the whole Kingdom of G[reat] Britain.[52]

Another warning came the following year from Charles Garth, the agent for South Carolina:

Very sorry I am to observe that the Contents of many of the papers particularly from the Northern Colonies, touching the Legislative Authority of Parliament, for Language and Expression, together with the accounts of the Tumultuous Proceedings, the Nature and Extent thereof, were received by the Committee [of the whole House] with an impression far from favourable to the great Object in View.[53]

Thus the key political issue in the entire revolutionary struggle had been introduced by 1765. In form, this debate was "constitutional." It was superficially a controversy over the jurisdiction of Parliament over America. Yet the term *constitutional* hardly conveys what was really at stake. It was whether and to what extent Parliament's power extended as far as the colonies. If Parliament did not have such power or if it was restricted to only as much power as the colonies were willing to consent to, the implication was that the colonies were declaring themselves to be de facto independent. This in any case was how the British saw it. The Americans were long loath to admit even to themselves that this was what they were aiming at.

This issue was crucial because Parliament was the only overall legislative body in the British system. If Parliament could not legislate for the American colonies, they were effectively cut adrift from that system. When the colonists hit on the idea of being attached to the British empire only through the king, they never faced the question of what powers the king would have over them. Once the power of Parliament over the colonies was "controverted," the American Revolution was set in motion.

[52] Jackson to Gov. Thomas Fitch, June 5, 1765, Fitch Papers, *Collections of the Connecticut Historical Society* (Hartford, 1920), vol. 18, p. 350.
[53] Letter from Garth, January 19, 1766, in Joseph W. Barnwell, "Hon. Charles Garth, M.P., the last Colonial agent of South Carolina in England, and some of his work," *South Carolina Historical and Genealogical Magazine*, April 1925, p. 76.

11

"Patchwork Government"

· 1 ·

THUS FAR, THE STAMP ACT crisis was only a battle of words. In the summer of 1765, the struggle moved to actions. The first acts of violence took place in Boston.

Boston was notorious for its organized street violence. One such outbreak had erupted in 1747, when Boston mobs prevented British naval press-gangs from forcibly obtaining conscripts for their ships. An enraged mob ruled the town until the men were released. Governor Shirley blamed the "populace assembled in their Town Meetings" as "the principal cause of the Mobbish turn in this Town." He believed that a "factious and Mobbish Spirit is cherished" by the "working Artificers, Seafaring Men, and low sort of people."[1]

On every November 5, known as Pope's Day in commemoration of the defeat of the Guy Fawkes plot of 1605 to blow up the House of Lords and bring about a Catholic restoration, gangs from the South and North ends of the town celebrated by staging bloody battles. In 1764, the fighting was so violent that the militia was called out; a wagon bearing an effigy of the pope ran over and killed a five-year-old child without deterring the warring factions from their free-for-all.

The victory that year had gone to the South End, whose leader, Ebenezer

[1] Shirley to the Lords of Trade, December 1, 1747, *Correspondence of William Shirley*, ed. Charles Henry Lincoln (Macmillan, 1912), vol. 1, p. 418.

Mackintosh, had molded his troops into a disciplined, semimilitary organization. Mackintosh was a fourth-generation descendant of Scottish prisoners
sent to the colonies by Oliver Cromwell. He was arrested for disturbing
the peace but let off. He was a shoemaker by trade, and the stamp tax
would not have affected him directly. He apparently enters the history of
the Revolution because he and his followers were useful to another, more
politically minded group.

This group, first known as the Loyal Nine, later, as they increased in
numbers, took on the name of Sons of Liberty, after the phrase tossed
out in Parliament by Isaac Barré and adopted throughout the colonies by
anti-British extremists. The Boston Nine included, occupationally, a distiller
or merchant, another distiller, two braziers or brass fabricators, a house
painter, a printer, a shipmaster, and a jeweler. The most prominent among
them was John Avery, Jr., the distiller or merchant, and Benjamin Edes,
the coprinter of the *Boston Gazette,* the paper to which James Otis, Samuel
Adams, and other radical figures contributed. The original nine, then, were
with one or two exceptions of middling status in the community. At a later
date, John Adams spent an evening in their company; Samuel Adams had also
met with the group at "a very Genteel Supper," during which they discussed
one of their exploits. Thus this incipient movement was made up of the street
fighters led by Mackintosh, the conspiratorial activists of the Loyal Nine, and
the ideological lawyers, such as the Adamses.[2]

This state of affairs led up to the first acts of prerevolutionary violence
on August 14, 1765. They seem to have been set off by the fortuitous
circumstance that it was customary to celebrate the birthday of the prince
of Wales, which happened to fall on August 12. The Loyal Nine met and
decided to celebrate in their own way two days later by hanging two effigies—
the burning of which was in the British tradition a symbolic way of staging
a political protest—from a great tree near the entrance of the town. One
effigy represented Andrew Oliver, who had been appointed the local stamp
distributor if there were to be any stamps to distribute. The other was the
replica of a boot, probably made by Mackintosh, that was emblematic of the
earl of Bute, the former chief British minister, to whom all the trouble was
mistakenly attributed. Despite official orders to remove the effigies, they
hung untouched all day. Taken down that evening, they were carried at the
head of a march through the town.

Whether planned or not, the marchers turned into a violent mob, with

[2] George P. Anderson, "Ebenezer Mackintosh: Stamp Act Rioter and Patriot," *Publications of the Colonial Society of Massachusetts, Transactions* (Boston, 1927), vol. 26,
pp. 16–50, 354–61.

Mackintosh and his South End street fighters in the vanguard. The mood turned ugly as the mob, shouting, "Liberty, Property and No Stamps," passed a building allegedly intended to be the office for the distribution of the stamps. The building was destroyed, after which Oliver's house was also severely damaged. The rampaging crowd crossed town until it came to Lt. Gov. Thomas Hutchinson's dwelling, which escaped with slight damage only because a neighbor said, mistakenly, that Hutchinson himself was not at home. Oliver resigned as stamp distributor the next day.

This was only the first phase of the outbreak. On August 26, a more serious outburst occurred. Just before dark, a bonfire was lit in front of the town office, and a large crowd gathered. The ominous cry "Liberty and Property" went up. Soon the crowd marched towards the house of Charles Paxton, the hapless customs officer, but it was deflected by a landlord who distributed free drinks, probably strong Madeira wine. As the crowd grew and drank, it became more belligerent and headed towards the houses of William Story, the register of the Admiralty's House, and Benjamin Hallowell, comptroller of customs. After their houses were looted, the mob was truly fired up and decided to take revenge on Hutchinson. The lieutenant governor and his children took refuge in a neighboring house just before his own was broken down with axes. Hutchinson later described the carnage:

> Not contented with tearing off all the wainscot and hangings and splitting the doors to pieces they beat down the Partition walls and altho that alone cost them near two hours they cut down the cupola or lanthern and they began to take the plate and boards from the roof and were prevented only by the approaching daylight from a total demolition of the building. The garden fence was laid flat and all my trees &c broke down to the ground. Such ruins were never seen in America. Besides my plate and family Pictures household furniture of every kind my own my children and servants apparel they carried off about £900 sterling in money emptied the house of everything whatsoever except a part of the Kitchen furniture not leaving a single book or paper in it and have scattered or destroyed all the manuscript and other papers I had been collecting for 30 years together besides a great number of Publick Papers in my custody.[3]

Gov. Francis Bernard was luckier. He escaped the vengeance of the mob

---

[3] Hutchinson to Richard Jackson, August 30, 1765, Massachusetts Archives, xxvi, pp. 146–47, cited in *Prologue to Revolution*, ed. Edmund S. Morgan (University of North Carolina Press, 1959), pp. 108–9.

by fleeing to the fort at Castle William, about three miles out of town, and his house was not touched. He wrote to Gen. Thomas Gage the next day:

> The Mob was so general & so supported, that all civil power ceased in an instant, & I had not the least authority to oppose or quiet the Mob. You are sensible how extreamly weak an American Governor is in regard to popular tumults, without a file of Men at his Command, & having no regular troops, at present, within call. . . . In short, The Town of Boston is in the possession of an incensed & implacable Mob; I have no force to oppose them; I know not whether I shall be able to preserve this Castle, which is threatened to be attacked, if the stamped papers from England should be, as is designed, placed here. The Garrison, when Compleat, amounts but to 60 men; & I dare not reenforce them out of the Country, for fear it should be the Means of betraying the place.[4]

Mackintosh was again arrested, charged with having led the mob in the destruction of Hutchinson's house, and again discharged without a trial. Others were jailed, but "in the dead of night, a large number of men entered the house of the prison keeper; compelled him to deliver the keys; opened the prison doors; and set every man free who had been committed for this offence." Hutchinson thought that Mackintosh went untouched because those behind him did not want him to divulge "who employed him," and because Governor Bernard thought that "the state of the province would not bear the execution of the law."[5] Bernard offered a reward of £300, a considerable sum, for information leading to the arrest of the leaders, but no one came forward, though hundreds must have known who they were.

Mackintosh soon married the daughter of an "eminently respectable" family. The wedding was performed in the eminently respectable New North Church in Boston by the Reverend Andrew Eliot, who had picked up the manuscripts from Hutchinson's house scattered in the mud by Mackintosh and his cohorts. Mackintosh himself was elected from 1766 to 1768 to the local board and was known as the First Captain General of Liberty Tree, in satirical imitation of Governor Bernard, who was officially captain general of the Massachusetts colony.

---

4 *Bernard Papers,* vol. 4, pp. 62–64, cited by Anderson, "Ebenezer Mackintosh," pp. 35–36.
5 *The Diary and Letters of His Excellency Thomas Hutchinson,* ed. Peter Orlando Hutchinson (London, 1883), vol. 1, pp. 70–71.

An important question is just how broad the support for the mob action of August 14 was. Hutchinson wanted to believe that "the rabble of the town of Boston headed by one Mackintosh" was "controuled by a superior set consisting of the master-masons[,] carpenters, &c. of the town," while "anything of more importance" than hanging effigies or pulling down houses was "under the direction of a committee of merchants Mr. Rowe at their head." For "all affairs of a general nature" in the law courts, Hutchinson noted, "Otis with his mobbish eloquence prevails in every motion."[6] The lieutenant governor also claimed that the mob had been led by "forty or fifty tradesmen, decently dressed."[7] He seemed to believe that everyone from "the rabble" to the merchants was behind the excesses.

The reality was more complex. John Rowe was one of Boston's foremost merchants, one of the town's "very rich men," according to John Adams.[8] Rowe kept a diary and dispassionately recorded in some detail the events of August 14, 1765, the first outbreak. When he came to "some Mischief to Mr. Andrew Oliver's house," he registered disapproval—"I think they were very much to blame."[9] Political sympathy was one thing, but physical violence was too much for merchants like Rowe.

John Adams also kept a most revealing diary of these events. On August 15, 1765, he meditated over the "strange Conduct of Yesterday and last Night, at Boston." At first, he questioned whether Andrew Oliver had ever done anything to deserve having "the blind undistinguishing Rage of the Rabble" do him "irreparable Injustice." What happened to Oliver, Adams thought, "is a very attrocious Violation of the Peace and of dangerous Tendency and Consequence."

But immediately afterwards, Adams adopted a different attitude towards Hutchinson. He accused him of "a very ambitious and avaricious Disposition," holding too many offices at once and with too many relatives in official positions, even that his son had married the daughter of a judge of the Superior Court. After more such complaints, Adams asked whether it would not be prudent for "those Gentlemen at this alarming Conjuncture" to "remove these Jealousies from the Minds of the People by giving an easy

---

[6] Hutchinson to Thomas Pownall, March 8, 1766, *Massachusetts Archives*, vol. 26, pp. 211–13.

[7] Thomas Hutchinson, *The History of the Colony and Province of Massachusetts-Bay*, ed. Lawrence Shaw Mayo, vol. 3, p. 87.

[8] *The Works of John Adams*, ed. Charles Francis Adams (Boston, 1861), vol. 2, p. 296.

[9] *Letters and Diary of John Rowe*, ed. Anne Rowe Cunningham (W. B. Clarke, 1903), pp. 88–89.

solution of these Difficulties."[10] Thus Adams started by disapproving of the "Rabble" and ended by denouncing its victims.

Samuel Adams was also divided in his response to the extraordinary events. He approved the peaceful march on August 14, 1765, but considered its violent aftermath to be "high-handed outrages," which, he noted with satisfaction, a town meeting had condemned the next day. But given the "greatest uneasiness," which the Stamp Act had evoked "even to the most judicious men of the Colony," Adams thought, "it was not to be wondered at, that among the common people such steps should be taken as could not be justified, it being frequent in populous towns when grievances are felt."[11] This is no unqualified repudiation.

James Otis was another who did not expect the protests to turn violent and indicated that he did not approve of the riot. He was the moderator of a town meeting in Boston the day after the riot and asked it to send "dutiful and loyal Addresses to his Majesty and his Parliament, who alone under God can extricate the Colonies from painful Scenes of Tumult, Confusion and distress."[12] Towards the end of 1765, he wrote to William Samuel Johnson, "We are much surprised at the violent proceedings at New York, as there has been so much time for people to cool, and the outrages on private property are so generally detested."[13]

From these testimonies, it seems clear that the August 1765 riots in Boston were inspired by political figures who had been working up protests against the Stamp Act but did not expect them to go so far. That the earl of Bute, who had resigned his office two years before, should have been made the butt of effigy hanging suggests that the rioters had only a vague idea of who was responsible for the tax. John Adams contemptuously referred to the "Rabble," and Sam Adams to the "common people." Hutchinson also blamed the "rabble," and Bernard the "mob." Yet the rabble, the common people, and the mob had little direct stake in the stamp tax, which struck mainly at merchants, lawyers, and printers. The merchants had well-known grievances against the customs and Admiralty officers, which would account for the latter as targets of the mob. Benjamin Hallowell, the comptroller of

[10] *The Diary and Autobiography of John Adams*, ed. L. H. Butterfield (Harvard University Press, 1961), vol. 1, pp. 259–61.

[11] William V. Wells, *The Life and Public Services of Samuel Adams* (Little, Brown, 1865), vol. 1, pp. 62–63.

[12] Cited by Alice Vering, *James Otis* (diss., University of Nebraska, 1955), p. 172; John C. Miller, *Origins of the American Revolution* (Little, Brown, 1943), p. 145.

[13] E. Edwards Beardsley, *Life and Times of William Samuel Johnson, LL.D.* (New York, 1876), p. 33. For the "violent proceedings," see p. 256.

customs, and Governor Bernard were sure that merchants were behind the rioters.[14]

The violence of August 1765 was unprecedented in its fury and raises the question of what had motivated the Boston "mob." Was it protesting solely against the Stamp Act, or was it responding to deeper social resentments? Recent American historians have believed that Hutchinson and Oliver were singled out because they had long represented a hateful, power-hungry upper class.[15] Governor Bernard was an early believer in this view. He reported that, after the demolition of Oliver's house,

> the government was obliged to look on, without being able to take one step to prevent it, and the principal people of the town publicly avowed and justified the act; the mob, both great and small, became highly elated, and all kinds of ill-humours were set on foot; everything that, for years past, had been the cause of any unpopular discontent, was revived; and private resentments against persons in office worked themselves in, and endeavoured to exert themselves under the mask of the public cause.

When Hutchinson's house was torn apart, Bernard added, "It was now becoming a war of plunder, of general levelling, and taking away the distinction of rich and poor."[16]

Social discontent was a latent ally of political rebelliousness. It is hard to believe that the ferocity with which the "mobs" destroyed the houses of Oliver and Hutchinson was brought on merely by a protest against paying the stamp tax; many, if not most, of its members were not likely to be affected by the tax. This was not the first time— far from it—that colonists had resorted to force to redress grievances. "Popular uprisings," an American historian notes, "were, then, an integral part of eighteenth-century American life."[17] But most of these "uprisings" had been aimed at customs officials or informers and naval officers sent to impress local recruits. These incidents of social violence were local and sporadic; they soon subsided and left no long-term mark on the society. Above all, they were not accompanied by

[14] Edmund S. Morgan and Helen M. Morgan, *The Stamp Act Crisis* (University of North Carolina Press, 1953), pp. 183–84.

[15] Gary B. Nash, *Race, Class, and Politics* (University of Illinois Press, 1986), pp. 231–33; G. B. Warden, *Boston, 1689–1776* (Little, Brown, 1970), pp. 165–69; Dirk Hoerder, *Crowd Action in Revolutionary Massachusetts 1765–1780* (Academic Press, 1977), pp. 99–101, 108–9.

[16] Bernard to Board of Trade, August 31, 1765, in William Cobbett, ed., *The Parliamentary History of England* (London, 1813), vol. 16, cols. 129–31.

[17] Pauline Maier, *From Resistance to Revolution* (Routledge & Kegan Paul, 1973), p. 12.

a larger program; they were, more than anything else, exhibitions of rage.

The mechanics and laborers who probably made up the majority of the rampaging mob in Boston were apparently filled with a mixture of motives. They had been brought out into the street by the agitation against the Stamp Act and used the opportunity to punish two of the best-known members of the local governing elite—Americans, not British. The lawyers and merchants who may have instigated the mob in the first place held their noses at the violence but did nothing to prevent it or help punish those responsible for it. The militia could not be used against the house wreckers. Bernard, Hutchinson, and Oliver were helpless to prevent or punish the perpetrators. No such mob action had ever before struck the property of persons so high in the governmental hierarchy.[18]

The anti–Stamp Act riots were a warning that a new stage of colonial violence had been reached. This stage was all the more dangerous to constituted authority because it combined social discontent with political insurgency. Hutchinson and Oliver were stand-ins for the British instigators of the stamp tax, but they were also local magnates whose wealth and influence were widely envied or disapproved of. The lesson for the British might have been that the political opposition was not going to be limited to intellectual lawyers or profit-hungry merchants; it was a lesson not well learned.

Nevertheless, the real continuity of the struggle against British rule was contributed by an upper colonial stratum that had a political program or was working one out step by step. The mobs had no program and merely added violence to the upper stratum's resistance. But the riots showed that an anti-British political program could unite colonists of all social levels for a variety of reasons. The helplessness of the British against the Stamp Act riots was the beginning of the end of British rule in the colonies.

[18] No one really knows who made up the mobs of August 14 and 26, 1765. Pauline Maier thinks that the events of August 14 were "prepared" by the Loyal Nine. But she differentiates them from the events of August 26, which were "inspired" by merchants who allegedly feared they had been named in depositions about smuggling, and, therefore, this latter eruption was not a Stamp Act riot. She also states: "Where resistance to the Stamp Act was at issue, the uprisings of August 1765 demonstrated a remarkable political extremism on the part of colonial crowds. Everywhere, 'followers' proved more ready than their 'leaders' to use force so as to assure that the Stamp Act would not go into effect" (*From Resistance to Revolution*, pp. 58–59).

Dirk Hoerder says there were 2,500 to 5,000 spectators during the day and 3,000 in the evening of August 14. At an early stage, the "gentlemen" left and "laborers" committed most of damage to Oliver's house. On August 26, young persons, probably indentured servants and apprentices, were said to be "extraordinarily active" (*Crowd Action in Revolutionary Massachusetts*, pp. 102–8).

· 2 ·

Violence was contagious. Newport, Rhode Island, followed Boston.

When news of the hanging of the effigies in Boston reached Newport, word spread that a similar scene was planned there for August 27. That morning, effigies of Augustus Johnston, the appointed stamp distributor, Dr. Thomas Moffat, a physician and known proponent of British authority, and Martin Howard, Jr., author, as previously seen, of a pro-British pamphlet hotly denounced by James Otis, were hanged from a gallows erected in front of the courthouse. Three leading merchants, Samuel Vernon, William Ellery, and Robert Crook, armed with clubs, marched back and forth under the scaffold. To encourage a crowd to assemble, the three merchants "sent into the streets strong Drink in plenty with Cheshire cheese and other provocatives to intemperance and riot," as the local paper reported. After sunset, the merchants cut down the effigies and flung them into a bonfire. No one was hurt and no property was damaged.

The next day was worse. A mob, with painted faces and axes in hand, marched to Howard's house and wrecked it. All the furniture and china in it were destroyed, and what could not be demolished was carried off. The mob then went to Dr. Moffatt's house and smashed paintings, medical and scientific instruments, fine china, and valuable books. Augustus Johnston's house was also looted. Not satisfied, the mob returned to Howard's house and finished the job there by tearing up floors, hearths, and chimney, and, still later, went back a third time to cut down young locust trees in the yard. Moffat's house was also visited a second time and given the same treatment as Howard's.

Then something unexpected happened. On the third day, August 29, the merchants lost control to a twenty-one-year-old brawler, John Webber, who had not had enough excitement. He turned against those merchants who had used him to demolish the houses and refused to let them call off the rioting. Part of the mob went with him and threatened to terrorize the entire town, including those who had originally instigated the violence. Frightened, the merchants and sheriff succeeded in seizing Webber and forcing him aboard a British vessel in the harbor. Webber's band retaliated by vowing to destroy the houses of the original, more respectable ringleaders if their leader was not released. Some merchants rowed out to the British ship and brought Webber back with them, apparently by telling its captain that Webber was not the right man.

The contretemps was still not over. The historian of Rhode Island in this period relates:

> The riot which had begun with the express purpose of manifesting revenge against men who defended Parliamentary supremacy and execution of the Stamp Act had developed into an aimless and half-ludicrous brawl between two factions of the rioters. The original leaders were scared out of their wits. They begged and entreated Webber to give up, bribed him with money and a new suit of clothes, in fact, promised him anything he pleased. Sheriff Joseph G. Wanton groveled and cringed before the rabble-rouser. "What would you have of me," the sheriff supplicated; "I will do every thing to satisfy you; I will lay myself down, and let you tread on my neck, if that will satisfy you."[19]

Webber did not give up so easily. He strutted around town, threatening revenge against those who had used and betrayed him. Finally, he encountered Augustus Johnston, the most marked man of all the original victims. As Webber abused him, Johnston "heroically seized upon him," and, with the help of others, carried him off to jail. At last Newport was peaceful again.

Throughout this turmoil, Gov. Samuel Ward behaved cravenly. He slipped out of Newport after the first effigies were burned and did not return until order had been restored. The only one ever apprehended was John Webber. The General Assembly gave assurances that no "Person of Consequence" had had anything to do with the riotous events.[20]

In Newport, even more than in Boston, it is clear that merchants were responsible for the violent protests. In Newport, too, they could not have staged the events by themselves. They needed the support of the same sort of "rabble," "mob," or "common people" that figured in the Boston riots. Again, even more than in Boston, this unruly element could not be controlled and almost turned a limited political action into an incipient social revolt. It did not go so far in this case, because Webber's little mob had no social or political program and was motivated by little more than primitive resentment or the excitement of the moment.

At one point, Captain Leslie of the British vessel was told that the crowd's ringleaders planned to take control of the local fort and fire its guns at the ship holding Webber. A mid-nineteenth-century historian of early Rhode Island

---

[19] David S. Lovejoy, *Rhode Island Politics and the American Revolution, 1760–1776* (Brown University Press, 1958), pp. 108–9.

[20] Ibid., pp. 100–110; and Morgans, *Stamp Act Crisis*, pp. 144–51.

was so carried away by this prospect that he thought "the revolution [would] have commenced" if this plan had been carried out, "but better counsels for the time prevailed."[21] If so, it would have been a quite different kind of revolution.

· 3 ·

In New York City, the Sons of Liberty made their appearance in the fall of 1765, at first secretly but by the beginning of 1766 openly. When branches sprang up in other New York towns, they banded together through committees of correspondence. As elsewhere, the New Yorkers were led by merchants and lawyers, and the rank and file consisted of "lower-class" elements—mechanics, artisans, and day laborers.[22]

Their first action came in October 1765, two months after the disturbances in Boston. It was reported that 2,000 people rallied to prevent the landing of stamps, but British officials foiled the effort by taking the stamps ashore at nightfall, after the crowd had dispersed. Signs were quickly put up threatening to "take care of [the] House, Person and Effects" of anyone caught distributing the stamps. On November 1, a crowd made up of 400 to 500 seamen, 300 carpenters, and many others destroyed the house of Major James, a British officer, who had boasted that he would "cram the stamps down [the people's] throats with the end of his sword." Lt. Gov. Cadwallader Colden's coach house was broken into and his "chariot," or state carriage, burned.[23] Other demonstrations followed, until Colden surrendered the stamps to militiamen, who decided to burn them. Stamp Distributor McEvers was forced to resign, as were a Maryland stamp distributor who had fled to New York, and the distributor for Canada and Nova Scotia. The house of a prospective stamp distributor was pulled down, whereupon he promised to give up all thought of the job. By the end of the year, the "Liberty Boys" had virtually established themselves as a dual power in New York, and nothing could be done of which they disapproved.[24]

Colden later explained in a message to the secretary of state in charge

<hr/>

[21] Samuel Greene Arnold, *History of the State of Rhode Island and Providence Plantations* (Appleton, 1860), vol. 2, p. 259.

[22] Herbert M. Morais, "The Sons of Liberty in New York," in *The Era of the American Revolution*, ed. Richard B. Morris (Columbia University Press, 1939), pp. 272–73.

[23] Lieutenant Governor Colden to Secretary Conway, June 24, 1766, *Documents relative to the Colonial History of the State of New-York*, ed. E. B. O'Callaghan (Albany, 1856), vol. 7, p. 832. [Hereafter cited as *New York Documents*.]

[24] Morais, "Sons of Liberty," pp. 274–76.

of the colonies, Henry Seymour Conway, why he had surrendered the stamps:

> No man in the administrat[io]n would support me, and a Governors authority must be weak when it is expected to be at an end [the] next day. On the contrary I was informed that some of the Council called me an obstinate old man in opposing the violent spirit of the people as I had done, and that such an opinion was every where propagated in Town. My whole fortune was exposed to the Mob, and they openly threatened to destroy every thing I had both in Town and Country. My eldest son who lives in Town, was obliged to bring all his Household Goods & effects into the Fort, came into it himself for security of his Person and sent his wife and children on board the Coventry for their protection, tho' he had done nothing to incur the displeasure of the People. The Fort was not then in a sufficient state of Defence. . . . It is true I had sufficient Force to disperse the Mob, but when neither the Council would advise nor the Magistrates ask assistance to do it, I must have done it on my single authority: the doing of it might have been fatal to many innocent people, and I did not think it prudent to risque the dangerous consequences which might have ensued.[25]

The newly arrived governor, Sir Henry Moore, reported to London that he could get no backing from the council, whose "apprehensions of future disturbances have influenced all the opinions they have given me on this occasion." He confessed why all semblance of authority had broken down: "In consequence of their resolutions, I am obliged to suspend a Power which I am not able to exert without their Assistance, and to make a merit of acting in a manner which carries no other recommendation with it but that of not exposing the Weakness of our Government."[26] As for the resignations of the stamp distributors, he explained:

> The Tumults which have been raised in different parts of the Continent and which have been artfully fomented by ill designing people, have spread so much terror, that the Officers appointed for the execution of the Act, have resigned their posts, and I am sorry to observe, that the Power of Govern[men]t was too weak to protect them from the insults they were threat[e]ned with; this is our unhappy situation at present, and the tranquillity we now enjoy, is owing to nothing but

[25] New York Documents, vol. 7, p. 812.
[26] Moore to Secretary Conway, November 21, 1765, ibid., p. 789.

the suspension of those powers, we are not able to employ to any effect.[27]

The Maryland distributor, who fled to New York, had a similar story to tell. He was Zachariah Hood, a merchant. In Annapolis, the ceremony was imaginative. The local paper reported that a crowd had gathered and "curiously dress'd up the Figure of a Man, which they placed in a One-Horse Cart, Malefactor-like, with some sheets of Paper in his Hands before his Face: In this Manner they Paraded thro' the Streets of the Town, till noon." A bell tolled solemnly, as if for a funeral. The effigy was burned, Hood's house torn down, and he was forced to flee. When the Sons of Liberty in New York learned of his presence at the King's Arms Tavern, they went after him; he escaped to the fort; they found him and compelled him to resign. Hood later returned to Maryland but, spurned, gave up and went to the West Indies.[28]

The Pennsylvania distributor, John Hughes, was, as previously noted, Benjamin Franklin's personal choice for the job. That Franklin should have chosen him indicates that Franklin was willing to go along with the tax, once it had been decided. By September 1765, Hughes wrote to Franklin in desperation about his predicament. Each letter might be the last from him, he said, because "the Spirit or Flame of Rebellion is got to a high Pitch amongst the North Americans; and it seems to me that a Sort of Frenzy or Madness has got such hold of the People of all Ranks, that I fancy some Lives will be lost before this Fire is put out." He did not expect to "escape the Storm of Presbyterian Rage." When he heard rumors that his house was going to be torn down, he armed himself and prepared "to stand a Siege." Almost 800 "sober Inhabitants" mobilized to resist the "Rabble" and "Mob." After holding out for days, Hughes resigned. Nevertheless, Franklin was advised by his old printing partner, James Parker, that "a black Cloud seems to hang over us," and "it appears to me, that there will be an End of all Government here" if "the Storm blows not over."[29] Gov. John Penn thought that "we are not more than one degree from open Rebellion."[30]

In Charleston, South Carolina, the distributor, Caleb Lloyd, and the inspector of stamps, George Saxby, took refuge in a nearby fort, where they were held prisoner for two days. Saxby was burned in effigy; his house

[27] Sir Henry Moore to the earl of Dartmouth, November 21, 1765, ibid.

[28] Janet Bassett Johnson, *Robert Alexander, Maryland Loyalist* (G. P. Putnam's Sons, 1942), pp. 20–21.

[29] Hughes to Franklin, September 8, 1765, pp. 264–65; Joseph Galloway to Franklin, September 20, 1765, p. 227; Parker to Franklin, October 10, 1765, p. 310 (*The Papers of Benjamin Franklin,* ed. Leonard W. Labaree, Yale University Press, 1961, vol. 12).

[30] Richard Penn, Jr., to Thomas Penn, December 15, 1765, cited by Morgans, *Stamp Act Crisis,* p. 198.

was made uninhabitable. They informed London that they had resigned "to prevent Murther and the destruction of the town."[31] Henry Laurens, a rich merchant and planter, was one of those who opposed the Stamp Act but, like Otis, believed that it had to be obeyed so long as it remained in force. "I would give, I would do," he wrote, "a great deal to procure a repeal of the Law which imposes it upon us, but I am sure that nothing but a regular, decent, becoming representation of the inexpediency & inutility of that Law will have the desir'd effect & that all irregular seditious practices Will have an evil tendency, even perhaps to perpetuate that & bring upon us other Acts of Parliament big with greater mischiefs."[32] A few days later, he was a victim of "irregular seditious practices." A "croud of Men chiefly in disguise," many of them drunk and armed with clubs and cutlasses, knocked at his door in search of stamped papers. He succeeded in convincing them that he was an enemy of the tax, whereupon they gave him three cheers and departed without doing any damage.[33] Evidently this crowd simply roved through the town and indiscriminately sought the enemy but could be turned off as well as on. Laurens supported independence in 1776, though with a broken heart— "even at this Moment I feel a Tear of affection for the good Old Country & for the People in it whom in general I dearly Love."[34]

In Virginia, the elite participated in the protests. Col. George Mercer, the distributor of stamps, was hanged in effigy and left for England. Gov. Francis Fauquier reported that a mob of "mercantile people," chiefly made up of gentlemen of property in the colony, had forced Mercer to resign. "Dissatisfaction of the people in this colony is too strong for my poor abilities to overcome," Fauquier explained to the secretary of state in London.[35]

· 4 ·

So it went in colony after colony. When all the protests were over, not a single stamp distributor was left in office. These events were unprecedented in the entire century and a half of previous colonial history. There had never been such a mass outbreak of violence and coercion. There had never been such unified action in virtually every colony from north to south. The old,

[31] Ibid., p. 156.

[32] Laurens to Joseph Brown, October 11, 1765, *The Papers of Henry Laurens*, ed. George C. Rogers, Jr., and David R. Chesnutt (University of South Carolina Press, 1976), vol. 5, p. 25.

[33] Ibid., pp. 29–31.

[34] Henry Laurens to his son, John Laurens, August 14, 1776, ibid., vol. 1, p. xvii.

[35] Terrance Leon Mahan, *Virginia Reaction to British Policy, 1763–1776* (diss., University of Wisconsin, 1960), pp. 96, 100.

comforting British assumption that the colonies were too self-interested and too far apart to act together was swept away. Divide and rule was no longer a useful principle of imperial control. The orchestration of all these hangings of effigies and smashing of houses was accomplished by a process of imitation. Once the news of the Boston riots of August 14 and 26 reached other colonies, the antistamp activists knew what to do. Sons of Liberty sprang up in one colony after another, linked by committees of correspondence or personal visitations. The delay in getting the news from Boston or Newport accounted for the delay in contributing to the upheavals, so that the disturbances continued like a rolling barrage, lasting from August 1765 to January 1766, and extending as far away as Georgia.

Gov. William Franklin of New Jersey informed his father, Benjamin, that "it is said the Presbyterians of N. England have wrote to all their Brethren throughout the Continent, to endeavor to stir up the Inhabitants of each Colony to act as they have done, in hopes of thereby making it appear to the Ministry too difficult a Matter to call them to account for their late outrageous Conduct."[36] Gov. William Bull of South Carolina believed that the *South Carolina Gazette* of Charleston was the "conduit Pipe" for subversive northern propaganda, which had "poisoned" the minds of South Carolina with principles "imbibed and propagated from Boston and Rhode Island."[37]

Yet as outrageous as the conduct and as poisoned as the minds may have been, or at least seemed to embattled governors, they were not symptomatic of a truly revolutionary uprising. For one thing, no one was killed, though many were threatened. There were no confrontations between rioters and officialdom or armed forces. No blood was shed, in part because the protesters met with no opposition. Governors fled to forts; stamp distributors ignominiously resigned; houses were torn down with impunity. In fact, governors such as Bernard of Massachusetts could not have used force, even if they had been disposed to do so. At the time of the anti–Stamp Act rampages, the British commander, Gen. Thomas Gage, had only fifteen understrength regiments available to him. They were spread out through Nova Scotia, Cape Breton, Canada, the Illinois country, Florida, and elsewhere, hundreds of miles from the scene of the action. "This was their situation at the time of the Stamp Act," Gage explained, "when no Governor would ask, it

[36] William Franklin to Benjamin Franklin, September 7, 1765, *Franklin Papers*, vol. 12, p. 262.
[37] Robert M. Weir, *"A Most Important Epocha": The Coming of the Revolution in South Carolina* (University of South Carolina Press, 1970), p. 16.

might be said dared to ask, for the aid of troops, nor any Council advise it."[38]

For a century and a half, the British had ruled the American colonies without the need to use or even display force. This line was crossed as a result of the antistamp riots. The very success of the rioters in taking over control of the leading towns, even temporarily, worked against such temerity the next time. The anti–Stamp Act outbursts overwhelmed those in authority, because the protesters benefited from surprise. After the events of 1765, the British could not claim that they had not been forewarned.

· 5 ·

Despite their rage, Americans still believed that the Stamp Act was the problem, not British rule itself. They denounced the tax as unfair and unconstitutional, the former because it inflicted an onerous burden on colonial businesses, the latter because Parliament did not have the right to impose it on unrepresented British subjects. Taxation was the issue, not any other traditional British prerogative, such as jurisdiction over trade and customs.

But British officials who had suddenly found themselves helpless in the face of riotous mobs did not take such a limited view. Frantic and sometimes desperate messages from the colonies told ministers that something far more serious and menacing had occurred. Appeals and alarms from governors were read by men in London who had been reared in a tradition which had long warned that colonies with extraordinary rates of increased population and unprecedented commercial growth were bound one day to break away from the mother country. For decades past, worried colonial administrators had been seeing these very signs of colonial self-determination but had been repeatedly ignored by their ministerial superiors. The reports of the Stamp Act riots gave reason to fear that more was at stake than the sale of stamps. Nothing less than the doomsday of the eighteenth-century British empire was said to be at hand.

Yet governors clamored for troops without success. In August 1765, Governor Bernard of Massachusetts lamented: "Surely it is not known at Whitehall how weak and impotent the Authority of American Governors is in regard to Popular Tumults." He soon declared regretfully: "It is a shocking Thing that British Troops should be used against British Subjects,

---

[38] Queries of George Chalmers, with the Answers of General Gage, *Massachusetts Historical Society Collections*, 4th ser., vol. 4, 1858, p. 370.

but a defection of the Colonies is a greater Evil even to the Colonists."39 In February 1766, Governor Moore of New York advised Secretary of State Conway that his armed force did not exceed 160 men and that "nothing at present but a superior Force [would] bring the people to a sense of their Duty."40 But British policy feared and distrusted the use of troops. When Governor Wright of Georgia distributed stamps for a short time with the aid of troops, he was rebuked by Secretary of State Shelburne on the ground that "the Reverence and Affections of the Governed" were better than the "lesser and more narrow Means of Government."41

Bernard was so depressed that he sent word to London on October 28, 1765, that "if things do not take another turn before the first of November, the appearance of Government will cease; as the real authority has ever since the first riot." He lamented that the mob violence had "left the cause of the King and Parliament almost without an advocate."42

A month later, he sent an extended report of the British predicament to the secretary at war, Lord Barrington, who was also the cousin of Bernard's wife and in whom he could confide freely. It exposes the British dilemma so clearly that it deserves to be cited at some length. Bernard was no wholehearted supporter of the Stamp Act. To begin with, he tried to explain why the act was so obnoxious to the colonies:

> It must have been supposed that such an Innovation as a Parliamentary Taxation would cause great Alarm & meet with much Opposition in most parts of America; It was quite new to the People, & had no visible Bounds set to it; The American's [sic] declared that they would not submit to it before the Act passed; & there was the greatest probability that it would require the utmost Power of Government to carry it into Execution.

Then he went into the reasons for British helplessness in the face of colonial opposition:

> Whereas at this Time the Governments were weak & impotent to an amazing Degree; The Governors & the Officers of the Crown in several of the cheif Provinces intirely dependent upon the People for Subsistence; The Popular Scale so much weig[h]tier than the Royal,

---

39 Bernard to Thomas Pownall, August 18, 1766; Bernard to Richard Jackson, August 24, 1765, cited by Maier, *From Resistance to Revolution*, p. 142.

40 Moore to Conway, February 20, 1766, *New York Documents*, vol. 7, p. 810.

41 Maier, *From Resistance to Revolution*, p. 144.

42 Francis Bernard, *Select Letters on the Government of America and the Principles of Law and Polity Applied to the American Colonies* (London, 1774), p. 27.

that it required Address & management & frequent temporizing to preserve a tolerable ballance; The Persons of the Governors & Crown-Officers quite defenceless, & exposed to the Violence of the People without any possible Resort for Protection. Was this a Time to introduce so great a Novelty as a Parliamentary inland Taxation into America!?

Bernard did not think so. The real question, he maintained, was not the Stamp Act:

Since the Insurrections against the Stampt-Act, The Americans have found the Governments so contemptibly weak & the People so superior to the Royal Authority, that they are not a little elated upon their Triumphs over the defenceless Officers of the Crown; & seem to be resolved that their Idea of their Relation to Great Britain, however extravagant[,] various & inconsistent shall be the standard of it. So that it is to be feared that it will cost much time & Treasure to bring America to that Degree of Submission, which the Parliament will think it necessary to require of them. The Question will not be whether there shall be a Stamp Act or not; but whether America shall or shall not be Subject to the Legislature of Great Britain.

Bernard was persuaded that the old colonial regime was doomed; it was necessary to put it on a new foundation by giving the Americans what they were demanding—representation in Parliament:

But tho the Parliament of Great Britain does not stand in Need of a Real or Virtual Representation to ground its Authority over the Colonies, it may now be worth Consideration whether Admitting Representatives from the Colonies may not be a Proper expedient for the present Exigencies. Two Years ago a proposal of this Kind would not have bore an [sic] hearing: But so much is America altered by the late financial Acts, that a New System of Policy is now become needful. The Patchwork Government of America will last no longer: The Necessity of a Parliamentary establishment of the Government of America upon fixed Constitutional Principles is brought on with a Precipitation which could not have been foreseen but a Year ago; & is become more urgent by the very Incidents which make it more difficult. The Circumstance of the Americans justifying their Disobedience by their not being represented points out a Method to inforce their Obedience upon their own Principles. Take them at their Word; let them send Representatives for the present Time & for the present Purposes: 30 for the Continent & 15 for the Islands would be sufficient.

But Bernard's plan was limited to holding an extraordinary session of Parliament—with American representatives—to work out a new "general uniform system of American Government & Established by Act of Government, by which the Americans according to their own Principles will be bound." Once this new constitutional arrangement was agreed on, the American representatives were to be dismissed and the American legislatures would take over in the colonies within the agreed "Bounds of their own Authority."

Bernard was not giving much away. He really wanted what British officialdom had always wanted. He conceived of a single form of government in every colony, with an intermediate legislature, modeled on that of Ireland. He wanted all Crown officers in the colonies paid from the British civil list, "so that they may not be too much dependent upon the People." He suggested that the new colonial governments should pay for standing forces, to be allotted among them by the British Parliament. The first act of each new colonial legislature should be "a solemn Recognition of the Supremacy of the Parliament of Great Britain."

All this testified to the depth of the crisis into which the Stamp Act riots had thrown the British imperial system. It also revealed the hopelessness of such schemes to rescue the system. Bernard chose the Irish model, because, he said, it "is as perfect for a dependent, as that of Great Britain for a supreme Power." He himself recognized that Americans openly claimed that the colonies were "perfect States, not otherwise dependent upon Great Britain than by having the same King." Bernard realized that having the same king was almost useless to curb the colonies, and he suffered from the common British illusion that the colonies could be held in check by tying them in with Parliament. His assumptions were that the colonies could somehow be made content to remain "dependent" and that Parliament had some uncanny power over them. However futile Bernard's plan may have been, it recognized that the British system could not go on as before and that the hour for a change was already very late.[43]

Another colonial official, Sir William Johnson, the superintendent of Indian affairs in New York, a man notably broad in his sympathies, saw

---

[43] Governor Bernard to Lord Barrington, November 23, 1765, *The Barrington-Bernard Correspondence*, ed. Edward Channing and Archibald Cary Coolidge (Harvard University Press, 1912), pp. 93–102. There is another version of this letter in Bernard's *Select Letters on the Government of America*.

independence lurking behind the Stamp Act riots. He wrote to Cadwallader Colden,

> I fear ye Independent Gentry have resolved to make themselves conspicuous under the feigned name of Patriots, at the expence of their Country, for surely they cannot imagine that a serious act of both Houses of Parliament passed notwithstanding all ye Arguments of the Agents & freinds of the Colonies should be repealed thro' the Menaces of a few party Men, or that they recommend themselves to the Government by rioting & Insulting its officers.

Johnson thought that the colonies might have gained their point if they had acted moderately, but only "a verry Sanguine Party Man" could imagine that the British government "will be silent, or that they will allow so dangerous a precedent for the Independency of the Colonies." Johnson recommended that the governors work together to point out who the "Authors and Characters" responsible for the disturbances were, but he recognized that they were up against "Arguments in favour of that beloved Independency w[hic]h so strongly prevails amongst all Ranks of People."[44] Soon Johnson sent another letter to Colden about "the Extraordinary Tumult at New York, and the Extravagant Lengths to which the deluded Mob were led," and warned that "if something is not done here, or at Home in consequence thereof Adieu to their pretended Darling the British Constitution in America."[45] Johnson agreed with Bernard that the issue was no longer the Stamp Act; it was, he said, a point on which "the Dependency of America depends, for that, and not the Stamp Act is now the Struggle, and if England Lets Slip this opertunity [sic] they may never meet with another."[46]

The British commander, General Gage, also recognized that more than the Stamp Act was at stake. He wrote to Sir Henry Conway, the secretary of state in charge of the colonies, "The Question is not of the inexpediency of the Stamp Act, or of the inability of the Colonys to pay the Tax, but that it is unconstitutional, and contrary to their Rights, Supporting the Independency of the provinces, and not Subject to the Legislative Power of Great Britain."[47]

A highly placed British pamphleteer foretold what was sure to happen

---

[44] Johnson to Colden, September 13, 1765, *Colden Papers, Collections of the New-York Historical Society*, 1923, vol. 7, p. 76.

[45] Johnson to Colden, November 8, 1765, ibid., p. 93.

[46] Johnson to Colden, January 9, 1766, ibid., p. 102.

[47] Gage to Conway, October 12, 1765, *The Correspondence of General Thomas Gage with the Secretaries of State, 1763–1775* (Yale University Press, 1931), vol. 1, pp. 69–70. [Hereafter cited as *Gage Correspondence.*]

if the guilty were not punished: "I shall conclude with the following observation, that if Great-Britain can or will suffer such conduct in her colonies to pass unpunished, a man need not be a prophet, or the son of a prophet, to see clearly that her empire in North-America is at an end."[48]

Similar views were expressed in the British press. One writer declared, "The Americans imbibe Notions of Independence and Liberty with their very Milk, and will some Time or other shake off all subjection. If we yield to them by *repealing the Stamp Act,* it is all over; they will from that moment assert their freedom. Whereas if we enforce the Act, we may keep them in Dependance for some Years longer."[49]

Another evoked pity for the poor British and envy of the Americans:

> The Americans have been increasing in riches these thirty years; . . . they are become at our expense, and for which we are starving, proud, lordly, and ambitious. . . . When once they become independent, they will trade where, and with whom they please. Where then will be your trade? And how will you then get bread? . . . where will money be found to pay our taxes and the interest of our debt? . . . Shall those who have so lately made France and Spain tremble in every quarter of the globe . . . be afraid of chastising an American mob, a handful of rioters stimulated to rebellion by their lordly tyrants? Forbid it, Heaven! Shall we be eternally taxed even to the uttermost farthing for others? Would ye wish the Americans should lord it over you like the Egyptian task-masters?[50]

Towards the end of 1765, Benjamin Franklin engaged in a dispute over this very question in the London press. A contributor in *The Gazetteer* had written of the colonies that "their refusing submission to the stamp act, proceeds *only* from their *ambition* of becoming *independent;* and that it is plain the colonies have no other aim but a *total enfranchisement* from obedience to our Parliament." Franklin himself was far from ready to go so far and knew that few colonists were. Writing as if he were another Englishman, which was one of his journalistic disguises, he made a sweeping

---

[48] *The Conduct of the Late Ministry Examined* (London, 1766). This pamphlet has been attributed to Charles Lloyd, the secretary of George Grenville. The first portion was allegedly dictated to Lloyd by Grenville, and it is therefore assumed to represent Grenville (Thomas R. Adams, *The American Controversy,* Brown University Press, 1980, pp. 61–62). I have used a 1767 edition, p. 73 n. 86.

[49] "Anti-Sejanus," *The Public Advertiser,* February 12, 1766, cited in Mary A. M. Marks, *England and America, 1763 to 1783* (London, 1907), vol. 1, p. 46 n. 1.

[50] *London Chronicle,* February 25–27, 1766, cited by Marks, *England and America,* vol. 1, p. 53.

denial of the charge: "The Americans, I am sure, for I know them, have not the least desire of independence; they submit, in general, to all the laws we make for them; they desire only a continuance of what they think a *right*, the privilege of manifesting their loyalty by granting their own money, when the occasions of their prince shall call for it." Franklin thus made it seem that the only difference was between granting money at the behest of the British government and granting money of the colonists' own volition. In addition, he could not resist the opportunity to press the argument from consent and representation, though he professed to be uncertain of the outcome—" 'Tis fit for the discussion of wise and learned men, who will, I doubt not, settle it wisely and benevolently."[51] Franklin was not yet ready to cut the umbilical cord with Great Britain.

George III was also careful at this stage not to side with either of the extremes on what to do about the Stamp Act. He preferred modifying the act to repealing it but favored repealing it over enforcing it.[52] In any case, he said, he went along with the government, because "he would never influence people in their parliamentary opinions, and that he had promised to support his Ministers."[53] It was only later, when he was convinced that the Americans wanted independence, that he became their adamant opponent.

· 6 ·

In 1765, the Americans did not yet demand independence in principle. But they already demanded the essence of independence in practice. The real issue that tormented both sides for the next ten years emerged openly in Virginia.

This challenge had been formulated at the end of 1764. The House of Burgesses had drawn up three formal petitions against the proposed stamp tax for the king, Lords, and Commons. The petition to the king had declared that Virginians insisted on *"their ancient and inestimable Right of being governed by such Laws respecting their internal Polity and Taxation as are derived from their own Consent."*[54] This statement was repeated in the

[51] *Benjamin Franklin's Letters to the Press, 1758–1775*, ed. Verner W. Crane (University of North Carolina Press, 1950), pp. 43–44.

[52] February 10, 1766, *Correspondence of King George the Third*, ed. John Fortescue (London, 1927), vol. 1, pp. 268–70.

[53] January 1, 1766, *The Grenville Papers*, ed. William James Smith (London, 1852), vol. 3, p. 353.

[54] *Journals of the House of Burgesses of Virginia*, November 14, December 18, 1764, pp. 256–57, 302–4, cited by Jack P. Greene, *The Quest for Power* (University of North Carolina Press, 1963), p. 366 (italics in original).

famous Virginia Resolves introduced by Patrick Henry on May 29, 1765. A key passage read:

That his Majesty's liege People of this his most ancient and loyal Colony have without interruption enjoyed the inestimable Right of being governed by such Laws, respecting their internal Polity and Taxation, as are derived from their own Consent, with the Approbation of their Sovereign, or his Substitute; and that the same hath never been forfeited or yielded up, but hath been constantly recognized by the Kings and People of *Great Britain*.[55]

This resolution outbid the Massachusetts protests by explicitly adding "internal Polity" to "Taxation." It implied that Parliament had no business interfering in the internal affairs of Virginia in any way and that only the king's approval, which was merely a nominal restraint, was still recognized. The resolutions were passed by a rump House; they came at the end of the session, when only 39 out of 116 representatives were present; and they— or one of them—apparently passed by only a single vote. Patrick Henry was a new member who rallied the hill-country members against the judgment of the dominant tidewater elite, most of whom had left. Nevertheless, Governor Fauquier fumed and quickly dissolved the House. Not everyone agreed with Henry's tactics. James Otis was said to have considered the Resolves treasonable.[56] The Virginia leadership considered them premature and unnecessarily provocative.

But other contemporaries were highly impressed. The Virginia Resolves were published in newspapers all over the colonies. The Maryland, Connecticut, and Rhode Island assemblies passed similar resolutions, using the terms "taxation and internal polity" or "policy."[57] Thomas Hutchinson thought that their spirit "had a tendency to bring on those acts of violence which soon after were committed in Boston."[58] Governor Bernard had thought, two or three months earlier, that "this people would submit to the Stamp Act without actual opposition," but now "the publishing of the Virginia Resolves proved an alarm bell to the disaffected." General Gage called them "the signal for a general outcry over the Continent."[59]

[55] This is the version in *Journals of the House of Burgesses, 1761–1765*, p. 360. There were other versions, omitting "internal Polity," all given in *Prologue to Revolution*, pp. 47–50. The entire incident is fully treated in Morgans, *Stamp Act Crisis*, pp. 88–98.

[56] *Hutchinson's History*, vol. 3, p. 86.

[57] *Prologue to Revolution*, pp. 51, 53, 55, for texts.

[58] *Hutchinson's History*, vol. 3, p. 86.

[59] Cited from "British Papers Relating to the American Revolution" in the Harvard Library by Arthur M. Schlesinger, *Prelude to Independence* (Alfred A. Knopf, 1958), p. 71.

In 1766, Richard Bland, a member of the House of Burgesses, put out a notable pamphlet in which he developed the basic point of the Virginia Resolves. He maintained that the colonies "contend for no other Right but that of directing their internal Government by Laws made with their own Consent." His term, "internal Government," was somewhat more explicit than "internal Polity." He argued that "every Act of Parliament that imposes *internal* Taxes upon the Colonies is an Act of *Power,* and not of *Right.*" "*Rights* imply *Equality,*" he went on, which led him to question why Great Britain and the colonies were treated unequally. "Why is the Trade of the Colonies more circumscribed than the Trade of *Britain*? And why are Impositions laid upon the one which are not laid upon the other?" Bland was not yet ready to cut Parliament out of all jurisdiction over the colonies and agreed that "the Colonies are subordinate to the Authority of Parliament." But, he hastened to add, "not absolutely so." He had trouble deciding what Parliament could or could not do and what the colonies should do if "deprived of their civil Rights, if great and manifest Oppressions are imposed upon them by the State on which they are dependent." He lamely suggested that "their Remedy is to lay their Complaints at the Foot of the Throne, and to suffer patiently rather than disturb the publick Peace, which nothing but a Denial of Justice can excuse them in breaking." Finally, he fell back on Thucydides, who, he said, would have counseled that colonies "were not sent out to be the Slaves, but to be the Equals of those that remain behind."[60]

What the Virginia Resolves and Bland made clear, if it was not clear before, was that the Americans now had the framework of an ideology that would serve them almost to the outbreak of the Revolution. It ruled out all British— in practice, parliamentary—interference in American internal affairs and recognized a connection only with the king. It implied independence—or at least self-rule—in American domestic affairs. It took its stand on a platform of equality between Americans and British, within a still unified British empire. This principle was not recognized everywhere at once and still left questions about what remained for the British to decide. Nevertheless, in a remarkably short span of time, the Americans had found an intellectual base from which to conduct their struggle against British rule. As late as 1763, there had been no suspicion of such a stand on the part of the Americans. Two years later, the Stamp Act had brought it forth virtually full-fledged.

Seen by itself, this emergence of a program of at least internal independence in 1765 is one of the most startling developments of the American

[60] Richard Bland, *An Inquiry into the Rights of the British Colonies* (Williamsburg, 1766), pp. 22, 24–27.

struggle. It seemed to spring out of nowhere, brought on by the need to find a reason to deny the British the right to impose a fairly modest and limited tax. The response appeared to be out of all proportion to the provocation. Yet it had been foreshadowed in the seventeenth century. Massachusetts had been virtually self-governing in its first incarnation and had established the kind of self-rule that came back to haunt the British in 1765. This past lay quiescent in the early eighteenth century, only to flare up as if it had merely been dormant. The British were caught unprepared.

· 7 ·

It took some time for the colonists to devise a way to bring the colonies together to deal with the issue. The initiative came from Massachusetts in June 1765, three months after the Stamp Act had made its final passage through Parliament and five months before it was slated to become effective. The Massachusetts Assembly proposed holding a meeting of representatives from all the colonies in New York on October 1, to consult together on the problems facing them.

Now, for the first time in a century and a half, the colonies were going to line up in their own collective interest, despite all past agreement by both British and Americans that they could never do it. They did not know where they were going, but they were going somewhere they had never been before.

The Stamp Act Congress met in New York from October 7 to October 25, 1765. It was attended by twenty-seven delegates from nine of the thirteen colonies, two or three from each. Among the outstanding delegates were James Otis of Massachusetts, John Dickinson of Pennsylvania, Robert R. Livingston of New York, and Christopher Gadsden of South Carolina. In the group were ten lawyers, ten merchants, and seven landowners. All were men of considerable property and high social position. After deliberating for over two weeks, they drew up three documents—an address to King George III, a memorial to the House of Lords, and a petition to Parliament. They objected not only to the Stamp Act but to the other parliamentary legislation of the past two years—the Proclamation of 1763, prohibiting settlement beyond the Allegheny Mountains to the Mississippi River, the so-called Sugar Act of 1764, imposing a duty of threepence per gallon of imported molasses, and the new vice admiralty court in Halifax.

That the meeting was held at all showed how much British authority had weakened. British officials considered it illegal, because it had not been authorized by the British government or governors. Individual colonies had petitioned Parliament for redress of grievances, but collective action was unprecedented. Each colony was related to Great Britain through its individual charter, which differed from colony to colony; there was no general charter binding all the colonies to Great Britain. Without express permission from Parliament or the Crown, the colonies were not supposed to act in concert. That they had the temerity to do so was a demonstration of newfound self-assertion and self-confidence; that the British side did nothing to stop or punish them was a confession that it did not have the power or will to do so. One lesson of the Stamp Act Congress was that enough colonies acting together with enough popular support could not be made to back down without force, which the British could not yet bring themselves to use.

These delegates represented a colonial elite, far removed from the "mob" and the "rabble." The lawyers were legal minded and the merchants business minded. They had the problem of staking out claims that went far enough to satisfy the minimal colonial demands without going so far that they could be accused of insubordination or even treason.

To show that they were loyal British subjects, they assured the king of "the warmest Sentiments of Duty and Affection," the House of Lords of "a due Subordination," and the House of Commons of "all due Subordination to the Parliament of Great Britain." The formula generally used in the instructions of the individual colonies to the delegates was, as in the case of Connecticut, "united, Humble[,] Loyal and dutifull." When they got down to cases, however, it appeared that their subordination was not complete. They adopted a Declaration of Rights and Grievances consisting of thirteen points, of which the first six were most important:

> 1st That his Majesty's Subjects in these Colonies Owe the same Allegiance to the Crown of Great Britain, that is Owing from his Subjects born within the Realm, and all due Subordination to that August Body the Parli[a]ment of Great Britain.
>
> 2d That his Majestys liege Subjects in these Colonies are intituld to all the Inherent Rights and liberties of his Natural Bornd [*sic*] Subjects, within the Kingdom of Great Britain.
>
> 3d That it is inseparably essential to the Freedom of a People, and the Undoubted Right of Englishmen, that no Taxes be imposed on them, but by their own Consent, given personally or by their

Representatives.

4th That the People of these Colonies are not and from their local Circumstances cannot be Represented in the House of Commons in Great Britain.

5th That the only Representatives of the People of these Colonies are persons chosen therein, by themselves & that no Taxes ever have been or can be constitutionally imposed on them but by their respective Legislatures.

6th That all Supplies to the Crown, being free Gifts of the People, it is unreasonable, and inconsistent with the principles and Spirit of the British Constitution, for the People of Great Britain, to Grant to his Majesty, the property of the Colonists.

It followed from these premises that the colonists could be taxed only by their own legislatures and not by Parliament, which allegedly represented only the people of Great Britain. In effect, the assemblies claimed the same power in the colonies that Parliament possessed in Great Britain, at least in the sphere of taxation. Representation in Parliament was no longer the issue. The Americans now wanted to have it both ways—not to be taxed without representation in Parliament, and not to be represented in Parliament. "All due Subordination" did not include subordination to Parliament's taxing power. Parliament's power was not challenged in any other respect; the colonies still accepted all the old restrictions on trade and manufacturing. The struggle for power was limited to taxation; every other grievance, such as the Sugar Act or the vice admiralty court in Halifax, was protested on grounds of expediency or burdensomeness. This declaration amounted to a demand for conditional or partial colonial independence—independence chiefly from British taxation.

In fact, the colonies had always been free from such taxation, because it had never before been imposed on them. Whatever the justification, the Stamp Act was an innovation. The difference was that the colonies had never needed to take a stand against Parliamentary taxation and, therefore, had not needed to delimit the British sphere of power over them. A stamp or similar tax might have gone through more easily when the colonies were too young and weak to struggle against it. By 1765, it was too late.

· 8 ·

To conduct a struggle for power, a movement was necessary. Such a movement existed and already had a body of gifted ideologists, who gave it a political program in the form of resolutions and pamphlets. It had shown itself capable of inspiring direct action in the streets. It had a hard core of militants in the Sons of Liberty. It had brought together representatives from different colonies at the Stamp Act Congress. Soon after the congress came to an end, it had something else—a weapon that hit the British where it hurt the most.

This time the initiative came from New York. Better yet, it came from the merchants. Merchants were distinct from mere shopkeepers; merchants carried on a large-scale export and import business with British and foreign markets. They owned their own ships and sent them anywhere in the world to buy, sell, or exchange cargoes. They made fortunes during the Seven Years' War by getting lucrative victualing and money contracts.[61] They constituted a "mercantile aristocracy"—the only aristocracy in the northern colonies. Intimate family ties—the son of one merchant was likely to marry the daughter of another—bound them closely together. The richest had town houses, summer houses, estates, villas with a "solid comfort which approached luxury." They imitated their betters with footmen, maids, coachmen, suits made by English tailors, wigs from London. They were more influential in provincial politics than any other group. Lawyers were beholden to them, because the best-known lawyers depended on merchants for clients; James Otis, Oxenbridge Thacher, Daniel Dulany, John Dickinson, and many others were such lawyers. In New York, the merchants divided politically into a "court party," represented by the De Lanceys and identified with the Anglicans, and a moderately oppositionist "popular party," headed by the Livingstons and identified with the Presbyterians.[62] Presbyterians were often blamed for the entire colonial uproar.

Merchants in New York and elsewhere fell on hard times after the war. The wartime prosperity began to fade as early as 1760, the year Canada was surrendered to the British, and a deep depression had set in by 1763, the year of the peace treaty.[63] As their businesses suffered, New York merchants became more and more disturbed by any British legislation that threatened their dwindling profits. They had long been accustomed to getting around the 1733 Molasses Act, and now the Grenville ministry took steps to crack down on smuggling, on corrupt customs officials, and

---

[61] Lawrence H. Leder, "Military Victualing in Colonial New York," in *Business Enterprise in Early New York,* ed. Joseph R. Frese and Jacob Judd (Sleepy Hollow Press, 1979), pp. 41–44.

[62] Virginia D. Harrington, *The New York Merchant on the Eve of the Revolution* (Columbia University Press, 1935), pp. 16, 19, 23, 29–30, 37, 40–41, 54–55.

[63] Ibid., p. 316.

on complaisant colonial juries. Even before the stamp tax, the Sugar Act of 1764 was resented so much that little more was needed to set off a political conflagration. In his old age, John Adams saw the Revolution, at least in part, as a struggle over molasses. "I know not why we should blush to confess that molasses was an essential ingredient in American independence," he reminisced. "Many great events have proceeded from much smaller causes."[64]

Merchants did not passively accept policies of which they disapproved. They and their lawyers had long experience getting the kind of legislation that favored them or getting rid of the kind they opposed. To obtain what they wanted, they had one advantage that no other colonial class enjoyed— they were closely connected with important British trading and banking interests, which gave them credit and handled their business. If American merchants suffered, they could make their British counterparts feel pain. The Americans could fail—or threaten to fail—to pay their debts or hold back from the buying and selling on which Brittish interests depended. When John Watts complained about the Sugar Act, he made sure to warn that it "Stops up I beleive many of the Outlets to the British Manufactorys, & not a little disables the Colonys from paying for those they import, which must fall ultimately upon the Mother Country, & will have disagreeable effects both on one & tother."[65]

The New York merchants had never taken advantage of their British connection as they did now. Their campaign against the Sugar Act was hatched on January 27, 1764, at the usual meeting place—Burns's Long Room, a tavern. They appointed a committee to prepare a statement of protest that eventually went to the Board of Trade and Parliament. It maintained that the enforcement of the act or enactment of any other like it "must necessarily end not only in the Utter Impoverishment of H.M. Northern Colonies and the Destruction of their Navigation but in the grievous Detriment of British Manufacturers and Artificers and the great Diminution of Trade, Power, Wealth, and Naval Strength of Great Britain."[66]

The merchants were as good as their word. If British manufacturers failed to cooperate, merchants forced them into line by refusing to give them a single order for goods.[67] Businesses failed, debts went uncollected. By August 1765, three months before the Stamp Act went into effect, John

---

[64] John Adams to William Tudor, August 11, 1818, *Works of John Adams*, vol. 10, p. 345.

[65] Watts to Colonel Barré, January 21, 1763, *Letter Book of John Watts*, (The New-York Historical Society, 1928), p. 218.

[66] Harrington, *New York Merchant*, p. 320.

[67] Dora Mae Clark, *British Opinion and the American Revolution* (Yale University Press, 1930), p. 42.

Watts advised Sir William Baker, who handled his financial affairs in London, that "Business is here very languid, the weak must go to the Wall, frequent Bankruptcys & growing more frequent."[68] Four out of the five New York delegates to the Stamp Act Congress were outstanding merchants. To Secretary Conway, in charge of the colonies, General Gage wrote from his headquarters in New York that the merchants "having Countermanded the Goods they had Wrote for unless it was repealed, they make no Doubt that many Trading Towns and principal Merchants in London will assist them to accomplish their Ends." He added:

> The Lawyers are the Source from whence the Clamors have flowed in every Province. In this Province Nothing Publick is transacted without them. . . . The whole Body of Merchants in general, Assembly Men, Magistrates, &c. have been united in this Plan of Riots, and without the Influence and Instigation of these the inferior People would have been quiet. Very great Pains was taken to rouse them before they Stirred. The Sailors who are the only People who may be properly Stiled Mob, are entirely at the Command of the Merchants who employ them.[69]

This strategy paid off. In London, the Americans had a formidable lobby of provincial agents, many of whom were British merchants. One of the most influential was Barlow Trecothick, who was married to the daughter of an American merchant, Charles Apthorp of Boston, with whom the British firm of Thomlinson and Trecothick was associated. He was also a close friend of Lord Rockingham, Grenville's successor as head of the government. On December 4, 1765, a "Committee of the London Merchants, trading to North-America," of which Trecothick was chairman, met to discuss "the present State of the British Trade to North-America, and the Prospect of increasing Embarrassments, which threaten the loss of our depending Property there and even to annihilate the Trade itself."[70] These London merchants soon presented a petition to the House of Commons in which they called attention to the annual British export of

> very large Quantities of *British* Manufactures, consisting of Woolen Goods of all Kinds, Cottons, Linens, Hardware, Shoes, Hous[e]hold Furniture, and almost without Exception of every other Species of Goods manufactured in these Kingdoms, besides other Articles

[68] *Letter Book of John Watts*, p. 368.
[69] *Gage Correspondence*, vol. 1, p. 79.
[70] *Prologue to Revolution*, p. 130.

imported from abroad. ... and that, in return for these Exports, the Petitioners have received from the Colonies, Rice, Indico [*sic*], Tobacco, Naval Stores, Oil, Whale Fins, Furs, and lately Pot Ash, with other Commodities.

They also noted that the colonies owed British merchants "several Millions sterling," which they could not pay, because the colonies alleged that "the Taxes and Restrictions laid upon them" had "interrupted the usual and former most fruitful Branches of their Commerce" and had "brought on so great a Number of actual Bankruptcies." As a result, the committee entreated the House of Commons for relief "in order to secure themselves and their Families from impending Ruin."[71] They sent their petition to British trading and manufacturing towns, of which twenty-seven came through with similar petitions to Parliament. According to Horace Walpole, "In reality it was the clamour of trade, of the merchants, and of the manufacturing towns, that had borne down all opposition. A general insurrection was apprehended as the immediate consequence of upholding the bill; the revolt of America, and the destruction of trade, was the prospect in future."[72] Closer to home, William Smith, an eminent lawyer, the early historian of New York and confidant of governors, was of the same mind. In November 1765, he advised Gov. Robert Monckton that "Great Britain has indeed lost the Affection of all the Colonists, and I am very fearful not only of Discontent and partial Tumults amongst them, but that a general Civil War will light up and rage all along the Continent."[73]

American merchants did not necessarily support the nonimportation movement only for patriotic reasons. They had overbought during the good years and were now able to get rid of surplus goods at higher prices. A Philadelphia merchant, John Chew, made no mystery of their motives: "Indeed we are well convinced something of this sort is absolutely necessary at this time from the great much too large importation that has for sometime past been made. There will be no wanted goods for a twelve month."[74] It never hurt to have economic interest coincide with political correctness.

[71] "The Petition of the London Merchants to the House of Commons," January 17, 1766, ibid., pp. 130–31.
[72] Horace Walpole, *Memoirs of the Reign of King George the Third,* ed. G. F. Russell Barker (Lawrence and Bullen, 1894), vol. 2, pp. 211–12. Langford agrees with Walpole (p. 182).
[73] *Historical Memoirs from 16 March 1763 to 9 July 1776 William Smith,* ed. William H. W. Sabine (New York, 1956), p. 30.
[74] Chew to Samuel Galloway, November 7, 1765, cited by Marc Egnal and Joseph A. Ernst, "An Economic Interpretation of the American Revolution," *William and Mary Quarterly,* January 1972, p. 22.

In any case, this unprecedented political activity by American merchants and lawyers was the crowning achievement of the early prerevolutionary movement. It had matured with unprecedented speed. In 1763, there was little or no evidence of it. In 1765, the Americans had proved themselves capable of formulating a political program and platform; producing resolutions and pamphlets; bringing out mobs and rioters; creating a secret, militant organization, the Sons of Liberty; holding a congress to address the British government; organizing a mass boycott of British goods; uniting social strata from the lowliest artisan to the merchant elite. All this had been done with a minimum of coordination and planning; spontaneity and improvisation seemed to be enough to set these forces in motion. From this time onward, the British could not fail to know that their worst fears and most gloomy predictions could be realized.

· 9 ·

The war of words and the war in the streets went on concurrently. There had been other contentions in the past, but they had not led to the physical opposition that developed in 1765. The past complaints had seemed to pit governors against assemblies, with the British administration largely aloof and remote, or they had concerned financial and economic matters that could be arranged or evaded. Now the conflict had taken a far more serious turn; it put the British Parliament on a collision course with the colonial assemblies or the most radical elements in them and in the communities at large. If the expediency of the act had been the only issue, its potential for verbal and physical violence would not have gone so far. A clash of principles was far more difficult to compromise. The combination of expediency and principle was what made the stamp tax so explosive; pure expediency would have made the cost of large-scale resistance higher than the possible gain; pure principle would have made the struggle too abstract and rarefied to catch on popularly. Already by 1765, it was becoming increasingly difficult to think of anything essentially new in the clash of ideas. The main themes had emerged; the players now began to perform variations, which were to go on for another decade, until they had exhausted their patience and had begun fully to understand what they were really trying to say.

The American and British pamphleteers who conducted another and even greater debate in 1765 were largely agreed on what the main questions were: What was the right or power of Parliament over the American colonies? Was it total, partial, or none at all? Was it flawed for lack of colonial representation? If so, what if anything could be done about it? What did taxes have to do with the far larger question of parliamentary authority?

Yet the very framing of the main questions made it increasingly difficult for both sides to avoid taking extreme positions in the end. For some time the question of Parliament's power was masked by making it a question of Parliament's "right." Its right might be challenged on various grounds— from the specific nature of British jurisdiction over the colonies to a general claim arising from "natural" or universal principles. Whatever the rationale, however, power—over the colonies by the British government or by the colonies over themselves—was the ultimate prize. In the long debate, the subject changed in time from how the colonies were to fit into the British system to whether they fitted into it at all.

12

"The very foundations of this Kingdom are sinking"

❧

· 1 ·

T HE NEWS FROM AMERICA plunged British politics into turmoil. Never before had the British establishment been so obsessed with what was happening in the colonies. To make matters worse, the new British government was one of the weakest in the century.

George Grenville was followed in July 1765 by Charles Watson-Wentworth, second marquess of Rockingham. He was only thirty-five years old, a country gentleman who notoriously preferred horse races to politics. A coterie—described waspishly by Horace Walpole as "young and inexperienced men, unknown to the nation, and great by nothing but their rank and fortunes"[1]—enabled him to be chosen as a stopgap until someone weightier could be found. The new ministry seemed to be an accident arising from a political vacuum. Charles Townshend mocked it with the taunt "a Lutestring ministry; fit only for the summer."[2]

Appointed first lord of the Treasury in July 1765, Rockingham remained

---

[1] Horace Walpole, *Memoirs of the Reign of King George the Third*, ed. G. B. Russell Barker (Lawrence and Bullen, 1894), vol. 2, p. 135.

[2] Cited by P. Langford, *The First Rockingham Administration, 1765–1766* (Oxford University Press, 1973), p. 4.

in office for less than a year, just long enough to pick up the shattered pieces of Grenville's policy. His main weakness was that he could not get the support of the old, wounded lion of British politics, William Pitt, now afflicted with gout and depressed in spirit but not yet to be counted out. The American challenge could not have come at a worse time for Great Britain, with a ministry so unstable and inexperienced that it was not expected to survive without Pitt, who refused to save it. "All in all the new Ministry was not such as to inspire confidence in its ability to survive" was the judgment of its historian. "Every circumstance of its formation seemed to militate against its chances of success."[3]

The American uproar created such a crisis in British political life that for a time it crowded out everything else. In March 1766, Edmund Burke, who had been taken on as Rockingham's private secretary and was a new member of the House of Commons, explained to a friend that "our hands are so full of America" he did not see how the parliamentary session could deal with anything else.[4] This session, which opened on January 14 and continued until March 4, 1766, dealt day after day with the American problem, as no Parliament had ever done before. William Pitt said that the occasion was the most important in the history of Parliament since the Glorious Revolution of 1688.[5] Burke thought that "surely, since this monarchy, a more material point never came under the consideration of Parliament."[6] George III confided that the fate of the Stamp Act was "undoubtedly the most serious matter that ever came before Parliament."[7]

Most famous was the debate between Pitt and Grenville. Pitt came forth for the pro-American side. In his first speech, his view of the Stamp Act was contained in these words: "It is my opinion that this kingdom has no right to lay a tax upon the colonies. At the same time, I assert the authority of this kingdom over the colonies, to be sovereign and supreme, in every circumstance of government and legislation whatsoever."

But how could he reconcile these apparently contradictory principles? To achieve this seemingly impossible task, Pitt made a distinction between "legislation and taxation." He argued that "taxation is no part of the governing or legislative power." He scornfully denied that America was "virtually" represented in the House of Commons—"the most contemptible

---

[3] Ibid., p. 39.

[4] Burke to Charles O'Hara, March 29, 1766, *The Correspondence of Edmund Burke*, ed. Thomas W. Copeland (Cambridge University Press, 1958), vol. 1, p. 247.

[5] *The Parliamentary History of England (Hansard)*, vol. 16, col. 98.

[6] Burke to Charles O'Hara, December 31, 1765, *Burke Correspondence*, vol. 1, p. 229.

[7] Langford, *First Rockingham Administration*, p. 165.

idea that ever entered into the head of a man—It does not deserve a serious refutation."[8]

Grenville represented the anti-American side. He quickly struck back at Pitt's main contention: "That this kingdom has the sovereign, the supreme legislative power over *America*, is granted. It cannot be denied; and taxation is a part of that sovereign power. It is one branch of the legislation. It is, it has been exercised, over those who are not, who were never represented."

For Grenville, the Americans' near rebellion was born of ingratitude:

> Protection and obedience are reciprocal. *Great-Britain* protects *America; America* is bound to yield obedience. If not, tell me where the *Americans* were emancipated? When they want the protection of this kingdom, they are always very ready to ask it. That protection has always been afforded them in the most full and ample manner. The nation has run itself into an immense debt to give them their protection; and now they are called upon to contribute a small share towards the public expence, an expence arising from themselves, they renounce your authority, insult your officers, and break out, I might almost say, into open rebellion.

Grenville's rage rose. He attributed "the seditious spirit of the colonies" to pro-American "factions in this House." The Americans had held out because they expected their British friends to take power. He had done his best "to advance the trade of *America*" and had been maligned as having discouraged it.

Grenville subsequently gave this opinion why the Americans had been so recalcitrant: "America would not have been in this condition if they had believed that we would enforce the law. . . . Whoever advises the King to give up his sovereignty over America is the greatest enemy to this country and will be accused by all posterity. . . . he finds the Americans disputing the authority of this country and was willing to try how far their disobedience could reach."[9]

Grenville's earlier attack was so virulent that Pitt insisted on answering it immediately. He interpreted Grenville's remarks about "giving birth to sedition in America" as having been directed against him personally. Then Pitt made one of his most splendid defenses of American liberty:

[8] *Proceedings and Debates of the British Parliaments Respecting North America, 1754–1783,* ed. R. C. Simmons and P. D. G. Thomas (Kraus International, 1983), vol. 2, Jan. 14, 1766, pp. 85–86.

[9] Ibid., January 14, 1766, pp. 87–88; February 7, 1766, p. 171.

"The gentleman tells us, *America* is obstinate; *America* is almost in open rebellion. I rejoice that *America* has resisted. Three millions of people, so dead to all the feelings of liberty, as voluntarily to submit to be slaves, would have been fit instruments to make slaves of the rest."

He recalled that he had rejected a stamp tax when it had been proposed to him during the recent war. He gave as the reason for his refusal that "perhaps the Americans would have submitted" with the enemy at their back, "but it would have been taking an ungenerous, and unjust advantage." He reiterated his belief in American subjection to British rule:

> I am no courtier of *America,* I stand up for this kingdom. I maintain, that the Parliament has a right to bind, to restrain *America.* Our legislative power over the colonies, is sovereign and supreme. When it ceases to be sovereign and supreme, I would advise every gentleman to sell his lands, if he can, and embark for that country. When two countries are connected together, like *England* and her colonies, without being incorporated, the one must necessarily govern, the greater must rule the less; but so rule it, as not to contradict the fundamental principles that are common to both.

The fundamental principle in question was the distinction between internal and external taxes, between taxes levied for revenue and duties imposed to regulate trade. Pitt then explained why colonial trade came first. When in office, he had found that the profit to Great Britain from it came to £2 million a year—"This is the fund that carried you triumphantly through the last war." Now he stirringly warned what success against America, if it came to war, would entail: "*America,* if she fell, would fall like a strong man. She would embrace the pillars of the state, and pull down the constitution along with her. Is this your boasted peace? Not to sheath the sword in its scabbard, but to sheath it in the bowels of your countrymen?"

Finally, he stated more fully what should be done:

> It is, that the Stamp Act be *repealed absolutely, totally,* and *immediately.* That the reason for the repeal be assigned, because it was founded on an erroneous principle. At the same time, let the sovereign authority of this country over the colonies, be asserted in as strong terms as can be devised, and be made to extend to every point of legislation whatsoever. That we may bind their *trade,* confine their *manufactures,* and exercise every *power* whatsoever, except that of taking their money out of their pockets without their consent![10]

[10] Ibid., January 14, 1766, pp. 88–91.

Pitt's was a double-edged prescription. It gave the Americans what they immediately wanted—repeal of the Stamp Act—but held in reserve a price—admission of British rule over them in every other respect—that contained hidden dangers.

Edmund Burke made his parliamentary debut in this session. His view was not unlike that of Pitt, who praised his effort. Burke supported the repeal of the Stamp Act on the ground that taxation was excluded from "the system of government with respect to the plantations." It was enough that Great Britain enjoyed a monopoly of colonial trade. He gave as an example the duty of £300,000 a year which Great Britain received from tobacco imported from the colonies. This trade would be destroyed if an additional duty were placed upon the tobacco in America. For Burke, practical consequences determined what taxes were appropriate in the colonies. His basic view rested on a distinction between the ideal and the practical. Ideally, the colonies could be taxed, but practically, taxation was poor policy. He wrote down his main thought in this schematic form:

To state the right of Great Britain to Tax the Colonies.

This speculative Idea of a right deduced from the unlimited Nature of the supreme Legislative authority, very clear and very undeniable, but, when explained proved and admitted little to no purpose.

The Practical, executive, exertion of this Right may be impracticable, may be inequitable and may be contrary to the Genius and Spirit even of the Constitution which gives this right at least contrary to the principles of Liberty.

In this way, Burke opposed the Stamp Act without challenging the premise of Parliament's "supreme Legislative authority" over the colonies. In principle, he supported the right of Parliament to have "full power and Authority" over the colonies "in all cases whatsoever." But "subordination" had to be tempered with "freedom." By making authority "ideal" and "speculative," he watered it down so much that only the practical consequences really mattered.[11] Subsequently, Burke warned that "the very foundations of this Kingdom are sinking under us."[12]

Some of the other speeches were equally revealing. Secretary of State Conway admitted the right to tax America but thought that "policy and justice" were against it. He would never consent to enforcing the Stamp Act by military force. He subsequently declared: "If we enforce the Stamp

[11] There is no satisfactory text of Burke's speeches. The problem is fully discussed in *The Writings and Speeches of Edmund Burke,* ed. Paul Langford (Oxford University Press, 1981), vol. 2, pp. 30–40. My summary is based on pp. 47, 50–51, 53.

[12] *Proceedings and Debates,* February 7, 1766, p. 168.

Act, we shall have a war in America, and the Bourbon league [France and Spain] will take this advantage." Or again: "The rebellion in America would be subdued. The force of this country is equal to it. But the conflict is death to both countries."[13]

Hans Stanley, a follower of Grenville, wondered whether "we shall give up all authority over the Americans and can never possibly recover it without all the miseries of a civil war." He foresaw that Great Britain was only at the beginning of its colonial problem: "The repeal of the Stamp Act will not content the Americans. A few years, or rather a few months will bring them again before you with the same decent and respectful opposition to your whole system of laws of American legislation."[14]

Atty. Gen. Charles Yorke, who is said to have worked out the double-edged policy,[15] was alarmed for "the vital principle of your Empire, the sovereignty of this Country," and trembled "for the future consequences." He warned, "If the [British] supremacy is not assured, no friend will trust you, no enemy will fear you."[16] William Blackstone insisted that the colonies "are dependent upon us, and if they attempt to shake off our [their?] dependence, we shall I hope have firmness enough to make them obey."[17]

Colonel Barré, who had inspired the Sons of Liberty, made one of the most ominous speeches. As usual, he was the most militant advocate of the colonial cause, but he saw ahead with singular insight into what others were reluctant to contemplate:

> If you do mean to lay internal taxes, act prudently and draw the sword immediately. If you do not confine yourselves to general words, the repeal of the Stamp Act alone will not satisfy them. The ulcer will remain, and they will expect another Stamp Act the next year. If you enforce the Act, you must draw the sword. You will force them to submit, but the trade will be forced to submit likewise. If they submit with high words only, the discontent will remain. . . .
>
> All colonies have their date of independence. The wisdom or folly of our conduct may make it the sooner or later. If we act injudiciously, this point may be reached in the life of many of the members of this House.[18]

---

[13] Ibid., February 3, 1766, p. 135; February 7, 1766, p. 172; February 21, 1766, p. 281.
[14] Ibid., February 3, 1766, vol. 2, p. 136.
[15] Langford, *First Rockingham Administration*, p. 151.
[16] *Proceedings and Debates*, February 3, 1766, p. 139.
[17] Ibid., p. 140.
[18] Ibid., p. 144.

Grenville turned on Conway for having said that "there were those who were wild and mad enough to think of employing force but that he [Conway] would sooner cut off his hand than employ such means." But, Grenville charged, Conway had himself ordered General Gage to use force, though he knew that there was none available. Grenville added that he differed from Barré totally but respected his consistency, whereas he despised the conduct of the others as "so mean and so distasteful."[19]

In subsequent days, other opinions were voiced. Charles Townshend cautioned:

> If some proper plan is not formed for governing as well as quieting them at present and for the future, it will be extremely dangerous. The magistrates at present in many colonies elective, the judges dependent on the assemblies for their salaries. . . .
>
> We are now without forts or troops. Our magistrates without inclinations and without power. Would you raise this temper while you are the most unable to resist it? . . .
>
> A picture of America. No commerce, no trade, no legislature. A line of separation drawn between Great Britain and the colonies for ever more.[20]

The entire debate revealed that an amicable resolution was still far off. From Grenville, the Americans could expect no sympathy and no concessions. But they could draw too much comfort from Pitt's support. His implicit assumption was that the Americans wanted nothing more than to get the Stamp Act out of the way and were willing to accept British domination in everything else but taxation. Pitt can be excused for thinking that an understanding could be worked out on this basis; Americans were saying the same thing.

What emerged unmistakably from this extraordinary debate were its alarmist character and its apocalyptic premonitions. Again and again speakers spoke of a chasm that was opening and a catastrophe that loomed ahead—"open rebellion" (Grenville); "the very foundations of this Kingdom are sinking under us" (Burke); "if we enforce the Stamp Act, we shall have a war in America" (Conway); "the miseries of a civil war" (Stanley); "if you enforce the Act, you must draw the sword" (Barré); "a line of separation drawn between Great Britain and the colonies for ever more" (Townshend). The British side felt that it had to make a decision as if the entire future of relations with the colonies was at stake. It did not have

[19] Ibid., p. 145.
[20] Ibid., February 7, 1766, p. 167.

enough arms in the colonies to use force, and it had too much to lose in trade and manufactures to risk failure.[21]

The result was mixed. In the critical vote, repeal of the Stamp Act was carried by 275 to 167.[22] But a price was paid for the victory. Repeal was linked with a Declaratory Act, which specifically gave Parliament full authority to make laws binding on the colonies *"in all cases whatsoever."* The last four words were deliberately italicized to make sure that the message got through. Yorke had originally wanted to add "as well in cases of Taxation," but Rockingham had objected in order not to arouse Pitt. This combination had been worked out before the session, because Rockingham knew that he could not get repeal through by itself. In any case, the vote showed that the British were deeply divided. Most of the votes for the repeal of the Stamp Act were cast for reasons of expediency, not principle. Almost one-third of the House voted against repeal and almost none against the Declaratory Act.

The Declaratory Act shows that the colonies had won no more than a temporary, limited victory. It opened the door to future conflicts so long as the dread word *taxation* was avoided. In the long run, the Declaratory Act was more important than the repeal of the Stamp Act, because the former provided the lasting source of colonial disaffection. On this occasion, Benjamin Franklin's usual acumen failed him; he thought that the Declaratory Act had been passed "merely to save Appearances."[23] But the antirepeal opposition was convinced, as the historian of this Rockingham ministry points out, that "the Americans were seeking not the redress of specific grievances but ultimately independence," and this conviction merely hardened after repeal.[24] British public opinion, with the help of merchant lobbying and ministerial encouragement, favored repeal, but there was no telling how long this pro-American sentiment would last. Something had been done; nothing had been decided.

· 2 ·

The Americans were far behind the British in their forebodings and

---

[21] For all the speeches from Conway on, I have used the *Parliamentary Diaries of Nathaniel Ryder*, in *Camden Miscellany*, 4th seri., vol. 7, (Royal Historical Society, 1969), pp. 273–320, as the most accessible and reliable.

[22] *Proceedings and Debates*, February 21, 1766, vol. 2, p. 287.

[23] Franklin to Joseph Fox, March 1, 1766, *The Papers of Benjamin Franklin*, ed. Leonard W. Labaree (Yale University Press, 1961), vol. 13, p. 186.

[24] Langford, *First Rockingham Administration*, p. 174.

anxieties. The disparity between the two sides is one of the most striking aspects of this phase of the prerevolutionary struggle.

A telling reflection of the American state of mind was provided by Benjamin Franklin's extraordinary examination, in February 1766, before a committee of the whole of the House of Commons, convened to hear expert testimony on conditions in the colonies before the vote on the repeal of the Stamp Act. Only extended extracts can convey the full flavor and significance of the occasion.

Franklin was asked "What was the temper of America towards Great Britain before the year 1763?" His reply made it seem that all the trouble had come afterwards:

> The best in the world. They submitted willingly to the government of the Crown, and paid, in all their courts, obedience to acts of parliament. Numerous as the people are in the several old provinces, they cost you nothing in forts, citadels, garrisons, or armies, to keep them in subjection. They were governed by this country at the expence only of a little pen, ink and paper. They were led by a thread. They had not only a respect, but an affection, for Great-Britain, for its laws, its customs and manners, and even a fondness for its fashions, that greatly increased the commerce. Natives of Britain were always treated with particular regard; to be an Old-England man was, of itself, a character of some respect, and gave a kind of rank among us.

Franklin was questioned about the change that had taken place by 1766:

> Q. And what is their temper now?
> A. O, very much altered.
> Q. Did you ever hear the authority of parliament to make laws for America questioned till lately?
> A. The authority of parliament was allowed to be valid in all laws, except such as should lay internal taxes. It was never disputed in laying duties to regular commerce.

Franklin became fulsome in his description of how the colonists had in the past admired and respected Parliament: "They considered the parliament as the great bulwark and security of their liberties and privileges, and always spoke of it with the utmost respect and veneration. Arbitrary ministers, they thought, might possibly, at times, attempt to oppress them; but they relied on it, that the parliament, on application, would always give redress."

Now, he said, the respect for Parliament had "greatly lessened." Would they submit to a "moderated" stamp tax? He was unyielding: "No, never, unless compelled by force of arms. . . . No; they will never submit to it." They would react to a future stamp tax the same way—"They would not pay it." He did not see how the British could use military force—"They cannot force a man to take stamps who chooses to do without them." Here, Franklin uttered an implied threat: "They will not find a rebellion; they may indeed make one." At a later stage, he again insisted that the colonies would never repudiate their anti–stamp tax resolutions "unless compelled by force of arms."

Franklin more than once brought up the issue of representation, as if he still thought it was the basic factor—"whenever the subject [of taxes] has occurred in conversation where I have been present, it has appeared to be the opinion of every one, that we could not be taxed in a parliament where we were not represented." In 1754, he recalled, a British proposal had been made to tax the colonies for the general defense, but "the general opinion was, that the parliament neither would or could lay any tax on us, till we were duly represented in parliament, because it was not just, nor agreeable to the nature of an English constitution." He went so far as to give assurances that the colonies would send representatives to Parliament "whenever the occasion arises."

Franklin also made use of the distinction between internal and external taxes; the former could not be avoided, whereas the latter, by imposing a duty on commodities, could raise the price so high that they would not be bought. In this connection, he hit the British where they were most vulnerable; if the Stamp Act was not repealed, "they will take very little of your manufactures in a short time."

Then Franklin made a most telling observation. He was asked what the Americans would think of British motives for repealing the Stamp Act. He replied: "I suppose they will think that it was repealed from a conviction of its inexpediency; and they will rely on it, that while the same inexpediency subsists, you will never attempt to make such another." By "inexpediency," Franklin explained, he meant the colonial inability to pay the tax, the general discontent it had aroused, and the impracticality of enforcing it. By putting so much emphasis on "inexpediency," he implied that the Americans were able to defeat the tax by making it too costly for the British to enforce, and that, by continuing to pinch the British where they were most sensitive, the Americans were going to prevent any future tax. It was a formula for a suspension rather than a cessation of hostilities.

But Franklin was a master of mixing the sweet and sour. If the stamp tax was repealed, would the colonies recognize the authority of Parliament? "I don't doubt at all," he replied, "that if the legislature repeal the stamp-act, the Colonies will acquiesce in the authority." Would the colonies accept even a small tax? Again Franklin's answer implied a desire for representation: "But as to any internal tax, how small soever, laid by the legislature here on the people there, while they have no representatives in this legislature, I think it will never be submitted to. They will oppose it to the last." Yet Franklin had to admit that the colonies had never asked for representation before. He soon fell back on the Lockean principle that "one of the privileges of English subjects is, that they are not to be taxed but by their common consent."

One of Franklin's boldest challenges came in connection with the Seven Years' War. The British felt that they were entitled to get more out of the Americans because they had fought a war in the Americans' behalf which had plunged them into debt. Franklin would have none of this. He declared that the war "was really a British war," because it had been fought "for the defence of territories of the Crown, the property of no American, and for the defence of trade purely British." He also denied that it was necessary to send British troops into the newly conquered territory "to defend the Americans against the Indians." The Americans were well able to defend themselves, he insisted, thus cutting the ground from under the British case for increasing the number of their armed forces in North America.

Towards the end of his ordeal, Franklin struck back with another implied threat: "Many arguments have been lately used here to shew them that there is no difference [between internal and external taxation], and that if you have no right to tax them internally, you have none to tax them externally, or make any other law to bind them. At present they do not reason so, but in time they may possibly be convinced by these arguments."

Franklin's last words were equally threatening to the British economy:

Q. What used to be the pride of the Americans?
A. To indulge in the fashions and manufactures of Great-Britain.
Q. What is now their pride?
A. To wear their old cloaths over again, till they can make new ones.[25]

[25] I have used the text of Franklin's "Examination" in *Franklin Papers*, vol. 13, pp. 129–59. There is also a discussion of the various versions, pp. 124–29.

Franklin's was a bravura performance. It was published in London in 1767 as a shilling pamphlet, and long excerpts appeared in two London magazines. At least four pamphlet editions soon came out in the colonies. Franklin's London printer, William Strahan, passed on word that Rockingham himself had said "the *Repeal* was generally and absolutely determined" by Franklin's testimony, so great an impression had it made on the House. None of his other political writings equaled the fame of this pamphlet in America, Great Britain, or Europe. For years, British pamphleteers, including William Knox, found it necessary to argue against it.[26] In Philadelphia, coffeehouses gave presents to every man on the ship that brought news of Franklin's triumph. On the king's birthday in June 1766, salutes were fired from a barge named the *Franklin.*[27]

Franklin led the British to believe that the Stamp Act was the only thing that barred the way to a return of the good old days, when all the colonists had been supremely happy with British rule. He made a stamp tax, no matter how small, out of the question, now and forever. He reinforced the British apprehension that the tax could be collected only by using armed force. He made the British face the disastrous prospect of losing the American market, through both the nonimportation of British goods and the American ability to manufacture their own substitutes. He rather overdid the factor of representation, which had already been ruled out as "impracticable" by the Massachusetts Assembly the previous October. Grenville and others had hammered away at him hour after hour, without ever getting the best of him or breaking down his composure, though he showed his teeth two or three times.

The British were forced to accept the unhappy denouement, but they could never quite understand what made the colonies so violent and obstinate about the stamp tax. No British government had faced such a colonial rebellion before. There were no precedents for handling it and no way of knowing how serious it was. The distinction between internal and external taxes struck most British legislators as strained and far-fetched. They could never agree that taxation was not a legitimate subject of legislation. They told themselves that, at best, the stamp tax was going to pay for only a small portion of their military expenses in America. Since they could not make any other sense of the uncompromising opposition to the Stamp Act, the more intransigent anti-Americans suspected that the real purpose was something far more threatening—a step on the way to the ultimate

[26] *Benjamin Franklin's Letters to the Press,* 1758–1775, ed. Verner W. Crane (University of North Carolina Press, 1950), pp. 73–75.

[27] Carl Van Doren, *Benjamin Franklin* (Viking Press, 1938), pp. 353–54.

independence of the colonies.[28] This eventuality had been anticipated by them for so long that events merely seemed to confirm what theory and history told them to expect. One expression of this view appeared in a London newspaper, in which it was said that the Americans

> might indeed for a few months lay down their arms, but they would still be working underhand, and collecting strength daily; till at last the seditious flame would burst out afresh, and having been for a-while pent up, would rage afterwards with redoubled fury.
>
> The Americans imbibe notions of independence and liberty with their very milk, and will some time or other shake off all subjection. If we yield to them in this particular, by repealing the Stamp-Act, it is all over; they will from that moment assert their freedom.[29]

Above all, repeal of the Stamp Act signified a change in the balance of power between Great Britain and the colonies. For the majority of Commons did not vote for repeal because they thought it was the right thing to do. They acted under pressure of the colonies' ability to inflict widespread economic distress in Great Britain; they were far more impressed by the testimony of British merchants and manufacturers that the American boycott was having a disastrous effect on their businesses; the parliamentary debate was overcast by the specter of mass British unemployment. If Horace Walpole may be trusted, the tax was repealed for an even more ominous reason—"A general insurrection was apprehended as the immediate consequence of upholding the bill; the revolt of America, and the destruction of trade, was the prospect in future." Walpole referred to "the manufacturers of Bristol, Liverpool, Manchester, and such populous and discontented towns, who threatened to send hosts to Westminster to back their demand for repeal."[30] That the Americans should have been able—or even been thought able—to wreak such havoc in Great Britain itself was an extraordinary tribute to their power.

---

[28] American historians have agreed. "It was this unconscious desire for complete self-government, which could be realized only by political independence, that explains the intensity of the opposition aroused by Grenville's policy" (George Louis Beer, *British Colonial Policy, 1754–1765*, Macmillan, 1907, p. 309). "In this last idea, that of national independence, lies the secret spring of the revolt [against the Stamp Act]" (H. L. Osgood, "England and the Colonies," *Political Science Quarterly*, vol. 2, p. 441). "The first organized resistance in America [against the Stamp Act] to the financial policy of Great Britain and the real beginning of the movement for separation from the mother country" (Charles M. Andrews, *The Colonial Background of the American Revolution*, Yale University Press, 1924, p. 140).

[29] Signed "Anti-Sejanus," *London Chronicle*, February 13, 1766, in *Prologue to Revolution*, ed. Edmund S. Morgan (University of North Carolina Press, 1959), p. 134.

[30] Walpole, *Memoirs of the Reign of King George the Third*, p. 213. British historians have taken this explanation most seriously. P. D. G. Thomas comments that "Horace Walpole was scarcely exaggerating" (*British Politics and the Stamp Act Crisis*, Clarendon Press, 1975, p. 248).

Thus the struggle over the Stamp Act was essentially a test of strength. The British and Americans stared at each other, and the British blinked first.

Yet the opportunistic nature of the settlement did not bode well for the future. Its great defect was that it told British politicians what not to do, not what to do. The next stage was sure to hinge on the question whether the repeal of the Stamp Act or the adoption of the Declaratory Act was more likely to influence future British policy. Once the British recovered their nerve, the answer was not long in coming.

The struggle over the Stamp Act was the defining phase of the ten years before the Revolutionary War. In effect, the struggles that came after it basically produced variations on the themes announced in 1765–66. The two sides wrestled to get the better of each other, all the while fearing the ultimate outcome and succeeding only in putting it off. The early American historian David Ramsay commented:

> The repeal of the stamp act, in a relative connexion with all its circumstances and consequences, was the first direct step to American independency. The claims of the two countries were not only left undecided, but a foundation was laid for their extending it at a future period, to the impossibility of a compromise. . . .
>
> Elevated with the advantage they had gained, from that day forward, instead of feeling themselves dependent on Great-Britain, they conceived that, in respect to commerce, she was dependent on them. It inspired them with such high ideas of the importance of their trade, that they considered the Mother Country to be brought under greater obligations to them, for purchasing her manufactures, than they were to her for protection and the administration of civil government. The freemen of British America, impressed with the exalting sentiments of patriotism and of liberty, conceived it to be within their power, by future combinations, at any time to convulse, if not to bankrupt the nation, from which they sprung.[31]

Significantly, the loyalist historian Peter Oliver, the former chief justice of the Massachusetts superior court, wrote about the repeal of the Stamp Act in a manner not unlike that of Ramsay. Oliver set down his thoughts in 1781, eight years before Ramsay, but his work was not published until 1961.

> In 1766 the Act was repealed. Illuminations & Sky-rockets proclaimed the general Joy. But it was not the Joy of Gratitude, but the

---

[31] David Ramsay, *The History of the American Revolution* (Philadelphia, 1789), vol. 1, pp. 74–75.

Exultation of Triumph. *America* had now found a Way of redressing her own Grievances, without applying to a superior Power. She felt her own Superiority, & has uninterruptedly applied the same Remedy. . . .

They were swelled with their own Importance, & had felt so little from british Power, that they now hugged themselves in Security, regardless of what a Power at 3000 Miles distant could do unto them.[32]

Ramsay, a participant in the struggle for independence, was also a hardheaded historian, who recognized how patriotism and liberty intersected with commerce and power. They did so with thunderous effect at the time of the Stamp Act, and the British-American connection was never the same. Oliver was a much more prejudiced writer, suffering from exile and disappointment. When these two men agree that the repeal of the Stamp Act gave the colonies a new sense of their own power and of the limitations of British power, they cannot be easily brushed aside.

· 3 ·

On the surface, the rejoicing was great in both America and Great Britain at the repeal of the stamp tax. The governor and assembly of Rhode Island sent a typical message of thanks to the king, though it contained a disturbing allusion to what might have happened if the colonies had not had their way: "It was with the deepest Concern we reflected upon the fatal Consequences we conceived would inevitably attend the Operation of that Act not only to your Majesty's loyal Subjects in America but also to those in Great Britain: And it is with equal Joy and Gratitude that we find an Act so destructive in our humble Opinions to the Interests of both Countries repealed."[33] If this message did come to the attention of the king, one wonders what he thought of having avoided "fatal Consequences" by capitulating to the colonies.

The repeal of the Stamp Act was not the only symptom of a British retreat. In 1766, the equally obnoxious Sugar Act was withdrawn. The threepence duty on molasses imported by the colonies was repealed and a duty of onepence per gallon on all molasses, British as well as foreign, substituted. One colonial agent, Joseph Sherwood, was so euphoric that he wrote to Gov.

---

[32] *Peter Oliver's Origin and Progress of the American Revolution*, ed. Douglass Adair and John A. Schutz (orig. ms., 1781; Huntington Library, 1961), pp. 55–56.

[33] "The Governor and Company of Rhode Island to the King," June 14, 1766, *The Correspondence of the Colonial Governors of Rhode Island*, ed. Gertrude Selwyn Kimball (Houghton Mifflin, 1903), vol. 2, pp. 388–89.

Samuel Ward of Rhode Island: "Every Grievance of which you Complained is now Absolutely and totally removed, a joyfull and a happy Event for the late Disconsolate Inhabitants of America."[34]

American merchants became the toast of London. In April 1766, a "City feast" was held for them. The *Annual Register* commemorated the occasion: "The company last Wednesday at Draper's-hall was very numerous, and the most brilliant almost ever seen in the city of London. It is said there were about 240 who dined, amongst whom were nine Dukes, and a very considerable number more of the nobility, and the members of the House of Commons, who honoured the American merchants with their company."[35] It was a case of making merry while the opportunity lasted.

William Pitt was the greatest hero of the moment. Medals, with his head in relief, bore the words "The man who, having saved the parent, pleaded with success for her children."[36] American towns put up statues in his honor. British ship captains and crews, weavers, ironworkers, shoemakers, hat manufacturers, window-glass makers, and others hurried back to their jobs. British merchants and manufacturers savored their moment of triumph, as if they had been saved from inevitable ruin. Unwittingly, they testified to the hold that American consumers had gained over them.

The colonial victory over the Stamp Act was paid for later. The British retreat gave the colonists the feeling that the British could not withstand the boycott of their goods and thus emboldened the colonists to repeat the strategy. If the colonists had been less successful, they might have been more cautious in future struggles. In this sense, the anti–Stamp Act movement set its stamp on the next ten years of colonial disaffection.

It did not take long for another colonial crisis to make its appearance. This one took its name from the Quartering Act, which aroused the same conflict between Parliament and the colonial assemblies as the Stamp Act. British troops had to be quartered whenever barracks were lacking or inadequate. It had long been customary to put them up in inns and public houses in England and Wales, where there was no shortage of such establishments. The colonies, however, did not have the same facilities, and the problem was not faced until forced on the British commander, Lord Loudoun, during the Seven Years' War. He soon discovered that he had to browbeat local

---

[34] Sherwood to Ward, May 15, 1766, ibid., p. 384.

[35] *Burke Correspondence*, vol. 1, p. 251, n. 1.

[36] Dora Mae Clark, *British Opinion and the American Revolution* (Yale University Press, 1930), p. 46. But hostile verses appeared in the *Gentleman's Magazine* of February 1766. They represented Pitt as having forced "Goody Bull" to her knees to ask her daughter's pardon:

No thanks to you, mother, the daughter reply'd:
But thanks to my friend here, I've humbled your pride.

assemblies to provide quarters for his troops, as if they had the sole power to give or deny them. The consent of the colonists to the quartering of troops, even in wartime, had become an issue at that time as it was later to become in the case of the stamp tax. In 1757, Loudoun vainly complained that "this last act of your assembly attempts to take away the king's undoubted prerogative and the rights of the mother country and the act of parliament."[37]

Belatedly, Parliament passed an act in 1765 requiring colonial assemblies to provide and furnish quarters for British troops. It was ill-timed, coinciding as it did with the anti–Stamp Tax agitation. A showdown occurred in New York, which was the headquarters of General Gage. On December 1, 1765, he requested provision for troops stationed there or passing through. Gage complained that the assembly was frustrating him "by Evasions." Only after the Stamp Act was repealed was the governor willing to put the matter to the assembly again. Finally, in July 1766, the assembly made provision for quartering troops but in such a way that it arrogated to itself authority over the procedure. This assumption of power was not lost on the British government. The secretary of state for the colonies enjoined the governor that it was "the indispensable Duty of His [Majesty's] Subjects in *America* to obey the Acts of the Legislature of *Great Britain.*" The assembly was not intimidated; it complained that New York was bearing a disproportionate share of the burden of the Quartering Act and refused to submit. The nonimportation tactic of 1765–66 was replaced by the noncompliance mode of 1766–67. The assembly took the stand that "we find it impossible to comply with what is now demanded, consistent with our Obligation to our Constituents" and could only agree to what was "most suitable to the Circumstances of the People we represent."[38]

The New York case against the Quartering Act was based mainly on its cost to the colonists and on the need for the local assembly to ratify it. But Sam Adams in Boston thought of an even better way to denounce the measure. He made the Quartering Act a form of taxation and thus stretched the old bugaboo against taxes to cover the seemingly different problem of putting up British troops. "Tell me Sir," he wrote to Christopher Gadsden of South Carolina, whether providing for the troops "is not taxing the Colonys as effectually as the Stamp Act & if so, either we have complain[e]d without Reason, or we still have reason to complain."[39] In this way, Adams succeeded

---

[37] Stanley McCrory Pargellis, *Lord Loudoun in America* (Yale University Press, 1933), pp. 187–208.

[38] Lawrence Henry Gipson, *The British Empire Before the American Revolution* (Alfred A. Knopf, 1965), vol. 11, pp. 43–52.

[39] Adams to Gadsden, December 11, 1766, *The Writings of Samuel Adams*, ed. Harry Alonzo Cushing (G. P. Putnam's Sons, 1906), vol. 1, p. 110.

in prolonging the life of the campaign against taxes by extending it to apply to whatever might cost the colonists money in behalf of British policies.

By January 1767, Gage thought it necessary to tell the secretary at war, Lord Barrington, what was really at stake: "I think I may tell Your Lordship in a private letter with great truth, that the Colonists are taking large strides towards Independency; and that it concerns Great Britain by a speedy and spirited Conduct to shew them that these provinces are British Colonies dependent on her, and that they are not independent States."[40]

The new contretemps spoiled the good feeling brought on by the stamp tax repeal. Israel Mauduit, the Massachusetts agent, informed Lieutenant Governor Hutchinson in April 1767: "The open disobedience of the Assembly at N[ew] York to the Act for Quartering the Soldiers, has raised a Spirit in parliament, w[hi]ch I have not seen before. All now agree that the Governm[en]t w[oul]d be no more, if it suffer'd any of its Subjects to dispute its supreme Authority."[41] Even Pitt, now the earl of Chatham, was disenchanted. He declared that the disobedience of the New York Assembly was "a matter so weighty, and big with consequences, which may strike so deep and spread so wide," that it should be brought before Parliament for "whatever steps shall be found necessary to be taken in this unfortunate business."[42]

At junctures like this one, Benjamin Franklin was ever ready with an anonymous article in the London press, written as if by an Englishman and subsequently reprinted in the colonies, to explain away some colonial action or inaction. In April 1767, he first testified to how much the British mood had changed, though with characteristic exaggeration:

> Every step is now [taken] to enrage us against *America*. Pamphlets and news papers flie about, and coffee-houses ring with lying reports of its being in rebellion. Force is call'd for. Fleets and troops should be sent. Those already there should be called in from the distant posts, and quartered on the capital towns. The principal people should be brought here and hang'd, &c.—And why?
>
> Why!—Do you ask why?
>
> Yes. I beg leave to ask why?

[40] *The Correspondence of General Thomas Gage with the Secretaries of State, 1763–1775* (Yale University Press, 1931), vol. 2, p. 406.

[41] Hutchinson Correspondence, *Massachusetts Archives*, vol. 25, p. 177, cited by Gipson, *British Empire Before the American Revolution*, vol. 11, p. 56.

[42] Chatham to the earl of Shelburne, February 17, 1767, *Pitt Correspondence*, vol. 3, p. 215.

Why they are going to throw off the government of *this country*, and set up for themselves.

Franklin pooh-poohed the whole affair. Only New York had refused to comply with the Quartering Act, he wrote, and its assembly was justified in refusing to comply, because it would otherwise have no reason for existence. "If they were oblig'd to make laws right or wrong in obedience to a law made by a superior legislature, they would be of no use as a parliament, their nature would be changed, their constitution destroyed." He did not cope with the implication that the superior legislature would also be of no use as a parliament if it could be overruled by a presumably inferior legislature. He put forth another Franklinesque argument:

> Our coffee-house orators, however, would have it declared, that this refusal of full compliance with the act, is REBELLION, and to be punished accordingly. . . . This is, besides, a new kind of *Rebellion*. It used to be thought that Rebellion consisted in *doing* something; but this is a Rebellion that consists of *not doing* something, or in doing nothing. If every man who neglects or refuses to comply with an act of parliament is a rebel, I am afraid we have many more rebels among us than we were aware.[43]

Franklin's main aim was to minimize the latest upset by saying, "molehills are often magnify'd to mountains." In fact, the Revolution was brought about by a succession of such "molehills," each higher than the last. But what was noteworthy in all of them was the same ready British suspicion that the colonies were just waiting to rebel and "set up for themselves."

In any case, "this unfortunate business" was referred to Parliament, which was increasingly determined to take drastic action. In June 1767, the New York Assembly had enough of the standoff and voted £3,000 to pay for the troops. The news took so long to filter back to London that, in October, the New York Assembly was punished by having all its laws declared null and void. It took a little while for the mix-up to be resolved.

But Lt. Gov. Cadwallader Colden, who had had his house vandalized in the Stamp Act riots and had never been reimbursed by the British government, warned that nothing had essentially changed. Colden aimed at the lawyers, towards whom he felt a particular animosity. In November 1767, he wrote to the earl of Shelburne, then secretary of state for the colonies:

---

[43] *London Chronicle*, April 9, 1767, reprinted in *Pennsylvania Chronicle, New-York Mercury*, and *Newport Mercury*, text in *Benjamin Franklin's Letters to the Press*, pp. 83–87. It was signed "A Friend to both Countries." This letter appears in *Franklin Papers*, vol. 14, pp. 103–7, quotations on pp. 104, 106–7.

The Assembly in the last Act they passed for Providing for the Troops quarter'd in this Province, have carefully avoided to acknowledge the Authority of Parliament. An opinion is industriously infused into the Minds of the People, that the legislative authority of Great Britain does not extend to the Colonies, by Men who from their Profession are supposed to understand the Constitution best. When this opinion prevails generally among the People, no jury will form a verdict on a Law which they think has no authority in the Colonies. I have heard some men place their confidence in this, that no man can be punished in the Colonies for his disobedience of an Act of Parliament.[44]

It was not the last time that a Quartering Act was to come between the British and the Americans. The fracas in New York was another stage in the displacement of Parliament by colonial assemblies on the legislative side of the struggle for power.

· 4 ·

Charles Townshend represented a new generation of British ministers. He was born into a family long accustomed to share in ruling Great Britain. His father, the third viscount Townshend, was an intimate of the previous generation of Walpole and Newcastle. Charles, the second son, had been handicapped since adolescence by epilepsy and other ills. Horace Walpole's opinion of him suggests a person combining peculiar gifts and frailties. To Walpole, he was someone with "prodigious parts" that were "so superior to rivals," yet he was "infinitely jealous." Walpole confessed to his "own futility when Charles Townshend was present. Yet such alloy did he bear with him to those marvellous parts, that children and women had more discretion and fewer weaknesses." Among his weaknesses was a disposition to be "restless in any situation, fond of mischief."[45] As an orator, he was considered second only to Pitt, but he never approached Pitt's influence. He was described by Sir Lewis Namier and John Brooke as possessing "wonderful abilities, inordinate vanity, and poverty of heart."[46] Townshend was the youngest of the new British generation, which included Grenville, born 1712, Halifax, 1716, and Townshend, 1725.

---

[44] Colden to Shelburne, November 23, 1767, *Documents relative to the Colonial History of the State of New-York*, ed. E. B. O'Callaghan (Albany, 1856), vol. 7, p. 996.
[45] Walpole, *Memoirs of the Reign of King George the Third*, vol. 2, pp. 6–7, 285.
[46] Lewis Namier and John Brooke, *Charles Townshend* (St. Martin's Press, 1964), p. 2.

As befitted one of his station, Townshend was elected to one of the safe seats in the House of Commons in 1747 at the age of twenty-two. Only two years later, he attached himself to Halifax, then president of the Board of Trade, who made a place for Townshend on the board.[47] Under Halifax's tutelage, Townshend embraced the view that the colonies had been too freewheeling during the Walpole era and needed to be brought under tighter control. By 1754, Townshend had learned enough to conclude that the weak link in British colonial rule was the assemblies' power of the purse:

> It is well known to those who have attended to the affairs of America that the provinces have for many years been engaged in a settled design of drawing to themselves the ancient and established prerogatives wisely preserved in the Crown as the only means of supporting and continuing the superintendency of the mother country, and their manner of doing this has been by their annual bills of supply, in which they have appointed all the officers of the Crown by name to be employed in the Exchequer, substituted warrants for drawing out public money in the place of the Governor's, and in one word dispossessed the Crown of almost every degree of executive power ever lodged in it.[48]

This distrust of the colonies was deeply ingrained in Townshend. His political career went forward erratically—from the Board of Trade to the Admiralty Board in 1754, privy councillor in 1757, secretary at war in 1761–62, president of the Board of Trade 1763–1765, paymaster 1765–66, though he was also accustomed to go in and out of opposition. In 1765, he again demonstrated his animus against the colonists by making the most notorious speech in favor of Grenville's Stamp Act ("And now will these Americans, children planted by our care . . . grudge to contribute their mite to relieve us from the heavy weight of that burden which we lie under?") and had brought down on his head the famous rebuke by Barré ("They planted by your care? No! your oppressions planted them in America"). His greatest opportunity to shine came with the fall of Rockingham's ministry and its replacement by the Chatham administration.

The new ministry was another unstable, makeshift affair—the sixth in seven years. Ever since he had resigned from office in 1761, Pitt had been a disruptive force in British politics, refusing to support any other ministry or take upon himself responsibility for governing. Ever more weary and

---

[47] Steven Gregory Greiert, *The Earl of Halifax and British Colonial Policy: 1748–1756* (diss., Duke University, 1976), p. 70.
[48] Namier and Brooke, *Charles Townshend*, p. 40.

unpredictable, he still dominated the political scene, as if no government could get along with him or without him. In July 1766, when the Great Commoner, as he was called, agreed to leave the House of Commons to become the earl of Chatham, he shocked many of his followers, who felt he had betrayed them; Horace Walpole said, "That fatal title blasted all the affection which his country had borne to him, and which he deserved so well."[49] He was then almost sixty, in very poor health, and an enigma to his colleagues.

With the fall of Rockingham, the British political structure was so shaken and demoralized that only the newly anointed Chatham seemed able to win back popular confidence and ministerial authority. Despite his infirmities, he was called to form the next government. He chose to hold the relatively minor office of lord privy seal, apparently because his health would not have permitted him to attend Commons regularly. There is something about his behavior in this period that defies easy explanation; his last years were fit for a drama about the tragic breakdown of a once great figure. A British historian of this phase has been moved to write:

> The tale of Chatham's Administration is curious and melancholy: never was so much expected from a statesman and so little fulfilled. The great war Minister, who rallied the nation round his measures and brought them to triumphant success, failed miserably where men of less ability would have succeeded. It will be clear as the story develops that he was suffering from some mental disturbance which paralyzed his will and action.[50]

Whatever the reason, the Chatham administration was put together with a strange assortment of misfits. First lord of the Treasury, the prime office, went to Augustus Henry Fitzroy, third duke of Grafton, then thirty-one, "indolent and bored by business, he preferred the turf to the Cabinet; he had a justified diffidence in his own abilities, and no standards by which to measure those of others."[51] The only appointment which Chatham allowed Grafton to make was chancellor of the Exchequer; Grafton chose Townshend, against Chatham's better judgment, a choice Grafton also lived

---

[49] Walpole, *Memoirs of the Reign of King George the Third*, vol. 2, p. 254. "The City of London had prepared to illuminate their public buildings as a sign of rejoicing on his return to power, but when it was known that Pitt was made Earl of Chatham the orders for illuminations were countermanded" (Walford David Green, *William Pitt, Earl of Chatham*, [G. P. Putnam's Sons, 1901] p. 273).

[50] John Brooke, *The Chatham Administration, 1766–1768* (Macmillan, 1956), p. xii.

[51] Ibid., p. 8. Horace Walpole wrote of his "extreme indolence," "disgusting coldness," "imperiousness," "levity," "inactivity," "moody and capricious temper" (*Memoirs of the Reign of King George the Third*, vol. 3, pp. 66, 76, 88, 91, 135, 179).

to regret.[52] The leader in Commons was Gen. Henry Seymour Conway, an old soldier who preferred the army to politics, for which he was not in any case cut out. Chatham, who was supposed to orchestrate the cabinet from the House of Lords, was stricken with his most serious illness in December 1766 and could hardly function at all physically by the following March. The Chatham administration was a misnomer; the earl gave it its name and little more.

Since the British side of every crisis was at least as important as the American, this succession of weak, unstable British governments came at the worst possible time for the survival of British rule in America.

· 5 ·

The extreme disorder in the British body politic made it possible for the next stage of the American crisis to take the form of the notorious Townshend Acts.

With the exception of Townshend, the chief ministers—Chatham, Grafton, Conway, and Shelburne, secretary of state of the Southern Department in charge of the colonies—had earned the reputation of being pro-American in the fight over the stamp tax. Yet Townshend was able to carry through a measure which seemingly should have been rejected in the cabinet. Instead, the disarray in the administration was so great that he made a personal commitment to do something about getting more revenue out of the colonies. He gave this pledge, without cabinet authorization, in Parliament in January 1767 and began to carry it out in April. In effect, he turned the clock back to Grenville's policy, except that Townshend knew that he had to resort to something other than a stamp tax. When the cabinet met the day after his pronouncement, Townshend was asked how he had presumed to depart from the policy set by the others. According to Grafton's later account, he "turned to Mr. Conway, appealing to him whether the House was not bent on obtaining a revenue of some sort from the colonies."[53] Townshend, then, was acting from strength, but in Commons, not in the cabinet.

For all his irresponsibility, Townshend was being consistent. Thirteen years earlier, he had expressed the view that the colonies had been getting away with actions that threatened "the ancient and established prerogatives

---

[52] Brooke, *Chatham Administration*, p. 9.
[53] *Autobiography and Political Correspondence of Augustus Henry Third Duke of Grafton* (John Murray, 1898), pp. 126–27.

wisely preserved in the Crown." It was not a large step from this general conviction to actions which struck back at the colonies for refusing to do what was expected of them.

The Chatham ministry had early agreed to try to make the colonies contribute more revenue to the British Treasury. This was not the issue and showed that the colonies were likely to face new demands from almost any British government. But nothing had been decided about how to do it, leaving the way open for Townshend, who alone had the temerity and ideological motivation, to precipitate the next great colonial crisis by taking it upon himself to make the colonies pay—and more.

There were three main Townshend Acts. One was the Restraining Act, to punish New York for its refusal to provide for British troops by nullifying all its legislation. Another made a number of administrative changes to tighten British control of American commerce.[54] Most important was the Duty Act, which called for import duties on glass, lead, paints, paper, and tea.

These duties were estimated to bring in £43,420 annually for the purpose of defending the colonies, which was estimated to cost a total of £405,607. The amount was modest, but Townshend hinted that it could serve as a first installment. The items were carefully chosen; with the exception of tea, they did not figure largely in colonial imports. The bill, however, also called for "defraying the charge of the administration of justice, and the support of civil government" in America. The intention here was to free governors and other British officials in the colonies from financial dependency on colonial assemblies—just what the assemblies were sure to resist at all costs, because it stripped them of their most effective hold over British officialdom. In their ultimate effect, the package of bills was designed to do no more than pay for a part of the cost of British soldiery; it was clearly aimed at tightening British control of the American economy and governance.

Townshend was apt, as in this case, to be overclever in his political games. He used duties to finesse the old distinction between internal and external taxation. After all, Pitt had previously blessed all kinds of taxes with the exception of internal ones. Had not the great man said, according to one version: "We may bind their trade, confine their manufactures, and exercise every power whatsoever, except that of taking money out of their pockets without their consent"?[55] The new duties sought to take advantage of this apparent license to do by other means what the Stamp Act had tried to do.

---

[54] Superior or supreme court justices were given power to issue writs of assistance to customs officers in all the colonies; new vice admiralty courts were established; and an American Board of Commissions, directly responsible to the British Treasury, was set up in Boston.

[55] Peter D. G. Thomas, *The Townshend Duties Crisis* (Oxford University Press, 1987), p. 3.

In effect, the Townshend duties flowed from the principle of the Declaratory Act in order to negate the policy implied by the repeal of the Stamp Act.

External taxes had previously been understood to be duties on commodities only for the purpose of regulating trade. By explicitly using duties to raise revenue, Townshend violated the regulatory purpose and made his duties merely another manner of squeezing money out of the colonies. Thus he virtually obliterated the old distinction between internal and external taxes, which now began to lose its relevance. As one British historian put it, "Townshend was merely changing the mode of payment rather than the incidence of taxation."[56]

Yet his proposals had little trouble getting through Parliament, receiving the royal assent, and going into effect in November 1767. As if the political paroxysm brought on by the stamp tax had never occurred or had been totally forgotten, the Townshend duties passed through the Commons Committee on Ways and Means without opposition and almost without debate.[57] One reason for Townshend's success was the state of the Chatham administration:

> At this time it presented a spectacle of weakness and division rare, if not unique, in British political history. The nominal head of the Ministry [Chatham] had retired from business altogether; the leader of the House of Commons [Conway] had voted against the two principal ministerial measures; the Chancellor of the Exchequer [Townshend] had also voted against one of these, and in addition seemed to regard the House merely as a stage on which he could exhibit himself in public; while the Secretary of State for the Southern Department [Shelburne], with the American colonies and British foreign policy towards France and Spain under his control, was disliked and distrusted by his colleagues. Grafton neglected his work for horse-racing and was openly living with a woman of loose morals; Northington [lord president of the council] was thought to be dying; Camden [lord chancellor] was timid and ineffectual; while Granby [commander in chief] and Hawke [first lord of the Admiralty] were ciphers outside their departments.[58]

With this conglomeration, Townshend had no trouble getting his way. Because they have been called Townshend Acts, he has been made to appear responsible for them, but he could not have pushed them through Parliament alone, and there were deeper reasons for their easy passage.

[56] Ibid., p. 24.
[57] Namier and Brooke, *Charles Townshend*, p. 179; Thomas, *Townshend Duties Crisis*, p. 31.
[58] Brooke, *Chatham Administration*, p. 139.

British public opinion had changed since the repeal of the stamp tax. The change was reflected in Parliament, which resented the failure to punish the stamp tax rioters in Massachusetts and the refusal to provision troops in New York. British merchants and manufacturers had gone back happily to their accustomed ways. The memory of the Stamp Act's repeal was humiliating, and a need to recover prestige or self-respect nagged at many British consciences.

In the mid-nineteenth century, George Bancroft made a bête noire of Townshend along with Grenville. Townshend, in his view, had "proclaimed a war of extermination against American Charters" and "assumed to dictate to the Ministry its colonial policy."[59] In fact, Townshend could have accomplished little if it had not been for a change in British public and parliamentary opinion. With or without him, the colonies were due to get an unwelcome surprise after their smashing victory over the Stamp Act.

The change in the British mood was reflected by the one American in London who was best able to judge—Benjamin Franklin. He had expected an era of good feeling to follow the repeal of the Stamp Act in March 1766. Less than one year later, he wrote worriedly to his friend Lord Kames: "But nothing is more common here than to talk of the *Sovereignty of Parliament,* and the *Sovereignty of this Nation* over the Colonies; a kind of Sovereignty the Idea of which is not so clear, nor does it clearly appear on what Foundations it is established."

Franklin was so depressed by the situation that he contemplated the prospect of separation and a turnabout whereby America would shackle Great Britain:

> [America] may suffer at present under the arbitrary Power of this Country; she may suffer for a while in a Separation from it; but these are temporary Evils that she will outgrow. . . . But America, an immense Territory, favour'd by Nature with all Advantages of Climate, Soil, great navigable Rivers and Lakes, &c. must become a great Country, populous and mighty; and will in a less time than is generally conceiv'd be able to shake off any Shackles that may be impos'd on her, and perhaps place them on the Imposers.[60]

In April 1767, Franklin reported on a debate in the House of Lords: "The word *Rebellion* was frequently used. . . . There are great Heats on American Affairs."[61] Thomas Pownall, the former British governor of Massachusetts,

[59] George Bancroft, *History of the United States* (Little, Brown, 1854), vol. 6, pp. 10, 63.
[60] Franklin to Kames, February 25, 1767, *Franklin Papers*, vol. 14, pp. 69–70.
[61] Franklin to Kames, April 11, 1767, ibid., pp. 108–9.

who was considered friendly to the American cause, informed Franklin at this period: "I find some People are Determined to decide that NA [North America] is in Rebellion, and to come to an open rupture."[62]

Also in April, Franklin confided to Joseph Galloway, his chief lieutenant in Philadelphia:

> The Current strong against America in general, which our Friends in the ministry are oblig'd a little to give way to. . . . But after all, I doubt People in Government here will never be satisfied without some Revenue from America, nor America ever satisfy'd with their imposing it; so that Disputes will, from this Circumstance besides others, be perpetually arising, till there is a consolidating Union of the whole.[63]

Again to Galloway in May: "The general Rage against America."[64] To Galloway in June: "the general Prejudice against the Colonies so strong in the House, that any thing in the Shape of a Favour to them all, was like to meet with great Opposition."[65] And a lengthy report to Galloway in August:

> It is already given out . . . that it is high time to put the Right and Power of this Country to tax the Colonies, out of dispute, by an Act of Taxation effectually carried into Execution, and that all the Colonies should be oblig'd explicitly to acknowledge that Right. Every Step is taking [sic] to render the Taxing of America a popular Measure, by continually insisting on the Topics of our Wealth and flourishing Circumstances, while this Country is loaded with Debt, great Part of it incurr'd on our Account the Distress of the Poor here by the Multitude and Weight of Taxes, &c. &c. And tho' the Traders and Manufacturers may possibly be kept in our Interest, the Idea of an American Tax is very pleasing to the landed Men, who therefore readily receive and propagate these Sentiments wherever they have Influence. If such a Bill should be brought in, it is hard to say what would be Event of it, or what would be the Effects. Those who oppose it, tho' they should be strong enough to throw it out, would be stigmatiz'd at the next Election as Americans, Betrayers of Old England, &c.[66]

Franklin did not mention Townshend in any of these tidings. He well knew

[62] Pownall to Franklin (the date of this letter is uncertain, but sometime between February and May 1767), ibid., p. 72.
[63] Franklin to Galloway, April 14, 1767, ibid., p. 125.
[64] Franklin to Galloway, May 20, 1767, ibid., p. 164.
[65] Franklin to Galloway, June 13, 1767, ibid., p. 182.
[66] Franklin to Galloway, August 8, 1767, ibid., pp. 229–30.

that the problem was British public and political opinion, not Townshend personally. As Burke later put it, Townshend "conformed exactly to the temper of the House; and he seemed to guide it, because he was always sure to follow it."[67] Once the shift of feeling from relief to revenge took place, no British politician could with impunity have made life easy for the colonies.

Townshend put into words what others thought. When he presented his proposals in Commons, he made no secret of his ulterior motives. One of those present made the following record of his words:

> That he believes there are in several of the assemblies a set of factious men closely cemented together upon a fixed plan from motives of self interest to establish their popularity in their own country upon the ruin of the dependency of the colonies upon Great Britain. . . .
>
> That he desires therefore to take some steps which by showing the Americans that this country would not tamely suffer her sovereignty to be wrested out of her hands might give spirit to men under this description and strike an awe into the factious and turbulent.[68]

These views lurked beneath the Townshend Acts and gave them their ultimate purpose and meaning. They were expressed in the language of a struggle for power, which Townshend had foreseen at the very outset of his political career. It was this underground stream in British thought and policy, surfacing periodically, that enabled him to prevail over those around him.

Thomas Hutchinson looked back at this period and gave as his opinion that "the revolt of the colonies ought to be dated from this time, rather than from the declaration of independence."[69] He might just as well have dated the counterrevolt from this time, too. The two forces went hand in hand.

Townshend died suddenly on September 4, 1767. He never had to cope with the furies that he had unleashed or that were unleashed in his name.

[67] Speech on American Taxation, April 19, 1774, *Writings and Speeches of Edmund Burke*, vol. 2, p. 452.

[68] *Parliamentary Diaries of Nathaniel Ryder*, p. 344.

[69] Thomas Hutchinson, *The History of the Colony and Province of Massachusetts-Bay*, ed. Lawrence Shaw Mayo (Harvard University Press, 1936), vol. 3, p. 125. Hutchinson mentioned the year 1767 on the same page, but he seems to have been referring to various events around that year.

13

"*We* are therefore —SLAVES"

❦

· 1 ·

B<small>Y NOW, IT WAS DIFFICULT</small> to think of anything essentially new in the struggle between Great Britain and its colonies. The Townshend Acts were effectively a variant of the Stamp Act on a larger scale. And the colonial response to the Townshend Acts was effectively a variant of the response to the Stamp Act, also on a larger scale.

Again, Boston acted first. On October 28, 1767, a Boston town meeting, chaired by James Otis, voted "to prevent the unnecessary Importation of European Commodities, which threaten the Country with Poverty and Ruin." The resolution was sent to representatives throughout the colonies. Towns in Rhode Island, Connecticut, and elsewhere followed suit. A heated argument, pro and con, raged in the local papers.

The Connecticut agent in London, William Samuel Johnson, told Gov. William Pitkin how British enemies and friends of the colonies reacted to the Boston move. Enemies took it to mean that the colony intended to encourage colonial manufactures—"this was received by very many with great indignation, and at first seemed to threaten some mischief." Friends sought to calm the uproar by pleading that the reasons were wholly practical, such as the inability of the colony to pay its debts to British lenders. But Johnson and other agents were worried about something deeper in the dispute. They were always afraid that the agitation in Boston would bring out the latent British fear of American independence. "But why should there be these public associations, these votes and subscriptions?" Johnson asked. "Why make such a parade about it, which must unavoidably give umbrage here, and add strength to the enemies of that country,—whose constant theme it is, that all these steps are taken with a view very soon to renounce all dependence upon this kingdom?"[1]

At this point, the most successful of all the colonial pamphlets, with a political line that was not likely to pacify British umbrage, appeared. It was the work of John Dickinson, who had already distinguished himself with a pamphlet on the Stamp Act. This second pamphlet began life as a series of twelve *Letters from a Farmer in Pennsylvania, To the Inhabitants of the British Colonies,* which appeared in Philadelphia newspapers from December 2, 1767, to February 18, 1768. They were quickly reprinted in twenty-one of the twenty-five colonial newspapers. Less than a month after the newspaper series had ended, they came out as a pamphlet, of which there were seven editions in America and three in Europe. It was by far the most famous and influential of all the American pamphlets in the prerevolutionary period. It has even been described as "the political bible of the Americans, retaining that honoured place until it was displaced in 1776 by [Thomas Paine's] *Common Sense.*"[2] That it was something of a hoax did not hurt its popularity; the "Farmer in Pennsylvania" was a wealthy, fastidious Philadelphia lawyer. This "farmer" embellished his pages with erudite footnotes from Tacitus, Machiavelli, Locke, and many others. For his efforts, he earned the title "Penman of the Revolution."

There was very little that was original in Dickinson's work. He repeatedly evoked the revolt against the Stamp Act and mainly applied the old arguments to the new disputes. On the New York revolt against the Quartering Act, he said that if members of Parliament could order a colony to supply troops with provisions, they could "lay *any burthens* they please upon us," which was one of the stock points made against the Stamp Act. "How is this mode," he asked, "more tolerable than the *Stamp Act?*" He made the provisioning order a form of tax, which enabled him to bring

[1] Johnson to Pitkin, December 26, 1767, *Massachusetts Historical Society Collections,* 5th ser., vol. 9, p. 249. On June 9, 1767, Johnson had already reported about the government: "Though they wish to keep the Colonies disunited, yet they seem too ready to impute to *all* the transgressions of any one of them, and consider them as all alike disaffected to this country, and seeking an entire independency upon all Parliamentary restraint or authority" (p. 237).

[2] Lawrence Henry Gipson, *The British Empire Before the American Revolution* (Alfred A. Knopf, 1965), vol. 11, p. 148. But Gipson notes that the "Letters" did not cause much stir in Dickinson's home colony, Pennsylvania (p. 148).

up the argument about representation—that the colonists could be taxed only by their own representatives, not by Parliament.

Dickinson also argued against the Townshend duties by making them a tax. That they were so small, he said, alarmed him the most, because they were intended "to establish a *precedent* for future use." His rhetoric could be shrill:

> These duties, which will inevitably be levied upon us—which are now levying upon us—are *expressly* laid FOR THE SOLE PURPOSE OF TAKING MONEY. This is the true definition of "*taxes.*" They are therefore *taxes.* This money is to be taken from *us. We* are therefore *taxed. Those* who are *taxed* without their own consent, expressed by themselves or their representatives, are *slaves. We are taxed* without our own consent, expressed by ourselves or our representatives. *We* are therefore—SLAVES.[3]

Dickinson was wrathful about the intention to make the colonial legal system and civil government financially dependent on the British Treasury rather than on the assemblies. "No free people ever existed, or can ever exist," he insisted, "without keeping, to use a common, but strong expression, "the purse strings,' in their own hands." A prominent lawyer, Dickinson was particularly anxious that the British Treasury should not pay the salaries of judges. Paradoxically, the colonists were willing to pay for judges but not for soldiers, because they could control the one but not the other by keeping the purse strings in their hands.

Nevertheless, Dickinson was ambivalent about how far to go in the challenge to British rule. He objected to the "parliamentary assertion of the *supreme authority* of the *British* legislature over these colonies." But he came out strongly against "turbulence and tumult," as well as "hot, rash, disorderly proceedings," and advised the colonists to act "*peaceably— prudently—firmly—jointly.*" He was, at bottom, a conservative and possibly even a "reluctant Revolutionary," as he has been called.[4] Dickinson stopped well short of calling for anything implying separation or independence. He recognized the authority of Parliament to "regulate" the trade of the colonies and denied that the colonies were "states distinct from the *British Empire.*" He told them that "the prosperity of these provinces

---

[3] *The Writings of John Dickinson,* ed. Paul Leicester Ford (Historical Society of Pennsylvania, 1895), letter 7, vol. 1, pp. 356–57.

[4] H. Trevor Colbourn, *The Lamp of Experience* (University of North Carolina Press, 1965), p. 107.

is founded in their dependence on *Great-Britain*" and urged them to "promote her welfare by all the means in their power" as soon as Great Britain returned to her "old good humour, and her old good nature."

On the other hand, he warned of dire consequences if the colonists did not resist British impositions immediately. Civil discord, he explained, was less likely "if every disgusting measure is opposed *singly,* and *while it is new.*" If not, "oppressions and dissatisfactions being permitted to accumulate—*if ever* the governed throw off the load, they will do more. A people does not reform with moderation." He called on the colonists to "take alarm on any addition being made to the power exercised over them." He told them to act promptly, because the question was "not, what evil *has actually attended* particular measures— but, what evil, in the nature of things, *is likely to attend* them." It was necessary for the colonists to act cautiously in order not to per- mit their current differences to get out of control: "When feuds have reached that fatal point, all considerations of reason and equity vanish; and a blind fury governs, or rather confounds all things. A people no longer regards their interest, but the gratification of their wrath." Dickinson never directly threatened Great Britain with anything like colonial revolt; he preferred more subtly to get the message across that it was bound to come if British policy were not immediately reversed. From one paragraph to the next, he blew hot and cold, he ranted and reasoned.

Concretely, Dickinson advised the colonies to start protesting with petitions of the assemblies to the British government against the Townshend duties. If they were ignored, his next step was to prevent *"the oppressors reaping advantage from their oppressions"* by "withholding from *Great- Britain* all the advantages she had been used to receive from us." Instead, he cautioned, always "behave like dutiful children, who have received unmerited blows from a beloved parent."

Dickinson's "Letters" seem to have been so successful because they represented a transitional, midway position against British policy. He objected to it, but in a manner most appealing to those who did not wish to ally themselves with either extreme. An early biographer may have stated best what gave Dickinson his attraction: "He writes not as an angry controversialist, but as a judicious counsellor or guide, free from the slightest heat or partisan excitement, treating the subject with a certain calm dignity and self-composure which seem to suggest that he can offer a remedy for evils from which the people around him are suffering, unknown to helpless and self-seeking politicians."[5] Dickinson offered no such remedy; he studiously avoided mentioning nonimportation or noncompliance. He somehow managed to be in the battle and above it. Anyone could read almost anything into his circuitous prose. Meanwhile, in early 1768, he encouraged engaging in the struggle against British policy and doing so in the least offensive way.

• 2 •

It was not received that way in British official circles. The new British secretary of state for the colonies, Wills Hill, first earl of Hillsborough, was one reader of Dickinson's "Letters." He told Benjamin Franklin that they were "well written" but that the doctrines were "extremely wild."[6] Wild was one thing Dickinson's "Letters" were not, but the word indicated that they had touched a raw nerve in the British imperial establishment. The "Letters'" popular reception persuaded the British authorities that a reply was necessary. Another pamphlet war was set off with the publication of *The Controversy between Great Britain and her Colonies Reviewed* by William Knox, the author of an earlier anti-American pamphlet. Knox's anti-Dickinson pamphlet took so long to prepare that it was not published until 1769, a year after Dickinson's, but it is best considered here, because the two are closely related.

Knox aimed at the weakest link in the colonial argument: What was the power of Parliament over the colonies? It went to the heart of the matter, because the colonial attack was not yet focused on British rule as such or on the colonies' attachment to the Crown. Instead, the colonial case was still directed squarely at Parliament. Parliament had passed the Stamp Act, and it was assailed on the ground that Parliament did not have the right to impose a tax on the colonies. Parliament had passed the Townshend duties, and Dickinson had attacked them on the ground that they were another illegitimate tax. The entire colonial case had been cast in the form

---

[5] Charles J. Stillé, *The Life and Times of John Dickinson* (J. B. Lippincott, 1891), p. 82. By the end of the nineteenth century, Dickinson's "Letters" had taken on heroic stature. Moses Coit Tyler celebrated them as "the most brilliant event in the literary history of the Revolution. . . . No other serious political essays of the Revolutionary era quite equaled the 'Farmer's Letters' in literary merit, including in that term the merit of substance as well as of form." But Tyler recognized "the reason, and the moderation, and the filial tenderness of Dickinson's arguments" (*The Literary History of the American Revolution*, G. P. Putnam's Sons, 1897, vol. 1, pp. 234, 236, 239).

[6] Benjamin Franklin to William Franklin, March 13, 1768, *The Papers of Benjamin Franklin*, ed. Leonard W. Labaree (Yale University Press, 1961), vol. 15, p. 75.

of Parliament versus the assemblies. To cut the ground from under the colonial case, Knox set himself the task of defending Parliament's authority as an orthodox British official saw it.

He ridiculed the distinction between "taxes for the regulation of trade, and taxes for the purpose of revenue." American consumers were not the only ones who were required to pay duties on goods that also yielded a revenue; British consumers had long paid such duties. If the colonists were exempt, so were the British themselves. The colonies, he maintained, were not really opposed to duties; they were opposed to the British ability to collect them. As long as the colonies were able to evade duties, such as the old one on molasses, they were content. The reason they were so bitter against Grenville was that he "took measures for the Colonies to pay."

As Knox saw it, either Parliament's authority to legislate was "equally supreme over the Colonies as . . . over the people of England" or the colonies were not "of the same community with the people of England." Knox was adamant on this point:

> All distinctions destroy this union; and if it can be shewn in any particular to be dissolved, it must be so in all instances whatever. There is no alternative: either the Colonies are a part of the community of Great Britain, or they are in a state of nature with respect to her, and in no case can be subject to the jurisdiction of that legislative power which represents her community, which is the British parliament.

With this, Knox explained why Dickinson's "Letters" were considered so subversive in British official circles:

> If the Farmer's Letters were indeed to be considered as mere speculative essays upon civil government, neither the justness or elegance of the composition, the knowledge of the subject handled, or the constitutional learning displayed in them, would give them much authority, or intitle them to the notice I have taken of them; but their purpose being to excite resentment in the Colonies against their parent country, and to push them on to a separation from her, tenderness for my deluded fellow-subjects engaged me to expose the fallacies and absurdities attempted to be imposed upon them for demonstrative truths.

Dickinson may have excited resentment against the treatment of the colonies by the mother country, but he surely did not "push them to a separation from her." In fact, he had tended to push them in the opposite direction. But it was characteristic of British polemicists that they insisted on reading more into colonial arguments than was actually there, because they were primed to expect the colonies to separate one day. Just as Dickinson argued that the Townshend duties were small but had to be opposed because they were a *"precedent* for future use," so Knox argued that any excitement of resentment against British treatment was intended to push the colonies towards separation. It was this inclination to envision the worst possible case that led him to insist, "If Great Britain does not possess the right of taxing the Colonies, she has no right to exercise any jurisdiction over them."

Knox also engaged in a lengthy defense of the British system of virtual representation and enlisted Locke in behalf of it. He twitted the colonies for both complaining that they were not represented in Parliament and declaring that they did not want to be represented in it. But, for Knox, the moral was always the same: "The truth however is, that they are determined to get rid of the jurisdiction of parliament *in all cases whatsoever,* if they can."

Knox did a great deal of research for his work—really a book of over 200 pages. He took on both Franklin and Dickinson for having denied that the British had fought the war against the French in behalf of the colonies and for having claimed that it had been waged for British interests only. To turn the argument around, Knox cited pages of anguished appeals in 1754 for the British to protect the colonies against the French menace. In this pamphlet war, history was fought over by both sides to score political points. When Knox came to the end of his historical lessons, he issued this challenge: "And let me now ask the advocates for their independency, upon which period of this history it is, that they would fix, as the epocha of the Colonies emancipation from the sovereign authority of the supreme legislature of the realm, or where will they carry us for those pretended rights and privileges which exempt them from its jurisdiction?" Whatever those advocates might say, someone like Knox was sure that they were advocating "independency."[7]

Yet the British case was beginning to make headway, even in the mind of Benjamin Franklin. The problem for him and his generation was whether the power of Parliament over the colonies could be bifurcated. Were there things that Parliament could do and others it could not do? Ever since the Stamp Act crisis of 1765, colonial advocates had made a crucial distinction

7 [William Knox], *The Controversy between Great Britain and her Colonies Reviewed* (London, 1769), pp. 35, 50–52, 200.

between internal and external taxes or between taxes for revenue and duties on commercial commodities. Franklin himself had exploited the distinction in his examination before the parliamentary committee in 1766. Dickinson had agreed to the Parliament's regulation of colonial trade but not to the raising of a revenue.

While Knox was preparing his reply in 1768, Franklin had second thoughts. In a letter to his son, William, then governor of New Jersey, in which he mentioned Hillsborough's disparaging remarks about Dickinson's "Letters," he went on in a new vein about the basic problem:

> I know not what the Boston people mean by the "subordination" they acknowledge in their Assembly to Parliament, while they deny its power to make laws for them, nor what bounds the Farmer sets to the power he acknowledges in Parliament to "regulate the trade of the colonies," it being difficult to draw lines between duties for regulation and those for revenue, and if the Parliament is to be the judge, it seems to me that establishing such principles of distinction will amount to little. The more I have thought and read on the subject the more I find myself confirmed in opinion, that no middle doctrine can be well maintained, I mean not clearly with intelligible arguments. Something might be made of either of the extremes; that Parliament has the power to make *all laws* for us, or that it has a power to make *no laws* for us; and I think the arguments for the latter more numerous and weighty than those for the former. Supposing that doctrine established, the colonies would then be so many separate states, only subject to the same King[,] as England and Scotland were before the Union. And then the question would be, whether a union like that with Scotland would or would not be advantageous to *the whole.* I should have no doubt of the afffirmative, being fully persuaded that it would be best for *the whole,* and that though particular parts might find particular disadvantages in it, they would find greater advantages in the security arising to every part from the increased strength of the whole. But such union is not likely to take place while the nature of our present relation is so little understood on both sides of the water, and sentiments concerning it remain so widely different.

Franklin now saw the colonial grievance in a different light. It was not, he wrote, "that Britain puts duties upon her own manufactures exported to us, but that she forbids us to buy the like manufactures from any other country." He recognized that Dickinson had allowed Great Britain "to regulate the commerce of the whole empire" but thought that this admission could be disputed "upon firmer ground." Yet Franklin ended inconclusively: "But my reasons are too many and too long for a letter."[8]

Until the outbreak of the Revolutionary War the haunting question was: Was there "a middle doctrine," a middle ground? Knox and the British extremists said it was either all or nothing. If all, Parliament could legislate for the colonies as it pleased; if nothing, it was tantamount to colonial separation and independence. Franklin saw the dilemma clearly, but even he dared to bring it up only in a private letter to his son.

In public, Franklin was circumspect. Towards the end of 1768, he went into print against the alarming reasoning of an English Quaker and merchant, Thomas Crowley, who advocated a federation, including the colonies, to hold the empire together, not unlike the idea that Franklin had proposed fifteen years earlier, at the time of the Albany Conference. Crowley warned of the colonies' "dangerous and vain Expectations of becoming independent" if a federation was not achieved. One way or another, this prospect was in the air whenever the colonial crisis was brought up in England. On this occasion, Franklin gave the orthodox colonial answer that "you are *certainly* mistaken, and that there is not a single Wish in the Colonies to be free from Subjection to their amiable Sovereign *the King* of Great Britain, and the constitutional Dependance then arising."[9] By this time, he knew that anything else carried with it dangerous implications of colonial independence, which neither he nor the pamphleteers back in the colonies were yet willing to avow.

· 3 ·

In the struggle between Great Britain and the colonies, 1768 was another turning point.

When Charles Townshend died in September 1767, his successor was Frederick North, better known as Lord North, a courtesy title.[10] He was considered an amiable young man of no considerable abilities when, at the age of twenty-two in 1754, he started his political career with an uncontested seat in the House of Commons as another beneficiary of the custom of putting younger sons of peers in Commons. In 1759, he

---

[8] Benjamin Franklin to William Franklin, March 13, 1768, *Franklin Papers,* vol. 15, pp. 75–77.

[9] *The Public Advertiser,* October 21, 1768; *Franklin Papers,* vol. 15, p. 239.

[10] Alan Valentine, *Lord North* (University of Oklahoma Press, 1967), p. 21.

received his first appointment as a junior official in the Treasury, where he spent the next six years, a stepping-stone to greater things. In Commons, he revealed something of his political inclinations by voting against the repeal of the Stamp Act. That vote apparently did him no political harm, because he was offered and accepted the more lucrative post of joint paymaster to the armed forces in the new Chatham administration. By this time, he was obviously a coming man. After Townshend's death, his great chance came—he was chosen to replace him as chancellor of the Exchequer. At the age of thirty-six, he had done nothing notable but had also made few political enemies and had gained a reputation for sobriety and soundness.

For a long time, North's reputation was based on the misfortune that he had held the highest office during the years when the American colonies were lost. More recently, a British historian has described him as "the antithesis of the dazzling Townshend" but "no dullard" and possessor of "charm, wit, and intelligence, as well as industry and a conscientious concern to do his duty by his King and country." North's promotion as chancellor of the Exchequer is seen as "the political turning-point of the decade, and the chief reason for the sea change in British politics that began at this time."[11]

North's arrival in a seat of real power was only the beginning of the change. With Chatham hors de combat, the ineffectual Grafton was willy-nilly thrust into filling the vacuum and taking charge of the government. To save it from immediate collapse, he brought in members of the opposition—a usual maneuver in such circumstances. They were identified with the colonial bête noire, George Grenville, and John Russell, fourth duke of Bedford, who as lord president of the council had been allied with Grenville during the latter's term of office. Ever since their downfall, they had tenaciously opposed any concessions to the colonies and now saw their chance to make a comeback. Of the two, the Bedfordites were considered to be less provocative than the Grenvilleites but equally hard-line, and the Bedfordites benefited most from the shake-up.

The full change came in January 1768. In addition to his post as chancellor of the Exchequer, North replaced Conway as leader of the House of Commons. A Bedfordite, Thomas Thynne, third viscount Weymouth, replaced Conway as northern secretary of state. William Fitzmaurice Petty, second earl of Shelburne, remained as southern secretary of state, but responsibility for the American colonies was removed from his office and given over to a new, third secretary of state. The first secretary of state

[11] Peter D. G. Thomas, *The Townshend Duties Crisis* (Oxford University Press, 1987), pp. 36–37.

for the colonies was the earl of Hillsborough, who soon made the "extremely wild" remark about Dickinson's "Letters" to Benjamin Franklin.

This reshuffle moved the center of gravity of the cabinet to a much harder line with the colonies. Shelburne was known as their friend, but he was no longer in charge of them. Hillsborough was Grenville's former president of the Board of Trade and much closer to his old leader than to his new one, Grafton. William Wildman Barrington, second viscount Barrington, had been secretary at war under Grenville and still held that office.

Only in retrospect is it possible to see that a major change had taken place in 1768. At the time, North, Hillsborough, Barrington, and others had not fully shown their hands, and much depended on how they would react to the fast-changing situation in the colonies. More than the movement of political chairs was going on; the political climate in Great Britain, which had been favorable to the colonies in 1765–66, was turning against them.

• 4 •

Our best informant in London was Benjamin Franklin, who was delaying his return home in order to do what he could to get the repeal of the Townshend duties. He was increasingly pessimistic.

When the Boston resolutions of October 28, 1767, became known in England, Franklin reported in January that there arose a "prodigious clamour" against them.[12] In March, he called attention to the British press campaign against the colonies, which, he said, made it seem "as proper now to make war on Boston, as ever it was to make war against France or Spain"—an exaggeration, no doubt, which he later softened by making the hostile articles "the productions of a few unknown angry writers." Nevertheless, the British press was full of "invective and abuse."[13] By 1769, Franklin was even gloomier. He deplored "the Prejudices that have so universally prevail'd here with regard to the Point of Right [to impose duties], and the Resentment at our disputing it."[14]

Meanwhile, the action-reaction cycle went on. The most definitive reaction again came in Boston. The assembly first sent instructions to its agent in London, Dennys De Berdt, on how to handle the new crisis.

[12] Benjamin Franklin to William Franklin, *Franklin Papers*, January 9, 1768, vol. 15, p. 15. To Joseph Galloway that same day, Franklin used the term *immense clamour* (p. 17).
[13] March 8, 1768, ibid., pp. 64–65.
[14] Franklin to Noble Wimberly Jones, June 7, 1769, ibid., vol. 16, p. 152.

They were drafted by Samuel Adams and were gone over line by line for seven days before they were approved.

One passage shows that the authors were keenly aware of what the British had in their minds and of the need to take precautions to counter it:

> When we mention the rights of the subjects in America, and the interest we have in the British constitution, in common with all other British subjects, we cannot justly be suspected of the most distant thought of an independency on Great Britain. Some, we know, have imagined this of the colonists, and others may, perhaps, have industriously propagated it, to raise groundless and unreasonable jealousies of them; but it is so far from the truth, that we apprehend the colonies would refuse it if offered to them, and would even deem it the greatest misfortune to be obliged to accept it.

The instructions went on to give the familiar reason why Parliament did not have the right to impose internal or external taxes on the colonies— "because, they cannot be represented, and therefore, their consent cannot be constitutionally had in Parliament." It was argued that there was no real difference between the stamp tax and the Townshend duties. Great Britain already had imposed the equivalent of an indirect tax by giving itself a monopoly on exports to the colonies, which was estimated to increase the price of manufactured goods by at least 20 percent. If corrupt governors were freed from financial dependence on the assemblies, the result would be "absolute government in America." The dispute was between "power and liberty in America," because "there is danger that the greatest credit will always be given to officers of the Crown, who are the men in power." There was no need for British soldiers in America; the *"English* affection in the colonists" for the mother country was enough to keep them connected for every valuable purpose, "unless it shall be erased by repeated unkind usage on her part." One more specter was the danger that "when the spirits of the people shall be depressed by the military power, another Caesar should arise and usurp the authority of his master." The punishment of the New York legislature was "political death and annihilation."

The instructions came close to envisaging an open struggle by speculating about the results of a total capitulation to British demands:

> Would it be possible for them to conciliate their constituents to such measures? Would not the attempt suddenly cut asunder all confidence and communication between the representative body and the people? What, then, would be the consequence? Could any

thing be reasonably expected but discontent, despair and rage, against their representatives, on the side of the people, and on the part of government, the rigorous exertion of civil and military power? The confusion and misery, after such a fatal crisis, cannot be conceived, much less described.[15]

These instructions to De Berdt reflected the most militant colonial thinking. They challenged British policy on every issue uncompromisingly. For the first time, they produced a scenario of a "fatal crisis," as if to warn the British that they could not get their way without bloodshed.

Next came a petition to the king. Significantly, it was sent to him, not to Parliament. It protested, however, that "your Parliament, the rectitude of whose intentions is never to be questioned," had imposed taxes for "the express purpose of raising a revenue." If Commons continued "to exercise the power" of taking away property, the colonists were "free subjects" in name only. Since colonial representation in Parliament, "considering their local circumstances, is utterly impracticable," the king was advised to ask the assembly, not Parliament, for funds.[16]

Finally, a circular letter of February 11, 1768, was sent to all other assemblies, calling on them to join in the protest movement. It was one of three or four fateful statements of the colonial case before the Declaration of Independence.

This document still faced two ways; it acknowledged the power of Parliament in theory only to undermine it in practice. It agreed that "his Majesty's high court of Parliament is the supreme legislative power over the whole empire" but immediately interpreted that power so that it did not apply to anything to which the colonists did not consent. It emphasized the concept of a "natural right" of an "absolute" nature—"that what a man has honestly acquired is absolutely his own, which he may freely give, but cannot be taken from him without his consent." By this doctrine, which it said had been "engrafted into the British constitution," the colonies could inferentially cut themselves off from any financial or economic link to Great Britain by not consenting to it. They had to agree to the connection

---

[15] Letter from the House of Representatives to D. De Berdt, January 12, 1768, *Speeches of the Governors of Massachusetts from 1765 to 1775; and the Answers of the House of Representatives to the Same* (Boston, 1818; reprint, Da Capo Press, 1971), pp. 124–33. This collection is also called *Massachusetts State Papers, 1765–1775*, which is how it will be cited hereafter. The instructions were drafted by Samuel Adams but were considered so important that the assembly discussed them for seven days and revised them carefully (William V. Wells, *The Life and Public Services of Samuel Adams*, [Little, Brown, 1865], vol. 1, pp. 152–53).

[16] Petition to the King, January 20, 1768, ibid., pp. 121–23. Other letters were sent to Shelburne, January 15, 1768, Rockingham, January 22, 1768, and others (pp. 137–41, 142–44).

with Great Britain freely or not at all. The circular letter reiterated "the utter impracticability of their ever being fully and equally represented in Parliament," so that consent could come only from the assemblies, which claimed to have the same power in the colonies that Parliament had in Great Britain. Again, however, it was considered necessary to deny charges that the colonies had any inclination to be independent:

> These are the sentiments and proceedings of this House; and as they have too much reason to believe that the enemies of the colonies have represented them to his Majesty's ministers, and to the Parliament, as factious, disloyal, and having a disposition to make themselves independent of the mother country, they have taken occasion, in the most humble terms, to assure his Majesty, and his ministers, that, with regard to the people of this province, and, as they doubt not, of all the colonies, the charge is unjust.[17]

At this stage, the Massachusetts leaders could not bring themselves to sever the imperial connection. They were willing to keep it, however, only on their own terms. They told themselves that they were rebelling against the authority of Parliament, not the king or the British empire in general. In effect, they wanted to deal with their British counterparts as if they were equals, basing themselves on "natural rights" or the "British constitution." This sense that they were "free" because they were British enabled them to strain the link to the utmost and yet feel connected by something that they did not wish to sever. This inhibition against formally breaking away took time to overcome and delayed the outbreak of the Revolution. In every practical respect, however, an implicit doctrine of practical independence was already in being and waiting to be used.

This aspect of the assemblies' actions against the Townshend Acts alarmed Governor Bernard of Massachusetts most of all. He was worried by rumors that the "prevailing opinion" in British circles was that "*America, if let alone, will come to herself, and return to the same sense of duty and obedience to Great Britain* which she professed before." To disabuse his superiors in London, he undertook to tell them what the struggle was all about:

> But when the dispute has been carried so far as to involve in it matters of the highest importance to the *imperial Sovereignty;* when it has produced questions which the *Sovereign* State cannot give up, and the *Dependent* States insist upon as the terms of a

[17] Circular Letter, February 11, 1768, ibid., pp. 134–36.

reconciliation; when the *Imperial* State has so far given way as to let the *Dependent* States flatter themselves that their pretensions are admissible; whatever terms of Reconciliation time, accident or design may produce, if they are deficient in settling the true Relation of *Great Britain* to her *Colonies,* and ascertaining the bounds of the *Sovereignty* of the one, and the *Dependence* of the other, Conciliation will be no more than a suspension of animosity; the seeds of which will be left in the ground ready to start up again whenever there shall be a new occasion for the *Americans* to assert their independence of the authority of *Parliament;* that is, whenever the *Parliament* shall make ordinances which the *Americans* shall think not for their interest to obey.

Bernard was not an orthodox British hard-liner. He favored "incorporating *America* with *Great Britain* in an Union" to prevent the two from separating. He wanted American representatives in Parliament, so that "there could be no dispute about the rights and privileges of *Americans* in contradiction to those of *Britons; and an opposition by force to the Government of Great Britain* would have but one name." He thought that Americans in general were not interested in getting parliamentary representation but still believed that it was the only way to "take away all pretences for disputing the ordinances of *Parliament.*" It was all the more necessary to solve the problem of representation, he reasoned, because the Americans, if frustrated, were bent on nothing less than "independence of the authority of *Parliament.*"[18] For his trouble, Bernard was told by Barrington that "the proposed expedient is impracticable, as no Influence could make ten Members of either House of Parliament to agree to such a Remedy."[19]

By this time, the British authorities had other things on their minds than colonial representation in Parliament and a new type of imperial union with the colonies. They were immediately concerned with the challenge to parliamentary authority which they read into the Boston circular letter. Hillsborough, the new American secretary, wrote to Bernard that it was "inflammatory" and might tend "to create unwarrantable combinations, and to excite an unjustifiable opposition to the constitutional authority of

---

[18] Letter to the Lord ——— ———, January 28, 1768, Francis Bernard, *Select Letters on the Government of America and the Principles of Law and Polity Applied to the American Colonies* (London, 1774), pp. 53–60.
[19] Barrington to Bernard, March 12, 1768, *The Barrington-Bernard Correspondence*, ed. Edward Channing and Archibald Cary Coolidge (Harvard University Press, 1912), p. 140.

Parliament." Bernard was ordered to dissolve the assembly if the circular letter was not withdrawn.[20]

The Massachusetts agent, Dennys De Berdt, reported that some members of the administration "say it is little better than an incentive to rebellion." Hillsborough told De Berdt that he and North had already decided on the repeal of the Townshend Acts but that the type of opposition to them "rendered it absolutely necessary to support the authority of Parliament."[21] In another meeting with De Berdt, Hillsborough was no longer sure that the Townshend Acts could be repealed, because everyone in the ministry was united on one point—when Parliament passed a law, it must be obeyed. De Berdt himself, an old hand at this game, was shaky on the arguments in the circular letter. "I wish," he wrote, "you had left the matter of right out of question, and only applied for a repeal of the laws, as prejudicial to the colonies and mother country."[22] This was always the sticking point; as soon as both sides dug themselves in as a matter of principle, they were locked in a combat which could not be resolved unless one or the other gave way.

Franklin, still in London, analyzed with his usual acuteness and subtlety the British problem with honor and principle. The ministry, he believed, was "a good deal embarrass'd and puzzled how to act with America." The majority really wished that the Townshend duties had never been imposed and considered them "equally prejudicial to this Country as to America." But, Franklin went on:

> they think the National Honour concern'd in supporting them, considering the Manner in which the Execution of them has been oppos'd. They cannot bear the Denial of the Right of Parliament to make them, tho' they acknowledge they ought not to have been made. They fear being despis'd by all the Nations round if they repeal them; and they say it is of great Importance to this Nation that the World should see it is Master of its Colonies, otherwise its Enemies on a Conceit of its Weakness, might be encourag'd to insult it.[23]

It was in the British interest that the Americans should argue against the Townshend Acts on purely practical or expedient grounds, not as a matter of "right," and wait for the British to repeal the measures in their own way.

[20] The substance of Hillsborough's order of April 22, 1768, to rescind the resolution is given in the Massachusetts Assembly's letter to Hillsborough, June 30, 1768, *Massachusetts State Papers*, p. 151.

[21] Letter from De Berdt, July 29, 1768, ibid., p. 161.

[22] Letter of De Berdt to the Speaker of the House of Representatives, August 29, 1786, ibid., p. 162.

[23] Franklin to Joseph Galloway, January 9, 1769, *Franklin Papers*, vol. 16, p. 11.

But both sides were prisoners of principles so often avowed that they could not retreat from them now. The anti–Townshend Acts movement took the same course as the anti–Stamp Act movement. All through 1768, other assemblies—Virginia, New Hampshire, Rhode Island, Connecticut, New York, New Jersey, Pennsylvania—passed more or less similar resolutions. Another united front was forming and needed only another provocative British action to bring on a more provocative colonial reaction.

· 5 ·

The colonists already thought of themselves as a "free people." Their problem was how to enjoy their freedom within the bounds set by limiting British legislation, especially the trade and navigation acts. By their very vocation, the merchants were hardest put to conduct their business as they pleased without running afoul of British restrictions, such as not being able to sell and buy anywhere in the world without stopping first at a British port to pay duties. One of the most cherished colonial freedoms had been the freedom to smuggle. For many decades, it had made both sides happy—the British kept the legislation on the books, and the colonists ignored it without getting caught. This was the old Walpolian system of "salutary neglect" that had become so obnoxious to the next British political generation. By smuggling, the Americans were only being British. Entire British fleets and about 40,000 people were said to be engaged in it. Favorite items in this underground trade were tea and wines—7,500,000 pounds of tea and £3,000,000 worth of wine annually. Adam Smith regarded the practice as a venial sin.[24]

Americans had smuggled for so long that they had reduced it to a system. The master of a ship usually landed his freight on a wharf while the customs officials were being entertained in the cabin.[25] A little bribery went a long way. Then came the Townshend Acts, which had the temerity not only to raise duties but to seek to collect them. One of the acts had provided for a more efficient method of collection through an American Board of Commissioners, located at Boston and directly responsible to the British Treasury. These newly appointed commissioners played by the new rules.

As tension was building as a result of the Boston circular letter, Governor Bernard on March 4, 1768, sent a panicky message to Barrington, the

---

[24] Arthur Lyon Cross, *Eighteenth Century Documents relating to the Royal Forests, the Sheriffs, and Smuggling* (Macmillan, 1928), pp. 22, 26 n. 13, 27.
[25] John Gorham Palfrey, *History of New England* (Little, Brown, 1905), vol. 5, p. 386.

war secretary. The merchants were organizing again; worse still, "violent
Methods of Opposition are every Day expected"; plans for a "Tumult" had
been reported in the last ten days; one merchant had unloaded cargo at night
without going through customs. The new commissioners were so jittery that
they had asked Bernard what support he could give them "if there should
be an Insurrection"; he answered, "none at all." Bernard was so afraid of
the council that he did not even dare to ask for more troops. He went on
tremulously:

> The present Suspence is a very disagreeable one: the Commissioners
> see that they must wait till a violent Opposition is made to their Officers;
> & yet they dread the Experiment. I must be involved with them more
> or less: I have promised them an Asylum at the Castle [fort], & possibly
> may want it myself. Tho' the more moderate of the Opponents to the
> Laws of Trade say that they will hurt No body; but when they find that
> they are not like to be redressed, they will put the Commissioners &
> all other Officers on board a Ship & send them back to England. This
> is the Talk used to prevent Riots: a Short Time will determine it.[26]

On May 9, he sent another frantic message to Barrington: "I am well
assured that it is the intention of the Faction here to cause an Insurrection
against the Crown Officers, at least of the Custom house, as soon as any
Kind of Refusal of their extravagant Demands against Great Britain shall
furnish a Pretense for so extraordinary a Step."[27]

In this tense atmosphere—at least as Bernard saw it or wanted it to be seen
in London—a famous incident in revolutionary lore occurred in Boston. On
June 10, the *Liberty,* a vessel owned by John Hancock, reputed to be the
richest merchant in the town and long suspected of smuggling, was seized
by customs officers. As usual, versions differ about the exact details, but there
is no doubt that a nasty riot broke out. One American historian reconstructed
the incident as a British conspiracy to "plunder" rich American merchants;
others suggest that Hancock had brought the trouble upon himself by trying
to evade the regulations.[28] In any case, the vessel was seized and taken near

---

[26] Bernard to Barrington, March 4, 1768, *Barrington-Bernard Correspondence,* p. 149.
[27] Bernard to Barrington, May 9, 1768, ibid., pp. 158–59.
[28] The conspiracy theory was advanced by Oliver M. Dickerson, *The Navigation Acts and the
American Revolution* (University of Pennsylvania Press, 1951), pp. 236–42. For Gipson, *British
Empire Before the American Revolution,* vol. 11, pp. 152–53, it was the result of a false entry
by Hancock. Herbert S. Allan, one of Hancock's biographers, told a story of how a customs
officer was forcibly confined in a cabin while an illicit cargo of wine was brought out of the
hold (Allan, *John Hancock,* Macmillan, 1948, p. 105). There seem to be as many versions as
there are books about the incident.

a British warship, the *Romney,* which had recently arrived in Boston harbor. A mob gathered onshore and attacked the customs officers, "not without wounds and bruises & a narrow escape with life," forcing them to flee to the Boston fort, Castle William—or so Bernard reported to Barrington.[29]

Bernard was so shaken that he asked for a leave of absence. On June 29, he feared the worst: "I expect great resentment from England against this Town & province, & that much confusion will arise here & perhaps there may be an actual insurrection."[30] In July, Bernard told Barrington that "Death has been denounced against those who are concerned in bringing Troops here."[31] The difficulty was that General Gage, the commander in North America, refused to send troops unless they were requested by the "civil power" in Massachusetts, which required the advice and consent of the council. Since Bernard could not get it, he wanted someone else to take the responsibility and let him off the hook. Besides, he was convinced it would be necessary to quarter the troops in the town permanently, because the threat was long range: "In Short, my Lord, Troops are not wanted here to quell a Riot or a Tumult, but to rescue the Government out of the hands of a trained mob, & restore the Activity of the Civil Power, which is now entirely obstructed." On July 30, Bernard realized that a struggle for power had been going on for the past three years:

> It is now 3 Years since the popular Power, which now prevails first raised its head: I have constantly give[n] Notice of every Step it has made, & have given my Opinion that there was no internal Power in this Government which could prevent its gaining all real Power. . . . But it is all over now: the indifference which has been shown in England to the checking the Demagogues of America for so long a Time has at length so effectually discouraged the Friends of Government, that they have been gradually falling off, 'till at length the Cause is become desperate.[32]

In August, Barrington finally informed him that the time had come to send troops to Massachusetts to maintain peace and law.[33] Later, he worried how Bernard would quarter them and indirectly confided his worst fear: "I long to hear that things are quiet, I mean *permanently* quiet in your part of the world, & I wish it may be without any bloodshed."[34] Two regiments from Halifax

[29] Bernard to Barrington, June 18, 1768, *Barrington-Bernard Correspondence,* p. 160.
[30] Bernard to Barrington, June 29, 1768, ibid., p. 163.
[31] Bernard to Barrington, July 11, 1768, ibid., p. 165.
[32] Bernard to Barrington, July 30, 1768, ibid., p. 170.
[33] Barrington to Bernard, August 11, 1768, ibid., p. 164.
[34] Barrington to Bernard, October 3, 1768, ibid., p. 171.

arrived in Boston on September 28, 1768, with two more from Ireland on the way.[35]

Meanwhile, from his headquarters in New York, General Gage was sending equally disturbing messages to Hillsborough. In late June, he advised Hillsborough of the reaction to the Boston events: "The Reports spread in this Place of the Outrageous Behavior, the licentious and daring Menaces, and Seditious Spirit of the People of all Degrees in Boston, are alarming; those of the lower Sort inflamed by Many, who should know, and act better."[36]

By September, as two British regiments were moving from Halifax to Boston, Gage expected to have to deal with treason and rebellion. He assured Hillsborough that he was taking measures "to defeat any Treasonable Designs," but "if open and declared Rebellion makes it's Appearance, I mean to use all the Powers lodged in my Hands, to make Head against it." He claimed to know that the American extremists relied on British merchants and especially manufacturers to work in their behalf, even hoping that they "will commit Riots and Tumults in their favor." Afraid that the British authorities might not approve of strong enough measures, he exhorted that nothing "can so effectively quell the Spirit of Sedition, which has so long and so greatly prevailed here, and bring the People back to a Sense of their Duty, as Speedy, vigorous, and unanimous Measures taken in England to suppress it" and "reduce them to their Constitutional Dependence, on the Mother Country."[37]

In October, Gage discovered that a "Spirit of Disaffection" had also appeared in New York. He went to Boston that month and found that every effort was being made to prevent the quartering of the troops. Quartering divided friends from foes: "Every Art and Evasion has been tryed, by the Major part of the People of every Degree, to force the Troops to quit the Town for want of Quarters; whilst those who may have acted, or made known their Sentiments in favor of Government, declared, they durst not stay in the Town, but must remove with their Familys and Effects, if the Troops should leave it." Gage saw the Boston events as part of a larger political threat:

> The Town has been under a kind of Democratical Despotism for a considerable time, and it has not been safe for People to act or Speak contrary to the Sentiments of the ruling Demagogues; and

[35] Gage to Hillsborough, *The Correspondence of General Thomas Gage with the Secretaries of State, 1763–1775* (Yale University Press, 1931), vol. 1, p. 201.
[36] Gage to Hillsborough, June 28, 1768, ibid., pp. 182–83.
[37] Gage to Hillsborough, September 26, 1768, ibid., pp. 196–97.

Surprizing as it may Appear, those Fears are not yet annihilated. . . . From what has been said, your Lordship will conclude, there is no Government in Boston. There is in Truth very little at present, and the Constitution of this Province leans so much to the Side of Democracy, that the Governor has not Power alone to remedy the Disorders which happens in it.[38]

By early November, Gage was pleased to report that the troops had restored peace and quiet in Boston.[39] It had taken almost six months. The chances are that Bernard and Gage were exaggerating the extreme danger. The Boston leaders themselves took the view that there were extenuating circumstances to explain the rioting on June 10; they attributed it to the "violence and unprecedentedness" of the boat's seizure but declared "their utter abhorrence and detestation" of the "criminal nature" of the "riotous proceedings."[40]

The way Sam Adams personally dealt with the incident shows how far he was willing and able to go to justify the rioting. His contribution to the affair appeared in the *Boston Gazette,* the radical organ, and illustrates the kind of public agitation that was driving Governor Bernard to distraction:

Can any one be surprized, that when property was violently seized, under a pretence of law, at an unseasonable time, at or after sunset, by the aid of military power, a power ever dreaded by all the lovers of the peace and good order of the province, and without any reason assigned or apparent: Is it at all surprizing that such ill-timed, violent and unheard of proceedings, should excite the resentment even of the better sort of people in the town[?].

He was "no friend to *Riots, Tumults and unlawful Assemblies,*" but he knew why they occurred:

But when the People are oppress'd, when their Rights are infring'd, when their property is invaded, when taskmasters are set over them, when unconstitutional acts are executed by a naval force before their eyes, and they are daily threatened with military troops, when their legislative is dissolv'd! and what government is left, is as secret as a *Divan,* when placemen and their underlings swarm about them, and Pensioners begin to make an *insolent* appearance—in such circumstances the people will be discontented, and they are not to

[38] Gage to Hillsborough, October 31, 1768, ibid., pp. 204–5.
[39] Gage to Hillsborough, November 3, 1768, ibid., p. 206.
[40] Report and Resolutions of the Council, June 30, 1768, *Massachusetts State Papers,* p. 157.

be blamed—their minds will be irritated as long as they have any sense of honor, liberty and virtue—In such Circumstances, while they have the spirit of freedom, they will *boldly assert* their freedom; and they are to be justify'd in so doing—I know very well that to murmur, or even to *whisper* a complaint, some men call a riotous spirit. But they are in the right of it to complain, and complain ALOUD. And they *will* complain, till they are either redress'd, or become poor deluded miserable ductile Dupes, fitted to be made the slaves of dirty tools of arbitrary power.[41]

In London, Benjamin Franklin did not find the rioting very shocking. He passed it off as "sudden unpremeditated things, that happened only among a few of the lower sort." Riots, in any case, were an old English custom. He himself had recently witnessed some of the worst riots in English history in behalf of the election of John Wilkes. "That in a Country so frequent in mischievous Mobs and murderous Riots as this is," Franklin calmly commented, " 'tis surprising to find such Resentment of a trifling Riot in Boston."[42] He seemed unmoved by an essential difference; the pro-Wilkes rioters did not intend to set up a separate state with Wilkes at the head of it; people like Bernard and Gage saw every American rioter as a carrier of "the Seditious Spirit of the People."

One of the Bostonians' characteristics was that they never tired of arguing. James Otis and Sam Adams were compulsive controversialists, equal to any on the British side. As the British troops settled in, their presence was challenged on the ground that it was "inconsistent with the spirit of a free constitution, and the very nature of government." One argument made the people of the colony the only judge of just and unjust laws: "The very supposition of an unwillingness in the people in general, that a law should be executed, carries with it the strongest presumption, that it is an unjust law; at least, that it is unsalutary. It cannot be their law; for, by the nature of a free constitution, the people must consent to laws, before they can be obliged, in conscience, to obey them."

The logic of consent, always the sine qua non of the revolutionary ideology, put the colonies in the position of having the last word in any dispute with British legislation or policy. At this time, the only thing the Bostonians could think of doing was to "lay their fervent and humble petition before their

[41] Signed "Determinatus," *Boston Gazette,* August 8, 1768, in *The Writings of Samuel Adams,* ed. Harry Alonzo Cushing (G. P. Putnam's Sons, 1906), vol. 1, pp. 236–40.
[42] Franklin to Jean-Baptiste LeRoy, January 31, 1769, *Franklin Papers,* vol. 16, p. 33; Franklin to Joseph Galloway, January 9, 1769, ibid., p. 12. On the Wilkes riots, ibid., vol. 15, pp. 98–99, 127–28.

gracious Sovereign."43 But they were up against a sovereign who knew his constitutional limitations and refused to act without or against the will of Parliament. The king could have answered their prayers only by going over the head of Parliament and, in effect, turning the clock back to the days before the Glorious Revolution. The colonial radicals undoubtedly did not intend to push him in that direction; they considered themselves good Whigs, even descendants of Real Whigs. But they were forced into putting their faith in him alone, because he was the only leg of the British triad— king, Lords, and Commons—left after their alienation from Parliament. They had no chance to win in a system that had arrived at the esoteric formula of king-in-Parliament, because the Americans needed him outside of Parliament. Their repeated pleas to the king to save them from Parliament did not do them any good in Parliament.

· 6 ·

Boston was the vanguard. For one reason, it had the most disciplined, sophisticated cadre of ideological lawyers. They controlled the legislature and were backed by wealthy merchants like John Hancock. Some of them spent so much time and energy countering every British move that they can be likened to professional revolutionaries. Sam Adams in particular had little more to do than carry on a war of words against the British. Governor Bernard was puzzled by what a few dedicated radicals could accomplish. "It has been a Subject of Wonder," he confessed, "how the Faction which harrases [sic] this Town and through it the whole Continent, which is known to consist of very few of the lowest kind of Gentry and is directed by 3 or 4 Persons bankrupt in Reputation as well as in Property, should be able to keep in Subjection the Inhabitants of such a Town as this, who possess an hundred Times the Credit & Property (I might say much more) of those who rule them with a Rod of Iron."44 But the "faction" had a mass base in a floating population that could be counted on to take the struggle into the streets and strike fear in British guardians. The British exposed their weakness by bringing in outside military force, which only succeeded in further enraging the populace.

Boston alone could have been isolated. But the lesson of the Stamp Act campaign had sunk in. The time was past when the British could count on

43 Answer of the House of Representatives to the Governor's Message, May 31, 1769, *Massachusetts State Papers*, pp. 170–71.

44 May 19, 1768, cited by Ralph Volney Harlow, *Samuel Adams* (Henry Holt, 1923), p. 115, from *Bernard Papers*, vol. 6, pp. 300–304.

colonial separateness and rivalry to work in their favor. At an early stage of the new crisis, General Gage advised Hillsborough that "all the Assembly's will not only follow the Example of that of the Massachusett's Bay, by preferring Petitions, Memorials, Remonstrances &c to the King, Lords, and Commons, upon the Subject of the new Dutys" but "invite the rest to combine with them in those Measures."[45]

The effectiveness, methods, and timing of the nonimportation movement differed from colony to colony, but on the whole it was successful. By the end of 1769, only New Hampshire had failed to respond. Colonial imports from Great Britain fell from £2,153,000 in 1768 to £1,332,000 in 1769. The drop was especially sharp in New York, from £482,000 to £74,000.[46] Some of the motives went beyond achieving repeal of the duties. George Washington, one of the prime movers in Virginia, thought that nonimportation was also going to encourage local manufactures and cut down indebtedness to Great Britain.[47] He was not the only one who viewed nonimportation as a blessing in disguise. Franklin went further and saw it as the road to economic self-sufficiency. "I hope my Country-folks will remain as fix'd in their Resolutions of Industry and Frugality till those Acts are repeal'd," he wrote home. "And if I could be sure of that, I should almost wish them never to be repeal'd; being persuaded that we shall reap more solid and extensive Advantages from the steady Practice of those two great Virtues, than we can possibly suffer Damage from all the Duties the Parliament of this Kingdom can levy on us." He wanted nothing so much as to show the British that they were wrong to "flatter themselves that you cannot long subsist without their Manufactures."[48] He wrote to the Philadelphia merchants that "to manufacture for themselves, or use colony manufactures only" was "the means, under God, of recovering and establishing the freedom of our country entire, and of handing it down compleat to our posterity."[49] Franklin, who was not yet ready for political independence, was already a prophet of economic independence.

For all of its early success, the anti-Townshend movement lacked staying power. It did not have the organization of the Stamp Act movement, which had been able to gather representatives in a congress and give them a sense of acting together. The anti-Townshend movement was

[45] Gage to Hillsborough, August 19, 1768, *Gage Correspondence,* vol. 1, p. 189.
[46] Lawrence Henry Gipson, *The British Empire Before the American Revolution* (Alfred A. Knopf, 1965), vol. 11, p. 266.
[47] George Washington to George Mason, April 5, 1769, *The Papers of George Mason,* ed. Robert A. Rutland (University of North Carolina Press, 1970), vol. 1, p. 97.
[48] Franklin to Samuel Cooper, April 27, 1769, *Franklin Papers,* vol. 16, p. 118.
[49] Franklin to the Philadelphia Merchants, July 9, 1769, ibid., p. 174.

individualistic, each colony going off on its own to do the same thing but with different methods and timing. Gradually, merchants in the three main centers, Boston, Philadelphia, and New York, saw their immediate interests differently and came to a parting of the ways. When New York dropped out in mid-1770, the movement began to fall apart and was effectively finished by the end of the year.

The lesson was not lost on George Mason, with Washington the moving spirit in Virginia, who made an acute analysis of the partial victory—or partial failure. He realized that the fault had been with the lack of organization and a general plan. The colonies had expected that it would take no more than a year to force the British government to capitulate and repeal the duties. When it had taken longer, the colonial merchants could not hold out and quarreled among themselves.

But Mason was not discouraged. "Time has pointed out our Mistakes, & Errors well known are more than half corrected," he wrote. Mason himself protested that throwing off dependence on Great Britain was "the wildest Chimera that ever disturbed a Madman's Brain." All he wanted was not "to have our own Money taken out our Pockets without our Consent." But even he did not know "what may be the effect of Violence & Oppression."[50]

The American Revolution moved forward in waves. The anti-Townshend nonimportation movement was the second wave. It represented a halting progress, which prepared the way for the struggle next time.

[50] George Mason to [George Brent?], December 6, 1770, *Papers of George Mason*, vol. 1, pp. 128–29.

14

''Flattering whispers
of independency''

· 1 ·

I**N ALL THIS TIME,** one factor in the relations between Great Britain and the American colonies was preeminent for the British. It rested on a question: What were colonies for?

In its simplest form, the early British empire was based on two main propositions—that colonies should provide the mother country with raw materials and that they should serve as a market for the mother country's manufactures. This system made commerce the key to national greatness, or, as one British authority put it: "A Nation cannot be safe without Power; Power cannot be obtained without Riches; nor Riches without Trade."[1] It followed that control of the colonies' trade in favor of the mother country was an essential element of the system; that was just what the Navigation Acts had sought to achieve ever since 1651. At the same time, the growth of British manufactures, especially in the woolen and iron industries, created a need for markets, particularly those that could be depended upon. For this purpose, colonies were ideal, because they were understood to be appendages of the mother country.

[1] William Mildmay, *The Laws and Policy of England Relating to Trade* (London, 1765), p. 3, cited by Klaus E. Knorr, *British Colonial Theories, 1570–1850* (University of Toronto Press, 1944), p. 23.

This colonial system implied that colonies were good to have only so long as they contributed to the mother country's interests, and that they were useless or even dangerous if they did not. But this did not mean that the mother country was oblivious to the colonies' interests; the more prosperous the colonies, the more raw materials they could supply, and the more manufactures they could consume.

This ideal relationship was, however, inherently unstable. It was workable so long as the colonies were young and undeveloped, and even then not without tensions and rivalries. To succeed, it required that the colonies should feel themselves so dependent on the mother country that they could not or did not wish to challenge their subservient status. For this reason, the French threat in Canada had been a useful means of keeping the Americans in their place. Without such an external inducement to accept their dependency, the colonies were free to see their interests differently and to act on what was best for them.

As the conflict between Great Britain and the American colonies began to heat up after the peace treaty with France in 1763, it became increasingly clear that the main weapon in the hands of the colonists was economic. This was necessarily so, because the raison d'être of the colonies for the British was economic. The colonists knew that the weak link in the British colonial chain was the need to hold on to the American market for British manufactures. This phase of the struggle for power had been coming on for a long time, but it broke out into the open only after the peace with France.

· 2 ·

The British had begun to worry about colonial competition as early as 1661. The Council for Foreign Plantations had complained of New England that "their Trade is in no way managed to ye Advantage of His Maj[es]ties Crown." In particular, New England, despite previous regulations, had increased its stock of sheep to almost 100,000, though the number was almost certainly exaggerated. As a result, the council pointed out, "This Nation & ye manufacture thereof are become less necessary to them." Worse still, the New Englanders were likely to supply the Dutch, with whom they then traded freely, with their excess wool and threaten to invade British wool markets by enabling the Dutch to mix the coarser New England wool with the finer Dutch-favored varieties. Any threat to Britain's greatest industry, especially one from the British colonies, was intolerable. Even at that early date, the British authorities were quick to see the political implications in Massachusetts's sheep. The council accused Massachusetts of refusing to give it information on its flocks "or having their Affairs judg'd, or disposed of in England, as if they intended to suspend their absolute obedience to His Ma[jes]ties Authority, until time shall farther discover how far Necessity or their Interests shall compell them thereunto." But the higher-up Privy Council refused to send a letter of rebuke and pursued a conciliatory course, which did nothing to lessen the number of Massachusetts's sheep, whatever it was.[2]

Another early precedent shows why British efforts to inhibit or stop the growth of colonial industry were futile. In 1699, English manufacturers and merchants succeeded in getting an act passed prohibiting colonial wool, woolen yarn, and cloth from being transported anywhere, even from one colony to another. But such an edict was unenforceable and at most encouraged colonial farmers to concentrate on fleeces instead of raw wool.[3] Another act in 1732 gave the colonies more to complain about. It prohibited their exportation of hats, especially those made of fur, which had figured in trade with Spain and the West Indies. Yet the hat-making industry in the colonies could not be discouraged and continued to add its bit to colonial manufacturing.

The most important and revealing of these prohibitory acts was directed against the colonial iron industry. In 1709, when the colonies were still in their first century, British manufacturers of ironwares complained that the Americans were producing too much iron and steel, mainly in Massachusetts, Pennsylvania, and New Jersey. They succeeded in forcing the Americans to pay higher prices for imported Swedish and Spanish bar iron as a way to cut down their competition. As American iron production refused to give up, British "ironmasters soon saw that the colonists, if permitted to continue the establishment of ironworks, might become serious competitors in the production of pig iron and bar iron, and therefore they demanded high duties on the importation of colonial iron."[4]

As the iron trade overtook woolen goods as Britain's foremost industry, the Board of Trade began to worry about American competition in many manufactures, including iron. In 1732, it reported that

---

[2] *Colonial Papers, America and West Indies, 1661–1668* (London, 1969), p. 79. On the probability that the numbers were exaggerated, see Victor S. Clark, *History of Manufactures in the United States* (Carnegie Institution of Washington, 1929), vol. 1, p. 81. What is most important here is how the Council for Foreign Plantations interpreted the threat.

[3] Clark, *History of Manufactures*, vol. 1, pp. 22–23.

[4] Arthur Cecil Bining, *British Regulation of the Colonial Iron Industry* (University of Pennsylvania Press, 1933), pp. 35–36.

there are more Trades carry'd on, and Manufactures set up in the Provinces on the Continent of *America* to the Northward of *Virginia,* prejudicial to the Trade and Manufactures of *Great Britain,* particularly in *New England,* than in any other of the *British* colonies, which is not to be wonder'd at; for their Soil, Climate and Produce being pretty near the same with ours, they have no Staple Commodities of their own Growth to exchange for our Manufactures, which puts them under a greater Necessity, as well as under a greater Temptation of providing for themselves at home.[5]

Towards the end of the decade, Joshua Gee, a major writer on trade and an investor in iron manufacture, testified before a parliamentary committee that if the Americans made bar iron, they were sure to make other iron manufactures and attract skilled British workers:

That if the *Americans* are suffered to make Bar Iron, it may be impossible and unreasonable to hinder them from manufacturing also. . . . That if their Forges and Manufactures are suffered to increase in the manner they now do, they will constantly drain this Kingdom of great Numbers of our People; which, as our Works of all Kinds must decline here, Want of Work at home, and a Prospect of higher Wages under new Masters abroad, they will be continually going from us to them, to the great Depopulation of their Mother Country.[6]

By 1747, a British writer complained that the colonies were making their own ironware and driving out British imports:

Formerly our Colonies were entirely supplied with Iron and Iron-ware from hence. But since the Erection of Iron-works there, *New-England* now not only furnishes herself, but other Colonies likewise with sundry sorts of Iron-wares. . . . The Erection of more [colonial] Forges, will naturally produce more Manufactories; and the *Americans* will soon supply themselves with every thing in that Way, which now they have from *Great Britain.*[7]

Yet the British iron makers were not united against their American counterparts. Makers of finished goods wanted to buy American pig and

[5] *Historical Register,* vol. 18, pp. 47–48, cited by Bining, *British Regulation,* p. 53.
[6] *Journals of the House of Commons,* vol. 23, p. 113, cited by Bining, *British Regulation,* pp. 99–100.
[7] *Interest of Great Britain in Supplying Herself with Iron Impartially Considered* (London, 1747, 1750), cited by Bining, *British Regulation,* p. 109.

bar iron cheaply, whereas forge owners wanted to forbid the importation of all American iron. In 1750, a compromise was reached. Iron manufacturers were permitted to receive colonial bar iron duty free, but the colonies were prohibited from erecting slitting mills, plating mills, and steel furnaces. These strictures were easily evaded; the colonies did not report the forbidden facilities or lied about having them. In 1764, an act was passed requiring colonial producers to send their iron to Great Britain; it failed to deter the colonists, as had all its predecessors.[8]

After all this agitation and legislation, little was accomplished to hold down American production. The British could keep the Americans from competing in the British market, but they could not prevent them from keeping pace with the growing demands of the American market, because the British had no means to enforce their edicts there. In fact, the Americans never produced much for the British market and did not need it to thrive. As Adam Smith noted, the regulations did "more to encourage the erection of furnaces in America" than to discourage it.[9]

The futility of the British campaign against colonial iron production was paradigmatic. The colonies were irked by laws that were not enforced or enforceable. By 1775, there were more forges in the colonies than in Great Britain. One reason the colonies were successful in the Revolution was the existence of so many blast furnaces producing weapons. Colonial tools were even generally superior to the British.[10]

The three main British efforts against colonial wool, hats, and iron did little or nothing to hinder the Americans. Yet they taught the Americans an invaluable lesson—that the British were most vulnerable in their trade in manufactures. Wherever American production paralleled British production, or even threatened to do so, the British regarded the Americans as dangerous rivals, not as partners in a common enterprise. At the core of the early British empire was this fatal antagonism; it ate away at the deference and loyalty which the colonists had been willing to grant in the years of their immaturity. In 1769, Benjamin Franklin expressed the colonial credo in a way that revealed the gulf between the Americans and British. Parliament, he said, should make laws "for the Evident Good of the Colonies themselves, or of the whole British Empire; never for the Partial Advantage of Britain to their Prejudice."[11] But British trade policy had

---

[8] Bining, *British Regulation*, pp. 69–72, 82, 86–87.

[9] Adam Smith, *An Inquiry into the Nature and Causes of the Wealth of Nations*, ed. Edwin Cannan (Modern Library ed., 1937), p. 547.

[10] Bining, *British Regulation*, pp. 27, 95, 106.

[11] Franklin to William Strahan, November 29, 1769, *The Papers of Benjamin Franklin*, ed. Leonard W. Labaree (Yale University Press, 1961), vol. 16, p. 244.

always been skewed to the advantage of Great Britain and to the prejudice of the American colonies.

The threat of the colonies to British manufacturing even led some to advocates' giving up the colonies as a bad bargain. As early as 1738, doubt was expressed that the colonists could be kept from establishing manufacturing industries rivaling those of the mother country.[12] By the 1760s, the feeling of "jealousy" was becoming increasingly bitter. In 1769, one writer maintained that "a Colony, incapable of producing any other commodities than those produced by its Mother Country, would be more dangerous than useful; it would be proper to call home its inhabitants and give it up. . . . This maxim cannot be contested."[13] In 1774, the *Monthly Review* commented on the view of Josiah Tucker that it would be best for Great Britain to rid itself of the American colonies. The *Review* said that Tucker's proposal was "not a new idea." Others had thought that "we can neither *govern* the Americans, nor be *governed by them;* that we can neither *unite* with them, nor ought to think of *subduing* them, and . . . that nothing remains but to part with them on as friendly terms as we can."[14]

The dispute over colonial manufactures was also a debate over colonial independence. If the British could not maintain their monopoly of selling manufactures to the colonies, there was no reason to maintain the colonies at all. This is a red thread that runs throughout the prerevolutionary period, though it was obscured by the more dramatic political excitement over the Stamp Act and the like.

· 3 ·

The Sugar Act of 1764, not the Stamp Act of 1765, first brought out the colonial threat to British manufactures. Discussion of this threat appeared in print more than once that year and suggests that it was not a sudden improvisation by any one ingenious colonial mind. To see how the colonial counterattack developed, it is necessary to go back to the American pamphlets of 1764–1768.

One of the first of the great prerevolutionary pamphlets, *Considerations*

---

[12] *Reflections and Considerations Occasioned by the Petition Presented to the Honourable House of Commons, for Taking off the Drawbacks on Foreign Linens, &c.* (London, 1738), pp. 15 ff, cited by Knorr, *British Colonial Theories*, p. 15.

[13] *St. James's Chronicle*, February 23, 1769, cited by Fred Junkin Hinkhouse, *The Preliminaries of the American Revolution As Seen in the English Press, 1763–1775* (Columbia University Press, 1926), p. 102.

[14] Cited by Hinkhouse, *Preliminaries of the American Revolution*, p. 114.

upon the Act of Parliament, came out anonymously in Boston in early 1764.[15] Its target was the Sugar Act, the main provision of which had imposed a duty of threepence a gallon on foreign molasses. Since turning molasses from the West Indies into rum was one of the most profitable occupations in New England, most of the protests originated in Massachusetts.

The most persuasive argument against the duty followed a simple line of reasoning. If the colonists could not make a profit on their production of rum, they could not use that money to provide a market for British manufactures. The duty on molasses was, therefore, a threat not only to an important branch of the colonial economy but to the entire British economy. If the colonists could not buy their manufactures from Great Britain, they were bound to make their own. Thus the Sugar Act was an inducement to increase colonial manufactures—a result far more costly to Great Britain than any revenue that could be expected to come from the molasses duty.

The *Considerations* put this case starkly. It contended that the Sugar Act "will lessen the ability of these colonies to pay for those British manufactures for which they have so increasing a demand and oblige them to turn their thoughts, though at first very unwillingly, upon the improvement of their own." The author pleaded that the colonies did not want to go in for manufactures. Alas, they were being forced to produce them against their will. If only the British knew their own best self-interest, they would do everything in their power to prevent the colonists from substituting colonial for British manufactures.

> Necessity has no law; it presses those supposed insuperable difficul-
> ties the surmounting of which often creates resolution to proceed fur-
> ther and to undertake to remove still more and greater obstacles. . . .
> Experience of this sort among the colonies should in all good policy be
> prevented as it might very much affect the British interest respecting
> both commerce and manufactures; and therefore we have reason to
> expect that the wisdom of Great Britain will permit and even encour-
> age any branch of trade (not interfering with her products or manufac-
> tures) to divert the colonies from all thoughts of manufacturing, even
> for their own use, those rough materials which their various soils and
> climates are so capable of producing, iron excepted.[16]

[15] Reprinted in Bernard Bailyn, ed., *Pamphlets of the American Revolution, 1750–1776* (Harvard University Press, 1965), pp. 361–77.

[16] *Considerations upon the Act of Parliament,* reprinted in Bailyn, *Pamphlets of the American Revolution,* pp. 372–73.

This argument was entirely economic; the colonial pamphleteers had not yet thought of challenging British policy on political or constitutional grounds.

Another pamphlet in 1764 came from a committee in New Haven, headed by Gov. Thomas Fitch. It was largely political in character but did not fail to make the economic case. Its target was the stamp tax, which had been announced but not yet passed, and which it called a duty, as if it were similar to the molasses duty. The authors stressed that a stamp tax was bound to be just as "prejudicial" to Great Britain as to the colonies but mentioned that they would have to obtain the "necessaries of life" in some other way:

> In the colonies there is a vent for and a consumption of almost all sorts of British manufactures, and of many and various kinds of goods of the produce of other countries first imported into Britain and from thence brought into the plantations, whereby the revenue of the crown and wealth of the nation are much increased at the expense of the colonies. . . . If the plantations are encouraged and prosper, this will be an increasing interest and become more and more of importance; but if measures should be taken which, in regard to them, would have a natural tendency to abate their vigor, spirit, and industry, or to turn them into some other channel to supply the necessaries of life, what can be expected but a decrease of the colonies' wealth and prosperity, and consequently a decay of an important national interest?[17]

The most famous pamphlet of that year by James Otis was less squeamish about what the colonies would do to take revenge on British manufactures. Otis left nothing to the British imagination, if Parliament persisted in passing laws to which the Americans objected:

> I am sure these colonies have the natural means of every manufacture in *Europe,* and some that are out of their power to make or produce. It will scarcely be believed a hundred years hence that the American manufactures could have been brought to such perfection as they will then probably be in if the present measures are pushed. . . .
>
> Manufactures we must go into if our trade is cut off; our country is too cold to go naked in, and we shall soon be unable to make returns to England even for necessaries.

Otis made the British dependent on the Americans: "Without the

---

[17] Thomas Fitch et al., *Reasons Why the British Colonies in America Should Not Be Charged with Internal Taxes* (New Haven, 1764), ibid., pp. 396–97.

American trade, would Britain, as a commercial state, make any great figure at this day in Europe?" If the colonists could not pay for British manufactures, he asked: "What will follow?" He answered: "One of these two things, both of which it is the interest of Great Britain to prevent. (1) The northern colonists must be content to go naked and turn savages. Or (2) become manufacturers of linen and woolen to clothe themselves, which, if they cannot carry to the perfection of Europe, will be very destructive to the interests of Great Britain."

Otis returned to a favorite theme—what Great Britain owed the American colonies:

> That the trade with the colonies has been of surprising advantage to Great Britain notwithstanding the want of a good regulation is past all doubt. Great Britain is well known to have increased prodigiously both in numbers and in wealth since she began to colonize. To the growth of the plantations Britain is in a great measure indebted for her present riches and strength. As the wild wastes of America have been turned into pleasant habitations and flourishing trading towns, so many of the little villages and obscure boroughs in Great Britain have put on a new face, and suddenly started up and become fair markets and manufacturing towns and opulent cities.[18]

Oxenbridge Thacher argued that the British were sure to lose by inhibiting American trade:

> The exports to the colonies wholly stopped or greatly diminished, the demands for those manufactures in Great Britain must be in proportion lessened. The substance of those [British] manufacturers, merchants, and traders whom this [American] demand supports is then gone. They who live from supplying these manufacturers, etc., must decay and die with them. Lastly, as trade may be compared to a grand chain made up of innumerable links, it is doubtful whether the British trade, great as it is, can bear the striking out so many without greatly endangering the whole.[19]

In 1765, Stephen Hopkins struck a familiar note from Providence, Rhode Island, which was particularly hard hit by the duty on molasses: "The genius of the people in these colonies is as little turned to manufacturing goods for their own use as is possible to suppose in any people whatsoever; yet

[18] James Otis, *The Rights of the British Colonies Asserted and Proved* (Boston, 1764), reprinted in Bailyn, *Pamphlets of the American Revolution*, pp. 460–62, 479–80.
[19] [Oxenbridge Thacher], *The Sentiments of a British American* (Boston, 1764), reprinted in Bailyn, *Pamphlets of the American Revolution*, p. 497.

necessity will compel them either to go naked in this cold country or to make themselves some sort of clothing, if it be only the skins of beasts."

Hopkins was so upset by the duty that he accused the British of being able to impose it on the colonies only because Canada was no longer French: "Better for them Canada still remained French, yea far more eligible that it ever should remain so than that the price of its reduction should be their slavery."[20]

Otis came back to the problem in two pamphlets in 1765. In one, he argued that the British protection of the colonies was fully repaid by "the immense commercial advantages resulting to Great Britain from her plantations, the revenues arising to the crown, the taxes we pay by the consumption of an infinity of British manufactures."[21] In the other, he produced a kind of declaration of independence for American manufactures, with particular reference to iron products: "Can any one tell me why trade, commerce, arts, sciences and manufactures, should not be as free for an American as for an European? Is there any thing in the laws of nature and nations, anything in the nature of our allegiance that forbids a colonist to push the manufacture of iron much beyond the making a horse-shoe or a hob nail?"[22]

Daniel Dulany's 1765 pamphlet made manufactures a patriotic duty— for Americans:

> Let the manufacture of America be a symbol of dignity, the badge of virtue, and it will soon break the fetters of distress. A garment of linsey-woolsey, when made the distinction of real patriotism, is more honorable and attractive of respect and veneration than all the pageantry and the robes and the plumes and the diadem of an emperor without it. Let the emulation be not in the richness and variety of foreign productions, but in the improvement and perfection of our own.

Dulany spotted the one colonial weapon that could bring the British to beg for mercy: "By a vigorous application to manufactures, the consequence of oppression in the colonies to the inhabitants of Great Britain would strike home, and immediately. None would mistake it."[23]

[20] [Stephen Hopkins], *The Rights of Colonies Examined* (Providence, 1764), reprinted in Bailyn, *Pamphlets of the American Revolution*, pp. 515, 520.

[21] James Otis, *A Vindication of the British Colonies* (1765), reprinted in Bailyn, *Pamphlets of the American Revolution*, p. 577.

[22] James Otis, *Considerations On Behalf of the Colonists in a Letter to a Noble Lord*, reprinted in *University of Missouri Studies*, October 1, 1929, p. 116.

[23] Daniel Dulany, *Considerations on the Propriety of Imposing Taxes in the British Colonies* (Annapolis, 1765), reprinted in Bailyn, *Pamphlets of the American Revolution*, pp. 649-50.

Of all those who dealt with the economic weapon, the most effective and influential was probably John Dickinson of Philadelphia in his pamphlet of 1765. It was not that he thought of anything particularly new, but, unlike the more hotheaded Bostonians, he adopted a more judicious tone to put the colonial case in the best light.

Dickinson first struck a defensive pose. The Americans did not really want to make their own manufactures. He said, they "have not time nor any temptation to apply themselves to manufactures." He proceeded to explain why Great Britain was dependent on the Americans: "Her prosperity depends on her commerce; her commerce on her manufactures; her manufactures on the markets for them; and the most constant and advantageous markets are afforded by the colonies." The Americans had not previously been unhappy with the rules, though Dickinson expressed specific displeasure with the iron restrictions. Unfortunately, the British had presented the Americans with a difficult choice:

> We have our choice of these two things—to continue our present limited and disadvantageous commerce—or to promote manufactures among ourselves, with a habit of economy, and thereby remove the necessity we are now under of being supplied by *Great-Britain*. . . . Necessity will teach us two ways to relieve ourselves. The one is, to keep *British* manufactures we purchase longer in use for wear than we have been accustomed to do. The other is, to supply their place by manufactures of our own.

The Americans, he pointed out, were already making colonial cloth. They were paying a heavy tax by buying such quantities of British goods that they could make more cheaply themselves. Dickinson warned the British not to drive the Americans into a corner and suffer even greater consequences: "A branch of trade once lost, is lost for ever. In short, so strong a spirit is raised in these colonies by late measures, and such successful efforts are already made among us, that it cannot be doubted, that before the end of this century, the modern regulations will teach *America*, that she has resources within herself, of which she never otherwise would have thought."

Dickinson also ventured to touch on the delicate subject of independence. "We are informed," he remarked, "that many persons at home affect to speak of the *colonists,* as of a people designing and endeavoring to render themselves independent, and therefore it may be said to be proper as much as possible to depress them." But repression could not work for the British any more than it had for other empires. There was one way the colonies might become independent, but they would have to thank the British for it: "In short, we never can be made an independent people, except by *Great-Britain* herself; and the only way for her to do it, is to make us frugal, ingenious, united and discontented." As his authority for the way this independence might come about, Dickinson cited at length from *Cato's Letters.* But, of course, he hoped to Providence that this would never happen, and it could not happen while the present generation and its filial sentiments existed.[24]

Three years later, in his most famous work, *Letters from a Farmer in Pennsylvania, to the Inhabitants of the British Colonies,* Dickinson dropped his judicious tone. By this time, the Townshend duties rather than the stamp tax were the enemy, and Dickinson began to sound like the Bostonians:

> Here then, my dear countrymen, ROUSE yourselves, and behold the ruin hanging over your heads. If you ONCE admit, that *Great-Britain* may lay duties on her exportations to us, *for the purpose of levying money on us only,* she then will have nothing to do, but to lay those duties on the articles which she prohibits us to manufacture— and the tragedy of *American* liberty is finished. We have been prohibited from procuring manufactures, in all cases, any where but from *Great-Britain* (excepting linens, which we are permitted to import directly from *Ireland*). We have been prohibited, in some cases, from manufacturing for ourselves; and may be prohibited in others. We are therefore exactly in a situation of a city besieged, which is surrounded by the works of the besiegers in every part *but one.* If *that* is closed up, no step can be taken, *but to surrender at discretion.* If *Great-Britain* can order us to come to her for necessaries we want, and can order us to pay what taxes she pleases before we take them away, or when we land them here, we are as abject slaves as *France* and *Poland* can shew in wooden shoes, and with uncombed hair.[25]

The interested British public read these words because Benjamin Franklin arranged to have Dickinson's *Letters* reprinted in London and wrote a preface for them.

It is clear, then, that the outburst of colonial protest that erupted after the Sugar Act and the Stamp Act was far more than an ideological, constitutional, and political struggle. That kind of struggle went on

---

[24] John Dickinson, *The Late Regulations respecting the British Colonies on the Continent of America considered* (Philadelphia, 1765), reprinted in *The Writings of John Dickinson,* ed. Paul Leicester Ford (Historical Society of Pennsylvania, 1895), vol. 1, pp. 213–15, 217, 226, 235–37, 241–43.
[25] Ibid., pp. 320–21.

interminably, and British spokesmen answered in kind. On both sides it was curiously bloodless and hyperintellectual. It resembled a debate between lawyers, as indeed much of it was. By itself, it could never have persuaded the British to repeal the Stamp Act in 1766. Something more forceful and pragmatic was necessary.

· 4 ·

We know how British merchants and manufacturers felt about the Stamp Act crisis, because the House of Commons took the trouble to find out. The House turned itself into an American Committee in February 1766 and listened hour after hour for several days to testimony of leading British and American merchants, including the famous examination of Benjamin Franklin.

The British witnesses were not worried merely about the loss of American trade and replacement by American manufactures; they were also troubled by a huge American debt. The colonists bought British goods on credit of a year or more. According to Barlow Trecothick of London, one of the wealthiest and most reputable of merchants, they owed £2,900,000 in London, at least £800,000 in Bristol, £500,000 in Glasgow, £150,000 in Liverpool, and £100,000 in Manchester, for a total of £4,450,000—in addition to debts in five other cities and towns. The colonists had stopped all payments, and nothing could be expected until the Stamp Act was repealed. He summed up the situation: "We find America in confusion, our property in danger, our remittances uncertain and the trade in danger of annihilation."[26]

Masses of British workers were being dismissed. Robert Lawson of Leeds reported that "great numbers" were out of work; he himself had recently dismissed almost 1,000 and intended to dismiss the rest if business did not pick up. Since August 1765, he had not received a single order from America. For lack of trade, goods in Great Britain were so cheap that he could buy them more cheaply than he could manufacture them. Benjamin Farrar, near Leeds, said that three out of ten manufacturing workers had been discharged. Robert Hamilton of Manchester had dismissed 400 weavers and expected to dismiss 2,000 more workers. William Reeve of

[26] Barlow Trecothick, *Proceedings and Debates,* vol. 2, pp. 192–93. Trecothick had been born in Boston and moved to London, where he became a wealthy merchant, trading with America. He was at that time alderman of London, and an adviser to Lord Rockingham, first lord of the Treasury.

Bristol had dismissed 300 nail makers in one day. John Hose, who made shoes in Cheapside, had formerly employed as many as 300 men; now the number was down to 45.

Americans, they said, were making or going to make their own manufactures. Barlow Trecothick thought that the high wages of British workers would lead to an increase of colonial manufactures. More British craftsmen would go to America from "want of work at home." Richard Oswald, another British merchant, was asked whether British workers would go to America if unemployed. He replied: "They would live better there." Capel Hanbury remarked on what was going on in the colonies: "There is now a spirit of emulation for wearing their own manufactures. . . . If the [British] merchants discontinue they [colonists] must manufacture." James Balfour, a Virginia merchant specializing in tobacco, explained: "If anything should interrupt that commerce the hands employed in tobacco would be employed in manufactures. There are already manufactures which I have seen and worn and are to be seen in every house there. . . . I believe the people can live with the greatest [ease?] without the British manufactures." William Kelly, a merchant from New York, reported that British goods could be manufactured there. "Cabinet ware they may make in New York. . . . Thinks they have the means for iron ware for they can make steel and have iron. There is a great plenty of wood and of streams of water so proper for making forges that many are erected." He foresaw two consequences if the Stamp Act remained in force: "First, they will avoid intercourse with this country. Second, they will go into manufactures."

Emanuel Elam of Leeds, who had recently visited all the colonies from Massachusetts to Virginia, gave a detailed, firsthand account of what he had seen and heard:

> It will put them to some inconvenience to manufacture their own goods at first but they go on very far in breeding sheep and working wool in their own families. . . . I have been told by some manufacturers that they can work it on equal terms with ours. . . . The turn of the country seems to be to manufacture. . . . Heard of embarrassments laid on their trade and that made them turn to manufactures. . . . Has seen linen goods manufactured in North America, and woollen goods manufactured there and brought to market and a great stocking manufactory at Philadelphia. . . . They were striving to wear their own manufacture.

A favorite question dealt with potential American independence. Trecothick was asked: "What effects on the stocks will the independency of North

America have?" He replied: "A very fatal one." Next question: "Which will establish the independency sooner, the enforcing the Stamp Act or repealing it?" Reply: "The enforcing it." A question to Capel Hanbury: "If America is made independent of Great Britain will she come here for her manufactures?" His answer: "I don[']t know how the mutual intercourse can be kept up." Hanbury also declared: "If this act should be enforced it can[']t be without military force and it would throw them into confusion. . . . On account of the uneasiness of the inhabitants, so great that if force was used they would repel force by force."

None of the witnesses thought that a compromise was possible; it was all or nothing for the Stamp Act. Hanbury's attitude was typical. Question: "What will be the remedy for the evils you have described?" Answer: "First a repeal of the act. Anything short of a total repeal will be inadequate. A modification would not answer." This was exactly what Franklin also told the committee: "Do you think the people of America would submit to pay the stamp-duty, if it was moderated? No, never, unless compelled by force at arms." Yet all were sure that everything would return to normal as soon as the act was repealed. Hanbury was asked: "Will the Americans consider the repeal of the Stamp Act as making them independent?" He thought not. Repeal of the act would be considered by the Americans as "an act of grace and favour and express their gratitude." Franklin said much the same thing in answer to the question: "Considering the resolutions of parliament, as to the right, do you think, if the stamp-act is repealed, that the North-Americans will be satisfied?" Franklin replied: "I believe they will."

But Franklin himself may have done most to warn the British of what they were up against in his "Examination" before the House of Commons in 1766. "I do not know," he told one of his tormentors, "a single article imported into the Northern Colonies, but what they can either do without, or make themselves." Wouldn't British cloth be absolutely necessary to them? "No, by no means absolutely necessary; with industry and good management, they may very well supply themselves with all they want." In three years, they might have enough wool and woolen manufactures, wool that is "very fine and good." If the stamp tax, which was still in force, was not repealed, "they will take very little of your manufactures in a short time." Would repeal of the Stamp Act discourage colonial manufactures? "Yes, I think [it] will."[27]

It is little wonder, then, that the British decided to repeal the Stamp Act.

[27] The testimony is taken from the transcript of evidence in ibid., pp. 185–276.

Their best customers were in revolt, and their merchants and manufacturers were faced with ruin. They were assured that the issue was limited to one thing only—the tax on stamps. Without withdrawing the right to levy that tax, the British decided as a matter of practical policy to waive the right in this case. Franklin assured them that "the resolutions of right will give them very little concern, if they are never attempted to be carried into practice." The colonies disposed of the tax in exchange for the declaration of a British right that was never supposed to be used against them again.

It was the specific, single-issue character of the anti–Stamp Act movement that made it possible for it to succeed by economic means alone. Once the act was repealed, everything else was expected to revert to the status quo ante. In fact, this was only the first stage of the struggle. As the colonies went from rejecting a single act of Parliament to challenging the right of Parliament to pass any act affecting them, the stakes increased, and there was less room for retreat.

The stamp tax was doomed when British merchants and manufacturers were convinced that it was not worth huge losses in the American market. The menace of colonial manufactures was more intimidating than a bushelful of colonial pamphlets. If giving up the stamp tax was all that was needed to calm down the Americans, the way was open to the compromise of 1766—repeal of the Stamp Act and passage of the Declaratory Act. It was only later, after British merchants and manufacturers decided that the Americans wanted much more, that British public opinion turned against the Americans and supported a harder line.

The fate of the Sugar and Stamp acts was decided by who would get hurt the most, and most quickly. The British, richer and more highly developed, were more vulnerable. The colonies had no employers who could dismiss 1,000 or more workers at one swoop. In this first test of strength, the weaker was the stronger.

· 5 ·

The British merchants and manufacturers who gave evidence to the American Committee were interested in little more than profit and loss. But the issue was essentially economic also for British spokesmen and observers who took part in the controversy on a more intellectual level. Two of these best represent the thinking of British officialdom.

One of the first to state the British case was Thomas Whately, secretary of the Treasury under Grenville. In 1765, he put out a tract of over one hundred pages designed to defend the policy of the Grenville administration.

He immediately emphasized what was important about the colonies:

> And the trade from whence its greatest Wealth is derived, and upon which its Maritime Power is principally founded, depends upon a wise and proper use of the Colonies: From them we are to expect the Multiplication of Subjects; the Consumption of our Manufactures; the Supply of those Commodities which we want; and the Encrease of our Navigation: To encourage their Population and their Culture; to regulate their Commerce; and to cement and perfect the necessary Connection between them and the Mother Country, should therefore be the principal Objects of a British Minister's care.

He acknowledged that Great Britain relied on the American colonies for the consumption of its manufactures. But Whately did not yet worry about competition from American manufactures. He thought that colonists who went in for manufactures would turn to farming as soon as they had accumulated enough money to buy land, because land was more profitable. For this reason, he foresaw no "flourishing and established" manufacturing activity in the colonies. In any case, he reassured his readers, the British could always step in to "thwart all their Endeavours."

The most striking thing about Whately's outlook—and not only his— was how British-centered it was. Trade was everything and defined what colonies were for: "Colonies are only Settlements made in different Parts of the World, for the Improvement of Trade." Colonies were not for prestige or for geopolitical advantage.

In peculiar ways, Whately evoked the old suspicion of American independence. He referred to "the industrious and frugal Republican of *America*," an allusion which did not escape the American pamphleteer Daniel Dulany. Since *Republican* was not a word in good repute in British official circles and Americans were not yet willing to admit it into their political vocabulary, Dulany angrily protested that "it implies that they are enemies to the government and ought therefore to be regarded with a jealous eye."[28]

More seriously, Whately referred to

> that Increase of Wealth, People, and Territory, which raises Appre- hensions in many Persons that the Colonies may break off their

[28] Dulany, *Considerations on the Propriety of Imposing Taxes,* p. 626.

Connections with *Great Britain:* That Connection is actually broken already, wherever the Acts of Navigation are disregarded; and for so much of their Trade as is thereby diverted from its proper Channel, they are no longer *British* Colonies, but Colonies of the Countries they trade to. . . . The extent of this Commerce, as it is in its Nature private, cannot be certainly known; but that it is now carried to a dangerous Excess, is an indisputable Fact.

Instead of agreeing or disagreeing with these "Apprehensions," Whately made the notorious colonial addiction to smuggling a form of independence, because it violated the hallowed British trade laws. According to this reasoning, the colonies were already independent to the extent that they did not give full and willing obedience to those laws.

Whately devoted most of his pages to Great Britain's need to get a revenue from the colonies. Only towards the end did he turn his attention to the stamp tax, which he regarded as a fair exchange for British protection. Most significant, he was already worried that excluding this tax from the authority of Parliament endangered everything else, including the acts of trade and navigation—"they are not obligatory if a Stamp Act is not, and every Argument in support of an Exemption from the Superintendance of the *British* Parliament in the one Case, is equally applicable to the others."[29]

A year later, Whately put out another weighty booklet. It showed the effect of colonial agitation by emphasizing how much the colonies had benefited from British policy. He went so far as to claim that the colonies have been "of late the darling object of their mother country's care." He cited British concessions to colonial whale fishery, rice, timber, hemp and flax. "The destribution [*sic*] is too unequal," he complained, "of benefits only to the colonies, and of all the burthens upon the mother country; and yet no more was desired, than they should contribute to the preservation of the advantages they have received, and take upon themselves a small share of the establishment necessary for their own protection."

Whately pointed out that a third of colonial imports came from foreign countries, not Great Britain. British manufactures did not amount in value to one-half of American consumption. The colonies carried on an extensive traffic with the West Indies, Africa, and all parts of Europe south of Cape Finisterre. By giving up the stamp tax, Great Britain had lost £100,000 in revenue. Impost duties had been reduced, bringing American revenues

---

[29] [Thomas Whately], *The Regulations Lately made concerning the Colonies, and the Taxes Imposed upon Them, considered* (London, 1765), pp. 3–4, 6, 67–68, 89, 92, 104.

down from £160,000 as planned to a mere £30,000 a year. He denied that the Stamp Act had caused the colonies to be distressed: "It was owing entirely to the refractory spirit which had gone abroad in the colonies." He made no concessions on manufactures—they "more peculiarly belong to the mother country."[30]

Whately was addressing a British audience, which wanted to know most of all what was in it for them from the colonial connection. The trade laws in favor of the mother country were a given that did not need to be justified; every other empire pursued the same course with even more determination and rigidity. Far from apologizing for British policy, Whately emphasized how liberal it was and how much the colonies got out of it. Above all, the context of the struggle with the colonies was, he thought, basically economic, and the larger significance of the stamp tax was that its fate threatened to bring down the whole structure of British economic interests in the colonies.

Until about 1768, the British still hoped to avoid a full-scale collision with the colonists. By this time, it was clear that the Declaratory Act had been far more important than the repeal of the Stamp Act two years earlier. The Stamp Act was a one-time imposition of a specific tax; the Declaratory Act was a statement of a general principle—that Parliament had the right to legislate for the colonies *"in all cases whatsoever."* The colonists had imagined that this declaration was merely a face-saving maneuver to cover the retreat on the stamp tax and had made little protest against it. But as events now demonstrated, the Declaratory Act had gone to the heart of the struggle.

One of those who saw it this way was Lord Hillsborough, who had become secretary of state for the colonies in January 1768. He had quickly shown that he intended to take a hard line with the colonies by the way he responded to a circular letter in February 1768 from Massachusetts to the other colonies calling for joint protest against the Townshend duties. Hillsborough, who learned of the letter in April, viewed it as an effort "to excite and encourage an unjustifiable Opposition to and Denial of the constitutional Authority of Parliament."[31] He instructed Governor Bernard to get the Massachusetts House to rescind the letter or to dissolve the House immediately. At that time, he had been made aware of the disturbing opinion of General Gage:

[30] [Thomas Whately], *Considerations on the Trade and Finances of this Kingdom* . . . (London, 1766); reprinted in *A Collection of scarce and interesting tracts* (London, 1787), vol. 2, pp. 144, 146, 150–51, 155, 182, 195.

[31] Hillsborough to Colony of Connecticut, *Pitkin Papers, Collections of the Connecticut Historical Society* (Hartford, 1921), vol. 19, p. 121.

That they will struggle for independency, if the good folks at home are not already convinced of it, they soon will be convinced. From denying the Right of internal taxations, they next deny the Right of duties on Imports, and thus they mean to go on step by step, 'till they throw off all subjections to your laws. They will acknowledge the King of Great Britain to be their King, but soon deny the prerogatives of the Crown, and acknowledge their King no longer than it shall be convenient for them to do so.[32]

This line of reasoning permeated British official circles in 1768 and made it difficult for them to repeal the Townshend duties in toto. Hillsborough explained his position to William Samuel Johnson, the London agent for Connecticut, in October 1768:

The colonies have rendered it impossible, by imprudently uniting to dispute the right of Parliament, which, since the declarative act especially, we cannot permit to be called in question. I am sorry that your Colony, which you have so often represented to me in so favorable a light, have listened to the factious suggestions of the Massachusetts Bay. Had they petitioned on the ground of inexpediency only, they would have succeeded; but while you call in question the right, we cannot hear you. It is essential to the constitution to preserve the supremacy of Parliament inviolate.[33]

Benjamin Franklin also saw that the British were caught in a quandary. They did not want the Townshend duties anymore, but they did not want to get rid of them to please the Americans:

The majority really wish the Duty Acts had never been made; they say they are evidently inconsistent with all sound commercial and political principles, equally prejudicial to this country as to America; but they think the national honour in supporting them, considering

---

[32] Gage to the earl of Barrington, March 10, 1768, *The Correspondence of General Thomas Gage with the Secretaries of State, 1763–1775* (Yale University Press, 1931), vol. 2, p. 450.

[33] William Samuel Johnson to William Pitkin, October 20, 1768, *MHS Collections*, 5th ser., vol. 9, p. 296.

Grenville was told that Hillsborough had informed the colonial agents that "if they would *waive* the point of right, and petition for a repeal of the duties as *burdensome and grievous*, Administration were disposed to come into it. The agents, however, declared they could not leave out the point of right, consistent with their present instructions, but should inform their respective colonies, and so it rests" (Knox to Grenville, December 15, 1786, *Grenville Papers*, vol. 4, pp. 400–401). Also see Charles Garth to South Carolina Committee of Correspondence, *South Carolina Historical and Genealogical Magazine*, vol. 30 (1929), p. 234; Johnson to Pitkin, January 3, 1769, *MHS Collections*, 5th ser., vol. 9, pp. 304–5.

the manner in which the execution of them has been opposed. They cannot bear the denial of the right of Parliament to make them, tho' they acknowledge they ought not to have been made.[34]

From this time on, the sides were clear. Whenever a colony called "in question the right" of Parliament to decide matters for the colonies, official British opinion refused to budge. Massachusetts was the bête noire, but other colonies were not far behind. In June 1768, Gov. William Pitkin of Connecticut tried to reason with Hillsborough about the colonial attitude. This instance is such a classical example of the colonial case that it deserves to be noted at some length.

Pitkin began by buttering up Hillsborough on his appointment as secretary of state. He expressed satisfaction that "we have a Person appointed of your Lordship's real Worth, known Ability, and approved Integrity, as well as great Humanity and benevolent Disposition." But he quickly switched over to the heavy burdens imposed by the Townshend duties and to "other Considerations which make them peculiarly greivious [*sic*] and afflicting, that the Parliament of Great Britain, whom we revere as the great Council of the Nation, should impose these Duties upon the American Colonies for the sole purpose of raising a Revenue in America." He left no doubt that the only difference was over how such revenue measures were to be decided—by the "free Gift" of the colonies or by the ukase of Parliament. He brought up the charter of Charles II, which had promised to treat the colonists as if they "were born within the Realm of England." This meant, according to Pitkin, that the colonists could not be taxed without their consent, which they could not give because they were not represented in Parliament. In effect, the argument had not moved much since the time of the Stamp Act.[35]

In November 1768, Hillsborough answered Pitkin uncompromisingly. He merely stated that Pitkin's contentions "tend to deny and draw into question the supreme Authority of the Legislature of Great Britain to enact Laws binding upon the Colonies in all cases whatever." He also enclosed the king's speech opening the current session of Parliament.[36]

In the king's speech on November 8, 1768, Pitkin and other colonists would have found a denunciation of Boston for having "a Disposition to throw off their Dependance on *Great Britain*."[37] This declaration

---

[34] Franklin to Joseph Galloway, January 9, 1769, *Franklin Papers*, vol. 16, p. 11.

[35] Pitkin to Hillsborough, June 10, 1768, *Collections of the Connecticut Historical Society*, vol. 19, 1921, pp. 132–35.

[36] Hillsborough to Pitkin, November 15, 1768, ibid., pp. 153–54.

[37] *Proceedings and Debates*, vol. 3, p. 1.

represented the view of the British government. It charged the colonies with the one thing they could not accept.

Not much had changed in the hard-line view by the time another literary counterattack was launched by William Knox in 1769. In his first pages, he called up the specter of colonial independence and denounced the colonial strategy of using the Crown as a means of eluding the grip of Parliament:

> Shall we see our fellow-subjects in the Colonies intoxicated with a fond conceit of their own importance, and charged by the flattering whispers of independency, forsaking the *guide of their youth,* the sure stay of all their liberties, and the protector of all their rights and possessions, the parliament of Great Britain; and throwing themselves into the arms of prerogative, and putting all their confidence in the good pleasure of the crown?

Knox could not let these whispers of independency pass unmentioned and took them up again in his last pages: "And let me now ask the advocates for their independency, upon which period of this history it is, that they would fix, as the epocha of the Colonies emancipation from the sovereign authority of the supreme legislature of the realm, or where will they carry us for those pretended rights and privileges which exempt them from its jurisdiction?"

He was also upset by the prospect of unfair competition by American manufactures: "Are your manufactures to rival her's in every market, from your manufacturers being exempt from taxes, whilst British manufacturers pay taxes upon everything they consume?"

Finally, Knox's indignation against what he took to be the one-sided demands of the colonies rose to such a pitch that he resorted to threats of force:

> There is a spirit rising in this country, which will make you to know its strength and your own weakness, that will convince you of its authority and of your dependence. ... If you do not avail yourselves of the information I have given you, perhaps the people of England may be led by it to conceive more justly of their *Rights,* and of your *Intentions,* than they have hitherto done; and may compel you to submit, if they unhappily find no argument, but force can induce you to obey. It is time indeed for my countrymen to bestir themselves, and to vindicate the honour of the state, and the rights of its legislature.

On his very last page, Knox made clear what the connection was between the economic and political sides of British policy. He called on the people of England to unite in behalf of their own interests and "the trading part especially, *whose property and commercial interests so much depend upon the power of parliament to bind the Colonies."*[38]

Without political control over the colonies, which in the existing system could be vested only in Parliament, economic control was unhinged. Though the system demanded that the colonies be politically dependent on the mother country, economically the position was reversed. By having permitted themselves to become so dependent on colonial trade, the British found themselves in desperate straits to continue to control the terms of that trade—a control that could be maintained only by political means. In effect, the British told themselves that they could not afford to lose colonial trade, whereas the colonies had come to believe that they would be better off trading freely with the rest of the world. Taxes in themselves did not count all that much in the bookkeeping of British economic relations with the colonies, for which reason they could be given up as not worth the trouble. But taxes raised the central issue of control and acted as surrogates for every other type of control. Once control had escaped from this Pandora's box, it could not be recaptured by repealing the Stamp Act and pretending to go back to the status quo ante.

6

Whately and Knox were British extremists who gave no quarter and asked none. But there were others who genuinely sought to find a peaceful way out of the impasse and realized that the old ways were no longer tenable. Of these thoughtful, knowledgeable, and well-intentioned British observers, none tried harder to find a solution fair to both sides than Thomas Pownall. Why his efforts were futile tells as much as the others' intransigence.

Unlike most British commentators on the colonial crisis, Pownall knew the colonies at first hand and wrote about them with special authority. After a short apprenticeship as clerk in the Board of Trade, he came to New York in 1753 at the age of thirty-one as the private secretary of the newly appointed governor, Sir Danvers Osborne, who soon committed suicide. Thomas's younger brother, John, had preceded him at the Board of Trade and rose to be its chief secretary. Ambitious and well placed, Thomas was appointed lieutenant governor of New Jersey in 1755 and governor of Massachusetts in 1757. Two years as governor during the ups

[38] [William Knox], *The Controversy between Great Britain and her Colonies Reviewed* (London, 1769), pp. 3–4, 200, 203–5 (italics in original).

and downs of the Seven Years' War—mainly downs before there were any ups—taught him the facts of life in colonial politics and shaped his later views on imperial reform. In November 1759, Pownall was shifted to the governorship of South Carolina, where he stayed only a short time. After he returned to England in 1760, no place was found for him in which to make use of his colonial experience, and he marked time in subordinate posts, mainly in Germany, in the closing years of the Seven Years' War.[39]

Even the bare bones of Pownall's colonial career indicate that he had an unusual background to advise on British policy. He thrust himself into colonial policy making by putting out a work, *The Administration of the Colonies,* which first appeared in 1764 as an anonymous essay of 132 pages. It reappeared five times in the next thirteen years in enlarged editions, the second edition, in 1765, carrying his name and the last, in 1777, enlarged to two substantial volumes.

Pownall was moved to write in 1764 because he recognized that the end of the Seven Years' War with France had created a new situation, not because an acute colonial crisis had already broken out. By the time he came to the fourth edition in 1768, he knew the worst and expressed himself fully on what had brought it on and what to do about it.[40]

Pownall approached these questions historically. His purpose was to show that much of what the colonies labored under in the present had come from a past long gone and was no longer suitable to what the colonies had become. The laws of trade had been enacted when the colonies were mere plantations, raising nothing but raw materials solely for British benefit. But the colonies had outgrown their original function and had entered a more advanced stage of commercial development:

> But the spirit of commerce, operating on the nature and situation of these external dominions, beyond what the mother country or the Colonists themselves ever thought of, planned, or even hoped for, has *wrought up these plantations to become objects of trade;* has enlarged and combined the intercourse of the barter and exchange of their various produce, into a very complex and extensive commercial spirit.

Pownall undertook the delicate task of explaining to British readers why the old commercial system was so unsatisfactory and unfair to the colonies—

[39] Pownall has had two biographies: Charles A. W. Pownall, *Thomas Pownall* (London, 1908), and John A. Schutz, *Thomas Pownall* (Arthur H. Clark, 1951).

[40] The fourth edition is the only one that has been reprinted and is, therefore, the most easily available (Da Capo Press, 1971).

and, in the end, harmful to the British. He located the source of the trouble in the northern colonies. They imported most British manufactures but had few natural resources to export. They were forced to trade in order to get the money or specie with which to pay for British goods. They obtained money or bills of exchange chiefly from trade with Spain, Portugal, and Italy. They brought back gold, ivory, and slaves from Africa in exchange for British manufactures. New England fisheries depended on sales to the French West Indies in return for molasses. Trade was New England's lifeblood as much as it was Great Britain's. The old imperial system could not cope with the new realities.

As a result, these colonies could no longer be content with a two-way British-American trade. They had to trade freely elsewhere if they were to buy British manufactures and pay their British debts. In this fashion, Pownall made his case as much in Britain's interest as in that of the colonies.

After all this, Pownall brought out his heavy artillery—the threat of colonial manufactures. If commerce of the colonies were checked, he exhorted, they "must, from inevitable necessity, betake themselves to manufactures of their own, which will be attended with consequences very detrimental to those of Great Britain." He elaborated:

> Nothing does at present, with that active and acute people, prevent their going into manufactures except the proportionate dearness of labour, as referred to the terms on which they can import; but encrease the price of their imports to a certain degree, let the extent of their settlements, either by policy from home or invasion of Indians abroad, be confined, and let their foreign trade and navigation be, in some measure suppressed;—their paper currency limited within too narrow bounds, and the exclusion of that trade which hath usually supplied them with silver-money too severely insisted upon;—this proportion of the price of labour will much sooner cease to be an object of objection to manufacturing there than is commonly apprehended. . . . If the colonists cannot on one hand purchase foreign manufactures at any reasonable price, or have not money to purchase with, and there are, on the other hand, many hands idle which used to be employed in navigation, and all these, as well as the husbandmen, want employment; these circumstances will soon overbalance the difference of the rate of labour in Europe and in America.

Whereupon Pownall brought out the heaviest gun of all: "And if the

Colonies, under any future state of administration, which they see unequal to the management of their affairs, *once come to feel their own strength in this way*, their independence on government, at least on the administration of government, will not be an event so remote as our leaders may think, which yet nothing but such false policy can bring on."

Pownall's thinking was based on three central factors—trade, manufactures, and independence. If the colonies could not trade enough, they needed to manufacture, in which case they were bound to move towards independence. Pownall was still a good enough Englishman to want to avoid independence by reforming the British system. His problem was how to reconcile the older imperial rule with the newer reality of colonial economic development.

He attempted to arrive at such a reconciliation by advocating a new system of imperial government. It was based on the idea that "Great Britain may be no more considered *as the kingdom of this Isle only, with many appendages of provinces, colonies, settlements, and other extraneous parts, but as A GRAND MARINE DOMINION CONSISTING OF OUR POSSESSIONS IN THE ATLANTIC AND AMERICA UNITED INTO A ONE EMPIRE, IN A ONE CENTER, WHERE THE SEAT OF GOVERNMENT IS.*" Unlike Chatham and Burke, Pownall saw clearly that either the Americans were to be given a semblance of equality within the British empire or they would burst the bonds that had been woven to keep them subordinate within it.[41]

From 1769 on, Pownall was convinced that Great Britain had to retreat or face a rebellious America. "The ground you are upon will lead if not to civil war," he warned in the House of Commons, "to a total disunion and alienation." The colonies did not wish to rebel, "but if you go to enforce these revenue laws by military execution, you will drive them to a madness that will be unconquerable." Britain's power would not be enough: "Nothing but power can operate, and that can operate to nothing but mischief. A further exertion of that power would press them together."[42] By 1770, he was resigned to the failure of peaceful persuasion. He admitted that "whatever may be my opinion of that right [to impose duties], as now stated, I know it *never* will be decided by arguments, reasonings, resolutions, or even Acts of Parliament—It will be decided by *power*. And I know that we never shall have any power which we shall think reasonable to hazard

---

[41] Thomas Pownall, *The Administration of the Colonies* (London, 1768; reprint, Da Capo Press, 1971), pp. 10, 282–83, 286, 289, 315–16. In a preface, written later, he was willing to give the colonies representation in Parliament as a token of their equal status (pp. xiv–xv).

[42] April 19, 1969, ibid., p. 148. Pownall was elected to the House of Commons in 1767.

by exerting—while the colonies will every day grow more and more into the capacity of disarming, if not of resisting, that power."[43] His foreboding began to take on an almost apocalyptic character: "If you attempt to force the troops upon them under the present establishment, you may drive the people to rebellion. . . . You may draw them not into a rebellion, but a civil war."[44]

Pownall was not at his best as a practical politician and usually managed to annoy all sides. He was a man of no party or faction and described himself as "inconsiderable, unconnected, independent."[45] Once the war broke out, a new Pownall appeared. He became a loyal British patriot and zealously supported the British war effort. But by 1780, he recognized that American independence could not be held back and that the British were doomed to fail. He predicted a grandiose future for the United States and characteristically called for a European congress to work out a code of free trade with the new nation.[46] He is best remembered for his independent judgment; his analysis of how trade, manufactures, and independence intersected; his vision of an enlarged British empire in which the colonies would be treated as equals. He saw what others resisted seeing—that tinkering would not do, that taxes were not the real problem, that there was no substitute for American independence short of a drastic transformation of the British imperial system.

[43] March 5, 1770, ibid., p. 230.
[44] May 8, 1770, ibid., p. 273.
[45] April 19, 1769, ibid., p. 148.
[46] [Thomas Pownall], A Memorial, most humbly addressed to the sovereigns of Europe, on the present state of affairs between the old and new World (London, 1780), preface.

15

"Blood in the Streets"

• 1 •

The one thing that had been lacking so far in the struggle for power was blood in the streets. The colonists had resorted to economic sanctions and to bursts of prerevolutionary propaganda. They had scored two bloodless victories, over the stamp tax and most of the Townshend duties. But both sides knew that nothing had changed fundamentally, and they girded for further battle.

Again, Boston was the tinderbox. When the British moved troops into the city at the end of 1768, they admitted that they had exhausted political options and that only force could hold their system in place. Though the immediate effect of putting in the troops had been reassuring, Benjamin Franklin knew better. "I am glad to hear that Matters were yet quiet at Boston," he wrote from London, "but fear they will not continue long so. Some Indiscretion on the part of their warmer People, or of the Soldiery, I am extreamly apprehensive may occasion a Tumult; and if Blood is once drawn, there is no foreseeing how far the Mischief may spread."[1]

Franklin had more than a year to wait before his premonition became a reality. The British garrison in Boston in early 1770 numbered 600, of whom only 400 could be used effectively. The civilian population numbered 16,000.[2] The British had put enough troops in Boston to stir up the

---

[1] Franklin to Joseph Galloway, January 9, 1769, *The Papers of Benjamin Franklin*, ed. Leonard W. Labaree (Yale University Press, 1961), vol. 16, p. 10.
[2] Hiller B. Zobel, *The Boston Massacre* (W. W. Norton, 1970), p. 181.

maximum resentment and not enough to contain it if it overflowed into violence. For months, the papers had been full of dark warnings to expect the worst from the troops. When an election to the assembly was called in May 1769, the commanding general was told to get the troops out of town, and his concession to confine them to barracks was not considered good enough.[3] A "standing army" was an old British bogey, which the colonists took over for their own purposes. Whenever the troops marched through Boston, they ran the risk of taunts and provocations from onlookers. "It is with Astonishment & Indignation that the Americans contemplate the folly of the British Minister, in employing Troops which have heretofore been the Terror of the Enemies of Liberty, only to parade the Streets of Boston; & by their ridiculous merry Andrew Tricks to become the objects of the Contempt even of Women and Children," Sam Adams wrote to Dennys De Berdt towards the end of 1769.[4]

Whatever grievances the lower orders—as John Adams called them—may have had, they were mainly expressed against the British rather than their own elite. This deflection was one of the most significant factors in the increasingly militant revolutionary movement. It served to divide the colonists into pro- and anti-British far more than to set one social rank against another.

This combustible material finally flared into violence. The circumstances show how broad the anti-British feeling was and how a little incident could escalate into full-fledged street warfare, as Franklin had foreseen.

The worst outbreak of violence began with name-calling in front of John Gray's rope works. Soldiers often took casual jobs during off-duty hours to supplement their meager pay. Pvt. Patrick Walker walked by the premises on March 2, 1770. The following dialogue ensued:

"Soldier, do you want work?" asked ropemaker William Green.

"Yes, I do, faith," said Walker.

"Well," said Green, in a triumph of ready wit, "then go and clean my shithouse."

"Empty it yourself," said Walker.

After more such exchanges, Walker, swearing "by the Holy Ghost" that he would have revenge, swung wildly at the ropemakers. Nicholas Ferriter, a one-day employee, "knocked up his heels"; a naked cutlass dropped from beneath his coat. Humiliated, drubbed, and disarmed,

---

[3] *The Writings of Samuel Adams,* ed. Harry Alonzo Cushing (G. P. Putnam's Sons, 1906), vol. 1, p. 341.

[4] Adams to De Berdt, November 6, 1769, ibid., p. 446.

the soldier fled. In a few moments he was back, reinforced by eight or nine other soldiers.5

Thus began what was called the Boston Massacre. On March 5, a mob attacked a British sentry. The commanding officer, Capt. Thomas Preston, led a relief party to rescue him. In the melee, the crowd taunted the soldiers and dared them to fire. Someone, not Preston, shouted "Fire," and shots rang out from the outnumbered soldiers. Three townspeople died, two others were so badly wounded that they later died. Nine soldiers, including Captain Preston, were arrested and jailed. Within days, the Boston radicals had a pamphlet out, *A Short Narrative of the Horrid Massacre in Boston*. After the incident, Boston was not the same. The two British regiments were quickly removed to Castle William, on an island in the harbor.

In the end, the heroes of the story were John Adams and Josiah Quincy, Jr. They, together with a conservative lawyer, defended Captain Preston at his trial in November 1770. In the still charged atmosphere, they succeeded in showing that Preston had not ordered the troops to fire, and he was found not guilty. Six of the other soldiers on trial received the same verdict, and two more were released on a technicality. In effect, the trial was a triumph for colonial lawyers, who were willing to defend a British officer despite their political sympathies. Nevertheless, the Boston Massacre was what most people remembered, and its memory was carefully cultivated for years to come. As late as 1970, its bicentennial was celebrated in Boston with a publication entitled *Blood in the Streets: The Boston Massacre.*6

General Gage reported to the earl of Hillsborough as if the end of British rule had come: "In Matters of Dispute with the Mother Country, or relative thereto, Government is at an End in Boston, and in the Hands of the People, who have only to assemble to execute any Designs. No Person dares to oppose them, or call them to Account; the whole Authority of Government, the Governor excepted, And Magistracy supporting them."7

The exception was Lt. Gov. Thomas Hutchinson. Governor Bernard had left Boston in the summer of 1769, never to return, leaving Hutchinson

---

5 Zobel, *Boston Massacre*, p. 182.

6 Published by the Revolutionary War Bicentennial Commission and the Trustees of the Boston Public Library. It should be said that this publication tried to give a fair account of the affair. It mainly contains photographs of documents.

7 Gage to Hillsborough, April 10, 1770, *The Correspondence of General Thomas Gage with the Secretaries of State, 1763–1775* (Yale University Press, 1931), vol. 1, p. 249. This letter contains an account of the incident from the British point of view.

in charge. Gage was so shaken that he wanted to get the troops out of Massachusetts altogether. Too late, he realized that in those conditions the soldiers were not able to defend themselves. "They were there contrary to the Wishes of the Council, Assembly, Magistrates and People," he wrote to Hillsborough, "and seemed only offered to Abuse and Ruin, And the Soldiers were either to suffer ill usage, and even Assaults upon their Persons till their Lives were in Danger, or by resisting and defending themselves, to run almost a Certainty of Suffering by the Law."[8]

Hillsborough was another of those British politicians who had hardened their line as unrest in the colonies had increased. In May 1770, after the "Boston Massacre," he made a statement of his political faith which showed how far he had gone in opposition to the Americans and what the idée fixe of British hard-liners had become. He explained that he never wanted to lose sight of the "constitutional point" respecting the mother country and colonies, namely, "the supremacy which the former should always possess over the latter." He then asked:

> But who, my lords, will take upon him to assert, that when the colonies rise up in a daring opposition to all legal authority; when they deny their dependence upon this kingdom; when they attack the lives of such among them as seem well affected to the parent state, and when they will not suffer English vessels to carry on a peaceable commerce, nor indeed any commerce at all with English ports in America; who, I say, in such a case, will assert, that the mother country should quietly sit down under the flagitious insolence of her dependencies, that she should tamely suffer injury after injury, and allow the colonies to rule her with a rod of iron, for fear of being charged with a severity of conduct towards the colonies?

After accusing the American friends in Parliament for encouraging colonial rebelliousness, he cried:

> This poor kingdom may be sacrificed to her dependencies, and the British Parliament be reduced to a necessity of rescinding its laws, at the command of a provincial Assembly. Can you, my lords, restrain your indignation at the bare idea of so mortifying, so abject a proposition? Is not the whole Englishman maddened in your bosoms, at the remotest thought of crouching to the creatures of your own

[8] Ibid., p. 251.

formation? Have you erected colonies to be your masters, not to be your dependents—and will you suffer that insolence to assume the name of patriotism, which arraigns the warrantable exercise of your own authority?"[9]

This was the true voice of the British hard-liners. By 1770, this position was set in political concrete. It was based as much on a fear of American mastery as on a habit of British imperiousness. It was maddening for many British politicians and officials to think that they were being manipulated by American agitators and provincial assemblies. Yet they did not quite know what to do about it, because the use of force was still repugnant and the absence of enough force ruled out a crackdown.

· 2 ·

While tension was building in Boston, the British government still had to struggle with the disposition of the Townshend duties. Again it had to decide whether to fight the colonies to a finish or give in to them, as it had done in the case of the Stamp Act.

The main British problem was to decide what was good for the British economy in general and British merchants and manufacturers in particular. But their interest could not be separated from that of American merchants and consumers of British goods. The Americans, in turn, had come to count on the support of British merchants and manufacturers, to whom they owed much for their victory in the Stamp Act crisis. As George Mason pointed out, the Americans had expected to win the battle of the Townshend duties by bringing about "such a sudden Stagnation in Trade, & such Murmurs among the Manufacturers of Great Britain that the Parliament wou'd not only see but feel the Necessity of immediately repealing the American Revenue Acts." The Americans, he said, had guessed wrong, because an unusual increase in demand from northern Europe made up for the loss of

---

[9] May 18, 1770, *Proceedings and Debates of the British Parliament Respecting North America, 1754–1783*, ed. R. C. Simmons and P. D. G. Thomas (Kraus International, 1983), vol. 3, pp. 334, 337. When Hillsborough took office in 1768, even Grenville did not know "whether the new Secretary of State for the Colonies [Hillsborough] will be reconciled to the ideas of their *dependence* and obedience, agreeably to the letter and intention of the British Acts of Parliament, or whether their independence is to be openly avowed: if the former is determined upon, a firm and temperate conduct must be steadily pursued; if the latter, appearances of resentment against the Americans, which you suspect, will only expose the honour of the King and kingdom to fresh insults and contempt" (George Grenville to Lord Trevor, December 31, 1767, *The Grenville Papers*, ed. William James Smith, London, 1852, vol. 4, p. 206).

American trade.[10] A threefold connection entered into the British-American equation, in which economics and politics were inextricably interwoven.

From a purely economic point of view, the British were faced with the fact that the Townshend duties had backfired. They brought in very little revenue because so few were paying them; they had resulted in a massive loss of trade in America; and they encouraged American manufactures to take the place of British products. Lord North and other British ministers recognized early on that the duties would have to go. They were, as North later put it, "teasing the Americans for a trifle."[11] On May 1, 1769, a first step had been taken by the government with a promise to levy no more taxes on the colonies and to propose the partial repeal of the Townshend duties in the next session of Parliament. These concessions did little to placate the rebellious colonies, which saw them as a sign of British weakness and were actually encouraged to go on with the boycott.

At the end of 1769, the Connecticut agent William Samuel Johnson interpreted the official British position to the new Connecticut governor, Jonathan Trumbull. British ministers were caught between wanting to repeal the Townshend duties because they were "anti-commercial" and fearing to repeal all of them and lose the colonies altogether:

> The apprehension of endangering the supremacy of Parliament, of which they have formed the most exalted ideas, seems to have absorbed all other considerations. They affect to imagine, that, by giving way in any measure to the claims of the Colonies, they should hazard the loss of all their hold of them; that one indulgence would require another, and one relaxation induce still farther concessions, until the Colonies would become totally independent of this country.[12]

Thus giving up the supremacy of Parliament was seen ultimately as equivalent to recognizing American independence. If Parliament surrendered

---

[10] Mason to [George Brent?], December 6, 1770, *The Papers of George Mason,* ed. Robert A. Rutland (University of North Carolina Press, 1970), vol. 1, p. 126.

[11] March 5, 1770, *Proceedings and Debates,* vol. 3, p. 212.

[12] Johnson to Trumbull, December 5, 1769, *Massachusetts Historical Society Collections,* 5th ser., vol. 9, p. 383.

In 1768, Johnson made a tour of France, during which he recorded in his journals: "The People of France give much attention to the Controversy between Britain & her Colonies, & entertain the Idea that tho' the Acquisitions which Britain made in the last war are for the present extremely advantageous to her, yet in the end she will be weakened by them as they imagine there will be a separation between her & her colonies" (George C. Groce, Jr., *William Samuel Johnson,* Columbia University Press, 1937, p. 80).

its power to tax the colonies and to impose duties on them, it virtually relinquished its hold over them. Parliamentary power was equated with British power and took precedence over purely commercial considerations, however important the latter might be.

The British government dithered through the rest of 1769. Nothing was decided until North replaced Grafton as the formal head of the government in January 1770. The North era of British colonial policy had arrived, to last the next twelve years. Not until March was North ready to make good the pledge of the previous May. In effect, he superficially repeated the strategy that had worked in Parliament in the case of the Stamp Act—the equivalent of repealing the tax and passing the Declaratory Act. In these different circumstances, however, North came out for repealing all the Townshend duties with the exception of the one on tea. The exception enabled him to show that the colonies could not have all they wanted, which was total repeal, and that the British government still insisted on its right to impose at least one tax on the colonies. Paradoxically, the East India Company, which had most at stake in the sale of tea, was opposed to the duty and preferred to stay out of the squabble. But North was determined to live up to the spirit of the Declaratory Act by keeping at least one duty, because, he vowed, "upon my word, if we are to run after America, in search of reconciliation in this way [repealing all the duties], I do not know one Act of Parliament will remain."[13] The key vote in Parliament was 204 to 142 against repealing tea, too.[14] The British political establishment was still divided on colonial policy, but the center of gravity had shifted ominously against the colonies.

The way the repeal of four out of five of the Townshend duties was handled testified to the peculiar contradictions that had come over British policy. As Hutchinson later pointed out, "Though the ostensible reason was, that such duties were hurtful to commerce, yet few doubted the real reason to be, a desire to comply with the demands of the colonies, without renouncing a right, which it was not intended further to exercise."[15] If the real reason was to comply with the demands of the colonies, it could not have been accomplished without renouncing the "right" to impose such measures, and it was an odd "real reason" that could never again have a practical application.

The issue was purely symbolic. There was no more practical significance

[13] March 5, 1770, *Proceedings and Debates*, vol. 3, p. 213.
[14] Ibid., p. 228.
[15] Thomas Hutchinson, *The History of the Colony and Province of Massachusetts-Bay*, ed. Lawrence Shaw Mayo (Harvard University Press, 1936), vol. 3, p. 238.

in maintaining the duty on tea than there had been in the case of the other duties. The importance of keeping the duty on tea was simply to show that the British Parliament was still able "to draw a line," as North put it, beyond which it was not willing to make any more concessions.[16] Opposition to the tea duty was also symbolic or, as it was commonly put, a matter of principle. In 1769, Charles Thomson of Philadelphia wrote to Benjamin Franklin: "It is true, the impositions already laid are not very grievous; but if the principle is established, and the authority by which they are laid is admitted, there is no security for what remains."[17]

For this reason, the struggle was sure to go on. North's decision had decided nothing of substance. Tea became a stand-in for maintaining the last shred of British power. The colonies did not rebel against the duty on tea because it was so onerous; they rebelled against it because it was a duty that had come to be viewed as equivalent to a tax. Taxes, no matter on what, were anathema to the Americans under North just as they had been under Grenville.

· 3 ·

The Americans were caught in their own contradictions. They never tired of protesting their eternal fidelity to and affection for the British Crown. They even professed to believe that "Parliament is the supreme legislative power over the whole empire."[18] But they quickly went on to maintain that Parliament had no power if the assemblies did not consent to its legislation. No effort was made to explain how a power could be supreme if another body had the power to override it.

In 1770, this dilemma took a peculiar turn, that was indirectly connected with the Boston Massacre. One result of the incident was that Lieutenant Governor Hutchinson was persuaded that it was safer to hold meetings of the General Court at Harvard College in nearby Cambridge than in Boston. Hutchinson protected himself by saying that he had been ordered by the king—probably more exactly by the king's ministers—to make the change. Every move by Hutchinson was sure to bring protests, but this one had a special ideological interest.

Until now, the colonial theorists had aimed their fire at the House of

[16] March 5, 1770, *Proceedings and Debates*, vol. 3, p. 213.
[17] Thomson to Franklin, November 26, 1769, *Franklin Papers*, vol. 16, p. 238.
[18] This phrase appears in the Massachusetts Assembly's "Circular Letter" of February 11, 1768, *Speeches of the Governors of Massachusetts from 1765 to 1775; and the Answers of the House of Representatives to the Same* (Boston, 1818; reprint, Da Capo Press, 1971), p. 134.

Commons and not at the king. In fact, they had exempted him from their complaints and had often appealed to him to rescue them from parliamentary decisions. When Hutchinson announced the change of venue from Boston to Cambridge, he was duly accused of violating the charter and constitution. He replied archly that "I must consider myself as a servant of the King, to be governed by what appears to me to be his Majesty's pleasure in those things."[19]

That did it. Since Hutchinson had based himself on the pleasure of the king, the assembly found it necessary to deal directly with the king's prerogative or power. It took this stand:

> And as the prerogatives of the Crown, however salutary, when they are exerted for the good of the people, have the most pernicious tendency, when exerted to their prejudice; and such exertions, unchecked, may overthrow the constitution itself; we cannot view the present situation of the General Assembly, in any other light, than as truly alarming. And it is become our indispensable duty, as the guardians of the people's rights, now to make a constitutional stand.[20]

Inevitably, Hutchinson answered back, and the assembly came back at him. As the argument became more heated, the assembly's repudiation of the king's power took on a sharper edge and more strident tone. Another salvo from the assembly deepened the dispute:

> Such is the imperfection of human nature, as to render discretionary power, however necessary, always in a greater or less degree dangerous; and the wickedness of men has very often prompted them to make ill use of it. If it should be admitted that the Governor of this province has still, by law, the power of convening, holding and keeping the General Court in any town, out of Boston, yet the House have as clear a right, by law, to inquire into the exercise of this power, and to judge for themselves, whether it be wisely and beneficially, or imprudently and arbitrarily exercised. And it is their duty, as well as their right, to remonstrate against all undue and oppressive exertions of a legal, as much as against a claim and exercise of an usurped prerogative. There are prerogatives in the Crown, which may be exercised to the destruction of the constitution, and the ruin of the

---

[19] Message, March 21, 1770, ibid., p. 198. Hutchinson reiterated the point on May 31, 1770, pp. 210–11.
[20] Report and Resolutions, June 6, 1770, ibid., p. 214.

people. . . . the democratical branch is, at least, as important to the people and the constitution, as the monarchical or aristocratical; and they have, at least, as clear a right to judge the proper time for them to do their part of the business of the province, as the Governor has to judge of his.[21]

Hutchinson quickly recognized what was at stake. He retorted that "you have explained away all the prerogative, and removed it from the King and his representative, and made yourselves and the people the judges, when it shall be exercised; and, in the present case, have determined that it is not fit it should be exercised."[22]

Still another counterblast, attributed to Sam Adams, raised the temperature of the dispute to the boiling point. It virtually accused Hutchinson of lying about his instructions from the king. It totally denied that the British attorney general and solicitor general "have any authority or jurisdiction over us" or even that "His Majesty in Council, has any constitutional authority to decide such questions, or any controversy whatever, that arises in this province, excepting only such matters as are reserved in the charter." It contended that "the people and their Representatives, have a right to withstand the abusive exercise of a legal and constitutional prerogative of the Crown." If any royal instructions injured the people, they ceased to be binding. The House of Representatives had "the same inherent rights in this province, as the House of Commons has in Great Britain." It was necessary "to prevent the most valuable of our liberties from being wrested from us, by the subtle machinations of wicked Ministers."[23]

At bottom, the question raised by an ostensibly minor dispute over whether to meet in Boston or Cambridge was this: Who was to decide whether the Crown was abusing its prerogative or the people were being injured? The Bostonians now took the position that the decision was always to be made by the colony's representatives. Never before had the Crown been explicitly made subordinate to the colonial assemblies. An American historian, who made a noted study of royal government in America, recognized how far-reaching these declarations were:

Hitherto no one had ventured to deny the right of the king to instruct his governor within the limits of the constitution or to question the

[21] Reasons of the House of Representatives, June 12, 1770, ibid., pp. 218, 222.
[22] Message from Hutchinson, June 15, 1770, ibid., p. 227.
[23] Message of House of Representatives to Lieutenant Governor Hutchinson, August 1, 1770, ibid., pp. 240–48. It is published in Writings of Samuel Adams but dated August 3, 1770, vol. 2, pp. 19–35. There are some differences in the wording of the two versions.

governor's duty to obey such instructions. But Adams dared to enter upon this forbidden ground. Instructions which were injurious to the people were not binding, he said, adding, in effect, that it made no difference whether such orders were legal and constitutional or not. Therefore the governor must not be permitted to obey them. From this position the conclusion seems inescapable, although Adams avoided its frank declaration, that the assembly and not the governor must be the interpreters of such documents and the judges of whether or not they constituted an "abusive exercise" of the prerogative. To have permitted such a privilege to the assembly would have meant that the British government had abandoned its fundamental claim to authority in America and had delegated to the assembly the sole right of controlling the provincial executive. No more sweeping challenge than this was made to the system of royal government in the provinces before the actual expulsion of the governors upon the outbreak of the Revolution. And so, though the meeting-place of the assembly was not in itself a vital point in the colonial system, it gave rise to controversies which went to the heart of the provincial constitution.[24]

Adams did not make these claims for himself alone. He wrote the words, but they were sent in the name of the House of Representatives. And Adams was not the only one who was thinking along these lines. Another was Benjamin Franklin.

· 4 ·

The idea of differentiating between "within the realm" and outside of it—the realm being Great Britain itself—had implicitly taken shape in Franklin's mind years before. It made a definite appearance in his examination before the parliamentary committee in 1766. Franklin was asked to explain the right of Parliament to levy money for the Crown. He had already answered this question back in 1754, in his letter to Governor Shirley. He now restated his position with a corollary about the geographic limits of parliamentary power:

They [colonists] understand that clause to relate to subjects only within the realm; that no money can be levied on them for the Crown,

[24] Leonard W. Labaree, *Royal Government in America* (Yale University Press, 1930), pp. 198–99.

but by consent of parliament. The Colonies are not supposed to be within the realm; they have assemblies of their own, which are their parliaments, and they are in that respect, in the same situation as Ireland. When money is to be raised for the Crown upon the subject in Ireland, or in the Colonies, the consent is given in the parliament of Ireland, or in the assemblies of the Colonies. They think the parliament of Great-Britain cannot properly give that consent till it has representatives from America; for the petition of right expressly says, it is to be by common consent in parliament; and the people of America have no representatives in parliament, to make a part of that common consent.

This answer contains the idea of parliamentary authority "only within the realm." If the realm did not include the colonies, parliamentary authority did not reach that far. But this delimitation had been expressed in the context of the stamp tax, which was the subject of the examination. By the time Franklin came to the end of his exposition, he reverted to the idea that all could be made right if the colonies were represented in Parliament. Nevertheless, the distinction between parliamentary authority within and outside the "realm" contained the seeds of a doctrine that denied Parliament the authority to legislate for the colonies.

In January 1768, Franklin alluded to the same problem but in a different context. He saw fit to reply to an article in a British magazine which had attacked the Boston nonimportation resolutions. The writer assailed the resolutions on the ground that they were aimed at ruining British trade as well as spreading "vain pernicious ideas of independance and separate dominion."

Franklin took the position that the British king and Parliament were able to legislate for Great Britain and its contiguous islands but not for the "provinces of America, which lie at a great distance." He explained:

But not withstanding this state of separate assemblies, the allegiance of the distant provinces to the crown will remain for ever unshaken, while they enjoy the rights of Englishmen; that is, with the consent of their sovereign, the right of legislation each for themselves; for this puts them on an exact level, in this respect, with their fellow subjects in the old provinces, and better than this they could not be by any change in their power. But if the old provinces should often exercise the right of making laws for the new, they would probably grow as restless as the Corsicans, when they perceived they were no longer fellow subjects, but the subjects of subjects.

As Franklin showed by pursuing the subject, he was still thinking in terms of consent doctrine:

> Upon the whole, the point in dispute does not depend on *gratitude* or *defence,* but on the right of Englishmen to give their own money with their own consent. While the Americans were in possession of that right, or thought themselves in possession of it, every requisition for that purpose by the king, or his ministers was chearfully complyed with; but since that right, by the mistaken *policy of one man* [Grenville], has been brought in question; murmuring and discontent have succeeded, and every artifice is now practiced to withhold sums levied *by a new mode;* which had they been demanded in the *old way,* would have been willingly granted.[25]

Here again, Franklin was struggling with a thought that needed more elaboration to be fully satisfying. He still based his thought on "the rights of Englishmen," not of separated Americans. Yet he gave the colonies the right to legislate for themselves, on the "exact level" of British subjects in the "old provinces," but only with "the consent of their sovereign." He was still primarily concerned with the principle of giving "their own money with their own consent." The *"old way"* was still the right way, as if this were what the colonies wanted and not a new way to govern themselves. In any case, the colonies had hardly "chearfully complyed with" every British requisition.

The next stage of Franklin's thinking is known from a peculiar source— his comments written in the margins of pamphlets he was reading.

Towards the end of 1769 or the beginning of 1770, on one such page he wrote: "The King only is sovereign in both Countries." Another page moved him to comment that "All this Argument of the Interest of Britain and the Colonies being *the same* is fallacious and unsatisfactory." In the margins of another pamphlet, he asserted: "The British State is only the Island of G. Britain. The British Legislature are undoubtedly the only proper Judges of what concerns the Welfare of that State; . . . and the American Legislatures of what concerns the American States respectively." In a third pamphlet, he held forth: "It is doubted whether any Act of Parliament should *of right* operate in the Colonies: *in fact* [however] several of them have and do operate." In response to an assertion that statutes and customs based on the special and local circumstances of "the Realm" did not apply to the colonies, where the circumstances differed, Franklin would have no such

[25] This article appeared in *The Gentleman's Magazine* in January 1768, signed by "S.N." It has been assigned to Franklin in *Franklin Papers,* vol. 15, pp. 36–38.

distinction: "These Laws have no Force in America; not merely because local circumstances differ; but because they have never been adopted, or brought over by Acts of Assembly or by Practice in the Courts." Another sharpened the significance of being out of or "within the Realm":

> When an American says that he has a Right to all the Privileges of a British Subject, he is an American Subject of the King; the Charters say they shall be entitled to all the Privileges of Englishmen as if *they had been* born *within* the Realm. But they were and are *without* the Realm, therefore not British Subjects; and tho' within the King's Dominions, because they voluntarily agreed to be his Subjects when they took his Charters, and have created those Dominions for him, yet they are not within the Dominion of Parliament which has no Authority, but *within* the Realm.

When the author said that the colonists were "faithful *subjects of Great Britain,*" Franklin protested: "They are Subjects of the King." In an allusion to the Mother Country, he retorted: "They us'd to call her by that endearing Appellation; but her late Conduct entitles rather to the Name of *Stepmother.*"[26]

We have here the equivalent of Franklin's musing to himself. Yet the remarks came out of his growing conviction that it was necessary to sever Parliament's link to the colonies and leave nothing more of the connection than an intangible loyalty to the king. The idea of "the realm" and what was in it and out of it cut the traditional British sovereignty in two, with nothing more to replace it than a vague association between the king and the colonial assemblies. After the Glorious Revolution and the laborious process of establishing parliamentary supremacy over the better part of a century, the new colonial theory was not likely to be persuasive in "the realm."

It took some time for Franklin to get news of the Boston Massacre, and then he learned about it from the highly biased pamphlet *A Short Narrative of the Horrid Massacre in Boston.* On June 8, 1770, just when Sam Adams was engaging in his extended dispute with Thomas Hutchinson, Franklin gave his reaction to the Boston incident to a Boston minister, Samuel Cooper. In this letter, Franklin went far afield and made Cooper privy to his latest thoughts on the British-American relationship. His ruminations are so telling that they are worth citing at some length:

> That the Colonies originally were constituted distinct States, and intended to be continued such, is clear to me from a thorough

[26] These marginal notes appear in *Franklin Papers,* vol. 16, pp. 278–326.

Consideration of their original Charters, and the whole Conduct of the Crown and Nation towards them until the Restoration. Since that Period, the Parliament here has usurp'd an Authority of making Laws for them, which before it had not. We have for some time submitted to that Usurpation, partly thro' Ignorance and Inattention, and partly from our Weakness and Inability to contend.

I hope when our Rights are better understood here, we shall, by a prudent and proper Conduct be able to obtain from the Equity of this Nation a Restoration of them. And in the mean time I could wish that such Expressions as, *The supreme Authority of Parliament; the Subordinacy of our Assemblies to the Parliament* and the like (which in Reality mean nothing if our Assemblies with the King have a true Legislative Authority) I say, I could wish that such Expressions were no more seen in our publick Pieces. They are too strong for Compliment, and tend to confirm a Claim [of] Subjects in one Part of the King's Dominions to be Sovereigns over their Fellow-Subjects in another Part of his Dominions; when [in] truth they have no such Right, and their Claim is founded only on Usurpation, the several States having equal Rights and Liberties, and being only connected, as England and Scotland were before the Union, by having one common Sovereign, the King.

Franklin went on to explain his conception of a new relationship in more detail:

This kind of Doctrine the Lords and Commons here would deem little less than Treason against what they think their Share of the Sovereignty over the Colonies. To me those Bodies seem to have been long encroaching on the Rights of their and our Sovereign, assuming too much of his Authority, and betraying his Interests.

By our Constitution he is, with [his] Plantation Parliaments, the sole Legislator of his American Subjects, and in that Capacity is and ought to be free to exercise his own Judgment unrestrain'd and unlimited by his Parliament here. And our Parliaments have Right to grant him Aids without the Consent of this Parliament, a Circumstance which, by the [way] begins to give it some Jealousy. Let us therefore hold fast [our] Loyalty to our King (who has the best Disposition toward us, and has a Family-Interest in our Prosperity) as that steady Loyalty is the most probable Means of securing us from the arbitrary Power of a corrupt Parliament, that does not like us, and conceives itself to have an Interest in keeping us down and fleecing us.

If they should urge the *Inconvenience* of an Empire's being divided into so many separate States, and from thence conclude that we are not so divided; I would answer, that an Inconvenience proves nothing but itself. England and Scotland were once separate States, under the same King. The Inconvenience found in their being separate States, did not prove that the Parliament of England had a Right to govern Scotland. A formal Union was thought necessary, and England was an hundred Years soliciting it, before she could bring it about. If Great Britain now thinks such an Union necessary with us, let her propose her Terms, and we may consider of them.[27]

Franklin's present doctrine differed from Adams's. Franklin made Parliament the enemy, Adams both Parliament and the Crown. Adams looked forward to complete colonial self-rule, Franklin to a partnership between the king and the colonial assemblies at the expense of Parliament. By implication, Franklin thought of limiting the power of Parliament to Great Britain alone and stripping it of all power in the colonies, where, in his view, Parliament had usurped power. Franklin could not yet contemplate breaking away from the British connection and desperately sought to keep the old tie by means of the Crown alone.[28] If he had not been so anxious to use any stick with which to beat Parliament, he could be taken here to be an ultra-Tory, devoted to the king more than to anything else in the British

[27] Franklin to Cooper, June 8, 1770, *Franklin Papers*, vol. 17, pp. 162–64.

This letter was too much for the American editors, who pointed out: "Ever since the Glorious Revolution and the Act of Union the course of constitutional development had increasingly emphasized the sovereignty of the crown in Parliament. Any sphere of royal influence outside the purview of Parliament was suspect, as appeared soon afterward in the controversies over reforming the government of India." It was also false to say, as Franklin did, that England had solicited union with Scotland for more than a century (see nn. 5 and 6, pp. 163–64).

I have added paragraph breaks to the original, which had only a single paragraph.

[28] One interpretation has been that Franklin did not take the tie to the king very seriously. "For Franklin, the king was only a symbolic link between England and America. Such a bond could easily be broken if necessary" (Cecil B. Currey, *Road to Revolution: Benjamin Franklin in England, 1765–1775* [Anchor Books, 1968], p. 176). Yet Franklin had written in 1769, only the year before: "I hope nothing that has happened or may happen will diminish in the least our Loyalty to our Sovereign, or Affection for this Nation in general. I can scarcely conceive a King of better Dispositions, of more exemplary Virtues, or more truly desirous of promoting the Welfare of all his Subjects" (Franklin to Samuel Cooper, April 27, 1769, *Franklin Papers*, vol. 16, p. 118). This was not written for publication but to a minister in Boston. This letter goes on to contrast the king with Parliament to the latter's disadvantage. I am inclined to think that Franklin clutched on to the Crown in a desperate effort to find a British link other than Parliament and because he had a genuine affection for Great Britain, whatever its shortcomings. Currey goes on even more dubiously: "Franklin was thus, by 1765 or early 1766, the foremost American exponent of separatism" (p. 178). Franklin needed more years to get to "separatism." Verner W. Crane is more trustworthy: "Pragmatically, Franklin was willing that the empire should be saved on any tolerable terms" (*Benjamin Franklin and a Rising People* [Little, Brown, 1954], p. 131).

system. The idea of concocting a new legislative authority out of the king
and assemblies was a will-o'-the-wisp in the eighteenth century, however
much it may have anticipated the later development of the British empire
in decline.[29]

The real interest in Franklin's scheme is its effort to find a way to make
the American colonies into "distinct States" that did not have to obey
Parliament.[30] To this extent, Franklin was trying to do the same thing
as Adams at approximately the same time. Yet Franklin's inability to go
the whole way in 1770 indicates why the Revolution was delayed for five
more years. Many more colonists, however fed up with British rule, were
not ready to go so far. Adams and his Boston cohort were out in front, but
even they did not go far enough to make a revolution.

It is fascinating to watch minds like Franklin's and Adams's struggling
again and again with the problem of the colonial connection with Great
Britain. It was as if the colonists could not work up the determination to
separate themselves from Great Britain until they had convinced themselves
that they had the right to do so, all the while thinking in traditional British
terms of reference. This inhibition against departing from familiar ground
rules made it difficult for Franklin and others in this period to strike out
into uncharted territory. They felt it necessary to go back to the founding
of the colonies for arguments, a procedure which gave their disputations a
somewhat archaic character. As in other revolutions, they had to go one
step back in order to go two steps forward.

· 5 ·

There was another Boston. It was typified at the highest level by Thomas
Hutchinson. For a long time, he was one of the most vilified characters in
the story of the American Revolution. George Bancroft gave him credit for
being "complaisant, cultivated, and truly intelligent," only to turn on him

[29] Later, Lord Mansfield, the main legal authority and a hard-line advocate, described the
colonial preference for the king: "They would allow the King of Great Britain a nominal
sovereignty over them, but nothing else. They would throw off the dependency on the crown
of Great Britain, but not on the person of the King, whom they would render a cypher"
(*Proceedings and Debates*, November 15, 1775, vol. 6, p. 254).

[30] The closest I have been able to come to an earlier claim that the colonies were "distinct states"
appears in Richard Bland's *An Inquiry into the Rights of the British Colonies* (Williamsburg,
1766). But Bland referred to the first colonists, who were "respected as a distinct State,
independent, as to their *internal* Government, of the original Kingdom, but united with her,
as to their *external* Polity, in the closest and most intimate LEAGUE AND AMITY, under
the same Allegiance, and enjoying the Benefits of a reciprocal Intercourse" (p. 20). He did
not carry this term forward to the conditions prevailing in his own time.

as one who "did not scruple to conceal truth, to equivocate, and to deceive," whose "sordid nature led him to worship power" and who "excelled in the art of dissimulation."[31] Bancroft was only following the example set by John Adams and other colonial figures, who detested Hutchinson. More recently Hutchinson's reputation has been rescued with compassion and fairness by a distinguished American historian, Bernard Bailyn.[32]

Hutchinson's background was as authentically American as that of any of those who came to hate him. There had been Hutchinsons as long as there was a Massachusetts Bay colony. One of his forebears was Anne Hutchinson, the early-seventeenth-century heroine of the antinomian controversy. Most Hutchinsons had been merchants. Col. Thomas Hutchinson, the father, was another well-to-do merchant who had made it into the colony's council. Thomas, the son, was born in 1711 and, unlike the other Hutchinsons, made his way into politics at the early age of twenty-six. He served in both houses of the legislature until he was appointed lieutenant governor in 1758 and chief justice in 1760. If he had been judged before 1760, he would have received high marks.

Hutchinson had not been an uncritical servant of the traditional British system. He showed his independence in 1754, when he cooperated with Franklin in the Plan of Union at the Albany Conference. But to get ahead he increasingly became enmeshed in colonial politics; in the 1760s he had to choose between the established order and its critics. His position as chief justice led him to take sides against James Otis and Oxenbridge Thacher in the writs of assistance case in 1761. It did not help that Otis had a personal grievance against him for having taken the office that had been previously promised to his father. Otis was a ferocious enemy and made Hutchinson his favorite victim.

The Stamp Act was Hutchinson's undoing. Yet he had opposed it and had written an essay and letters against it. His essay, composed in 1764, gave all the standard arguments against the tax—the colonies had long taxed themselves by their own representatives in the assemblies; Americans were not represented in Parliament; the act was economically harmful to both sides. He even rejected the idea of virtual representation. There was little difference between his views and Otis's, even to their agreement that, whatever the rights and wrongs of the issue, Parliament was supreme. Hutchinson's chief sin at this time was to tone down a petition to Parliament protesting the tax.

Yet so despised and reviled had Hutchinson become that no other house

[31] George Bancroft, *History of the United States* (Little, Brown, 1852), vol. 4, pp. 27–28.
[32] Bernard Bailyn, *The Ordeal of Thomas Hutchinson* (Harvard University Press, 1974).

in Boston was so much the target of attack as his in the riots of August 1765. Why was he singled out? Two American historians have given this answer:

> Hutchinson would certainly have been justified in thinking that he deserved better at the hands of Massachusetts. And yet in a perverse way the mob had been right. Mobs never act reasonably, for they would not be mobs if they did. The mob which destroyed Hutchinson's house was right in attacking him, because he was a man of strength: the people of Massachusetts had sensed a showdown was near and that when it came, the strength of Thomas Hutchinson would be against them. Whatever his feelings about the expediency or constitutionality of the Stamp Act, he would be found defending law and order. When the barricades were up, Thomas Hutchinson would be on the other side. And in the summer of 1765 it looked as though the barricades were going up. It was his prudence, his moderation, his fundamental conservatism that made Hutchinson an enemy of the people in 1765, because the time for prudence had suddenly passed. The face of revolution had appeared; he who was not a friend was an enemy; and Hutchinson was an enemy not to be dealt with lightly.[33]

For his part, Hutchinson was mystified by what had hit him. In 1764, he reasoned, no one would have disobeyed Parliament. A year later, a furor had gripped the populace and made it do the unthinkable. Hutchinson attributed the transformation to demagogues and opportunists acting for their own profit and advancement. For one of his intelligence and experience to think so suggests how difficult it must have been for others to digest the almost incredible transformation. It does seem, however, that Boston had an extraordinary group of prerevolutionary propagandists without whom events could not have moved so quickly. By 1766, Hutchinson saw the colonies approaching "very near to independence."[34]

The interesting debate was not between those who wanted change and those who did not. It was between those who wanted a revolutionary change and those who wanted to reform the existing system to prevent a revolution. Hutchinson was one of the latter, and this is what got him into trouble. When he woke up to the seriousness of the crisis in 1766, he started from the premise that the American colonies could not survive alone. Professor Bailyn has given this summary of his position:

---

[33] Edmund S. Morgan and Helen M. Morgan, *The Stamp Act Crisis* (University of North Carolina Press, 1953), p. 215.

[34] Bailyn, *Ordeal of Thomas Hutchinson*, p. 74.

Everything flowed from one simple but inescapable and undeniable fact: the American colonies were too weak to survive independently in a world of rival nation-states. Perhaps in a hundred years the colonies would be strong enough to maintain their independence, though he was glad he was "not like to live to see that time." But since they could not now strike out for themselves, they must seek protection from some power, and they did so from England, the freest state in the world. As a consequence of this necessary dependence, compounded by the colonists' remoteness, certain privileges enjoyed by Englishmen could not be held by them. It was simply a matter, he wrote in letter after letter in this period, of what was and what was not possible, not of what was theoretically good or bad.[35]

But, Hutchinson believed, dependence did not mean oppression. On the contrary, he told a correspondent in 1769, the colonies should be freed from taxes and indulged in every possible way. To achieve this balance, Hutchinson rejected structural change, such as combining colonies to make fewer and larger ones. He put his faith rather in a more permissive, responsive, flexible adaptation of the existing system. In 1770, he recommended a policy which would

> bear with their disorderly behavior until they have distressed themselves so as to bear their distresses no longer. Encourage the animosities already begun between the colonies, and distinguish one colony from another by favor for good behavior and frowns for the contrary. Lay aside taxation, not upon the principle that it is to be distinguished from legislation in general but because it is inexpedient. Keep up every other part of legislation and familiarize every colony to acts of Parliament. This may in time bring the colonies to their old state.[36]

Their old state—this was Hutchinson's real goal; it was what made him a political ogre to the embattled American radicals. He was wrong in his insistence that America could not subsist without British protection. He blamed each side for provoking the other but reserved most of his anguish for the British. In the end, Hutchinson made a last-ditch case for a status quo that was rooted in the past, while the other side was looking forward to a different future. No matter how much he regretted what Great Britain had done to deserve its American crisis, he could only think

35 Ibid., p. 91.
36 Ibid., p. 95.

as far as a change of policy, while the situation demanded a recognition that a new nation was striving to come into being. He could not permit himself to accept that prospect, because it meant giving up his identity as an Englishman, an identity which Franklin, in another way, was also holding on to desperately—but was able to shed bit by bit as events foreclosed a return to the past.

After serving about six months as lieutenant governor, Hutchinson was appointed governor in March 1770. He took on the governorship knowing full well that it would bring him even more woe: "In Boston they say nothing to my charge but my bad principles of government."[37] At this very time he embroiled himself in the change of venue from Boston to Cambridge. Why did Hutchinson persevere? His most recent and most sympathetic biographer thinks that he could not resist "influence, authority, profit, and position" or "gauge the grip of the evolving revolutionary ideology on the minds of his fellow New Englanders and hence the dimensions of the problem he faced."[38] His desire for influence, profit, and position did not set him apart; it was his political allegiance to British authority that made him a defeated, tragic figure. From 1766 on, he was fighting a rearguard action, knew it, yet carried on. The Hutchinsons in the struggle for power made it a civil as well as an anti-imperial war. They had too much to lose to have persisted for so long without a genuine residue of loyalty and conviction.

[37] James K. Hosmer, *The Life of Thomas Hutchinson* (Houghton Mifflin, 1896), p. 204.
[38] Bailyn, *Ordeal of Thomas Hutchinson*, pp. 141–42. But also that his deepest instincts were "acquisitiveness, public concern, prudence, honesty, and a deferential acceptance of constituted authority," a list that is somewhat less derogatory (p. 151).

16

"If this be not a Tyranny"

✣

· 1 ·

T HE NEXT STAGE IN THE struggle for power was a curious inversion
of the old disputes about governors' salaries. The colonists, who did not
often want to part with their money, were now determined to pay the
salaries of governors and judges. The British, who had long tried to rule
the colonies on the cheap by making the colonists support their officials,
reversed themselves and decided to gain control of the salaries—but still
without spending their own money, if they could help it.

So long as governors and judges owed their salaries to colonial assemblies,
they were open to monetary pressures that made them responsive to the
assemblies rather than to their superiors in London. Governors who
officially took their orders from the Crown had in fact acted as intermedi-
aries between their British taskmasters and their American paymasters. The
reality of the system was very different from its formal arrangements.

It had long been a British aim to liberate the governors and other
appointed officials from this colonial constraint. As early as 1754, Charles
Townshend had drawn attention to the assemblies' annual bills of supply,
"in which they have appointed all the officers of the Crown by name to be
employed in the Exchequer, substituted warrants for drawing out public
money in the place of the Governor's, and in one word dispossessed the
Crown of almost every degree of executive power ever lodged in it."[1] In

---

[1] Lewis Namier and John Brooke, *Charles Townshend* (St. Martin's Press, 1964), p. 40.

1768, Gov. Francis Bernard pleaded to be paid from an official "civil list" that guaranteed incomes, as was the case in Great Britain. "In this Province particularly," he wrote to Lord Barrington, "the Want of Pay for proper Officers will be found among the cheif Causes of the Imbecillity of Government." Trade officials in the colonies were paid with British funds and, therefore, carried out their orders. "But in all other Departments of civil Policy the Service of the Crown will be defeated," he went on, "for it cannot be expected that Officers should act in Opposition to the Humours of the People on the Behalf of the Crown, when they are left by the Crown to the People for scanty & precarious Salaries."[2]

Thanks to the Townshend duties, the British were able at long last to make inroads on this system. In Massachusetts, the duties enabled the British Treasury to pay all the top officials, including the governor. In New York, the attorney general was similarly paid in 1768, the governor in 1770, and the chief justice in 1772.[3] In New Jersey, the chief justice was paid by the Treasury by 1771.[4] With enough time, the British were going to put all the colonial governors and officials on the British payroll.

The tea duty provided most of the money for these salaries, and all of it after the other Townshend duties were rescinded. Despite all the smuggling, the tea duty brought in enough to begin to change the character of the imperial system, most of all in Massachusetts. Duty was paid on 786,000 pounds in 1768, the first full year of the tea tax, and 151,842 pounds in 1772, a steep drop as a result of the nonimportation movement but still a substantial figure.[5] One Philadelphia merchant estimated the American consumption of tea at nearly 6 million pounds a year.[6] In effect, the duty forced the colonists, primarily in Massachusetts, to pay for some part of the British colonial establishment but in a way that evaded their control, since the duty went into the British Treasury before disbursement.

This transfer of power over the governors and judges in Massachusetts did not escape the watchful eye of Sam Adams. In April 1771, he said that he had long suspected that "a Design has been on foot to render ineffectual the Democratical part of this Government." The design, he now saw, was being carried out

[2] Bernard to Barrington, October 20, 1768, *The Barrington-Bernard Correspondence*, ed. Edward Channing and Archibald Cary Coolidge (Harvard University Press, 1912), pp. 178–79.

[3] Peter D. G. Thomas, *The Townshend Duties Crisis* (Oxford University Press, 1987), pp. 245–46.

[4] Larry R. Gerlach, *Prologue to Independence* (Rutgers University Press, 1976), p. 172.

[5] Oliver M. Dickerson, *The Navigation Acts and the American Revolution* (University of Pennsylvania Press, 1951), p. 99 n. 79.

[6] Benjamin Woods Labaree, *The Boston Tea Party* (Oxford University Press, 1964), p. 74.

by making the Governor altogether independent of the People for his Support; this is depriving the House of Representatives of the only Check they have upon him & must consequently render them the Objects of the Contempt of a Corrupt Administration. Thus the peoples Money being first taken from them without their Consent, is appropriated for the Maintenance of a Governor at the Discretion of *one in the Kingdom* of Great Britain upon whom he absolutely depends for his Support. If this be not a Tyranny I am at a Loss to conceive what a Tyranny is.7

Who was to pay the governor was thus transformed into who was to control the governor. The colonists wanted to pay the governor directly in order to control him, instead of paying for him indirectly through the tea duty.

From 1770 to 1772, Adams stormed against "a *Governor independent* of the free grants of the assembly."8 He broadened the issue by demanding "what weight remains in the scale of the *democratick* part of the constitution to check the *monarchick* in the hands of the governor, if the king has not only an uncontroulable power to nominate and appoint a governor, but may pay him too?"9 Finally, on October 5, 1772, Adams thought the time ripe for action. He outdid himself in his call for another wave of resistance:

> To what a State of Infamy, Wretchedness and Misery shall we be reduc'd if our Judges shall be prevail'd upon to be thus degraded to *Hirelings,* and the *Body of the People* shall suffer their free Constitution to be overturn'd and ruin'd. Merciful God! Inspire Thy People with Wisdom and Fortitude, and direct them to gracious Ends. In this extreme Distress, when the Plan of Slavery seems nearly compleated, O save our Country from impending Ruin— Let not the iron Hand of Tyranny ravish our Laws and seize the Badge of Freedom, nor avow'd Corruption and the murderous Rage of lawless Power be ever seen on the sacred Seat of Justice!

After this passage, Adams appealed to everyone in Massachusetts to "consider what is best to be done": "Let us converse together upon this most interesting Subject and open our minds freely to each other. Let it be

7 Adams to Arthur Lee, April 19, 1771, *The Writings of Samuel Adams,* ed. Harry Alonzo Cushing (G. P. Putnam's Sons, 1906), vol. 2, pp. 164–66.

8 Article signed "Candidus," *Boston Gazette,* October 7, 1771, reprinted in *Writings of Samuel Adams,* vol. 2, p. 247.

9 Article signed "Cotton Mather," *Boston Gazette,* November 25, 1771, reprinted in *Writings of Samuel Adams,* vol. 2, p. 278.

the topic of conversation in every social Club. Let every Town assemble. Let Associations & Combinations be everywhere set up to consult and recover our just Rights."[10]

A town meeting was held in Boston on October 28, 1772, for just this purpose. Adams was not content with mere talk. He was ready with a plan for organizing "committees of correspondence" throughout the colonies to act in concert against the British "Plan of Slavery." A Boston Committee of Correspondence was appointed on November 2. It was such a far-reaching step that some of Adams's old allies, most notably John Hancock, who had been wavering for some time, refused to go along with it. Hancock had evidently resented being taken for granted by Adams or not having been given enough recognition; he now showed his independence by declining to serve on the committee. The breach was later healed, but it reveals that there were differences within the opposition camp.[11]

The conflict over paying the official salaries came to a head in 1773. It was rumored that the British government intended to pay the salaries from the customs duties. At the opening of the 1773 term, the General Court made Crown salaries for judges the focal point of its assault; it warned Governor Hutchinson that "the people without doors are universally alarmed" about the threat. Hutchinson maintained that the North ministry had given orders that the justices should be paid from customs receipts. The House of Representatives replied: "We conceive that no Judge who had a due regard to Justice, or even to his own Character, would chuse to be placed under such an undue bias as they must be under, in the Opinion of the House, by accepting of and becoming dependent for their Salaries upon their Crown." The House decided to grant £300 to Chief Justice Oliver for a year's service already passed, and £200 to the associate justices for the same term. Oliver and the three associate justices used only half the grant. The General Court warned that, should the justices accept a Crown salary instead of the assembly grant, they would violate "the most important Clause in the Charter," by which the assembly was allegedly empowered to pay for services of government. On February 14, 1774, the General Court voted to impeach Oliver as "an enemy" to the "constitution." Hutchinson took the position that he could not try the chief justice and ended by proroguing the General Court.[12]

Meanwhile, committees of correspondence spread quickly, first through

[10] Article signed "Valerius Poplicola," *Boston Gazette*, October 5, 1772, reprinted in *Writings of Samuel Adams*, vol. 2, pp. 332–37.

[11] Herbert S. Allan, *John Hancock* (Macmillan, 1948), pp. 130–32.

[12] Peter Charles Hoffer and N. E. H. Paul, *Impeachment in America* (Yale University Press, 1984), pp. 50–55.

the Massachusetts towns, then from colony to colony. By February 1774, all the colonies except North Carolina and Pennsylvania had named committees. It did little good for Governor Hutchinson to disapprove of the committees; he was told that it was not "unreasonable" for the colonists to correspond with one another, since the governor and other Crown officials corresponded with British ministers, as if the committees were on the same plane as the British government. Hutchinson at first underestimated the importance of the committees—"a foolish scheme that they must necessarily make themselves ridiculous," he wrote.[13] Later he changed his mind: "This was too serious an affair to be treated ludicrously, and it soon after appeared to be sporting with firebrands, arrows, and death."[14]

The committees of correspondence transformed the struggle for power from agitation to organization. They were a radical innovation in the colonial struggle, extralegal if not illegal. They represented the prototype of a dual power outside the regular official channels. Governors could—and did—dismiss or refuse to convene councils and assemblies, but they had no authority over committees of correspondence, which, in effect, existed outside the British imperial system. They again belied the old British assumption that the colonies were not to be feared because they were so diverse that they could not act together. From 1773 on, the colonies were prepared to meet any British threat with organized, collective opposition.

· 2 ·

Colonial ideology kept pace with colonial organization. The original resistance to the Stamp Act had objected to an act of Parliament, not to the authority of Parliament to act. Colonial ideology now progressed from the first proposition to the second.

That the fault was with Parliament, not merely with Parliament's acts, had occurred to the ever-fertile brain of Benjamin Franklin as early as 1771. Hutchinson later accused Franklin of having been the source of the Boston radicals' ideas and actions—"their great director in England, whose counsels they obeyed, and in whose wisdom and dexterity they had an implicit faith."[15] Whether or not the Bostonians needed to be

[13] Hutchinson to Pownall, November 10, 1772, *Proceedings of Massachusetts Historical Society*, vol. 19 (1881–82), p. 140.
[14] Thomas Hutchinson, *The History of the Colony and Province of Massachusetts-Bay*, ed. Lawrence Shaw Mayo (Harvard University Press, 1936), vol. 3, p. 286.
[15] Ibid., p. 262.

directed from abroad, Franklin as agent for Massachusetts gave them some inspiration in 1771.

In February, in a letter to Thomas Cushing, Speaker of the House of Representatives, Franklin expressed the view that the colonies should be "considered in the light of *distinct states,* as I conceive they really are."[16] This term, *distinct states,* was something new, though Franklin did not spell out what implications it had for him.

As the weeks went by, Franklin seemed to become increasingly pessimistic about the chances for a peaceful British settlement with the colonies, though he still devoutly hoped for it to be possible. In May 1771, he wrote to the Boston committee of Thomas Cushing, James Otis, and Samuel Adams: "I think one may clearly see, in the system of customs to be exacted in America by act of Parliament, the seeds sown of a total disunion of the two countries, though, as yet, that event may be at a considerable distance." He could also see how "the British nation and government will become odious, and subjection to it will be deemed no longer tolerable; war ensues, and the bloody struggle will end in absolute slavery in America, or ruin to Britain by the loss of her colonies; the latter most probable, from America's growing strength and magnitude." Hoping against hope, he ended on this ominous note: "I do not pretend to the gift of prophecy. History shows, that, by these steps, great empires have crumbled heretofore; and the late transactions we have so much to complain of show, that we are in the same train, and that, without a greater share of prudence and wisdom, than we have seen both sides to be possessed of, we shall probably come to the same conclusion."[17]

In June, in a letter to Thomas Cushing, Franklin struggled to clarify his thoughts on what was wrong in the relationship with Great Britain. As usual, he looked both ways. He was sure that the British had given up getting any considerable revenue from the colonies and would never try it again. But he was worried about a loss of British prestige, as foreign powers saw the British show weakness in the face of colonial demands. Further on, Franklin dealt in a new way with the authority of Parliament:

And in this View, whether it will not be better gradually to wear off the assum'd Authority of Parliament over America, which we have in too many Instances given countenance to, with our indiscrete

[16] Franklin to Cushing, February 5, 1771, *The Papers of Benjamin Franklin,* ed. Leonard W. Labaree (Yale University Press, 1961), vol. 18, p. 28.
[17] Franklin to the Massachusetts House of Representatives, May 15, 1771, ibid., pp. 102–4.

Acknowledgement of it in Publick Acts, than by a general open
Denial and Resistance to it, bring on prematurely a Contest, to
which, if we are not found equal, that Authority will by the Event
be more strongly establish'd; and if we should prove superior, yet
by the Division the general Strength of the British Nation must be
greatly diminished. ... In the mean time, while we are declining
the usurped Authority of Parliament, I wish to see a steady dutiful
Attachment to the King and his Family maintained among us. ...
My Opinion has long been that Parliament had originally no Right to
bind us by any kind of Law whatever without our Consent. We have
indeed in a manner consented to some of them, at least tacitly: But
for the future methinks we should be cautious how we add to those
Instances, and never adopt or acknowledge an Act of Parliament but
by a formal Law of our own.[18]

Here Franklin had arrived at the idea of denying that Parliament had
any authority over the colonies, though he admitted it was something new.
He regretted that the "usurpation" had not been caught earlier and advised
adopting a policy of gradualism to undo the damage. He saw that a head-on
collision might backfire if the colonies were not yet strong enough to prevail.
He did not want to weaken Great Britain or loyalty to the king, and he did
not want to give up the goal of breaking the link between Parliament and
the colonies, but he did not quite know how to make the two compatible.
He fell back on a strategy of caution, which was easier for him to propose
in London than to carry out in Boston. Yet the essential point was the denial
that Parliament had any right to make laws for the colonies.

Cushing undoubtedly showed Franklin's letter to his closest colleagues,
one of whom soon questioned—in his own way—Parliament's authority
to make laws for the colonies. In October 1771, Sam Adams published
an article in which he expounded the same idea and embellished it with
some revolutionary mythology, which had been lacking in Franklin's letter.
Adams first contended that the early colonists had made a "compact" with
the king of England, in which they had agreed to "become his voluntary
subjects, not his slaves." But, Adams asked, "did they enter into an express
promise to be subject to the controul of the parent state? What is there
to show that they were in any way bound to obey the acts of the British
parliament, but those very acts themselves?" Since the first colonists had
not consented to obey the laws of Parliament, their successors were not
required to do so. Adams warmed to his argument:

[18] Franklin to Cushing, June 10, 1771, ibid., p. 123.

No body can have a power to make laws over a free people, but by their own consent, and by authority receiv'd from them: It follows then, either that the people of this province have consented & given authority to the parent state to make laws over them, or that she has no such authority. No one I believe will pretend that the parent state receives any authority from the people of this province to make laws for them, or that they have ever consented she should. If the people of this province are a part of the body politick of Great Britain, they have as such a right to be consulted in the making of all acts of the British parliament of what nature soever. If they are a separate body politick, and are free, they have a right equal to that of the people of Great Britain, to make laws for themselves, and are no more than they, subject to the controul of any legislature but their own.[19]

The "compact" to which Adams referred was none other than the charter which King James I had granted in 1620, "according to our princely Inclination," to "certain Knights, Gentlemen, and Merchants" at their "humble Request."[20] James had given them permission to invest in the New England colonies on terms determined by him. No doubt the knights, gentlemen, and merchants would have been surprised to learn that they had made a "compact" with the king, as if they been in a position to negotiate on equal terms with him. The New England colonies in the seventeenth century had been singularly independent in their conduct, despite what the charters said, but this alleged compact with a divine-right king was a newly minted revolutionary myth.

The important advantage of the compact theory was that it went back to a time long before the Glorious Revolution of 1688–89, which had brought about parliamentary supremacy in the British political order. That supremacy had been recognized by the colonies for almost a century, for which reason Franklin now regretted "our indiscrete Acknowledgement of it in Publick Acts." When the compact theory was wedded to the consent theory, the colonies had an ideology that implicitly made them free from Great Britain.

How far the Franklin-Adams theory of parliamentary authority diverged from the British view may be shown by Hutchinson's observation that he knew "no line that can be drawn between the supreme authority of

[19] Article signed "Valerius Poplicola," *Boston Gazette*, October 28, 1771, reprinted in *Writings of Samuel Adams*, vol. 2, pp. 260–61.

[20] Ben Perley Poore, First Charter of New England, *The Federal and State Constitutions, Colonial Charters, and other Organic Laws of the United States* (Washington, 2d ed., 1878), pt. 1, p. 921.

Parliament and the total independence of the colonies."[21] If so, declaring that Parliament lacked supreme authority over the colonies was equivalent to declaring that the colonies were totally independent.

Not all of the Boston leaders wanted to push the issue of parliamentary supremacy to a showdown in 1773. One of those who held back was Thomas Cushing, the Speaker of the Massachusetts Assembly. His reasons are as interesting as his opinion:

> You possibly observe that the government at home are daily growing weaker, while we in America are continually growing stronger. Our natural increase in wealth and population will in a course of years effectually settle this dispute in our favour; whereas, if we persist in strenuously denying the right of parliament to legislate for us in any case whatever, and insist upon their yielding up this right, they may think us very extravagant in our demands, and hence there will be great danger of bringing on a rupture fatal to both countries; whereas, if these high points about the supreme authority of parliament, were to fall asleep, and administration would desist from the exercise of this right, and the present system of American laws and regulations adopted on the idea of raising a revenue in America, were abolished, I should think Great Britain would regain the affection of the people of America, retrieve her commerce, and recall that confidence in her wisdom and justice, which is so necessary for the mutual interests of both countries.[22]

This view managed to combine a confidence in the ultimate American victory owing to "our natural increase in wealth and population," a reluctance to precipitate "a rupture fatal to both countries," and the recovery by Great Britain of "the affection of the people of America." It reflects the difficulties that still beset the more extreme Boston leaders in working out their strategy for dealing with British demands.

By a strange twist of logic, the more extreme leaders, who called themselves Whigs, were theoretically more royalist than the king in their rejection of Parliament. Before they made Great Britain the enemy, they made the British Parliament the enemy. According to this view, the only

---

[21] Governor Hutchinson's speech to the two houses, January 6, 1773, *Speeches of the Governors of Massachusetts from 1765 to 1775; and the Answers of the House of Representatives to the Same* (Boston, 1818; reprint, Da Capo Press, 1971), p. 340. [Hereafter cited as *Massachusetts State Papers.*].

[22] Cushing to Arthur Lee, September 20, 1773, Richard Henry Lee, *Life of Arthur Lee, LL.D.* (Boston, 1929), vol. 2, pp. 237–38.

tie that bound them to Great Britain was the king. This was still short of full ideological independence, yet the Bostonians were coming close.

In 1770, in the argument over the movement of the meeting place of the assembly from Boston to Cambridge, the radical leaders had contended that the charter was no more than "a compact between the Crown and this people" and had not provided for instructions from the king to the governor.[23] As Hutchinson later commented: "It is a new doctrine advanced by the last Assembly, that the King, by reserving to himself the power of nominating and appointing a Governor, hath divested himself of the right of instructing him."[24] If Parliament could make no laws for the colonies, and if the king could not send instructions to the governors, the only sources of power in the colonies were their own assemblies. Whatever the tie that still bound the colonies to Great Britain, it was purely nominal or intangible. These ideas were floating about in 1770–71 and represented an ideological break with the British connection long before even the most radical colonists were ready to put them into practice.

· 3 ·

In 1772, a notable but long forgotten book appeared in London. Its author was Arthur Young, famous for works on his tours of England, Ireland, and France and known as "the greatest of English writers on agriculture."[25] He corresponded with Washington, Lafayette, and other celebrated men of his time. *Political Essays concerning the Present State of the British Empire* dealt with British history, institutions, and economy, often in a very critical vein. It was also concerned with the relations between Great Britain and the American colonies. Young never visited the colonies himself, but he closely studied the work of the best authorities on them and knew as much about America as anyone on either side of the Atlantic.

Young boldly plunged into the question of American independence. He asserted: "There is no point in the modern politics of this country that has been more debated, or that has occasioned a greater contrariety of opinions, than this of the continuance of the colonies under the power of the mother-country." He then posed the critical question: "It may certainly be asked, Whether a colony, or a chain of colonies, who are

---

[23] Message from the Council to the Lieutenant Governor, June 19, 1770, *Massachusetts State Papers*, p. 229.
[24] Speech of the Governor to the Two Houses, July 5, 1771, ibid., p. 311.
[25] *Dictionary of National Biography*, vol. 21, pp. 1272–78.

very populous, possess a flourishing agriculture, and consequently the *necessaries* of *life;* numerous manufactures, an extensive commerce, and a beneficial circulation of internal wealth: it may be asked, I say, whether such a set of colonies are as likely to throw off the obedience to a mother-country, as another set in every respect the reverse?" He quickly replied: "Does not this question answer itself? Is it not very clear, that the first are infinitely nearer independency than the latter?"

In effect, Young considered the question of American independence from the point of view of the traditional British premonitions. He expressed them in this way: "The great pillars and foundations of independency are a *numerous* people, possessing, through agriculture and manufactures, the *necessaries of life.*" He went into greater detail:

> They form a territory which, in respect of agriculture, possesses all the necessaries of life—and that to so complete a degree, as always to have a superfluity ready for the demand of those that want; but never are in want themselves. In every thing respecting food they are perhaps the most independent people in the universe. As to manufactures, they possess most of those which are real necessaries, being supplied by Britain only to the amount of less than one eleventh part of their consumption; and as they trade to the West Indies in manufactures to the extent of above a million sterling, there is great reason to believe that even this eleventh consists of scarce any *necessaries,* as it supposes the amount of their consumption of European imports to be chiefly superfluous manufactures and India goods.

In agriculture, manufactures, and commerce, Young concluded, "our colonies are so nearly independent of their mother-country." Their commerce went far beyond necessity; "they are, to colonies, those of superfluity and *power.*" Colonial navigation was potentially dangerous; it had "been more than once exerted in actual feats of power, in carrying on a war—against the enemies of Britain indeed; but the same power might be exerted against her; and, in case of a revolt, most certainly would." Young was impressed with the military prowess of the colonies, probably more than it deserved: "During the last war they kept an army of about thirty thousand men on foot. They have foundaries of cannon, magazines of war, arsenals, forts, and fortifications; and even victorious generals among their own troops.— They have a standing militia; and constantly have the means of raising and arming a formidable body of forces."

After all this, Young asked another question: Why, in these circumstances, "do they not throw off the dominion of Britain;—or rather, why did they not, when they were so exasperated at the act of parliament which taxed them in stamps?" His answer turned on the factor of population. Independent agriculture and manufactures were necessary, but only population was a sufficient condition. He could not see how 2 or even 3 million people, spread over an immense territory, could rebel now: "All I have attempted to prove is, that these circumstances combined, most undoubtedly may enable our colonies, when arrived at a *certain* degree of population, to become an independent nation."

So Young put off the American Revolution for a while. But not for too long. He calculated that the Americans would need 5 or 6 million people to "very easily become *totally* independent." Ten thousand or even 20,000 British troops would not be enough to hold them back. Moreover, the Americans had another advantage: "It is impossible to state exactly the balance of power between Great Britain and North America; but the latter enjoys some peculiar advantages, which are of very great consequence. In case of a rupture between them, it is the interest of all those powers in Europe, whom Britain rivals either in general power, naval dominion, trade, commerce, or manufactures, that the colonies should become independent."

Young was not a proponent of American independence. Though he believed that Great Britain could not hold on to the colonies forever, he wanted to put off the evil day of their loss as long as possible. His advice was to encourage the colonies to concentrate on selling raw materials, especially staples; to make them dependent on Great Britain for manufactures; and to get them to spread out instead of to collect in towns. He thought in terms of power: "But when once (from whatever cause) towns arise, and manufactures are introduced, that people, whose only weakness consisted in the want of connection, would at once feel that power which policy had kept even from their imagination." Britain's "present system tends immediately to render them independent: That the longer this system is continued, the less will it be possible ever to retrieve the mistake."

In the end, he agreed with those who saw that Great Britain was fatally dependent on the colonies:

We are now at a crisis. Formerly it mattered but little, whether our statesmen were asleep or awake: And why? Because the increase of the colonies did the business for them: their increase occasioned the national trade to increase, and all went on silently, but prosperously. But late ill-judged measures have irritated the colonists, and at the same time, by confining them, forced them into those manufactures which their anger made them wish for. Their scheme, according to the present conduct of Britain, must succeed, and will end in the ruin of a vast part of our commerce and manufactures; so that for the future, trade will not increase, as it has done, of itself, and without attention; because the cause which operated such good effects will every day be turning against it. May we not therefore call this a crisis in the British Commerce? We have hitherto defied the rivalship of foreigners; let our American trade decline instead of increasing, and the case will be greatly changed.[26]

The main interest of Young's work is the reasoning behind his belief in ultimate American independence. In 1772, he went all the way back to the kind of thinking the "speculative reasoners" had used in the seventeenth century. Young knew all about "the ill-judged measures," such as the stamp tax and the Townshend duties, which had so irritated the colonists in his own day. Yet he barely touched on them to account for the British crisis. His view was based on purely objective factors, such as population, commerce, manufactures, power. His own recipes for holding back the colonial tide were already much too late and merely counted as counsels of desperation. Yet he was as close a student of colonial conditions as Great Britain had. He was divided in his intellectual allegiance—that the Americans were bound to become independent and that the best the British could do was to delay that outcome as long as possible. It was not the best frame of mind for a country about to take on the risks of war. Above all, his work testifies to the long duration of the British view that colonies, when they grew strong and prosperous enough, were not going to be colonies willingly.

· 4 ·

The British government was now dedicated to the policy of forestalling the movement for American independence. If the American radicals had prayed for the British government to make the wrong move, their prayers were about to be answered.

By 1773, the North ministry was solidly entrenched. The procolonial parliamentary opposition was dispersed and discouraged. After every previous wave of colonial ferment, a relative calm had settled. Each wave

[26] [Arthur Young], *Political Essays concerning the Present State of the British Empire* (London, 1772; reprint, Research Reprints, 1970), pp. 416–33, 552.

had been broken by a British initiative, first the repeal of the Stamp Act, then that of most of the Townshend Acts, after which an uneasy truce had prevailed. Action and counteraction were again the pattern of the third wave.

The new British challenge was the by-product of a policy that was primarily intended for another purpose. In May 1773, Parliament passed a Tea Act to rescue the East India Company from threatened bankruptcy. Tea had previously been imported into the colonies by colonial merchants, much of it smuggled from Holland, which undersold British exporters. British tea was expensive because it was heavily taxed by the British government, which depended on this tax for revenue. As Governor Hutchinson reported in 1771, five-sixths of the tea consumed in Massachusetts in the past two years was judged to have been illegally imported, nine-tenths in Philadelphia and New York. Hutchinson added: "The Custom-house officers on shore have strong inducements to do their duty but they are really afraid of the rage of the people."[27] Tea smuggling was not an American phenomenon; in Great Britain, an estimated 7,500,000 pounds of a total consumption of 13,000,000 pounds of tea was smuggled in annually from the continent.[28] Smuggling tea was so common that it did not rate as a serious crime; it was more like a gamble, in that the worst that could happen to a smuggler was confiscation of his goods.

The Tea Act was intended to help the East India Company in two ways. It was now to be permitted to sell to the American market, though through American merchants acting as consignees. The only ones to be cut out were the smugglers. The price of East India tea was also set at 2 shillings a pound in order to undersell the smuggled tea, which was going at 2s. 7d. At that price, it was believed that tea drinkers in Massachusetts alone were going to save £2,000 a year.[29] The company was supposed to make more money in the American market, drive out the Dutch competition, and benefit the American consumers.

But there was a flaw in the plan. Tea smuggling was big business. New York, Boston, and Philadelphia were havens of merchant smugglers. According to a well-informed Tory view, the British made the mistake of underestimating the smuggling business in America, which "was so universal, that the Smugglers Interest had engrossed so great a Power" it would have

[27] Hutchinson to Hillsborough, August 25, 1771, Davies, ed., *Documents of the American Revolution* (Irish University Press, 1973), vol. 3, pp. 172–73.

[28] Labaree, *Boston Tea Party*, p. 6.

[29] *Peter Oliver's Origin and Progress of the American Revolution*, ed. Douglass Adair and John A. Schutz (orig. ms., 1781; Huntington Library, 1961), p. 101.

required ten British soldiers to protect every chest of tea.[30] New York merchants who had been appointed consignees for the East India tea warned that the smugglers were "a formidable body among the merchants, and will of themselves be able to raise a considerable mob, including a great number of retainers, such as boatmen, alongshoremen, etc. who are all paid highly for their services."[31] The issue divided merchant from merchant, those willing to cooperate with the East India Company as consignees and those who saw their businesses, based largely on smuggling, as ruined.

The British neglected something else. Duty still had to be paid on imported tea, and the Americans considered the duty to be no better than another tax. When North was asked in the Commons to do away with the tea duty, he replied that "I must see very substantial reason before I part with a fund so applicable to the support of the civil [government]."[32] What he saw no reason to part with was anathema to the colonists for precisely the reason that the tea duty not only was a hateful tax but was used to pay some British colonial officials—and in time all of these officials—hitherto dependent on colonial largesse. North also revealed that another motive for holding on to the tea duty was rancor. It came out when he said: "No doubt there are political reasons. . . . I know the temper of the people there is so little deserving favour from hence, unless the reasons are very great."[33] This drastic step in British history went almost unnoticed—"perhaps no bill of such consequences has ever received less attention upon passage in Parliament."[34]

At this moment, the final stage of the prerevolutionary struggle hung in the balance. Yet the real stakes were comparatively minor. The tea duty to which North and his ministers were determined to cling brought in a pittance of £9,790 after 1770, little more than enough to pay for a couple of governors.[35] It was a derisory sum on which to base a policy that at best was sure to annoy the Americans and at worst to enrage them. It is clear from what North said that he was fed up with the Americans and wanted to pay them back for their insubordination and insolence. Yet what is most

[30] Ibid. Peter Oliver was the chief justice of the Superior Court of Massachusetts and brother of the lieutenant governor, Andrew Oliver. He went into exile and wrote his book in London after the Revolution.

[31] Cited by Labaree, *Boston Tea Party*, p. 91.

[32] April 26, 1773, *Proceedings and Debates of the British Parliaments Respecting North America, 1754–1783*, ed. R. C. Simmons and P. D. G. Thomas (Kraus International, 1983), vol. 3, p. 489.

[33] Ibid., p. 492.

[34] Labaree, *Boston Tea Party*, p. 73.

[35] Ibid., p. 52. Another figure was £400 a year after the costs of collection were deducted (p. 71).

revealing about North's action is that it was taken in the belief that the Americans were not going to do much about it. "Teas may be exported cheap enough to find a market in America, and preserve the duty," said North. "You will have your market, and your revenue."[36] Even Hutchinson was surprised by the American reaction.[37] At first the news attracted little attention in America, but soon the newspapers and their usual contributors found a way to represent the tea duty as an assault on the economic fabric of the colonies.

That the colonies should have objected to the new British tea policy is one thing. That it should have set off a political convulsion is something else. It could have been seen as little more than a matter of commercial competition—the monopolistic British East India Company versus colonial tea merchants. This approach had the advantage of concentrating attention on the relatively small and affluent portion of the colonial population that had brought on the confrontation by engaging in widespread smuggling and now could not meet the cheaper price of British tea. On the other hand, the colonial merchants could well complain against unfair competition and the prospect of higher tea prices once they had been driven out of business.

Here again, the campaign against the Stamp Act showed the way. Once more the successful strategy converted a matter of money into a question of principle. The Stamp Act had been beaten because it had come to symbolize the principle of taxation without consent, on which the colonists would not compromise. The Townshend Acts had brought out the same fundamental principle, and, except for tea, the colonists had won again. This well-rehearsed strategy was used once more against the tea duty and the introduction of the East India Company into the colonial tea trade.

News of the Tea Act reached the colonies in October 1773. A meeting in New York on October 15 denounced the "insidious Purpose of levying the Duty in America . . . being nothing less than to establish the *odious* Precedent of *raising a Revenue in America.*" Another meeting in Philadelphia the next day declared that the "Claim of Parliament to tax America is, in other Words, a Claim of Right to levy Contributions on us at Pleasure." Such a tax without American consent had "a direct Tendency to render Assemblies useless, and to introduce arbitrary Government and Slavery." Anyone who aided or abetted the sale of tea "while it remains subject to the Payment of a Duty here, is an Enemy to his Country."[38]

[36] April 26, 1773, *Proceedings and Debates,* vol. 3, p. 490.
[37] *Hutchinson's History,* vol. 3, p. 303.
[38] Lawrence Henry Gipson, *The British Empire Before the American Revolution* (Alfred A. Knopf, 1965), vol. 12, pp. 75–76.

Meanwhile, the Boston Committee of Correspondence warned the other committees that East India shipments of tea were intended "to destroy the Trade of the Colonies & increase the revenue." The British government was determined to make the colonies "absolutely dependent on the Crown, which will, if a little while persisted in, end in absolute Despotism." This message also contained a peculiar sidelight. Great Britain, it advised, was expected to find itself in a war in the near future. In this case the colonies were urged "to withhold all kinds of Aid in a general War, untill the Rights & Liberties which *they ought to enjoy* are restored, & secured to them upon the most permanent foundation."39 On November 5, a town meeting in Boston asserted that the tea tax had "a direct tendency to render Assemblies useless, and to introduce Arbitrary Government and Slavery" into the colonies.40 In effect, all the old bugbears—taxation, revenue, economic disaster, destruction of the assemblies, slavery—were resurrected in the cause of fighting a mere duty on the importation of tea by the East India Company— a duty that did not bring in enough revenue to justify the effort to collect it and a trade that could not have done much to rescue the East India Company. Tea itself was attacked as a poisonous substance. One medical extremist, Dr. Thomas Young of Boston, contributed an article designed to show that tea was the cause in Europe of "spasms, vapors, hypochondrias, apoplexies of the serious kind, palsies, dropsies, rhumatisms, consumptions, low nervous, miliary and petechial fevers."41

Action followed words. On November 28, a tea ship with 114 chests on board arrived in Boston harbor and was forced to depart without landing its cargo. A notice went up warning "public enemies of this country," the local tea consignees, that they would be treated "as wretches, unworthy to live, and made the first victims of our resentment." When three tea ships lingered in the harbor, they were boarded by colonists disguised as Mohawk Indians. They methodically spilled the contents of 342 chests of tea, worth about £10,000, into the water and triumphantly marched through the town accompanied by pipes and drums. This was not the first time that such an operation had been carried out. In 1771, a customhouse schooner patrolling off the coast of Philadelphia had intercepted a boat loaded with

39 "The Committee of Correspondence of Massachusetts to Other Committees of Correspondence," October 21, 1773, text in *Writings of Samuel Adams*, vol. 3, pp. 62–67. The idea of taking advantage of a war to force Great Britain to yield to American demands seems to have originated with Samuel Adams (Adams to Joseph Hawley, October 13, 1773, ibid., pp. 60–61). Adams's expectation of a war was probably derived from the tension between Great Britain and Spain over the Falkland Islands.

40 "Resolutions of the Town of Boston, November 5, 1773," text in *Writings of Samuel Adams*, pp. 67–69.

41 *Boston Evening-Post*, October 25, 1773, and *Massachusetts Spy*, December 30, 1773.

smuggled tea; the schooner had been boarded by masked men, the officers attacked and locked up below, and the cargo taken off. As the historian of the Boston Tea Party observed, "Not until Parliament finally provided for stricter enforcement of the laws did the smugglers claim their activities to be patriotic. Then they succeeded in convincing the American public that their search for illegal profit was somehow a part of the common fight for freedom."[42]

The Boston Tea Party had been prepared for at least a month by propaganda threatening bodily harm to anyone who helped to bring in the hateful tea. A "Committee for Tarring and Feathering" in New York put up warnings to the captain of a tea ship: "What think you, Captain, of a Halter around your Neck, then Gallons of Liquid Tar decanted on your pate—with the Feathers of a dozen live Geese laid over that to enliven your Appearance?"[43] As in the case of the stamp distributors, tea consignees in Boston were summoned to appear at the Liberty Tree and resign their commissions. A mob broke into the offices of one consignee who refused to appear, tore the outer door off its hinges, broke all the windows and window frames, and drove him to an upper floor for safety.[44] John Hancock conducted a special town meeting, which denounced the tea duty and demanded the resignation of the consignees. Despite mob intimidation, the consignees refused to give way.[45] "I am in a helpless state," Governor Hutchinson wrote to Governor Tryon of New York, "no person who shares any part of the Authority of Government concurring with me in Measures for the support of it."[46] Notices posted all over Boston read:

> Friends! Brethren! Countrymen!
>
> That worst of Plagues The Detestable Tea, ship'd for this Port by the East India Company is now arriv'd in this Harbour, the Hour of Destruction or manly Opposition to the Machinations of Tyranny stares you in the Face: every Friend to his Country to himself & to Posterity is now called upon to meet at Fanewell [Faneuil] Hall at nine of Clock this Day (at which time the Bells will begin to ring) to make a United & Successful Resistance to this last worst & most Destructive Measure of Administration
>
> Boston Nov[embe]r 29, 1773[47]

[42] Labaree, *Boston Tea Party*, pp. 55–56.
[43] Ibid., p. 101.
[44] Ibid., p. 110; *Letters and Diary of John Rowe*, ed. Anne Rowe Cunningham (W. B. Clarke, 1903), p. 254.
[45] Labaree, *Boston Tea Party*, p. 110.
[46] Hutchinson to Tryon, November 21, 1773, cited by Labaree, *Boston Tea Party*, p. 118.
[47] *Letters and Diary of John Rowe*, p. 255.

About 1,000 people attended this meeting and voted to return the tea. About 2,500 came to another meeting that afternoon. A committee made up of Sam Adams, John Hancock, and two merchants, Jonathan Williams and John Rowe, was chosen to represent the protesters. By December 2, all the consignees, except those in Boston, had agreed to resign.[48]

The raid on the three ships was not a spontaneous act. The plan was worked out at a meeting in the home of Benjamin Edes, part owner of the *Boston Gazette,* and the signal was given by Samuel Adams to a crowd at the Old South Church.[49] Between thirty and sixty men apparently participated in the operation, while as many as 2,000 people looked on. Its historian concluded: "The undertaking had all the signs of a well-planned operation."[50]

No government authority interfered, though a regiment of troops was stationed at nearby Castle William. Hutchinson later defended his decision to abstain from using force on the ground that he could not have saved the tea without landing marines from nearby British warships. He saw no point in this course, because it would have "brought on a greater convulsion than there was any danger of in 1770 [after the Boston Massacre], and it would not have been possible, when two regiments were forced out of town, for so small body of troops to have kept possession of the town." Hutchinson was totally isolated, unable to get support from any quarter.[51] John Rowe wrote in his diary that he was named "much against my will but I dare not say a word."[52] The local consignees of the tea fled from Boston and did not return for months.[53]

In effect, Boston was lost to the British empire in December 1773. The significance of the event was not lost on another Adams, though he had engaged in little political activity for the past three years.

The Boston Tea Party, wrote John Adams in his diary for December 17, the day after the incident, was "an Epocha in History." His reaction shows how far the estrangement from Great Britain had gone. The "Party" was elevated to the dignity of the "most magnificent Movement of all. There is a Dignity, a Majesty, a Sublimity, in this last Effort of the Patriots, that I greatly admire." Adams foresaw that worse might follow: "This however is but an Attack upon Property. Another similar Exertion of popular Power, may produce the destruction of Lives. Many Persons wish, that as many dead Carcasses were floating in the Harbour, as there are Chests of Tea:—a much less Number of Lives however would remove the Causes of all our Calamities."

[48] Labaree, *Boston Tea Party*, p. 125.
[49] Letter of Peter Edes, *MHS Proceedings*, ser. 1, 1871–1873, pp. 174–75.
[50] Labaree, *Boston Tea Party*, p. 144.
[51] *Hutchinson's History*, vol. 3, p. 313.
[52] *Letters and Diary of John Rowe*, p. 256.
[53] Thomas Hutchinson to the earl of Dartmouth, March 9, 1774, Davies, *Documents of the American Revolution*, vol. 8, p. 63.

He speculated on what form British retaliation might take: "What Measures will the Ministry take, in Consequence of this?—Will they resent it? will they dare to resent it? will they punish Us? How? By quartering Troops upon Us?—by annulling our Charter?—by laying on more duties? By restraining our Trade? By Sacrifice of Individuals, or how."

Adams asked himself whether the destruction of the tea was necessary. He answered that it was "absolutely and indispensably so." Otherwise, he said, the colonists "would be giving up the Principle of Taxation by Parliamentary Authority, against which the Continent have struggled for 10 years, it was loosing [losing] all our labour for 10 years and subjecting ourselves and our Posterity forever to Egyptian Taskmasters—to Burthens, Indignities, to Ignominy, Reproach and Contempt, to Desolation and Oppression, to Poverty and Servitude."[54] Little had changed in the rhetoric since the Stamp Act a decade earlier.

John Adams's attitude was typical. "At and near Boston," Hutchinson confided to Lord Dartmouth, "the people seem regardless of all consequences." "We are in a perfect jubilee," rejoiced a letter from Boston printed in a New York newspaper. The repercussions were felt throughout the colonies. When tea was landed in Charleston, it was not dumped into the ocean, but it could not be distributed, and no duty was paid on it. In Philadelphia, the inhabitants persuaded the captain of a tea ship to take the tea back to England. A winter storm caused a tea ship to delay its arrival in New York for four months, and even then it was forced to leave without disposing of the tea. Everywhere governors found themselves helpless. Tea, the once favorite beverage, suffered such bad repute that drinking it became an offense. By the end of 1774, some type of violent anti-tea demonstration had been staged in virtually every colony. What had started as a protest against the East India Company turned into a general revolt against paying duty on any tea.[55]

Samuel Adams sent word to Arthur Lee in London about the real meaning of the Boston Tea Party: "The Destruction of the Tea is the pretence for the unprecedented Severity shown to the Town of Boston but the real Cause is the opposition to Tyranny for which the people of that Town have always made themselves remarkable & for which I think this Country is much obliged to them."[56] The revolutionary move was to make tyranny, and not merely tea, the issue. The opposition to tea could

[54] *The Diary and Autobiography of John Adams*, ed. L. H. Butterfield (Harvard University Press, 1961), vol. 2, pp. 85–86.
[55] Labaree, *Boston Tea Party*, pp. 152–69; Gipson, *British Empire Before the American Revolution*, vol. 12, pp. 86–100.
[56] Adams to Lee, January 25, 1774, *Writings of Samuel Adams*, vol. 3, p. 79.

have been strong or weak, but the opposition to tyranny could never be strong enough.

In a letter to their London agent, the Boston leadership contended that the Tea Party was preferable to "a second Effusion of Blood"—the first having been the Boston Massacre—which would have resulted if the customs officers had attempted to land the tea from the ships.[57] If the local British officials had been made of stronger stuff, the war of the American Revolution might well have started on December 16, 1773, at Long Wharf in Boston, instead of on April 19, 1775, at Lexington and Concord.

· 5 ·

The point of no return arrived in 1774. It was reflected by two leading figures, one American, the other British.

The American was again Benjamin Franklin. For almost a decade, Franklin had struggled to resolve the duality in his thinking about the connection between his native land and its mother country. At the political heart of that struggle was the question of Parliament's authority to make laws for the Americans, inasmuch as Parliament was the only lawmaking body in the British system of government. To reject Parliament's jurisdiction over America was to bifurcate the empire into a British realm, for which Parliament made the laws, and an American domain that floated free from parliamentary control and at best maintained tenuous links to the Crown.

Franklin's struggle with himself went through several phases. In 1767, he still believed that "a fair and equal Representation of all the Parts of this Empire in Parliament, is the only firm Basis on which its political Grandeur and Stability can be founded."[58] This stage implied no challenge to Parliament's authority over the colonies, merely American representation in Parliament. By 1768, he had come to believe that there was no "middle doctrine"—Parliament had the right to make either all laws for America or none at all. He had inclined towards the latter, without being able to shake off his British pride and loyalty. He managed to hold on to them by putting his faith in the king, who, he argued, was the only link that held the entire empire together. Though Franklin had a soft spot for the Crown, his willingness to make it supreme in the colonies was merely a way of escaping the clutches of Parliament, which had become his particular bête noire. Not

[57] Gipson thinks that this letter was sent to Benjamin Franklin, though it was attributed to Arthur Lee in *Massachusetts Historical Society Collections*, 4th ser., vol. 4, 1858, p. 377.
[58] Franklin to Lord Kames, February 25, 1767, *Franklin Papers*, vol. 14, p. 65.

until 1773 was Franklin able to bring himself to entertain the thought that the king himself was one of the hard-liners and approved of harsh measures to put the Americans in their place. "Between you and I," he wrote to his son, William, on July 14, "the late Measures have been, I suspect, very much the King's own, and he has in some Cases a great Share of What his Friends call *Firmness*."[59] Increasingly pessimistic, Franklin was still unable to cut the umbilical cord. As he admitted in 1774, "I have been thought here [England] too much of an American, I have in America been deem'd too much of an Englishman."[60]

Yet in all this time of increasing doubt and despondency, Franklin had a fallback position that enabled him to differ tactically from the more militant Bostonians. He repeatedly urged them "to keep our People quiet." His reasoning was that "Insurrections" would give America's enemies a pretext for using more military force and imposing "more severe Restraints." His optimism about ultimate colonial victory was based on his long-term outlook: "And it must be evident to all that by our rapidly increasing Strength we shall soon become of so much Importance, that none of our just Claims of Privilege will be as heretofore unattended to, nor any Security we can wish for our Rights be deny'd us."[61]

Then Franklin did something that upset his optimistic calculus and freed him from his final inhibitions. He sent off a delayed-action political bomb to Thomas Cushing, the Speaker of the Massachusetts House, in the form of a collection of purloined letters. They were thirteen letters sent by Thomas Hutchinson, then lieutenant governor, and Andrew Oliver, then province secretary, and some of their allies, mainly to Thomas Whately, the former secretary of the Treasury in London. The letters had been sent in 1767–1769 and, therefore, did not deal with the current situation. How Franklin had come into possession of them remains a mystery. In his letter in December 1772, Franklin enjoined Cushing to show them to some leading Bostonians and return them in a few months.[62]

The letters largely confirmed what everyone already knew—that Hutchinson and his friends sided with the British view of colonial dependence. The revelation was evidence of the panic that had taken hold of them as early as 1768–69 and the lengths to which they had gone to encourage a British

---

[59] Benjamin Franklin to William Franklin, July 14, 1773, ibid., vol. 20, p. 308. But Franklin added: "Yet, by some Painstaking and proper Management, the wrong Impressions he has received may be removed, which is perhaps the only Chance America has for obtaining *soon* the Redress she aims at. This entirely to yourself" (p. 309).

[60] "Tract Relative to the Affair of Hutchinson's Letters," ibid., vol. 21, p. 417.

[61] Franklin to Thomas Cushing, March 9, 1773, ibid., vol. 20, p. 99.

[62] Franklin to Cushing, December 2, 1772, ibid., vol. 19, p. 412.

crackdown on the colonies. Hutchinson's most explicit letter was dated
January 20, 1769:

> This is most certainly a crisis. I really wish that there may not have
> been the least degree of severity beyond what is absolutely necessary
> to maintain, I think I may say to you the *dependance* which a colony
> ought to have upon the parent state; but if no measures shall have
> been taken to secure this dependance, or nothing more than some
> declaratory acts or resolves, *it is all over with us.* The friends of
> government will be utterly disheartened, and the friends of anarchy
> will be afraid of nothing be it ever so extravagant.

Hutchinson later claimed that his letters had done no more than reiterate
what he had said in his speeches.[63] In fact, he had never publicly called on
the British government to take whatever measures were necessary to secure
the dependence of the colonies or *"it is all over with us."* Hutchinson was
blamed for the hardening of British policy, as if British ministers could not
have made up their own minds. Franklin had exaggerated the importance
of the letters by advising the Bostonians that they had "laid the foundation
of most if not all our present grievances."

The Boston leaders received the letters some months before they decided
what to do with them. The delay came about because Franklin had sent the
originals on the "express Conditions, that they should not be printed, that
no Copies should be taken of them; that they should be shown only to a few
of the leading People of the Government, and that they should be carefully
returned." He had agreed to these conditions, he explained, because
publication might "occasion some Riot of mischievous Consequence."[64]
He was, therefore, in no doubt about the explosiveness of the revelations.

All these conditions were violated. The Bostonians divulged the contents
through a series of subterfuges. Their problem was that they had the originals
and wanted to circulate copies for maximum effect. On June 2, 1774, Sam
Adams informed the House of Representatives that "he had perceived the
Minds of the People to be greatly agitated with a prevailing Report that
Letters of an extraordinary Nature had been written and sent to *England,*
greatly to the Prejudice of this Province."[65] Somehow, word had been let
out that there were such letters. A committee was appointed to consider the
letters, after which John Hancock reported that they had the "Tendency and

---

[63] *Hutchinson's History,* vol. 3, p. 289.

[64] "Tract Relative to the Affair of Hutchinson's Letters" (1774), *Franklin Papers,* vol.
21, p. 420.

[65] *Journals of the House of Representatives of Massachusetts, 1773–1774,* p. 26.

Design" to "overthrow the Constitution of this Government, and to introduce arbitrary Power into the Province."[66] Hutchinson vainly protested that he had never sent letters of such a character.

On June 9, Hancock made the next move to get copies of the letters out. He informed the House that he had already received copies and moved that they be compared with the originals, which was so ordered.[67] By this time, if Hancock can be believed, someone had made unauthorized copies. The next day, the House was informed that Adams had received permission from Franklin, who was still in London and could not have known what was happening to the letters in Boston, "to print, copy, or make what other Use of them they please."[68] On June 15, the official printers were ordered to make copies of the letters for the members of the House, numbering over a hundred.[69] Finally, the House passed resolutions to the effect that the letters were "highly injurious to this Province," "*insidious*," designed to "alienate the Affections of our most gracious Sovereign King George the Third, from his loyal and affectionate Province" and "suppress the very Spirit of Freedom." In conclusion, the king was asked to punish Hutchinson and Oliver by removing them from office.[70] For days afterwards, the imbroglio was kept alive by pretending that it was necessary to compare the copies with the originals and by ordering a petition for dismissing Hutchinson and Oliver to be sent to Franklin for him to present to the king.[71] The affair had preoccupied the House for the better part of a month.

The letters appeared in pamphlet form with a title that left nothing to the imagination:

> *Copy of Letters Sent to Great-Britain, by His Excellency Thomas Hutchinson, the Hon. Andrew Oliver, and Several Other Persons, Born and Educated among Us in which (Notwithstanding His Excellency's Declaration to the House, That the Tendency and Design of Them Was Not To Subvert the Constitution, But rather To Preserve It Entire) the Judicious Reader Will Discover the Fatal Source of the Confusion and Bloodshed to Which This Province Especially Has Been Involved, and Which Threatned Total Destruction to the Liberties of All America*[72]

Franklin defended his role on the ground that he had acted with "good

66 Ibid., p. 27.
67 Ibid., p. 41.
68 Ibid., p. 44.
69 Ibid., p. 56.
70 Ibid., pp. 58–61.
71 Ibid., pp. 72, 75.
72 Printed Boston, 1773.

Intentions," though not successfully. He had had no "Scruple in sending them," he explained, "for as they had been handed about here to prejudice that People, why not to [use] them for their Advantage?"[73] His apologia then took a peculiar turn. He had grown "resentful" of British treatment of the colonies, but was still loyal to the empire as a whole, when he had been pleased to learn from "a Gentleman of Character and Distinction" that the British government had not been principally at fault. This single source had assured him that the American grievances "took their Rise, not from Government here, but were projected, proposed to Administration, solicited, and obtained by some of the most respectable among the Americans themselves, as necessary Measures for the welfare of that Country." When Franklin had expressed some doubt, the Gentleman of Character and Distinction had convinced him by showing him the letters.

It took some time for Franklin to admit that he had been the source of the letters. By chance, suspicion was cast on two others—John Temple, a former commissioner of customs in Boston, and William Whately, brother of Thomas Whately, to whom the letters had been addressed. In the exchange of charges, they fought a duel in which Whately was injured. When Franklin heard that they might fight another duel as soon as Whately had recovered, he thought that the contretemps had gone far enough and cleared both by confessing his own role. Whately was not appeased and sued Franklin for having appropriated his brother's letters and for having had them published.[74]

Whatever the handling of the letters tells about Franklin, it is even more revealing about the temper of the Bostonians. They knew they were playing with fire by making the letters public and maneuvered to get them out step by step in the House of Representatives, which they controlled. They believed that Hutchinson and Oliver were such enemies that any means of disgracing and getting rid of them were justified. They behaved with ruthlessness and determination, as revolutionaries might be expected to do.

The repercussions in England of Franklin's role in the affair made it far more than a tempest in a colonial teapot. Franklin passed on the petition for the removal of Hutchinson and Oliver to Dartmouth, as if he did not anticipate that it was sure to send shock waves through the British establishment. Israel Mauduit asked for a hearing on the petition before the Privy Council. The hearing took place on January 29, 1774, with Alexander Wedderburn, the solicitor general, as Mauduit's counsel. Unluckily, news of

---

[73] "Tract Relative to the Affair of Hutchinson's Letters," *Franklin Papers*, vol. 21, p. 420. A complete copy substituted "use" for "to."

[74] Ibid., pp. 430–35.

the Boston Tea Party had reached London nine days earlier and did not make the British mood any less belligerent.

Wedderburn came thirsting for blood. His attack on Franklin's character was so scurrilous that it became a classic of legal invective. He accused Franklin of having obtained the letters by "fraudulent or corrupt means, for the most malignant of purposes; unless he stole them, from the person who stole them." He charged that Franklin had become responsible for having "nearly occasioned the murder" of William Whately. He made Franklin, "the inventor and first planner of the whole contrivance," the head of a conspiracy against Hutchinson. But Wedderburn's personal attack has somewhat obscured what he also said about Franklin's motives: "My Lords, Dr. Franklin's mind may have been so possessed with the idea of a Great American Republic, that he may easily slide into the language of the minister of a foreign independent state."

After vilifying Franklin, Wedderburn turned his fire on the Bostonians: "These men are perpetually offering every kind of insult to the English nation. Setting the King's authority at defiance; treating the parliament as usurpers of an authority not belonging to them, and flatly denying the Supreme Jurisdiction of the British empire." He accused them of having found that mobs could "establish their power, and make all future Governors bow to their authority. They wish to erect themselves into a tyranny greater than the Roman." This invective delighted the packed chamber, filled with the leading lords and other dignitaries of the land. Only North is said to have restrained himself. Franklin bitterly described the scene—"all the courtiers were invited as to an entertainment."[75] To get the maximum publicity for Wedderburn's assault, his speech was quickly published, but it was so coarse that some passages were omitted. A British newspaper reported that he had "decked his Harangue with the choicest Flowers of Billingsgate."

In the end, the committee of the Privy Council denounced the Massachusetts petition as "Vexatious and Scandalous and calculated only for the Seditious Purpose of keeping up the Spirit of Clamour and Discontent in the said province."[76]

It was a strange end to Franklin's English years. When he had arrived in London in 1767 as agent for Pennsylvania, he was already known for his scientific experiments. Soon he was recognized as the most famous American in Europe. Seven years later, he left his beloved England ignominiously. He had suffered public denunciation by a minister as a thief and traitor. The British press was filled with vituperation and abuse against him. It

75 Franklin to Cushing, February 15 [19], 1774, ibid., p. 92.
76 For the entire proceedings, ibid., pp. 19–70.

was even hinted to him that he was going to be arrested and thrust into jail.

Franklin was not the only victim. "I suppose," he wrote to Cushing in March 1774, "we never had since we were a People, so few friends in Britain."[77]

That Franklin should have been accused of betraying the British empire was the unkindest cut of all. He had long insisted that he intended to advance the cause of reconciliation between Great Britain and the colonies by showing that Americans like Hutchinson and not the British government had been responsible for the anticolonial policy.[78] It was a strange explanation, because Hutchinson could not have had such immense influence unless his letters had been received by very receptive and impressionable ministerial minds, even supposing one could be sure that the right ministers had read the letters.[79] The decisions, after all, had been made by British ministers who hardly needed to be brainwashed by panicky Massachusetts officials into taking an increasingly strong line against the colonies. The entire affair was not Franklin's finest hour. Yet his explanation attests that he held on to his policy of reconciliation until the exposure of the letters unexpectedly disillusioned him in January 1774.

Within days of the ghastly "entertainment," Franklin confided, "I am at a loss to know how peace and union is to be maintained or restored between the different parts of the empire."[80] In March 1774, he wrote an article for a British newspaper—in his usual style, as if he were an Englishman—in which he protested the warlike, anticolonial propaganda that he attributed to "Ministerial Writers." They were calling the American struggle for rights a "REBELLION" and the Americans "REBELS." They were using their utmost effort "to persuade us that this War with the Colonies (for a War it will be) is a *national* Cause when in fact it is merely a *ministerial* one." Franklin still played his old role of pacifier: "The Quarrel is about a paltry threepenny Duty on Tea. There is no real Clashing of Interests between Britain and America." He blamed "ministerial Pique and Obstinacy."[81] He

---

77 Franklin to Cushing, March 22, 1774, ibid., p. 152. To the Massachusetts Committee of Correspondence, Franklin had already written on February 2, 1774, that "it is impossible to justify with People so prejudiced in favour of the Power of Parliament to tax America, as most are in this Country" (p. 76).

78 "I was convinced accordingly, by perusing those Letters, and thought it might have a good Effect, if I could convince the Leaders there [New England] of the same Truth, since it would remove much of their Resentment against Britain as a harsh unkind Mother, lay the blame where it ought to lay, and by that means promote a Reconciliation" (Franklin to Joseph Galloway, February 18, 1774, ibid., p. 109).

79 Franklin merely alleged that the letters had been shown "here to several Persons" (ibid.).

80 Franklin to Cushing, February 15 [19?], 1774, ibid., pp. 93–94.

81 To the *Public Ledger*, after March 9, 1774, ibid., pp. 134–35.

did not explain why the Americans had made such a fuss about the duty if it was such a paltry matter. But, significantly, he now accused British ministers, not Hutchinson-type Americans, of causing all the trouble. Above all, he acknowledged such an acute intensification of the crisis that "war" could be threatened.

The year 1774 was the end of the peaceful road for Franklin—and not only for him. If even Franklin could not hold on to his yearning for reconciliation, there was little hope.

· 6 ·

The British point of no return was reflected by the American secretary, William Legge, the second earl of Dartmouth.

Dartmouth was known as the Americans' only friend in the North cabinet. Franklin had recently described him as "truly a good Man," who "wishes sincerely a good Understanding with the Colonies, but does not seem to have Strength equal to his Wishes."[82] He was North's stepbrother and moved in the same social circles. With the help of the old duke of Newcastle, Dartmouth did not have to work his way up in British politics. In 1765, at the age of thirty-four, he had stayed in the second rank as head of the Board of Trade in the short-lived Rockingham ministry. Since much of the board's business was with the colonies, Dartmouth had received a quick education in what was going on there. He had strongly supported the repeal of the Stamp Act in 1766, from which time the colonies had recognized him as their well-wisher. In Massachusetts, the House of Representatives had voted unanimously to thank him for his "noble and generous patronage of the British colonies."[83]

Dartmouth spent only a year at the Board of Trade. After six years out of office, he came back in 1772 as secretary of state for the colonies, the American secretaryship, in North's ministry. The test of how friendly he was to the colonies came in the following year. Dartmouth was just as much a believer in the principle of parliamentary authority over the colonies as anyone in the ministry, except that he wanted no unnecessary difficulties with the colonies over it. Events soon made it increasingly difficult for him to straddle the issue. In 1773, when the divide opened between Hutchinson and the Boston radicals over the authority of Parliament, Dartmouth backed

[82] Benjamin Franklin to William Franklin, July 14, 1773, ibid., vol. 20, p. 308.
[83] B. D. Bargar, *Lord Dartmouth and the American Revolution* (University of South Carolina Press, 1965), pp. 15–33.

Hutchinson in rejecting "doctrines subversive of every principle of the constitutional dependence of the colonies upon this kingdom."[84] In January 1774, when Franklin was caught up in the imbroglio over the purloined letters, Dartmouth could not "applaud his conduct."[85]

Dartmouth still reflected the view of London that a relatively few "enemies of government" were responsible for creating distrust and inflaming minds. He sensed that the use of military force might be necessary but warned Hutchinson that "the aid of the military except in cases of actual rebellious insurrection cannot be brought forward but upon the requisition of the civil magistrate and for his support in cases of absolute necessity when every other effort has failed."[86]

At this point, Dartmouth engaged in a unique correspondence with an American. That two such people could become estranged tells much about why the Revolution came about. The American was Joseph Reed, a successful Philadelphia lawyer. Like many well-born colonists, he had studied at one of the Inns of Court in London, a finishing school for those who could afford the best legal education. He was married to the daughter of Dennys De Berdt, the London merchant who doubled as agent for Massachusetts. Through De Berdt, Reed was put forward to be Dartmouth's secretary in 1766, when Dartmouth was up for the post of American secretary. When Dartmouth failed to get the post, Reed stayed in Philadelphia and attended to his flourishing career. Seven years later, when Dartmouth became the American secretary, Reed took the unusual step of offering his services to Dartmouth as a more trustworthy informant on colonial affairs than the secretary's official sources. His first letter was dated December 22, 1773, soon after the Boston Tea Party. The twelfth and last was sent on February 13, 1775, two months before the battle of Lexington. Only one letter seems to have been sent from Dartmouth to Reed.[87]

Reed wrote from a point of view very different from that of the Boston "maximalists." If they can be considered the colonial "left wing," he belonged to the "right wing." Like Franklin, he wanted nothing so much as a restoration of the old ties, which in retrospect had become invested with an idealized perfection. "No king ever had more loyal subjects; or any country more affectionate colonists than the American *were*," he assured Dartmouth.

[84] Dartmouth to Hutchinson, April 10, 1773, in Bargar, *Lord Dartmouth,* p. 87.

[85] Dartmouth to Joseph Reed, July 11, 1774, in William B. Reed, *Life and Correspondence of Joseph Reed* (Philadelphia, 1847), vol. 1, p. 74.

[86] Dartmouth to Hutchinson, January 8, 1774, Davies, *Documents of the American Revolution,* vol. 8, pp. 24–25.

[87] For Reed's background, see John F. Roche, *Joseph Reed* (Columbia University Press, 1957), pp. 3–37.

"I, who am but a young man, well remember when the former was always mentioned with a respect approaching to adoration, and to be an *Englishman* was alone a sufficient recommendation for any office of friendship and civility." Sadly, those days had passed.[88]

In his first letter, he pleaded with Dartmouth to get "the Mother Country to relax, and adopt lenient measures." Repeal of the Tea Act was sure to bring about "the future submission of the inhabitants of this part of America."[89] His next letter, warning of the consequences, reflected the opinion of the social circles to which he belonged: "Any further attempt to enforce this act, I am humbly of opinion, must end in blood. We are sensible of our inability to contend with the Mother Country by force, but we are hastening fast to desperate resolutions, and unless internal peace is speedily settled, our most wise and sensible citizens dread the anarchy and confusion that must ensue."[90]

In a later letter, Reed assured Dartmouth that he spoke "not only my own sentiments, but the sentiments of the most respectable in this city when I say that there is nothing they so much lament as these unhappy differences, and that they will rejoice to see the old union and affection restored." But Reed was clear about one thing: The colonies, whatever their differences, agreed on these same principles, "and your lordship, I think, may consider it as a fixed truth, that all the dreadful consequences of civil war will ensue before the Americans will submit to the claim of taxation by Parliament."[91]

Dartmouth was not impressed. He first assured Reed that "there is not in any part of the King's dominions a more real friend to the constitutional rights and liberties of America than myself." But he went on to state in no uncertain terms what he thought the struggle was about:

What then is the present case? The Supreme Legislature of the whole British Empire has laid a duty (no matter for the present whether it has or has not the right so to do, it is sufficient that we conceive it has), on a certain commodity, on its importation into America. The people of America, at Boston, particularly, resist that authority, and oppose the execution of the law in a manner clearly treasonable. Upon the principles of every government upon earth, the Mother Country, very unwilling to proceed to extremities, passes laws (indisputably within its power) for the punishment of the most flagrant offenders, for the reformation of abuses, and for the prevention of like extremities in

[88] Reed, *Life and Correspondence of Joseph Reed*, p. 77.
[89] Reed to Dartmouth, December 22, 1773, ibid., p. 53.
[90] Reed to Dartmouth, December 27, 1773, ibid., p. 55.
[91] Reed to Dartmouth, June 10, 1774, ibid., pp. 69–70.

future. The question then is whether these laws are to be submitted to? If the people of America say no, they say in effect that they will no longer be a part of the British Empire; they change the whole ground of the controversy,—they no longer contend that Parliament has not a right to enact a particular provision,—they say that it has no right to consider them as at all within its jurisdiction.[92]

Reed's response to a friend was "Such is Lord Dartmouth's confession of faith,—bad enough, God knows." Reed's reply to Dartmouth indicated that time was running out. "Unless some plan of accommodation can be speedily formed," he warned, "the affection of the colonists will be irrecoverably lost." Americans were ready for anything, "should it be war itself." The way "all ranks of people" were speaking, he wrote, "I am convinced, my Lord, that if blood be once spilled, we shall be involved in all the horrors of a civil war." Such a war "will require a greater power than Great Britain can spare, and it will be one continued conflict, till depopulation and destruction follow your victories, or the Colonies establish themselves in some sort of independence." Reed invoked the specter of a civil war again and again—"we are on the verge of a civil war not to be equalled in history for its importance and fatal consequences . . . the most dreadful of all calamities, a civil war."[93] In his last letter, Reed tried vainly to convince Dartmouth that the Americans were determined to fight—"this country will be deluged with blood, before it will submit to any other taxation than by their own Legislature."[94]

The significance of this correspondence is that both Dartmouth and Reed represented men of goodwill on both sides. They were the kinds of people who were needed to make a "plan of accommodation" possible. Reed's efforts were futile because he could not surmount the colonial objection to parliamentary taxes or overcome Dartmouth's insistence that Parliament was "the Supreme Legislature of the whole British Empire." Reed once tried to make a distinction between "supreme and absolute" power and challenged Dartmouth to say "whether this supremacy might not be accurately defined, and its operation limited by some certain bounds so as to leave no room for future disputes."[95] But the time had passed for linguistic niceties. The struggle had entered into its yes-or-no phase; either Parliament could make laws for America or it could not, in which case America was splitting the British empire and the British were determined to hold it together.

[92] Dartmouth to Reed, July 11, 1774, ibid., p. 72.
[93] Reed to Dartmouth, September 25, 1774, ibid., pp. 76–80.
[94] Reed to Dartmouth, February 10, 1775, ibid., p. 95.
[95] Reed to Dartmouth, September 25, 1774, ibid., p. 77.

· 7 ·

As Reed's letters to Dartmouth show, some colonial moderates wanted nothing so much as a way out of the increasingly dangerous impasse. But others, especially in Boston, seized every opportunity to increase the distance between Great Britain and the Americans.

American extremist denunciation of British rule found free expression in the colonial newspapers, of which there were twenty-one in 1763 and forty-two in 1775.[96] Most of them were anti-British, some militantly so. Boston had three newspapers: the fiery *Boston Gazette,* printed by Benjamin Edes and John Gill; from 1770 to 1775, the *Massachusetts Spy,* published by Isaiah Thomas; and the *Boston Evening-Post,* issued by Thomas Fleet. Only the last tried to be nonpartisan. At the height of the revolutionary ferment in 1774–75, the *Boston Gazette* claimed that it sold 2,000 copies weekly. The political line of the *Gazette* was set by Sam Adams, who rarely permitted an issue to come out without one of his articles, signed with a Roman pseudonym. John Adams once revealed how the newspaper was put out; he spent an evening with Gill, Sam Adams, and James Otis, and wrote in his diary: "The Evening spent in preparing for the Next Days Newspaper—a curious Employment. Cooking up Paragraphs, Articles, Occurrences, &c.— working the political Engine!"[97]

Intimations of coming American independence appeared openly in the colonial press. One of the first, if not the first, was published in the *Boston Gazette* of October 2, 1769. Signed by "Alfred," it dealt with the post–Stamp Act tension. It reads in part:

> For tho' it was soon repeal'd, it yet created such a jealousy between the mother country and the colonies, as it is to be fear'd will never wholly subside; and for aught the promoters of it can tell will finally end in the ruin of the most glorious Empire the sun ever shone upon, or at least may accelerate consequences, arising from American independence, which, whenever they happen, will be fatal to Britain herself.

Seventeen seventy-two was a banner year for omens of American independence. One of the most revealing articles that year appeared in the

---

[96] Philip Davidson, *Propaganda and the American Revolution, 1763–1783* (University of North Carolina Press, 1941), pp. 225–26.

[97] *Diary and Autobiography of John Adams,* September 2, 1769, vol. 1, p. 343.

Essex Gazette of Salem on February 25 and was reprinted in the *Providence Gazette* of March 7. The author, who signed himself FORESIGHT and ostensibly came from New Hampshire, reproduced many of the leading ideas:

> The reason why the people in the several provinces have not of late sent home petitions, remonstrances, &c. and continued their publications in favour of liberty, as frequent as heretofore, is, they have already sufficiently informed the Parliament, and people of Great Britain, what their sentiments and intentions are, and are now waiting to see whether Great Britain will restore their liberties—if she will not, they will soon put in practice their meditated plan, of the United Provinces, after the example of the Dutch, and form an independent commonwealth.— This plan may be easily executed whenever necessity shall require it; and such a period will soon arrive, unless Britain immediately gives up her pretensions to tax the Americans. It is evident, to every discerning eye, that perilous times are coming on in Europe, and that Britain is in imminent danger. Nothing in the nature of things, can preserve Great-Britain, but the affection and union of the Americans with her; and nothing can preserve this union, but a firm and speedy establishment of American liberty, and thereby making it the *interest* of the colonies to be united with the parent country. . . .
>
> Let it be the study of all the colonies, to establish that union between them, which is the sure foundation for freedom; and prepare to act as joint members of the Grand American Commonwealth. That these colonies will, in some future time, be an independent state, is morally certain; the only question is, how long will it be before that event takes place. But by all the signs of the times, and appearance of things, it is very near—'tis not probable that it is at the distance of fifteen years.

Most of the more daring advance notices appeared in the *Boston Gazette*. They undoubtedly came from the circle around Samuel Adams, who wrote some of them himself.

> *January* 6, 1772: If the Americans are disunited from her, and allied with another nation, it will be such a diminution of Britain's wealth and power, as must prove fatal to her. The Americans well know their weight and importance in the political scale; that their alliance, and in the privilege of a free trade with them, will be courted by all the powers in Europe; and will turn the balance in favour of any nation that enjoys it. Their situation is such, their natural advantages so great,

and so immense will be their sources of wealth and power, that instead of being subject to any foreign power (as some have vainly imagined) they may soon become the arbiters among nations, and set bounds to kingdoms—be the patrons of universal liberty, and the guardians of the rights of mankind.

The most eligible course for the Americans, and that which they will probably take, is to form a government of their own, similar to that of the United Provinces in Holland, and offer a free trade to all the nations of Europe. . . . If she [Great Britain] still pursues false maxims and arbitrary measures, the Americans will soon dissolve their union with Great Britain. They have all the advantages for independence, and every temptation to improve them that ever a people had.

November 2, 1772: The people in every town must immediately instruct their Representatives, to send a remonstrance to the King of Great Britain, and assure him, that they will (unless their liberties are immediately restored whole and entire) form an independent common wealth, after the example of the Dutch provinces—And to secure our sea ports, offer a free trade to all nations—This is the only method that affords any prospect of success; and this, will undoubtedly preserve our freedom.

Should any one province begin the example, the people in the other provinces will immediately follow; and the people of Britain must comply with our demands, or sink under the united force of all their enemies, the French and Spaniards.

December 16, 1772: What sentiments must arise in their [American] minds when they behold their enemies exalted to rule over them, and men crowned with royal favours, who ought to be committed into the hands of the executioner?—This, is sowing dangerous seed in America, and if it is not covered by future clemency, demonstrations of royal, & parliamentary, love and favour, may produce effects that will shake your throne, and kingdom; and bury both in final ruin!—Many and great are the motives that induce the Americans to look forward with eager expectation to an independent state.

Similar articles continued to appear in the *Boston Gazette* in 1773:

January 11, 1773: Truth and common sense will at last prevail, and if the Britons continue their endeavors much longer to subject us to their government and taxation, we shall become a separate State.— This is as certain as any event that has not already come to pass; for the people from every quarter of the world are coming to this country, of all trades, arts and sciences, soldiers and seamen, and in a short time the Americans will be too strong for any nation in the world.

October 11, 1773: How shall the colonies force their oppressors to terms? This question has often been answered by our politicians; viz., "Form an independent State—an American Commonwealth." This plan has been proposed, and I can't find that any other is likely to answer the great purpose of preserving our liberties. I hope, therefore, it will be well digested and forwarded, to be in due time put into execution, unless our political fathers can secure American liberties in some other way. As the population, wealth, and power of this continent are swiftly increasing, we certainly have no cause to doubt our success in maintaining liberty by forming a commonwealth, or whatever measure wisdom may point out for the preservation of the rights of America.

These voices were not weak or whimpering. Even in the relatively calm period 1772–73, they were boastful and combative. Whether or not there was much substance behind their warnings and self-glorification, they reflect a leadership willing to take chances and hit the British where it could hurt the most.

No wonder, then, that British governors were furious at the press and blamed it for their troubles. Governor Bernard traced the riots of August 14, 1765, to the *Boston Gazette* and accused it of "raising that flame in America which has given so much trouble."[98] Yet he did not dare arrest the editors or close down the office of the paper. Hutchinson later wrote to Bernard: "The misfortune is that seven eighths of the people read none but this infamous paper, and so are never undeceived."[99] In 1767, Grenville tried to get Parliament to censure "certain papers, published at Boston" as "libellous and treasonable." He was talked out of the effort, because "it was below the dignity of Parliament to pay any regard to angry newspaper writers, who were as frequent and as impudent here as they could be in any country."[100] Grenville's motion shows that the writings in the Boston papers were well known in London and enraged anti-American opinion.

Much in these articles is bluster and bravado. Yet they express ideas that helped to sustain patriotic colonial circles and give them a sense of irresistible

[98] Cited by Davidson, *Propaganda and the American Revolution*, p. 228.

[99] Hutchinson to Bernard, August 12, 1770, cited by William V. Wells, *The Life and Public Services of Samuel Adams* (Little, Brown, 1865), vol. 1, p. 206.

[100] William Samuel Johnson to William Pitkin, December 26, 1767, *MHS Collections*, 5th ser., vol. 9, p. 247. The event occurred on November 27, 1767 (*Proceedings and Debates*, vol. 3, p. 523).

destiny. These advanced groups were not diffident in their propaganda; they challenged the British with unrestrained audacity. It was commonly believed that another war with France and Spain was imminent, in which case the British would have to come on bended knee to get American help. The British needed the Americans so much that their very survival as a great power depended on American support and goodwill. The idea of American independence was the final threat if the British did not give way. In the propaganda war, the British did not have the means to fight back on equal terms. They were beaten in the press before they were defeated on the field of battle.

· 8 ·

Another sign of the times was the Boston Massacre orations. Until the incident in March 1770, the colonists had paid little attention to the units of the British army stationed among them.[101] But the Boston leadership decided that the "massacre" lent itself to a campaign against a British "standing army" in the colonies. It mattered little that the altercation had been set off by nothing more than an exchange of insults between a colonial ropemaker and a British private, that a colonial mob had attacked a British sentry, that no official order was given to the soldiers to fire, that John Adams and Josiah Quincy, Jr., had defended the commanding officer, Capt. John Preston, and that a colonial jury had found him and the other soldiers not guilty of the deaths of the five townspeople. This "massacre" became the first annual commemoration celebrated in Boston from 1771 to 1783, after which it was replaced by the Fourth of July. The annual orations were put out as pamphlets and circulated far beyond their local audiences. They were an occasion for setting forth the political line of the Boston leadership and show how far it was willing to go publicly in the six years before the Declaration of Independence.

The first oration in 1771 was given by James Lovell, a prominent schoolmaster. He quickly made clear what the memory of the "massacre" was supposed to do: "Make the bloody 5th of March the aera of the resurrection of your birthrights which have been murdered by the very strength that nursed them in their infancy." He called on the colonists to "behave with the propriety and dignity of free men and thus exhibit to the world, a new character of a people, which no history describes." He saw no

---

[101] John Shy, *Toward Lexington* (Princeton University Press, 1965), p. 376.

reason to fear separation from Great Britain: "It is said that disunited from *Britain* 'we should bleed at every vein.' I cannot see the consequence."[102]

The Boston Massacre oration the following year went even further. It was given by Joseph Warren, a Boston physician who was a member of the inner circle of the most radical leaders. Despite his profession, he was probably the most fiery in his words and actions. By this time, he was already a recognized leader of the most extreme faction.

Warren was a descendant of a seventeenth-century family in Roxbury, outside Boston. His father, of the same name, was a selectman and treasurer of his church. After graduating from Harvard, the son served his medical apprenticeship and emerged as Dr. Joseph Warren in 1763, at the age of twenty-two. Warren practiced in Boston, where he soon joined politically with some of his patients, the two Adamses, James Otis, John Hancock, and others. In 1765, he was drawn into the movement against the Stamp Act and was fully engaged in local politics, sharing the leadership with Sam Adams. In his first letter to the press against the Stamp Act, Warren struck a characteristic note: "Awake! Awake, my countrymen, and by a regular and legal opposition, defeat the designs of those who would enslave us and our posterity."[103] His biographer says that he subsequently directed "the destruction of property, tarring and feathering, and intimidation became standard political techniques" of the Warren–Sam Adams faction.[104]

After the Stamp Act crisis, Warren lived a dual existence. He conducted his medical practice with increasing success and spent whatever time was left on his growing political passion. The "well spoken, charming, and handsome doctor" was a leading advocate of violent methods against British rule.[105] In 1770, Warren urged the colonists to develop "the more martial virtues" in preparation for the time they might have to "hazard all."[106] Two years later, he made the second Boston Massacre oration in his most inflammatory style.

For Warren, the colonists were not only slaves; they were absolute slaves:

> Whoever pretends that the late acts of the British parliament for taxing America ought to be deemed binding upon us, must admit at once that we are absolute slaves, and have no property of our own, which is

[102] Hezekiah Niles, *Principles and Acts of the Revolution in America* (reprint, A. S. Barnes, 1876), pp. 17–20.
[103] John Cary, *Joseph Warren* (University of Illinois Press, 1961), for Warren's life and career.
[104] Ibid., p. 52.
[105] Ibid., pp. 54, 79.
[106] Ibid., p. 100.

entirely at the disposal of another. . . . for, if they may be taxed without their consent, even in the smallest trifle, they may also, without their consent, be deprived of every thing they possess, although never so valuable, never so dear.

He cried out against the "ruinous consequences of standing armies," which he denounced as "the ready engines of tyranny and oppression." He luridly recalled the day in 1770 "when our streets were stained with the blood of our brethren—when our ears were wounded by the groans of the dying, and our eyes were tormented with the sight of the mangled bodies of the dead." Nothing could be done on earth about the acquittal of the British soldiers, but he advised them to "be prepared to stand at the bar of an omniscient judge!"

Warren called upon their colonial ancestors to inspire the present generation to make every sacrifice to prevent "your liberties to be ravished from you by lawless force, or cajoled away by flattery and fraud." His oratorical style left nothing to the imagination: "The voice of your fathers' blood cries to you from the ground, *my sons scorn to be slaves!* in vain we met the frowns of tyrants— in vain we crossed the boisterous ocean, found a new world, and prepared it for the happy residence of liberty—in vain we toiled—in vain we fought— we bled in vain, if you, our offspring, want valor to repel the assaults of her invaders."

Warren's last words breathed the noble ambition and vast aim of a new country: "May our land be a land of liberty, the seat of virtue, the asylum of the oppressed, a name and a praise in the whole earth, until the last shock of time shall bury the empires of the world in one common undistinguished ruin!!"[107]

Such was the rhetoric that was common in Boston by the early 1770s. British governors felt themselves helpless against it. Sam Adams, Joseph Warren, and others went as far in their denunciations of British rule as they could go, short of calling for an American breakaway. When British officials learned of them in London, they were in no doubt about what they signified.

[107] Niles, *Principles and Acts of the Revolution,* pp. 20–24.

17

"The dye is now cast"

❧

ONCE THE BEST FRIEND OF the American colonies in the British government, Lord Dartmouth found himself in the position of defending the British empire against them. He changed sides as soon as he made up his mind that the fate of the empire was at stake. His choice was symptomatic of where even the most sympathetic British politicians drew the line.

In February 1774, soon after the Boston Tea Party, Dartmouth asked Atty. Gen. Edward Thurlow and Solicitor Gen. Alexander Wedderburn to pass judgment on the seriousness of the colonial infractions—insulting Parliament and obstructing lawful commerce. They replied that the offenses amounted to "the crime of high treason, namely to the levying of war against His Majesty."[1] The verdict laid the groundwork for taking the severest measures to punish Boston for its defiance.

The king, Dartmouth told Governor Hutchinson, was determined "to pursue such measures as should be effectual for securing the dependence of the said colonies upon this kingdom and for the protection of the subject in the exercise of his lawful commerce." The term *dependence* reveals the deeper spring of British motivation; it was the antithesis of what the British considered the American goal to be—independence. In practice, the issue was whether the Americans should obey the "insulted authority of this

---

[1] Attorney and Solicitor General to Dartmouth, February 11, 1774, K. G. Davies, *Documents of the American Revolution* (Irish University Press, 1975), vol. 8, p. 47.

kingdom," as Dartmouth put it, or decide for themselves whether there was any authority over them. The king, according to Dartmouth, wanted to punish Boston by suspending "all the privileges enjoyed by the town of Boston as the seat of government and a place of trade," but he had decided to lay the whole matter before both houses of Parliament in order "to vindicate the authority of Parliament."[2]

The British acted on the assumption that Boston's rebellion was the root of the evil and that by extirpating it they could return to the status quo ante. There was enough truth in this to be misleading. Boston's example was contagious and set a model for the other colonies, but they had their own radicals and militants, who needed little urging to swing into action.

Boston's punishment was mainly laid out in three bills. In March 1774, Lord North introduced a bill closing the port of Boston as "an example to the other parts of America, which will prevent them from imitating the town of Boston in various insults and outrages which from time to time have been there committed against the subjects and the laws of this country." He recognized that America as a whole was likely to go the way of Boston and sought to head it off. But North also gave a much larger reason for the crackdown on Boston. It was, he held, a move against those who maintained that Great Britain and America were "two independent states under the same Prince." The dispute was not merely over internal and external taxes, representation and taxation, or legislation and taxation; it was "whether we have or have not any authority in that country." A few days later, North served notice that it would be necessary to find "some methods by which the military force of this country may act with effect" against Massachusetts. This threat was first made in March 1774, but it was not immediately acted on.[3]

The Boston Port Bill encountered no resistance in Commons. It was even supported by such staunch defenders of the colonies as Colonel Barré, who had contributed the name to the Sons of Liberty. He freely admitted that "the country in general are against America."[4] It was this turn of British public opinion that enabled North to carry out an increasingly hostile anticolonial policy.

The North strategy to make Boston the test case of American resistance was no aberration. Everything depended on how the other colonies reacted to Boston's punishment, and there was reason to believe that Boston would

---

[2] Dartmouth to Hutchinson, March 9, 1774, ibid., p. 61.

[3] *Proceedings and Debates of the British Parliament Respecting North America, 1754–1783*, ed. R. C. Simmons and P. D. G. Thomas (Kraus International, 1983), vol. 4, pp. 57, 63–93.

[4] Ibid., p. 103.

not drag them into a wider conflict. A credible witness and participant, David Ramsay, recalled:

> The other provinces were but remotely affected by the fate of Massachusetts. They were happy, and had no cause, on their own account, to oppose the government of Great-Britain. That a people so circumstanced, should take part with a distressed neighbour, at the risque of incurring the resentment of the Mother Country, did not accord with the selfish maxims by which states, as well as individuals, are usually governed. The ruled are, for the most part, prone to suffer as long as evils are tolerable, and in general they must feel before they are roused to contend with their oppressors, but the Americans acted on a contrary principle.[5]

The Boston Port Bill effectively closed Boston harbor to commercial traffic by prohibiting the loading or unloading of ships in any part of it. In May, an Administration of Justice Act sought to protect Crown officials in Massachusetts from standing trial before hostile provincial courts. It revised the judicial system by enabling the governor to appoint and remove inferior judges, sheriffs, and justices of the peace. Next, a Massachusetts Government Bill sought to show that the colony was not going to be governed as before. It partially abrogated the Massachusetts charter of 1691 by giving the London government the power to appoint all members of the council, whose approval of the governor's actions had previously been required. These Coercive Acts, as they were known, were intended to break Boston's will to resist.

North openly avowed what he hoped to achieve by them. Boston, he said, "has been the ringleader of all violence and opposition to the execution of the laws of this country. New York and Philadelphia grew unruly on receiving the news of the triumph of the people of Boston. Boston has not only therefore to answer for its own violence but for having incited other places to tumults."

The real struggle, he contended, was no longer about taxation. It was about who was going to submit to whom: "They deny our legislative authority. Not all the places but there are those who hold and defend that doctrine. If they deny authority in one instance it goes to all. We must control them or submit to them."[6]

---

[5] David Ramsay, *The History of the American Revolution* (Philadelphia, 1789), vol. 1, p. 113.

[6] March 14, 1774, *Proceedings and Debates*, vol. 4, pp. 75–76.

North's political objective was spelled out. "I propose in this bill," he said of the Massachusetts Government Bill, "to take the executive power from the hands of the democratic part of government."[7] He later declared: "The Americans have tarred and feathered your subjects, plundered your merchants, burnt your ships, denied all obedience to your laws and authority; yet so clement, and so long forbearing has our conduct been, that it is incumbent on us now to make a different course. *Whatever may be the consequence, we must risk something; if we do not, all is over.*"[8] He insisted that the bill was the dividing line: "We are now to establish our authority, or give it up entirely."[9] On the other side, the colonists' friend Lord Camden replied: "This Bill will either produce War or Slavery, both equally bad for this country, since they must both be supported by violence."[10]

Yet North was criticized in the Commons debate for not cracking down on Boston hard enough. The government majority was one-sided—239 to 64. One reason was that sentiment in the country had turned sharply against the colonies. Even past American defenders agreed that Boston deserved punishment.

In May, Hutchinson was finally saved from further torment and humiliation. He gave up the governorship, went to England, from which he never returned, and was replaced by Gen. Thomas Gage, who doubled as governor and commander in chief. Hutchinson soon met with North, who confided to him what was behind British policy. North thought that the Coercive Acts should have come earlier, at the previous session of Parliament, when both the Massachusetts Council and House had made their "Declaration of Independence." North said that he had acted as soon as he could get all parties to unite "in the necessity of a change, in order to prevent the Colony from entirely throwing of[f] their dependence."[11]

Again and again the stress was put on the main point—colonial dependence. Boston had dared to challenge it and could not be forgiven until it acknowledged that Parliament had the rightful power to legislate for the colonies. By this time the crisis had gone so far that the British began to make plans for the use of force. In April, Dartmouth gave instructions to General Gage to employ "Troops with effect, should the madness of

[7] March 28, 1774, ibid., p. 150.
[8] April 22, 1774, ibid., p. 276.
[9] May 4, 1774, ibid., p. 383.
[10] May 11, 1774, ibid., p. 422.
[11] Hutchinson related his conversation with North in a letter of July 8, 1774, to a friend in America, *Diary and Letters of His Excellency Thomas Hutchinson*, ed. Peter Orlando Hutchinson (London, 1883), vol. 1, p. 181.

the People on the one hand, or the timidity or want of Strength of the peace officers on the other hand, make it necessary to have recourse to their assistance." Gage, who had four regiments at hand, was told "to use every endeavour to avoid it," but he was not to be satisfied without "a full and absolute submission." Dartmouth was not optimistic—"The last Advices from Boston are of a nature to leave but little room to hope, that order and obedience are seen likely to take the place of Anarchy and Usurpation."[12]

When Gage reached Boston in May, he reported that Hutchinson, Chief Justice Peter Oliver, the commissioners of customs, and the tea consignees had taken refuge at Castle William in the harbor, "not daring to reside at Boston." By this time, Gage added, a town meeting had decided to ask the other colonies to cease all exports and imports to and from Great Britain, Ireland, and the West Indies until the Boston Port Bill was repealed.[13]

Yet, as each side moved inexorably towards a test of strength, Dartmouth was still regarded as the least anti-American of North's ministers. He even seems to have entertained the thought that the tea duty might be repealed, if the Bostonians showed signs of behaving themselves. If they did not, he was resigned to going to the bitter end, agonizing all the way.[14]

· 2 ·

The Bostonians showed no signs of backing down, and they were not alone.

The text of the Port Act reached Boston in May 1774. The Committee of Correspondence immediately went into action. The British crackdown was made to order for Sam Adams. The town meeting, to which Gage alluded, appointed Adams to compose an appeal for the support of the other colonies:

> The Town of Boston is now Suffering the Stroke of Vengeance in the Common Cause of America. I hope they will sustain the Blow with a becoming fortitude; and that the Effects of this cruel Act, intended to intimidate and subdue the Spirits of all America will by the joynt Efforts of all be frustrated.

[12] Dartmouth to Gage, April 9, 1774, *The Correspondence of General Thomas Gage with the Secretaries of State, 1763–1775* (Yale University Press, 1931), vol. 2, pp. 159–62.
[13] Davies, *Documents of the American Revolution*, vol. 8, pp. 115–16.
[14] Benjamin Woods Labaree, *The Boston Tea Party* (Oxford University Press, 1964), pp. 182–83.

The People receive this Edict with Indignation. It is expected by their Enemies and fear[e]d by some of their Friends, that this Town singly will not be able to support the Cause under so severe a Tryal. As the very being of every Colony, consider[e]d as a free People depends upon the Event, a Thought so dishonorable to our Brethren cannot be entertained, as that this Town will now be left to struggle alone.[15]

The immediate response to the Bostonians was mixed. Many of the colonies were still divided in their sympathies; resolute support came mainly from Virginia. There another remarkable cohort of colonial leaders—George Washington, Richard Henry Lee, Richard Bland, Peyton Randolph, Thomas Jefferson, George Mason, Patrick Henry, and others—went as far as the Bostonians could have wished. By July, Washington and Mason had put together twenty-four "Resolves," one of which threatened the use of force if King George went so far as "to reduce his faithful Subjects in America to a State of Desperation."[16] Philadelphia, New York, and other places elsewhere still held back.

By June 1774, Dartmouth had given up hope of placating the rebellious colonists. To Gage, he confided his darkest fears, especially about what was at stake for Great Britain: "not only its dignity and reputation but its power."[17] Gage dissolved the Boston legislature soon after receiving Dartmouth's message.[18]

In mid-1774, opinion in Massachusetts was still fairly fluid. "The ideas of the people," John Adams's diary in June 1774 reads, "are as various as their faces."[19] Even on the pro-American side, they varied from the extremism of Sam Adams to the moderation of John Rowe, the merchant. Rowe, like others caught in the middle, did not approve of destroying private property—in this case, tea—without compensation. Benjamin Franklin repeatedly urged the Bostonians to pay for it. When Rowe learned of the Massachusetts Government Act annulling the old charter, he entered these words in his diary on June 2, 1774: "I am afraid of the Consequences that this Act will Produce. I wish for Harmony & Peace between Great Britain Our Mother Country & the Colonies— but the Time is far off. The People have done amiss & no sober man

[15] *The Writings of Samuel Adams*, ed. Harry Alonzo Cushing (G. P. Putnam's Sons, 1906), vol. 3, p. 108.

[16] "Fairfax County Resolves," no. 23, July 18, 1774, *The Papers of George Mason*, ed. Robert A. Rutland (University of North Carolina Press, 1970), vol. 1, p. 209.

[17] Dartmouth to Gage, June 3, 1774, Davies, *Documents of the American Revolution*, vol. 8, p. 124.

[18] Gage to Dartmouth, June 26, 1774, ibid., p. 136.

[19] June 20, 1774, *The Works of John Adams*, ed. Charles Francis Adams (Boston, 1861), vol. 2, p. 338.

can vindicate their Conduct but the Revenge of the Ministry is too severe."[20]

On June 15, more than 800 Boston merchants met "to Consult on the Distress of this Place." Nothing came of it, those in attendance "being much Divided in Sentiment." On June 17, Rowe recorded: "The People at present seem very averse to Accommodate Matters, I think they will Repent of their Behaviour, sooner or later." On June 28: Another meeting to discuss the actions of the Committee of Correspondence—"The Merchants have taken up against them, they have in my Opinion exceeded their Power & the Motion was Put that they should be dismissed." It was voted down four to one. On July 14: Some ministers recommended a day of fasting. "I cannot Reconcile this measure & should much Rather the People would do Justice & Recommend the Payment for the Tea instead of losing a Day by fasting."[21] Rowe was on the losing side in this argument; payment for the tea was cried down.

In this still indecisive climate of opinion, Boston clearly could not hold out alone. The remedy obviously required it to get the other colonies to act in concert with Massachusetts. Towards this end, the Bostonians called for a "Solemn League and Covenant," pledging all to cease the import, export, or consumption of British goods and to boycott anyone who refused to sign it.

The covenant effort was not a success, but it led to something much larger. In Boston itself, many merchants protested that it went too far or was premature. Other colonies were reluctant to ruin their own merchants to rescue Boston's. Philadelphia replied that *"moderate prudent* Measures" should be tried first.[22] The measure on which almost all the colonies could agree was a continental congress to take up the various grievances and decide what to do about them. It was considered moderate and prudent, because no one could be sure what would come of it, and in any case it postponed the day of decision. Sam Adams, who had previously advocated some such gathering and still wanted it, now worried that it could not act "speedily enough to answer for the present Emergency."[23] The covenant and the congress were not in conflict, but the limited success of the one encouraged the other to go forward.

For Gage, however, the covenant was too much to bear. He issued

---

[20] *Letters and Diary of John Rowe*, ed. Anne Rowe Cunningham (W. B. Clarke, 1903), p. 274.

[21] Ibid., pp. 275–78.

[22] John C. Miller, *Sam Adams* (Little, Brown, 1936), p. 305.

[23] Adams to Silas Deane, May 18, 1774; Adams to Charles Thomson, May 30, 1774, *Writings of Samuel Adams*, vol. 3, pp. 115, 123–24.

a proclamation denouncing it as a "traitorous combination" and the correspondence about it as "a scandalous, traitorous, and seditious Letter," and he ordered the arrest of anyone publishing or signing it.[24] About all this fury did was to make everyone who signed the letter swell the ranks of putative "traitors."

By June 1774, Dartmouth and Gage had more to worry about. This time the lead came from Virginia. As Thomas Jefferson later related, the Virginians at the end of May deliberately provoked the governor, John Murray, fourth earl of Dunmore. The younger leaders, such as Jefferson, were, in his words, seeking a way to arouse "our people from the lethargy into which they had fallen as to passing events" in order to "boldly take an unequivocal stand in the line with Massachusetts." They hit on a scheme to declare a day of "fasting, humiliation & Prayer" as most likely to "call up & alarm their attention." Then they "cooked up a resolution"—Jefferson's words—for the House of Burgesses to pass. Dunmore took it as an insult to the king and Parliament that gave him reason to dissolve the House. His move invited the vast majority of the House to go him one better.[25]

Eighty-nine members quickly met separately and formed an "association" that was itself an extralegal challenge to the established political system, which did not provide for unauthorized, competitive political bodies. They issued a statement expressing the opinion that "an attack, made on one of our sister colonies, to compel submission to arbitrary taxes, is an attack made on all British America"—which was just what the Bostonians hoped for. They instructed the local Committee of Correspondence to sound out the other colonial committees on the advisability of meeting annually in a general congress "to deliberate on those general measures which the united interests of America may from time to time require."[26]

In mid-June 1774, the decision was made to hold the proposed congress in Philadelphia on September 1. All the colonies except Georgia voted to attend.

Even before the congress assembled, the reaction to these events in London and by the colonial governors was a mixture of outrage and

---

[24] Labaree, Boston Tea Party, p. 227; Lawrence Henry Gipson, The British Empire Before the American Revolution (Alfred A. Knopf, 1965), vol. 12, p. 154. Gipson differs from Miller on the outside support given to the covenant, but Miller's evidence is very strong (Gipson, vol. 12, 1965, p. 154; Miller, pp. 304–6).

[25] Autobiography, The Works of Thomas Jefferson, ed. Paul Leicester Ford (G. P. Putnam's Sons, 1904), vol. 1, pp. 11–13.

[26] "Resolution of the House of Burgesses Designating a Day of Fasting and Prayer," May 24, 1774, ibid., pp. 107–8.

consternation. From New York, Lt. Gov. Cadwallader Colden, in charge in the absence of a governor, wrote Dartmouth:

> These transactions are dangerous, my lord, and illegal but by what means shall government prevent them? An attempt by the power of the civil magistrate would only show their weakness, and it is not easy to say upon what foundation a military aid should be called in. Such a measure would involve us in troubles which it is thought much more prudent to avoid, and to shun all extremes while it is yet possible things may take a favourable turn.[27]

From Lt. Gov. William Bull of South Carolina, Dartmouth received more bad news:

> I had expectation that the measures taken by the Parliament relative to Boston would have had some happy effect towards composing the disturbances in this province which seemed to have subsided a little last winter, but it has taken a contrary turn. Their own apprehensions and thoughts confirmed by the resolutions and correspondence from other colonies have raised an universal spirit of jealousy against Great Britain and of unanimity towards each other. I say universal, my lord, for few who think otherwise are hardy enough to avow it publicly. . . .[28]

As the congress convened, the newly appointed Lt. Gov. Thomas Oliver of Massachusetts sent a panic-stricken letter to Dartmouth. Oliver thought that he was safe from attack but learned better as soon as he took the oath of office. He was able to withstand a crowd of 1,500 in the morning, but the afternoon was different. It is best to give the rest of the story in his own words, even if at some length, to get a sense of the terror that gripped the second-highest official in the colony:

> But in the afternoon I observed such companies pouring in from all quarters, and those of a lower class, I began to apprehend they would become unmanageable, and fearing some troubles would arise wherein I should be called upon, I chose to get out of the way. I was just going into my carriage [in Cambridge] to proceed to Boston when a vast crowd advanced and in a short time my house was surrounded by 4000 people and one-4th part in arms. Not apprehending any

[27] Colden to Dartmouth, July 6, 1774, Davies, *Documents of the American Revolution*, vol. 8, p. 147.
[28] Bull to Dartmouth, July 31, 1774, ibid., pp. 153–54.

abuse designed to me I waited in my hall, where 5 persons entered with a decent appearance who informed me they were a committee from the body of the people to demand my resignation as a Councillor [Oliver's other official position]. I reproached them with ingratitude and false dealings and refused to hear them. They answered that the people were dissatisfied with the votes of their committee in the morning and now demanded my resignation as drawn up in a paper which they held in their hands. I absolutely refused to sign any paper. They desired me to consider the consequences of refusing the demands of an outraged people. I told them they might put me to death but I would never submit.

Oliver held out as long as he could:

The populace, growing impatient, began to press up to my windows, calling for vengeance against the foes of their liberty. The five persons appeared anxious for me and, impressed with some humanity, endeavoured to appease the people; but in vain. I could hear them from a distance swearing that they would have my blood. At this time the distresses of my wife and children, which I heard in the next room, called up feelings, my lord, which I confess I could not suppress. I found myself giving way, and at that instant nature ingenious in forming new reasons suggested to my mind the calamities which would ensue if I did not comply.

A desperate Oliver finally broke down:

I cast about to find some means of preserving my reputation, I proposed that the people should take me by force, but they urged the danger of such an expedient. I told them I would take the risk but they would not consent. Reduced to this extremity I took up the paper and, casting my eyes over it with a hurry of mind and conflict of passion which rendered me unable to remark the contents, I wrote underneath the following words "My house being surrounded with four thousand people, in compliance with their commands I sign my name Tho. Oliver."

This is how his ordeal ended:

The five persons taking it carried it out to the people and found great difficulty in getting it accepted. I had several messages sent me informing me it would not do. But I declared I would do nothing else if they put me to death. The more respectable farmers used all their endeavours to reconcile the rest and finally prevailed, when they all marched off in their several companies wishing me well but cautioning not to break my promise. Thus, my lord, I have given you a plain narrative of the proceedings of this day.[29]

Such were the messages that Dartmouth received as the preparations for the congress proceeded. They gave the impression of a complete breakdown of the imperial structure in the colonies. Gage explained why he had "experienced much timidity and backwardness, which finding in those pointed to me as staunch friends to government surprised me a good deal." Many tradespeople feared the loss of customers "should they appear too openly in favour of government." Many loyal merchants did not want to see smuggling totally prevented. Government employees were afraid that the vigorous policy might be relaxed and "they should be left as they have been before to the mercy of their opponents and their mobs."[30] Gage blamed Boston more than Virginia. As the congress neared, he reported: "It is agreed that popular fury was never greater in this province than at present and it has taken its rise from the old source at Boston, though it has appeared first at a distance." Past government weakness was responsible: "Those demagogues trust their safety in the long forbearance of government and an assurance that they can't be punished here. They chicane, elude, openly violate or passively resist the laws as opportunities serve, and opposition to authority is of so long standing that it is become habitual."[31]

By the time the congress convened, Gage was distraught. The courts were immobilized "as no jurors would appear." The entire system had broken down: "It was considered that the whole is now at stake." Connecticut and Rhode Island were "as furious as they are in this province [Massachusetts]." As Gage went on, he became more and more desperate: "Civil government is near its end, the courts of justice expiring one after another." He meant "to avoid any bloody crisis as long as possible unless forced into it by themselves, which may happen," but he had no faith that it could be avoided:

Nothing that is said at present can palliate; conciliating, moderation, reasoning is over; nothing can be done but by forcible means. Though the people are not held in high estimation by the troops, yet they are numerous, worked up to a fury, and not a Boston rabble but the

[29] Oliver to Dartmouth, September 3, 1774, ibid., pp. 182–84.
[30] Gage to Dartmouth, July 27, 1774, ibid., p. 152.
[31] Gage to Dartmouth, August 27, 1774, ibid., p. 166.

freeholders and farmers of the country. A check anywhere would be fatal and the first stroke will decide a great deal. We should therefore be strong and proceed on a good foundation before anything decisive is tried, which it's to be presumed will prove successful.[32]

The popular "fury" in 1774 that followed the Boston Tea Party needs explanation. For three years, after most of the Townshend Acts had been repealed, the colonies, including Massachusetts and Virginia, had been relatively quiet and had given little warning of the future outburst. This calm was one reason why the British had not expected the single exception of tea to cause so much uproar. Yet the "lethargy," as Jefferson had called it in Virginia, was deceptive. All the revolutionary leaders had to do in Massachusetts and Virginia was touch the right buttons, and the pent-up resentment and rebelliousness again broke loose. The years from the Stamp Act to the First Continental Congress were not an unbroken chain of events; they went through a number of ups and downs, depending largely on British policy. But an underground stream of revolutionary energy flowed throughout the decade and gave continuity to the periodic eruptions of protest and fury. After 1774, it was only a matter of time before Gage's fatalism that "nothing can be done but by forcible means" brought about the last eruption.

By now, the British felt themselves to be hopelessly on the defensive. The main question was not what they could do to put down the colonial unrest, short of using force, but whether the colonists themselves were sufficiently united to carry on a sustained offensive. The question was still open as the meeting of the First Continental Congress approached.

· 3 ·

The great question that confronted the sixty-four delegates to the Continental Congress on September 5, 1774, was: To what extent were they willing to break the bonds with Great Britain?[33] Almost two months later, when they adjourned on October 26, they had not yet come to a decision—but it was much closer.

---

[32] Gage to Dartmouth, September 2, 1774, ibid., pp. 180–82.

[33] The list appears in Edmund C. Burnett, ed., *Letters of Members of the Continental Congress* (Carnegie Institution of Washington, 1921), pp. xli–lxvi. The numbers present at any one time fluctuated.

The delegates made up a fair cross section of the most eminent and representative colonial figures on both sides of the issue. Among those present were John Adams, Samuel Adams, James Bowdoin, and Thomas Cushing of Massachusetts; Roger Sherman, Silas Deane, and William Samuel Johnson of Connecticut; James Duane, John Jay, Philip Livingston, and Robert R. Livingston of New York; John Dickinson and Joseph Galloway of Pennsylvania; Stephen Hopkins and Samuel Ward of Connecticut; Christopher Gadsden and Edward Rutledge of South Carolina; Patrick Henry, Richard Henry Lee, Peyton Randolph, and George Washington of Virginia. Since the decision was made to keep the proceedings secret, we are dependent on diaries, notes, letters, and memories of participants. Just what happened, however, is sufficiently clear.

In effect, two schools of thought—or "parties," as Joseph Galloway later called them[34]—struggled for supremacy. They emerged on the very first day and persisted throughout the congress. Patrick Henry immediately talked as if the colonial bonds were already broken: "Government is dissolved, Fleets and Armies and the present State of Things shew that Government is dissolved. . . . We are in a State of Nature, Sir. . . . I am not a Virginian, but an American."[35] But John Jay objected: "I can[']t yet think that all Government is at an End. The Measure of arbitrary Power is not full, and I think it must run over, before We undertake to frame a new Constitution."[36]

Henry's extreme views were premature. The Boston delegation, although as militant as any, was determined to avoid a split in the congress. It quickly learned that a break could not be avoided if anything that implied independence was insisted on. "Absolute Indepen[den]cy etc.," John Adams found, "are Ideas which Startle People here."[37] John Jay declared: "War is by general Consent to be waived at present," and everyone realized that independence without war was not likely.[38] George Washington assured a correspondent that "it is not the wish or interest of that Government [Massachusetts], or any other upon this continent, separately or collectively, to set up for independency." But, he quickly added, "you may at the same time rely on [it], that none of them will ever submit to the loss of those

[34] [Joseph Galloway], *Historical and Political Reflections on the Rise and Progress of the American Rebellion* (London, 1780), p. 66.

[35] *The Diary and Autobiography of John Adams*, ed. R. H. Butterfield (Harvard University Press, 1961), vol. 2, pp. 124–25.

[36] Ibid., p. 126.

[37] John Adams to Joseph Palmer, September 26, 1774, Burnett, *Letters of Members of the Continental Congress*, vol. 1, p. 48.

[38] *Diary and Autobiography of John Adams*, vol. 2, p. 139.

valuable rights and privileges, which are essential to the happiness of every free state and without which, life, liberty, and property are rendered totally insecure."[39] He still could or would not say "where the line between Great Britain and the Colonies should be drawn."[40] This was the easy, middle-of-the-road formula which enabled Washington and others at the congress as late as the end of 1774 to avoid facing the ultimate question— for or against independence?

Yet the specter of war hovered over the meetings. "They have drawn the Sword," said Eliphalet Dyer of Connecticut, "in order to execute their Plan, of subduing America. I imagine they will not sheath it, but that the next Summer will decide the Fate of America." Thomas Cushing agreed that Great Britain "has drawn the sword against Us, and nothing prevents her sheathing it in our Bowells but Want of Sufficient Force." Patrick Henry was most pessimistic: "I am inclined to think the present Measures lead to War."[41]

Early in the congress, war cries almost sounded. A false report was received that Boston had been bombarded by British warships. John Adams wrote to his wife: "War! War! War! was the Cry, and it was pronounced in a Tone, which would have done Honour to the Oratory of a Briton or a Roman. If it had proved true, you would have heard the Thunder of an American Congress."[42] When this rumor proved to be false, the tone changed. Adams informed a correspondent: "They will not, at this session, vote to raise men or money, or arms or ammunition. Their opinions are fixed against hostilities and rupture, except they should become absolutely necessary; and this necessity they do not yet see. They dread the thoughts of an action, because it would make a wound which would never be healed; it would fix and establish a rancor which would descend to the latest generations; it would light up the flames of war, perhaps through the whole continent, which might rage for twenty years, and end in the subduction of America as likely as in her liberation."[43]

Nevertheless, the congress sent General Gage a message which evoked

[39] Washington to Capt. Robert Mackenzie, October 9, 1774, *The Writings of George Washington*, ed. John C. Fitzpatrick (Government Printing Office, 1931), vol. 3, p. 246.

[40] Washington to Bryan Fairfax, August 24, 1774, ibid., p. 242.

[41] *Diary and Autobiography of John Adams*, vol. 2, pp. 140, 143.

[42] John Adams to Abigail Adams, September 18, 1774, *Adams Family Correspondence*, ed. L. H. Butterfield (Harvard University Press, 1963), vol. 1, p. 159. The bombardment rumor seems to have been factually wrong; the false rumor that set off all the excitement in Boston itself was about a fight between British soldiers and colonists in which the soldiers killed six persons (*The Literary Diary of Ezra Stiles*, ed. Franklin Bowditch Dexter [Charles Scribner's Sons, 1901], vol. 1, pp. 477–85).

[43] Adams to William Tudor, October 7, 1774, Burnett, *Letters of Members of the Continental Congress*, vol. 1, p. 65.

"the horrors of civil war" if he continued to behave in a hostile manner.[44] This letter was a toned-down version of one submitted by Samuel Adams, whose language was far more threatening: "Your Situation Sir is extremely critical. A rupture between the Inhabitants of the Province over which you preside and the Troops under your Command would produce Consequences of the most serious Nature: A Wound which would never be heald! It would probably establish Animosities between Great Britain & the Colonies which time would never eradicate!"[45]

Another indication of the mood that dominated the congress was the reception of the so-called Suffolk Resolves. While the larger Continental Congress was meeting, local conventions were organized in Massachusetts, orchestrated by Joseph Warren. One convention in Suffolk County produced resolutions that went further in revolutionary letter and spirit than anything of the kind before. They denounced a "licentious minister," "the parricide which points the dagger at our bosoms," and "the endless and numberless curses of slavery upon us." They still recognized the king as the colonies' rightful sovereign but rejected every other connection in the most provocative terms—Parliament was guilty of "attempts of a wicked administration to enslave America," all British-appointed officers who refused to resign were "obstinate and incorrigible enemies to this country," the present government was "tyrannical and unconstitutional." They told inhabitants of towns and districts to "use their utmost diligence to acquaint themselves with the art of war as soon as possible" and "appear under arms at least once every week." They urged the stoppage of all commercial intercourse with Great Britain. These resolves were unanimously approved, with praise for "the wisdom and fortitude, with which opposition to these wicked ministerial measures has hitherto been conducted."[46]

But with independence and war in fact ruled out, the great debate in Philadelphia was set off by a "Plan of Union" presented by Joseph Galloway. Galloway was supported by several others and confronted the majority of the congress with the ultimate question—what price were they were willing to pay for peace?

Galloway's credentials were as impressive as anyone else's in that distinguished company. His family went back to the mid-seventeenth century. He had been brought up in affluent circumstances and, like most of the others, practiced law. In Philadelphia, Galloway married into one of

[44] *Journals of the Continental Congress, 1774–1789,* ed. Worthington C. Ford (Washington, 1904), vol. 1, pp. 60–61.

[45] "The Continental Congress to General Gage," October 10, 1774, *Writings of Samuel Adams,* vol. 3, pp. 161–62.

[46] *Journals of the Continental Congress,* vol. 1, pp. 32–39.

the richest families and came to possess a large town house and five country estates. When he entered Pennsylvania politics in the 1750s, he gravitated to the faction headed by Benjamin Franklin and for the next twenty years served as Franklin's first lieutenant. After Franklin went to England in 1757, Galloway minded his political interests at home. Franklin—older by almost a quarter of a century—was his mentor, and in the turbulent politics of Pennsylvania they were more than allies; they operated as a team, with Franklin the senior partner. From London, Franklin kept Galloway abreast of what was happening and what his thoughts were about people and events, as if they were two of a kind. As late as January 1774, only a few months before the congress, Franklin assured his son, William, that he "always had the strongest reliance on the steadiness of his [Galloway's] friendship, and on the best grounds, the knowledge I have of his integrity, and the often repeated disinterested services he has rendered me."[47] There does not seem to have been a breach between them until Galloway presented his "Plan of Union" at the Continental Congress.

That someone so close to Franklin for so many years should have been the bugbear of the congress is one of the anomalies of the revolutionary process. Galloway's plan was a desperate attempt to reconcile the irreconcilable. His introductory statement at the congress, in the sometimes cryptic notes of John Adams, was designed to put the best face on his proposals for the benefit of those who, he later claimed, wanted "to throw off all subordination and connexion with Great-Britain."[48] He said that he had always thought the colonies were exempt from all laws made by the British Parliament. This much agreed with the extremists, who were content to stop there. But Galloway continued: "I am well aware that my Arguments tend to an Independency of the Colonies, and militate against the Maxim that there must be some absolute Power to draw together all the Wills and strength of the Empire."[49] Yet he protested: "I am as much a friend of liberty [as] exists—and No Man shall go further, in Point of Fortune, or in Point of Blood, than the Man who now addresses you." He went even further: "We are independent States. The Law of Great Britain don[']t bind us in any Case whatever." Nevertheless, the colonies needed the assistance and protection of Great Britain, and protection went together with allegiance. He therefore proposed to divide the problem in two—laws for internal policy in each colony, and laws for more than one colony, such as raising

[47] Benjamin Franklin to William Franklin, January 5, 1774, *The Papers of Benjamin Franklin*, ed. Leonard W. Labaree (Yale University Press, 1961), vol. 21, pp. 7–8.

[48] Galloway, *Historical and Political Reflections on the American Rebellion*, p. 66.

[49] *Diary and Autobiography of John Adams*, vol. 2, p. 130.

money for war. His formula to cover both cases was this: "No one Act can be done, without the Assent of Great Britain.—No one without the Assent of America. A British American Legislature."

Galloway then sought a tie that could still bind Great Britain and the colonies. He found it in the area of trade, which the colonies had previously accepted as a British prerogative, so long as it was fairly based on the interests of the entire empire. To the objection that the British Parliament and ministry would take advantage of British control over trade to continue to tax and increase their power over the colonies, Adams had him say: "We shall not be bound further than We acknowledge it." In this and other respects, Galloway seemed to lean over backward to give the colonies the last word, short of cutting all ties with Great Britain—or at least that is how Adams understood him. Adams described Galloway as a "sensible and learned" but cold speaker. Evidently Adams did not immediately regard his ideas as beyond serious consideration. In Adams's version, Galloway seems to want to have the best of both worlds—American "independence" of some sort and allegiance to Great Britain.[50] But beneath the surface, each side may well have suspected that the other was hiding its true goal—Galloway that the radicals were really committed to independence but could not admit it, and the radicals that Galloway was really bent on dragging the colonies into British subjection but would not admit it.

The organizational details of Galloway's plan were reminiscent of Franklin's old plan of 1754. Galloway proposed that a "British and American legislature" should regulate the administration of the "general affairs" of America. The administration would include a president general, appointed by the king, and a Grand Council, chosen by the colonial assemblies. The Grand Council was to possess all the rights, liberties, and privileges of the House of Commons. In addition, the president and Grand Council were to be "an inferior and distinct branch of the British legislature, united and incorporated with it," but both bodies would need to approve laws passed by either one.[51]

The plan posed at least as many questions as it answered. Galloway explained

[50] Ibid., pp. 141–44, 150. Some years later, Galloway reconstructed his introductory statement in *Historical and Political Reflections on the American Rebellion*, pp. 70–81. But he reconstructed it for a very different British audience; Adams's account tells what his American listeners got out of it at the time. Julian P. Boyd pointed out the differences between the two with the comment "If we accept the Adams version as being the substance of what he actually said, the speech was as well tempered and as conciliatory as the *Arguments on Both Sides* from much of it was drawn" (*Anglo-American Union: Joseph Galloway's Plans to Preserve the British Empire, 1774–1788* [University of Pennsylvania Press, 1941], pp. 35–36). There is no doubt that Galloway attempted to give the most moderate version of his plan in his introductory statement, and this is what the delegates had to consider.

[51] "A Plan of A Proposed Union between Great Britain and the Colonies," reprinted in Joseph Galloway, *Selected Tracts* (Da Capo Press, 1974), vol. 1, pp. 27–29.

that he did not consider it perfect and had merely intended it to serve as a basis for discussion or negotiation. It was hardly clear how the Grand Council could be an inferior branch of the British Parliament if it had as much right as Parliament to approve laws. Nevertheless, Galloway's basic purpose was sufficiently clear—to give the colonies a new setup they would largely control without breaking the umbilical cord to Great Britain and its Parliament.

The reception of Galloway's plan at the congress tells as much as anything else about the doubts and divisions that still beset the colonists on the way to the final break. He received substantial support. Edward Rutledge said that he thought "the Plan may be freed from almost every objection. I think it almost a perfect Plan." John Dickinson came out for the regulation of colonial trade by Parliament. John Jay was "led to adopt this Plan." He suggested that it gave the colonies much and took away nothing by asking: "Does this Plan give up any one Liberty?—or interfere with any one Right?" To a correspondent at this time, Jay confided: "God knows how the Contest will end. I sincerely wish it may terminate in a lasting Union with Great Britain."[52] James Duane was a particularly zealous advocate for Galloway; he seconded the motion to adopt the plan. Isaac Low of New York declared: "We ought not to deny the just Rights of our Mother Country. We have too much Reason in this Congress, to suspect that Independency is aimed at."[53] Stephen Hopkins also favored the plan.[54] The vote—by colonies— on whether to give it further consideration went in favor of Galloway by six to five. He later claimed that he had been supported by "men of the best fortunes" and "all the men of property."[55]

But Richard Henry Lee and Patrick Henry—their names are the only ones specifically mentioned by Adams—spoke up against the plan, and they were supported by the majority of delegates. In the end, the opposition succeeded—though how is not entirely clear—not merely in voting it down but expunging it from the record.[56] In the internecine struggle among the colonists, the victors no longer dealt gently with the losers.

52 Jay to John Vardill, September 24, 1774, Paul H. Smith, ed., *Letters of Delegates to Congress, 1774–1789* (Library of Congress, 1976), vol. 1, p. 95.

53 *Diary and Autobiography of John Adams*, vol. 2, pp. 133 (Dickinson), 142–43 (Duane), 143 (Edward Rutledge), 143 (John Jay), 148 (Low).

54 Diary of Samuel Ward, October 22, 1774, in Smith, *Letters of Delegates to Congress*, vol. 1, p. 234.

55 *Examination of Joseph Galloway by a Committee of the House of Commons*, ed. Thomas Balch, the Seventy-six Society, 1855, p. 48; Galloway, *Historical and Political Reflections*, p. 81.

56 [Joseph Galloway], *A Candid Examination of the Mutual Claims of Great-Britain and the Colonies* (New York, 1775), p. 52. In his diary, Ward merely said that the plan was "dismissed" (Smith, *Letters of Delegates to Congress*, vol. 1, p. 234). But see the editorial discussion, pp. 112–17 n. 1. Also see *Journals of the Continental Congress*, vol. 1, p. 51 n. 1. There is no mention of Galloway's plan in the *Journals*.

After disposing of Galloway's plan, the delegates still had to decide on what positive actions to take. They adopted a nonimportation agreement to begin December 1, 1774. They halted exports to Great Britain, Ireland, and the West Indies as of September 10, 1775. They set up an "Association" to enforce the economic sanctions against Great Britain. They decided to reconvene on May 10, 1775, if their grievances were not redressed by that time.

Of all the actions of the congress, the association may have been the most significant. It was dual power par excellence put in place before the actual Revolution. The councils and assemblies no longer served the purpose of representing the colonial rebels, because governors prevented them from meeting. The association was a permanent, policy-enforcing body that represented the colonists alone and was set up to punish the British at their weakest economic link. It was clearly an organ of struggle, far beyond the bounds of the committees of correspondence, which were designed merely to exchange information.

The congress also sent forth "Addresses" that stated its case to both the colonists and the outside world. An "Address to the People of Great-Britain" was most interesting for its intrusion into domestic British politics. It sought to convince the British people that they were faced with the same fate as the Americans. "May not a Ministry with the same armies inslave you!" it warned. If that happened, the colonists could not be expected to "refuse to assist in reducing you to the same abject state," as if in an act of revenge. "Take care," the British people were exhorted, "that you do not fall into the pit that is preparing for us." Yet hope was not lost. "You have been told that we are seditious, impatient of government and desirous of independency." Nothing was further from the truth: "Be assured that these are not facts, but calumnies.—Permit us to be free as yourselves, and we shall ever esteem a union with you to be our greatest glory and our greatest happiness." What would it take? "Place us in the same situation that we were at the close of the last war, and our former harmony will be restored."[57]

A "Memorial to the Inhabitants of the Colonies" also located the trouble with Great Britain to "soon after the conclusion of the late war." It rehearsed all the familiar grievances and blamed Parliament and the administration for having been "equally injurious, and irritating to this devoted country." It especially defended Massachusetts against the charge of having been "particularly disrespectful to Great-Britain" and stressed that all the colonies

[57] *Journals of the Continental Congress*, vol. 1 pp. 82–90.

had equally opposed "the power assumed by parliament." Now the British aim was "to extinguish the freedom of these colonies, by subjecting them to a despotic government." A veiled threat of something more than economic measures followed—"if the peaceable mode of opposition recommended by us, be broken and rendered ineffectual, as your cruel and haughty ministerial enemies, from a contemptuous opinion of your firmness, insolently predict will be the case, you must inevitably be reduced to chuse, either a more dangerous contest, or a final, ruinous, and infamous submission."[58]

A "Petition to the King" blamed Parliament for all the "unhappy differences between Great-Britain and these colonies," which, it said, "fly to the foot of his throne and implore his clemency for protection against them." It assured him that he had no British subjects with more "affectionate attachment to your majesty's person, family and government" and that the petitioners did not wish "a diminution of the prerogative, nor do we solicit the grant of any new right in our favour." Again they pleaded that all they wanted was relief from "the system and regulations adopted since the close of the late war" and that, if that relief was granted, "our future conduct will prove us not unworthy of the regard, we have been accustomed, in our happier days, to enjoy."[59]

The most devious message was addressed to the "Inhabitants of the Province of Quebec." It was occasioned by the Quebec Act of 1774, which gave the French-Canadian majority the free exercise of their Catholic religion and the retention of French-Canadian civil law. The act also avoided the problem of political rivalry between the large French majority and small British minority by postponing the establishment of a popularly elected assembly and substituting a council appointed by the king. By chance, one of the Coercive Acts against Massachusetts had been passed at the very time the Quebec Bill was introduced in Parliament, with the result that the two came to be closely associated at a critical moment. The American Protestant colonies were so enraged that they even considered the Quebec Bill one of the Coercive Acts. The "Memorial to the Inhabitants of the Colonies" went so far as to charge that the British government intended to use Quebec to assist "in the oppression of such, as differ from them in modes of government and faith," namely, the American Protestant colonies.[60] The "Address to the People of Great-Britain" expressed astonishment that "a British Parliament

58 Ibid., pp. 90–101.
59 Ibid., pp. 115–21.
60 Ibid., p. 99.

should ever consent to establish in that country a religion that has deluged your island in blood, and dispersed impiety, bigotry, persecution, murder and rebellion through every part of the world."[61]

The "Address to the Inhabitants of the Province of Quebec" did not, of course, take this line. Instead, it assailed the Quebec Act for having failed to give the Canadians their "irrevocable rights" in the form of an assembly, though it was the opposition of the French Canadians to an assembly that had helped to convince the British government to do without it.[62] For the most part, this address sought to win over the French Canadians by instructing them how much more fortunate they would be if they adopted the same form of government as the American colonies. The Canadians were invited to join with the Americans in one union and to send delegates to the Second Continental Congress. Paradoxically, all this was proposed to them in order to preserve "a happy and lasting connection with Great-Britain."[63]

These addresses were clearly calibrated for maximum effect on different and even conflicting recipients. The varying emphases testified to the political adroitness of the American leaders, who were more interested in gaining short-term advantages than in pursuing a consistent, impeccable political line. As late as 1774, they were still willing to avow their loyal subservience to the king in order to make Parliament and the ministry the sole enemies to be overcome. They emphasized again and again that they merely wanted to go back to the status quo ante of 1763, as if they had no objection to the way the British government had dealt with them in all the years prior to the end of the last war.

Resolutions adopted by the congress gave more evidence of its ambivalence. One claimed the "free and exclusive power of legislation" in "all cases of taxation and internal polity." But it made this power "subject only to the negative of their sovereign, in such manner as has been heretofore used and accustomed." In addition, it volunteered that "we cheerfully consent to the operation of such acts of the British parliament" for the regulation of trade, so long as they benefited the entire empire and all its members.[64] These demands and concessions were designed to appeal to the greatest

---

[61] Ibid., p. 88. The Suffolk Resolves denounced the Quebec Act in much the same language (pp. 34–35).

[62] The French-Canadian representative, Francis Maseres, had argued that "it would be a representative of only the 600 new English settlers and an instrument in their hands of domineering over 90,000 French" (R. Coupland, *The Quebec Act* [Oxford University Press, 1925], p. 85).

[63] *Journals of the Continental Congress*, vol. 1, pp. 105–13.

[64] Resolution no. 4, ibid., pp. 68–69.

number in and out of the congress and did not necessarily reflect the view of the revolutionary vanguard.

But no inhibitions entered into the handling of Galloway. His proposals were not all that new or original; they came from positions which the revolutionary colonists had held in the past and from which they had been hastily disentangling themselves. When Galloway pleaded for giving Parliament supervision of imperial trade and the colonies control of their own internal affairs, he was saying no more than what had been commonly accepted in recent years and in the congress's own resolutions. But his enemies would not accept it from him. Moreover, there is a problem with what Galloway's position really was. What he said at the congress, at least as reported by John Adams, was deliberately moderate and defensible; what he wrote after the congress was insufferably provocative and offensive. Yet the delegates had to react to what he actually said, and they could have made it the basis of a possible compromise or negotiation, which is all he said he wanted. The rough handling of Galloway shows what the majority of delegates thought he really stood for or shows that they did not want negotiation so much as a British backdown. Whatever his words, he was looked on as a man of the past, and his enemies were men of the future.

One such man who had to choose between the past and future was Benjamin Franklin, Galloway's confidant for two decades. But Galloway had gone off on his own in the formulation of his plan, even if it was in large part based on Franklin's plan of 1754. Franklin, still in London, did not give Galloway his reaction to the plan until February 1775, four months after the congress had adjourned. Galloway was not the only problem for Franklin; his relations with his son, Gov. William Franklin of New Jersey, who agreed with Galloway, were also at stake. Father and son represented the same great divide in the revolutionary road that Galloway's plan presented—one took the revolutionary, the other the antirevolutionary, turn. For the older Franklin, it was almost the last moment in which to make the choice.

Franklin let Galloway down gently. Franklin wrote that he did not know what objections had been made to the plan in the congress, but he himself had only one. It had less to do with the plan than with his own deep alienation from British ruling circles following his ordeal at the hands of Solicitor General Wedderburn over a year earlier. Franklin now saw "more Mischief than Benefit from a closer Union" with Great Britain, owing to "the extream Corruption prevalent among all Orders of Men in this old rotten State" compared with "the glorious publick Virtue so predominant in our rising Country." Franklin had worked up a boiling indignation against Great Britain: "Here Numberless and needless Places, enormous Salaries, Pensions, Perquisites, Bribes, groundless Quarrels, foolish Expeditions, false Accompts or no Accompts, Contracts and Jobbs devour all Revenue, and produce continual Necessity in the Midst of natural Plenty." Nevertheless, he still could not bring himself to contemplate a war that might result from a break in relations: "However I would try any thing, and bear any thing that can be borne with Safety to our just Liberties rather than engage in a War with such near Relations, unless compelled to it by dire Necessity in our own Defence."

Franklin had given much thought to the nature of a plan he could approve, because he went on to propose six points requiring preliminary agreement. They included repeal of the detested Declaratory Act and of all acts restraining colonial manufactures. But he was willing to accept those parts of the Navigation Acts that were "for the Good of the whole Empire" and to tolerate duties so long as they were collected by colonial officials and not by "unprincipled Wretches generally appointed from England." But, as if he did not wish to go too far, Franklin quickly added, "These are hasty Thoughts, submitted to your Consideration."[65]

Franklin's struggle with himself continued into the first months of 1775. It is critically significant, because it shows how difficult the final break with Great Britain was for a preeminent American who had gone to the very limit of encouraging his fellow Americans to unite and resist. But the final step was the hardest; it was what separated Americans who were not so very different in other respects. On his return home in May 1775, Franklin still wrote to Galloway in the friendliest vein and tried to persuade him not to resign as a delegate to the Second Continental Congress.[66] We know of the final stage of Franklin's road to Damascus only from a conversation which Galloway had with Thomas Hutchinson when they were both exiles in England four years later. Galloway recalled that Franklin had come to see him soon after his return. Galloway said he hoped that Franklin had come "to promote a reconciliation." Franklin replied noncommittally: "Well, Mr. Galloway, you are really of a mind that I ought to promote a reconciliation?" Galloway answered, "Yes." That was all on that occasion. During the next five or six weeks, Franklin kept to himself and even aroused suspicions that he had come to spy for the British. William Franklin told Galloway that his father had avoided talking to him about what the colonies should do. Suspecting his father's intention, however, William warned him that "if he designed to set the Colonies in a flame, he would take care to run away by the light of it." Soon after, Galloway and the two Franklins met, drank a

[65] Franklin to Galloway, February 25, 1775, *Franklin Papers,* vol. 21, pp. 508–10.
[66] Franklin to Galloway, May 8, 1775, ibid., vol. 22, pp. 33–34.

bit too much, and, at a late hour, Benjamin "opened himself, and declared in favour of measures for attaining to Independence:—exclaimed against the corruption and dissipation of the Kingdom, and signified his opinion, that from the strength of Opposition, the want of union in the Ministry, the great resources in the Colonies, they would finally prevail." After that, Franklin "broke away from Galloway."[67]

This, sometime in mid-1775, was Franklin's Rubicon. The sympathetic editors of his papers note that the evidence does not "throw much light on the two personal crises in which he was involved after he landed, his alienation from Joseph Galloway and from William Franklin."[68] Historians have differed about the degree of Franklin's hesitation.[69]

As for Galloway, he seems to have become unhinged as a result of his treatment at the First Continental Congress. In 1775, he put out a pamphlet filled with extraordinary vituperation. The colonies, he raged, were "now governed by the barbarian rule of frantic folly, and lawless ambition." A "lawless power" was "inflicting penalties more severe than death itself." It was pushing the colonies "in the highroad of sedition and rebellion, which must ultimately terminate in their misery and ruin." A particularly feverish passage warned against what America might be about to endure:

> What think you, O my countrymen, what think you will be your condition, when you shall see the designs of these men carried a little farther into execution?—Companies of armed, but undisciplined men, headed by men unprincipled, travelling over your estates, entering your houses—your castles—and sacred repositories of safety for all you hold dear and valuable—seizing your property, and carrying havock and devastation wherever they head—ravishing your wives and daughters, and afterwards plunging the dagger into their tender bosoms, while you are obliged to stand the speechless, the helpless spectators.[70]

[67] *Diary and Letters of Thomas Hutchinson,* vol. 2, pp. 237–38. A somewhat later version by Galloway has Franklin say "that *America would be united,* and always able to draw her powers into exertion, while the British nation, and its public councils, *were, and would be yet more, divided and distracted.* That the *friends to the American cause in Britain, would incessantly maintain and increase that division and distraction, by opposing the measures of Government;* and consequently, that though he confessed the resources of Great Britain, from whence the supplies of war must be drawn, were very great, yet that *she never would be able to command them, nor to make the exertions necessary to reduce the Colonies*" (Joseph Galloway, *Letters from Cicero to Cataline the Second* [London, 1781], pp. 47–48).

[68] *Franklin Papers,* vol. 22, pp. xliii–xliv.

[69] Benjamin H. Newcomb thinks Galloway did not realize that Franklin was already "cooperating with the revolutionaries" (*Franklin and Galloway: A Political Partnership* [Yale University Press, 1972], p. 282). Carl Van Doren seems to credit Galloway's version (*Benjamin Franklin* [Viking Press, 1938], pp. 527–28).

[70] [Galloway], *Candid Examination of the Mutual Claims,* pp. 1, 2, 32–33.

All this was imaginary. From then on, Galloway was a marked man. He continued to argue his case in the Pennsylvania Assembly, which reappointed him a delegate to the next Continental Congress. To make sure that he understood the risks he was running by trying to hold back the revolutionary tide, he was sent a halter to which a letter was attached threatening to put him to death if he did not make use of it. He alleged that he "remained several months in the utmost danger of mobs" who wanted to hang him by his own door.[71] In December 1776, he left his home and joined the British forces under Gen. William Howe, whom he served as an adviser. In 1778, he left for England, where he sent forth one pamphlet after another defending his past actions and denouncing the colonial rebellion. He never forgave and was never forgiven.

From all that we know of the First Continental Congress, two things stand out—it stopped short of an open break with Great Britain at the same time that it brought the break closer, so much closer that some delegates went away with the approach of war in their heads. Charles Thomson of Pennsylvania, the secretary of the congress, in a letter to Benjamin Franklin, blamed the "cursed schemes of [British] policy" for "dragging friends and brothers into the horrors of civil War and involving their country in ruin." He ended with these words: "Even yet the wounds may be healed and peace and love restored; But we are on the very edge of the precipice."[72] John Dickinson had the same premonition. On his return from the congress, he wrote: "Colonists have now taken such Ground, that Great Britain must relax, or inevitably involve herself in a Civil War, likely in all human probability to overwhelm her with a Weight of Calamities. ... I wish for peace ardently; but must say, delightful as it is, it will come more grateful by being unexpected. The first Act of Violence on the Part of Administration in America, or the Attempt to reinforce General Gage this Winter or next Year, will put the whole Continent in arms from Nova Scotia to Georgia."[73] Galloway agreed: "As to the unfortunate Dispute between The Mother Country & her Colonies, I fear it is now arrived to such an Height that It will be with great Difficulty accomodated."[74]

While the congress was sitting, an ominous statement appeared in the *Boston Evening Post* of September 19, 1774. It was addressed "To the Officers and Soldiers of His Majesty's Troops in Boston" and began:

[71] *Examination of Joseph Galloway by a Committee of the House of Commons*, pp. 55, 59.

[72] Thomson to Franklin, November 1, 1774, *Franklin Papers*, vol. 21, p. 345.

[73] Dickinson to Arthur Lee, October 27, 1774, Smith, *Letters of Delegates to Congress*, vol. 1, p. 250.

[74] Ibid., p. 255.

"It being more than probable that the King's standard will soon be erected from rebellion breaking out in this Province, it's proper that you soldiers should be acquainted with the authors thereof, and of all the misfortunes brought upon the Province." Then followed fifteen names of the outstanding oppositionists, beginning with Samuel Adams. The statement continued: "The friends of your King and country and of America hope and expect it from you soldiers, the instant rebellion happens, that you will put the above persons to the sword, destroy their houses, and plunder their effects!"[75]

By the end of 1774, Massachusetts, army and people, was preparing for war. John Adams informed a correspondent: "Our People, thro the Province, are every where learning the military Art—exercising perpetually—So that, I suppose, if occasion should require, an Army of Fifteen Thousand Men from this Province alone, might be brought into the Field in one Week."[76] The news of arming in Massachusetts traveled fast. Thomas Johnson, Jr., of Maryland received a letter from Boston saying that its inhabitants "are formed in Companies, are well armed and have a Magazine."[77] Samuel Ward of Rhode Island expressed the familiar thought that the British ministers were guilty of provoking hostilities, but "All the Horrors of a Civil War and even Death itself in any form whatever will be infinitely preferable to Slavery."[78] Galloway, as might be expected, held the "Frenzy of America" to be responsible for the determination to "plunge into Rebellion and subject her People to all the Horrors of a civil War, in which she must be infallibly subdued."[79] In October 1774, Elbridge Gerry told Sam Adams that a civil war was "almost unavoidable," and John Dickinson advised Josiah Quincy, Jr., that "a civil war is unavoidable, unless there be a quick change in British measures."[80]

Galloway, all hope of compromise gone, summed up the position at the end of the year: "Thus the Issue is join'd between the two Countries—The one asserting her Supremacy in all Cases whatever, and the other denying it in all."[81]

[75] *Boston Evening Post,* September 19, 1774, cited by William V. Wells, *The Life and Public Services of Samuel Adams* (Little, Brown, 1865), vol. 2, p. 250.

[76] Adams to Edward Biddle?, Smith, *Letters of Delegates to Congress,* vol. 1, p. 265.

[77] Johnson to Horatio Gates, December 14, 1774, ibid., p. 268.

[78] Ward to John Dickinson, December 14, 1774, ibid., p. 269.

[79] Galloway to Samuel Verplanck, ibid., p. 287.

[80] Gerry to Adams, October 15, 1774, cited by Pauline Maier, *From Resistance to Revolution* (Routledge & Kegan Paul, 1973), p. 244; Dickinson to Quincy, October 28, 1774, *Memoir of the Life of Josiah Quincy Jun.* (Boston, 1825), p. 193.

[81] Galloway to Samuel Verplanck?, December 30, 1774, Smith, *Letters of Delegates to Congress,* vol. 1, p. 284.

· 4 ·

For the British government, the Continental Congress itself was illegal. That it could not be prevented from meeting showed how far the decline of British power had gone. As the congress neared, the advices from governors added to the gloom and tension in London. Massachusetts and Virginia were far from being the only trouble spots.

Lt. Gov. William Bull of South Carolina decided to tell Lord Dartmouth the bitter truth:

> I beg your lordship's permission to observe, and I do it with great concern, that this spirit of opposition to taxation and its consequences is so violent and so universal throughout America that I am apprehensive it will not be soon or easily appeased. The general voice speaks discontent, and sometimes in a tone of despair, as determined to stop all exports to and imports from Great Britain and even to silence the courts of law, foreseeing but regardless of the ruin that must attend themselves in that case, content to change a comfortable for a parsimonious life, to be satisfied with the few wants of nature if by their sufferings they can bring Great Britain to feel [*sic*]. This is the language of the most violent, others think it going too far; and the most violent too often prevail over the moderate.[82]

Lt. Gov. Cadwallader Colden of New York was only somewhat less depressing:

> The meeting of the delegates [to the Continental Congress], I am of opinion, cannot be prevented. . . .
> From a view of the numerous resolves of the people in all the colonies which appear in every newspaper, your lordship might be led to think a stupid, fatal hardiness intoxicated the whole. But there are everywhere many people who are seriously alarmed at the critical posture of the contention between Great Britain and her colonies.[83]

Colden also explained why "gentlemen of property," who did not want

---

[82] Bull to Dartmouth, July 31, 1774, Davies, *Documents of the American Revolution*, vol. 8, p. 154.

[83] Colden to Dartmouth, August 2, 1774, ibid., pp. 155–56.

trouble, thought they had to go along with a new committee in New York, formed to enforce the decisions of the congress:

> In the present Committee of this place there are several gentlemen of property and who are esteemed to favour moderate and concili-atory measures. I was surprised to find such men joining with the Committee whose design is to execute the plan of the Congress. I have at length discovered that they act with a view to protect the city from the ravages of the mob. For this purpose they say they are obliged at present to support the measures of the Congress; that if they did not, the most dangerous men among us would take the lead and under the pretence of executing the dictates of the Congress would immediately throw the city into the most perilous situation; that however considerable the numbers may be who disapprove of violent riotous measures, yet the spirit of mobbing is so much abroad it is in the power of a few people at any time to raise a mob and that the gentlemen and men of property will not turn out to suppress them. I fear, my lord, there is too much truth in this representation. It is a dreadful situation. If we are not to be rescued from it by the wisdom and firmness of Parliament, the colonies must soon fall into distraction and every calamity annexed to a total annihilation of government.[84]

Gov. James Wright of Georgia, not a colony from which much gloom might be expected, reported that

> the licentious spirit in America has received such countenance and encouragement from many persons, speeches and declarations at the time of the Stamp Act and ever since in Great Britain, and has now gone to so great a length and is at such a height that neither coercive or lenient measures will settle matters and restore any tolerable degree of cordiality and harmony with the mother country; and in short, things and circumstances in America have increased so fast and at this time so amazingly exceed what at the first settling and planting the colonies could possibly have been supposed or expected, and America is now become or indisputably ere long will be such a vast, powerful and opulent country or dominion, that I humbly conceive in order to restore and establish real and substantial harmony, affection and confidence, and that Great Britain may receive that benefit and advantage which she has a right to expect from the colonies, it

[84] Colden to Dartmouth, December 7, 1774, ibid., pp. 237–38.

may be found advisable to settle the line with respect to taxation etc. by some new mode of constitution, and without which my real and candid opinion is that, however matters may be got over at present and whatever appearances there may be of amity and union, the flame will only be smothered for a time and break out again at some future day with more violence.[85]

Dep. Gov. John Penn of Pennsylvania sent much the same advice. He told Dartmouth that

> the resolution of opposing the Boston Acts and the Parliamentary power of raising taxes in America for the purpose of a revenue is in a great measure universal throughout the colonies and possesses all ranks and conditions of people. They persuade themselves there is a formed design to enslave America, and though the Act for regulating the government of Canada does not immediately affect the other provinces it is nevertheless held up as an irrefragable argument of that intention. General however as the resolution is to oppose, there is great diversity of opinions as to the proper modes of opposition.[86]

Gov. John Wentworth of New Hampshire had the least bad news for Dartmouth: "I think this province is much more moderate than any other to the southward, although the spirit of enthusiasm is spread and requires the utmost vigilance and prudence to restrain it from violent excess."[87]

Equally alarming private intelligence reached influential British figures. Charles Lee, who in 1774 still enjoyed the reputation of having achieved an outstanding military career in Europe and America but who was later to be one of Washington's greatest disappointments, assured Edmund Burke that he had traveled up and down the colonies, had talked with every type of colonist,

> and cannot express my astonishment at the unanimous, ardent spirit reigning through the whole. They are determined to sacrifice everything, their property, their wives, children, and blood, rather than cede a tittle of what they conceive to be their rights. The tyranny exercised over Boston, indeed, seems to be resented by

[85] Wright to Dartmouth, August 24, 1774, ibid., pp. 162–63.
[86] Penn to Dartmouth, September 5, 1774, ibid., pp. 186–87.
[87] Wentworth to Dartmouth, August 29, 1774, ibid., p. 168.

the other colonies in a greater degree than by the Bostonians themselves.[88]

General Gage had already intimated that all was lost in Massachusetts if stronger measures were not employed:

It is agreed that popular fury was never greater in this province than at present and it has taken its rise from the old source at Boston, though it has appeared first at a distance. Those demagogues trust their safety in the long forbearance of government and an assurance that they can't be punished here. They chicane, elude, openly violate or passively resist the laws as opportunities serve, and opposition to authority is of so long standing that it is become habitual.[89]

Dartmouth did not need much persuasion and had written off the congress in advance. One month before it met he had condemned its premises as "propositions that lead to inevitable destruction."[90] Afterwards he made sure that the colonists knew that they could not depend on the king to save them from the decrees of Parliament. Towards the end of 1774, he circulated copies of the king's speech to Parliament expressing "His firm & steadfast Resolution to withstand every attempt to weaken or impair the Authority of the Supreme Legislature." Dartmouth intended it "to remove those false Impressions, which have been made upon the Minds of His Majesty's Subjects in America, & put an end to those Expectations of Support, in their unwarrantable Pretensions, which have been held forth by artful & designing Men."[91] This was the answer to the long-held colonial belief that the king could be their benefactor.

By the time the congress met, North knew that the king had hardened his views against the American colonies. In July 1774, about two months before the congress, the king had had a talk with Hutchinson, now in London, and had been led to believe that "they will soon submit."[92] If so, there was no need to worry too much. A few days into the congress, the king decided there was reason to go beyond worrying. He gave his opinion to North that "the dye is now cast, the Colonies must either submit or triumph." He said he did not wish "severer measures, but we must not retreat." He did not

---

[88] Lee to Burke, December 16, 1774, Lee Papers, *Collections of the New-York Historical Society*, 1871, vol. 1, p. 145.

[89] Gage to Dartmouth, August 27, 1774, Davies, *Documents of the American Revolution*, vol. 8, p. 166.

[90] Dartmouth to Governor Dunmore (Virginia), August 3, 1774, cited by B. D. Bargar, *Lord Dartmouth and the American Revolution* (University of South Carolina Press, 1965), p. 147.

[91] Circular letter, December 10, 1774, *Gage Correspondence*, vol. 2, p. 178.

[92] King George to North, July 1, 1774, *Correspondence of King George the Third*, ed. John Fortescue (London, 1927), vol. 3, p. 116.

object to letting the colonies know that "there is no inclination to lay fresh taxes on them." But he insisted that "there must always be one tax to keep up the right, and as such I approve of the Tea Duty."[93] Two months later, after the congress, he worried that "the New England Governments are in a state of rebellion, blows must decide whether they are to be subject to this country or independent."[94] The next day, he repeated that "we must either master them or totally leave them to themselves and treat them as aliens."[95]

Dartmouth could do little more than to wish that "all hope of Peace & Union with the Mother Country" would not be cut off by the congress and to lament that the colonial grievances were not coming from individual colonies instead of from all of them collectively.[96] After the congress was over, Dartmouth opened his mind to the possible use of force in Massachusetts. So far, military reinforcements had not worked. He told Gage that "it looks not only as if the people were determined at all events to refuse obedience to the Law but that, notwithstanding the assistance of so large a Military Force sent purposely to support the authority of Civil Government, they have it still in their power to trample upon it with impunity and to bid defiance to all control." He was seriously worried about "what may happen, should the madness of the people urge them to a continuation of the violences they have committed, or lead them to more desperate measures." But he had bad news: "The State of this Kingdom will not admit of our sending more Troops from Great Britain." Gage had to depend on his "fortitude, & discretion" to deal with "the present critical situation of The King's Affairs in North America, and more particularly in New England."[97]

Before the end of 1774, Gage's messages took an increasingly ominous turn: "The people would cool, was not means taken to keep up their enthusiasm. Truths or falsehoods equally serve the purpose for they are so besotted to one side that they will not believe or even hear what is said to convince them of their errors."[98] Soon he reported a "secret determination," to be put into effect at the Second Continental Congress in 1775, "to form as complete a government as they can and to have, as

---

[93] King George to North, September 11, 1774, ibid., p. 131.

[94] King George to North, November 18, 1774, ibid., p. 153.

[95] Ibid., November 19, 1774, p. 154.

[96] Dartmouth to Gage, September 8, 1774, *Gage Correspondence*, vol. 2, p. 172; Dartmouth to John Penn, September 7, 1774, Davies, *Documents of the American Revolution*, vol. 8, p. 193.

[97] Dartmouth to Gage, October 17, 1774, *Gage Correspondence*, vol. 2, pp. 174–75.

[98] Gage to Dartmouth, October 30, 1774, Davies, *Documents of the American Revolution*, vol. 8, p. 220.

they say, a vast army in the field in the spring at the continental expense."[99] By this time, the British were getting alarming reports of arms and arming on the colonial side, though all importation of arms and ammunition into the colonies had already been prohibited.[100] Dutch gunpowder was being imported clandestinely in New York.[101] Dartmouth sent word of "large quantities of Gunpowder exported from Holland to North America" and of "Americans purchasing large Quantities of Arms and Ammunition in the different Ports of Europe."[102] At the end of 1774, Thomas Cushing described how the Americans were "adopting the most effectual methods to defend themselves against any hostile invasion of the enemies to America." He told Josiah Quincy, Jr., then in London: "The people of Rhode-Island have used the precaution to remove the powder, cannon, and other military stores from the fort at Newport, into the country. The people at Portsmouth, in New Hampshire, have done the like by their cannon and other military stores at the fort at New Castle, at the entrance of their harbour."[103]

Thus, by the end of 1774, the "dye is now cast," as the king had put it. Both sides tried to avoid responsibility by making demands that neither had the intention of meeting. The British said that they were prepared to relent if the colonies showed proper deference to the authority of Parliament. The colonies said that they were ready to go back to the status quo ante of 1763 if the British retracted everything they had done afterwards. Yet neither wanted to show weakness in the face of the other's perseverance. As usual in such circumstances, they spoke of peace and prepared for war.

· 5 ·

The year 1774 was also notable for the efforts made to rethink the British-American relationship. It was another year of great speeches, pamphleteering, and theorizing of various kinds. The approaching crisis helped to concentrate men's minds and crystallize the issues they were fighting about; it was the last chance to think through the nature of the conflict before the first shots were fired.

---

99 Ibid., pp. 220–21.

100 Circular Letter by Dartmouth, October 19, 1774, *Colden Papers, Collections of the New-York Historical Society, 1923*, vol. 7, p. 252.

101 Cadwallader Colden to Dartmouth, November 2, 1774, Davies, *Documents of the American Revolution*, vol. 8, p. 225.

102 Dartmouth to Colden, November 2, 1774, *Colden Papers*, vol. 7, p. 254.

103 Cushing to Quincy, December 30, 1774, *Memoir of the Life of Josiah Quincy Jun.*, pp. 211–12.

On the American side, it was the year of Thomas Jefferson's ideological coming of age. Jefferson had been elected to the House of Burgesses in 1769 at the age of twenty-five and was still serving his political apprenticeship. He represented a new generation in American colonial politics, a generation that had not gone through the fires of the opposition to the Stamp Act but had inherited those traditions and outlook. In his first days in office, he had aligned himself with the militant majority and had signed his name to the local nonimportation, nonconsumption agreement. After that, he had not done much politically, for one reason because the House of Burgesses was suspended much of the time.

Jefferson's first opportunity to assert himself politically came in July 1774, in conjunction with the Virginia delegation to the First Continental Congress. Jefferson was not a delegate, but he submitted a number of resolutions intended as instructions to the delegation. These were printed without his knowledge as a pamphlet entitled *A Summary View of the Rights of British America.* It was his first important political contribution to the oncoming Revolution.

The pamphlet is mainly significant for showing the way the new American political generation reworked and reinforced the old grievances and demands. Jefferson's great biographer found it necessary to caution that the pamphlet contained so many inaccuracies that it "bordered on recklessness" and that it "is more noteworthy for boldness and fervor than for historical precision or literary grace."[104] Jefferson denounced the British prohibition of fur hats made by Americans as "an instance of despotism to which no parrallel can be produced in the most arbitrary ages of British history." As a particularly outrageous act by the British Parliament, he cited the establishment of a post office. Such "acts of tyranny" plainly proved "a deliberate, systematical plan of reducing us to slavery."

The chief interest in the pamphlet is how Jefferson treated the roles of Parliament and the king. He simply dismissed Parliament as having "no right to exercise authority over us." But he did not fail to criticize the king. He took him to task for never having rejected a law passed by the two houses of Parliament, whereas laws of the American legislatures were commonly disapproved. He wanted the king to "dissolve" Parliament if he disapproved of it, as colonial legislatures had been dismissed. He berated the king for having sent "among us large numbers of armed forces, not made up of the people here, nor raised by the authority of our laws." Jefferson addressed the king directly and told him how to behave: "Open your breast Sire, to

---

[104] Dumas Malone, *Jefferson the Virginian* (Little, Brown, 1948), p. 182.

liberal and expanded thought. Let not the name of George the third be a blot in the page of history. . . . Only aim to do your duty, and mankind will give you credit where you fail. No longer persevere in sacrificing the rights of one part of the empire to the inordinate desires of another: but deal out to all equal and impartial right."

Nevertheless, Jefferson still sought "that harmony which alone can continue both to Great Britain and America the reciprocal advantages of their connection."

> It is neither our wish nor our interest to separate from her. We are willing on our part to sacrifice every thing which reason can ask to the restoration of that tranquillity for which all must wish. On their part let them be ready to establish union on a generous plan. Let them name their terms, but let them be just. Accept of every commercial preference it is in our power to give for such things as we can raise for their use, or they make for ours. But let them not think to exclude us from going to other markets, to dispose of those commodities which they cannot use, nor to supply those wants which they cannot supply. Still less let it be proposed that our properties within our own territories shall be taxed or regulated by any power on earth but our own.[105]

Jefferson's way of addressing the king was novel for the time, because it was no longer reverential. Yet he berated the king less for what he did than for what he did not do; Jefferson seemed to demand an increase in royal power, even to the point of overriding parliamentary legislation and dissolving Parliament itself. In the heat of ideological battle, Jefferson let himself get carried away, but this was his first try as an ideological warrior. His contribution to the cause was not adopted by the Virginia delegation to the Continental Congress and might have remained in obscurity if its author had not been Thomas Jefferson. Though its main distinctions were the "intemperance" of its language and the temerity of its approach, it is still significant for demonstrating how the revolutionary cause was taken up by a younger generation.

· 6 ·

Far more precocious was another member of the younger revolutionary generation. The antecedents of Alexander Hamilton are so obscure that

---

[105] *The Papers of Thomas Jefferson*, ed. Julian P. Boyd (Princeton University Press, 1950), vol. 1, pp. 125–35.

historians have had trouble deciding when he was born. One gives the date as 1755, another 1757.[106] He was born on Nevis, one of the British Virgin Islands in the Caribbean, but was brought up on the Danish island of St. Croix. He was an illegitimate child of a mother who had been divorced on charges of adultery and James Hamilton, a ne'er-do-well Scot who had abandoned her. The stigma of his birth never left the son. Long after his death, two old men, John Adams and Thomas Jefferson, entered into a famous correspondence in the course of which Adams referred to Hamilton as that "bastard Bratt of a Scotch Pedlar."[107]

Not the least of the remarkable aspects of Hamilton's life is how he managed to overcome the greatest odds. What, if any, formal education he had as a child is unknown; in his early teens, he had been apprenticed to a firm of merchants. At the age of fifteen (or seventeen, depending on the source), he left to make his fortune in New York. After attending a preparatory school, he was admitted to King's College (predecessor of Columbia) in the spring of 1774 and was soon swept into the city's revolutionary currents. At the age of seventeen, after only a few months at the college, he was ready to begin his political career as a revolutionary pamphleteer.

Hamilton was inspired by a pamphlet by Samuel Seabury, the Anglican rector of St. Peter's Church in Westchester, later bishop of Connecticut and Rhode Island, a man more than twice Hamilton's age. In November 1774, soon after the proceedings of the First Continental Congress were published in New York, Seabury came out with a counterattack entitled *Free Thoughts On The Proceedings of The Grand Continental Congress.*[108] It was ostensibly addressed to "The Farmers and other inhabitants of North America" by "A. W. Farmer." Seabury was no more a New York farmer than John Dickinson had been a "Pennsylvania Farmer," but such was the convention of the times.

Seabury accused the congress of having "either ignorantly misunderstood, carelessly neglected, or basely betrayed the interests of all the Colonies." The nonexportation and nonconsumption agreements were probably going to set off "clamours, discord, confusion, mobs, riots, insurrections, rebellions, in Great-Britain, Ireland and the West Indies."

[106] Broadus Mitchell, *Alexander Hamilton: Youth to Maturity, 1755–1788* (Macmillan, 1957), p. 1, and John C. Miller, *Alexander Hamilton: Portrait in Paradox* (Harper, 1959), choose 1755; Robert Hendrickson, *Hamilton I* (Mason/Charter, 1976), p. 1, gives 1757.

[107] Adams to Jefferson, July 12, 1813, *The Adams-Jefferson Letters,* ed. Lester J. Cappon (University of North Carolina Press, 1959), vol. 2, p. 354.

[108] It was reprinted, together with three other pamphlets by Seabury, in *Letters of a Westchester Farmer, 1774–1775,* ed. Clarence H. Vance (Da Capo Press, 1970).

He exclaimed: "Good God! can we look forward to the ruin, destruction, and desolation of the whole British Empire, without one relenting thought?" Nevertheless, Seabury also warned that England could "ruin us effectually" in a single campaign should she exert her force. By using less violent means, she could even "humble us without hurting herself."

Most of Seabury's argument was economic. The colonies were sure to suffer the most. "Should our mad schemes take place, our sailors, shipcarpenters, carmen, sail-makers, riggers, miners, smelters, forge-men, and workers in bar-iron, &c. would be immediately out of employ; and we should have twenty mobs and riots in our own country before one would happen in Britain or Ireland." People would go mad for want of food, invade farms, and take by force what they could not buy. Prices were bound to rise disastrously for years to come. Only merchants were going to benefit from the higher prices. Farmers faced the worst. "The farmer that is in debt, will be ruined: the farmer that is clear in the world, will be obliged to run in debt, to support his family: while the proud merchant, and the forsworn smuggler, riot in their ill-gotten wealth; the laborious farmers, the grand support of every well-regulated country, must all go to the dogs together.—Vile! Shameful! Diabolical Device!"

The idea of revolutionary committees enforcing the congress's decisions revolted Seabury. He assured his readers that they would be forced to

open your doors to them,—let them examine your tea-cannisters, and molasses-jugs, and your wives and daughters petty-coats,— bow, and cringe, and tremble, and quake,—fall down and worship our sovereign Lord the Mob.—But I repeat it, by H——n, I will not.—No, my house is my castle: as such I will consider it, as such I will defend it, while I have breath. . . . Before *I* submit, I will die; live *you,* and be slaves.

More noteworthy than anything else in Seabury's pamphlet is its nearly hysterical tone. His was the voice of traditionalists who knew they were facing revolutionary forces determined to have their way at all costs.

· 7 ·

Before the year 1774 was out, Hamilton took it upon himself to publish a reply to Seabury entitled *A Full Vindication of the Measures of the Congress, from the Calumnies of their Enemies, etc.* It was less hysterical than Seabury's and shows that Hamilton had already mastered the familiar arguments from natural rights, consent, and the rest. But he announced that the time for resting the American case on "rights" was over. The only recourse left was "a restriction of our trade" or "a resistance *vi & armis.*" He blamed Parliament and did not even mention George III. But he enlarged the circle of British enemies by maintaining that "the manufacturers of Great Britain and Ireland, and the Inhabitants of the West Indies" may "in a political view, be esteemed criminals" and "in some measure accomplices." They were guilty because they had permitted their rulers "to abuse and tyrannize over others." His invective was by this time standard—"popery and arbitrary dominion in Canada," "system of slavery," "despotism," "vassals."

Hamilton claimed to know what was behind the British insistence on maintaining the tax on tea. It was to enable the British House of Commons to have complete control over American lives and properties. He scorned any other view: "How ridiculous then it is to affirm, that we are quarrelling for the trifling sum of three pence a pound on tea; when it is evidently the principle against which we contend."

At another point, Hamilton touched on a deeper motive for the British Parliament's oppression of America:

Jealousy would concur with selfishness; and for fear of the future independence of America, if it should be permitted to rise to too great a height of splendor and opulence, every method would be taken to drain it of its wealth and restrain its prosperity. We are already suspected of aiming at independence, and that is one principal cause of the severity we experience. The same cause will always operate against us, and produce an uniform severity of treatment.

In the end, Hamilton could not go as far as "force and arms." The First Continental Congress, to which he was committed, had decided on economic measures only—nonimportation and nonexportation. Hamilton argued that Great Britain could not withstand them. The reasoning flowed from the alleged dependence of Great Britain on the Americans:

Reason and experience teach us, that the consequences would be too fatal to Great Britain to admit of delay. There is an immense trade between her and the colonies. The revenues arising from thence are prodigious. The consumption of her manufactures in these colonies supplies the means of subsistence to a vast number of her most useful inhabitants. The experiment we have made heretofore, shews us of how much importance our commercial connexion is to her;

and gives us the highest assurance of obtaining immediate redress by suspending it.

With so much at stake, Hamilton was sure that it would be "the grossest infatuation of madness" for Britain "to enforce her despotic claims by fire and sword." He contended that "it would be hard, if not an impracticable task to subjugate us by force." In such an "unnatural war," he saw only "dreadful consequences" for the British—the decay of commerce, the decrease of revenues, "insupportable" expense, attack by foreign enemies; "ruin, like a deluge, would pour in from every quarter." If the British rulers were mad enough to behave inflexibly, he held out an even greater punishment for them—the revolt of their own people. Either the British ministry would change its American policy or the Continental Congress intended "to affect the inhabitants of Great-Britain, Ireland and the West-Indies in such a manner, as to rouse them from their state of neutrality, and engage them to unite with us in opposing the lawless hand of tyranny, which is extended to ravish our liberty from us, and might soon be extended for the same purpose against them.

Hamilton gave assurances that the British people would rise up, because they would realize that "the calamities, that threaten them, proceed from the weakness, or wickedness of their own rulers." In that case, it was "most reasonable to believe, they will revenge the evils they may feel on the true authors of them, on an aspiring and ill-judging ministry; not on us, who act out of melancholy necessity, and are the innocent causes in self-defence." Ireland and the West Indies could also be expected "to escape the miseries they are in danger of" from their loss of the American market and American supplies.[109]

With such reasoning, Hamilton sought to convince his readers that the Americans could not lose. He was not the only one who was sure that the British had to capitulate. From London in February 1774, Arthur Lee assured James Warren that British policy "must eventually operate the ruin of this country."[110] At the First Continental Congress later that year, Richard Henry Lee had been "absolutely certain, that the same Ship which carries home the [nonimportation] Resolution will bring back the Redress."[111] The British were reported to entertain the same misplaced optimism. William Lee sent word from London that "the King and his friends" expected no

[109] *The Papers of Alexander Hamilton,* ed. Harold C. Syrett (Columbia University Press, 1961), vol. 1, pp. 46–48, 54, 56, 60.

[110] Lee to Warren, February 20, 1774, Richard Henry Lee, *Life of Arthur Lee, LL.D.* (Boston, 1929), vol. 1, p. 265. Arthur Lee later admitted that he had been mistaken about the effect of the nonimportation agreement on Great Britain (p. 265 n).

[111] *Diary and Autobiography of John Adams,* September 3, 1774, vol. 2, p. 120.

more resistance in Boston, and that the other colonies "will look on quietly and see Boston destroyed." He thought they were wrong on both counts but considered the opinion worth reporting.[112] A statement by Henry Ellis, the former governor of Georgia, bore out these tidings: "We know the real inability of the Americans to make any effectual resistance to any coercive method which might be employed to compel their obedience . . . we know their weakness as well as their want of bravery."[113] One reason both sides moved towards war was that each half-expected to overawe the other and win without a war.

Hamilton's pamphlet was a remarkable work for a college sophomore, but he had undoubtedly picked up arguments and counterarguments that were already common in revolutionary circles. Notably absent was any accusation against—or even mention of—King George III. The enemy was still Parliament and specifically the House of Commons.

· 8 ·

A much weightier argument against Parliament also appeared in 1774. It was the work of one of the most admired eighteenth-century American legal minds, James Wilson, one of the six men who signed both the Declaration of Independence and the Constitution, and one of the original justices of the Supreme Court of the United States. Wilson wrote his *Considerations on the Nature and Extent of the Legislative Authority of the British Parliament* in 1768 but did not publish it until 1774. He was a Scot who at the age of twenty-three had arrived in America in 1765, only three years before he composed this pamphlet on a fundamental theme. He was another of the extraordinary young men who entered into the controversy at this late prerevolutionary stage.

Wilson immediately stated the supreme question of the hour—"does the legislative authority of the British parliament extend over" the colonies? He had none of Jefferson's or Hamilton's youthful militancy. He was all judiciousness and sobriety. He started out by glorifying the House of Commons as the protector and defender of British liberties. But, he went on, it was able to perform its lofty duties because it was an elected body and acted in conformity with the wishes of those who elected it. Foremost among the power of Commons over the Crown was its command of taxes,

[112] William Lee to Richard Henry Lee, March 17, 1774, *Letters of William Lee*, ed. Worthington Chauncey Ford (Brooklyn, 1891), vol. 1, p. 84.
[113] Cited by Alan Valentine, *Lord North* (University of Oklahoma Press, 1967), vol. 1, p. 310.

by which it could refuse to provide supplies and thus "check the progress of arbitrary power." Wilson was almost ecstatic about the beauty of the system: "Such is the admirable temperament of the British constitution! such the glorious fabrick of Britain's liberty—the pride of her citizens—the envy of her neighbours—planned by her legislators—erected by her patriots— maintained entire by numerous generations past! may it be maintained by numerous generations to come!"

At this point, however, he turned the argument on its head. He had extolled the British system only to limit it to Great Britain. The authority of the Commons could not be transferred to America for the very reason that gave legitimacy to the Commons in Great Britain—Americans did not vote for members of the House of Commons and had no control over them. British voters did. By making voting a fundamental requirement for the "glorious fabrick of Britain's liberty," he tore a gaping hole in that fabric, through which Americans could escape from British control. The British, he conceded, could well be happy with their wonderful system; to the Americans it brought only grief:

> While the happy commons of Great Britain congratulate themselves upon the liberty which they enjoy, and upon the provisions—infallible, as far as they can be rendered so by human wisdom—which are made for perpetuating it to their latest posterity; the unhappy Americans have reason to bewail the dangerous situation to which they are reduced; and to look forward, with dismal apprehension, to those future scenes of woe, which, in all probability, will open upon their descendants.

Wilson was another Philadelphia lawyer and cast his argument almost solely in legalistic terms. He finally came to the determining question: If the American colonies were not bound by the acts of the British Parliament, were they not throwing off all dependence on Great Britain? Wilson would not or could not go that far. His solution shows how little the Americans still blamed the king for their plight. He maintained that they owed their obedience and loyalty to the king, on whom they were dependent, not to Parliament. For confirmation, he appealed to the authority of Lord Bacon in the Jacobean age. Just how the king in the eighteenth century could exercise his authority in the colonies without money granted to him by Parliament and with an entire system of governance dependent on Parliament, Wilson did not say.[114]

---

[114] *The Works of James Wilson*, ed. Robert Green McCloskey (Harvard University Press, 1967), vol. 2, pp. 731, 735, 742–43.

• 9 •

Of far greater moment at the time was the famous exchange of articles between "Novanglus" and "Massachusettensis." Novanglus (or New Englander) was John Adams; Massachusettensis was Daniel Leonard. Adams thought that his opponent was Jonathan Sewall, the Massachusetts attorney general and close ally of Governor Hutchinson. Instead, Leonard was a friend of Adams; it was a striking case of friends falling out in the heat of the political struggle just before the outbreak of the Revolutionary War. Sewall was also an old friend of Adams, but they had parted company just before the First Continental Congress and did not see each other until after the war, when they embraced and made up.[115]

Leonard started the exchange with an article in the *Boston Gazette* of December 12, 1774. After six articles had appeared, Adams could stand no more and decided to write one reply after another. They went at each other in successive issues of the paper until April 1775, when the first shots were fired at Lexington and Concord and arms took the place of argument.

The two differed on almost everything. Leonard tried to convince his readers that the colonists did not stand a chance against British force. Adams was sure that the Americans could defend themselves. Leonard complained that the local press favored the American opposition and had been responsible for inflaming the mobs to commit outrages. Adams claimed that the press had "uniformly" been pro-British. Leonard maintained that the British administration had always been devoted to "the good of the whole." Adams charged that the Americans had suffered "cruel insults, distresses and provocations, as the history of mankind cannot parallel." Adams knew enough about the history of mankind to know better, but this was not an occasion for punctiliousness.

The main interest in the debate was what they thought of British-American relations on the eve of the armed struggle. To Leonard, there was no middle ground: "There is no possible medium between absolute independence, and subjection to the authority of parliament." This principle was central to the British case; it had been stated by Governor Hutchinson back in January 1773: "I know of no line that can be drawn between

---

[115] Preface by John Adams to *Novanglus, and Massachusettensis; or Political Essays, etc.* (Boston, 1819), pp. vi, vii. This book is a reprint of the original articles; owing to Adams's mistake, it attributed the articles of Massachusettensis to Sewall.

the supreme authority of Parliament and the total independence of the colonies." Leonard now elaborated:

> If the colonies are not subject to the authority of parliament, Great Britain and the colonies must be distinct states, as completely so, as England and Scotland were before the union, or as Great Britain and Hanover are now. The colonies in that case will owe no allegiance to the imperial crown, and perhaps not to the person of the king, as the title to the crown is derived from an act of parliament, made since the settlement of this province, which act respects the imperial crown only. Let us wa[i]ve this difficulty, and suppose allegiance due from the colonies to the person of the king of Great Britain. He then appears in a new capacity, of king of America, or rather in several new capacities, of King of Massachusetts, king of Rhode Island, king of Connecticut, &c. &c.

In reply to this challenge, Adams gradually evolved a clear statement of the prerevolutionary American position. He first insisted that the Americans had "the utmost abhorrence of treason and rebellion." He recoiled from Leonard's implication that the colonies wanted to be "independent of the crown of Great Britain, and [wanted] an independent republic in America, or a confederation of independent republics." Adams protested hotly— "nothing can be more wicked, or a greater slander on the [American] Whigs; because he knows there is not a man in the province, among the Whigs, nor ever was, who harbours a wish of that sort."

This disclaimer appeared in his article of February 13, 1775. A month later, however, Adams seems to have decided on a somewhat different approach. Instead of denying the view attributed to him by Leonard, he emphasized how he saw the future relationship. He seized on Leonard's charge that the colonies wanted to be "independent states" and, in view of what he had been protesting against, surprisingly agreed:

> There is no need of being startled at this consequence. It is very harmless. There is no absurdity at all in it. Distinct states may be united under one king. And those states may be further cemented and united together, by a treaty of commerce. This is the case. We have, by our own express consent, contracted to observe the navigation act, and by our implied consent, by long usage and uninterrupted acquiescence, have submitted to the other acts of trade, however grievous some of them may be. This may be compared to a treaty of commerce, by which those distinct states are cemented together, in

perpetual league and amity. And if any further ratifications of this pact or treaty are necessary, the colonies would readily enter into them, provided their other liberties were inviolate.

Adams went on to explain: The king was the only connection between Great Britain and the American colonies. But the allegiance was to "the person of the king, not to his crown: to his natural, not his politic capacity." It was not absurd at all, Adams urged, for the British king to be the king of Massachusetts, king of Rhode Island, king of Connecticut. But Adams acknowledged one difficulty brought out by Leonard: How could the king govern the colonies if each colony was free to do as it pleased in its own particular interest? He first played around with the idea of a "union of the colonies" that would be allotted a quarter of all members of the House of Commons, which would meet once in every four sessions in the colonies instead of in London. But on reflection, he suggested that it was impractical to send American representatives to London and preferred "letting parliament regulate trade, and our own assemblies all other matters." In the end he settled for this: "Our houses of Representatives have, and ought to exercise, every power of the House of Commons."

This view was not original with John Adams. Its seeds had been planted in the struggle against the Stamp Act, and it was implicit in the reply the Massachusetts Council had made to Governor Hutchinson in March 1773. But Adams had hardened the previous American position. He came out for "independent states" in the colonies linked to Great Britain only by "the person of the king." Even the concession to Parliament that it was empowered to regulate trade was now likened to a "treaty of commerce." Yet Adams still stopped short of calling for outright independence.

It has been noted that Adams's concept anticipated the twentieth-century British Commonwealth, in which Canada, Australia, New Zealand, India, and other former colonies have been completely autonomous in domestic and foreign affairs, as well as equal in status, and united only by "a common allegiance to the crown," expressed mainly on ceremonial occasions. To an eighteenth-century British mind, however, such an arrangement was unthinkable, and almost two centuries had to pass before it could be accepted.

Much of Adams's argument went back to the original settlement of the colonies. It eliminated about two centuries of British political development, the main achievement of which had been the institution of parliamentary supremacy. As a result of that achievement, William and Mary had been put on the throne through an act of Parliament and had sworn a coronation oath to govern the kingdom "and the dominions thereto belonging according to the statutes of Parliament agreed on." By cutting the umbilical cord with Parliament and particularly with the House of Commons, Adams severed the connection with the British political system. Paradoxically, he could do so only by making obeisance to the king, soon to be made the bête noire of the Declaration of Independence. But he also recalled James Harrington's words of 120 years earlier and seized on them to press home the point that "the colonies are now nearer manhood than ever Harrington foresaw they would arrive, in such a period of time."[116]

Intellectually, the American Revolution came of age in 1774–75. But without the growth of population, the sense of British economic dependence on colonial trade, the expansion of far-flung colonial economic interests straining to be released from imperial restraints, the military experience gained in the Seven Years' War, and the rise of a new colonial generation unburdened by attitudes of deference and obedience, it would have mattered little who was right or wrong in the ideological, constitutional, and political arguments of the years after the Stamp Act.

[116] *Novanglus, and Massachusettensis,* pp. 25–26, 38, 41, 82, 89–91, 108–9, 170–71, 174.

18

"To raise a Flame"

❧

· 1 ·

By 1774, THE APPROACH OF war was palpable. Both sides were locked in a battle of wills. The Boston Tea Party and the Coercive Acts—known in America as the Intolerable Acts—had set up a confrontation that could be resolved only if one side or the other backed down. If neither drew back, the struggle for power was bound to move from the political stage to the military.

If any one act was most responsible for setting off the drift towards war, it was the British decision in March 1774 to close down the port of Boston until reparation was made for the destroyed tea. The punishment was incommensurate with the crime. The Boston raiders had dumped 342 chests of tea, worth about £10,000, into the harbor. It was a crime against property, which many Americans did not condone. But Boston and its environs were so dependent on the port and outlet to the ocean for fishing, commerce, and every kind of livelihood that the closure amounted to economic strangulation. The British government could justify it only on the assumption that Boston could not hold out for long and that its capitulation was the key to gaining control of all the colonies.

The practical implications on the spot were the particular problem of Gen. Thomas Gage, the commander in chief of the British forces in North America from 1763 to 1775 and governor of Massachusetts from 1774 to 1776. He was the best placed of British observers to know what was going on, with a direct line to the earl of Dartmouth, the American secretary, and to Viscount Barrington, the secretary at war. Gage's reports to both of them tell what the British problems were and how he tried to cope with them.

Gage knew the American colonies as well as almost any American. Lieutenant Colonel Gage had come to America for the first time in 1754 and had fought under Major General Braddock the following year in the first disastrous battle of the Seven Years' War. After the war, Gage had spent three years as governor of Montreal, gaining political experience in dealing with a recalcitrant civilian population. In 1764, Gage, now lieutenant general, was appointed commander in chief of all the British forces in North America, a post which he held for the next twelve years. With only about 5,000 men, he was expected to safeguard British interests in all thirteen colonies. When Thomas Hutchinson retired to England in 1774, Gage was additionally made governor of Massachusetts. He had had two decades of service in the colonies; he was married to an American woman; he was well liked and unthreatening. When he was appointed, Benjamin Franklin reported from London that Gage was considered "a cool prudent Man."[1]

Gage was the eyes and ears of the British government in America. Yet even he seems to have misjudged the colonial temper. He told King George in February 1774 that he could control Boston with only four regiments and that the Americans "will be Lyons [lions], whilst we are Lambs but if we take the resolute part they will undoubtedly prove very meek."[2] This was not the first time that Gage had given such advice, which is open to misinterpretation. He had always stressed "the resolute part" as a condition of American meekness. In 1770, after the Boston Massacre, he had advised Barrington in unmistakable terms:

> No Laws can be put in Force; for those who shou'd execute the Laws, excite the People to break them, and defend them in it. Nothing will avail in so total an Anarchy, but a very considerable Force, and that Force empower'd to act. If that is done at once, with a determined Resolution to reduce them, Matters may still end without Bloodshed. But if you pursue another Conduct, and make a Shew only of Resistance, it is the Opinion of many you will draw them into Arms. Better therefore to do nothing. Every Body must have observed how they have gone Step by Step to their present Degree

[1] Franklin to Thomas Cushing, October 10, 1774, *The Papers of Benjamin Franklin*, ed. Leonard W. Labaree (Yale University Press, 1961), vol. 21, p. 329.

[2] *Correspondence of King George the Third*, ed. Leonard W. Fortescue (London, 1927), vol. 3, p. 59.

of Licentiousness, and the same Conduct towards them continued, will carry them still higher.[3]

This message embodies the British dilemma and shows that it was not new. While the Americans were fulminating against Gage's "standing army" and British brutality, Gage was faced with an indecisive British government and minimal forces at his command. He saw that the Americans were bound to reach out for more power until there was nothing left of the British empire in America. For him, the choice before British policy makers was stark—either treat the Americans with "determined Resolution," including the use of force, or resign themselves to steady disintegration.

Gage was not the only one who had thought that overcoming colonial resistance would be relatively easy. He later admitted that the colonial reaction to the Coercive Acts had caught the British by surprise. In October 1774, he confessed: "Nobody here or at home could have conceived, that the Acts made for the Massachusett's Bay, could have created such a ferment throughout the Continent, and united the whole in one common Cause, or that the Country People could have been raised to such a pitch of Phrenzy as to be ready for any mad attempt they are put upon."[4] In August 1775, he again retrospectively acknowledged that the British government had not been prepared for the colonial revolt.[5]

Whatever Gage may have said to the king before he returned to America on May 13, 1774 (and we have only the king's version of it), he soon learned better. He found that a dual colonial power had taken over and virtually superseded the British administration. From this time on, we can follow the erosion of British power as recorded in his voluminous correspondence. On July 5, he informed Dartmouth:

> Your Lordship is acquainted with the Usurpation and Tyranny establish'd here by Edicts of Town Meetings enforced by Mobs, by assuming the sole Use and Power of the Press, and influencing the Pulpits; by nominating and intimidating of Juries, and in some Instances threatening the Judges. And this Usurpation has by Time acquired a Firmness that I fear is not to be annihilated at once, or by ordinary Methods.[6]

Later that month, he explained why the British were isolated politically and could not even count on their sympathizers. He reported that he

---

[3] Gage to Barrington, July 6, 1770, *The Correspondence of General Thomas Gage with the Secretaries of State, 1763–1775* (Yale University Press, 1931), vol. 2, p. 547.

[4] Gage to Dartmouth, October 30, 1774, ibid., vol. 1, p. 380.

[5] Gage to Dartmouth, August 20, 1775, ibid., p. 413.

[6] Gage to Dartmouth, July 5, 1774, ibid., p. 359.

had experienced much Timidity and Backwardness; which finding in those pointed to me as staunch Friends of Government, surprised me a good deal.

I have endeavoured to find out the Motives of their Timidity, and various Causes are assigned for it; I am told that many in Trade fear the loss of Custom, shou'd they appear too openly in Favor of Government, that many Merchants, tho' they wish to see the Power of their Oppressors annihilated, yet wou'd not chuse that the Laws were so far enforced, as totally to prevent smuggling; and finally that Men who hold Employmants and receive Salaries under Government, fear that the Administration might relax from the Vigour now adopt'd, and that there might be a Change of Measures, when they should be left as they had been before, to the Mercy of their Opponents and their Mobs.[7]

In London, events seemed to be driving to a test of power. In June 1774, Dartmouth confided to Gage:

To what further Extravagance the People may be driven, it is difficult to say. Whatever Violences are committed must be resisted with firmness; the Constitutional Authority of this Kingdom over its Colonies must be vindicated, and its Laws obeyed throughout the whole Empire.

It is not only it's [sic] Dignity & Reputation, but it's power, nay it's very existence depends upon the present moment; for should those Ideas of Independence, which some dangerous & ill-designing Persons here are artfully endeavouring to instil into the Minds of the King's American Subjects, once take root, that Relation between this Kingdom and its Colonies, which is the Bond of Peace & Power, will soon cease to exist and Destruction must follow Disunion.

It is not the mere Claim of Exemption from the Authority of Parliament in a particular Case that has brought on the present Crisis: it is actual Disobedience & open Resistance that have compelled coercive Measures.[8]

Boston was Gage's worst trial, but it was far from the only one. In July 1774, from far-off South Carolina, Lieutenant Governor Bull advised Dartmouth that "resolutions and correspondence from other Colonies, have raised an universal spirit of jealousy against *Great Britain,* and of unanimity

[7] Gage to Dartmouth, July 27, 1774, ibid., p. 363.
[8] Dartmouth to Gage, June 3, 1774, ibid., vol. 2, p. 165.

towards each other; I say universal, my Lord, for few who think otherwise are hardy enough to avow it publicly."[9]

In August, Gage was instructed to form a new council for Massachusetts and to appoint Thomas Oliver as his lieutenant governor. He was also told firmly to resist "Whatever Violences" were committed. In the same month, these instructions were put to the test.

Gage dutifully appointed new members of the council. But a number of them found it unhealthy to serve. Gage explained why:

> Several of the New Counsellors who dwell at a Distance had fled from their Houses, and been obliged to seek Protection amongst the Troops in Boston. . . . The Object of the People was to force them to give up their Seats in Council, which has taken Effect with Mr Paine, who was seized and roughly treated . . . but Mr Willard was grievously maltreated first in Connecticut when he went on Business, and every Township he passed through in his way home in this Province had previous Notice of his Approach, and ready to insult him, Arms were put to his Breast with Threats of instant Death, unless he signed a Paper, the Contents of which he did not know nor regard. He went home after making me that Report, but the News is that a large Body was marching to his House in Lancaster to force him to some other Concessions.[10]

Other resignations followed. Gage ordered the remaining members to meet at Salem, but they pleaded that "they shou'd be watched, stopped, and insulted on the Road to Salem" and wanted the meeting moved to Boston.[11] In Boston, however, government no longer functioned. No court could conduct business, no jurors would appear. "Civil Government is near it's End," Gage lamented.[12] Samuel Cooper reported to Benjamin Franklin: "Sheriffs, Justices, Clerks &c have either made their Peace with the People by solemnly promising not to act upon the new Laws, or have fled to this poor proscribed Town as an Asylum."[13] By 1774, a dual power had superseded British civil government in Massachusetts; in this sense, the Revolution there had already begun.

To punish Boston, the capital of Massachusetts had been moved northward to Salem. Meetings were prohibited without Gage's authorization. In

---

[9] Bull to Dartmouth, July 3, 1774, *American Archives*, ed. Peter Force (Washington, 1837), 4th ser., vol. 1, col. 662.

[10] Gage to Dartmouth, September 2, 1774, *Gage Correspondence*, vol. 1, p. 370.

[11] Ibid.

[12] Ibid., p. 371.

[13] Cooper to Franklin, September 9, 1774, *Franklin Papers*, vol. 21, pp. 298–99.

August 1774, however, the town's Committee of Correspondence called a meeting in defiance of his orders. That morning Gage issued a proclamation banning it. A British regiment was encamped about a mile from Salem, and two of its companies were sent marching to the site of the meeting. Undaunted, it went on and finished its business before the soldiers could get to it. To save face, Gage had two leaders arrested but soon released them. The judge who issued the warrants of arrest was soon compelled to rescind them. The Salem committee showed that it could defy Gage with impunity. He swallowed the indignity, because he knew that he did not have the means to do otherwise.[14]

A week later, Gage professed to see this incident as evidence of an alarming colonial plan. From Salem, he reported to London that "forceable Opposition and Violence is to be transferred from the Town of Boston to the Country." It was intended "to raise a Flame not only throughout this Province, but also in the Colony of Connecticut," while "Boston affects Quiet and Tranquillity." In Worcester, in central Massachusetts, "they keep no Terms, openly threaten Resistance by Arms, have been purchasing Arms, preparing them, casting Ball, and providing Powder, and threaten to attack any Troops who dare to oppose them."[15]

Just such an attack was narrowly avoided in September. By this time, Gage was most worried that the colonists were accumulating arms and supplies in provincial storehouses. In September, when he sent soldiers to move gunpowder from Charleston, near Boston, to the British fort at Castle William in Boston harbor, he almost precipitated a clash. The operation was a success, but it set off an alarm that showed how ready the colonists were to take on the British.[16] A rumor began that a small battle had taken place in which six colonists were killed, and that the British fleet had bombarded Boston. As word spread, armed militiamen began to collect, and their number gradually assumed mythical proportions—20,000, 30,000, 40,000, or even more.[17] Caesar Rodney, a Delaware delegate to the First Continental Congress, passed on the news that there had been "upwards of fifty thousand men, well armed, actually on their march to

<hr />

[14] For Gage's versions, Gage to Dartmouth, *Gage Correspondence*, August 27, 1774, vol. 1, p. 367; October 29, 1774, vol. 1, p. 382. A colonial version is in *American Archives*, 4th ser., vol. 1, col. 730.

[15] Gage to Dartmouth, August 27, 1774, *Gage Correspondence*, vol. 1, p. 366.

[16] The incident is related in Robert P. Richmond, *Powder Alarm 1774* (Auerbach, 1971).

[17] For 20,000, Dr. Thomas Young to Samuel Adams, September 4, 1774, William V. Wells, *The Life and Public Services of Samuel Adams* (Little, Brown, 1865), vol. 2, p. 238; the same source has 30,000 men under arms marching towards Boston (p. 237); for "at least forty thousand New Englanders," Lawrence S. Mayo, *Commonwealth History of Massachusetts*, ed. Albert Bushnell Hart (States History, 1928), vol. 2, p. 548.

Boston, for the relief of the inhabitants; and that every farmer who had a cart or wagon, (and not able to bear arms), was with them, loaded with provisions, ammunition, &c., all headed by experienced officers, who had served in the late *American* war; and that vast numbers more were preparing to march. Upon the news being contradicted, they returned peaceably to their several places of abode."[18] Other reports had them marching twenty to thirty miles before they learned that the rumor was false and turned back. Joseph Warren told Sam Adams that the war might have broken out then and there: "Had the [British] troops marched only five miles out of Boston, I doubt whether a man would have been saved of their whole number."[19]

This false alarm taught Gage a lesson—that the colonists were determined to fight at the first sign or rumor of a British crackdown. His report carried the message to London:

> We hear of Nothing but Extravagancies in some Part or other, and of military Preparations from this place [Boston] to the Province of New York, in which the whole seems to be united. Upon a Rumor propagated with uncommon Dispatch thro' the Country, that the Soldiers had killed six People, and that the Ships and Troops were firing upon Boston, the whole Country was in Arms, and in Motion, and numerous Bodies of the Con[n]ecticut People had made some Marches before the Report was contradict'd.[20]

Gage faced another trial. When he tried to build more barracks for new arrivals, he found that he could not get carpenters in Boston to do the work. He sent to New York for carpenters, but posters were put up there to prevent help coming. Gage even appealed to the governor of New Hampshire, John Wentworth, to send workers to Boston. Wentworth went about hiring them surreptitiously but could not keep the secret and found himself denounced as "cruel and unmanly" and "an enemy of the community."

Worse soon befell Wentworth. On December 14, 1774, a crowd

---

[18] Force, *American Archives,* 4th ser., vol. 1, col. 793. Another report came to Franklin in London from Samuel Cooper in Boston: "Reports flew thro the Country that He [Gage] was disarming the Inhabitants of Boston, and seizing all the Ammunition thro the Province; and that the Fleet and Army had attack'd the Town. These false Reports being credited for a while, many Thousands of People especially in the Western Parts of the Province were immediately in Arms and in full March for this place, to relieve their Brethren or share their Fate: Thousands were in motion from Connecticut (for the N. England Provinces are one in Sentiment and Spirit upon these Matters) but being inform'd of Facts they quietly return'd home, sending their Messengers from all Quarters signifying their Determination to act unitedly upon any warrantable Occasion" (Cooper to Franklin, September 29, 1774, *Franklin Papers,* vol. 21, p. 300).

[19] Cited by Richmond, *Powder Alarm 1774,* p. 24.

[20] Gage to Dartmouth, September 25, 1774, *Gage Correspondence,* vol. 1, pp. 376–77.

assembled to make an assault on Fort William and Mary, at the entrance to the harbor of Portsmouth, with the intention of seizing and carrying off munitions stored there. The chief justice read the riot act and warned that a rebellion was about to be committed. With reinforcements from other towns, about 400 men attacked the five defenders in the fort. Capt. John Cochran and his few men were taken prisoner, the king's colors hauled down, and a hundred barrels of powder carried off in boats. The raiders returned to the fort the next day and removed cannon and muskets. Wentworth's government was helpless. A similar action took place in Rhode Island, where arms stored at Fort George on Goat Island were seized and brought to Providence.[21]

Early in September, Gage shared his innermost thoughts with Dartmouth: "Nothing that is said at present can palliate, Conciliating, Moderation, Reasoning is over, Nothing can be done but by forceable Means. . . . A Check any where wou'd be fatal, and the first Stroke will decide a great deal. We shou'd therefore be strong and proceed on a good Foundation before any thing decisive is tried, which it's to be presumed will prove successfull."[22]

Later that month, Gage was even more pessimistic, if that were possible. He wrote to Barrington from Boston:

> Affairs here are worse than even in the Time of the Stamp-Act, I don't mean in Boston, but throughout the Country. The New England Provinces, except part of New Hampshire, are I may say in Arms, and the Question is not now whether you shall quell Disturbances in Boston, but whether those Provinces shall be conquered, and I find it is the general Resolution of all the Continent to support the Massachusett's Bay in their Opposition to the late Acts. . . . From Appearances no People are more determined for a Civil War, the whole Country from hence to New York armed, training and providing Military Stores. Every Man supposed averse to their Measures so molest'd & oppressed, that if he can get out of the Country, which is not an easy Matter, he takes shelter in Boston.[23]

Another sign of the times in late September resulted from a London suggestion that Gage should arrest some of the colonial ringleaders. It

[21] Lawrence S. Mayo, *John Wentworth* (Harvard University Press, 1921), pp. 138–42; Gipson, *The British Empire Before the American Revolution* (Alfred A. Knopf, 1965), vol. 12, pp. 169–71 (New Hampshire), 172 (Rhode Island).

[22] Gage to Dartmouth, September 2, 1774, *Gage Correspondence*, vol. 1, p. 371.

[23] Gage to Barrington, September 25, 1774, ibid., vol. 2, pp. 654–55.

"wou'd have been a very proper Measure some Time ago," Gage responded, "but at present it wou'd be the Signal for Hostilities, which they seem very ripe to begin."[24] He was taking no chances so long as he did not have the reinforcements he was asking for.

The British in Massachusetts felt as if they were a besieged garrison. In October 1774, Gage reported that his "Moderation and Forbearance" were being sorely tested—straw for the army burned, boats sunk with bricks, wood carts overturned. When he heard that a ship was delivering twelve pieces of cannon, he expressed the hope that they would not fall into "bad Hands." By the end of October, he was so apprehensive that he might not be able to get supplies and provisions that he told contractors "to lay in large Quantities in Time." If anything worse happened, he was sure that he could not get provisions from other colonies. In November, he was relieved to get flour that had been stopped in Maryland because it was known to be going to the troops in Boston; but he was able to report that he could get provisions for his troops to last about six months. At about the same time, however, he was left without colonial-owned transports, previously used to carry troops and supplies, because "no Persons in any of the Provinces dared to let out a ship for the use of Troops." In December, despite the cold weather, his barrack master general still could not get materials to put up quarters for recently arrived reinforcements.[25]

By the fall of 1774, then, the British commander in chief in North America and governor of Massachusetts had just about given up hope of a peaceful settlement. He portrayed himself and his forces as beset by enraged colonial forces bent on humiliating and isolating them. His entire demeanor was defensive, his strategy one of gaining time until his superiors in London decided to send him the vastly larger forces he thought he needed to go on the offensive. While he seethed inwardly against the Americans, he held his fire, even at the cost of losing face, in order to avoid a premature test of strength. His political base among the colonists had evaporated; he was penned up in Boston; his only remaining authority was over his still inadequate army.

Between his assurance to King George in February 1774 that he could handle the Americans with four regiments and his cries of alarm to Dartmouth and Barrington in September 1774, Gage went through a conversion experience. Within four months after his return to America in May 1774, he came to realize that he was in no position to take on

[24] Gage to Dartmouth, September 25, 1774, ibid., vol. 1, p. 376.
[25] Gage to Dartmouth, October 17, October 30, November 15, December 15, 1774, ibid., pp. 379, 382, 384, 388; Gage to Barrington, November 20, 1774, vol. 2, p. 662.

the Americans. If the British had had a general with less coolness and prudence than Gage in America in 1774, the Revolution might easily have broken out in the last half of that year.

• 2 •

While Gage was edging towards the inescapability of war, the Americans were doing the same. They were not acting as if they were forced into a war with Great Britain; they seemed to be inviting it.

Something happened to the Americans in 1774. The Boston Port Bill appears to have made a qualitative difference in the way they reacted to British policy. When the bill went into effect in May of that year, John Scollay of Boston wrote to Arthur Lee in London, describing the change that had taken place—"in short we have all, from the cobbler up to the senator, become politicians." Scollay himself was not an extremist. He wrote, "We have too great a regard for our parent state (although cruelly treated by some of her illegitimate sons) to withdraw our connexion; of her we have no idea of an independency, and the colonies are too precious a jewel for the crown to part with." He still thought that some plan of conciliation might succeed.[26]

Earlier in the year, Arthur Lee—the youngest of the four Lee brothers of Virginia—had been fearful that the Americans would go too far, because he assumed that they were the weaker party. A lawyer in London who replaced Franklin as agent for the Massachusetts Assembly, Arthur gave this advice to his brother Richard Henry Lee in Virginia about protesting the Boston Port Bill:

> Great care, therefore, should be taken to word them unexception-ably and plausibly. They should be prefaced with the strongest professions of respect and attachment to this country; of reluctance to enter into any dispute with her; of the readiness you have always shown, and still wish to show, of contributing according to your ability, and in a constitutional way, to her support; and of your determination to undergo every extremity rather than submit to be enslaved. These things tell much in your favour with moderate men, and with *Europe*, to whose interposition *America* may yet owe her salvation, should the contest be serious and lasting. In short, as we are the weaker, it

[26] Scollay to Lee, May 31, 1774, in Richard Henry Lee, *Life of Arthur Lee, LL.D.* (Boston, 1929), vol. 2, pp. 213–15.

becomes us to be *suaviter in modo,* however we may be determined to act *fortiter in re.* There is a persuasion here that *America* will see, without interposition, the ruin of *Boston.*[27]

Arthur Lee was mainly concerned with opinion in Great Britain and Europe. In April, however, he received from Samuel Adams a letter which shows that his view from abroad was far from that of kindred spirits in Boston:

> And if the British administration and government do not return to the principles of moderation and equity, the evil which they profess to aim at preventing by their rigorous measures, will the sooner be brought to pass, viz:—*the entire separation and independence of the colonies.* . . . I wish for a permanent union with the mother country, but only on the principles of liberty and truth. No advantage that can accrue to America from such an union can compensate for the loss of liberty. The time may come sooner than they are aware of it, when the being of the British nation, I mean the being of its importance, however strange it may now appear to some, will depend on her union with America. It requires but a small portion of the gift of discernment for any one to foresee, that providence will erect a mighty empire in America; and our posterity will have it recorded in history, that their fathers migrated from an *island* in a distant part of the world, the inhabitants of which had long been revered for wisdom and valour. They grew rich and powerful; these emigrants increased in numbers and strength. But they were at last absorbed in luxury and dissipation; and to support themselves in their vanity and extravagance they coveted and seized the honest earnings of those industrious emigrants. This laid a foundation of distrust, animosity and hatred, till the emigrants, feeling their own vigour and independence, dissolved every former band of connexion between them, and the *islanders* sunk into obscurity and contempt.[28]

This private communication by Adams was more revealing than anything he was as yet willing to say publicly or put into print in his own name. It broached the prospect of *"the entire separation and independence of the colonies,"* though it put the onus on the British. To avoid this fate, the British would be required to accept the conditions presented to them by

[27] Arthur Lee to Richard H. Lee, March 18, 1774, *American Archives,* 4th ser., vol. 1, col. 229.

[28] Adams to Lee, April 4, 1774, *The Writings of Samuel Adams,* ed. Harry Alonzo Cushing (G. P. Putnam's Sons, 1906), vol. 3, pp. 100–102.

the Americans. The British were seen as the weaker party; they needed the Americans more than the Americans needed them. America was destined to become "a mighty empire," grown "rich and powerful," always increasing in "numbers and strength." But the Americans, whose "honest earnings" had been "coveted and seized," had been made to pay for British "vanity and extravagance." Economic exploitation was the root of American "distrust, animosity and hatred." The Americans were now feeling their own "vigour and independence," which explained why they were ready to cut themselves loose from Great Britain. Without the Americans, the British were doomed to sink "into obscurity and contempt."

In this letter Samuel Adams used the phrase "a mighty empire." Later that year, Joseph Warren congratulated John Adams on what was happening in Braintree: "I am pleased to find your Town makes such a Figure in a military way. The Spirit is catching, and spreads into every Corner, and bids fair to cherish the seeds, and support the Stock of a rising Empire."[29]

These phrases, "a mighty empire" and "a rising empire," reverberated through the later history of the new American nation. They suggested that the Revolution was made in behalf of the future and not only for the sake of the present. Adams and Warren reflected a sense of destiny that had long prevailed in the colonies and was now about to take off.

Adams was not the only one to think that the British needed the Americans too much to risk losing them. John Dickinson, a far more moderate mind, wrote to Arthur Lee in August:

> Is it possible that the people of our mother country, so beloved and revered by us, can seriously think of sheathing their swords in bosoms so affectionate to them? Of engaging in a war that must instantly produce such deficiencies in her revenue, expose her to her natural enemies, and, if she conquers, must, in its consequences, drag her down to destruction; and, if she fails of success, as, if the Colonists have common sense, she certainly must, will involve her in immediate ruin?[30]

These sentiments must be taken into account to explain why the

---

[29] Warren to Adams, December 19, 1774, *Warren-Adams Letters* (Massachusetts Historical Society, 1917), vol. 1, p. 34.

[30] Dickinson to Lee, August 20, 1774, *American Archives*, 4th ser., vol. 1, col. 726. Two months later, Dickinson again wrote to Lee: "The colonists have now taken such grounds, that Great Britain must relax, or inevitably involve herself in a civil war, likely in all probability to overwhelm her with a weight of calamities, in comparison of which, the contentions between the houses of York and Lancaster, or the distractions of the last century, were gentle misfortunes" (October 27, 1774, in Lee, *Life of Arthur Lee*, vol. 2, p. 306).

Americans were not backward in their challenges to the British in 1774. Advanced American opinion could not understand why Britain should want to engage in a ruinous war with its colonies. At the same time, the British made themselves believe that the Americans could not stand up to British economic and military pressure. In April 1774, Benjamin Franklin advised Boston that the British were taking great pains to foster the conviction that "Boston must immediately submit, and acknowledge the Claim of Parliament, for that none of the other Colonies will adhere to them."[31] Each side moved towards a war that it hoped to avoid by proving to itself that the other side could not possibly want it.

As early as April 9, 1774, the British anticipated the use of force. Dartmouth had authorized Gage to employ troops "should the madness of the People on the one hand, or want of Strength of the peace officers on the other hand, make it necessary to have recourse to their assistance."[32] Gage did not have the force to take advantage of this authorization, but it was an early omen of how serious the crisis was considered to be in London.

· 3 ·

The most militant colonial expression came in September 1774 with the Suffolk County Resolves, which amounted to a call for military mobilization. They could not have come from the side which considered itself the weaker one. If Gage had been less prudent and had arrested some colonial leaders, as his superiors in London had advised him to do, and the Massachusetts colonists had retaliated by seizing "every servant of the present tyrannical and unconstitutional Government, through the county and Province," as the thirteenth resolve threatened, war could no longer have been avoided.

When the resolves were published in London, they were received as open declarations of rebellion. Dartmouth told Hutchinson: "Why, if these Resolves of your people are to be depended on, they have declared War against us: they will not suffer any sort of Treaty."[33] When the First Continental Congress soon voted to approve the Suffolk County Resolves, Joseph

[31] Franklin to Thomas Cushing, April 2, 1774, *Franklin Papers*, vol. 21, p. 182.

[32] Dartmouth to Gage, April 9, 1774, *Gage Correspondence*, vol. 2, p. 159. But Dartmouth held back in December 1774 from authorizing the use of military force to prevent violence in a matter involving conflicting land claims in the town of Bennington (Dartmouth to Cadwallader Colden, December 10, 1774, *Colden Papers, Collections of the New-York Historical Society, 1923*, vol. 7, p. 256).

[33] *Diary and Letters of His Excellency Thomas Hutchinson*, ed. Peter Orlando Hutchinson (London, 1883), vol. 1, p. 284.

Galloway later recalled, "the foundation of military resistance throughout America was effectually laid."[34]

Bravado was not a monopoly of Suffolk County. Other counties and towns soon followed its example. Boston, Marblehead, Plymouth, Roxbury, Cambridge, Newburyport, and Charlestown held town meetings to pass similar denunciations of British rule. An Essex County convention at Ipswich on September 6 and 7, 1774, resolved that any officers or magistrates who cooperated with England to restrict American liberties "are and will be considered its unnatural and malignant enemies." At Worcester County in August–September 1774, a resolution stated: "If there be an invasion, or danger of an invasion, in any town in this county, then, such town shall, by their Committee of Correspondence, or some other proper persons, send letters by post immediately to the Committees of the adjoining towns, who shall send to the other Committees in the towns adjoining them, that they all come properly armed and accoutred to protect and defend the place invaded."[35] In the end, one-third of all the towns in Massachusetts took similar action.[36]

Gage reacted defensively to these challenges. Boston was then almost an island, connected with the mainland by a narrow strip of land called Boston Neck. In September 1774, the same month as these conventions and town meetings, Gage took steps to fortify the neck in case of an attack on Boston. It was an action that clearly revealed how defensive minded the general was; fortifying the neck was a protective measure, not a means of breaking out of Boston and seizing the military initiative. John Adams, at this time in Philadelphia for the First Continental Congress, wrote to William Tudor in Boston that it was the "universal opinion here" that Gage "means to act only on the defensive."[37]

Meanwhile, Massachusetts prepared for war. A Massachusetts Provincial Congress was held at Salem in October 1774. It put into practice what the Suffolk County Resolves had called for. It set up a "Committee for the Defence and Safety of the Province" (in short, Committee of Safety), consisting of nine members, including three from Boston and six from elsewhere. Its business was "most carefully and diligently to inspect and observe all and every such person and persons as shall, at any time, attempt or enterprise the destruction, invasion, detriment, or annoyance of this Province, &c." It was also given the power

---

[34] [Joseph Galloway], *Historical and Political Reflections on the Rise and Progress of the American Rebellion* (London, 1780), pp. 68–69.

[35] *American Archives*, 4th ser., vol. 1, col. 795.

[36] Gipson, *British Empire Before the American Revolution*, vol. 12, p. 50.

[37] Adams to Tudor, September 29, 1774, *The Works of John Adams*, ed. Charles Francis Adams (Boston, 1861), vol. 9, p. 347.

whenever they shall judge it necessary for the safety and defence of the inhabitants of this Province, and their property, against such person or persons aforesaid, to alarm, muster, and cause to be assembled, with the utmost expedition, and completely armed, accoutred, and supplied with provisions sufficient for their support in their march to the place of rendezvous, such and so many of the militia of this Province, as they shall judge necessary for the ends aforesaid, and at such place or places as they shall judge proper, and to discharge them as soon as the safety of the Province shall permit.

It was instructed to form companies with at least fifty privates; each company to choose a captain and two lieutenants; nine companies in each battalion; and field officers to command regiments. A committee of three, made up of Joseph Warren, Capt. [later Maj. Gen.] William Heath, and Benjamin Church, another doctor, was directed to put in a safe place the "warlike stores now in the Commissary General's office, and that the matter be conducted with the greatest secrecy." It authorized the purchase of arms and ammunition to the considerable sum of £20,837. This congress for the first time attempted to give a collective name to what it called the "United American Colonies."[38] Gage futilely issued a proclamation "strictly prohibiting" compliance with the resolves of the Salem congress.[39]

John Dickinson wrote to Josiah Quincy, Jr., on October 28, 1774: "The most peaceable provinces, are now animated; and a civil war is unavoidable, unless there be a quick change of British measures."[40] Gage informed Dartmouth, November 2, 1774: "This Province, without Courts or Legislature, the whole Country in a Ferment, many parts of it, I may say, actual[l]y in arms, and ready to unite."[41] Joseph Warren told Josiah Quincy, Jr., November 21, 1774: "If the late acts of Parliament are not to be repealed, the wisest step for both countries is fairly to separate, and not spend their blood and treasure in destroying each other."[42] Gage advised Dartmouth, December 15, 1774: "Your Lordship's Idea of disarming certain Provinces would doubtless be consistent with Prudence and Safety, but

[38] *American Archives*, 4th ser., vol. 1, cols. 834–53. Church was later shown to be in British pay; he was the first American traitor.

[39] Ibid., cols. 973–74.

[40] Dickinson to Quincy, October 28, 1774, *Memoir of the Life of Josiah Quincy Jun.* (Boston, 1825), p. 193. Dickinson could not see how Great Britain could come out ahead: "The usual events, no question, will take place if that happens;—victories and defeats. But what will be the final consequence? If she fails, immediate distress; if not ruin. If she conquers, destruction at last."

[41] Gage to Dartmouth, November 2, 1774, *Gage Correspondence*, vol. 1, p. 383.

[42] Warren to Quincy, November 21, 1774, *Memoir of the Life of Josiah Quincy Jun.*, p. 208.

it neither is nor has been practicable without having Recourse to Force, and being Masters of the Country."[43] Thomas Cushing wrote to Josiah Quincy, Jr., December 30, 1774: "The late order of the King in Council, prohibiting the exportation of Powder, or any sort of Arms or Ammunition, from *Great Britain,* unless by special license, has alarmed the people in *America;* it forebodes the most vigorous exertions of martial force. They are therefore adopting the most effectual methods to defend themselves against any hostile invasion of the enemies to *America.*"[44]

In effect, Massachusetts was transforming its militia into a rudimentary army. Only an occasion for using it was lacking. By the end of 1774, both sides expected war.

· 4 ·

A question arises: Why didn't the British under Gage preemptively put down the colonial threat in Massachusetts in 1774?

The short answer is that the balance of forces did not favor the British. Gage was all for teaching the rebellious colonists a bloody lesson, but he refused to act until conditions changed in the British favor. They did not change fast enough.[45]

By the fall of 1774, Gage was so alarmed that he began to press for a huge increase in his forces. He wanted more men quickly, because he believed that the more he had "at the beginning" the quicker and easier it would be to put down the incipient rebellion. On October 30, he sent word that force must be used; he had fewer than 3,000 men and needed 20,000, a figure soon increased to 32,000.[46] "I have Nothing good to send your Lordship from this Continent," he wrote to Barrington, "there is Nothing going on but Preparations for War, and Threats to take Arms, & they affect to despise our small Numbers, and to overwhelm us with forty or fifty Thousand Men."[47]

Gage repeatedly begged the British government to act quickly and with superior force:

[43] Gage to Dartmouth, December 15, 1774, *Gage Correspondence,* vol. 1, p. 387.
[44] Cushing to Quincy, December 30, 1774, *American Archives,* 4th ser., vol. 1, col. 1080.
[45] David Hackett Fischer in *Paul Revere's Ride* (Oxford University Press, 1994) gives a somewhat different interpretation of Gage's reluctance to use force. Fischer emphasizes that "Thomas Gage was an English gentleman who believed in decency, moderation, liberty, and the rule of law" (p. 64). All this may be true, but Gage clearly held back from using force because he did not have enough force to use.
[46] Gage to Dartmouth, October 30, 1774, *Gage Correspondence,* vol. 1, p. 383; June 12, 1775, p. 404.
[47] Gage to Barrington, October 3, 1774, ibid., vol. 2, p. 656.

If Force is to be used at length, it must be a considerable one, and Foreign Troops must be hired, for to begin with Small Numbers will encourage Resistance and not terrify; and will in the End cost more Blood and Treasure. An Army on Such a Service should be large enough to make considerable Detachments to disarm and take in the Counties, procure Forrage Carriages &ca and keep up Communications, without which little Progress could be made in a Country, where all are Enemies.[48]

By early November, he was almost frantic with anxiety that the British government's response would be too little and too late:

This Province [Massachusetts] and the neighboring ones, particularly Con[n]ecticut, are preparing for War; if you will resist and not yield, that Resistance should be effectual at the Beginning. If you think ten Thousand Men sufficient, send Twenty, if one Million [pounds] is thought enough, give two; you will save both Blood and Treasure in the end. A large Force will terrify and engage many to join you, a middling one will encourage Resistance, and gain no Friends.[49]

In December he tried again to wake up London: "I hope you will be firm, and send me a sufficient Force to command the Country, by marching into it, and sending off large Detachments to secure obedience thro' every part of it; affairs are at a Crisis, and if you give way it is for ever."[50]

But in London, the government was not prepared to make a quick decision. The only immediate action in 1774 was the dispatch of three ships filled with ten companies of British marines to American waters, far fewer than what Gage had asked for.[51] In Boston, where the first test of strength was taking place, Gage had only 4,000 men in 1774 and could get only 2,000 more in 1775.[52] His few regiments were decidedly under strength. The British navy could close the port of Boston, but it could not change the balance of power on land, where it counted the most.

The British commander had reason to be reluctant to take on the Americans. They had always had a military force in their militia, which had originated in the earliest settlements. After the Revolution, John

---

[48] Gage to Dartmouth, October 30, 1774, ibid., vol. 1, p. 380.
[49] Gage to Barrington, November 2, 1774, ibid., vol. 2, p. 659.
[50] Gage to Barrington, December 14, 1774, ibid., p. 663.
[51] Bernard Donoughue, *British Politics and the American Revolution* (London, 1964), p. 205.
[52] Ira D. Gruber, *Military History of the American Revolution* (Office of Air Force History and United States Air Force Academy, 1976), p. 46. These figures vary in different sources but not by much.

Adams named the militia as one of the four institutions that had made the Revolution possible—the other three were towns, congregations, and schools. Every male between the ages of sixteen and sixty was nominally enrolled in a company and required to keep in his house, at his own expense, a firelock in good order, a powder horn, a pound of powder, twelve flints, twenty-four balls of lead, a cartridge box, and a knapsack.[53] Virtually every male American possessed a musket at a time when muskets and bayonets were still the main British weapons.[54] In times of peace, the provincial militias declined in numbers and discipline, so that they hardly counted as a fighting force. By mid-1774, however, a new spirit, leadership, and training took over. An elite corps, the "Minutemen," consisting of members of the militia "ready to act at a minute's warning," was organized. By September 1774, Gage referred to the militia around Boston with new respect. "Tho' the People are not held in high Estimation by the Troops," he noted, "yet they are numerous, worked up to a Fury, and not a Boston Rabble but the Freeholders and Farmers of the Country."[55]

Logistics also favored the Americans. The British had to bring men and supplies, even oats for horses, across 3,000 miles of ocean. The Americans were accustomed to fighting in the wilderness, where much of the action was likely to take place. They had far greater reserves of manpower and did not have to bring them from afar. They could live off the land far more easily than the British or their German mercenaries. An American military historian of the Revolution notes the "outburst of enthusiasm in the spring of 1775" and "the naive optimism of 1775" on the American side.[56] This enthusiasm and optimism arose from the early American advantages, before the British brought over much larger forces. The initial British inferiority induced the British government to hire 18,000 German mercenaries, but they did not arrive until the summer of 1776.[57]

Gage's dispatches to London reveal how seriously he took the colonial mobilization in the latter half of 1774:

> *September* 12, 1774: The Country People are exercising in Arms in this Province [Massachusetts], Connecticut, and Rhode Island, and getting Magazines of Arms and Ammunition in the Country, and such

[53] Adams to Abbé de Mably, 1782, *Works of John Adams*, vol. 5, pp. 495–96.
[54] Frey, *The British Soldier in America* (University of Texas Press, 1981), pp. 100–101.
[55] Gage to Dartmouth, September 2, 1774, *Gage Correspondence*, vol. 1, p. 371.
[56] John Shy, *A People Numerous and Armed* (University of Michigan Press, rev. ed., 1990), pp. 20–21, 25.
[57] Piers Mackesy, *The War for America, 1775–1783* (Harvard University Press, 1965), pp. 62, 70.

Artillery, as they can procure good and bad. They threaten to attack the Troops in Boston, and are very angry at a Work throwing up at the Entrance of the Town [Boston Neck].[58]

September 25, 1774: The New England Provinces, except part of New Hampshire, are I may say in Arms . . ., From Appearances no People are more determined for a Civil War, the whole Country from hence to New York armed, training and providing Military Stores."[59]

Yet so long as the British government could not make up its mind about how far to go in suppressing the colonies, Gage felt that he had to stay on the defensive. It is conceivable, perhaps even probable, that war might have been avoided—or at least postponed—if the British had had enough military superiority in the colonies to make colonial resistance seem hopeless. Instead, the government decided on a policy of coercion without having sufficient powers of coercion to back it up—until it was too late. Gage later admitted that the British government had been "unprepared to oppose so general a Revolt."[60]

The decisive British blunder in this opening phase was strategic. It resulted from the assumption in London that Boston was the key to breaking American resistance and that the colonies were too divided for Boston to get support from others. In part, this was wishful thinking based on the kind of advice the British were getting from their leading adherents in Boston. Governor Hutchinson was one of those who misled the British the most. As late as July 1773, he sent word to London that all the anti-British moves in Massachusetts were the work of "half a dozen or half a score."[61] In September he told Dartmouth that "the body of the people of the province are far from a perverse disposition" but were "deluded by a few men."[62] In June 1774, Dartmouth again referred to "a few desperate Men" who created "in the people Ideas of a more general Resistance."[63]

But Boston, as Gage later realized, was the worst possible place for a showdown; it was where colonial power and determination were maximal. Too late, Gage admitted to Barrington that he had been forced to attack "the Enemy in their Strong parts" and that it was "the worst place either

[58] Gage to Dartmouth, September 12, 1774, *Gage Correspondence*, vol. 1, p. 374.
[59] Gage to Barrington, September 25, 1774, ibid., vol. 2, pp. 654–55.
[60] Gage to Dartmouth, October 15, 1775, ibid., p. 420.
[61] Hutchinson to John Pownall (private), July 3, 1773, Davies, *Documents of the American Revolution*, vol. 6, p. 180.
[62] Hutchinson to Dartmouth, September 16, 1773, ibid., p. 220.
[63] Dartmouth to Gage, June 3, 1774, *Gage Correspondence*, vol. 2, p. 166.

to act Offensively from, or defencively."[64] Dartmouth later admitted that he had misgauged the Americans. "I was willing to suppose," he said,

> that the disorders in that country were local, and had chiefly pervaded the hearts of an inconsiderable number of men, who were only formidable, because they possessed the power of factious delusion and imposition. I all along expected, that the *body* of the people, when they came to view the consequences closely, and consider them attentively, would soon perceive the danger in which they were precipitating themselves, and of course return to their duty.[65]

One of the most self-deluded was the king. He persistently took the hardest line against the Americans, because he thought that "once vigorous measures appear to be the only means left of bringing the Americans to a due Submission to the Mother Country that the Colonies will Submit."[66]

British policy in 1774 was based on multiple misunderstandings of the American reality. The nagging question is whether anything would have been different if the king, Dartmouth, Gage, and other British officials had known the Americans better. They went to war thinking that they would not have to fight.

Instead of isolating Boston, British strategy united the colonies as never before. "I find it is the general Resolution of all the Continent to support the Mas[s]achusett's Bay in their opposition to the late Acts," Gage reported to Barrington in September 1774. "You supposed in England that the Port-Bill regarded Boston alone, as well as the Acts for regulating their Government, but they have contrived to get the rest of their Brethren in every Province to be as violent in their Defense as themselves."[67] To Dartmouth, Gage confessed that "it is somewhat surprising that so many in the other Provinces interest themselves so much in behalf of this [Massachusetts]."[68] At one point in 1774, Gage almost lost his nerve; he entertained the idea of suspending the Coercive Acts, though, he added, in order to be better prepared.[69] The king thought that this proposal was "the most absurd that can be suggested" and insisted that "we must either master them or totally

---

[64] Gage to Barrington, June 26, 1775, ibid., p. 687.

[65] *Proceedings and Debates of the British Parliaments Respecting North America, 1754–1783*, ed. R. C. Simmons and P.D.G. Thomas (Kraus International, 1983), March 14, 1776, vol. 6, pp. 469–70.

[66] *Correspondence of King George the Third*, vol. 3, p. 175.

[67] Gage to Barrington, September 25, 1774, *Gage Correspondence*, vol. 2, p. 654.

[68] Gage to Dartmouth, September 12, 1774, ibid., vol. 1, p. 374.

[69] Gage to Dartmouth, September 25, 1774, ibid., p. 375.

leave them to themselves and treat them as aliens."[70] By December 1774, the British had decided that Massachusetts was guilty of "open rebellion and war."[71]

By the end of 1774, peaceful maneuvering was clearly coming to an end. In November, Charles Thomson of Philadelphia informed Benjamin Franklin, still in London, that the Americans were being dragged "into the horrors of civil War" and that "we are on the very edge of the precipice."[72] In December, John Adams explained what was happening to James Burgh, a sympathetic British author:

> We are, in this province, Sir, at the brink of a civil war. We have no council, no house, no legislative, no executive. Not a court of justice has sat since the month of September. Not a debt can be recovered, nor a trespass redressed, nor a criminal of any kind brought to punishment. . . . New England alone has two hundred thousand fighting men, and all in a militia, established by law; not exact soldiers, but all used to arms.[73]

The War of the Revolution was not a sudden eruption of violence. By 1774, both sides were straining to break out of the impasse into which the Boston Tea Party and its aftermath, the Coercive Acts, had driven them. General Gage's biographer says that "the War of Independence could have begun at any time between September, 1774, and April, 1775, through some unfortunate incident."[74] What happened in the next two years developed as a consequence of the way both sides behaved in 1774. Any turning back would have had to come in 1774. Later, it was too late.

· 5 ·

Early in 1775, but from letters sent in late 1774, the British press made known that war was coming. Most of the news about America in the British press was quoted from the American press or took the form of

[70] King to North, November 19, 1774, *Correspondence of King George the Third*, vol. 3, p. 154.
[71] Attorney and Solicitor General to Earl of Dartmouth, December 13, 1774, Davies, *Documents of the American Revolution*, vol. 8, p. 240.
[72] Thomson to Franklin, November 1, 1774, *Franklin Papers*, vol. 21, p. 345.
[73] Adams to Burgh, December 28, 1774, *Works of John Adams*, vol. 9, pp. 351–52.
[74] John Richard Alden, *General Gage in America* (Louisiana State University Press, 1948), p. 222.

letters written by Americans to British friends or correspondents or by Englishmen temporarily stationed in America and writing to friends back home.[75]

On January 12, 1775, the *London Chronicle* published this excerpt from a letter sent from Boston, evidently by a British sympathizer, on November 8, 1774:

> War, that evil, look all around us; the country expect it, and are prepared to die freemen, rather than live what they call slaves. ... I hope, on your side the water, measures of prudence will be proceeded on; here they seem to consider all prudence as pusillanimous; multitudinous are the curses, and manifold the daily prayers raised by this praying people, for the eternal destruction of N[orth] and H[utchinson]; what will be the consequence heaven knows; if England gives up, we must sacrifice all her friends here, and render the Americans still more daring; if she persists, the first hour of blood will be her last of glory in this country: I think she may destroy it, but never conquer it.[76]

Another letter from Boston, dated November 15, 1774, appeared in the *Bristol Gazette.* It sought to convey the state of mind of the Americans:

> The shock of the port-bill lasted but a few days, from which they rose superior to all their former feelings. They now felt themselves willing to endure any hardships, to encounter any dangers, to sacrifice ease, health, wealth, and even life itself to the sacred calls of their country. ... They will therefore in safety to themselves, and from the dictates of an enlightened conscience, cheerfully give up the friendship of that man who is not a friend to his country; renounce that family alliance—those ties which would bind them with the galling chains of slavery, detest, thoroughly detest, that official dependence which is opposed to the blessings of freedom, and the eternal and indefensible rights of mankind; and ultimately, if reduced to the sad necessity, take the sword, and appeal to the God of battles—the great general of the universe.[77]

On January 19, 1775, the *Gazetteer and New Daily Advertiser* brought

[75] *Letters on the American Revolution, 1774–1776,* ed. Margaret Wheeler Willard (Houghton Mifflin, 1925), p. xiii.
[76] Ibid., p. 6.
[77] Ibid., pp. 8, 10.

this news of the American attitude, written in Boston on November 20, 1774:

> In short, Sir, the Americans are contending for power, and that I think is manifest, notwithstanding all their art and cunning. . . . Nothing will satisfy them [New England] or conciliate them to your government, and nothing but force can extort submission and obedience from them. . . . Such, however, is the influence of the faction which presides at the head of affairs, that nine tenths of the people will greedily swallow the most glaring fictions which they shall think proper to propagate, and nothing can get the better of their infatuation, but a spirited exertion of power, which all good men are waiting to see take place.[78]

A letter of December 8, 1774, printed in the *Morning Chronicle and London Advertiser* of January 17, 1775, claimed to show how close the Americans had come to war:

> This country is now in open rebellion; but we have not yet come to the last act, that of fighting. Those of the rebels, who are most moderate and conversible, say, that they expect a civil war in the spring, as they cannot bring themselves to believe that Great Britain will ever comply with their demands, and therefore they all lay their account with being conquered, and of course ruined. . . . You will see in the papers the villainous resolve of the blacksmiths of Worcester County not to work for the gentlemen appointed Counsellors, who have long been obliged to quit the country and take shelter in Boston. The Provincial Congress, which consists of between two and three hundred members, have taken the whole Government of the country into their hands; the General Gage with his troops, has the care of Boston and the Tories only, a name given by the rebels to all the loyal and peaceable part of the community. . . . People travelling the high roads and seized, and obliged to declare themselves Whigs, their name for rebels, and to CURSE *the* KING *and the* PARLIAMENT, and to wish the island of Great Britain SUNK *in the* SEA, before they are permitted to pass; to such a height of phrenzy have the common people got thro' the delusions of the chief conspirators. . . . All the towns in the province, Boston excepted, are, at the desire of the Congress exercising their militia every fair day, and are also chusing

[78] Ibid., pp. 10–14.

their own militia officers; another open act of treason, in order to prepare themselves for the spring, when they boast they will take the field, and that fifty thousand regulars would make no impression upon them.[79]

More military intelligence came from New York in a letter of December 17, 1774, published in the *Morning Chronicle and Daily Advertiser* of January 31, 1775: "The militia throughout America are now constantly exercised three times a week; a number of troops under the command of Gen. Gage have lately deserted; a few days since upwards of forty left the regiments they belonged to, taking with them their muskets, bayonets, etc."[80]

The letters of a gentleman in Philadelphia to a member of the British Parliament, dated December 24 and 26, 1774, appeared in the *London Chronicle* of April 25 to 27, 1775. They warned that the proclamation forbidding exportation of gunpowder and firearms to America would not work, because the colonists were manufacturing their own gunpowder. They had enough gunsmiths to make 100,000 stand of arms in a single year:

> It may not be amiss to make this intelligence as public as possible, that our rulers may see the impossibility of enforcing the late acts of parliament by arms. Such is the wonderful martial spirit which is enkindled among us, that we begin to think the whole force of Britain could not subdue us. We trust no less to the natural advantages of our country than to our numbers and military preparations. . . .
>
> Nothing but a total repeal of the acts of parliament of which we complain can prevent a civil war in America. . . . We tremble at the thoughts of a separation from Great Britain. All our glory and happiness have been derived from you. But we are in danger of being shipwrecked upon your rocks. To avoid these, we are willing to be tossed, without a compass or a guide, for a while upon an ocean of blood.[81]

Finally, a pro-British writer in a letter of December 28, 1774, appearing in the *Morning Chronicle and Daily Advertiser* of February 2, 1775, told how difficult it had become to be a British partisan:

> Every man who will not drink "destruction to his King," is a Tory, and liable to tar and feathers. In the east and southern provinces

79 Ibid., pp. 25–26.
80 Ibid., p. 36.
81 Ibid., pp. 40–41.

they are in actual rebellion, raising troops, and seizing ammunition in the most daring manner; the common people are mad, they only hear one side of the question, and believe they are oppressed because they are told so, which is all they know of the matter. As the fever is very high, a little bleeding is absolutely necessary.[82]

The letters sent from America in early 1775 were even more concrete and frightening. British sympathizers warned that a rebellion was coming in the spring. They left no doubt that they were overwhelmed by colonial zealots:

> *Boston, January* 16, 1775: Our insurgents are making great preparations for opening their rebellion in the Spring with a numerous body of troops (*Gazetteer and New Daily Advertiser,* March 1, 1775).
>
> *Charleston, South Carolina, January* 17, 1775: Parties run so high here, or rather a very great majority being of one opinion, that it is dangerous for the friends of government (who are very few in number) to speak or write their sentiments (*London Evening Post,* March 23–25, 1775).
>
> *Norfolk, Virginia, January* 30, 1775: The gentlemen, who stile themselves Whigs and Patriots, carry every thing with a high hand, while those of more moderate principles, especially in this Province, [do not] dare to avow them (*Morning Chronicle and London Advertiser,* March 18, 1775).
>
> *Colchester, Virginia, February* 9, 1775: All the counties in Virginia are forming companies of men, and committees are daily meeting who distress those merchants who sell goods at a higher rate than before the non-importation scheme took place (*Gazetteer and New Daily Advertiser,* March 29, 1775).
>
> *Boston, March* 1, 1775: It is impossible to give you a better description of the bulk of the people on this Continent (and particularly in the province of Massachusetts Bay) than every English history gives of the principles of the Independents in Oliver's [Cromwell's] time. There their pictures are justly drawn (*Farley's Bristol Journal,* April 29, 1775).
>
> *Virginia, April* 16, 1775: The New-England provinces have at this day 50,000 of as well trained soldiers as any in Europe, ready to take the field at a day's warning, it is as much as the more prudent and moderate among them can do, to prevent the more violent from

[82] Ibid., p. 46.

crushing General Gage's little army (*London Chronicle*, June 1–3, 1775).[83]

Meanwhile, Gage was telling his superiors in London that more offensive measures were necessary. He still did not have enough troops to act aggressively and told Barrington on February 10, 1775, that "to keep quiet in the Town of Boston only, will not terminate Affairs; the Troops must March into the Country."[84] On March 28, Gage still awaited orders to march. As far as he knew, "nothing had been resolved upon," but he thought, "you are now making your final Efforts respecting America." His advice was "If you yield, I conceive that you have not a spark of Authority remaining over this Country. If you determine on the contrary to Support your Measures, it should be done with as little delay as possible, and as Powerfully as you are able, for its easier to crush Evils in their Infancy than when grown to Maturity."[85]

· 6 ·

Gage's reference to "final Efforts respecting America" alluded to a so-called plan of conciliation, put forward by Lord North in February 1775. North had been under increasing pressure from the king to treat the New England colonies as rebellious and been told in November 1774 that "blows must decide whether they are to be subject to this country or independent."[86] That month North used the same kind of language in a conversation with the recently arrived former Massachusetts governor, Thomas Hutchinson: "Parliament would not—could not—concede. For aught he could see it must come to violence."[87] At the end of the year, North informed the king of a plan "for carrying on a War in America."[88] Yet, as the tension increased throughout 1774 and North professed to believe that only force could subdue the colonies, he hesitated.

In January 1775, the British cabinet authorized a "plan of conciliation," which North presented on February 20, 1775.[89] In effect, his plan turned

[83] Ibid., pp. 53–75.

[84] Gage to Barrington, February 10, 1775, *Gage Correspondence*, vol. 2, p. 669.

[85] Gage to Barrington, March 28, 1775, ibid., pp. 671–72.

[86] King George to Lord North, November 18, 1774, *Correspondence of King George the Third*, vol. 3, p. 153.

[87] November 12, 1774, *Diary and Letters of Thomas Hutchinson*, vol. 1, p. 293.

[88] North to King, [?] December 1774, *Correspondence of King George the Third*, vol. 3, p. 158.

[89] *The Manuscripts of the Earl of Dartmouth*, Royal Commission on Historical Manuscripts (Her Majesty's Stationery Office, 1887; reprint, Gregg Press, 1972), vol. 1, pp. 372–73.

the clock back to the debate over the Stamp Act of 1765. The proposal was simple. It offered to put an end to British taxation of the colonies, with the exception of duties for the regulation of commerce, in return for an agreement by each colony to pay for its own civil government, courts of law, and defense.[90]

North's plan assumed that taxation was still the essential colonial complaint. But by 1775, the issue was whether Parliament had the right or power to legislate for the colonies at all. Even in the latter case, North insisted that Parliament had the right in principle to tax the colonies but agreed only "to the suspension of the exercise of our right" if the Americans contributed their share to the common defense in some other way. The suspension, he added, was no more than an "indulgence."[91]

North presented the plan in such a way that he made its rejection by the colonies almost a matter of course. By this time the First Continental Congress had shown that the colonies could act as one in a common interest. North deliberately presented his plan to each colony individually, with the clear intention of separating them from Massachusetts, which he declared to be in rebellion. Barré accused him of founding his plan on "that wretched, low, shameful abominable maxim . . . of *divide & impera*." North admitted that he was "using that principle which will thus divide the good from the bad." During the debate, some thought it conceded too much to the colonies, some not enough. The vote was 274 in favor, 88 against.[92]

It is a question whether North was more interested in making a show of doing something to placate the colonies than in satisfying them. He made no secret that his purpose was at least partially tactical and would change nothing in principle. The *London Evening Post* interpreted his speech in the worst possible light, from the point of view of the colonies: "Lord North confessed that he rather imagined this proposition would not be to the *Taste* of the Americans; and would not be complied with by several of the colonies. However, if but ONE of them submitted, that ONE Link of the chain would be broken; and if so, the whole world [would] inevitably fall to pieces. This separation would restore our Empire; and *divide et impera* was a maxim never held unfair or unwise in government. If this hope should be frustrated, and that the proposition should do *no Good in America, it will not however fail of doing Good in England.*" Moreover, this proposition was an *"Ultimatum."*[93]

[90] *Proceedings and Debates*, vol. 5, p. 435.
[91] Ibid., pp. 440, 448.
[92] Ibid., pp. 440, 448–50.
[93] *London Evening Post*, February 25, 1775, in *Proceedings and Debates*, vol. 5, p. 436.

North himself told the king that he hoped "for great utility (if not in America, at least on this side of the water)" and thought his plan "would give general satisfaction here," if nowhere else.[94] His object was clearly to make some gesture of giving way on taxation, as if to put the onus on the colonies if they did not accept his proposals. On February 27, 1775, he let the colonies know that he had made them an offer on the basis of take-it-or-leave-it and suffer-the-consequences. "Among other things," he said, "if the colonies reject the conditions, they must be reduced to unconditional obedience."[95] By that time, it was clear that all pretense of conciliation had been replaced by a resort to force. A bill was introduced to cut off the trade and fishing of all New England, not merely Massachusetts. He hoped, North said on March 8, 1775, "when they began to feel the weight of the power of this country, and to see the force of it was ready to strike the blow, they would be convinced that their leaders and false friends had deceived them, and that they would return to their duty, so that all these evils might be avoided."[96] Between February 20 and March 8, the "weight of the power" had replaced the "plan of conciliation." The one thing that North could not and would not tamper with was the core issue— parliamentary supremacy over the colonies; Hutchinson heard that North had said "such Ministers as should concede it, would bring their heads to the Block."[97] It was even an illusion to think that what Parliament said or did still mattered very much. One week before North presented his plan in Commons, King George was so out of touch with colonial realities that he assured North "nothing can be more calculated to bring the Americans to a due Submission than the very handsome Majority that at the outset have appeared in both Houses of Parliament."[98]

If parliamentary majorities could have brought the Americans to submit, the Americans would have submitted long before. A hard core in Parliament, previously North's main supporters, scorned his plan and could not wait for a showdown. So many speakers rejected any concessions that they seemed to have him on the defensive. He was saved by the intervention

[94] North to King, February 19, 1775, *Correspondence of King George the Third*, vol. 3, p. 177. His object was clearly to make some gesture of giving way on taxation, as if to put the onus on the colonies if they did not accept his proposals. On February 27, 1775, he let the colonies know that he had made them an offer on the basis of take-it-or-leave-it and suffer-the-consequences. "Among other things," he said, "if the colonies reject just conditions, they must be reduced to unconditional obedience."

[95] *Proceedings and Debates*, vol. 5, February 27, 1775, p. 475.

[96] March 8, 1775, ibid., p. 513.

[97] *Diary and Letters of Thomas Hutchinson*, vol. 1, p. 389.

[98] King to North, January 23, 1775, *Correspondence of King George the Third*, vol. 3, p. 168.

of Sir Gilbert Elliot, close to the king, who found an acceptable formula by combining "measures of force, with power, with arms" and a policy of "humanity."

• 7 •

If anything more were needed to show that Parliament was war minded, it was provided by the reception of another plan of conciliation, by Edmund Burke. On March 22, 1775, Burke made one of his most famous speeches on America. He argued that North had opened the door to concessions to the colonies but had not gone far enough. Burke deplored governing America "by abstract ideas of right" or "mere general theories of government." He emphasized the population of America, which he estimated at about 2.5 million. He went on to stress American commerce, grown from about £500,000 in 1704 to about £6 million in 1772. He attributed colonial growth and prosperity to "a wise and salutary neglect" by Great Britain, not to British care and encouragement. Instead of using force to keep America, he pleaded for "prudent management." If force was used, "the thing you fought for is not the thing which you recover; but depreciated, sunk, wasted, and consumed in the contest." He celebrated the "fierce spirit of liberty" as "stronger in the English colonies probably than in any other people of the earth."

Then Burke turned to the question of taxation, as if it were still the main issue. He agreed with the colonies that the people must "possess the power of granting their own money, or no shadow of liberty could subsist." The colonies had their own legislative assemblies and "a strong aversion from whatever tends to deprive them of their chief importance." Another cause of the colonies' "disobedient spirit" was the distance—"three thousand miles of ocean lie between you and them." Nothing could prevent government from being weakened when "seas roll, and months pass, between the order and the execution."

Burke then drew back a bit. Perhaps the colonial spirit was excessive. But there it was, and the question was "what, in the name of God, shall we do with it?" The British had not been prepared for a trial of strength; they had thought that "the utmost which the discontented colonies could do, was to disturb authority; we never dreamt they could of themselves supply it." Somehow "a new government [had] originated directly from the people" and had instilled "order, in the midst of a struggle for liberty."

Burke faced three possible courses—to change the colonial spirit, to prosecute it as criminal, or to "comply with it as necessary." He assumed that a fourth course—giving up the colonies—was out of the question. He found practical and political reasons for dismissing the first two. For him the third way was the only possible one. In practice, he knew, it meant giving up all right of taxation by Parliament. But Burke tried to avoid going down this beaten path—"I am resolved this day to have nothing at all to do with the question of the right of taxation." Nevertheless, he continued to dwell on the implications of taxation, if not the right, as if he could not extricate himself from the subject. He discussed the British fear that the Americans would attack the trade laws if they succeeded in getting rid of taxation, to which he answered that the trade laws were just as "useless" as the revenue laws were "mischievous."

Burke put forward thirteen resolutions, including the substitution of grants by colonial assemblies for taxes imposed by Parliament. He wanted to repeal the Boston Port Bill, restore Massachusetts's charter, and permit the assemblies to settle the pay of chief justices and judges. These proposals embodied the Burkean ideals of government—"compromise and barter," "balance inconveniences," "give and take." He pleaded for freedom for the colonies as the way to bind their commerce to Great Britain and "through them secure to you the wealth of the world." In the end, he uttered words good not for that time alone: "Magnanimity in politics is not seldom the truest wisdom; and a great empire and little minds go ill together."[99]

In this justly celebrated speech, Burke made as persuasive a case as possible for "pacifying" the colonies—in the ultimate interest of the British empire. But that was just the trouble, because the time had passed for compromise and pacification. Although Burke said that he did not want to be "overwhelmed" in the "bog" of taxation, to his adversaries his position boiled down to giving the power of taxation to the assemblies instead of to Parliament. Lord George Germain, who had recently gone over to North's side, maintained that it was necessary to enforce obedience in America. Lord Frederick Campbell, a Scottish hard-liner, declared that colonial assemblies could not grant revenue "without subverting the constitution." Charles Jenkinson, later first earl of Liverpool, one of George III's chief favorites, insisted that the right of taxation was inherent in the supreme power, which was what those who made the British decisions believed was at stake.[100]

Burke made the last, desperate attempt to stave off the war. He failed

[99] *Proceedings and Debates*, vol. 5, pp. 598–631.
[100] Ibid., pp. 595 (Germain), 598 (Campbell), 597 (Jenkinson).

because the particulars of how the colonies were ruled from London no longer mattered. The issue was whether they should be ruled from London at all, and this was no longer amenable to argument. Burke's proposals never had a chance. They were voted down 270 to 78.

But it would be a mistake to think that the war on the British side was brought on solely by ministerial machinations. Burke himself knew better. In August 1774, he explained to the New York Assembly, which employed him as its agent:

> This unhappy disposition in the colonies was, by the friends of the coercive measures, attributed to the pride and presumption arising from the rapid population of these colonies, and from their lax form and more lax exercise of government. I found it in general discourses and even in public debates, the predominant and declared opinion, that the cause of this resistance to legal power ought to be weakened, since it was impossible to be removed; that any growth of the colonies which might make them grow out of the reach of the authority of this kingdom ought to be accounted rather a morbid fulness than a sound and proper habit. All increase of the Colonies which tended to decrease their advantage to this country they considered as useless and even mischievous.[101]

In September of that year, he reported to the earl of Rockingham: "The insensibility of the Merchants of London is of a degree and kind scarcely to be conceived. Even those merchants who are most likely to be overwhelmed by any real American confusion, are among the most supine. The Character of the ministry, either produces, or perfectly coincides with the disposition of the publick."[102]

In June 1775, the duke of Richmond wrote to Burke: "Your accounts are most melancholy to a thinking man, but I agree with you in opinion that the good People of England will not much care whether America is lost or not till they feel the Effects in their purses or in their bellies."[103] Even in 1777, Burke admitted that his parliamentary group "oppose the more considerable part of the Landed and mercantile Interests."[104] Towards the end of that year, Burke was astounded: "In Liverpool they

[101] Burke to the Committee of the New York Assembly, August 2, 1774, ed. Ross J. Hoffman, *Edmund Burke, New York Agent* (American Philosophical Society, 1956), pp. 254–55.
[102] Burke to Rockingham, September 18, 1774, *The Correspondence of Edmund Burke*, vol. 3, ed. George H. Guttridge (University of Chicago Press, 1861), p. 29.
[103] Richmond to Burke, June 16, 1775, ibid., p. 170.
[104] Burke to Rockingham, January 6, 1777, ibid., p. 312.

are literally almost ruined by this American War; but they love it as they suffer from it."[105]

Other sources tell the same story. Edward Gibbon, the great historian, later recalled: "The American War had once been the favourite of the country; the pride of England was irritated by the resistance of her Colonies; and the executive power was driven by national clamour into the most vigorous and coercive measures."[106] As early as March 1774, Benjamin Franklin wrote from London: "The violent Destruction of the Tea seems to have united all Parties here against our Province, so that the Bill now brought into Parliament for shutting up Boston as a Port till Satisfaction is made, meets with no Opposition."[107] In September 1774, William Lee also wrote from London to Richard Henry Lee in Virginia: "The merchants are almost universally your enemies."[108] In January 1775, Josiah Quincy, Jr., reported from London: "America might sink in bondage, and long drag the load of misery and shame, before either of these orders [merchants and manufacturers], as a body of men, would feel one generous sentiment, or make one feeble effort, unless their own immediate and obvious interest prompted the exertion."[109] In February 1775, the British industrialist Josiah Wedgwood told his partner, Richard Bentley: "I do not know how it happens, but a general infatuation seems to have gone forth, & the poor Americans are deemed Rebels, now the Minister has declared them so, by a very great majority wherever I go."[110] And in September of that year, John Norton, an important merchant in London, advised his eldest son in Virginia: "The People here seem resolute to support the Dignity of Parliament and by the Americans (after receiving Lord Norths plan) not proposing any thing towards a Reconciliation Many People here are of opinion that they only desire an Independency."[111]

Thus George III and Lord North were largely backed by British public opinion. The coming war was not merely against the king and his ministers; it was against the bulk of the British people, who had come to believe that the Americans were bent on splitting the British empire and establishing

[105] Burke to Charles James Fox, October 8, 1777, ibid., p. 382.

[106] *The Autobiographies of Edward Gibbon*, ed. John Murray (London, 1890), p. 324.

[107] Franklin to Thomas Cushing, March 22, 1774, *Franklin Papers*, vol. 21, p. 152.

[108] William Lee to Richard H. Lee, September 10, 1774, *Letters of William Lee*, ed. Worthington Chauncey Ford (Brooklyn, 1891), vol. 1, p. 96.

[109] Josiah Quincy to Mrs. Quincy, January 11, 1775, *Memoir of the Life of Josiah Quincy Jun.*, p. 300.

[110] Josiah Wedgwood to Richard Bentley, February 6, 1775, cited by J. H. Plumb, *In the Light of History* (Houghton Mifflin, 1973), p. 79.

[111] John Norton to John Hatley Norton, September 5, 1775, *John Norton & Sons* (Augustus M. Kelley, 1968), p. 388.

a rival power of their own. For most people, the details were lost in the general impression that British power and prestige were at stake.

· 8 ·

Meanwhile, the Americans expected the British to attack and prepared to defend themselves.

In November 1774, the Connecticut Assembly instructed the towns to double their stock of powder, balls, and flints.[112] In December 1774, the Rhode Island Assembly appointed a major general (for the first time) and formed several companies of light infantry, fusiliers, hunters, and so on; it ordered the militia "to be disciplined and the Commanding Officers empowered to march the troops to the assistance of any sister Colony." Samuel Ward, the delegate to the First Continental Congress, confided to Richard Henry Lee: "The idea of taking up arms against Great Britain is shocking, but if we must become slaves or fly to arms, I shall not hesitate one moment which to choose."[113] In December 1774, the Maryland Provincial Convention decided that all males between the ages of sixteen and fifty should form themselves into companies and that all counties should purchase arms for the militiamen. The Maryland radical leader Samuel Chase exceeded the New Englanders in militancy. In a message to John Adams, he said he thought that the British were soon going to invade the colonies. He proposed immediately outfitting ships to war on the British merchant marine and favored the prompt destruction of the British army in Boston: "In short I would adopt every Scheme to reduce G[reat] B[ritain] to our Terms."[114]

Another Massachusetts Provincial Congress took place in February 1775. It decided that large quantities of straw were needed "in case we should be driven to the hard necessity of taking up arms in our own defence." It urged "every preparation for your necessary defence." It organized a Committee of Supplies "to provide Ordnance, Stores, Provisions, and Arms." It resolved "That the great law of self-preservation calls upon the inhabitants of this Colony immediately to prepare against every attempt that may be made to attack them by *surprise;* and it is, upon serious deliberation, most earnestly

---

[112] *American Archives,* 4th ser., vol. 1, col. 858.

[113] Ward to Lee, December 14, 1774, cited by David Ammerman, *In the Common Cause* (University Press of Virginia, 1974), pp. 142–43.

[114] Chase to Adams, December 12, 1774, cited by Ammerman, *In the Common Cause,* p. 143.

recommended to the Militia in general, as well as the detached part of it in Minute-men, that they spare neither time, pains, nor expense, at so critical a juncture, in perfecting themselves forthwith in military discipline."[115]

On April 16, 1775, James Warren wrote from Concord to his wife, Mercy: "All things wear a warlike appearance here. This Town is full of Cannon, ammunition, stores, etc., and the Army long for them and they want nothing but strength to Induce an attempt on them. The people are ready and determine[d] to defend this Country Inch by Inch."[116]

War was imminent.

[115] *American Archives*, 4th ser., vol. 1, cols. 1323–41.
[116] James Warren to Mercy Warren, *Warren-Adams Letters*, vol. 1, p. 45.

19

"The Rubicon passed"

❧

• 1 •

T HE BREAK IN THE DEADLOCK came from the British side. On January 27, 1775, Lord Dartmouth sent General Gage a fatal message that, in effect, told him to take preemptive action against the rebellious colonists.

Gage's own reports, Dartmouth said, demonstrated that they were in "actual Revolt, and shew a determination to commit themselves at all Events to open Rebellion." In such a situation, "Force should be repelled by Force." It was impossible, without putting the British army on a full war footing, to satisfy Gage's demand for a force of 20,000 men to conquer Massachusetts, Connecticut, and Rhode Island. But this extreme measure was unnecessary. Dartmouth called for a change in strategy. Gage's policy had been "to act upon the Defensive, & to avoid the hazard of weakening your Force by sending out Detachments of your Troops upon any Occasion whatsoever." This defensiveness was not necessary, because the colonists were not strong enough or organized enough to resist a smaller force:

> I have stated that the violences committed by those who have taken up arms in Massachusetts Bay, have appeared to me as the acts of a rude Rabble without plan, without concert, & without conduct, and therefore I think that a smaller Force now, if put to the Test, would be able to encounter them with greater probability of Success than might be expected from a greater Army, if the people should be suffered to form themselves upon a more regular plan, to acquire confidence from

discipline, and to prepare those resources without which every thing must be put to the issue of a single Action.

Now, with fewer than 4,000 men, Gage was told "to take a more active & determined part." Dartmouth wanted him "to arrest and imprison the principal actors & abettors in the Provincial Congress (whose proceedings appear in every light to be acts of treason & rebellion)." But not immediately—only if "they should presume again to assemble for such rebellious purposes." He did not expect a regular British force to encounter much resistance, but even if it came to hostilities, "it will surely be better that the Conflict should be brought on, upon such ground, than in a riper state of Rebellion." The purpose of the exercise was to make "a Test of the People's resolution to resist." In addition, if Connecticut and Rhode Island showed any intention to support Massachusetts, their fortifications and armaments should be dismantled and stored in a safe place. In the end, however, Dartmouth left the "Expediency and Propriety" of carrying out these measures to Gage.[1]

This message pushed Gage over the brink. He had previously taken a hard line against the colonies but had demanded as many as 20,000 troops before striking out. Now Dartmouth told him to act with what he had at hand. Dartmouth went as far as he could go to force Gage's hand and get him to take some offensive action, without accepting full responsibility for the means and timing.

Dartmouth was not the only one on the British side who thought that the American rebels were too few to need more than a British push to fall over. In November 1774, Lord North told Thomas Hutchinson that "the Kingdom was able to do it"—to subdue the colonies. North said that he was willing to employ Hessians and Hanoverians if necessary, but he thought that "there was no need of a foreign force."[2] In December 1774, Josiah Quincy, Jr., wrote from London to his wife in Boston: "The people of this country have too generally got an idea that Americans are all cowards and poltro[o]ns."[3] In February 1775, Col. James Grant rose in the Commons to say that he had served in America and "knew the Americans very well, was certain they would not fight; they would never dare to face an English army, and that they did not possess any of the qualifications necessary to

[1] Dartmouth to Gage, January 27, 1775, *The Correspondence of General Thomas Gage with the Secretaries of State, 1763–1775* (Yale University Press, 1931), vol. 2, pp. 179–83.

[2] North to Hutchinson, November 19, 1774, *Diary and Letters of His Excellency Thomas Hutchinson*, ed. Peter Orlando Hutchinson (London, 1883), vol. 1, p. 297.

[3] Quincy to Mrs. Quincy, December 7, 1774, *Memoir of the Life of Josiah Quincy Jun.* (Boston, 1825), p. 256.

make a good soldier."[4] In March 1775, the earl of Sandwich, first lord of the
Admiralty, gave assurances that the British forces faced "raw, undisciplined,
cowardly men. . . . Believe me, my Lords, the very sound of a cannon would
carry them off . . . as fast as their feet could carry them."[5] In April 1775,
Richard Rigby, paymaster of the forces, still insisted: "The Americans will
not fight. They would never oppose General Gage with force of arms."[6] At
about this time, Gen. Sir William Howe wrote that "I may safely assert that
the insurgents are very few, in comparison with the whole of the people."[7]
In a letter from London of April 8, 1775, Hutchinson alluded to the opinion
of Lieutenant-Governor Oliver of Massachusetts that "the people will not
resist the King's troops." Hutchinson himself thought that "very powerful
resistance" must be "irrational, for nothing can be gained, and everything
may be lost."[8]

Only a small minority disagreed with this optimistic view.[9] Writing after
the outbreak of hostilities, William Knox, then an undersecretary of state
for the colonies, recalled: "When Troops were first sent to America for
the purpose of carrying the Laws of Great Britain into Execution, it was
generally expected that large Bodies of the Inhabitants would flock to the
Royal Standard and that those who were averse to the British Government
would be found inconsiderable and quickly subdued." But nothing like this
happened.[10] The British still thought of the American soldiers as they had
allegedly behaved in the Seven Years' War and not as they were likely
to behave over a decade later. In any case, the British did not have
existing forces in the colonies for more than a blow by "a smaller Force
now."[11]

For various reasons, Dartmouth's message of January 27, 1775, did not

---

[4] February 2, 1775, *Proceedings and Debates of the British Parliaments Respecting North America, 1754–1783*, ed. R. C. Simmons and P.D.G. Thomas (Kraus International, 1983), vol. 5, p. 347.

[5] March 16, 1775, ibid., pp. 546–47.

[6] April 5, 1775, ibid., vol. 6, p. 10.

[7] Anderson, *Command of the Howe Brothers* (Oxford University Press, 1936), p. 49.

[8] *Diary and Letters of Thomas Hutchinson,* vol. 1, 427.

[9] In December 1774, Hutchinson heard from Adj. Gen. Edward Harvey that more troops should be ordered to America as soon as possible or those already there should be withdrawn (*Diary and Letters of Thomas Hutchinson,* vol. 1, p. 297). Barrington was also less sure about British readiness to take on the Americans. On January 3, 1775, he advised Gage that the colonists should be subdued by a naval blockade, or a great army should be sent to America if troops were to be used (John Richard Alden, *General Gage in America* [Louisiana State University Press, 1948], p. 235).

[10] William Knox, "Considerations on the great Question, what is to be done in America," ed. Jack P. Greene, *William and Mary Quarterly,* April 1973, p. 297.

[11] Britain had no more than 10,975 infantry of all ranks in England and Scotland, of whom 1,500 were invalids fit for light duty only (Piers Mackesy, *The War for America, 1775–1783* [Harvard University Press, 1965], p. 39).

leave England immediately and Gage did not receive it until April 14. The general now had to decide how to carry it out. He had Dartmouth's advice to arrest and imprison colonial leaders on charges of treason and rebellion. But Gage was a prudent man and knew that taking such action was looking for maximum trouble. Instead, he chose to take a minimal action in such a way that it might be slipped over before the colonists were ready to do anything about it.

Back in October 1774, Dartmouth had ordered all American governors to take measures "for arresting, detaining & securing" any arms or ammunition imported by colonists without a British license.[12] In February 1775, Gage had already tried to confiscate eight field pieces that he had reason to believe had been brought to Salem. He had sent out 200 men to seize them, only to find that they were old ship guns that had been carried away from Salem some time before. At that time he had reported to Dartmouth that "the people assembled in great Numbers with Threats and abuse" before the troops came back empty-handed.[13]

Instead of arresting colonial leaders, Gage decided to make another attempt at capturing colonial military stores. He acted five days after receiving Dartmouth's message.

• 2 •

Gage decided to send out an armed force to destroy a colonial arms and supply depot in Concord, about sixteen miles away. He hoped to carry out the mission so secretly and quickly that his force could get back before the colonists knew what was happening. From informants in the colonial ranks, Gage was able to give Lt. Col. Francis Smith, his senior regimental commander, a map of Concord on which were marked the houses and barns in which artillery, ammunition, provisions, tents, small arms, and other military stores were allegedly kept. In the early morning hours of April 19, 1775, about 700 men commanded by Smith set out for Concord. They went without baggage and artillery and carried only thirty-six rounds of ammunition per man in an attempt to make the colonists believe that it was just another training march. But it was impossible for a relatively large force to assemble without giving the preparations away. Surprise and secrecy were lost even before the operation began.

One detachment, commanded by Maj. John Pitcairn, went through

[12] October 19, 1774, *Gage Correspondence*, vol. 2, p. 176.
[13] Gage to Dartmouth, March 4, 1775, ibid., vol. 1, p. 394.

Lexington on the way to Concord. In Lexington, Pitcairn's group encountered about 75 armed colonial Minutemen commanded by Capt. John Parker. Each side later blamed the other for having fired first. Eight Americans were killed, and one British soldier was wounded. By this time, Smith realized that the American countryside was up in arms and sent word to Gage for reinforcements. About 1,000 men under Lord Percy went out to support Smith.

At Concord, the British force met with about 450 militiamen. Again each side claimed that the other had fired first. When Smith retreated to Lexington, he joined with Percy's reinforcements. They had to fight their way back to Boston; over half the British losses came during the retreat. When the engagements were over, the British losses were 73 killed, 174 wounded, and 26 missing. The American losses were 49 killed, 41 wounded, and 5 missing. If Percy had not come in time, Smith's force would probably have been wiped out. In the last stage of the retreat, so many new militiamen entered the battle that the British were outnumbered.[14]

That the war broke out at Lexington and Concord was an almost inevitable concomitant of the total situation. The Americans had been storing arms and ammunition for months. Gage's order to Smith stated that the stores had been "collected at Concord, for the Avowed Purpose of raising and supporting a Rebellion against His Majesty."[15] Whether this purpose was avowed or not, they were stored for the purpose of being used, if necessary. For Gage, destroying these stores was a way of postponing, not provoking, a war. As he had been telling Dartmouth and Barrington for months, he did not have the forces to wage a real war. At Dartmouth's urging, he was willing to destroy colonial military stores, but he expected to get away with it by means of surprise and speed—neither of which he really had. Yet his decision to destroy the American stores at Concord was an act of preemption the Americans could not permit without resistance. In any case, owing to the advance knowledge of Gage's intentions, many of the colonial stores had already been removed and concealed elsewhere by the time the British reached Concord.

Another reason the clash broke out at Lexington and Concord may have

---

[14] The battles of Lexington and Concord have, of course, been described many times. They may be followed in great detail in Harold Murdock, *The Nineteenth of April 1775* (Houghton Mifflin, 1925); Allen French, *The Day of Concord and Lexington* (Little, Brown, 1925); Christopher Ward, *The War of the Revolution* (Macmillan, 1952), vol. 1, pp. 32–51; Don Higginbotham, *The War of American Independence* (Macmillan, 1971), pp. 58–65. The latest and fullest account is in *Paul Revere's Ride* by David Hackett Fischer (Oxford University Press, 1994).

[15] The entire order is given in John R. Galvin, *The Minute Men* (Hawthorn, 1967), pp. 112–13.

been the decision of Joseph Warren. He gave orders to William Dawes and Paul Revere to ride to Lexington, where Sam Adams and John Hancock were staying, to warn them to get out of there. But Revere also spread the word that "the Regulars are coming!" and thus helped to whip up the alarm that eventually brought out hundreds and even thousands of militiamen. Warren's most modern biographer had no doubt of his subject's purpose: "Talking with Revere on the evening of April 18, Warren realized that the time had come to act. At that moment the decision of war or peace presented itself to him as clearly as it ever does to any man, and Warren instructed Revere to arouse the militia on his ride to Lexington, a step which he was virtually certain would mean war before sunrise."[16]

By this account, Warren was more set on war than Gage or the Massachusetts Congress. The latter had, on March 30, sitting at Concord, resolved that "whenever the Army under command of General Gage, or any part thereof to the Number of Five Hundred, shall march out of the Town of Boston, with Artillery and Baggage, it ought to be . . . opposed; and therefore the Military Force of the Province ought to be assembled."[17] This was probably the reason that Gage sent out Smith's force without artillery and baggage. It also suggests that Warren went beyond the Massachusetts Congress's instructions. But, whatever Warren's responsibility, the congress was willing and ready to assemble "the Military Force of the Province" and "oppose" the British if certain conditions were fulfilled.

Whatever Gage may have intended in response to Dartmouth's call for action, it was not to start a war. He sought to stir up the colonists as little as possible by trying to camouflage his real purpose as a training march. As a result, Smith's men found themselves helpless when they had exhausted their ammunition and were saved only by Percy's timely appearance with reinforcements.

A report to Arthur Lee in London by Joseph Warren, now a general, suggests how trigger-ready the colonists were:

> The first brigade of the army marched about four miles out of town three days ago, under the command of a brigadier general (Earl Percy), but as they marched without baggage or artillery, they did not occasion so great an alarm as they otherwise would. Nevertheless great numbers, completely armed, collected in the neighbouring towns; and it is the opinion of many, that had they marched eight or ten miles, and

[16] John Cary, *Joseph Warren* (University of Illinois Press, 1961), p. 183.
[17] *The Journals of Each Provincial Congress of Massachusetts in 1774 and 1775* (Boston, 1838), p. 12.

attempted to destroy any magazines, or abuse the people, not a man of them would have returned to Boston.[18]

Nevertheless, the pro-American press took advantage of the engagement to portray the British troops as murderers and robbers:

AMERICANS! forever bear in mind the BATTLE OF LEXINGTON! where British Troops, unmolested and unprovoked, wantonly and in a most cruel manner fired upon and killed a number of our countrymen, then robbed them of their provisions, ransacked, plundered and burnt their houses! nor could the tears of defenceless women, some of whom were in the pains of childbirth, the cries of helpless babes, nor the prayers of old age, confined to beds of sickness, appease their thirst for blood!—or divert them from their DESIGN of MURDER and ROBBERY![19]

The chief lesson of Lexington and Concord is that the tension between the British and Americans had now become so great that any threatening British behavior could start a war. The mere appearance of British troops marching out of Boston was enough to bring out hundreds, if not thousands, of militiamen from miles around. Gage was still trying to wait for large-scale reinforcements before taking on the Americans and yet to do something to satisfy Dartmouth's call for action. Gage's fundamental error was in failing to realize that any military action could bring out armed colonial resistance on a scale with which he was unprepared to deal.[20]

The major responsibility for Lexington and Concord was the belief of Dartmouth and others in the British administration that the colonists were a "rude Rabble without plan, without concert, & without conduct." As such, they were not supposed to be able to resist a British test of their resolution.[21] Far from being a rabble, they were in this first test able to

[18] Warren to Lee, April 3, 1775, in Richard Henry Lee, *Life of Arthur Lee, LL.D.* (Boston, 1929), vol. 2, p. 266. Earlier, Warren had written to Lee: "But I am of opinion that if once Gen. Gage should lead his troops into the country with a design to enforce the late acts of parliament, Great Britain may take her leave, at least of the New-England colonies; and if I mistake not, of all America" (February 20, 1775, vol. 2, p. 265).

[19] *Massachusetts Spy,* May 3, 1775.

[20] There is a rough draft of Gage's order to Smith that states: "If any body ['of men' inserted above the line] dares ['attack' written, then crossed out] oppose you with arms, you will warn them to disperse ['and' written, then crossed out] or attack them" (Galvin, *Minute Men,* p. 113). Galvin believes that Gage told Smith in private "what actions were expected of him," but even so Gage was remiss in limiting the soldiers' ammunition and therefore their ability to fight if necessary.

[21] Gage later acknowledged: "These People Shew a Spirit and Conduct against us, they never shewed against the French, and every body has Judged of them from their former Appearance and Behavior, when joyned with the Kings Forces in the last war; which has led many into great mistakes" (Gage to Barrington, June 26, 1775, *Gage Correspondence,* vol. 2, p. 686).

outshoot British soldiers, who did not expect to receive such treatment and, like the militiamen, had never fought before.[22] Gage's second in command, Maj. Gen. Frederick Haldimand, may have come closer to pointing out some of the underlying causes that had provoked the first military engagement. In his private notebook, he wrote: "Revolts which have happened in other nations have been occasioned by tyranny; here it is the ease of rapid fortunes and the indolence of England which have brought one on."[23]

· 3 ·

From the British side, we have a series of letters written by Hugh, Earl Percy, who commanded the reinforcements that saved the British from suffering a total disaster at Lexington. These letters to correspondents in England tell most vividly how a high-ranking British officer saw the Americans from the spring of 1774 to the battles at Lexington and Concord, a year later.

Percy was opposed to the American war but embarked for Boston in the spring of 1774 to share in the command there. While Gage stayed in Salem, Percy commanded the British troops in Boston. On April 17, 1774, before leaving England, he wrote a letter to the Reverend Thomas Percy, a distinguished scholar,[24] in which he remarked: "Surely the People of Boston are not Mad enough to think of opposing us."

On July 5, 1774, after taking command of the British troops in Boston, Percy gave his first impression of the colonists to the duke of Northumberland, his father: "The people, by all accounts, are extremely violent & wrong headed, so much so that I fear we shall be obliged to come to extremities." Later that month, he took a hard line against the colonists: "One thing I will be bold to say, which is, that till you make their Committees of Correspondence and Congress with the other Colonies high treason, & try them for it in England, you never must expect perfect obedience & submission from this to the Mother Country." By August 1774, he was even more hostile: "The people here are a set of sly, artful, hypocritical rascals, cruel, & cowards. I must own I cannot but despise them completely."

He continued to think, however, that the colonists were not likely to be

[22] John R. Galvin, *Minute Men*, argues that "the minute men and militia were not an armed rabble but a well-organized, well-equipped, and relatively well-trained army of 14,000 men" (p. 255).

[23] Allan French, "Haldimand in Boston 1774–1775," *Proceedings of the Massachusetts Historical Society*, vol. 66, 1942, p. 87.

[24] He was the author of *Reliques of Ancient English Poetry*.

troublesome. He reported that "they are arming & exercising all over the country. Yet I am still convinced that nothing but either drunkenness or madness can force [?] them to molest us. If, however, they once begin, I fear there will be some bloodshed." By September 1774, he was more alarmed:

> Things here are now drawing to a crisis every day. The People here openly oppose the New [Coercive] Acts. They have taken up arms in almost every part of this Province, & have drove in the Gov[erno]r & most of the Council. The few that remain in the country, they have not only obliged to resign but to take up arms with them. A few days ago, they mustered about 7000 men at Worcester, to wh[ich] place they have conveyed about 20 pieces of cannon.
>
> In short, this country is now in as open a state of rebellion as Scotland was in the year '45. . . .
>
> What makes an insurrection here always more formidable than in other places, is that there is a law of this Province wh[ich] obliges every inhabitant to be furnished with a firelock, bayonet, & pretty considerable quantity of ammunition. Besides wh[ich], every township is obliged by the same law to have a large magazine of all kinds of military stores.

In October 1774, he was almost frantic:

> Our affairs here are in the most Critical Situation imaginable; Nothing less than the total loss or Conquest of the Colonies must be the End of it. Either indeed is disagreeable, but one or the other is now absolutely necessary.

Towards the end of November 1774, he almost gave up hope for a peaceful solution:

> I really begin now to think that it will come to Blows at last; For They are most amazingly encouraged by our having done nothing as yet.
>
> In short they have now got to such lengths that nothing can secure the Colonies to the Mother Country, but the Conquest of them. The People here are the most designing, Artfull Villains in the World. They have not the least Idea of either Religion or Morality. Nor have they the least Scruple of taking the most solemn Oath on any Matter that can assist their Purpose, tho' they know the direct contrary can be clearly & evidently proved in half an Hour.

Thereafter, Percy complained that Gage was not receiving instructions from London, "so that [on] our side no steps of any kind can be taken as yet." On April 20, 1775, he gave Gage his version of what had happened in the retreat from Lexington—"there was not a stone-wall, or house, though before in appearance evacuated, from whence the Rebels did not fire upon us." He mistakenly believed that the "Rebels" had suffered greater losses than the British forces. In another account, he gave the colonists their due:

> Whoever looks upon them as an irregular mob, will find himself much mistaken. They have men amongst them who know very well what they are about, having been employed as Rangers ag[ain]st the Indians & Canadians, & this country being much cov[ere]d w[ith] wood, and hilly, is very advantageous for their method of fighting.
>
> Nor are several of their men void of a spirit of enthusiasm, as we experienced yesterday, for many of them concealed themselves in houses, & advanced within 10 yds. to fire at me & other officers, tho' they were morally certain of being put to death themselves in an instant.
>
> You may depend upon it, that as the Rebels have now had time to prepare, they are determined to go thro' with it, nor will the insurrection here turn out so despicable as it is perhaps imagined at home. For my part, I never believed, I confess, that they w[oul]d have attacked the King's troops, or have had the perseverance I found in them yesterday.

Percy's conversion from believing that there was no danger of the colonists fighting the British troops to giving the colonists credit for bravery and determination was an essential element in the coming of the war. The British in both London and Boston were caught by surprise by the colonial willingness to fight, and their miscalculation helps to explain the procrastination of the North administration in preparing for the armed struggle. The British talked war before they realized that they had to wage it.[25]

• 4 •

Thus began the War for Independence. It began in April 1775 at Lexington and Concord because both sides, after rubbing each other the wrong way for about ten years, were spoiling for a fight. In May, American militiamen

[25] All the excerpts from Percy's letters come from *Letters of Hugh Earl Percy from Boston and New York, 1774–1776,* ed. Charles Knowles Bolton (Charles E. Goodspeed, 1902).

under Benedict Arnold and Ethan Allen attacked and overcame a small British garrison at Ticonderoga on Lake Champlain. That month, the Second Continental Congress met in Philadelphia and resolved to put the colonies in a state of defense. On June 15, the congress named George Washington as commander in chief of the American force. Two days later, British and American forces fought the battle of Bunker Hill, near Boston, at which the British suffered 228 dead and 826 wounded, or 42 percent of the 2,500 British troops.[26] The Americans lost 115 dead, one of whom was Joseph Warren, and 271 wounded. The disparity again shows that the British forces were outfought in the opening phases of the Revolution. Gage was recalled to England at the end of September 1775 and replaced by Sir William Howe, who moved the British forces out of Boston to Halifax in March 1776.

But the War of Independence began with Lexington and Concord. The reaction in England was fatalistic. On July 1, 1775, Dartmouth gave Gage his view of the events—that

> there was no longer any room to doubt of the Intention of the People of Massachuset's Bay, to commit themselves in open Rebellion;—the other three New England Governments have taken the same part, and in fact all North America (Quebec, Nova Scotia and the Floridas excepted) is in Arms against Great Britain, and the People involved in the Guilt of levying War against the King, in every sense of that Expression.[27]

But Gage could not expect to get more help in 1775. George III was adamently belligerent. "I have no doubt but the Nation at large sees the conduct of America in its true light," he wrote to North on July 5, "and, I am certain, any other conduct but compelling obedience would be ruinous and culpable, therefore no consideration could bring me to swerve from the present path which I think Myself in Duty bound to follow."[28] The nation at large supported the king. But officially little changed. North made no effort to keep his ministers in London during that summer and gave the impression that there was still plenty of time to deal seriously with the American explosion.

In Boston, British sympathizers were hysterically fearful. From there on June 1, Thomas Hutchinson, Jr., wrote to his father in London:

[26] Higginbotham, *War of American Independence*, p. 76.
[27] Dartmouth to Gage, July 1, 1775, *Gage Correspondence*, vol. 2, p. 200.
[28] George III to North, July 5, 1775, *Correspondence of King George the Third*, ed. John Fortescue (London, 1927), vol. 3, p. 233.

You can have no idea of the state we have been in ever since the 19th of April. The fears and apprehensions of what might be the consequence of that skirmish, before the arrival of the Irish fleet, has occasioned people to fly to all quarters for safety. Everything that has hapned [*sic*] has afforded matter of triumph to the people, and I believe them to be ripe for any undertaking: they appear to be desperate and determined throughout the continent.[29]

On June 10, Chief Justice Peter Oliver wrote to Hutchinson:

You who riot in pleasure in London, know nothing of the distress in Boston: you can regale upon delicacies, whilst we are in the rotations of salt beef and salt pork one day, and the next, chewing upon salt pork and salt beef. The very rats are grown so familiar that they ask you to eat them, for they say that they have ate up the sills already, and they must now go upon the clapboards.[30]

After Lexington and Concord, American leaders had lost no time preparing for a full war. A circular issued by the Committee of Safety on April 20 stated:

The barbarous murders committed on our innocent brethren, on Wednesday the 19th instant, have made it absolutely necessary that we immediately raise an army to defend our wives and our children from the butchering hands of an inhuman soldiery, who, incensed at the obstacles they met with in their bloody progress, and enraged at being repulsed from the field of slaughter, will, without the least doubt, take the first opportunity in their power to ravage this devoted country with fire and sword.[31]

After talking with the main American military leaders a few days later, John Adams wrote in his diary: "There was great confusion and much distress. Artillery, arms, clothing were wanting, and a sufficient supply of provisions not easily obtained. Neither the officers nor men, however, wanted spirits or resolution." As he rode along the scene of the recent action, he was convinced that "the die was cast, the Rubicon passed."[32] As soon as rumors of the fighting reached London, William Knox, the undersecretary of the American Department in the British government, used almost the

---

[29] Thomas Hutchinson, Jr., to Thomas Hutchinson, June 1, 1775, *Diary and Letters of Thomas Hutchinson,* vol. 1, p. 461.

[30] Peter Oliver to Thomas Hutchinson, June 10, 1775, ibid., vol. 1, p. 469.

[31] Richard Frothingham, *Life and Times of Joseph Warren* (Little, Brown, 1865), p. 466.

[32] *The Works of John Adams,* ed. Charles Francis Adams (Boston, 1861), vol. 2, p. 406.

same words—"the die is cast, and more mischief will follow."[33] On May 8, Benjamin Franklin wrote to his British friend David Hartley: "You will have heard before this reaches you of the Commencement of a Civil War; the End of it perhaps neither myself, nor you, who are much younger, may live to see."[34]

The first battles were curiously atypical of the rest of the war. They were entered into by the militia with an eagerness that soon evaporated. By 1776, popular enthusiasm began to wane, and by 1777 little was left of it. Once the British held out and reinforcements started to come in, Washington's army began to experience acute problems of recruitment, pay, and morale. In September 1775, the commander in chief warned that "the greater part of the Army [is] in a state not far from mutiny" and that, if conditions did not improve, "the Army must absolutely break up."[35] Washington wanted nothing so much as to get rid of the militia and form a conventional, regular army based on enlistments and discipline.

After Lexington and Concord, eight years of war, with many ups and downs, were necessary before the Americans were officially free from British rule. But they belong to the story of the war, not why and how it came about.

[33] Mackesy, *War for America*, p. 2.
[34] Franklin to Hartley, May 8, 1775, *The Papers of Benjamin Franklin*, ed. Leonard W. Labaree (Yale University Press, 1961), vol. 22, p. 34.
[35] Washington to the President of Congress, September 21, 1775, *The Writings of George Washington*, ed. John C. Fitzpatrick (Government Printing Office, 1931), vol. 3, p. 512.

20

"A degree of importance"

❧

· 1 ·

AS ONE LOOKS BACK AT the prerevolutionary period, some things stand out.

The end of the Seven Years' War in 1763 opened the revolutionary road by giving the British a rationale to tax the Americans and by relieving the American colonists of the French threat. Whether the Revolution might have broken out even if the French were still in Canada is something we will never know. But there is good reason to believe that it would at least have come much later in time and in different circumstances.

Long after 1763, the Americans claimed that all they had ever wanted was a return to the status quo ante. In effect, they were satisfied with their status in 1763, because they effectively managed their own lives and dominated the governors sent to rule over them. They were growing spectacularly in population and commerce, whatever the obstacles put in their path. They were protected by the British navy in a still dangerous and treacherous world. They enjoyed thinking of themselves as part of the British empire, and their elite imitated the ways of their counterparts in England. There is no reason to doubt that the Americans really wanted to preserve the status quo before 1763, because it worked largely in their favor.

But the new British legislation of 1764–65, culminating in the Stamp Act, brought about a sudden, unexpected, explosive change in the American ethos. It is hard to believe that the cost of the stamps could have made so great a difference that a revolutionary trend was set in motion by it.

The Stamp Act represented something much larger and more threatening than a tax. What that was is the secret of the American Revolution.

In large part, the ensuing struggle was one between British sovereignty and American autonomy. British sovereignty was the guiding British principle from the beginning to the end of the struggle. But once the Americans discovered how to fight against parliamentary taxation, they had a fatal stranglehold on that sovereignty. Again and again they invoked the old Lockean doctrine that they must give consent before parting with their money. The colonists presented the British with a paradox—consent meant that they had to be represented in Parliament, yet the colonies said that they could not be meaningfully represented there. The British could not hold on to their sovereignty if they gave up their right to taxation, and the Americans could not hold on to the right to tax themselves without fatally impairing British sovereignty over them.

For ten years, the argument went round and round, always ending in the same place. But why did it take ten years to settle the matter? For one thing, the British long did not have the force in the colonies to compel obedience. For another, the British were filled with illusions about the colonies—that they were too different from one another to unite against British rule, that the Americans needed British protection against other predatory powers, that there were enough British well-wishers in the colonies to prevent a total British collapse. These misconceptions had just enough truth in them to be misleading. If we can believe John Adams, at least one-third of the colonial population opposed the Revolution.[1] A later estimate has put the figure at about one-fifth.[2] In any case, the pro-British opposition was large enough to give the British reason to expect substantial aid from inside the colonies.

As for the Americans, they had been part of the British empire for so long—a century and a half for the oldest colonies—that breaking away seemed to go against their very nature. They needed time and goading to develop an ideology and a leadership that brought them to the full realization that they were aiming at independence. In fact, they engaged in some extraordinary intellectual gymnastics to hold on to some shred of attachment to the British empire. First they objected to taxation, not trade; then they held on almost to the very end to a loyalty to the king, not Parliament. When the Declaration of Independence of July 4,

[1] John Adams to Thomas McKean, August 31, 1813, *The Works of John Adams*, ed. Charles Francis Adams (Boston, 1861), vol. 10, p. 63; John Adams to James Lloyd, January 1815, ibid., pp. 110–11.

[2] Paul H. Smith, "The American Loyalists: Notes on Their Organization and Numerical Strength," *William and Mary Quarterly*, vol. 25 (April 1968), pp. 259–77.

1776, declared, "The history of the present King of Great Britain is a history of repeated injuries and usurpations, all having in direct object the establishment of an absolute Tyranny over these States," and went on to state at length all of his alleged "Oppressions," with barely a mention of Parliament, it forgot all that had been said in previous years about obeying the king and blaming Parliament.

The final stage of the revolutionary struggle against the tea tax was brought about by a relatively minuscule issue. As late as December 1774, the precocious Alexander Hamilton noted that it was ridiculous "to affirm, that we are quarrelling for the trifling sum of three pence a pound on tea; when it is evidently the principle against which we contend."[3] George Grenville had said essentially the same thing: "The question is not about paying of this sum, or that sum of money, but to establish your jurisdiction, and power of every kind within the words of the Act of Parliament over the colonies."[4] They agreed that the specific issue could not have had revolutionary implications if it had not embodied principle, jurisdiction, and power.

The entire colonial case against British rule had been largely negative—against taxation, against a "standing army," against the importation of tea, against the Coercive Acts. In all the mountain of words against the British from 1765 to 1775, few—if any—have anything to do with changing the political and certainly not the social structure as it had developed under British rule. The Revolution was not fought to bring about democracy or any kind of egalitarianism. Before 1776, very few—if any—Americans expected to bring about a republic.[5] The British gave the colonists a revolutionary program long before the Americans were willing to admit that this was their goal. "It is something of a paradox of the American Revolution," J. R. Pole, a British historian, has observed, "that its leaders knew what they were against before they were absolutely sure about what they were for."[6]

Once the war broke out, it was obvious that the new American states could not reorganize themselves in a monarchical fashion or substitute an

---

[3] Alexander Hamilton, *A Full Vindication of the Measures of the Congress, & c.,* in *The Papers of Alexander Hamilton,* ed. Harold C. Syrett (Columbia University Press, 1961), vol. 1, p. 48.

[4] January 26, 1769, *Proceedings and Debates of the British Parliaments Respecting North America, 1754–1783,* ed. R. C. Simmons and P. D. G. Thomas (Kraus International, 1983), vol. 3, p. 73.

[5] W. Paul Adams, "Republicanism in Political Rhetoric Before 1776," *Political Science Quarterly,* September 1970, pp. 397–421.

[6] J. R. Pole, "The Ambiguities of Power," in *The American Revolution: Its Character and Limits,* ed. Jack P. Greene (New York University Press, 1987), p. 124; "Republican government was scarcely mentioned in the colonies until the very eve of the revolution" (Richard L. Bushman, *King and People in Provincial Massachusetts* [University of North Carolina Press, 1985], p. 6).

American monarchy for a British monarchy. The result was the creation of a republic, with all the political changes that implied. But the term itself was not an issue in the prewar period; it was realized only as a result of the war. In 1775, for example, that inveterate ideologist John Adams, as *Novanglus,* had only gone so far as wanting an American state united with a British state "under one king." It was not until 1776 that Adams turned his mind to what the next stage would be and decided that "all good government is republican."[7] In fact, Adams was astounded that the change in attitude had come so suddenly. "Idolatry to Monarchs, and servility to Aristocratical Pride," he wrote to his wife, Abigail, in July 1776, "was never so totally eradicated from so many Minds in so short a Time."[8]

In October 1774, the First Continental Congress still gave assurances that "our connexion with Great Britain we shall always carefully and zealously endeavour to support and maintain."[9] The following year, even after Lexington and Concord and the appointment of George Washington as commander in chief, the Second Continental Congress declared that "we mean not to dissolve that union which has so long and so happily subsisted between us" and "we have not raised armies with ambitious designs of separating from Great-Britain and establishing independent states."[10] The popular turn to independence came after the publication of Thomas Paine's *Common Sense* in January 1776. Independence meant that the Americans wanted to have the power to determine their own fate, but just what that fate was going to be was still an open question.

Were the Americans sincere in their long denials of the goal of independence, or did they play a double game of seeming to reject it publicly while wanting it privately? It is difficult to be sure of the answer, because none of the American Founders ever discussed it publicly and historians have not been much more helpful. The connection with Great Britain was so deeply ingrained in the American consciousness that it was broken only with the greatest difficulty. American extremists came close to advocating a semblance of independence in 1774–75, but only in the form of equality within the empire. On this score, too, the British were the first to recognize what they were fighting against. They had been prepared to expect an American breakaway for decades before it became a practical

---

[7] Adams to John Penn, *Works of John Adams,* vol. 4, p. 204. The letter was probably written in March 1776.

[8] John Adams to Abigail Adams, July 1776, *The Adams Family Correspondence,* ed. L. H. Butterfield (Harvard University Press, 1963), vol. 2, p. 28.

[9] *Journals of the American Congress,* vol. 1, p. 49.

[10] Ibid., p. 103.

issue. In any case, it appears that the Americans made the Revolution only as a last resort and by telling themselves that they were aiming at something else—not an unusual occurrence in great historic events.

Another tantalizing question is what might have happened if the British had not deceived themselves that the Americans were too weak and divided to fight. When it was too late, at least two British ministers admitted that they had been "misled and deceived."[11] Lord North himself confessed that "he had been deceived in events" and had not imagined that "all America would have armed in the cause."[12] In fact, the British government blundered into a war which it did not think it would have to fight. Yet it is hard to believe that it would have capitulated to the Americans without a struggle, even if it had been more foreknowing. After all, it would have had to agree to a cringing dissolution of the empire and the expected ruination of Great Britain itself. More likely, a less deluded British government might have taken more resolute military measures earlier to head off the coming challenge. In this case, the question is whether the Americans would have been so headstrong if Gage had had 24,000 troops instead of about 4,000.

Yet to overemphasize the grievances and self-deceptions that ostensibly brought about the Revolution is to lose sight of the underlying changes in the relationship between the colonies and the mother country. In the "pamphlet war" of 1759–1761, the premonitions of colonial independence had had nothing to do with those grievances and illusions, all of which came later. The British pamphleteers based themselves on objective factors that arose out of the growth and development of the colonies. They saw that Great Britain, 3,000 miles away, could not by itself hold the Americans back from wanting to determine their own fate. Only an external threat from the French in Canada could restrain the Americans from striking out on their own.

One of the peculiar aspects of the Revolutionary War was its outbreak. It began at Lexington and Concord at a time when the colonial militia was fired up with an inordinate sense of its advantage over the British regulars. This sense was fed by the disparity in casualties at Lexington and Concord in April 1775, the capture of Ticonderoga in May of that year, and the disparity of casualties at Bunker Hill in June. Gage's force was cooped up in Boston and did not dare offer opposition to a superior colonial force. The colonial advantage, however, began to evaporate in

[11] *Proceedings and Debates,* October 26, 1775, vol. 6, p. 78 (duke of Grafton), p. 84 (Earl Gower).
[12] Ibid., October 27, 1775, p. 127.

1776. One wonders whether the militia would have been so headstrong and confident if the early disparities had not existed. These had resulted wholly from the sluggishness with which the British side had prepared for a war. The British did not begin to take the war seriously until 1776, by which time it was too late. In fact, the war broke out even before the entire American side fully believed that independence was what it was fighting for. There is no telling what would have happened if the British had manifested more force earlier, but it is safe to say that British military policy in 1774–75 was partially responsible for setting off the war.

To some later British historians, British colonial policy made no sense. One attributed it to "a stupid generation of English politicians."[13] Another pointed out that the Stamp Act was never expected to bring in more than £100,000, the tax on tea never more than £30,000, and the war cost the British Treasury £128,000,000 and thousands of British lives. In the light of these figures, "one would think there was no man in Great Britain but would have run out into the streets crying for instant reconciliation with the Colonies."[14] But it was not merely "a stupid generation of English politicians" that wanted the war; the bulk of British people of that generation supported the war. The forces that led to the American Revolution were too large and too deep to be attributed to stupid British politicians.

· 2 ·

In the end, the Revolution was a struggle for power—between the power the British wished to exercise over the Americans and the power the Americans wished to exercise over themselves. The Declaration of Independence put it bluntly—the Americans in 1776 wanted nothing more than to assume a "separate and equal station" among "the Powers of the earth."

This struggle for power was masked for some time—by the issues of taxation, the authority of Parliament, the Coercive Acts. But all the while, the real question was which side would dictate to the other side. The British generation of the revolutionary period believed that Great Britain was faced with ruin and degradation if the American colonies were lost. It was willing to fight a war not merely to keep the American colonies but to prevent

---

[13] Basil Williams, *The Whig Supremacy, 1714–1760* (Clarendon Press, 1939; reprint 1952), p. 306.

[14] Mary A. M. Marks, *England and America, 1763 to 1783* (London, 1907), vol. 1, p. 23.

Great Britain from sinking into an economic and diplomatic morass. This outlook turned out to be wrong, and a new British empire, much stronger than the first, was created in the nineteenth century. But the future was a dark secret to the British people and politicians of 1774–75.

James Otis had stated the essential issue as early as 1762 in the preface to his first pamphlet: "*The world ever has been and will be pretty equally divided, between those two great parties, vulgarly called the* winners, *and the* loosers; *or to speak more precisely, between those who are discontented that they have no Power, and those who never think they can have enough.*"[15]

Otis and other Americans were soon busy arguing about the various differences that arose between Great Britain and the colonies. But increasingly, Americans saw that the British were responding to a rising American power. In 1768, a Philadelphia essayist, William Hicks, asked: "Shall we be reduced to the most abject state of dependence, because we may possibly become formidable rivals to our jealous British brethren?"[16] In 1774, Richard Wells wrote a pamphlet in which he exulted: "We look to manhood—our muscles swell out with youthful vigor; our sinews spring with elastic force; and we feel the *marrow of Englishmen in our bones*. The day of independent manhood is at hand—we feel our strength; and with a filial grateful sense of *proper* obedience, would wish to be esteemed the *friend* as well as the *child* of Britain."[17] In 1774, Thomas Jefferson explained the Boston Tea Party in terms of a new power relationship: "An exasperated people, who feel that they possess power, are not easily restrained within limits strictly regular."[18]

To get over the objection that British rule meant rule by Parliament, the revolutionary colonists long tried to substitute the king for Parliament. This strategy never impressed the British public or the king, because at least in this instance they knew their history better than Benjamin Franklin or the Massachusetts legislature did. According to the settlement of 1688–89, the king swore to rule by the laws of Parliament. For British Whigs, this compact

[15] James Otis, *A Vindication of the Conduct of the House of Representatives of the Province of the Massachusetts-Bay* (Boston, 1762), p. iv. I have let stand Otis's eighteenth-century spelling of "loosers."

[16] William Hicks, *The Nature and Extent of Parliamentary Power Considered*, reprinted in Merrill Jensen, ed., *Tracts of the American Revolution 1763–1776* (Bobbs-Merrill, 1967), pp. 171–72. Hicks's essays were first printed in the *Pennsylvania Journal*, January 21–February 25, 1768.

[17] Richard Wells, *A Few Political Reflections submitted to the Consideration of the British Colonies* (Philadelphia, 1774), p. 33.

[18] *A Summary View*, reprinted in *The Papers of Thomas Jefferson*, ed. Julian P. Boyd (Princeton University Press, 1950), vol. 1, p. 127.

was sacrosanct. In 1773, George III had Dartmouth tell Franklin that laws had to be made by Parliament in all cases whatsoever and that it was his duty to preserve this right "entire and inviolate."[19] One wonders whether the delegates in 1776 blamed the king for all their troubles because they had previously exempted him from them.

Both sides were victims of their own contradictions. The British maintained that Parliament had the right to legislate and tax the Americans because the Americans were British subjects. But the British also held that the colonies were and must remain "dependent" on Great Britain and, therefore, different from it. The Americans wanted to be British subjects but not for the purpose of being taxed or subject to parliamentary legislation. The two were incompatible.

One American contradiction concerned slavery. The Americans assailed a tax on stamps or on tea as the equivalent of nothing short of slavery, even absolute slavery. Yet they paid little attention to the real slavery of blacks that was all around them, mainly in the south but also in the north. There was some sentiment for abolition in the north before the American Revolution, but it never amounted to much, and some of the most eminent revolutionaries were slave owners. This discrepancy did not escape the notice of Dr. Johnson, who asked, "How is it that we hear the loudest yelps for liberty among the drivers of negroes?"[20]

The question arises how important the "constitutional" or "political" arguments between the British and Americans were. These arguments can be followed in the speeches, pamphlets, and resolutions that traditionally make up a good part of the American road to revolution. They are important because they tell of the intellectual struggle that preceded the outbreak of hostilities. In this struggle, however, the American political positions changed repeatedly over the critical ten years. They went from objecting to taxation only, to rejecting the legislation of Parliament in all cases, to accepting the weak link with the king, to declaring absolute independence. Something of longer range and deeper significance was driving the Americans to an ever more extreme resolution of the conflict.

It could well be found in the insight which James Harrington had expressed in *The Common-wealth of Oceana*, published in 1656—that colonies were "as yet babes that cannot live without suckling the breasts of their mother-Cities," but that "I mistake, if when they come of age

[19] From Lord Dartmouth, June 2, 1773, *The Papers of Benjamin Franklin*, ed. Leonard W. Labaree (Yale University Press, 1961), vol. 20, pp. 223–24.
[20] Samuel Johnson, *Taxation No Tyranny* (London, 1775), p. 89.

they do not wean themselves." Or, a century later, Francis Hutcheson's thought: "Large numbers of men cannot be bound to sacrifice their own and their posterity's liberty and happiness, to the ambitious views of their mother-country, while it can enjoy all rational happiness without subjection to it." Or the conviction that the British could not keep the Americans in subjection without a French Canada to frighten them, a proposition that was at the very heart of the Canada versus Guadeloupe debate a half decade before the Stamp Act. These views point to a "real cause" that, as Thucydides put it, "made war inevitable"—the growth of the power of the Americans, and the alarm this inspired in Great Britain. There was something in this conflict in the nature of a struggle between a British immovable body and an American irresistible force. Such an impasse could not persist indefinitely; one or the other force had to give way.

In 1776, one of the most acute British observers of the time, Adam Smith, cut through the old disputes to what he thought was the real American motivation. The American leaders, he wrote, "feel in themselves at this moment a degree of importance which, perhaps the greatest subjects in Europe scarce feel. From shopkeepers, tradesmen, and attornies, they are become statesmen and legislators, and are employed in contriving a new form of government for an extensive empire, which, they flatter themselves, will become, and which, indeed, seems very likely to become, one of the greatest and most formidable that ever was in the world." He continued: "Such has hitherto been the rapid progress of that country in wealth, population and improvement, that in the course of little more than a century, perhaps, the produce of America might exceed that of British taxation. The seat of the empire would then naturally remove itself to that part of the empire which contributed most to the general defence and support of the whole."[21] Smith wrote before the full impact of the Revolution was clear, but he clearly saw it in terms of "wealth, population and improvement" that promised to make the Americans more important than the British even if they stayed in the empire.

In 1777, Thomas Paine wrote: "America, by her own internal industry, and unknown to all the powers of Europe, was, at the beginning of the dispute, arrived at a pitch of greatness, trade and population, beyond which it was the interest of Britain not to suffer her to pass, lest she should grow too powerful to be kept subordinate."[22]

[21] Adam Smith, *An Inquiry into the Nature and Causes of the Wealth of Nations*, ed. Edwin Cannan (Modern Library ed., 1937), pp. 587–88, 590.
[22] *The American Crisis*, April 17, 1777, in *The Complete Writings of Thomas Paine*, ed. Philip S. Foner (Citadel Press, 1945), vol. 1, p. 78.

As the war dragged on, even Lord North frequently remarked that "the advantages of this contest could never repay the expence." This sign of weakness did not sit well with George III, who sent North a note to stiffen him and to explain what the stakes for Great Britain were. The king's view may seem overwrought in retrospect, but at the time it was shared by others and helps to explain why the British fought so long to prevent what much later came to be known as "falling dominoes":

> The present Contest with America I cannot help seeing as the most serious in which any Country was ever engaged[;] it contains such a train of consequences that they must be examined to feel its true weight; whether the laying a Tax was deserving all the Evils that have arisen from it, I should suppose no man could alledge that without being thought more fit for Bedlam than a Seat in the Senate; but step by step the demands of America have risen—independence is their object, that certainly is one which every man not willing to sacrifice every object to a *momentary and* inglorious Peace must concurr with me in thinking that this Country can never submit to; should America succeed in that, the West Indies must follow them, not independence, but must for its own interest be dependent on North America; Ireland would soon follow the same plan and be a separate State, then this Island would be reduced to itself, and soon would be a poor Island indeed, for reduced in Her Trade Merchants would retire their Wealth to Climates more to their Advantage, and Shoals of Manufacturers would leave this Country for the New Empire.[23]

From this point of view, the British stakes could not have been higher. If Great Britain lost the war, it was allegedly condemned to change from being the greatest power in the world to being but a "poor Island," from which her merchants and manufacturers would flee. This forecast proved to be overly pessimistic, but no one could have known it at the time. In effect, Great Britain was thought to be fighting for keeping its status as a great power or for retaining almost any power at all. By the same reasoning, the Americans were fighting to become the "New Empire."

If, as seems clear from the evidence, the Americans in 1774–75 were fighting against the king, the majority in Parliament, and most of the politically minded British public, no one of these three can be blamed for the War of Independence. When the Americans first put the responsibility

---

[23] King to North, June 11, 1779, *Correspondence of King George the Third*, ed. John Fortescue (London, 1927), vol. 4, p. 351.

for their plight on Parliament and then on the king, they were looking for a convenient scapegoat. In fact, the war was a struggle between the main bodies of leaders and people on both sides. The one wanted to keep what seemed to be essential to its welfare, and the other wanted to break away to release itself from external restraints and prohibitions.

Paradoxically, the Americans were lucky to have been *British* colonies. In no other empire of the time could the colonies have had the advantages that the Americans had under the British empire. Only the British could have permitted a colonial press to go so far in challenging and defying the mother country. Only the British could have allowed a substantial and vigorous part of their own upper class to sympathize with and support the American rebels. Only the British could have provided much of the theoretical underpinning of colonial ideology. There was no Locke or "Cato" in France or Spain to inspire its colonists and arm them with convenient arguments against its own rule. Almost to the end of the colonial period, the colonists pleaded for their rights as *British* subjects, not as Americans. The Americans may have deceived the British or themselves in their allegiance to what they considered to be the true British tradition, even if it was a dissident side of that tradition. Nevertheless, the Americans could not have obtained such political and psychological sustenance from anywhere else in the world at that time.

Who made the American Revolution? The best-known revolutionaries belonged to a relatively small American elite. Sometimes backing it and sometimes going its own way was a larger, anonymous mass of the poor to the middle stratum, sometimes called the "populace," the "rabble," or the "mob." From time to time, the latter's violence and lack of control frightened the revolutionary elite as well as British officialdom. In the end, the elite managed to hold on to its leadership and to direct the Revolution where it wanted it to go. The supreme political advantage of the elite was that it had a unifying program that was simple and manageable. It wanted freedom from British subjection without social turmoil and transformation. The mass support had no such large program and generally expressed itself in destructive local violence, which suddenly flared up and just as suddenly subsided. The most probable answer to the question is that the American Revolution was made by both strata but that the elite gave it its leadership, program, and continuity.

We may usefully go back to the pamphlet war of 1759–1761, with which we began. The main issue in those pamphlets was how the American colonies influenced the interests of Great Britain. The pro-Guadeloupe side held that it was better to leave Canada to the French, because "in process of Time" the American colonies would "care little about the Mother Country," since the colonies were sure to "increase infinitely from all Causes." As a British pamphlet of 1761 put it: "As America increases in people, so she must increase in arts and sciences, in manufactures and trade, while she has the same laws, liberties, and genius we have at home; the more she increases in these, the less she must want from Britain; the more she rises above a certain pitch, her utility and advantage to Britain must proportionately decline."

At that time nothing had yet happened to come between Great Britain and the American colonies. All this theorizing was based on long-held ideas about empires and colonies. The British government had ignored the warnings against taking Canada instead of Guadeloupe. Nevertheless, the long procession of British thinkers who had contributed such warnings had not labored in vain; they had produced a climate of opinion that had increasingly hardened the British resolve to make the showdown with the Americans hinge on the issue of sovereignty and power. There is no telling what the Americans would have done if the British had left well enough alone after 1763 or even 1766, but it is almost certain that the Revolution would not have come when and how it did. The struggle for power might have been delayed, but it could not have been indefinitely postponed.

· 3 ·

The struggle for American independence was a struggle for power because—most simply—the essential issue was this: Who would make the ultimate decisions? This question came to a head in the 1760s, but it had long haunted both the colonies and the mother country.

The decision-making power had worried the British as early as the seventeenth century. It had been at the bottom of all the British predictions and speculations about the tenuous hold the mother country had over the colonies. It had expressed itself in the unwavering insistence of the colonies that their charters gave them full control of their monies and expenditures. Money-power had prevailed in the incessant struggles between governors and assemblies. Only the laissez-faire British colonial policy in the first half of the eighteenth century and the daunting French threat from Canada had made it unnecessary or inopportune for the colonies to attempt to make any important change in the nominal relationship with Great Britain before the 1760s.

That the struggle was over the power of decision was shown in its most naked and unmistakable form in the first case, previously described, against Governor Bernard of Massachusetts, led by James Otis in 1762. Otis did not challenge the facts about Bernard's response to the demand of merchants and fishermen in Salem and Marblehead to protect them against an alleged threat from a French privateer. He based his entire case on Bernard's expenditure of funds to send out a colonial sloop. The issue was clear-cut for Otis—only the assembly had the power to authorize the expenditure. Nothing but the power of decision was at stake.

This precedent held for the rest of the colonial period. The stamp tax was fought so vehemently because it was imposed by Parliament and not the assemblies. For the first time, it violated the assemblies' monopoly of power over money. Once the assemblies were deprived of this preeminent power, they saw themselves as virtually powerless. They were mollified for a time by the repeal of the Stamp Act, and they tolerated the Declaratory Act as a face-saving gesture on the part of the British government. But the Declaratory Act was the true casus belli of the American Revolution. When it stated in unmistakable terms that Parliament had full power to make laws binding on the colonies *"in all cases whatsoever,"* it challenged the colonies to—as George III put it—"submit or triumph."

In these tumultuous years between 1765–66 and the outbreak of the war in 1775, the struggle for power was marked by various ideological, constitutional, and political issues. But these controversies invariably turned on who had the power of decision to settle them. They were not intellectual exercises between rival groups of ideologues. In the end, the issue was dependence versus independence—colonial dependence on Great Britain, meaning that Parliament would make the ultimate decisions, or American independence, meaning that the assemblies would make the ultimate decisions. A fundamental change in the American form of government had to wait for the end of the war and the new federal Constitution, drawn up in 1787.

In the end, the colonies had to wrest the power of decision from Great Britain before they could face the question of what to do with it. The struggle for power came first.

INDEX

Abercromby, James, 84–86

An Account of the European Settlements in America (William Burke), 122–23

Adams, John: on American Revolution, 271, 507, 509; and Boston Massacre, 358, 412; and Boston newspapers, 408; and Boston Tea Party, 395–96; and Canada versus Guadeloupe issue, 15–16; on colonial militia, 475–76; and First Continental Congress, 427, 428, 430, 431, 432, 436; on Hamilton, 449; on Harrington, 44, 45; on Hutchinson, 236, 247, 373; on independence of colonies, 44, 45, 427, 507; and Loyal Nine, 244; mentioned, 222, 413, 470, 491; on molasses tax, 270–71; on Otis, 186, 188, 194, 236; on population, 102–3; and preparations for war, 472, 504; on public opinion in Massachusetts, 420; and Stamp Act crisis, 247, 248; on war issue, 428, 507, 509; and writs of assistance, 183–84, 186–89

Adams, Samuel: and battle of Lexington and Concord, 498; and *Boston Evening Post* letter to British military, 440; and Boston newspapers, 408, 409–10; and Boston Tea Party, 396–97; on British military as standing army, 357; and change of venue from Boston to Cambridge, 365–66; and Coercive Acts, 419–20; on colonists as precipitating war, 469–71; "compact theory" of, 383–84; and covenant effort, 421; as extremist, 420; and First Continental Congress, 427, 429;

Franklin compared with, 371; and Hutchinson's purloined letters, 399; and Loyal Nine, 244; mentioned, 326, 413, 414, 465; on money-power of assemblies, 378–80; on parliamentary supremacy, 383–84; on population, 108; and Quartering Act, 292–93; on salaries of British officials, 378–80; and Stamp Act crisis, 218–19, 247–48; and Tea Act, 395; and Townshend Acts, 315–16, 324–25; on violence, 324–25

"Address to the People of Great-Britain" (First Continental Congress), 433, 434–35

administration of colonies: Bladen's views about, 100–101; and British Constitution, 139; British recommendation for centralization of, 140–41; by parliament, 216; and commerce/trade, 140; and Crown-parliament relations, 216; early, 30–33; and financial affairs, 140–41; French views about British, 79–80; and parliament, 63, 91–92, 94, 141; problems of, 32–33; and Walpole's administration, 90–92. *See also* assemblies; Board of Trade; councils, colonial; Privy Council; *specific commission, committee or board*

The Administration of Colonies (Thomas Pownall), 352

Administration of Justice Act. *See* Coercive Acts

Admiralty, British, 32

Aix-la-Chapelle, treaty of (1748), 134